Collins
COBUILD

Pocket
English-English-Marathi
Dictionary

इंग्रजी-इंग्रजी-मराठी

**Exclusively marketed by Ratna Sagar Pvt. Ltd.
in the Indian Subcontinent only**

HarperCollins Publishers
Westerhill Road
Bishopbriggs
Glasgow
G642QT

First Edition 2011

Reprint 10 9 8 7 6 5 4 3 2 1 0

© HarperCollins Publishers 2011

ISBN 978-0-00-743858-7

Collins® is a registered trademark of
HarperCollins Publishers Limited

www.collinslanguage.com

A catalogue record for this book is available from
the British Library

Typeset by Aptara in India
Artwork by Q2A Media

Printed in India by Gopsons Papers Ltd.

Acknowledgements

We would like to thank those authors and
publishers who kindly gave permission for
copyright material to be used in the Collins
Word Web. We would also like to thank Times
Newspapers Ltd for providing valuable data.

Contents

आशय

Editorial consultant   संपादकीय सल्लागार
Lilavati Vaidya

Translation co-ordination   भाषांतर सुसूत्रीकरण
Ajit Shirodkar
Shakti Enterprise

Translators   भाषांतरकार
Dinkar Dattatray
Waman Puranik

Computing support   संगणकीय आधार
Thomas Callan

Editors   संपादक
Gerry Breslin
Freddy Chick
Lucy Cooper
Kerry Ferguson

Editor-in-chief   मुख्य संपादक
Dr Elaine Higgleton

Abbreviations संक्षिप्त रूपे

abbr	abbreviation
adj	adjective
adv	adverb
conj	conjunction
det	determiner
excl	exclamation
n	noun
npl	plural noun
num	numeral
prep	preposition
pron	pronoun
US	American English
v	verb
vi	intransitive verb
vt	transitive verb

Using this Dictionary

Entry words
Entry words are printed in blue bold type.

> **abbreviation**

Inflected forms
The inflected forms of verbs, nouns, adjectives, abbreviations, and numerals are printed in black bold type in brackets.

> **abduct** (**abducts, abducting, abducted**)

Parts of speech
Parts of speech are abbreviated and printed in italics. When a word can be used as more than one part of speech, the change of part of speech is shown after an empty arrow.

> **about** *adv* **About** means near to something.
> सुमारे ▷ *prep* **About** means to do with.

Definitions
Definitions give the meaning of the word. In the definition, the entry word is printed in black bold.

> **abroad** *adv* If you go **abroad**, you go to a
> foreign country.

Usage and regional labels
Usage and regional labels are printed in italics in brackets after the definition.

> **consequently** *adv* **Consequently** means as a
> result. (*formal*)

Translations
Translations come after the definition and give the equivalent of the entry word in Marathi.

> **abolition** *n* The **abolition** of something is its
> formal ending. निर्मूलन

Examples
Example sentences are printed in italics and show how the word is used.

> **consist of** *v* Something that **consists of**
> particular things or people is formed from them.
> चे बनलेले असणे *The cabin consisted of two small rooms.*

शब्दकोशाचा वापर

नोंद शब्द

नोंद शब्द ठळक निळ्या ठशात छापले आहेत.

abbreviation

विकारी रूपे

क्रियापदे, नाम, विशेषणे, संक्षिप्त रूपे, आणि संख्यावाचक शब्द यांची विकारी रूपे कंसात ठळक काळ्या ठशात छापली आहेत.

abduct (**abducts, abducting, abducted**)

शब्दांच्या जाती

शब्दांच्या जाती संक्षिप्त रूपात व वक्राक्षरात छापल्या आहेत. जेव्हा एखादा शब्द एकाहून अधिक शब्दांच्या जातींत वापरला गेला असेल, त्यावेळी शब्दांच्या जातींत झालेला बदल एका रिकाम्या बाणानंतर दाखवला गेला आहे.

> **about** *adv* **About** means near to something.
> सुमारे ▷ *prep* **About** means to do with.

व्याख्या

शब्दाचा अर्थ व्याख्येत दिला आहे. व्याख्येत नोंद शब्द ठळक काळ्या ठशात छापला आहे.

> **abroad** *adv* If you go **abroad**, you go to a
> foreign country.

शब्दांच्या वापराची पद्धत आणि प्रादेशिक खूणपट्ट्या

शब्दांच्या वापराची पद्धत आणि प्रादेशिक खूणपट्ट्या व्याख्येनंतर असलेल्या कंसात वक्राक्षरात छापल्या आहेत.

> **consequently** *adv* **Consequently** means as a
> result. (*formal*)

भाषांतरे

नोंद शब्दांचे समानार्थ आणि मराठीतील भाषांतरे व्याख्येनंतर दिली आहेत.

> **abolition** *n* The **abolition** of something is its
> formal ending. निर्मूलन

उदाहरणे

उदाहरण वाक्ये वक्राक्षरात छापली असून, ती शब्द कसा वापरावा हे दाखवतात.

> **consist of** *v* Something that **consists of**
> particular things or people is formed from them.
> चे बनलेले असणे *The cabin consisted of two small rooms.*

a

a *det* You use **a** or **an** before a noun when people may not know which person or thing you are talking about. एक वस्तू दर्शविण्यासाठी वापरण्यात येणारे इंग्रजीमधील अनिश्चिततादर्शी उपपद *A waiter came in with a glass of water.*

abandon (**abandons, abandoning, abandoned**) *vt* If you **abandon** a thing, place, or person, you leave them permanently or for a long time. सोडून देणे, त्याग करणे

abbreviation (**abbreviations**) *n* An **abbreviation** is a short form of a word or phrase. संक्षिप्त रूप

abdomen (**abdomens**) *n* Your **abdomen** is the part of your body below your chest where your stomach is. *(formal)* पोट

abduct (**abducts, abducting, abducted**) *vt* If someone **is abducted**, he or she is taken away illegally. पळवून नेणे

ability (**abilities**) *n* Your **ability** is the quality or skill that you have which makes it possible for you to do something. क्षमता

able (**abler, ablest**) *adj* An **able** person is clever or good at doing something. सक्षम

abnormal *adj* Someone or something that is **abnormal** is unusual in a way that is worrying. *(formal)* असाधारण, अस्वाभाविक

abolish (**abolishes, abolishing, abolished**) *vt* If someone in authority **abolishes** a practice or organization, they put an end to it. निर्मूलन करणे

abolition *n* The **abolition** of something is its formal ending. निर्मूलन

about *adv* **About** means near to something. सुमारे ▷ *prep* **About** means to do with. संबंधी *This book is about history.*

above *prep* If something is **above** another thing, it is over it or higher than it. वर *Lift the ball above your head.*

abroad *adv* If you go **abroad**, you go to a foreign country. परदेश

abrupt *adj* An **abrupt** action is very sudden and often unpleasant. अचानक, एकाएकी आणि अनपेक्षित

abruptly *adv* If you do something **abruptly**, you do it in an abrupt manner. एकाएकी

abscess (**abscesses**) *n* An **abscess** is a painful swelling containing pus. गळू

absence (**absences**) *n* The **absence** of someone or something is the fact that they are not there. अनुपस्थिती

absent *adj* If someone or something is **absent** from a place or situation, they are not there. अनुपस्थित

absent-minded *adj* An **absent-minded** person is very forgetful or does not pay attention to what they are doing. विक्षिप्त, अनवधानी

absolutely *adv* **Absolutely** means totally and completely. संपूर्णतः, अगदी

abstract *adj* An **abstract** idea or way of thinking is based on general ideas rather than on real things and events. अमूर्त

absurd *adj* If you say that something is **absurd**, you think that it is ridiculous or that it does not make sense. निरर्थक, खुळचट, मूर्खपणाचा

Abu Dhabi *n* **Abu Dhabi** is an emirate in south-east Arabia, on the southern coast of the Persian Gulf. अबू धाबी

academic *adj* **Academic** means relating to life or work in schools, colleges, and universities. शैक्षणिक

academic year (**academic years**) *n* The **academic year** is the period of the year during which students attend school or university. शैक्षणिक वर्ष

academy (academies) n A school or college specializing in a particular subject is sometimes called an **academy**. अकादमी, विशेष प्रशिक्षण देणारी संस्था

accelerate (accelerates, accelerating, accelerated) v If the rate of something **accelerates**, or if something **accelerates** it, it gets faster. चालना/गती देणे

acceleration n The **acceleration** of a process is the fact that it is getting faster. गतिवर्धन

accelerator (accelerators) n In a vehicle, the **accelerator** is the pedal you press to go faster. ऐक्सलरेटर

accept (accepts, accepting, accepted) v If you **accept** something that you have been offered, you say yes to it or agree to take it. स्वीकार करणे

acceptable adj If a situation or action is **acceptable**, people approve of it. स्वीकाराई

access (accesses, accessing, accessed) n If you have **access** to a building or other place, you are able to go into it. एखाद्या ठिकाणी शिरण्याचा मार्ग ▷ vt If you **access** something, especially information held on a computer, you succeed in finding or obtaining it. (संगणकाकडून) माहिती मिळवणे

accessible adj If a place is **accessible**, you are able to reach it or get into it. उपलब्ध; सहज घेता येण्याजोगा वा वापरता येण्याजोगा

accessory (accessories) n **Accessories** are extra parts added to something to make it more useful or decorative. उपयुक्त पण आवश्यक नसलेली वस्तू

accident (accidents) n An **accident** is something nasty that happens, and that hurts someone. अपघात ▷ n If something happens by **accident**, you do not expect it to happen. योगायोग

accidental adj An **accidental** event happens by chance or as the result of an accident. अपघाती

accidentally adv If something happens **accidentally**, it happens by chance or as the result of an accident, and is not deliberately intended. नजरचुकीने

accident and emergency n **Accident and emergency** is the room or department in a hospital where people who have severe injuries or sudden illness are taken for emergency treatment. आपत्कालीन अपघात विभाग

accident insurance n **Accident insurance** is insurance providing compensation for accidental injury or death. अपघात विमा

accommodate (accommodates, accommodating, accommodated) vt If a building or space can **accommodate** someone or something, it has enough room for them. सामावून घेणे

accommodation n **Accommodation** is used to refer to rooms or buildings where people live, stay, or work. राहण्याची व्यवस्था

accompany (accompanies, accompanying, accompanied) vt If you **accompany** someone, you go somewhere with them. (formal)) सोबत करणे

accomplice (accomplices) n An **accomplice** is a person who helps to commit a crime. दुष्कृत्य करण्यातील साथीदार

accordingly adv You use **accordingly** to say that one thing happens as a result of another thing. त्यानुसार

according to prep You say **according to** somebody to show that you are only repeating what you have read or heard, and that it may not be true. अनुसार They drove away in a white van, according to the news. ▷ prep If somebody does something **according to** a set of rules, they follow those rules. -च्या अनुसार They played the game according to the rules.

accordion (accordions) n An **accordion** is a musical instrument in the shape of a box which you hold in your hands. You play it by pressing keys and buttons on the side, while moving the two ends in and out. ऐकॉर्डियन

account (accounts) n An **account** is a written or spoken report of something that has happened. अहवाल ▷ n If you have an **account** with a bank, you leave money with the bank and take it out when you need it. खाते

accountable adj If you are **accountable** for something that you do, you are responsible for it. जबाबदार

accountancy n **Accountancy** is the work of keeping financial accounts. अकाऊंटन्सी

accountant (accountants) n An **accountant** is a person whose job is to keep financial accounts. हिशेब ठेवणारी व्यक्ती

account for (accounts for, accounted for, accounting for) v If you can **account for** something, you can explain it or give the necessary information about it. खुलासा करणे *How do you account for the missing money?*

account number (account numbers) n Your **account number** is the unique number of your account with something such as a bank. खाते क्रमांक

accuracy n The **accuracy** of information or measurements is their quality of being true or correct. अचूकपणा

accurate adj Something that is **accurate** is correct to a detailed level. अचूक

accurately adv **Accurately** means in an accurate manner. अचूकपणे

accusation (accusations) n If you make an **accusation** against someone, you express the belief that they have done something wrong. आरोप

accuse (accuses, accusing, accused) vt If you **accuse** someone of something, you say that you believe they did something wrong or dishonest. आरोप ठेवणे

accused (accused) n The **accused** refers to the person or people charged with a crime. आरोपी

ace (aces) n An **ace** is a playing card with a single symbol on it. एक्का

ache (aches, aching, ached) n An **ache** is a steady, fairly strong pain in a part of your body. वेदना ▷ vi If you **ache** or a part of your body **aches**, you feel a steady, fairly strong pain. वेदना होणे

achieve (achieves, achieving, achieved) vt If you **achieve** a particular aim or effect, you succeed in doing it or causing it to happen, usually after a lot of effort. प्राप्त करणे

achievement (achievements) n An **achievement** is something which someone has succeeded in doing, especially after a lot of effort. महत्कृत्य, (मोठी) कामगिरी

acid (acids) n An **acid** is a chemical, usually a liquid, that can burn your skin and cause damage to other substances. आम्ल, ऍसिड

acid rain n **Acid rain** is rain that damages plants, rivers, and buildings because it contains acid released into the atmosphere from factories and other industrial processes. आम्लयुक्त/ऍसिडयुक्त पाऊस

acknowledgement n An **acknowledgement** of something is a statement or action that recognizes that it is true. कबुली, पोचपावती

acne n **Acne** is a skin disease which causes spots on the face and neck. मुरूम

acorn (acorns) n An **acorn** is a pale oval nut that is the fruit of an oak tree. ऍकॉर्न

acoustic adj An **acoustic** musical instrument is one which is not electric. विजेचा वापर न करणारे वाद्य

acre (acres) n An **acre** is a unit of area equal to 4840 square yards or approximately 4047 square metres. एकर

acrobat (acrobats) n An **acrobat** is an entertainer who performs difficult physical acts such as jumping and balancing, especially in a circus. कसरतपटू

acronym (acronyms) n An **acronym** is a word made of the initial letters of the words in a phrase, especially when this is the name of an organization such as NATO. बहुशब्दीय नावाचे संक्षिप्त रूप/शब्द

across prep If someone goes **across** a place, they go from one side of it to the other. पलीकडे *She walked across the road.*

act (acts, acting, acted) n An **act** is an action or thing that someone does. कृती ▷ vi When you **act**, you do something. कृती करणे ▷ vi If you **act** in a play or film, you pretend to be one of the people in it. अभिनय करणे

acting adj You use **acting** before the title of a job to indicate that someone is doing that job temporarily. हंगामी ▷ n **Acting** is the activity or profession of performing in plays or films. अभिनय

action n **Action** is doing something for a particular purpose. कारवाई

active adj An **active** person is energetic and always busy. सक्रिय

activity n **Activity** is a situation in which a lot of things are happening. उपक्रम, कार्यक्रम, धामधूम

actor (actors) n An **actor** is someone whose job is acting in plays or films. अभिनेता

actress (actresses) n An **actress** is a woman whose job is acting in plays or films. अभिनेत्री

actual adj **Actual** is used to emphasize that you are referring to something real or genuine. वास्तविक

actually adv You use **actually** to indicate that a situation exists or that it is true. खरोखर

acupuncture n **Acupuncture** is the treatment of a person's illness or pain by sticking small needles into their body. ऍक्यूपंक्चर

ad (ads) n An **ad** is an announcement in a newspaper, on television, or on a poster about something such as a product, event, or job. (informal) जाहिरात

AD abbr You use **AD** in dates to indicate a number of years or centuries since the year in which Jesus Christ is believed to have been born. इसवी सन

adapt (adapts, adapting, adapted) vi If you **adapt** to a new situation, you change your ideas or behaviour in order to deal with it. जुळवून घेणे

adaptor (adaptors) n An **adaptor** is a special device for connecting electrical equipment to a power supply, or for connecting different pieces of electrical or electronic equipment together. ऍडेप्टर

add (adds, adding, added) vt If you **add** one thing to another, you put it with the other thing. मिसळणे ▷ vt If you **add** numbers together, you find out how many they make together. बेरीज करणे

addict (addicts) n An **addict** is someone who cannot stop taking harmful drugs. व्यसनाधीन

addicted adj Someone who is **addicted** to a harmful drug cannot stop taking it. व्यसनी

additional adj **Additional** things are extra things apart from the ones already present. अतिरिक्त

additive (additives) n An **additive** is a substance which is added to food by the manufacturer for a particular purpose, such as colouring it. खाण्यायोग्य पूरक पदार्थ

address (addresses) n If you give an **address** to a group of people, you give a speech to them. भाषण ▷ n Your **address** is the number of the house, the name of the street, and the town where you live or work. पत्ता

address book (address books) n An **address book** is a book in which you write people's names and addresses. पत्तापुस्तिका

add up (adds up, adding up, added up) v If you **add up** numbers or amounts, or if you add them **up**, you calculate their total. मिळवणे, बेरीज करणे Add up the total of those six games.

adjacent adj If two things are **adjacent**, they are next to each other. संलग्न

adjective (adjectives) n An **adjective** is a word such as 'big' or 'beautiful' that describes a person or thing. Adjectives usually come before nouns or after verbs like 'be' or 'feel'. विशेषण

adjust (adjusts, adjusting, adjusted) v When you **adjust** to a new situation, you get used to it by changing your behaviour or your ideas. जुळवून घेणे

adjustable adj If something is **adjustable**, it can be changed to different positions or sizes. कमी-जास्त करता येण्याजोगे

adjustment (**adjustments**) *n* An **adjustment** is a change that is made to something such as a machine or a way of doing something. एखादी गोष्ट सुधारण्यासाठी केलेला बदल

administration *n* **Administration** is the range of activities connected with organizing and supervising the way that an organization functions. प्रशासन

administrative *adj* **Administrative** work involves organizing and supervising an organization. प्रशासकीय

admiration *n* **Admiration** is a feeling of great liking and respect. कौतुक

admire (**admires, admiring, admired**) *vt* If you **admire** someone or something, you like and respect them. स्तुती/ कौतुक करणे

admission (**admissions**) *n* If you gain **admission** to a place or organization, you are allowed to enter it or join it. प्रवेश

admit (**admits, admitting, admitted**) *vt* If someone **is admitted** to a place or organization, they are allowed to enter it or join it. प्रवेश देणे ▷ *v* If you **admit** that something bad or embarrassing is true, you agree, often reluctantly, that it is true. मान्य करणे

admittance *n* **Admittance** is the act of entering a place or institution or the right to enter it. प्रवेशाचा हक्क

adolescence *n* **Adolescence** is the period of your life in which you develop from being a child into being an adult. पौगंडावस्था

adolescent (**adolescents**) *n* An **adolescent** is a young person who is no longer a child but who has not yet become an adult. पौगंडावस्थेतील मूल

adopt (**adopts, adopting, adopted**) *vt* If you **adopt** someone else's child, you take it into your own family and make it legally your own. दत्तक घेणे

adopted *adj* An **adopted** child is one which has been adopted. दत्तक

adoption (**adoptions**) *n* **Adoption** is the act of adopting a child. दत्तक घेण्याची क्रिया

adore (**adores, adoring, adored**) *vt* If you **adore** someone, you love and admire them. पूज्य मानणे

Adriatic *adj* **Adriatic** means of or relating to the Adriatic Sea, or to the inhabitants of its coast or islands. ॲड्रिॲटिक

Adriatic Sea *n* The **Adriatic Sea** is an arm of the Mediterranean between Italy and the Balkan Peninsula. ॲड्रिॲटिक समुद्र

adult (**adults**) *n* An **adult** is a mature, fully developed person. An adult has reached the age when they are legally responsible for their actions. प्रौढ

adult education *n* **Adult education** is education for adults in a variety of subjects, most of which are practical, not academic. Classes are often held in the evenings. प्रौढ शिक्षण

advance (**advances, advancing, advanced**) *n* An **advance** is money which is lent or paid to someone before they would normally receive it. आगाऊ रक्कम ▷ *vi* To **advance** means to move forward, often in order to attack someone. आगेकूच करणे

advanced *adj* An **advanced** system, method, or design is modern and has been developed from an earlier version of the same thing. प्रगत

advantage (**advantages**) *n* An **advantage** is something that puts you in a better position than other people. फायदा

advent *n* The **advent** of something is the fact of its starting or coming into existence. *(formal)* आगमन

adventure (adventures) n An **adventure** is a series of events that you become involved in that are unusual, exciting, and perhaps dangerous. साहसी कारनामे

adventurous adj An **adventurous** person is willing to take risks and eager to have new experiences. साहसी

adverb (adverbs) n In grammar, an **adverb** is a word such as 'slowly' or 'very' which adds information about time, place, or manner. क्रियाविशेषण

adversary (adversaries) n Your **adversary** is someone you are competing with or fighting against. विरोधक

advert (adverts) n An **advert** is an announcement in a newspaper, on television, or on a poster about something such as a product, event, or job. जाहिरात

advertise (advertises, advertising, advertised) v If you **advertise**, or **advertise** something such as a product, event, or job, you tell people about it in newspapers, on television, or on posters. जाहिरात देणे

advertisement (advertisements) n An **advertisement** is an announcement in a newspaper, on television, or on a poster that tells people about a product, event, or job vacancy. *(written)* जाहिरात

advertising n **Advertising** is the business activity of encouraging people to buy products, go to events, or apply for jobs. जाहिरातबाजी

advice n If you give someone **advice**, you tell them what you think they should do. सल्ला

advisable adj If you tell someone that it is **advisable** to do something, you are suggesting that they should do it. *(formal)* सल्ला देण्याजोगे

advise (advises, advising, advised) vt If you **advise** someone to do something, you tell them what you think they should do. सल्ला देणे

aerial (aerials) n An **aerial** is a piece of metal equipment that receives television or radio signals. एरिअल

aerobics npl **Aerobics** is a form of exercise which increases the amount of oxygen in your blood and strengthens your heart and lungs. ऐरोबिक्स

aerosol (aerosols) n An **aerosol** is a small container in which a liquid such as paint is kept under pressure. When you press a button, the liquid is forced out as a fine spray or foam. एअरसोल

affair (affairs) n You refer to an event as an **affair** when you are talking about it in a general way. प्रकरण

affect (affects, affecting, affected) vt When something **affects** someone or something, it influences them or causes them to change. परिणाम करणे/होणे

affectionate adj If you are **affectionate**, you show your fondness for another person in your behaviour. ममताळू

afford (affords, affording, afforded) vt If you cannot **afford** something, you do not have enough money to pay for it. परवडणे

affordable adj If something is **affordable**, people have enough money to buy it. परवडण्याजोगे

Afghan (Afghans) adj **Afghan** means belonging or relating to Afghanistan, or to its people or language. अफगाणी ▷ n An **Afghan** is a person from Afghanistan. अफगाणी

Afghanistan n **Afghanistan** is a republic in central Asia. अफगाणिस्तान

afraid adj If you are **afraid** of someone or **afraid** to do something, you are frightened because you think that something horrible is going to happen. भयभीत

Africa n **Africa** is the second largest of the continents. It is located to the south of Europe. आफ्रिका

African (Africans) adj **African** means belonging or relating to the continent of Africa. आफ्रिकन ▷ n An **African** is someone who comes from Africa. आफ्रिकन

Afrikaans n **Afrikaans** is one of the official languages of South Africa. आफ्रिकान्स

Afrikaner (Afrikaners) n An **Afrikaner** is one of the white people in South Africa whose ancestors were Dutch. आफ्रिकानर (डच वंशाची गोरी आफ्रिकन व्यक्ती)

after conj If something happens **after** another thing, it happens later than it. नंतर He arrived after I had left. ▷ prep If something happens **after** another thing, it happens later than it. नंतर I watched television after dinner. ▷ prep If you go **after** a person or thing, you follow them or chase them. पाठीमागे They ran after her.

afternoon (afternoons) n The **afternoon** is the part of each day which begins at 12 o'clock lunchtime and ends at about six o'clock. दुपार

afters npl **Afters** is a dessert or sweet. (informal) आफ्टर्स (जेवणानंतर खायचे पक्वान्न)

aftershave n **Aftershave** is a liquid with a pleasant smell that men sometimes put on their faces after shaving. आफ्टरशेव्ह (दाढी केल्यानंतर लावण्याचा सुगंधी पदार्थ)

afterwards adv If something is done or happens **afterwards**, it is done or happens later than a particular event or time that has already been described. त्यानंतर

again adv If something happens **again**, it happens another time. पुन्हा

against prep If something is **against** another thing, it is touching it. टेकून He leaned against the wall. ▷ prep If you play **against** someone in a game, you try to beat them. विरुद्ध The two teams played against one another.

age (ages) n Your **age** is the number of years that you have lived. वय

aged adj You use **aged** followed by a number to say how old someone is. वयाचा

age limit (age limits) n An **age limit** is the oldest or youngest age at which you are allowed under particular regulations to do something. वयोमर्यादा

agency (agencies) n An **agency** is a business which provides services for a person or another business. व्यावसायिक संस्था, एजन्सी

agenda (agendas) n An **agenda** is a list of items to be discussed at a meeting. विषयपत्रिका

agent (agents) n An **agent** is someone who arranges work or business for someone else. प्रतिनिधी, एजन्ट

aggressive adj An **aggressive** person behaves angrily or violently towards other people. आक्रमक

AGM (AGMs) abbr The **AGM** of a company or organization is a meeting which it holds once a year in order to discuss the previous year's activities and accounts. **AGM** is an abbreviation for 'Annual General Meeting'. वार्षिक सर्वसाधारण सभा

ago adv You use **ago** to talk about a time in the past. पूर्वी

agree (agrees, agreeing, agreed) v If you **agree** with someone, you have the same opinion about something. मान्य करणे

agreed adj If people are **agreed** on something, they have reached a joint decision on it or have the same opinion about it. मान्य असलेले

agreement (agreements) n An **agreement** is a decision that two or more people, groups, or countries have made together. करार

agricultural adj **Agricultural** means involving or relating to agriculture. शेतीविषयक

agriculture n **Agriculture** is farming and the methods used to look after crops and animals. शेती

ahead adv Someone who is **ahead** of another person is in front of them. पुढचा

aid n **Aid** is money, equipment, or services that are provided for people, countries, or organizations who need them but cannot provide them for themselves. सहाय्य

AIDS n **AIDS** is an illness which destroys the natural system of protection that the body has against disease. **AIDS** is an abbreviation for 'acquired immune deficiency syndrome'. एड्स्

aim (aims, aiming, aimed) n The **aim** of something that you do is the purpose for which you do it. उद्दिष्ट ▷ v If you **aim** for something or **aim** to do it, you plan or hope to achieve it. उद्दिष्ट ठेवणे

air n **Air** is the mixture of gases which forms the earth's atmosphere and which we breathe. हवा

airbag (**airbags**) n An **airbag** is a safety device in a car which automatically fills with air if the car crashes, and is designed to protect the people in the car when they are thrown forward in the crash. एयर बेग

air-conditioned adj If a room is **air-conditioned**, the air in it is kept cool and dry by means of a special machine. वातानुकूलित

air conditioning n **Air conditioning** is a method of providing buildings and vehicles with cool air. वातानुकूलन

aircraft (**aircraft**) n An **aircraft** is a vehicle which can fly, for example a plane or a helicopter. विमान

air force (**air forces**) n An **air force** is the part of a country's military organization that is concerned with fighting in the air. हवाई दल

air hostess (**air hostesses**) n An **air hostess** is a woman whose job is to look after passengers in an aircraft. (old-fashioned) हवाई सुंदरी

airline (**airlines**) n An **airline** is a company which provides regular services carrying people or goods in aeroplanes. एअरलाइन (विमानसेवा पुरविणारी कंपनी)

airmail n **Airmail** is the system of sending letters, parcels, and goods by air. हवाई टपाल

airport (**airports**) n An **airport** is a place where aircraft land and take off, usually with a lot of buildings and facilities. विमानतळ

airsick adj If you are **airsick**, you are sick or nauseated from travelling in an aircraft. विमान लागणारा

airspace n A country's **airspace** is the part of the sky that is over that country and is considered to belong to that country. हवाई हद्द

airtight adj If a container is **airtight**, its lid fits so tightly that no air can get in or out. हवाबंद

air traffic controller (**air traffic controllers**) n An **air traffic controller** is someone whose job is to organize the routes

that aircraft should follow, and to tell pilots by radio which routes they should take. हवाई वाहतूक नियंत्रक

aisle (**aisles**) n An **aisle** is a long narrow gap that people can walk along between rows of seats in a public building such as a church, or between rows of shelves in a supermarket. मोकळी मार्गिका

alarm n **Alarm** is a feeling of fear or anxiety that something unpleasant or dangerous might happen. भयसूचक भावना

alarm clock (**alarm clocks**) n An **alarm clock** is a clock that you can set to make a noise so that it wakes you up at a particular time. गजराचे घड्याळ

alarming adj Something that is **alarming** makes you feel afraid or anxious that something unpleasant or dangerous might happen. भयसूचक

Albania n **Albania** is a republic in south-east Europe, on the Balkan Peninsula. अल्बेनिया

Albanian (**Albanians**) adj **Albanian** means belonging or relating to Albania, its people, language, or culture. अल्बेनियन ▷ n An **Albanian** is a person who comes from Albania. अल्बेनियन ▷ n **Albanian** is the language spoken by people who live in Albania. अल्बेनियन

album (**albums**) n An **album** is a CD, record, or cassette with music on it. संग्रह

alcohol n Drinks that can make people drunk, such as beer, wine, and whisky, can be referred to as **alcohol**. मद्य

alcohol-free adj Beer or wine which is **alcohol-free** contains only a trace of alcohol. मद्यरहित

alcoholic (**alcoholics**) adj **Alcoholic** drinks contain alcohol. मद्ययुक्त ▷ n An **alcoholic** is someone who is addicted to alcohol. मद्यपी

alert (**alerts, alerting, alerted**) adj If you are **alert**, you are paying full attention to things around you and are ready to deal with anything that might happen. सावध ▷ vt If you **alert** someone to a situation, especially a dangerous or unpleasant situation, you tell them about it. सावध करणे

Algeria *n* **Algeria** is a republic in north-west Africa, on the Mediterranean. अल्जीरिया

Algerian (**Algerians**) *adj* **Algerian** means belonging or relating to Algeria, or its people or culture. अल्जेरियन ▷ *n* An **Algerian** is an Algerian citizen or a person of Algerian origin. अल्जेरियन

alias *prep* You use **alias** when you are mentioning another name that someone, especially a criminal or an actor, is known by. उर्फ *...the defendant Pericles Pericleous, alias Peter Smith.*

alibi (**alibis**) *n* If you have an **alibi**, you can prove that you were somewhere else when a crime was committed. अलिबाय् (गुन्हा घडताना एखादी व्यक्ती अन्यत्र उपस्थित होती असे सिद्ध करणारा पुरावा)

alien (**aliens**) *n* An **alien** is someone who is not a legal citizen of the country in which they live. *(formal)* परकीय

alive *adj* If people or animals are **alive**, they are living. जिवंत

all *det* You use **all** to talk about everything, everyone, or the whole of something. सर्व *Did you eat all of it?* ▷ *pron* You use **all** to talk about everything, everyone, or the whole of something. सर्व *We make our own hair-care products, all based on herbal recipes.*

Allah *n* **Allah** is the name of God in Islam. अल्ला

allegation (**allegations**) *n* An **allegation** is a statement saying that someone has done something wrong. आरोप

alleged *adj* An **alleged** fact has been stated but has not been proved to be true. *(formal)* संशयित

allergic *adj* If you are **allergic** to something, or have an **allergic** reaction to it, you become ill or get a rash when you eat it, smell it, or touch it. वावडे असलेला, ॲलर्जिक

allergy (**allergies**) *n* If you have a particular **allergy**, you become ill or get a rash when you eat, smell, or touch something that does not normally make people ill. वावडे, ॲलर्जी

alley (**alleys**) *n* An **alley** or **alleyway** is a narrow passage or street with buildings or walls on both sides. गल्ली

alliance (**alliances**) *n* An **alliance** is a group of countries or political parties that are formally united and working together because they have similar aims. युती

alligator (**alligators**) *n* An **alligator** is a large reptile with short legs, a long tail and very powerful jaws. मगर

allow (**allows**, **allowing**, **allowed**) *vt* If someone **is allowed** to do something, it is all right for them to do it. परवानगी देणे

all right *adv* If something goes **all right**, it happens in a satisfactory manner. *(informal)* ठीक ▷ *adj* If you say that something is **all right**, you mean that it is good enough. *(informal)* ठीक

ally (**allies**) *n* An **ally** is a country, organization, or person that helps and supports another. तहाने मित्र झालेला देश वा माणूस

almond (**almonds**) *n* An **almond** is a kind of pale oval nut. बदाम

almost *adv* **Almost** means very nearly. बहुतेक

alone *adj* When you are **alone**, you are not with any other people. एकटा

along *prep* If you walk **along** a road or other place, you move towards one end of it. बाजूने *We walked along the street.* ▷ *adv* If you bring something **along** when you go somewhere, you bring it with you. सोबत

aloud *adv* When you speak or read **aloud**, you speak so that other people can hear you. मोठ्याने

alphabet (**alphabets**) *n* The **alphabet** is the set of letters in a fixed order which is used for writing the words of a language. वर्णमाला

Alps *n* The **Alps** are a mountain range in south central Europe. आल्प्स्

already *adv* You use **already** to show that something has happened before the present time. अगोदरच

also *adv* You use **also** to give more information about something. सुद्धा

altar (altars) *n* An **altar** is a holy table in a church or temple. अल्तार

alter (alters, altering, altered) *v* If something **alters**, or if you **alter** it, it changes. फेरफार करणे

alternate *adj* **Alternate** actions, events, or processes regularly occur after each other. आलटून पालटून

alternative (alternatives) *adj* An **alternative** plan or offer is different from the one that you already have, and can be done or used instead. पर्यायी ▷ *n* If one thing is an **alternative** to another, the first can be found, used, or done instead of the second. पर्याय

alternatively *adv* You use **alternatively** to introduce a suggestion or to mention something different from what has just been stated. पर्यायाने

although *conj* You use **although** to add information that changes what you have already said. जरी *They all play basketball, although on different teams.* ▷ *conj* You use **although** to start talking about an idea that is not what you would expect. जरी *I can remember seeing it on TV, although I was only six.*

altitude (altitudes) *n* If something is at a particular **altitude**, it is at that height above sea level. समुद्रसपाटीपासूनची उंची

altogether *adv* If you say that different numbers of people or things add up to something **altogether**, you mean that you have counted all of them. एकंदरित

aluminium *n* **Aluminium** is a lightweight metal used for making things such as cooking equipment and aircraft parts. ॲल्युमिनिअम

always *adv* If you **always** do something, you do it every time or all the time. नेहमी

Alzheimer's disease *n* **Alzheimer's disease** is a condition in which a person's brain gradually stops working properly. अल्झायमर्स रोग

a.m. *abbr* **a.m.** after a number indicates that the number refers to a particular time between midnight and noon. मध्यान्ह्पूर्व

amateur (amateurs) *n* An **amateur** is someone who does a particular activity as a hobby, not as a job. हौशी

amaze (amazes, amazing, amazed) *vt* If something **amazes** you, it surprises you very much. विस्मयचकित करणे

amazed *adj* If you are **amazed**, you are very surprised. आश्चर्यचकित

amazing *adj* If something is **amazing**, it is very surprising and makes you feel pleasure or admiration. आश्चर्यकारक

ambassador (ambassadors) *n* An **ambassador** is an important official living in a foreign country who represents the government of his or her own country. राजदूत

amber *n* **Amber** is a hard yellowish-brown substance used for making jewellery. तैलस्फटिक

ambition (ambitions) *n* If you have an **ambition** to achieve something, you want very much to achieve it. महत्त्वाकांक्षा

ambitious *adj* Someone who is **ambitious** wants to be successful, rich, or powerful. महत्त्वाकांक्षी

ambulance (ambulances) *n* An **ambulance** is a vehicle for taking people to and from hospital. रुग्णवाहिका

amenities *npl* **Amenities** are things such as shopping centres or sports facilities that are for people's convenience or enjoyment. सुविधा

America *n* **America** is the American continent, including North, South, and Central America. अमेरिका

American (Americans) *adj* **American** means belonging or relating to the United States of

America, or to its people or culture. अमेरिकन

▷ *n* An **American** is a person who comes from the United States of America. अमेरिकन

American football *n* **American football** is a game similar to rugby that is played by two teams of eleven players using an oval-shaped ball. अमेरिकन फूटबॉल

among *prep* Someone or something that is **among** a group of things or people has them around them. -च्या समवेत, -च्या मध्यभागी *There were children sitting among adults.*

▷ *prep* If something happens **among** a group of people, it happens in that group. समवेत, मधे समाविष्ट *Discuss it among yourselves.*

amount (amounts) *n* An **amount** of something is how much of it you have, need, or get. रक्कम

amp (amps) *n* An **amp** is a unit which is used for measuring electric current. ऍम्पिअर

amplifier (amplifiers) *n* An **amplifier** is an electronic device in a radio or stereo system, which causes sounds or signals to become louder. प्रवर्धी/ऍम्प्लिफायर

amuse (amuses, amusing, amused) *vt* If something **amuses** you, it makes you want to laugh or smile. करमणूक करणे

amusement arcade (amusement arcades) *n* An **amusement arcade** is a place where you can play games on machines which work when you put money in them. करमणुकीची जागा

an *det* **An** means the same as a, but you use an before words that begin with the sound of a, e, i, o, or **u**. इंग्रजीतील एक अनिश्चिततादर्शी उपपद *He started eating an apple.*

anaemic *adj* Someone who is **anaemic** suffers from a medical condition in which there are too few red cells in their blood, making them feel tired and look pale. रक्तक्षयी

anaesthetic (anaesthetics) *n* **Anaesthetic** is a substance used to stop you feeling pain during an operation. संवेदना वा शुद्ध हरवणारा पदार्थ

analyse (analyses, analysing, analysed) *vt* If you **analyse** something, you consider it or examine it in order to understand it or to find out what it consists of. विश्लेषण करणे

analysis (analyses) *n* **Analysis** is the process of considering something or examining it in order to understand it or to find out what it consists of. विश्लेषण

ancestor (ancestors) *n* Your **ancestors** are the people from whom you are descended. पूर्वज

anchor (anchors) *n* An **anchor** is a heavy hooked object at the end of a chain that is dropped from a boat into the water to make the boat stay in one place. जहाजाचा नांगर

anchovy (anchovies) *n* **Anchovies** are small fish that live in the sea. They are often eaten salted. अँकोही नावाचा मासा

ancient *adj* **Ancient** means very old, or having existed for a long time. प्राचीन

and *conj* You use **and** to join two or more words or ideas. आणि *She and her husband have already gone.*

Andes *n* The **Andes** are a major mountain system of South America. अँडीज

Andorra *n* **Andorra** is a small, mountainous country in south-west Europe, between France and Spain. अँडोरा

angel (angels) *n* **Angels** are spiritual beings that some people believe are God's messengers and servants in heaven. देवदूत

anger *n* **Anger** is the strong emotion that you feel when you think someone has behaved in an unfair, cruel, or unacceptable way. क्रोध

angina *n* **Angina** is severe pain in the chest and left arm, caused by heart disease. अँजायना

angle (angles) *n* An **angle** is the difference in direction between two lines or surfaces. Angles are measured in degrees. कोन

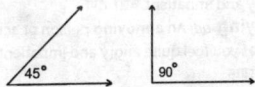

angler (anglers) *n* An **angler** is someone who fishes with a fishing rod as a hobby. गळ टाकून मासे पकडणारी व्यक्ती

angling n **Angling** is the activity of fishing with a fishing rod. मासे पकडण्यासाठी गळ टाकणे

Angola n **Angola** is a republic in south-west Africa, on the Atlantic. अँगोला

Angolan (**Angolans**) adj **Angolan** means belonging or relating to Angola or its people. अँगोलन ▷ n An **Angolan** is someone who comes from Angola. अँगोलन

angry (**angrier, angriest**) adj When you are **angry**, you feel strong emotion about something that you consider unfair, cruel, or insulting. क्रोधित

animal (**animals**) n Any living creature other than a human being can be referred to as an **animal**. प्राणी

aniseed n **Aniseed** is a substance made from the seeds of the anise plant. It is used as a flavouring in sweets, drinks, and medicine. बडीशेपपासून बनवलेला पदार्थ

ankle (**ankles**) n Your **ankle** is the joint where your foot joins your leg. घोटा

anniversary (**anniversaries**) n An **anniversary** is a date which is remembered or celebrated because a special event happened on that date in a previous year. वर्धापन दिन

announce (**announces, announcing, announced**) vt If you **announce** something, you tell people about it publicly or officially. जाहीर करणे

announcement (**announcements**) n An **announcement** is a public statement which gives information about something that has happened or that will happen. घोषणा

annoy (**annoys, annoying, annoyed**) vt If someone **annoys** you, they make you quite angry and impatient. त्रास देणे

annoying adj An **annoying** person or action makes you feel quite angry and impatient. तापदायक

annual adj **Annual** means happening or done once every year. वार्षिक

annually adv If something happens **annually**, it happens once every year. दरवर्षी

anonymous adj If you remain **anonymous** when you do something, you do not let people know that you were the person who did it. अनामिक

anorak (**anoraks**) n An **anorak** is a warm waterproof jacket, usually with a hood. अनोरॅक(डोके झाकण्याची सोय असलेला अंगरखा)

anorexia n **Anorexia** or **anorexia nervosa** is an illness in which a person refuses to eat enough because they have a fear of becoming fat. भूक न लागणे

anorexic adj If someone is **anorexic**, they are suffering from anorexia and so are very thin. भूक न लागणारा

another det You use **another** to mean one more. दुसरा She ate another cake.

answer (**answers, answering, answered**) n An **answer** is something that you say or write when you answer someone. उत्तर ▷ v When you **answer** someone who has asked you something, you say something back to them. उत्तर देणे

answering machine (**answering machines**) n An **answering machine** is a device which records telephone messages while you are out. उत्तर देणारे यंत्र

answerphone (**answerphones**) n An **answerphone** is a device which you connect to your telephone and which records telephone calls while you are out. संभाषण नोंदवून ठेवणारा दूरध्वनी

ant (**ants**) n **Ants** are small crawling insects that live in large groups. मुंगी

antagonize (**antagonizes, antagonizing, antagonized**) vt If you **antagonize** someone, you make them feel hostile towards you. वैर उत्पन्न करणे

Antarctic n The **Antarctic** is the area around the South Pole. अंटार्क्टिक

Antarctica n **Antarctica** is a continent around the South Pole. It is extremely cold and there is very little light in winter and very little darkness in summer. अंटार्क्टिका

antelope (**antelopes, antelope**) *n* An **antelope** is an animal like a deer, with long legs and horns, that lives in Africa or Asia. Antelopes are graceful and can run fast. काळवीट

antenatal *adj* **Antenatal** means relating to the medical care of women when they are expecting a baby. प्रसूतिपूर्व

anthem (**anthems**) *n* An **anthem** is a song or hymn written for a special occasion. स्तुतिगीत

anthropology *n* **Anthropology** is the study of people, society, and culture. मानववंशशास्त्र

antibiotic (**antibiotics**) *n* **Antibiotics** are drugs that are used in medicine to kill bacteria and to cure infections. प्रतिजैविक

antibody (**antibodies**) *n* **Antibodies** are substances which your body produces in order to fight diseases. प्रतिपिंड

anticlockwise *adv* If something is moving **anticlockwise**, it is moving in the opposite direction to the direction in which the hands of a clock move. अपसव्य

antidepressant (**antidepressants**) *n* An **antidepressant** is a drug which is used to treat people who are suffering from depression. नैराश्य दूर करणारे औषध

antidote (**antidotes**) *n* An **antidote** is a chemical substance that controls the effect of a poison. विषबाधेवरील उतारा

antifreeze *n* **Antifreeze** is a liquid which is added to water to stop it freezing. It is used in car radiators in cold weather. गोठनरोधी

antihistamine (**antihistamines**) *n* An **antihistamine** is a drug that is used to treat allergies. वावडेरोधी औषध, ॲंटिहिस्टमीन

antiperspirant (**antiperspirants**) *n* An **antiperspirant** is a substance that you put on your skin to stop you from sweating. घर्मरोधी

antique (**antiques**) *n* An **antique** is an old object which is valuable because of its beauty or rarity. मौल्यवान पुराण वस्तू

antique shop (**antique shops**) *n* An **antique shop** is a shop where antiques are sold. मौल्यवान पुराण वस्तू विकणारे दुकान

antiseptic (**antiseptics**) *n* **Antiseptic** kills harmful bacteria. जंतुनाशक

anxiety (**anxieties**) *n* **Anxiety** is a feeling of nervousness or worry. चिंता

any *det* You use **any** to mean some of a thing. काही *Is there any juice left?* ▷ *pron* **Any** is used in negative sentences to show that no person or thing is involved. कोणताही नाही *The children needed new clothes and we couldn't afford any.* ▷ *det* You use **any** to show that it does not matter which one. कोणताही *Take any book you want.*

anybody *pron* You use **anybody** to talk about a person, when it does not matter which one. कोणी *Is there anybody there?*

anyhow *adv* You use **anyhow** to give the idea that something is true even though other things have been said. कसेही

anymore *adv* If something does not happen or is not true **anymore**, it has stopped happening or is no longer true. अस्तित्वात नसणे

anyone *pron* You use **anyone** to talk about a person, when it does not matter who. कोणालाही *Don't tell anyone.*

anything *pron* You use **anything** to talk about a thing, when it does not matter which one. काहीही *I can't see anything.*

anytime *adv* You use **anytime** to mean a point in time that is not fixed. कोणत्याही वेळी

anyway *adv* You use **anyway** or **anyhow** to give the idea that something is true even though other things have been said. नाहीतरी

anywhere *adv* You use **anywhere** to talk about a place, when it does not matter which one. कोठेही

apart *adv* When things are **apart**, there is a space or a distance between them. दूर ▷ *adv* If you take something **apart**, you take it to pieces. तुकड्यांमध्ये विभागणे

apart from *prep* You use **apart from** when you are giving an exception to a general statement. शिवाय *The room was empty apart from one man sitting beside the fire.*

apartment (apartments) n An **apartment** is a set of rooms for living in, usually on one floor of a large building. बहुमजली घर, अपार्टमेंट

aperitif (aperitifs) n An **aperitif** is an alcoholic drink that you have before a meal. अपारिटिफ(भूकवर्धक मयमिश्रित पेय)

aperture (apertures) n An **aperture** is a narrow hole or gap. *(formal)* छोटे छिद्र

apologize (apologizes, apologizing, apologized) vi When you **apologize** to someone, you say that you are sorry that you have hurt them or caused trouble for them. क्षमा मागणे

apology (apologies) n An **apology** is something that you say or write in order to tell someone that you are sorry that you have hurt them or caused trouble for them. क्षमा, माफी

apostrophe (apostrophes) n An **apostrophe** is the mark (') that shows that one or more letters have been removed from a word, as in 'isn't'. It is also added to nouns to show possession, as in 'the girl's doll'. अपोस्ट्रफि

appalling adj Something that is **appalling** is so bad that it shocks you. भीषण

apparatus (apparatuses) n The **apparatus** of an organization or system is its structure and method of operation. उपकरण

apparent adj An **apparent** situation seems to be the case, although you cannot be certain that it is. स्पष्ट, उघड

apparently adv You use **apparently** to refer to something that seems to be the case although it may not be. स्पष्टपणे उघडपणे

appeal (appeals, appealing, appealed) n An **appeal** is a serious and urgent request. आवाहन ▷ vi If you **appeal** to someone to do something, you make a serious and urgent request to them. आवाहन करणे

appear (appears, appearing, appeared) vt If something **appears** to be the way you describe it, it seems that way. दिसणे

appearance (appearances) n When someone makes an **appearance** at a public

event or in a broadcast, they take part in it. उपस्थिती

appendicitis n **Appendicitis** is an illness in which a person's appendix is infected and painful. आंत्रपुच्छाचा रोग

appetite (appetites) n Your **appetite** is your desire to eat. भूक

applaud (applauds, applauding, applauded) v When a group of people **applaud** or applaud someone, they clap their hands to show that they have enjoyed a performance. टाळ्या वाजवणे

applause n **Applause** is the noise made by a group of people clapping their hands to show approval. टाळ्यांचा गजर

apple (apples) n An **apple** is a round fruit with a smooth skin and firm white flesh. सफरचंद

apple pie (apple pies) n An **apple pie** is a kind of pie made with apples. ऐपल् पाय् (सफरचंदापासून बनवलेले पक्वान्न)

appliance (appliances) n An **appliance** is a device such as a vacuum cleaner that does a particular job in your home. *(formal)* उपकरण

applicant (applicants) n An **applicant** for a job or position is someone who applies for it. अर्जदार

application (applications) n An **application** for something such as a job or a place at a college is a formal written request to be given it. अर्ज

application form (application forms) n An **application form** is a formal written request for something such as a job or membership of an organization. अर्जाचा नमुना

apply (applies, applying, applied) v If you **apply** for something or to something, you ask to be allowed to have it or do it. अर्ज करणे

appoint (appoints, appointing, appointed) vt If you **appoint** someone to a job or post, you formally choose them for it. नेमणूक करणे

appointment (appointments) n The **appointment** of a person to a particular job is the choice of that person to do it. नेमणूक

appreciate (appreciates, appreciating, appreciated) vt If you **appreciate** something, you like it because you recognize its good qualities. प्रशंसा करणे

apprehensive adj Someone who is **apprehensive** is afraid that something bad may happen. भयभीत

apprentice (apprentices) n An **apprentice** is a person who works with someone in order to learn their skill. शिकाऊ

approach (approaches, approaching, approached) v When you **approach** something, you get closer to it. जवळ जाणे

appropriate adj Something that is **appropriate** is suitable or acceptable for a particular situation. योग्य

approval n If a plan or request gets someone's **approval**, they agree to it. संमती

approve (approves, approving, approved) vi If you **approve** of something or someone, you like them or think they are good. संमती देणे

approximate adj **Approximate** figures are close to the correct figure, but are not exact. अंदाजित, जवळजवळ

approximately adv **Approximately** means close to, around, or roughly. अंदाजे

apricot (apricots) n An **apricot** is a small, soft, round fruit with yellow-orange flesh and a stone inside. जर्दाळू

April (Aprils) n **April** is the fourth month of the year in the Western calendar. एप्रिल

April Fools' Day n In the West, **April Fools' Day** is the 1st of April, the day on which people traditionally play tricks on each other. एप्रिल फूलचा दिवस

apron (aprons) n An **apron** is a piece of clothing that you put on over the front of your clothes to prevent them from getting dirty. ऍप्रन

aquarium (aquariums, aquaria) n An **aquarium** is a building, often in a zoo, where fish and underwater animals are kept. मत्स्यालय

Aquarius n **Aquarius** is one of the twelve signs of the zodiac. Its symbol is a person pouring water. People who are born between 20th January and 18th February come under this sign. कुंभ रास

Arab (Arabs) adj **Arab** means belonging or relating to Arabs or to their countries or customs. अरब ▷ n **Arabs** are people who speak Arabic and who come from the Middle East and parts of North Africa. अरब

Arabic n **Arabic** is a language that is spoken in the Middle East and in parts of North Africa. अरबी ▷ adj Something that is **Arabic** belongs or relates to the language, writing, or culture of the Arabs. अरबी

arbitration n **Arbitration** is the judging of a dispute between people or groups by someone who is not involved. मध्यस्थी

arch (arches) n An **arch** is a structure which is made when two columns join at the top in a curve. कमान

archaeologist (archaeologists) n An **archaeologist** is a person who studies the past by examining the remains of things such as buildings and tools. पुरातत्व शास्त्रज्ञ

archaeology n **Archaeology** is the study of the past by examining the remains of things such as buildings and tools. पुरातत्व शास्त्र

architect (architects) n An **architect** is a person who designs buildings. स्थापत्य शास्त्रज्ञ

architecture n **Architecture** is the art of designing and constructing buildings. स्थापत्य शास्त्र

archive (archives) n **Archives** are collections of documents that contain information about the history of an organization or group of people. पुराभिलेख

Arctic n The **Arctic** is the area of the world around the North Pole. It is extremely cold and there is very little light in winter and very little darkness in summer. आर्क्टिक

Arctic Circle n The **Arctic Circle** is an imaginary line drawn around the northern part of the world at approximately 66° North. आर्क्टिक वर्तूळ

Arctic Ocean n The **Arctic Ocean** is the ocean surrounding the North Pole, north of the Arctic Circle. आर्क्टिक महासमुद्र

area (areas) n An **area** is a particular part of a city, a country, or the world. क्षेत्र

Argentina n **Argentina** is a republic in southern South America. अर्जेंटिना

Argentinian (Argentinians) adj **Argentinian** means belonging or relating to Argentina or its people. अर्जेंटिनियन ▷ n An **Argentinian** is someone who comes from Argentina. अर्जेंटिनियन

argue (argues, arguing, argued) vi If you **argue** with someone, you disagree with them about something, often angrily. वाद घालणे

argument (arguments) n If people have an **argument**, they disagree with each other, often angrily. वादविवाद

Aries n **Aries** is one of the twelve signs of the zodiac. Its symbol is a ram. People who are born between 21st March and 19th April come under this sign. मेष रास

arm (arms) n Your **arms** are the two parts of your body between your shoulders and your hands. बाहू

armchair (armchairs) n An **armchair** is a comfortable chair with a support on each side for your arms. आरामखुर्ची

armed adj Someone who is **armed** is carrying a weapon. सशस्त्र

Armenia n **Armenia** is a republic in north-west Asia. आर्मेनिया

Armenian (Armenians) adj **Armenian** means of or relating to Armenia, its inhabitants, their language, or the Armenian Church. आर्मेनियन ▷ n An **Armenian** is a native or inhabitant of Armenia or an Armenian-speaking person elsewhere. आर्मेनियन ▷ n **Armenian** is the language spoken by people who live in Armenia. आर्मेनियन

armour n In former times, **armour** was special metal clothing that soldiers wore for protection in battle. चिलखत

armpit (armpits) n Your **armpits** are the areas of your body under your arms where your arms join your shoulders. काख

army (armies) n An **army** is a large organized group of people who are armed and trained to fight. सैन्यदल

aroma (aromas) n An **aroma** is a strong pleasant smell. सुगंध

aromatherapy n **Aromatherapy** is a type of treatment which involves massaging the body with special fragrant oils. सुगंधोपचार

around adv **Around** means surrounding, or on all sides of. सभोवती ▷ prep Things or people that are **around** a place or object surround it or are on all sides of it. भोवताली There were lots of people around her. ▷ prep You use **around** to say that something is in every part of a place. सगळीकडे His toys lay around the room. ▷ prep **Around** means near to something. जवळपास We left around noon.

arrange (arranges, arranging, arranged) v If you **arrange** something, you make plans for it to happen. आयोजित करणे ▷ vt If you **arrange** things somewhere, you put them in a way that looks tidy or pretty. व्यवस्थित लावणे

arrangement (arrangements) n **Arrangements** are plans and preparations which you make so that something can happen. व्यवस्था

arrears npl **Arrears** are amounts of money that someone owes. If someone is **in arrears** with regular payments, they have not paid them. थकबाकी

arrest (arrests, arresting, arrested) n An **arrest** is the act of taking a person into custody, especially under lawful authority. अटक ▷ vt If the police **arrest** you, they take charge of you and take you to a police station, because they think you may have committed a crime. अटक करणे

arrival (arrivals) n Your **arrival** at a place is the act of arriving there. आगमन

arrive (arrives, arriving, arrived) vi When you **arrive** at a place, you reach it at the end of a journey. आगमन होणे

arrogant adj If you say that someone is **arrogant**, you disapprove of them because they behave as if they are better than other people. उद्धट

arrow (arrows) n An **arrow** is a long, thin stick with a sharp point at one end. बाण ▷ An **arrow** is a sign that shows you which way to go. बाणाचे चिन्ह

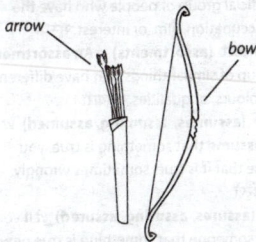

arrow

bow

arson n **Arson** is the crime of deliberately setting fire to a building or vehicle. जाळपोळ

art n **Art** is paintings, drawings, and sculpture which are beautiful or which express an artist's ideas. कला

artery (arteries) n Your **arteries** are the tubes that carry blood from your heart to the rest of your body. धमनी

art gallery (art galleries) n An **art gallery** is a building where paintings and other works of art are shown to the public. कला दालन

arthritis n **Arthritis** is a condition in which the joints in someone's body are swollen and painful. सांधेदुखी

artichoke (artichokes) n An **artichoke** or a **globe artichoke** is a round vegetable with thick green leaves arranged like the petals of a flower. आर्टिचोक

article (articles) n An **article** is a piece of writing in a newspaper or magazine. लेख

artificial adj **Artificial** objects, materials, or situations do not occur naturally and are created by people. कृत्रिम

artist (artists) n An **artist** is someone who draws, paints, or produces other works of art. कलाकार

artistic adj Someone who is **artistic** is good at drawing or painting, or arranging things in a beautiful way. कलात्मक

art school (art schools) n An **art school** is a college that specializes in art. कला महाविद्यालय

as conj If one thing happens **as** a different thing happens, it happens at the same time. जसे, जेव्हा, ज्यावेळी We shut the door behind us as we entered. ▷ prep You use **as** when you are talking about somebody's job. प्रमाणे, म्हणून He works as a doctor.

asap abbr **Asap** is an abbreviation for 'as soon as possible'. शक्य तेवढया लवकर

as ... as adv You use the structure **as ... as** when you are comparing things, or emphasizing how large or small something is. एवढे

ashamed adj If someone is **ashamed** of something or someone, they feel embarrassed about it or guilty because of it. लज्जित

ashtray (ashtrays) n An **ashtray** is a small dish in which people put the ash from their cigarettes and cigars. राखपात्र

Ash Wednesday n **Ash Wednesday** is the first day of Lent. ऐश वेनस्डे

Asia n **Asia** is the largest of the continents, bordering on the Arctic Ocean, the Pacific Ocean, the Indian Ocean, and the Mediterranean and Red Seas in the west. आशिया

Asian (Asians) adj **Asian** means belonging or relating to Asia. आशियन ▷ n An **Asian** is a person who comes from a country or region in Asia. आशिशन

aside adv If you move something **aside**, you move it to one side of you. बाजूला

ask (asks, asking, asked) vt If you **ask** someone a question, you say that you want to know something. विचारणे

ask for (asks for, asking for, asked for) v If you **ask for** something, you say that you want it. हवे असणे, मागणे *She asked for some sweets.*

asleep adj Someone who is **asleep** is sleeping. झोपलेला

asparagus n **Asparagus** is a vegetable with green shoots that you cook and eat. मुसळी नावाची वनस्पती

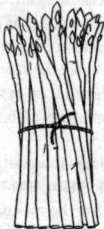

aspect (aspects) n An **aspect** of something is one of the parts of its character or nature. पैलू

aspirin (aspirins, aspirin) n **Aspirin** is a mild drug which reduces pain and fever. ऍस्पिरीन

assembly (assemblies) n An **assembly** is a group of people gathered together for a particular purpose. जमाव

asset (assets) n If something that you have is an **asset**, it is useful to you. मालमत्ता

assignment (assignments) n An **assignment** is a piece of work that you are given to do, as part of your job or studies. ठरावीक कामगिरी

assistance n If you give someone **assistance**, you help them. मदत

assistant (assistants) n Someone's **assistant** is a person who helps them in their work. सहायक

associate (associates) adj **Associate** is used before a rank or title to indicate a slightly different or lower rank or title. कनिष्ठ सहयोगी ▷ n Your **associates** are your business colleagues. भागीदार, सहकारी

association (associations) n An **association** is an official group of people who have the same occupation, aim, or interest. संस्था

assortment (assortments) n An **assortment** is a group of similar things that have different sizes, colours, or qualities. प्रतवारी

assume (assumes, assuming, assumed) vt If you **assume** that something is true, you suppose that it is true, sometimes wrongly. गृहीत धरणे

assure (assures, assuring, assured) vt If you **assure** someone that something is true or will happen, you tell them that it is the case, to make them less worried. खात्री देणे

asthma n **Asthma** is an illness which affects the chest and makes breathing difficult. दमा

astonish (astonishes, astonishing, astonished) vt If someone or something **astonishes** you, they surprise you very much. चकित करणे

astonished adj If you are **astonished** by something, you are very surprised about it. चकित झालेला

astonishing adj Something that is **astonishing** is very surprising. चकित करणारे

astrology n **Astrology** is the study of the movements of the planets, sun, moon, and stars in the belief that they can influence people's lives. ज्योतिषशास्त्र

astronaut (**astronauts**) n An **astronaut** is a person who travels in a spacecraft. अंतराळयात्री

astronomy n **Astronomy** is the scientific study of the stars, planets, and other natural objects in space. खगोलशास्त्र

asylum n If a government gives a person from another country **asylum**, they allow them to stay, usually because they are unable to return home safely for political reasons. राजाश्रय

asylum seeker (**asylum seekers**) n An **asylum seeker** is a person who is trying to get asylum in a foreign country. राजाश्रय मिळवू इच्छिणारी व्यक्ती

at prep You use **at** to say where or when something happens or where it is. -ला, -कडे, -वर, -ने I'll meet you at the information desk at seven o'clock.

atheist (**atheists**) n An **atheist** is a person who believes that there is no God. नास्तिक

athlete (**athletes**) n An **athlete** is a person who takes part in athletics competitions. कसरतपटू

athletic adj **Athletic** means relating to athletes and athletics. कसरत करणारा

athletics npl **Athletics** consists of sports such as running, the high jump, and the javelin. कसरतीचे खेळ

Atlantic Ocean n The **Atlantic Ocean** is the second largest ocean in the world. अटलांटिक महासमुद्र

atlas (**atlases**) n An **atlas** is a book of maps. नकाशापुस्तिका

at least adv **At least** means not less than. कमीत कमी

atmosphere (**atmospheres**) n A planet's **atmosphere** is the layer of air or other gas around it. वातावरण

atom (**atoms**) n An **atom** is the smallest possible amount of a chemical element. अणू

atom bomb (**atom bombs**) n An **atom bomb** is a bomb that causes an explosion by a sudden release of energy that results from splitting atoms. अणुबॉंब

atomic adj **Atomic** means relating to atoms or to the power produced by splitting atoms. अणुसंबंधी

attach (**attaches, attaching, attached**) vt If you **attach** something to an object, you join it or fasten it to the object. चिकटवणे, जोडणे

attached adj If you are **attached** to someone or something, you care deeply about them. लळा असलेला

attachment (**attachments**) n An **attachment** to someone or something is a love or liking for them. लळा

attack (**attacks, attacking, attacked**) n An **attack** is the act or an instance of attacking. हल्ला ▷ v To **attack** a person or place means to try to hurt or damage them using physical violence. हल्ला करणे

attempt (**attempts, attempting, attempted**) n If you make an **attempt** to do something, you try to do it, often without success. प्रयत्न ▷ vt If you **attempt** to do something, especially something difficult, you try to do it. प्रयत्न करणे

attend (**attends, attending, attended**) v If you **attend** a meeting or other event, you are at it. उपस्थित राहणे

attendance n Someone's **attendance** at an event or an institution is the fact that they are present at the event or go regularly to the institution. उपस्थिती

attention n If something has your **attention** or if you are paying **attention** to it, you have noticed it and are interested in it. लक्ष

attic (attics) n An **attic** is a room at the top of a house, just below the roof. पोटमाळा

attitude (attitudes) n Your **attitude** to something is the way you think and feel about it. दृष्टिकोन

attract (attracts, attracting, attracted) vt If something **attracts** people or animals, it has features that cause them to come to it. आकर्षित करणे

attraction (attractions) n **Attraction** is a feeling of liking someone. आकर्षण

attractive adj An **attractive** person or thing is pleasant to look at. आकर्षक

aubergine (aubergines) n An **aubergine** is a vegetable with a smooth purple skin. ओबर्जिन

auburn adj **Auburn** hair is reddish brown. तपकिरी केस

auction (auctions) n An **auction** is a sale where goods are sold to the person who offers the highest price. लिलाव

audience (audiences) n The **audience** is all the people who are watching or listening to a play, concert, film, or programme. श्रोते वा प्रेक्षक

audit (audits, auditing, audited) n An **audit** is an inspection, correction, and verification of business accounts, conducted by an independent qualified accountant. हिशेबतपासणी ▷ vt When an accountant **audits** an organization's accounts, he or she examines the accounts officially in order to make sure that they have been done correctly. हिशेबतपासणी करणे

audition (auditions) n An **audition** is a short performance given by an actor, dancer, or musician so that someone can decide if they are good enough to be in a play, film, or orchestra. स्वरचाचणी

auditor (auditors) n An **auditor** is an accountant who officially examines the accounts of organizations. हिशेबतपासनीस

August (Augusts) n **August** is the eighth month of the year in the Western calendar. ऑगस्ट

aunt (aunts) n Your **aunt** is the sister of your mother or father, or the wife of your uncle. मावशी, आत्या, चुलती

auntie (aunties) n Someone's **auntie** is the sister of their mother or father, or the wife of their uncle. (informal) मावशी, आत्या, काकू, मामी

au pair (au pairs) n An **au pair** is a young person who lives with a family in a foreign country in order to learn their language and help around the house. अव् पेर (एखाद्या कुटुंबात राहून त्यांची भाषा शिकणारी व त्यांच्या घरकामात मदत करणारी तरुण व्यक्ती)

austerity n **Austerity** is a situation in which people's living standards are reduced because of economic difficulties. दयनीयता, साधेपणा

Australasia n **Australasia** is Australia, New Zealand, and neighbouring islands in the South Pacific Ocean. ऑस्ट्रेलेशिया

Australia n **Australia** is a country located between the Indian Ocean and the Pacific. ऑस्ट्रेलिया

Australian (Australians) adj **Australian** means belonging or relating to Australia, or to its people or culture. ऑस्ट्रेलियन ▷ n An **Australian** is someone who comes from Australia. ऑस्ट्रेलियन

Austria n **Austria** is a republic in central Europe. ऑस्ट्रिया

Austrian (Austrians) adj **Austrian** means belonging or relating to Austria, or to its people or culture. ऑस्ट्रियन ▷ n An **Austrian** is a person who comes from Austria. ऑस्ट्रियन

authentic adj If something is **authentic**, it is genuine or accurate. अस्सल

author (authors) n The **author** of a piece of writing is the person who wrote it. लेखक

authorize (authorizes, authorizing, authorized) vt If someone **authorizes** something, they give their official permission for it to happen. अधिकृत परवानगी देणे

autobiography (**autobiographies**) *n* Your **autobiography** is an account of your life, which you write yourself. आत्मचरित्र

autograph (**autographs**) *n* An **autograph** is the signature of someone famous which is specially written for a fan to keep. सही, स्वाक्षरी

automatic *adj* An **automatic** machine or device is one which has controls that enable it to perform a task without needing to be constantly operated by a person. स्वयंचलित

automatically *adv* If you do something **automatically**, you do it without thinking about it. आपोआप

autonomous *adj* An **autonomous** country, organization, or group governs or controls itself rather than being controlled by anyone else. स्वायत

autonomy *n* If a country, person, or group has **autonomy**, they control themselves rather than being controlled by others. स्वायतता

autumn (**autumns**) *n* **Autumn** is the season between summer and winter. ऑटम

availability *n* The **availability** of something is the ease with which you can find it or obtain it. उपलब्धता

available *adj* If something is **available**, you can use it or obtain it. उपलब्ध

avalanche (**avalanches**) *n* An **avalanche** is a large mass of snow or rock that falls down the side of a mountain. डोंगरावरून कोसळणारा बर्फाचा कडा

avenue (**avenues**) *n* An **avenue** is a wide road, with shops or houses on each side. ऐव्हेन्यू (वृक्षाच्छादित व दोन्ही बाजूला इमारती असलेला रुंद रस्ता)

average (**averages**) *adj* If you describe a figure as **average**, you mean that it represents a numerical average. सरासरी ▷ *n* An **average** is the result that you get when you add two or more numbers together and divide the total by the number of numbers you added together. सरासरी

avocado (**avocados**) *n* An **avocado** is a fruit in the shape of a pear with a dark green skin and a large stone inside it. ऐव्हेकेंडो

avoid (**avoids, avoiding, avoided**) *vt* If you **avoid** something unpleasant that might happen, you take action in order to prevent it from happening. टाळणे

awake (**awakes, awaking, awoke, awoken**) *adj* If you are **awake**, you are not sleeping. जागे ▷ *v* When you **awake**, or when something **awakes** you, you wake up. (*literary*) जागे राहणे

award (**awards**) *n* An **award** is a prize or certificate you get for doing something well. पारितोषिक

aware *adj* If you are **aware** of a fact or situation, you know about it. जाणीव असलेले

away *adv* If someone moves **away** from a place, they move so that they are not there anymore. दूरवर ▷ *adv* If you put something **away**, you put it where it should be. जागेवर

away match (**away matches**) *n* When a sports team plays an **away match**, it plays on its opponents' ground. विरुद्ध संघाच्या मैदानावरचा सामना

awful *adj* If you say that someone or something is **awful**, you dislike that person or thing or you think that they are not very good. भयानक, वाईट

awfully *adv* You use **awfully** to emphasize how much of a quality someone or something has. अत्यंत

awkward *adj* An **awkward** situation is embarrassing and difficult to deal with. गैरसोयीचा

axe (**axes**) *n* An **axe** is a tool used for chopping wood. It consists of a blade attached to the end of a long handle. कुन्हाड

axle (**axles**) *n* An **axle** is a rod connecting a pair of wheels on a car or other vehicle. आस

Azerbaijan *n* **Azerbaijan** is a republic in north-west Asia. अझरबैजान

Azerbaijani (**Azerbaijanis**) *adj* **Azerbaijani** means belonging or relating to Azerbaijan. अझरबैजानी ▷ *n* An **Azerbaijani** is a native or inhabitant of Azerbaijan. अझरबैजानी

b

BA (BAs) *abbr* A **BA** is a first degree in an arts or social science subject. **BA** is an abbreviation for 'Bachelor of Arts'. बी. ए., कलाशाखेचा पदवीधर

baby (babies) *n* A **baby** is a very young child that cannot yet walk or talk. बालक

baby milk *n* Baby milk is a powder which you mix with water to make artificial milk for babies. दूधपावडर

baby's bottle (babies' bottles) *n* A **baby's bottle** is a drinking container used by babies. It has a special rubber part at the top through which they can suck their drink. लहान मुलांची बाटली

babysit (babysits, babysitting, babysat) *v* If you **babysit** for someone or **babysit** their children, you look after their children while they are out. पाळणाघर चालवणे

babysitter (babysitters) *n* A **babysitter** is a person who looks after someone's children while they are out. पाळणाघर चालवणारी व्यक्ती

babysitting *n* Babysitting is the action of looking after someone's children while they are out. पाळणाघर

baby wipe (baby wipes) *n* A **baby wipe** is a disposable moistened medicated paper towel, usually supplied in a plastic drum or packet, used for cleaning babies. लहान मुलांचा कागदी टॉवेल

bachelor (bachelors) *n* A **bachelor** is a man who has never married. अविवाहित

back (backs, backing, backed) *n* Back is used to refer to the part of something that is farthest from the front. मागील ▷ *n* Your **back**

is the part of your body from your neck to your bottom. पाठ ▷ *adv* If you move **back**, you move away from the way you are facing. मागे ▷ *vi* If a building **backs** onto something, the back of it faces that thing. पाठमोरी ▷ *n* The **back** of something is the side or part of it that is farthest from the front. मागील बाजू

backache (backaches) *n* Backache is a dull pain in your back. पाठदुखी

backbone (backbones) *n* Your **backbone** is the column of small linked bones along the middle of your back. पाठीचा कणा

backfire (backfires, backfiring, backfired) *vi* If a plan **backfires**, it has the opposite result to the one that was intended. मलतेच होणे, उलटणे

background (backgrounds) *n* Your **background** is the kind of family you come from and the kind of education you have had. पार्श्वभूमी

backing (backings) *n* Backing is money, resources, or support given to a person or organization. पठिंबा

back out (backs out, backing out, backed out) *v* If you **back out**, you decide not to do something that you previously agreed to do. अंग काढून घेणे *They backed out of the project.*

backpack (backpacks) *n* A **backpack** is a bag with straps that go over your shoulders, so that you can carry things on your back when you are walking or climbing. पाठीवर ठेवायची पिशवी, बॅगपॅक

backpacker (backpackers) *n* A **backpacker** is a person who goes travelling with a backpack. पाठीवर पिशवी ठेऊन प्रवास करणारा, बॅगपॅकर

backpacking *n* If you go **backpacking**, you go travelling with a backpack. पाठीवर पिशवी ठेऊन प्रवास करणे, बॅगपॅकिंग

back pain *n* Back pain is pain that you feel in your back. पाठीतील वेदना

backside (backsides) *n* Your **backside** is the part of your body that you sit on. *(informal)* पाठीमागची बाजू

backslash (backslashes) *n* A **backslash** is the mark (\ ). बॅकस्लेश

backstroke n **Backstroke** is a swimming stroke that you do on your back. पाठीवर पोहणे

back up (backs up, backing up, backed up, backups) v If someone or something **backs up** a statement, they show that it is true. समर्थन करणे *He didn't have any proof to back up his story.* ▷ n **Backup** consists of extra equipment or people that you can get help or support from if necessary. जादा आधार, बॅकअप

backwards adv If you move **backwards**, you move in the direction behind you. मागच्या बाजूला ▷ adv If you do something **backwards**, you do it the opposite of the usual way. उलट

bacon n **Bacon** is salted or smoked meat taken from the back or sides of a pig. बेकन (डुकराच्या पाठीचे वा बाजूचे खारावलेले वा जाळावर टांगून सुकवलेले० मांस

bacteria npl **Bacteria** are very small organisms which can cause disease. जीवाणू

bad (worse, worst) adj Something that is **bad** is not nice or good. खराब ▷ adj Someone who is **bad** does things they should not do. वाईट

badge (badges) n A **badge** is a small piece of metal or cloth showing a design or words, which you attach to your clothes. बिल्ला

badger (badgers) n A **badger** is a wild animal with a white head with two wide black stripes on it. बॅजर नावाचा प्राणी

badly adv If you do something **badly**, you do it with very little success or effect. वाईट रीतीने

badminton n **Badminton** is a game played on a rectangular court by two or four players. They hit a feathered object called a shuttlecock across a high net. बॅडमिंटन

bad-tempered adj If you are **bad-tempered**, you are not cheerful and get angry easily. चिडचिडा

baffled adj If you are **baffled** by something, you cannot explain or understand it. संभ्रमित, गोंधळलेला

bag (bags) n A **bag** is a container made of paper, plastic, or leather which you use to carry things. पिशवी

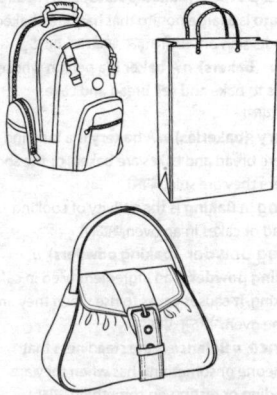

baggage n Your **baggage** consists of the suitcases and bags that you take with you when you travel. पेट्यांतून भरलेले सामान

baggy (baggier, baggiest) adj **Baggy** clothes hang loosely on your body. सैल कपडे

bagpipes npl **Bagpipes** are a musical instrument that are played by blowing air through a pipe into a bag, and then squeezing the bag to force the air out through other pipes. बॅगपाईप नावाचे वाद्य

Bahamas n The **Bahamas** are a group of over 700 coral islands in the Caribbean. बहामास

Bahrain n **Bahrain** is a country on the Persian Gulf that consists of several islands. बेहरेन

bail n **Bail** is a sum of money that an arrested person or someone else puts forward as a guarantee that the arrested person will attend their trial in a law court. If the arrested person does not attend it, the money is lost. जामीन

bake (bakes, baking, baked) *vi* If you **bake**, you spend some time preparing and mixing together ingredients to make bread, cakes, pies, or other food which is cooked in the oven. भाजणे

baked *adj* **Baked** food is cooked in the oven. भाजलेला

baked potato (baked potatoes) *n* A **baked potato** is a large potato that has been baked with its skin on. सालीसहित भाजलेले बटाटे

baker (bakers) *n* A **baker** is a person whose job is to bake and sell bread and cakes. बेकरीवाला

bakery (bakeries) *n* A **bakery** is a building where bread and cakes are baked, or the shop where they are sold. बेकरी

baking *n* **Baking** is the activity of cooking bread or cakes in an oven. भाजणे

baking powder (baking powders) *n* **Baking powder** is an ingredient used in cake making. It causes cakes to rise when they are in the oven. बेकिंग पावडर

balance *n* **Balance** is the steadiness that someone or something has when they are standing or resting on something. तोल

balanced *adj* A **balanced** account or report is fair and reasonable. संतुलित

balance sheet (balance sheets) *n* A **balance sheet** is a written statement of the amount of money and property that a company or person has, including amounts of money that are owed or are owing. ताळेबंद

balcony (balconies) *n* A **balcony** is a platform on the outside of a building with a wall or railing around it. सज्जा

bald (balder, baldest) *adj* Someone who is **bald** has little or no hair on the top of their head. टक्कल पडलेला

Balkan *adj* **Balkan** means of or relating to the Balkan Peninsula or the Balkan Mountains, or to the Balkan States or their inhabitants. बाल्कन

ball (balls) *n* A **ball** is a round object used in games such as football. चेंडू ▷ *n* A **ball** is a large formal dance. बॉल डान्स

ballerina (ballerinas) *n* A **ballerina** is a woman ballet dancer. महिला बैले नर्तिका

ballet *n* **Ballet** is a type of artistic dancing with carefully planned movements. बैले नृत्य

ballet dancer (ballet dancers) *n* A **ballet dancer** is a dancer who does ballet, especially as a profession. बैले नर्तक

ballet shoes *npl* **Ballet shoes** are special soft, light shoes that ballet dancers wear. बैले शूज

balloon (balloons) *n* A **balloon** is a small, thin, rubber bag that becomes larger when you blow air into it. फुगा

ballpoint (ballpoints) *n* A **ballpoint** or a **ballpoint pen** is a pen with a very small metal ball at the end which transfers the ink from the pen onto a surface. बॉलपॉईंट पेन

ballroom dancing *n* **Ballroom dancing** is a type of dancing in which a man and a woman dance together using fixed sequences of steps and movements. बॉलरूम नृत्य

bamboo (bamboos) *n* **Bamboo** is a tall tropical plant with hard hollow stems. बांबू

ban (bans, banning, banned) *n* A **ban** is an official ruling that something must not be done, shown, or used. बंदी ▷ *vt* To **ban** something means to state officially that it must not be done, shown, or used. बंदी घालणे

banana (bananas) *n* A **banana** is a long curved fruit with a yellow skin. केळे

band (bands) *n* A **band** is a group of people who play music together. बँडचे पथक ▷ *n* A **band** is a narrow strip of material that you put around something. पट्टी

bandage (bandages, bandaging, bandaged) *n* A **bandage** is a long strip of cloth that is tied around a wounded part of someone's body in order to protect or support it. मलमपट्टी ▷ *vt* If you **bandage** a wound or part of someone's body, you tie a bandage round it. मलमपट्टी करणे

bang (bangs, banging, banged) *n* A **bang** is a sudden loud noise such as an explosion. मोठा आवाज ▷ *v* If you **bang** something such as a door, or if it **bangs**, it closes suddenly with a loud noise. मोठा आवाज करणे

Bangladesh n **Bangladesh** is a republic in South Asia, formerly the Eastern Province of Pakistan. बांगलादेश

Bangladeshi (**Bangladeshis**) adj **Bangladeshi** means belonging to or relating to Bangladesh, or to its people or culture. बांगलादेशी ▷ n The **Bangladeshis** are the people who come from Bangladesh. बांगलादेशी

banister (**banisters**) n A **banister** is a rail supported by posts and fixed along the side of a staircase. जिन्याच्या कठड्याला असलेले गज

banjo (**banjos**) n A **banjo** is a musical instrument that looks like a guitar with a circular body, a long neck, and four or more strings. बँजो

bank (**banks**) n A **bank** is the ground beside a river. किनारा ▷ n A **bank** is a place where people can keep their money. बँक

bank account (**bank accounts**) n A **bank account** is an arrangement with a bank which allows you to keep your money in the bank and to take some out when you need it. बँकखाते

bank balance (**bank balances**) n Your **bank balance** is the amount of money that you have in your bank account at a particular time. बँकेतील शिल्लक

bank charges npl **Bank charges** are an amount of money that you have to pay to your bank, for example, if you have spent more money than you have in your account. बँक प्रभार

banker (**bankers**) n A **banker** is someone involved in banking at a senior level. बँकेतील वरिष्ठ अधिकारी

bank holiday (**bank holidays**) n A **bank holiday** is a public holiday. सार्वजनिक सुट्टी

banknote (**banknotes**) n A **banknote** is a piece of paper money. बँकनोट

bankrupt adj People or organizations that go **bankrupt** do not have enough money to pay their debts. दिवाळखोर

bank statement (**bank statements**) n A **bank statement** is a printed document showing all the money paid into and taken out of a bank account. बँक विवरण

banned adj If something is **banned**, it has been stated officially that it must not be done, shown, or used. बंदी घातलेले

bar (**bars**) n A **bar** is a long, thin piece of wood or metal. गज ▷ n A **bar** is a place where people buy and drink alcoholic drinks. मद्यपानगृह

Barbados n **Barbados** is an island in the Caribbean, in the east Lesser Antilles. बार्बाडोस

barbaric adj **Barbaric** behaviour is extremely cruel. रानटी

barbecue (**barbecues**) n A **barbecue** is a grill used to cook food outdoors. अन्नपदार्थ शिजवण्यासाठी असलेली लोखंडी जाळी

barbed wire n **Barbed wire** is strong wire with sharp points sticking out of it, which is used to make fences. काटेरी तार

barber (**barbers**) n A **barber** is a man whose job is cutting men's hair. न्हावी

bare (**barer, barest, bares, baring, bared**) adj If a part of your body is **bare**, it is not covered by any clothes. उघडा ▷ vt If you **bare** something, you show it. उघडे करणे ▷ adj If something is **bare**, it has nothing on top of it or inside it. उघडा

barefoot adj If you are **barefoot** or **barefooted**, you are wearing nothing on your feet. अनवाणी ▷ adv If you do something **barefoot**, you do it while wearing nothing on your feet. अनवाणी चालणे

barely adv You use **barely** to say that something is only just true or possible. जेमतेम

bargain (**bargains**) n Something that is a **bargain** is good value, usually because it has been sold at a lower price than normal. सौदा

barge (**barges**) n A **barge** is a narrow boat with a flat bottom, used for carrying heavy loads. सामानवाहू नौका

bark (**barks, barking, barked**) vi When a dog **barks**, it makes a short, loud noise. भुंकणे

barley n **Barley** is a crop which has seeds that are used in the production of food, beer, and whisky. बार्ली नावाचे धान्य

barn (barns) n A **barn** is a building on a farm in which crops or animal food are kept. शेतावरील झाप, कोठार

barrel (barrels) n A **barrel** is a large round container for liquids or food. Barrels are usually wider in the middle than at the top or bottom. पिंप

barrier (barriers) n A **barrier** is something such as a law or policy that makes it difficult or impossible for something to happen. अडथळा

base (bases) n The **base** of something is its lowest edge or part, or the part at which it is attached to something else. तळ

baseball n **Baseball** is a game that is played with a bat and a ball on a large field by two teams of nine players. Players must hit the ball and run around four bases to score. बेसबॉल

baseball cap (baseball caps) n A **baseball cap** is a close-fitting thin cap with a deep peak. बेसबॉल कॅप

based adj If one thing is **based** on another, the first thing is developed from the second one. आधारित

basement (basements) n The **basement** of a building is an area partly or completely below ground level, with a room or rooms in it. तळघर

bash (bashes, bashing, bashed) n A **bash** is a party or celebration. (informal) मेजवानी ▷ vt If you **bash** someone or something, you hit them hard in a rough way. (informal) चोप देणे

basic adj You use **basic** to describe things, activities, and principles that are very important or necessary, and on which others depend. मूलभूत

basically adv You use **basically** for emphasis when you are stating an opinion, or when you are making an important statement about something. मूलत:

basics npl The **basics** of something are its simplest, most important elements, ideas, or principles, in contrast to more complicated or detailed ones. मूलभूत बाबी

basil n **Basil** is a strong-smelling and strong-tasting herb that is used in cooking, especially with tomatoes. तुळशीच्या जातीची एक वनस्पती

basin (basins) n A **basin** is a deep bowl that you use for holding liquids, or for mixing food in. बेसिन, तसराळे

basis (bases) n If something happens or is done on a particular **basis**, it happens or is done in that way. आधार

basket (baskets) n A **basket** is a container made of thin strips of cane, metal or plastic woven together. टोपली

basketball n **Basketball** is a game in which two teams of five players each try to throw a large ball through a round net hanging from a high metal ring. बास्केटबॉल

Basque (Basques) adj **Basque** means relating to, denoting, or characteristic of the Basques or their language. बास्क ▷ n The **Basques** are a people of unknown origin living around the western Pyrenees in France and Spain. बास्क ▷ n **Basque** is the language spoken by the Basque people. बास्क

bass (basses) n A **bass** is a man with a deep singing voice. खर्जातील आवाज

bass drum (bass drums) n A **bass drum** is a large shallow drum of low and indefinite pitch. मोठ्या आवाजाचा ढोलक, बास ड्रम

bassoon (bassoons) n A **bassoon** is a large musical instrument of the woodwind family that is shaped like a tube and played by blowing into a curved metal pipe. खालच्या आवाजाचे फुंकून वाजवायचे एक वाद्य

bat (bats) n A **bat** is a special stick that you use to hit a ball in some games. बॅट ▷ n A **bat** is a small animal that looks like a mouse with wings. **Bats** come out to fly at night. पाकोळी, वटवाघूळ

bath (baths) n A **bath** is a container which you fill with water and sit in while you wash your body. आत बसून आंघोळ करण्यासाठी असलेला छोटा हौद

bathe (bathes, bathing, bathed) *vi* When you **bathe** in a sea, river, or lake, you swim or play there. *(formal)* आंघोळ करणे

bathing suit (bathing suits) *n* A **bathing suit** is a piece of clothing which people wear when they go swimming. पोहताना घालावयाचे कपडे

bathrobe (bathrobes) *n* A **bathrobe** is a loose piece of clothing made of the same material as towels. You wear it before or after you have a bath or a swim. आंघोळीपूर्वी किंवा नंतर घालावयाचा दिला झगा

bathroom (bathrooms) *n* A **bathroom** is a room in a house that contains a bath or shower, a washbasin, and sometimes a toilet. न्हाणीघर

baths *npl* A **baths** is a public building containing a swimming pool, and sometimes other facilities that people can use to have a wash or a bath. अत्याधुनिक सुविधांनी युक्त सार्वजनिक न्हाणीघर

bath towel (bath towels) *n* A **bath towel** is a very large towel used for drying your body after you have had a bath or shower. आंघोळीचा टॉवेल

bathtub (bathtubs) *n* A **bathtub** is a container which you fill with water and sit in while you wash your body. बाथटब

batter *n* **Batter** is a mixture of flour, eggs, and milk used to make pancakes. केक करण्यासाठी पीठ व अंडी फेटून केलेले मिश्रण

battery (batteries) *n* **Batteries** are the devices that you put in electrical items to provide the power that makes them work. बॅटरी

battle (battles) *n* In a war, a **battle** is a fight between armies or between groups of ships or planes. लढाई

battleship (battleships) *n* A **battleship** is a very large, heavily armoured warship. लढाऊ जहाज

bay (bays) *n* A **bay** is a part of a coastline where the land curves inwards. उपसागर

bay leaf (bay leaves) *n* A **bay leaf** is a leaf of an evergreen tree that can be dried and used as a herb in cooking. तमालपत्र

BC *abbr* You use **BC** in dates to indicate a number of years or centuries before the year in which Jesus Christ is believed to have been born. ख्रिस्तपूर्व

be (am, are, is, being, was, were, been) *v* You use **be** to say what a person or thing is like. असणे *She is very young.* ▷ *v* You use **be** to say that something is there. असणे *There is a tree in the garden.*

beach (beaches) *n* A **beach** is an area of sand or pebbles by the sea. समुद्रकिनारा

bead (beads) *n* **Beads** are small pieces of coloured glass, wood, or plastic with a hole through the middle which are used for jewellery or decoration. मणी

beak (beaks) *n* A bird's **beak** is the hard curved or pointed part of its mouth. चोच

beam (beams) *n* A **beam** of light is a line of light that shines from an object such as a torch or the sun. किरण

bean (beans) *n* **Beans** are the pods of a climbing plant, or the seeds that the pods contain, which are eaten as a vegetable. शेंग

beansprouts *npl* **Beansprouts** are small, long, thin shoots grown from beans. शेंगेतच मोड आणलेले धान्य

bear (bears, bearing, bore, borne) *n* A **bear** is a big, strong animal with thick fur and sharp claws. अस्वल ▷ *vt* If you **bear** something somewhere, you carry it there. *(literary)* वाहून नेणे

beard (beards) *n* A man's **beard** is the hair that grows on his chin and cheeks. दाढी

bearded *adj* A **bearded** man has a beard. दाढी असलेला

bear up (bears up, bearing up, bore up, borne up) *v* If you **bear up** when experiencing problems, you remain cheerful and show courage in spite of them. सहन करणे *How's she bearing up?*

beat (beats, beating, beaten) *n* A **beat** is a regular sound or rhythm. ठोका ▷ *vt* If you **beat** something, you keep hitting it. मारणे ▷ *vt* If you **beat** someone in a game or a competition, you do better than they do. पराभूत करणे

beautiful *adj* **Beautiful** means attractive to look at. सुंदर

beautifully *adv* If you do something **beautifully**, you do it in a beautiful manner. सुंदरपणे

beauty *n* **Beauty** is the state or quality of being beautiful. सौंदर्य

beauty salon (**beauty salons**) *n* A **beauty salon** is a place where women can go to have beauty treatments, for example to have their hair, nails or make-up done. सौंदर्यप्रसाधनगृह

beauty spot (**beauty spots**) *n* A **beauty spot** is a place in the country that is popular because of its beautiful scenery. सौंदर्यस्थळ

beaver (**beavers**) *n* A **beaver** is a furry animal like a large rat with a big flat tail. बिव्हर नावाचा प्राणी

because *conj* You use **because** to say why something happens. कारण की *I went to bed because I was tired.*

become (**becomes, becoming, became**) *v* If one thing **becomes** another thing, it starts to be that thing. होणे

bed (**beds**) *n* A **bed** is a piece of furniture that you lie on when you sleep. पलंग

bed and breakfast *n* **Bed and breakfast** is a system of accommodation in a hotel or guesthouse in which you pay for a room for the night and for breakfast the following morning. The abbreviation 'B&B' is also used. खाण्यापिण्याची व झोपण्याची सोय असलेली हॉटेलातील खोली

bedclothes *npl* **Bedclothes** are the sheets and covers which you put on a bed. अंथरूण

bedding *n* **Bedding** consists of sheets, blankets, and other covers used on beds. अंथरूण व पांघरूण

bed linen *n* **Bed linen** is sheets and pillowcases. चादर व उशांचे अभ्रे

bedroom (**bedrooms**) *n* A **bedroom** is a room which is used for sleeping in. शयनकक्ष

bedside lamp (**bedside lamps**) *n* A **bedside lamp** is a lamp that you have next to your bed. शयनकक्षातला दिवा

bedside table (**bedside tables**) *n* A **bedside table** is a small table usually with shelves or drawers, that you have next to your bed. शयनकक्षातले टेबल

bedsit (**bedsits**) *n* A **bedsit** is a room you rent which you use for both living in and sleeping in. राहण्यासाठी व झोपण्यासाठी भाड्याने घेतलेली खोली

bedspread (**bedspreads**) *n* A **bedspread** is a decorative cover which is put over a bed, on top of the sheets and blankets. अंथरायची शोभिवंत चादर

bedtime *n* Your **bedtime** is the time when you usually go to bed. झोपण्याची वेळ

bee (**bees**) *n* A **bee** is an insect with a yellow-and-black striped body that makes a buzzing noise as it flies. Bees make honey. मधमाशी

beech (**beeches**) *n* A **beech** or a **beech tree** is a tree with a smooth grey trunk. बीच नावाचा वृक्ष

beef *n* **Beef** is the meat of a cow, bull, or ox. गाय किंवा बैल यांचे मांस

beefburger (**beefburgers**) *n* A **beefburger** is minced meat which has been shaped into a flat circle. बीफ बर्गर

beeper (**beepers**) *n* A **beeper** is a portable device that makes a beeping noise, usually to tell you to phone someone or to remind you to do something. (*informal*) बीपर

beer (**beers**) *n* **Beer** is a bitter alcoholic drink made from grain. बीअर

beetle (**beetles**) *n* A **beetle** is an insect with a hard covering to its body. एक प्रकारचा कीटक

beetroot (**beetroots**) *n* **Beetroot** is a dark red root vegetable which can be cooked or pickled. बीट

before *adv* You use **before** when you are talking about a previous time. पूर्वी ▷ *conj* If you do something **before** someone else, you do it when they have not yet done it. आधी *Before I got to the ball, someone else kicked it away.* ▷ *prep* If one thing happens **before**

another thing, it happens earlier than it. अगोदर *My birthday is just before his.*

beforehand *adv* If you do something **beforehand**, you do it earlier than a particular event. अगोदरच

beg (begs, begging, begged) *v* If you **beg** someone to do something, you ask them anxiously or eagerly to do it. याचना करणे

beggar (beggars) *n* A **beggar** is someone who lives by asking people for money or food. भिकारी

begin (begins, beginning, began, begun) *vt* If you **begin** to do something, you start to do it. सुरुवात करणे

beginner (beginners) *n* A **beginner** is someone who has just started learning to do something and cannot do it well yet. नवशिक्या

beginning (beginnings) *n* The **beginning** of something is the first part of it. सुरुवात

behave (behaves, behaving, behaved) *vi* The way you **behave** is the way that you do and say things. वागणे ▷ *vt* If you **behave** yourself, you are good. चांगले वागणे

behaviour (behaviours) *n* A person's **behaviour** is the way they behave. वर्तणूक करणे

behind (behinds) *adv* **Behind** means in or to a position further back. पाठीमागे ▷ *n* Your **behind** is the part of your body that you sit on. पार्श्वभाग ▷ *prep* If something is **behind** another thing, it is at the back of it. च्या मागे *He stood behind his desk.*

beige *adj* Something that is **beige** is pale brown in colour. फिकट तपकिरी रंगाचे

Beijing *n* **Beijing** is the capital of the People's Republic of China. बिजिंग

Belarus *n* **Belarus** is a republic in eastern Europe. बेलारूस

Belarussian (Belarussians) *adj* **Belarussian** means of, relating to, or characteristic of Belarus, its people, or their language. बेलासरुसियन ▷ *n* A **Belarussian** is a native or inhabitant of Belarus. बेलासरुसियन ▷ *n*

Belarussian is the official language of Belarus. बेलासरुसियन

Belgian (Belgians) *adj* **Belgian** means belonging or relating to Belgium or to its people. बेल्जियन ▷ *n* A **Belgian** is a native or inhabitant of Belgium. बेल्जियन

Belgium *n* **Belgium** is a country in north-west Europe. बेल्जियम

belief (beliefs) *n* **Belief** is a feeling of certainty that something exists, is true, or is good. श्रद्धा

believe (believed, believing, believes) *vt* If you **believe** that something is true, you think that it is true. *(formal)* विश्वास वाटणे ▷ *vi* If you **believe** in things such as God, fairies, or miracles, you are sure that they exist or happen. श्रद्धा/विश्वास ठेवणे

bell (bells) *n* A **bell** is a device that makes a ringing sound which attracts people's attention. घंटा

belly (bellies) *n* A person's or animal's **belly** is their stomach or abdomen. पोट

belly button (belly buttons) *n* Your **belly button** is the small round thing in the centre of your stomach. *(informal)* बेंबी

belong (belongs, belonging, belonged) *vi* If something **belongs** somewhere, that is where it should be. योग्य जागी असणे ▷ *vi* If something **belongs to** you, it is yours. मालकीचे असणे *The book belongs to her.* ▷ *vi* If you **belong** to a group of people, you are one of them. मधील असणे

belongings *npl* Your **belongings** are the things that you own. स्वत:च्या मालकीच्या वस्तू

below *adv* **Below** means at or to a lower position or place. खाली ▷ *prep* If something is **below** another thing, it is lower down than it. च्या खाली *His shoes were below his bed.*

belt (belts) *n* A **belt** is a strip of leather or cloth that you fasten round your waist. पट्टा

bench (benches) *n* A **bench** is a long seat of wood or metal. बाकडे, बाक

bend (bends, bending, bent) *n* A **bend** in a road, river, or pipe is a curved part in it. वळण

▷ *vi* When you **bend**, you move the top part of your body downwards and forwards. झुकणे

bend down (bends down, bending down, bent down) *v* When you **bend down**, you move the top part of your body downwards and forwards. खाली झुकणे *He bent down to tie his laces.*

bend over (bends over, bending over, bent over) *v* When you **bend over**, you move the top part of your body downwards and forwards. खाली झुकणे *I bent over and kissed her cheek.*

beneath *prep* If something is **beneath** another thing, it is below it. च्या खाली *The dog was beneath the table.*

benefit (benefits, benefiting, benefited) *n* The **benefit** of something is the help that you get from it or the advantage that results from it. फायदा ▷ *vi* If you **benefit** from something or if it **benefits** you, it helps you or improves your life. फायदा होणे

bent *adj* Something that is **bent** is not straight. वाकलेला ▷ *adj* If you say that someone in a position of responsibility is **bent**, you mean that they are dishonest or do illegal things. अप्रामाणिक

beret (berets) *n* A **beret** is a circular, flat hat that is made of soft material and has no brim. मऊ गोल हॅट

berry (berries) *n* **Berries** are small round fruit that grow on a bush or a tree. बेरी

berth (berths) *n* A **berth** is a bed on a boat or train, or in a caravan. गाडीतील झोपण्याची जागा

beside *prep* If something is **beside** another thing, it is next to it. बाजूला *He sat down beside me.*

besides *adv* You use **besides** when you want to give another reason for something. शिवाय ▷ *prep* **Besides** means as well as. खेरीज, शिवाय *Besides being tall, they're strong and clever.*

best *adj* If you say that something is **best**, you mean that it is better than all the others. सर्वांत चांगला ▷ *adv* You use **best** to say

that something is better than all the others. सर्वोत्तम

best-before date (best-before dates) *n* The **best-before date** on a food container is the date by which the food should be used before it starts to decay. डब्यातील अन्न ज्या तारखेपूर्वी वापरावे ती तारीख

best man *n* The **best man** at a wedding is the man who assists the bridegroom. नव्या मुलाचा सहाय्यक

bestseller (bestsellers) *n* A **bestseller** is a book of which a very large number of copies have been sold. भरपूर विक्री होणारे पुस्तक

bet (bets, betting) *n* A **bet** is an agreement between two parties that a sum of money will be paid by the loser to the party who correctly predicts the outcome of an event. पैज ▷ *v* If you **bet** on the result of a horse race, football game, or other event, you give someone a sum of money which they give you back with extra money if the result is what you predicted, or which they keep if it is not. पैज लावणे

betray (betrays, betraying, betrayed) *vt* If you **betray** someone who trusts you, you do something which hurts and disappoints them. विश्वासघात करणे

better *adj* You use **better** to mean that a thing is very good compared to another thing. अधिक चांगला ▷ *adv* You use **better** to mean that someone or something does something very well compared to another person or thing. अधिक चांगला ▷ *adj* If you feel **better**, you do not feel ill anymore. अधिक बरे, सुधारलेले

between *prep* If you are **between** two things, one of them is on one side of you and the other is on the other side. मध्ये, दरम्यान *She stood between her two brothers.*

bewildered *adj* If you are **bewildered**, you are very confused and cannot understand something or decide what you should do. गोंधळलेला

beyond *prep* Something that is **beyond** a place is on the other side of it, or farther away than it. दुसऱ्या बाजूला, पलिकडे *On his right was a garden, and beyond it there was a large house.*

biased adj Someone or something that is **biased** towards one thing is more concerned with it than with other things. पक्षपाती

bib (bibs) n A **bib** is a piece of cloth or plastic which is worn by very young children to protect their clothes while they are eating. लहान मुलांना भरविताना त्यांच्या गळ्यात बांधावयाचे कापड

Bible n The **Bible** is the sacred book of the Christian religion. बायबल

bicarbonate of soda n **Bicarbonate of soda** is a white powder which is used in baking to make cakes rise, and also as a medicine for your stomach. बायकार्बोनेट सोडा

bicycle (bicycles) n A **bicycle** is a vehicle with two wheels which you ride by sitting on it and pushing two pedals with your feet. सायकल

bicycle pump (bicycle pumps) n A **bicycle pump** is a hand pump for pumping air into the tyres of a bicycle. सायकलच्या टायरमध्ये हवा भरण्याचा पंप

bid (bids, bidding, bade, bidden) n If you make a **bid** for something that is being sold, you say that you will pay a certain amount of money for it. बोली ▷ v If you **bid** for something that somebody is selling, you offer to pay a price that you think is fair. बोली लावणे

bifocals npl **Bifocals** are glasses with lenses made in two halves. The top part is for looking at things some distance away, and the bottom part is for reading and looking at things that are close. द्विकेंद्रक काच असलेला चष्मा

big (bigger, biggest) adj A person or thing that is **big** is large in size. मोठा

bigheaded adj If you describe someone as **bigheaded**, you disapprove of them because they think they are very clever and know everything. अतिशहाणा

bike (bikes) n A **bike** is a vehicle with two wheels which you ride by sitting on it and pushing two pedals with your feet. *(informal)* दुचाकी

bikini (bikinis) n A **bikini** is a two-piece swimming costume worn by women. स्त्रियांचा पोहण्याचा पोशाख

bilingual adj **Bilingual** means involving or using two languages. द्विभाषी

bill (bills) n A **bill** is a written statement of money that you owe for goods or services. देयक ▷ n In parliament, a **bill** is a formal statement of a proposed new law that is discussed and then voted on. विधेयक

billiards npl **Billiards** is a game played on a large table, in which you use a long stick called a cue to hit small heavy balls against each other or into pockets around the sides of the table. बिलियर्ड्स

billion (billions) num A **billion** is the number 1,000,000,000. अब्ज

bin (bins) n A **bin** is a container that you put rubbish in. केराची टोपली

bingo n **Bingo** is a game in which players aim to match the numbers that someone calls out with the numbers on a card that they have been given. बिंगो नावाचा खेळ

binoculars npl **Binoculars** consist of two small telescopes joined together side by side, which you look through in order to see things that are a long way away. दुर्बिण

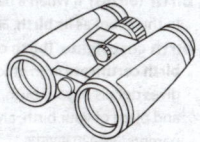

biochemistry n **Biochemistry** is the study of the chemical processes that happen in living things. जैवरासायनिक अभ्यास, जीवरसायन शास्त्र

biodegradable adj Something that is **biodegradable** breaks down or decays naturally without any special scientific treatment, and can therefore be thrown away without causing pollution. विघटनयोग्य

biography (biographies) n A **biography** of a person is an account of their life, written by someone else. चरित्र

biological adj **Biological** is used to describe processes and states that occur in the bodies and cells of living things. जैविक

biology n **Biology** is the science concerned with the study of living things. जीवशास्त्र

biometric adj **Biometric** tests and devices use biological information about a person to create a detailed record of their personal characteristics. जैवमितिक

birch (birches) n A **birch** is a tall tree with thin branches. बर्च नावाचे झाड

bird (birds) n A **bird** is a creature with feathers and wings. पक्षी

bird flu n **Bird flu** is a virus which can be transmitted from chickens, ducks, and other birds to people. बर्ड फ्लू नावाचा रोग

bird of prey (birds of prey) n A **bird of prey** is a bird such as an eagle or a hawk that kills and eats other birds and animals. शिकारी पक्षी

birdwatching n **Birdwatching** is the activity of watching and studying wild birds in their natural surroundings. पक्षीनिरीक्षण

Biro® (Biros) n A **Biro** is a pen with a small metal tip at its tip. बायरो नावाचे पेन

birth (births) n When a baby is born, you refer to this event as its **birth**. जन्म

birth certificate (birth certificates) n Your **birth certificate** is an official document which gives details of your birth, such as the date and place of your birth, and the names of your parents. जन्म प्रमाणपत्र

birthday (birthdays) n Your **birthday** is the anniversary of the date on which you were born. वाढदिवस

birthplace (birthplaces) n Your **birthplace** is the place where you were born. (written) जन्मठिकाण

biscuit (biscuits) n A **biscuit** is a small flat cake that is crisp and usually sweet. बिस्किट

bit (bits) n A **bit** of something is a small amount of it, or a small part of it. थोडा अंश

bitch (bitches) n A **bitch** is a female dog. कुत्री

bite (bites, biting, bit, bitten) n A **bite** of something, especially food, is the action of

biting it. घास ▷ v If you **bite** something, you use your teeth to cut into it, for example in order to eat it or break it. If an animal or person **bites** you, they use their teeth to hurt or injure you. चावा घेणे

bitter (bitterest) adj In a **bitter** argument, people argue very angrily. कडवट

black (blacker, blackest) adj Something that is **black** is of the darkest colour that there is, the colour of the sky at night when there is no light at all. काळा

blackberry (blackberries) n A **blackberry** is a small dark purple fruit. गौरीफळ, काळी तुती

BlackBerry® (BlackBerries) n A **BlackBerry** is a mobile computing device that allows you to send and receive email. ब्लॅकबेरी

blackbird (blackbirds) n A **blackbird** is a common European bird. The male has black feathers and a yellow beak, and the female has brown feathers. ब्लॅकबर्ड नावाचा पक्षी

blackboard (blackboards) n A **blackboard** is a dark-coloured board which teachers write on with chalk. फळा

black coffee (black coffees) n **Black coffee** has no milk or cream added to it. कोरी कॉफी

blackcurrant (blackcurrants) n **Blackcurrants** are very small, dark purple fruits that grow in bunches. ब्लॅककरंट नावाची फळे

black ice n **Black ice** is a thin, transparent layer of ice on a road or path that is very difficult to see. रस्त्यावर पसरलेला बर्फाचा अतिपातळ थर

blackmail (blackmails, blackmailing, blackmailed) n **Blackmail** is the action of threatening to reveal a secret about someone, unless they do something you tell them to do, such as giving you money. गुप्ति उघड करण्याची धमकी देऊन घेतलेला गैरफायदा ▷ vt If one person **blackmails** another person, they use blackmail against them. खोट्यानाट्या कंद्या पसरवण्याची धमकी देऊन गैरफायदा घेणे

blackout (blackouts) n A **blackout** is a period of time during a war in which the

b

buildings in an area are made dark for safety reasons. युद्धकाळातील प्रकाशबंदी

bladder (bladders) *n* Your **bladder** is the part of your body where urine is held until it leaves your body. मूत्राशय

blade (blades) *n* The **blade** of a knife, axe, or saw is the sharp edge of it that is used for cutting. पाते

blame (blames, blaming, blamed) *vt* If you **blame** a person or thing for something bad, you believe or say that they are responsible for it or that they caused it. दोषारोप ठेवणे ▷ *n* The **blame** for something bad that has happened is the responsibility for causing it or letting it happen. दोषारोप

blank (blanks) *adj* Something that is **blank** has nothing on it. कोरा ▷ *n* A **blank** is a space which is left in a piece of writing or on a printed form for you to fill in particular information. गाळलेली जागा

blank cheque (blank cheques) *n* If someone is given a **blank cheque**, they are given the authority to spend as much money as they need or want. रक्कम न लिहिलेला धनादेश

blanket (blankets) *n* A **blanket** is a large piece of thick cloth, especially one which you put on a bed to keep you warm. ब्लॅंकेट, घोंगडी

blast (blasts) *n* A **blast** is a big explosion. स्फोट

blatant *adj* If you describe something you think is bad as **blatant**, you mean that it is very obvious. उघड, निर्लज्ज

blaze (blazes) *n* A **blaze** is a large fire in which things are damaged. ज्वाला

blazer (blazers) *n* A **blazer** is a kind of jacket. ब्लेझर

bleach *n* **Bleach** is a chemical that is used to make cloth white, or to clean things thoroughly. कापड पांढरे स्वच्छ करण्यासाठी वापरण्यात येणारे रसायन

bleached *adj* Something that is **bleached** has been made lighter in colour. पांढरे फिके केलेले

bleak (bleaker, bleakest) *adj* If a situation is **bleak**, it is bad, and seems unlikely to improve. दुःखद, वाईट व सुधारण्याची शक्यता नसलेले

bleed (bleeds, bleeding, bled) *vi* When you **bleed**, you lose blood from your body as a result of injury or illness. रक्तस्राव होणे

blender (blenders) *n* A **blender** is an electrical kitchen appliance used for mixing liquids and soft foods together or turning fruit or vegetables into liquid. ब्लेंडर

bless (blesses, blessing, blessed) *vt* When a priest **blesses** people or things, he or she asks for God's favour and protection for them. आशीर्वाद देणे

blind *adj* Someone who is **blind** is unable to see because their eyes are damaged. आंधळा

blindfold (blindfolds, blindfolding, blindfolded) *n* A **blindfold** is a strip of cloth that is tied over someone's eyes so that they cannot see. डोळ्यांवर बांधलेली पट्टी ▷ *vt* If you **blindfold** someone, you tie a strip of cloth over their eyes. डोळ्यांवर पट्टी बांधणे

blink (blinks, blinking, blinked) *v* When you **blink** or when you **blink** your eyes, you shut your eyes and very quickly open them again. पापण्यांची उघडझाप करणे

bliss *n* **Bliss** is a state of complete happiness. परमानंद

blister (blisters) *n* A **blister** is a painful swelling containing clear liquid on the surface of your skin. काचफोड, त्वचेखाली येणारा पाणी असलेला फोड

blizzard (blizzards) *n* A **blizzard** is a storm in which snow falls heavily and there are strong winds. बर्फाचे जोरदार वादळ

block (blocks, blocking, blocked) *n* A **block** of a substance is a large rectangular piece of it. ठोकळा ▷ *n* In a town, a **block** is a group of buildings with streets on all four sides. चारही बाजूनी रस्त्यांनी वेढलेल्या इमारतींचे संकुल ▷ *n* A **block** is an obstruction or hindrance. अडथळा ▷ *vt* To **block** a road or channel means to put something across or in it so that nothing can go through it or along it. अडथळा निर्माण करणे

blockage (blockages) *n* A **blockage** in a pipe or tunnel is something that is blocking it. अडथळा

blocked adj If something is **blocked**, it is completely closed so that nothing can get through it. अडथळा निर्माण झालेले

blog (blogs, blogging, blogged) v When you **blog**, you update a website containing a diary or journal. ब्लॉगवर लिहिणे

bloke (blokes) n A **bloke** is a man. (informal) मनुष्य

blonde (blonder, blondest) adj Someone who has **blonde** hair has pale-coloured hair. भुऱ्या केसांची व्यक्ती

blood n **Blood** is the red liquid that flows inside your body. रक्त

blood group (blood groups) n Someone's **blood group** is the type of blood that they have in their body. There are four main types: A, B, AB, and O. रक्तगट

blood poisoning n **Blood poisoning** is a serious illness resulting from an infection in your blood. रक्तात विष निर्माण होणे

blood pressure n Your **blood pressure** is a measure of the force with which blood is pumped around your body. रक्तदाब

blood test (blood tests) n A **blood test** is a medical examination of a sample of your blood. रक्ताची चाचणी

blossom (blossoms, blossoming, blossomed) n **Blossom** is the flowers that appear on a tree before the fruit. बहर ▷ vi If someone or something **blossoms**, they develop good, attractive, or successful qualities. उत्कर्ष होणे

blouse (blouses) n A **blouse** is a kind of shirt worn by girls or women. पोलका

blow (blows, blowing, blew, blown) n Someone receives a **blow** when someone or something hits them. फटका ▷ vi When the wind **blows**, it moves the air. वाहणे ▷ vt When you **blow**, you push air out of your mouth. फुंकर मारणे

blow-dry n A **blow-dry** is a method of styling the hair while drying it with a hand-held hairdryer. यंत्राच्या सहाय्याने केसांना वळण देणे व सुकविणे

blow up (blows up, blowing up, blew up, blown up) v If someone **blows** something up, or if it **blows up**, it is destroyed by an explosion. फुटणे Their boat blew up.

blue (bluer, bluest) adj Something that is **blue** is the colour of the sky on a sunny day. निळा रंग

blueberry (blueberries) n A **blueberry** is a small dark blue fruit that is found in North America. ब्लूबेरी

blues npl The blues is a type of music which was developed by African-American musicians in the southern United States. It is characterized by a slow tempo and a strong rhythm. ब्लूज एक संगीत प्रकार

bluff (bluffs, bluffing, bluffed) n A **bluff** is an attempt to make someone believe that you will do something when you do not really intend to do it. भूलथापा ▷ v If you **bluff**, you try to make someone believe that you will do something although you do not really intend to do it, or that you know something when you do not really know it. थापा मारणे, ठकवणे

blunder (blunders) n A **blunder** is a stupid or careless mistake. घोडचूक

blunt (blunter, bluntest) adj If you are **blunt**, you say exactly what you think without trying to be polite. उद्धट, रोखठोक

blush (blushes, blushing, blushed) vi When you **blush**, your face becomes redder than usual because you are ashamed or embarrassed. लाजणे

blusher (blushers) n **Blusher** is a coloured substance that women put on their cheeks. गालावर लाली आणणारे प्रसाधन

board (boards) n The **board** of a company or organization is the group of people who control it. मंडळ ▷ n A **board** is a flat piece of wood, plastic, or cardboard which is used for a particular purpose. फळा

boarder (boarders) n A **boarder** is a pupil who lives at school during the term. शाळेत राहून शिकणारा विद्यार्थी

board game (board games) n A **board game** is a game such as chess or backgammon, which people play by moving small objects around on a board. पटावरचा खेळ

boarding school (boarding schools) n A **boarding school** is a school where the pupils live during the term. वसतीगृह असलेली शाळा

boast (boasts, boasting, boasted) vi If someone **boasts** about something that they have done or that they own, they talk about it very proudly, in a way that other people may find irritating or offensive. बढाई मारणे

boat (boats) n A **boat** is something in which people can travel across water. नौका

body (bodies) n Your **body** is all your physical parts, including your head, arms, and legs. शरीर

bodybuilding n **Bodybuilding** is the activity of doing special exercises regularly in order to make your muscles grow bigger. शरीर कमावणे

bodyguard (bodyguards) n Someone's **bodyguard** is the person or group of people employed to protect them. अंगरक्षक

bog (bogs) n A **bog** is a wet muddy area of land. दलदलीचा प्रदेश

boil (boils, boiling, boiled) vt When you **boil** food, you cook it in water that is boiling. उकडणे ▷ vi When water **boils**, it becomes very hot, and you can see bubbles in it and steam coming from it. उकळणे

boiled adj Food that is **boiled** is cooked in boiling water. उकडलेले

boiled egg (boiled eggs) n A **boiled egg** is an egg that has been cooked in its shell in boiling water. उकडलेले अंडे

boiler (boilers) n A **boiler** is a device which burns fuel to provide hot water. बंब

boiling adj Something that is **boiling** is very hot. उकळते

boil over (boils over, boiling over, boiled over) v When a liquid that is being heated **boils over**, it rises and flows over the edge of the container. उतू जाणे Heat the liquid in a large, wide container so it doesn't boil over.

Bolivia n **Bolivia** is an inland republic in central South America. बोलिव्हिया

Bolivian (Bolivians) adj **Bolivian** means belonging or relating to Bolivia or its people.

बोलिव्हियन ▷ n A **Bolivian** is a person who comes from Bolivia. बोलिव्हियन

bolt (bolts) n A **bolt** is a long metal object which screws into a nut and is used to fasten things together. अडसर, वस्तू घट्ट बसवण्यासाठी वापरायचे मळसूत्र व त्याची फिरकी

bomb (bombs, bombing, bombed) n A **bomb** is a device which explodes, damaging a large area or killing people. बॉंब ▷ vt When a place **is bombed**, it is attacked with bombs. बॉंब टाकणे

bombing (bombings) n **Bombing** is the action of attacking a place with bombs. बॉंबफेक

bond (bonds) n A **bond** between people is a close link between them, for example feelings of love, or a special agreement. बंध

bone (bones) n Your **bones** are the hard parts inside your body which together form your skeleton. हाड

bone dry adj If you say that something is **bone dry**, you are emphasizing that it is very dry indeed. कोरडा ठणठणीत

bonfire (bonfires) n A **bonfire** is a fire built outdoors, usually to burn rubbish. (कचऱ्याची) होळी

bonnet (bonnets) n The **bonnet** of a car is the metal cover over the engine at the front. बॉनेट

bonus (bonuses) n A **bonus** is an amount of money that is added to someone's pay, usually because they have worked very hard. लाभांश

book (books, booking, booked) n A **book** consists of pieces of paper, usually with words printed on them, which are fastened together and fixed inside a cover of strong paper or cardboard. पुस्तक ▷ vt When you **book** something such as a hotel room or a ticket, you arrange to have it or use it at a particular time. आरक्षित करणे

bookcase (bookcases) n A **bookcase** is a piece of furniture with shelves for books. पुस्तकांचे कपाट

booking (bookings) n A **booking** is the arrangement that you make when you book something such as a hotel room, a table at a restaurant, a theatre seat, or a place on public transport. आरक्षण

booklet (**booklets**) *n* A **booklet** is a small paperback book, containing information on a particular subject. पुस्तिका

bookmark (**bookmarks**) *n* A **bookmark** is a narrow piece of card or cloth that you put between the pages of a book so that you can find a particular page easily. पुस्तकातील खूण

bookshelf (**bookshelves**) *n* A **bookshelf** is a shelf on which you keep books. पुस्तकांचे कपाट

bookshop (**bookshops**) *n* A **bookshop** is a shop where books are sold. पुस्तकांचे दुकान

boost (**boosts, boosting, boosted**) *vt* If one thing **boosts** another, it causes it to increase, improve, or be more successful. चालना देणे

boot (**boots**) *n* **Boots** are strong heavy shoes that cover your whole foot and the lower part of your leg. पादत्राण, बूट

booze *n* **Booze** is alcoholic drink. *(informal)* बूझ, मद्यार्क असलेले पेय

border (**borders**) *n* The **border** between two countries is the dividing line between them. सीमा, सरहद्द

bore (**bores, boring, bored**) *vt* If someone or something **bores** you, you find them dull and uninteresting. कंटाळा आणणे

bored *adj* If you are **bored**, you feel tired and impatient because you are not interested in something or because you have nothing to do. कंटाळलेला

boredom *n* **Boredom** is the state of being bored. कंटाळा

boring *adj* If you say that someone or something is **boring**, you think that they are very dull and uninteresting. कंटाळवाणा

born *adj* You use **born** to describe someone who has a natural ability to do a particular activity or job. For example, a **born** cook has a natural ability to cook well. जन्मजात

borrow (**borrows, borrowing, borrowed**) *vt* If you **borrow** something that belongs to

someone else, you take it, usually with their permission, intending to return it. उसने घेणे

Bosnia *n* **Bosnia** is a region of central Bosnia-Herzegovina. बोस्निया

Bosnia-Herzegovina *n* **Bosnia-Herzegovina** is a country in south-west Europe, which was part of Yugoslavia until 1991. बोस्निया हरझेगोविना

Bosnian (**Bosnians**) *adj* **Bosnian** means of or relating to Bosnia or its inhabitants. बोस्नियन ▷ *n* A **Bosnian** is a native or inhabitant of Bosnia. बोस्नियन

boss (**bosses**) *n* Your **boss** is the person in charge of the organization or department where you work. मालक

boss around (**bosses around, bossing around, bossed around**) *v* If you say that someone **bosses** you **around**, you mean that they keep telling you what to do in a way that is irritating. हुकूम सोडणे

bossy (**bossier, bossiest**) *adj* If someone is **bossy**, they enjoy telling people what to do. हुकूम सोडणारी व्यक्ती

both *det* You use **both** to mean two people or two things together. दोन्ही *He put both books in the drawer.* ▷ *pron* You use **both** when you are saying that something is true about two people or things. दोचेही *The woman and her friend, both aged 50, were arrested.*

bother (**bothers, bothering, bothered**) *v* If you do not **bother** to do something or if you do not **bother** with it, you do not do it, consider it, or use it because you think it is unnecessary or because you are too lazy. मनावर घेणे

Botswana *n* **Botswana** is a republic in southern Africa. बोत्स्वाना

bottle (**bottles**) *n* A **bottle** is a glass or plastic container in which drinks and other liquids are kept. बाटली

bottle bank (**bottle banks**) *n* A **bottle bank** is a large container into which people can put empty bottles so that the glass can be used again. रिकाम्या बाटल्या टाकण्याची टाकी

bottle-opener (**bottle-openers**) *n* A **bottle-opener** is a metal device for removing caps or tops from bottles. बाटली उघडण्याचे साधन

bottom (**bottoms**) *adj* The **bottom** thing is the lowest one. खालचा भाग ▷ *n* The **bottom** of something is its lowest part. तळ, बूड ▷ *n* Your **bottom** is the part of your body that you sit on. पार्श्वभाग

bounce (**bounces, bouncing, bounced**) *v* When an object such as a ball **bounces** or when you **bounce** it, it moves upwards from a surface or away from it immediately after hitting it. उडणे, उसळणे

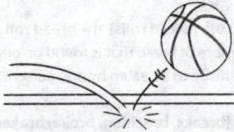

boundary (**boundaries**) *n* The **boundary** of an area of land is an imaginary line that separates it from other areas. सीमा

bouquet (**bouquets**) *n* A **bouquet** is a bunch of flowers arranged in an attractive way. पुष्पगुच्छ

bow (**bows, bowing, bowed**) *n* A **bow** is a long, curved piece of wood with a string stretched between its two ends, that is used to send arrows through the air. धनुष्य ▷ *vi* When you **bow**, you bend your body towards someone as a polite way of saying hello or thanking them. झुकणे ▷ *n* A **bow** is a knot that you use to tie laces and ribbons. बो

bowels *npl* Your **bowels** are the tubes in your body through which digested food passes through your stomach. मोठे आतडे

bowl (**bowls**) *n* A **bowl** is a circular container with a wide uncovered top that is used for mixing and serving food. वाटी

bowling *n* **Bowling** is a game in which you roll a heavy ball down a narrow track towards a group of wooden objects and try to knock down as many of them as possible. चेंडूफेक

bowling alley (**bowling alleys**) *n* A **bowling alley** is a building which contains several tracks for bowling. बोलिंग ऐली

bow tie (**bow ties**) *n* A **bow tie** is a tie in the form of a bow. Bow ties are worn by men, especially for formal occasions. बो टाय

box (**boxes**) *n* A **box** is a square or rectangular container with stiff sides and sometimes a lid. पेटी

boxer (**boxers**) *n* A **boxer** is someone who takes part in the sport of boxing. मुष्टियोद्धा

boxer shorts *npl* **Boxer shorts** are loose-fitting men's underpants that are shaped like the shorts worn by boxers. बॉक्सर शॉर्ट्स

boxing *n* **Boxing** is a sport in which two people wearing padded gloves fight, using only their hands. मुष्टियुद्ध

box office (**box offices**) *n* The **box office** in a theatre or cinema is the place where the tickets are sold. चित्रपटगृहाची तिकीट खिडकी

boy (**boys**) *n* A **boy** is a male child. मुलगा

boyfriend (**boyfriends**) *n* Someone's **boyfriend** is the man or boy with whom they are having a romantic relationship. प्रियकर

bra (**bras**) *n* A **bra** is a piece of underwear that a woman wears to support her breasts. काचोळी

brace (**braces**) *n* A **brace** is a device attached to a person's leg to strengthen or support it. पायाला आधार देणारे उपकरण

bracelet (**bracelets**) *n* A **bracelet** is a piece of jewellery that you wear round your wrist. मनगटातील शोभिवंत साखळी

braces *npl* **Braces** are a pair of straps that you wear over your shoulders to prevent your trousers from falling down. विजार खाली सरकू नये म्हणून गळ्यातून लावलेले पट्टे

brackets *npl* **Brackets** are a pair of written marks that you place round a word, expression, or sentence in order to indicate that you are giving extra information (). कंस

brain (**brains**) *n* Your **brain** is the organ inside your head that controls your body's activities and enables you to think and to feel things. मेंदू

brainy (**brainier, brainiest**) *adj* Someone who is **brainy** is clever and good at learning. *(informal)* बुद्धिमान

brake (**brakes, braking, braked**) *n* A vehicle's **brakes** are devices that make it go slower or stop. ब्रेक ▷ *v* When a vehicle or its driver **brakes**, or when a driver **brakes** a vehicle, the driver makes it slow down or stop by using the brakes. ब्रेक लावणे

brake light (**brake lights**) *n* A **brake light** is a red light attached to the rear of a motor vehicle that lights up when the brakes are applied, serving as a warning to following drivers. ब्रेक लाईट

bran *n* Bran consists of small brown flakes that are left when wheat grains have been used to make white flour. भूसा, कोंडा

branch (**branches**) *n* The **branches** of a tree are the parts that grow out from its trunk. फांदी

brand (**brands**) *n* A **brand** of a product is the version made by one particular manufacturer. व्यापारी चिन्ह

brand name (**brand names**) *n* A product's **brand name** is the name the manufacturer gives it and under which it is sold. व्यापारी चिन्हाचे नाव

brand-new *adj* Something that is **brand-new** is completely new. नवा कोरा

brandy (**brandies**) *n* Brandy is a strong alcoholic drink. ब्रँडी

brass *n* Brass is a yellow metal made from copper and zinc. पितळ

brass band (**brass bands**) *n* A **brass band** is a band that is made up of brass and percussion instruments. ब्रास बँड

brat (**brats**) *n* If you call a child a **brat**, you disapprove of their bad or annoying behaviour. *(informal)* ग्राम्य

brave (**braver, bravest**) *adj* Someone who is **brave** is willing to do dangerous things, and does not show fear in difficult or dangerous situations. शूर

bravery *n* Bravery is brave behaviour or the quality of being brave. शौर्य

Brazil *n* Brazil is a country in South America. ब्राझील

Brazilian (**Brazilians**) *adj* Brazilian means belonging or relating to Brazil, or to its people or culture. ब्राझिलियन ▷ *n* A **Brazilian** is a person who comes from Brazil. ब्राझिलियन

bread *n* Bread is a food made from flour, water, and often yeast. पाव

bread bin (**bread bins**) *n* A **bread bin** is a wooden, metal, or plastic container for storing bread. पाव ठेवण्याची टोपली

breadcrumbs *npl* Breadcrumbs are tiny pieces of dry bread. They are used in cooking. पावाचे तुकडे

bread roll (**bread rolls**) *n* A **bread roll** is a small piece of bread that is round or long and is made to be eaten by one person. पावांचा रोल

break (**breaks, breaking, broke, broken**) *n* A **break** is the result of breaking. तुटणे, फुटणे वा मोडण्याची क्रिया ▷ *v* When something **breaks**, or when you **break** it, it goes into pieces. फुटणे ▷ *v* If a machine **breaks**, or if you **break** it, it stops working. नादुरुस्त होणे

break down (**breaks down, breaking down, broke down, broken down, breakdowns**) *v* If a machine or a vehicle **breaks down**, it stops working. बिघडणे *Their car broke down.* ▷ *n* The **breakdown** of a system, plan, or discussion is its failure or ending. निष्फळ, यंत्रातील किंवा योजनेतील बिघाड

breakdown truck (**breakdown trucks**) *n* A **breakdown truck** is a truck which is used to pull broken or damaged cars and other vehicles. ब्रेकडाऊन ट्रक

breakdown van (**breakdown vans**) *n* A **breakdown van** is a motor vehicle which is used to pull broken or damaged vehicles. ब्रेकडाऊन व्हॅन

breakfast (**breakfasts**) *n* Breakfast is the first meal of the day, which is usually eaten early in the morning. न्याहारी

break in (**breaks in, breaking in, broke in, broken in, break-ins**) *v* If someone **breaks**

in, they get into a building by force. घुसणे *The robbers broke in and stole a valuable painting.* ▷ *n* When there is a **break-in**, someone gets into a building by force. घुसखोरी

break up (breaks up, breaking up, broke up, broken up) *v* When something **breaks up** or when you **break** it **up**, it separates or is divided into several smaller parts. तोडणे *Break up the chocolate and melt it.*

breast (breasts) *n* A woman's **breasts** are the two soft round pieces of flesh on her chest that can produce milk to feed a baby. स्तन

breast-feed (breast-feeds, breast-feeding, breast-fed) *v* When a woman **breast-feeds**, or **breast-feeds** her baby, she feeds her baby with milk from her breasts, rather than from a bottle. स्तनपान देणे

breaststroke *n* **Breaststroke** is a swimming stroke which you do lying on your front, and making circular movements with your arms and legs. ब्रेस्टस्ट्रोक पद्धतीने पोहणे

breath (breaths) *n* Your **breath** is the air which you take into and let out of your lungs when you breathe. श्वास

Breathalyser® (Breathalysers) *n* A **Breathalyser** is a bag or electronic device that the police use to test whether a driver has drunk too much alcohol. ब्रेदलायझर

breathe (breathes, breathing, breathed) *v* When people or animals **breathe**, they take air into their lungs and let it out again. श्वासोच्छ्वास करणे

breathe in (breathes in, breathing in, breathed in) *v* When you **breathe in**, you take some air into your lungs. श्वास घेणे *She breathed in deeply.*

breathe out (breathes out, breathing out, breathed out) *v* When you **breathe out**, you send air out of your lungs through your nose or mouth. श्वास सोडणे *Breathe out and bring your knees in toward your chest.*

breathing *n* **Breathing** is the passage of air into and out of the lungs to supply the body with oxygen. श्वासोच्छ्वास

breed (breeds, breeding, bred) *n* A **breed** of animal is a particular type of it. विशिष्ट वंश ▷ *vt* If you **breed** animals or plants, you keep them for the purpose of producing more animals or plants. निपज करणे

breeze (breezes) *n* A **breeze** is a gentle wind. वाऱ्याची झुळूक

brewery (breweries) *n* A **brewery** is a place where beer is made. बीअरचा कारखाना

bribe (bribes, bribing, bribed) *vt* If one person **bribes** another, they give them a bribe. लाच देणे

bribery *n* **Bribery** is the action of giving someone a bribe. लाच लुचपतपणा

brick (bricks) *n* **Bricks** are rectangular blocks of baked clay used for building walls. वीट

bricklayer (bricklayers) *n* A **bricklayer** is a person whose job is to build walls using bricks. गवंडी

bride (brides) *n* A **bride** is a woman who is getting married or who has just got married. नवरी

bridegroom (bridegrooms) *n* A **bridegroom** is a man who is getting married. नवरा

bridesmaid (bridesmaids) *n* A **bridesmaid** is a woman or a girl who helps a bride on her wedding day. करवली

bridge (bridges) *n* A **bridge** is a structure built over a river, road, or railway so that people or vehicles can cross from one side to the other. पूल

brief (briefer, briefest) *adj* Something that is **brief** lasts for only a short time. अल्प

briefcase (briefcases) *n* A **briefcase** is a case for carrying documents. ब्रीफकेस

briefing (briefings) n A **briefing** is a meeting at which information or instructions are given to people. थोडक्यात दिलेली माहिती

briefly adv Something that happens **briefly** happens for a very short period of time. थोडेसे

briefs npl Men's or women's underpants can be referred to as **briefs**. चड्डी

bright (brighter, brightest) adj A **bright** colour is very easy to see. भडक ▷ adj Something that is **bright** shines with a lot of light. तेजस्वी

brilliant adj If you describe people or ideas as **brilliant**, you mean that they are extremely clever. बुद्धिमान

bring (brings, bringing, brought) vt If you **bring** something, you take it with you when you go somewhere. आणणे

bring back (brings back, bringing back, brought back) v If something **brings back** a memory, it makes you start thinking about it. आठवण करून देणे, आठवणींना उजाळा देणे Your article brought back sad memories for me.

bring forward (brings forward, bringing forward, brought forward) v If you **bring forward** an event, you arrange for it to take place at an earlier time than had been planned. अगोदर आणणे/ठेवणे He had to bring forward an 11 o'clock meeting.

bring up (brings up, bringing up, brought up) v If you **bring up** a child, you look after it until it is grown up. संगोपन करणे She brought up four children.

Britain n **Britain** is the island consisting of England, Scotland, and Wales, which together with Northern Ireland makes up the United Kingdom. ब्रिटन

British adj **British** means belonging or relating to Great Britain. ब्रिटिश ▷ npl The **British** are the people who come from Great Britain. ब्रिटिश

broad (broader, broadest) adj Something that is **broad** is wide. विशाल, मोठे

broadband n **Broadband** is a method of sending many electronic messages at the same time by using a wide range of frequencies. ब्रॉडबँड

broad bean (broad beans) n **Broad beans** are flat round beans that are light green in colour and are eaten as a vegetable. एक प्रकारच्या भाजीच्या शेंगा

broadcast (broadcasts, broadcasting) n A **broadcast** is something that you hear on the radio or see on television. प्रक्षेपण ▷ v To **broadcast** a programme means to send it out by radio waves, so that it can be heard on the radio or seen on television. प्रक्षेपित करणे

broad-minded adj Someone who is **broad-minded** does not disapprove of actions or attitudes that many other people disapprove of. उदारमतवादी

broccoli n **Broccoli** is a vegetable with green stalks and green or purple flower buds. ब्रॉकोली नावाची छोटी कोबी

brochure (brochures) n A **brochure** is a booklet with pictures that gives you information about a product or service. माहितीपुस्तिका

broke adj If you are **broke**, you have no money. (informal) निर्धन

broken adj A **broken** line is not continuous but has gaps in it. खंडित

broken down adj A **broken down** vehicle or machine no longer works because it has something wrong with it. बिघडलेला

broker (brokers) n A **broker** is a person whose job is to buy and sell shares, foreign money, or goods for other people. दलाल

bronchitis n **Bronchitis** is an illness like a very bad cough which makes breathing painful. फुप्फुसाच्या नळ्यांची सूज

bronze n **Bronze** is a yellowish-brown metal made from copper and tin. कांस्य

brooch (brooches) n A **brooch** is a small piece of jewellery which can be pinned on a dress, blouse, or coat. बूच

broom (brooms) n A **broom** is a long-handled brush which is used to sweep the floor. झाडू

broth (broths) n Broth is a kind of soup. It usually has vegetables or rice in it. ब्रॉथ नावाचे भाजीपाला व तांदूळ यांपासून बनवलेले सूप

brother (brothers) n Your **brother** is a boy or a man who has the same parents as you. भाऊ

brother-in-law (brothers-in-law) n Someone's **brother-in-law** is the brother of their husband or wife, or the man who is married to their sister. मेहुणा, दीर

brown (browner, brownest) adj Something that is **brown** is the colour of earth or of wood. तपकिरी

brown bread n Brown bread is made from grains that have not had their outer layers removed. ब्राऊन ब्रेड

brown rice n Brown rice is unpolished rice, in which the grains retain the outer yellowish-brown layer (bran). पॉलिश न केलेले तांदूळ

browse (browses, browsing, browsed) vi If you **browse** in a shop, you look at things in a fairly casual way, in the hope that you might find something you like. डोकावणे, सहज पहाणे

browser (browsers) n A **browser** is a piece of computer software that you use to search for information on the Internet. ब्राऊझर

bruise (bruises) n A **bruise** is an injury which appears as a purple or dark mark on your body. खरचटल्याने झालेली जखम

brush (brushes, brushing, brushed) n A **brush** is an object with a large number of bristles fixed to it. You use brushes for painting, for cleaning things, and for tidying your hair. कुंचला ▷ vt If you **brush** something or **brush** something such as dirt off it, you clean it or tidy it using a brush. ब्रशने घासणे

Brussels sprouts npl Brussels sprouts are vegetables that look like tiny cabbages. छोट्या कोबीसारखी दिसणारी एक भाजी

brutal adj A **brutal** act or person is cruel and violent. क्रूर

bubble (bubbles) n Bubbles are small balls of air or gas in a liquid. फुगा

bubble bath n Bubble bath is a liquid that smells nice and makes a lot of bubbles when you add it to your bath water. बबल बाथ (आंघोळीचे पाणी फेसाळण्यासाठी असलेला द्रवपदार्थ)

bubble gum n Bubble gum is a sweet substance similar to chewing gum. You can blow it out of your mouth so it makes the shape of a bubble. बबलगम

bucket (buckets) n A **bucket** is a deep round metal or plastic container with a handle. बादली

buckle (buckles) n A **buckle** is a piece of metal or plastic attached to one end of a belt or strap, which is used to fasten it. बकल

Buddha n Buddha is the title given to Gautama Siddhartha, the religious teacher and founder of Buddhism. बुद्ध

Buddhism *n* **Buddhism** is a religion which teaches that the way to end suffering is by overcoming your desires. बौद्ध धर्म

Buddhist (**Buddhists**) *adj* **Buddhist** means relating or referring to Buddhism. बौद्ध ▷ *n* A **Buddhist** is a person whose religion is Buddhism. बौद्ध

budgerigar (**budgerigars**) *n* **Budgerigars** are small, brightly-coloured birds from Australia. बजेरिगर पक्षी

budget (**budgets**) *n* Your **budget** is the amount of money that you have available to spend. The **budget** for something is the amount of money that a person, organization, or country has available to spend on it. खर्चाचे अंदाजपत्रक

budgie (**budgies**) *n* **Budgies** are small, brightly-coloured birds from Australia. (*informal*) बजी नावाचा पक्षी

buffalo (**buffaloes, buffalo**) *n* A **buffalo** is a wild animal like a large cow with long curved horns. रेडा

buffet (**buffets**) *n* A **buffet** is a meal of cold food at a special occasion. Guests usually help themselves to the food. बुफे प्रकारचे जेवण

buffet car (**buffet cars**) *n* On a train, the **buffet car** is the carriage where food is sold. बुफे कार

bug (**bugs**) *n* A **bug** is a tiny insect, especially one that causes damage. (*informal*) एक हानिकारक लहान कीटक

bugged *adj* If a place or a telephone is **bugged**, tiny microphones have been hidden in it which transmit what people are saying. फोनला चोरून लावलेले ध्वनिग्राहक यंत्र

buggy (**buggies**) *n* A **buggy** is a small folding seat with wheels, which a young child can sit in and which can be pushed around. लहान मुलांना बसवून ढकलायची गाडी

build (**builds, building, built**) *vt* If you **build** a structure, you make it by joining things together. बांधणे

builder (**builders**) *n* A **builder** is a person whose job is to build or repair buildings. बांधकाम व्यावसायिक

building (**buildings**) *n* A **building** is a structure with a roof and walls, such as a house. इमारत

building site (**building sites**) *n* A **building site** is an area of land on which a building or a group of buildings is in the process of being built or altered. बांधकाम चालू असलेली जागा

bulb (**bulbs**) *n* A **bulb** is an onion-shaped root that grows into a plant. कंद ▷ *n* A **bulb** is the glass part of an electric lamp which gives out light when electricity passes through it. विजेवर चालणारा दिवा

Bulgaria *n* **Bulgaria** is a republic in south-east Europe, on the Balkan Peninsula on the Black Sea. बल्गेरिया

Bulgarian (**Bulgarians**) *adj* **Bulgarian** means belonging or relating to Bulgaria, or to its people, language, or culture. बल्गेरियन ▷ *n* A **Bulgarian** is a person who comes from Bulgaria. बल्गेरियन ▷ *n* **Bulgarian** is the main language spoken by people who live in Bulgaria. बल्गेरियन

bulimia *n* **Bulimia** or **bulimia nervosa** is a mental illness in which a person eats very large amounts and then makes themselves vomit. भस्म्यारोग

bull (**bulls**) *n* A **bull** is a male animal of the cow family. बैल

bulldozer (**bulldozers**) *n* A **bulldozer** is a large tractor with a broad metal blade at the front, used for moving earth or knocking down buildings. बुलडोझर

bullet (**bullets**) *n* A **bullet** is a small piece of metal which is fired from a gun. बंदुकीच्या गोळ्या

bulletin board (**bulletin boards**) *n* A **bulletin board** is a board which is usually attached to a wall in order to display notices giving information about something. सूचनाफलक

bully (**bullies, bullying, bullied**) *n* A **bully** is someone who uses their strength or power to hurt or frighten other people. पुंड ▷ *vt* If someone **bullies** you, they use their strength or power to hurt or frighten you. दडपशाही करणे

bum (bums) n Your **bum** is the part of your body which you sit on. (informal) पार्श्वभाग

bum bag (bum bags) n A **bum bag** consists of a small bag attached to a belt which you wear round your waist. You use it to carry things such as money and keys. कमरेला अडकवायची लहान बॅग

bumblebee (bumblebees) n A **bumblebee** is a large hairy bee. मोठी केसाळ माशी

bump (bumps) n A **bump** is an accidental knock or collision. धक्का वा ठोकर

bumper (bumpers) n **Bumpers** are bars at the front and back of a vehicle which protect it if it bumps into something. वाहनाचा बंपर

bump into (bumps into, bumping into, bumped into) v If you **bump into** someone you know, you meet them by chance. (informal) अचानक भेटणे I bumped into a friend of yours today.

bumpy (bumpier, bumpiest) adj A **bumpy** road or path has a lot of bumps on it. खाचखळगे असलेला

bun (buns) n A **bun** is a small round cake. छोटा गोल पाव

bunch (bunches) n A **bunch** of things is a group of them. (informal) समूह

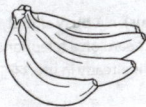

bungalow (bungalows) n A **bungalow** is a house with only one floor. बंगला

bungee jumping n If someone goes **bungee jumping**, they jump from a high place such as a bridge or cliff with a long piece of strong elastic cord tied around their ankles connecting them to the bridge or cliff. बंजी जंपिंग (घोट्याला दोरी बांधून उंच जागेवरून मारलेली उडी)

bunion (bunions) n A **bunion** is a large painful lump on the first joint of a person's big toe. पायाच्या अंगठ्यावर उठलेली दुखरी गाठ वा फोड

bunk (bunks) n A **bunk** is a bed fixed to a wall, especially in a ship or caravan. जहाजात भिंतीवर बसवलेले अंथरूण

bunk beds npl **Bunk beds** are two beds fixed one above the other in a frame. एकाच चौकटीत एकमेकांवर बसवलेली अंथरूणे

buoy (buoys) n A **buoy** is a floating object that shows ships and boats where they can go and warns them of danger. जहाजांच्या मार्गदर्शनासाठी ठेवलेली तरंगती खूण

burden (burdens) n Something that is a **burden** causes you a lot of worry or hard work. ओझे

bureaucracy (bureaucracies) n A **bureaucracy** is an administrative system operated by a large number of officials. नोकरशाही

bureau de change (bureaux de change) n A **bureau de change** is a place where foreign currencies can be exchanged. परदेशी चलन बदलून मिळण्याचे ठिकाण

burger (burgers) n A **burger** is a flat round mass of meat or vegetables, which is grilled or fried. बर्गर

burglar (burglars) n A **burglar** is a thief who breaks into houses and steals things. घरफोडी करणारा चोर

burglar alarm (burglar alarms) n A **burglar alarm** is an electric device that makes a bell ring loudly if someone tries to enter a building by force. अनोळखी माणूस घुसल्यास धोक्याची सूचना देणारी घंटा

burglary (burglaries) n If someone commits a **burglary**, they enter a building by force and steal things. घरफोडी

burgle (**burgles, burgling, burgled**) *vt* If a house **is burgled**, someone breaks in and steals things. घरफोडी करणे

Burmese (**Burmese**) *n* A **Burmese** is a person who comes from Myanmar. ब्रह्मदेशी ▷ *n* **Burmese** is the main language spoken by the people who live in Myanmar. ब्रह्मदेशी

burn (**burns, burning, burned, burnt**) *n* A **burn** is an injury caused by fire or something very hot. भाजून झालेली जखम ▷ *vi* If something is **burning**, it is on fire. जळणे ▷ *vt* If you **burn** something, you destroy it or damage it with fire. जाळणे ▷ *vt* If you **burn** yourself, you touch something that is hot and get hurt. जाळणे

burn down (**burns down, burning down, burned down, burnt down**) *v* If a building **burns down** or if someone **burns** it **down**, it is completely destroyed by fire. जाळून टाकणे

burp (**burps, burping, burped**) *n* A **burp** is a noise someone makes because air from their stomach has been forced up through their throat. ढेकर ▷ *vi* When someone **burps**, they make a noise because air from their stomach has been forced up through their throat. ढेकर देणे

burst (**bursts, bursting**) *v* When something **bursts** or when you **burst** it, it suddenly splits open, and air or some other substance comes out. फुटणे

bury (**buries, burying, buried**) *vt* If you **bury** something, you put it into a hole in the ground and cover it up, often in order to hide it. गाडणे

bus (**buses**) *n* A **bus** is a large motor vehicle which carries passengers. बस

bus conductor (**bus conductors**) *n* A **bus conductor** is a person on a bus whose job is to sell tickets to the passengers. बस कंडक्टर

bush (**bushes**) *n* The **bush** is a dense cluster of shrubs. झुडपांनी आच्छादलेला ▷ *n* A **bush** is a plant which is like a very small tree. झुडूप

business *n* **Business** is work relating to the production, buying, and selling of goods or services. व्यापार

businessman (**businessmen**) *n* A **businessman** is a man who works in business. व्यापारी

businesswoman (**businesswomen**) *n* A **businesswoman** is a woman who works in business. व्यापारी स्त्री

busker (**buskers**) *n* A **busker** is a person who sings or plays music for money in streets and other public places. रस्त्यावर गाणी गाऊन पैसे मागणारा

bus station (**bus stations**) *n* A **bus station** or **coach station** is a place where buses or coaches start a journey. बसस्थानक

bus stop (**bus stops**) *n* A **bus stop** is a place on a road where buses stop to let passengers on and off. बसथांबा

bust (**busts**) *n* A **bust** is a statue of someone's head and shoulders. अर्धपुतळा

bus ticket (**bus tickets**) *n* A **bus ticket** is a small, official piece of paper or card which shows that you have paid for a journey on a bus. बसचे तिकीट

busy (**busier, busiest**) *adj* If you are **busy**, you have a lot of things to do. व्यग्र, गुंतलेले ▷ *adj* A **busy** place is full of people. गजबजलेला

busy signal (**busy signals**) *n* A **busy signal** is a repeated single note heard on a telephone when the number called is already in use. व्यग्र संदेशयंत्रणा, बीझी सिग्नल

but *conj* You use **but** to say something that is different than what you have just said. परंतु *Heat the milk until it is very hot but not boiling.*

butcher (**butchers**) *n* A **butcher** is a shopkeeper who sells meat. खाटीक ▷ *n* A **butcher** or a **butcher's** is a shop where meat is sold. खाटकाचे दुकान

butter *n* **Butter** is a yellowish substance made from cream which you spread on bread or use in cooking. लोणी

buttercup (buttercups) n A **buttercup** is a small plant with bright yellow flowers. पिवळ्या फुलांचे रानटी झाड

butterfly (butterflies) n A **butterfly** is an insect with large colourful wings and a thin body. फुलपाखरू

buttocks npl Your **buttocks** are the two rounded fleshy parts of your body that you sit on. कुल्ले

button (buttons) n **Buttons** are small hard objects sewn on to pieces of clothing, which you use to fasten the clothing. बटन

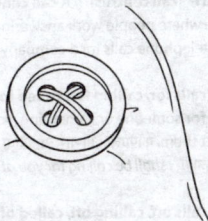

buy (buys, buying, bought) vt If you **buy** something, you obtain it by paying money for it. विकत घेणे

buyer (buyers) n A **buyer** is a person who is buying something or who intends to buy it. खरेदीदार

buyout (buyouts) n A **buyout** is the buying of a company, especially by its managers or employees. खरेदी केलेली कंपनी

by prep If something is done **by** a person or thing, that person or thing does it. ने Dinner was cooked by the children.

bye! excl **Bye!** is another way of saying goodbye. (informal) बरं निघू या

bye-bye! excl **Bye-bye!** is another way of saying goodbye. (informal) बरं निघू या

bypass (bypasses) n A **bypass** is a surgical operation performed on or near the heart, in which the flow of blood is redirected so that it does not flow through a part of the heart that is diseased or blocked. बायपास शश्रक्रिया

cab (cabs) n A **cab** is a taxi. टॅक्सी

cabbage (cabbages) n A **cabbage** is a round vegetable with green leaves. कोबी

cabin (cabins) n A **cabin** is a small room in a ship or boat, or one of the areas inside a plane. केबिन

cabin crew (cabin crews) n The **cabin crew** on an aircraft are the people whose job is to look after the passengers. विमानातील सेवकवर्ग

cabinet (cabinets) n A **cabinet** is a cupboard used for storing things or for displaying objects in. कपाट

cable (cables) n A **cable** is a thick wire which is used to carry electricity or electronic signals. केबल

cable car (cable cars) n A **cable car** is a vehicle for taking people up mountains or steep hills. It is pulled by a moving cable. केबल कार

cable television n **Cable television** is a television system in which signals are sent along wires rather than by radio waves. केबल दूरदर्शन

cactus (cactuses, cacti) n A **cactus** is a desert plant with a thick stem, often with spikes. निवडुंग

cadet (cadets) n A **cadet** is a young person who is being trained in the armed forces or police. सैन्यदल किंवा पोलीसदलातील प्रशिक्षणार्थी

café (cafés) n A **café** is a place where simple meals, snacks, and drinks are sold. उपहारगृह

cafeteria (cafeterias) n A **cafeteria** is a self-service restaurant in a large shop or workplace. स्वयंसेवा असलेले खान-पानगृह

caffeine n **Caffeine** is a chemical substance found in coffee, tea, and cocoa, which makes you more active. कॅफिन

cage (cages) n A **cage** is a structure of wire or metal bars in which birds or animals are kept. पिंजरा

cagoule (cagoules) n A **cagoule** is a lightweight usually knee-length type of anorak. टोपी जोडलेले जाकीट

cake (cakes) n A **cake** is a sweet food made by baking a mixture of flour, eggs, sugar, and fat. केक

calcium n **Calcium** is a soft white element found in bones and teeth, and also in limestone, chalk, and marble. कॅल्शिअम

calculate (calculates, calculating, calculated) vt If you **calculate** a number or amount, you work it out by doing some arithmetic. आकडेमोड करणे

calculation (calculations) n A **calculation** is something that you think about and work out mathematically. आकडेमोड

calculator (calculators) n A **calculator** is a small electronic device used for doing mathematical calculations. परिगणक, गणनयंत्र

calendar (calendars) n A **calendar** is a chart or device which displays the date and the day of the week, and often the whole of a particular year. दिनदर्शिका

calf (calves) n A **calf** is a young cow. वासरू ▷ n Your **calves** are the thick parts at the backs of your legs, between your ankles and your knees. पोटरी

call (calls, calling, called) n When you make a telephone **call**, you telephone someone. केलेला फोन ▷ vt If you **call** someone something, you give them a name. हाक मारणे ▷ v If you **call** something, you say it in a loud voice. मोठ्याने ओरडणे ▷ v If you **call** someone, you talk to them on the telephone. फोन करणे

call back (calls back, calling back, called back) v If you **call** someone **back**, you telephone them again or in return for a telephone call that they have made to you earlier. उतरादाखल फोन करणे OK, I'll call you back around three o'clock.

call box (call boxes) n A **call box** is a small shelter in the street in which there is a public telephone. सार्वजनिक दूरध्वनीची पेटी

call centre (call centres) n A **call centre** is an office where people work answering or making telephone calls for a company. कॉल सेंटर

call for (calls for, calling for, called for) v If you **call for** someone or something, you go to collect them. कोणाला आणायला किंवा काही घ्यायला जाणे I shall be calling for you at seven o'clock.

call off (calls off, calling off, called off) v If you **call off** an event, you cancel it. रद्द करणे The wedding was called off.

calm (calmer, calmest) adj A **calm** person does not show or feel any worry, anger, or excitement. शांत

calm down (calms down, calming down, calmed down) v If you **calm down** or if someone **calms** you **down**, you become less upset or excited. शांत होणे I'll try a herbal remedy to calm him down.

calorie (calories) n A **calorie** is a unit of measurement for the energy value of food. उष्मांक

Cambodia n **Cambodia** is a country in south-east Asia. कंबोडिया

Cambodian (Cambodians) adj **Cambodian** means of or relating to Cambodia or its inhabitants. कंबोडियन ▷ n A **Cambodian** is a native or inhabitant of Cambodia. कंबोडियन

camcorder (camcorders) n A **camcorder** is a portable video camera. वाहून नेण्याजोगा व्हिडिओ कॅमेरा

camel (camels) n A **camel** is a desert animal with one or two humps on its back. ऊंट

camera (cameras) n A **camera** is a piece of equipment for taking photographs or for making a film. कॅमेरा

cameraman (cameramen) n A **cameraman** is a person who operates a television or film camera. छायाचित्रकार

camera phone (camera phones) n A **camera phone** is a mobile phone that can also take photographs. कॅमेरा फोन

Cameroon n **Cameroon** is a republic in West Africa, on the Gulf of Guinea. कॅमेरून

camp (camps, camping, camped) n A **camp** is a place where people live or stay in tents or caravans. छावणी ▷ vi If you **camp** somewhere, you stay there in a tent or caravan. छावणी टाकणे

campaign (campaigns) n A **campaign** is a planned set of activities that people carry out over a period of time in order to achieve something such as social or political change. मोहीम

camp bed (camp beds) n A **camp bed** is a small bed that you can fold up. सोबत नेता येईल असे अंथरूण

camper (campers) n A **camper** is a person who goes camping. छावणीत राहणारी व्यक्ती

camping n **Camping** is the action of staying in a tent or caravan. छावणीतील वास्तव्य

campsite (campsites) n A **campsite** or a **camping site** is a place where people who are on holiday can stay in tents. छावणीची जागा

campus (campuses) n A **campus** is the area of land containing the main buildings of a college or university. महाविद्यालयीन परिसर

can (cans) v If you **can** do something, you are able to do it. शकणे I can swim. ▷ n A **can** is a metal container for food or drink. कॅन

Canada n **Canada** is a country in North America. कॅनडा

Canadian (Canadians) adj **Canadian** means belonging or relating to Canada, or to its people or culture. कॅनेडिअन ▷ n A **Canadian** is a Canadian citizen, or a person of Canadian origin. कॅनेडिअन

canal (canals) n A **canal** is a long, narrow, man-made stretch of water. कालवा

Canaries npl The **Canaries** are a group of islands in the Atlantic, off the northwest coast of Africa. कॅनरी लोक

canary (canaries) n **Canaries** are small yellow birds which sing beautifully. कॅनरी पक्षी

cancel (cancels, cancelling, cancelled) v If you **cancel** an order or an arrangement, you stop it from happening. रद्द करणे

cancellation (cancellations) n **Cancellation** is the fact or an instance of cancelling. रद्द करण्याची प्रक्रिया

cancer (cancers) n **Cancer** is a serious illness in which abnormal body cells increase, producing growths. कर्करोग

Cancer n **Cancer** is one of the twelve signs of the zodiac. Its symbol is a crab. People who are born between the 21st of June and the 22nd of July come under this sign. कर्क रास

candidate (candidates) n A **candidate** is someone who is being considered for a position. उमेदवार

candle (candles) n A **candle** is a stick of hard wax with a piece of string called a wick through the middle. You light the wick so the candle produces light. मेणबत्ती

candlestick (candlesticks) n A **candlestick** is a narrow object with a hole at the top which holds a candle. मेणबत्ती ठेवण्यासाठी भोक असलेला उभा स्टँड

candyfloss n **Candyfloss** is a large pink or white mass of sugar threads that is eaten from a stick. It is sold at fairs or other outdoor events. कँडीफ्लॉस

canister (**canisters**) *n* A **canister** is a metal container. धातूचा डबा

canned *adj* **Canned** music, laughter, or applause on a television or radio programme has been recorded beforehand and is added to the programme to make it sound as if there is a live audience. मूळ कार्यक्रमात वापरलेले आधीच ध्वनिमुद्रित केलेले हास्याचे, टाळ्यांचे आवाज|

canoe (**canoes**) *n* A **canoe** is a small narrow boat that you row using a paddle. पायाने चालवायची होडी

canoeing *n* **Canoeing** is the sport of using and racing a canoe. कॅनोईंग

can opener (**can openers**) *n* A **can opener** is a tool that is used for opening cans of food. डबे उघडणारे उपकरण

canteen (**canteens**) *n* A **canteen** is a place in a factory, office, or shop where the workers can have meals. उपाहारगृह

canter (**canters, cantering, cantered**) *vi* When a horse **canters**, it moves at a speed that is slower than galloping but faster than trotting. हळूहळू धावणे

canvas (**canvases**) *n* **Canvas** is strong heavy cloth used for making tents, sails, and bags. कॅनव्हास

canvass (**canvasses, canvassing, canvassed**) *vi* If you **canvass** for a person or political party, you try to persuade people to vote for them. प्रचार करणे

cap (**caps**) *n* A **cap** is a soft flat hat usually worn by men or boys. टोपी

capable *adj* If you are **capable** of doing something, you are able to do it. सक्षम

capacity (**capacities**) *n* Your **capacity** for something is your ability to do it, or the amount of it that you are able to do. क्षमता

capital (**capitals**) *n* **Capital** is money that you use to start a business. भांडवल ▷ *n* The **capital** of a country is the main city, where the country's leaders work. राजधानी ▷ *n* A **capital** is a big letter of the alphabet, for example A or R. मोठे अक्षर

capitalism *n* **Capitalism** is an economic and political system in which property, business, and industry are owned by private individuals and not by the state. भांडवलशाही

capital punishment *n* **Capital punishment** is the legal killing of a person who has committed a serious crime. फाशीची शिक्षा

Capricorn *n* **Capricorn** is one of the twelve signs of the zodiac. Its symbol is a goat. People who are born between the 22nd of December and the 19th of January come under this sign. मकर रास

capsize (**capsizes, capsizing, capsized**) *v* If you **capsize** a boat or if it **capsizes**, it turns upside down in the water. उलटणे

capsule (**capsules**) *n* A **capsule** is a small container with powdered or liquid medicine inside, which you swallow whole. औषधाचे बाह्य वेष्टन

captain (**captains**) *n* In the army, navy, and some other armed forces, a **captain** is an officer of middle rank. कॅप्टन

caption (**captions**) *n* The **caption** of a picture consists of the words printed underneath. मथळा

capture (**captures, capturing, captured**) *vt* If you **capture** someone or something, you catch them and keep them somewhere so that they cannot leave. पकडणे

car (**cars**) *n* A **car** is a motor vehicle with room for a small number of passengers. कार, गाडी

carafe (**carafes**) *n* A **carafe** is a glass container in which you serve water or wine. कराफे

caramel (**caramels**) *n* A **caramel** is a chewy sweet food made from sugar, butter, and milk. कॅरामेल

carat (**carats**) *n* A **carat** is a unit equal to 0.2 grams used for measuring the weight of diamonds and other precious stones. कॅरेट

caravan (**caravans**) n A **caravan** is a vehicle without an engine that can be pulled by a car or van. It contains beds and cooking equipment so that people can live or spend their holidays in it. केरावॅन

carbohydrate (**carbohydrates**) n **Carbohydrates** are energy-giving substances found in foods such as sugar and bread. कर्बोदक

carbon n **Carbon** is a chemical element that diamonds and coal are made of. कार्बन

carbon footprint (**carbon footprints**) n Your **carbon footprint** is a measure of the amount of carbon dioxide released into the atmosphere by your activities over a particular period. कार्बन फूटप्रिंट

carburettor (**carburettors**) n A **carburettor** is the part of an engine, usually in a car, in which air and petrol are mixed together to form a vapour which can be burned. कारब्युरेटर

card (**cards**) n A **card** is a folded piece of stiff paper that has a picture on the front and a message inside. You send **cards** to people at special times, like birthdays. शुभेच्छापत्र ▷ n **Card** is stiff paper. काई ▷ n **Cards** are pieces of stiff paper with numbers or pictures on them that you use for playing games. खेळातील पते

cardboard n **Cardboard** is thick stiff paper used to make boxes and other containers. कार्डबोर्ड

cardigan (**cardigans**) n A **cardigan** is a knitted woollen garment that fastens at the front. समोर बटणे असलेला लोकरी कपडा

cardphone (**cardphones**) n A **cardphone** is a public telephone operated by the insertion of a phonecard instead of coins. कार्डचा सहाय्याने वापरण्यात येणारा सार्वजनिक दूरध्वनी

care (**cares, caring, cared**) n **Care** is very careful attention. काळजी ▷ vi If you **care** about something, you think that it is important. पर्वा करणे ▷ vi If you **care** for a person or an animal, you look after them. काळजी घेणे

career (**careers**) n Your **career** is your job or profession. पेशा, व्यवसाय

careful adj If you are **careful**, you pay attention to what you are doing in order to avoid damage or mistakes. दक्ष

carefully adv If you do something **carefully**, you pay attention to what you are doing, in order to avoid damage or mistakes. सावधानतेने

careless adj If you are **careless**, you do not pay enough attention to what you are doing, and so you make mistakes. निष्काळजी

caretaker (**caretakers**) n A **caretaker** is someone who looks after a building and the area around it. इमारतीची देखभाल करणारी व्यक्ती

car ferry n A **car ferry** is a boat that transports vehicles and passengers, usually across rivers or short stretches of sea. फेरीबोट

cargo (**cargoes**) n The **cargo** of a ship or plane is the goods that it is carrying. विमानातून वा जहाजातून वाहून न्यायचे सामान

car hire n **Car hire** is the activity or process of hiring a car. भाड्याने दिलेली /घेतलेली गाडी

Caribbean n **Caribbean** means belonging or relating to the Caribbean Sea and its islands, or to its people. कॅरिबिअन ▷ n The **Caribbean** is the sea which is between the West Indies, Central America and the north coast of South America. कॅरिबअन समुद्र

caring adj A **caring** person is affectionate, helpful, and sympathetic. प्रेमळ

car insurance n **Car insurance** is an arrangement in which you pay money to a company, and they pay money to you if you have an accident in your car or if your car is stolen. कारविमा

car keys npl **Car keys** are a set of keys that you use to lock and unlock a car and to start and stop its engine. कारच्या चाव्या

carnation (**carnations**) n A **carnation** is a plant with white, pink, or red flowers. गुलनार

carnival (**carnivals**) n A **carnival** is a public festival with music, processions, and dancing. कानिव्हल

carol (**carols**) n **Carols** are Christian religious songs that are sung at Christmas. ख्रिस्ती धर्मपर गीत

car park (car parks) n A **car park** is an area or building where people can leave their cars. कार उभी करून ठेवण्याची जागा

carpenter (carpenters) n A **carpenter** is a person whose job is making and repairing wooden things. सुतार

carpentry n **Carpentry** is the activity of making and repairing wooden things. सुतारकाम

carpet (carpets) n A **carpet** is a thick covering for a floor or staircase, made of wool or a similar material. जाजम

car rental n **Car rental** is the activity or process of renting a car. कारचे भाडे

carriage (carriages) n A **carriage** is one of the separate sections of a train that carries passengers. रेल्वेमधील (प्रवाशांचा) डबा वा बोगी

carrier bag (carrier bags) n A **carrier bag** is a paper or plastic bag with handles. कागदाची किंवा प्लॅस्टिकची पिशवी

carrot (carrots) n **Carrots** are long, thin, orange-coloured vegetables that grow under the ground. गाजर

carry (carries, carrying, carried) vt If you **carry** something, you take it with you, holding it so that it does not touch the ground. वाहून नेणे

carrycot (carrycots) n A **carrycot** is a small bed for babies which has handles so it can be carried. कॅरिकॉट

carry on (carries on, carrying on, carried on) v If you **carry on** doing something, you continue to do it. हाती असलेले काम चालू ठेवणे *The assistant carried on talking.*

carry out (carries out, carrying out, carried out) v If you **carry out** a threat, task, or instruction, you do it or act according to it. दिलेल्या सूचनांनुसार काम करणे *The police carried out the arrests.*

cart (carts) n A **cart** is an old-fashioned wooden vehicle, usually pulled by an animal. बैलगाडी, घोडागाडी

carton (cartons) n A **carton** is a plastic or cardboard container in which food or drink is sold. खोका, डबा

cartoon (cartoons) n A **cartoon** is a funny drawing. व्यंगचित्र ▷ n A **cartoon** is a film that uses drawings, not real people or things. व्यंगपट

cartridge (cartridges) n In a gun, a **cartridge** is a tube containing a bullet and an explosive substance. काडतूस

carve (carves, carving, carved) v If you **carve** an object, you cut it out of stone or wood. You **carve** wood or stone in order to make the object. कोरणे

car wash (car washes) n A **car wash** is a place with special equipment, where you can pay to have your car washed. कार धुण्याची जागा

case (cases) n A **case** is a particular situation, especially one that you are using as an example. प्रकरण ▷ n A **case** is a container that is used to hold or carry something. डबी, पेटी

cash n **Cash** is money, especially money in the form of notes and coins. रोख रक्कम

cash dispenser (cash dispensers) n A **cash dispenser** is a machine built into the wall of a bank or other building, which allows people to take out money from their bank account using a special card. कॅश डिस्पेन्सर

cashew (cashews) n A **cashew** or a **cashew nut** is a curved nut that you can eat. काजू

cashier (cashiers) n A **cashier** is the person that customers pay money to or get money from in a shop or bank. रोखपाल

cashmere n **Cashmere** is a kind of very fine soft wool. उत्तम प्रकारची लोकर

cash register (cash registers) n A **cash register** is a machine in a shop, pub, or restaurant that is used to add up and record how much money people pay, and in which the money is kept. कॅश रजिस्टर

casino (casinos) n A **casino** is a place where people play gambling games. कसिनो (जुगार खेळण्याचे ठिकाण)

casserole (casseroles) n A **casserole** is a meal made by cooking food in liquid in an oven. कॅसेरोल (मंदाग्नीवर पातळ सूपात शिजवलेले जेवण)

cassette (**cassettes**) n A **cassette** is a small, flat, rectangular, plastic container with magnetic tape inside, which is used for recording and playing back sounds. ध्वनिफित

cast (**casts**) n The **cast** of a play or film is all the people who act in it. भूमिकेसाठी निवडलेला कलाकार

castle (**castles**) n A **castle** is a large building with thick, high walls that was built in the past to protect people during wars and battles. किल्ला

casual adj If you are **casual**, you are relaxed and not very concerned about what is happening. वरवरचे, सहज, अनौपचारिक

casually adv If you do something **casually**, you do it in a relaxed and unconcerned way. सहजपणे, अनौपचारिकरीत्या

casualty (**casualties**) n A **casualty** is a person who is injured or killed in a war or accident. युद्ध किंवा अपघातात मृत्यू किंवा जखमी होणे

cat (**cats**) n A **cat** is a small furry animal with a tail, whiskers, and sharp claws. मांजर

catalogue (**catalogues**) n A **catalogue** is a list of things, such as the goods you can buy from a company. तालिका, कॅटलॉग

catalytic converter (**catalytic converters**) n A **catalytic converter** is a device which is fitted to a car's exhaust to reduce the pollution coming from it. कॅटॅलेटिक कन्व्हर्टर

cataract (**cataracts**) n A **cataract** is a large waterfall or rapids. धबधबा ▷ n A **cataract** is a layer that has grown over a person's eye that prevents them from seeing properly. मोतिबिंदु

catarrh n **Catarrh** is a medical condition in which a lot of thick liquid is produced in your nose and throat. You may get catarrh when you have a cold. पडसे

catastrophe (**catastrophes**) n A **catastrophe** is an unexpected event that causes great suffering or damage. अनपेक्षित संकट/अरिष्ट

catch (**catches, catching, caught**) vt If you **catch** a person or animal, you capture them. पकडणे ▷ vt If you **catch** something that is moving, you take hold of it while it is in the air. झेलणे ▷ vt If you **catch** a bus or a train, you get on it. पकडणे ▷ vt If you **catch** an illness, you become ill with it. आजार होणे

catching adj If an illness or a disease is **catching**, it is easily passed on or given to someone else. संसर्ग

catch up (**catches up, catching up, caught up**) v If you **catch up** with someone, you reach them by moving faster than them. गाठणे I ran faster to catch up with him.

category (**categories**) n If people or things are divided into **categories**, they are divided into groups according to their qualities and characteristics. वर्ग

catering n **Catering** is the activity or business of providing food for people. खानपानसेवा

caterpillar (**caterpillars**) n A **caterpillar** is a small worm-like animal that eventually develops into a butterfly or moth. सुरवंट

cathedral (**cathedrals**) n A **cathedral** is a large important Christian church which has a bishop in charge of it. कॅथेड्रल

cattle npl **Cattle** are cows and bulls. गुरे

Caucasus n The **Caucasus** is a mountain range in south-west Russia. कॉकेसस

cauliflower (**cauliflowers**) n A **cauliflower** is a large, round, white vegetable surrounded by green leaves. कॉलिफ्लॉवर

cause (**causes, causing, caused**) n The **cause** of an event is the thing that makes it happen. कारण ▷ n A **cause** is an aim which a group of people supports or is fighting for. ध्येय ▷ vt To **cause** something, usually something bad, means to make it happen. कारणीभूत होणे

caution n **Caution** is great care taken in order to avoid danger. सावधानता

cautious adj A **cautious** person acts very carefully in order to avoid danger. सावध

cautiously adv If you do something **cautiously**, you do it very carefully in order to avoid possible danger. सावधपणे

cave (**caves**) n A **cave** is a large hole in the side of a cliff or hill, or under the ground. गुहा

CCTV abbr **CCTV** is an abbreviation for 'closed-circuit television'. सीसीटीव्ही

CD (**CDs**) n A **CD** is a small shiny disc on which music or information is stored. **CD** is an abbreviation for 'compact disc'. सीडी

CD burner (**CD burners**) n A **CD burner** is a piece of computer equipment that you use for copying data from a computer onto a CD. सीडी बर्नर

CD player (**CD players**) n A **CD player** is a machine on which you can play CDs. सीडी प्लेअर

CD-ROM (**CD-ROMs**) n A **CD-ROM** is a disc which can be read by a computer, and on which a large amount of data is stored. सीडी-रॉम

ceasefire (**ceasefires**) n A **ceasefire** is an arrangement in which countries at war agree to stop fighting for a time. युद्धबंदी

ceiling (**ceilings**) n A **ceiling** is the top inside surface of a room. छत

celebrate (**celebrates, celebrating, celebrated**) v If you **celebrate**, or **celebrate** something, you do something enjoyable because of a special occasion. साजरा करणे

celebration (**celebrations**) n A **celebration** is a special enjoyable event that people organize because something pleasant has happened or because it is someone's birthday or anniversary. उत्सव

celebrity (**celebrities**) n A **celebrity** is someone who is famous. सुप्रसिद्ध व्यक्ती

celery n **Celery** is a vegetable with long pale green stalks. सेलरी नावाची भाजी बनवण्यासाठी उपयुक्त वनस्पती

cell (**cells**) n A **cell** is the smallest part of an animal or plant. Animals and plants are made up of millions of cells. पेशी

cellar (**cellars**) n A **cellar** is a room underneath a building. तळघर

cello (**cellos**) n A **cello** is a musical instrument that looks like a large violin. You hold it upright and play it sitting down. सेलो नावाचे वाद्य

cement n **Cement** is a grey powder which is mixed with sand and water in order to make concrete. सिमेंट

cemetery (**cemeteries**) n A **cemetery** is a place where dead people are buried. दफनभूमी

census (**censuses**) n A **census** is an official survey of the population of a country. जनगणना

cent (**cents**) n A **cent** is a small unit of money in many countries. सेंट

centenary (**centenaries**) n A **centenary** is the one hundredth anniversary of an event. शताब्दी

centimetre (**centimetres**) n A **centimetre** is a unit of length equal to ten millimetres or one-hundredth of a metre. सेंटीमीटर

central adj Something that is **central** is in the middle of a place or area. मध्यवर्ती

Central African Republic n The **Central African Republic** is a country of central Africa. सेंट्रल आफ्रिकन रिपब्लिक

Central America n **Central America** is an area joining the continents of North and South America, extending from the south border of Mexico to the north-west border of Colombia. सेंट्रल अमेरिका

central heating n **Central heating** is a heating system in which water or air is heated and passed round a building through pipes and radiators. मध्यवर्ती उष्णता, सेंट्रल हिटिंग

centre (**centres**) n The **centre** of something is the middle of it. केंद्र

century (**centuries**) n A **century** is one hundred years. शतक

CEO (CEOs) *abbr* CEO is an abbreviation for 'chief executive officer'. मुख्य कार्यकारी अधिकारी, सी.ई.ओ.

ceramic *adj* Ceramic means of, relating to, or made of clay that has been heated to a very high temperature so that it becomes hard. कुंभारकाम वा त्याविषयी

cereal (cereals) *n* A cereal is a food made from grains that you eat with milk for breakfast. न्याहारीच्या वेळेस दुधाबरोबर खाल्ले जाणारे धान्य ▷ *n* A cereal is a kind of plant, for example wheat or rice. The seeds of cereals are used for food. तृणधान्याचे रोप

ceremony (ceremonies) *n* A ceremony is a formal event such as a wedding or a coronation. समारंभ

certain *adj* If you are certain about something, you know it is true. निश्चित, निःसंशय

certainly *adv* You can use certainly to emphasize what you are saying. निश्चितपणे

certainty (certainties) *n* Certainty is the state of having no doubts at all. निश्चितता

certificate (certificates) *n* A certificate is an official document which states that particular facts are true, or which you receive when you have successfully completed a course of study or training. प्रमाणपत्र

Chad *n* Chad is a republic in north central Africa. चाड

chain (chains) *n* A chain consists of metal rings connected together in a line. साखळी

chair (chairs) *n* A chair is a piece of furniture for one person to sit on, with a back and four legs. खुर्ची

chairlift (chairlifts) *n* A chairlift is a line of chairs that hang from a moving cable and carry people up and down a mountain or ski slope. चेअरलिफ्ट

chairman (chairmen) *n* The chairman of a meeting or organization is the person in charge of it. अध्यक्ष

chalk *n* Chalk is soft white rock. चुनखडक, खडू

challenge (challenges, challenging, challenged) *n* A challenge is something new and difficult which requires great effort and determination. आव्हान ▷ *vt* If you challenge ideas or people, you question their truth, value, or authority. आव्हान देणे

challenging *adj* A challenging job or activity requires great effort and determination. आव्हानात्मक

chambermaid (chambermaids) *n* A chambermaid is a woman who cleans and tidies the bedrooms in a hotel. हॉटेलात साफसफाई करणारी स्त्री

champagne (champagnes) *n* Champagne is an expensive French sparkling white wine. शँपेन

champion (champions) *n* A champion is someone who has won the first prize in a competition. विजेता

championship (championships) *n* A championship is a competition to find the best player or team in a particular sport. विजेतेपद

chance (chances) *n* If there is a chance of something happening, it is possible that it will happen. संधी

change (changes, changing, changed) *n* If there is a change in something, it becomes different. बदल ▷ *vi* When you change, you put on different clothes. कपडे बदलणे ▷ *v* When you change something, or when it changes, it becomes different. बदलणे ▷ *n* Change is the money that you get back when you pay too much for something. सुटे पैसे

changeable *adj* Someone or something that is changeable is likely to change many times. परिवर्तनशील

changing room (changing rooms) n A **changing room** is a room where you can change your clothes and usually have a shower, for example at a sports centre. कपडे बदलण्याची खोली

channel (channels) n A **channel** is a wavelength on which television programmes are broadcast. वाहिनी

chaos n **Chaos** is a state of complete disorder and confusion. गोंधळ, अनागोंदी

chaotic adj If a situation is **chaotic**, it is in a state of disorder and confusion. गोंधळाचा

chap (chaps) n A **chap** is a man or boy. (informal) माणूस

chapel (chapels) n A **chapel** is a part of a Christian church which has its own altar and which is used for private prayer. चर्चमधील चॅपेल

chapter (chapters) n A **chapter** is one of the parts that a book is divided into. प्रकरण

character (characters) n Your **character** is the kind of person you are. चरित्र ▷ n A **character** is a person in a story or a film. पात्र

characteristic (characteristics) n A **characteristic** is a quality or feature that is typical of someone or something. गुणधर्म

charcoal n **Charcoal** is a black substance used as a fuel and for drawing, obtained by burning wood without much air. कोळसा

charge (charges, charging, charged) n A **charge** is an amount of money that you have to pay for a service. आकारलेली किंमत ▷ n A **charge** is a formal accusation that someone has committed a crime. आरोप ▷ n An electrical **charge** is an amount of electricity that is held in or carried by something. प्रभरण, विद्युतभार ▷ v If you **charge** someone an amount of money, you ask them to pay that amount for something. किंमत आकारणे ▷ vt When the police **charge** someone, they formally accuse them of having done something illegal. आरोप ठेवणे ▷ vt To **charge** a battery means to pass an electrical current through it to make it more powerful or to make it last longer. प्रभरण करणे, विद्युतभारित करणे

charger (chargers) n A **charger** is a device used for charging or recharging batteries. चार्जर

charity (charities) n A **charity** is an organization which raises money to help people who are ill, disabled, or poor. धर्मादाय संस्था

charity shop (charity shops) n A **charity shop** is a shop that sells used goods cheaply and gives its profits to a charity. स्वस्तात वस्तू विकणारे व मिळणारा नफा धर्मादाय संस्थेला देणारे दुकान

charm n **Charm** is the quality of being attractive and pleasant. आकर्षकपणा

charming adj If someone or something is **charming**, they are very pleasant and attractive. आकर्षक

chart (charts) n A **chart** is a diagram or graph which displays information. तक्ता

chase (chases, chasing, chased) n A **chase** is the act of chasing someone. पाठलाग ▷ vt If you **chase** someone, you run after them or follow them in order to catch them or force them to leave a place. पाठलाग करणे

chat (chats, chatting, chatted) n A **chat** is informal conversation or talk conducted in an easy familiar manner. गप्पागोष्टी ▷ vi When people **chat**, they talk to each other in an informal and friendly way. गप्पागोष्टी करणे

chatroom (chatrooms) n A **chatroom** is a site on the Internet, or another computer network, where users have group discussions by electronic mail, typically about one subject. चेट रूम

chat show (**chat shows**) n A **chat show** is a television or radio show in which an interviewer and his or her guests talk in a friendly, informal way about different topics. चेट शो

chauffeur (**chauffeurs**) n A **chauffeur** is a person whose job is to drive and look after another person's car. शोफर

chauvinist (**chauvinists**) n A **chauvinist** is a man who believes that men are naturally better and more important than women. पुरुषवादी, दुराभिमानी

cheap (**cheaper, cheapest**) adj **Cheap** goods or services cost less money than usual or than you expected. स्वस्त

cheat (**cheats, cheating, cheated**) n Someone who is a **cheat** does not obey a set of rules which they should be obeying. फसवणूक करणारी व्यक्ती ▷ vi When someone **cheats**, they do not obey a set of rules which they should be obeying, for example in a game or exam. फसवणे

Chechnya n **Chechnya** is a republic that is part of south Russia. चेच्न्या

check (**checks, checking, checked**) n A **check** is a control, especially a rapid or informal one, designed to ensure accuracy, progress, etc. नियंत्रण ▷ v If you **check** something such as a piece of information or a document, you make sure that it is correct or satisfactory. खातरजमा करणे

checked adj Something that is **checked** has a pattern of small squares, usually of two colours. चौकडीचे

check in (**checks in, checking in, checked in**) v When you **check in** or **check into** a hotel or clinic, you arrive and go through the necessary procedures before staying there. (हॉटेल किंवा दवाखान्यात) आत येणे He checked in at the hotel and asked to see the manager.

check out (**checks out, checking out, checked out, checkouts**) v When you **check**

out of a hotel, you pay the bill and leave. (हॉटेल किंवा दवाखान्यात) बाहेर पडणे They packed and checked out of the hotel. ▷ n In a supermarket, a **checkout** is a counter where you pay for your goods. चेक-आऊट

check-up (**check-ups**) n A **check-up** is a routine examination by a doctor or dentist. तपासणी

cheek (**cheeks**) n Your **cheeks** are the sides of your face below your eyes. गाल

cheekbone (**cheekbones**) n Your **cheekbones** are the two bones in your face just below your eyes. गालफड

cheeky (**cheekier, cheekiest**) adj Someone who is **cheeky** is rude to someone they ought to respect, but often in a charming or amusing way. उद्धट

cheer (**cheers, cheering, cheered**) n A **cheer** is a shout or cry of approval, encouragement, etc. प्रोत्साहन ▷ v When people **cheer**, they shout loudly to show their approval or to encourage someone who is doing something such as taking part in a game. प्रोत्साहित करणे

cheerful adj A **cheerful** person is happy. आनंदी

cheerio! excl People sometimes say 'Cheerio!' as a way of saying goodbye. (informal) नमस्कार, पुन्हा भेटू या

cheers! excl **Cheers!** is a word that people say to each other as they lift up their glasses to drink. चीअर्स

cheese (**cheeses**) n **Cheese** is a solid food made from milk. चीझ

chef (**chefs**) n A **chef** is a cook in a restaurant or hotel. हॉटेलातील स्वयंपाकी

chemical (**chemicals**) n **Chemicals** are substances that are used in or made by a chemical process. रसायन

chemist (**chemists**) n A **chemist** is a specially qualified person who prepares and sells medicines. औषधविक्रेता ▷ n A **chemist** or a **chemist's** is a place where medicines are sold or given out. औषधांचे दुकान

chemistry *n* **Chemistry** is the scientific study of the characteristics and composition of substances. रसायनशास्त्र

cheque (**cheques**) *n* A **cheque** is a printed form on which you write an amount of money and say who it is to be paid to. Your bank then pays the money to that person from your account. धनादेश

chequebook (**chequebooks**) *n* A **chequebook** is a book containing detachable blank cheques, issued by a bank or building society to holders of cheque accounts. धनादेश पुस्तिका

cherry (**cherries**) *n* **Cherries** are small, round fruit with red or black skins. चेरी

chess *n* **Chess** is a game for two people played on a board with 64 black and white squares. Each player has 16 pieces including a King. The aim is to trap your opponent's King. बुद्धिबळ

chest (**chests**) *n* Your **chest** is the top part of the front of your body. छाती ▷ *n* A **chest** is a large heavy box, used for storing things. तिजोरी

chestnut (**chestnuts**) *n* A **chestnut** or **chestnut tree** is a tall tree with broad leaves. चेस्टनटचे झाड

chest of drawers (**chests of drawers**) *n* A **chest of drawers** is a low, flat piece of furniture with drawers in which you keep clothes and other things. कप्पे असलेले कपड्यांचे कपाट

chew (**chews, chewing, chewed**) *v* When you **chew** food, you break it up with your teeth and make it easier to swallow. चावून चोथा करणे, चावणे

chewing gum *n* **Chewing gum** is a kind of sweet that you can chew for a long time. You do not swallow it. च्युईंगगम

chick (**chicks**) *n* A **chick** is a baby bird. पक्ष्याचे पिल्लू

chicken (**chickens**) *n* A **chicken** is a bird that is kept on a farm for its eggs and meat. कोंबडी ▷ *n* **Chicken** is the meat that comes from chickens. कोंबडीचे मांस

chickenpox *n* **Chickenpox** is a disease which gives you a high temperature and red spots that itch. कांजिण्या

chickpea (**chickpeas**) *n* **Chickpeas** are hard round seeds that look like pale-brown peas. They can be cooked and eaten. लहान आकाराचा वाटाणा

chief (**chiefs**) *adj* **Chief** is used in the job titles of the most senior worker or workers of a particular kind in an organization. मुख्य ▷ *n* The **chief** of an organization or department is its leader or the person in charge of it. प्रमुख

child (**children**) *n* A **child** is a human being who is not yet an adult. मूल

childcare *n* **Childcare** refers to looking after children. बालसंगोपन

childhood (**childhoods**) *n* A person's **childhood** is the time when they are a child. बालपण

childish *adj* **Childish** means relating to or typical of a child. पोरकट

childminder (**childminders**) *n* A **childminder** is someone whose job it is to look after children when the children's parents are away or are at work. Childminders usually work in their own homes. आई-वडिलांच्या अनुपस्थितीत मुलांची काळजी घेणारी व्यक्ती

Chile *n* **Chile** is a republic in South America, on the Pacific. चिली

Chilean (**Chileans**) *adj* **Chilean** means of or relating to Chile or its inhabitants. चिलियन ▷ *n* A **Chilean** is a native or inhabitant of Chile. चिलियन

chill (**chills, chilling, chilled**) *v* To **chill** something means to make it cold. थंड करणे

chilli (**chillies, chillis**) *n* **Chillies** are small red or green seed pods with a hot, spicy taste. मिरची

chilly (**chillier, chilliest**) *adj* **Chilly** means uncomfortably cold. अति थंड

chimney (**chimneys**) *n* A **chimney** is a pipe above a fireplace or furnace through which smoke can go up into the air. धुराडे

chimpanzee (**chimpanzees**) *n* A **chimpanzee** is a kind of small African ape. चिंपांझी

chin (chins) *n* Your **chin** is the part of your face below your mouth and above your neck. हनुवटी

china *n* **China** or **china clay** is a very thin clay used to make cups, plates, and ornaments. चिनीमाती

China *n* **China** is a republic in East Asia. चीन

Chinese (Chinese) *adj* **Chinese** means relating to or belonging to China, or its people, languages, or culture. चिनी ▷ *n* The **Chinese** are the people who come from China. चिनी ▷ *n* The languages that are spoken in China, especially Mandarin, are often referred to as **Chinese**. चिनी

chip (chips, chipping, chipped) *n* A **chip** is a small piece which has been broken off something. कपची, टवका ▷ *n* A **chip** is a very small part that controls a piece of electronic equipment. चिप ▷ *vt* If you **chip** something, you break a small piece off it by accident. कपची/टवका उडणे

chips *npl* **Chips** or potato **chips** are thin pieces of potato fried in oil. पातळ कचऱ्या

chiropodist (chiropodists) *n* A **chiropodist** is a person whose job is to treat and care for people's feet. पायांवर उपचार करणारे डॉक्टर

chisel (chisels) *n* A **chisel** is a tool that has a long metal blade with a sharp edge at the end. It is used for cutting and shaping wood and stone. छिन्नी, पटाशी

chives *npl* **Chives** are the long, thin, hollow green leaves of a herb. Chives are cut into small pieces and added to food to give it a flavour similar to onions. चिव्हज वनस्पती

chlorine *n* **Chlorine** is a gas that is used to disinfect water and to make cleaning products. क्लोरिन

chocolate (chocolates) *n* **Chocolate** is a sweet food made from cocoa beans. चॉकलेट

choice (choices) *n* If there is a **choice** of things, there are several of them and you can choose the one you want. पर्याय

choir (choirs) *n* A **choir** is a group of people who sing together. गायकसमूह

choke (chokes, choking, choked) *v* When you **choke** or when something **chokes** you, you cannot breathe properly or get enough air into your lungs. गुदमरणे, घुसमरणे

cholesterol *n* **Cholesterol** is a substance that exists in the fat, tissues, and blood of all animals. Too much cholesterol in a person's blood can cause heart disease. कोलेस्टेरॉल

choose (chooses, choosing, chose, chosen) *v* If you **choose** someone or something from all the people or things that are available, you decide to have that person or thing. निवड करणे

chop (chops, chopping, chopped) *n* A **chop** is a small piece of meat cut from the ribs of a sheep or pig. मांसाचा तुकडा ▷ *vt* If you **chop** something, you cut it into pieces with a knife or axe. कापून तुकडे करणे

chopsticks *npl* **Chopsticks** are a pair of thin sticks which people in Asia use to eat their food. चॉपस्टिक्स

chosen *adj* Something that is **chosen** has been selected or picked out. निवडलेला

Christ *n* **Christ** is one of the names of Jesus, whom Christians believe to be the son of God and whose teachings are the basis of Christianity. ख्रिस्त

Christian (Christians) *adj* **Christian** means relating to Christianity or Christians. ख्रिस्ती ▷ *n* A **Christian** is someone who follows the teachings of Jesus Christ. ख्रिस्ती

Christianity *n* **Christianity** is a religion based on the teachings of Jesus Christ. ख्रिस्ती धर्म

Christmas (Christmases) *n* **Christmas** is the period around the 25th of December when Christians celebrate the birth of Jesus Christ. नाताळ

Christmas card (Christmas cards) *n* **Christmas cards** are cards with greetings, which people send to their friends and family at Christmas. ख्रिसमस कार्ड

Christmas Eve *n* **Christmas Eve** is the 24th of December. ख्रिसमस ईव्ह

Christmas tree (Christmas trees) *n* A **Christmas tree** is a real or artificial fir tree, which people put in their houses at Christmas and decorate with lights and balls. ख्रिसमस ट्री

chrome n **Chrome** is a hard silver-coloured metal, used to coat other metals. मुलामा देण्यासाठी वापरला जाणारा धातू, क्रोमिअम

chronic adj A **chronic** illness lasts for a very long time. जुनाट

chrysanthemum (**chrysanthemums**) n A **chrysanthemum** is a large garden flower with many long, thin petals. शेवंती

chubby (**chubbier, chubbiest**) adj A **chubby** person is rather fat. स्थूल

chunk (**chunks**) n A **chunk** of something is a thick solid piece of it. कशाची तरी जाड व मोठा तुकडा

church (**churches**) n A **church** is a building in which Christians worship. चर्च

cider (**ciders**) n **Cider** is an alcoholic drink made from apples. सायडर (सफरचंदाचे रसमिश्रित मद्य)

cigar (**cigars**) n **Cigars** are rolls of dried tobacco leaves which people smoke. सिगार

cigarette (**cigarettes**) n **Cigarettes** are small tubes of paper containing tobacco which people smoke. सिगरेट

cigarette lighter (**cigarette lighters**) n A **cigarette lighter** is a device which produces a small flame when you press a switch and which you use to light a cigarette or cigar. सिगरेट लायटर

cinema (**cinemas**) n A **cinema** is a place where people go to watch films. चित्रपटगृह

cinnamon n **Cinnamon** is a spice used for flavouring sweet food. दालचिनी

circle (**circles**) n A **circle** is a round shape. Every part of its edge is the same distance from the centre. वर्तुळ

circuit (**circuits**) n An electrical **circuit** is a complete route which an electric current can flow around. सर्किट

circular adj Something that is **circular** is shaped like a circle. वर्तुळाकार

circulation n The **circulation** of something is the passing of it around, or the spreading of it among a group of people. वाटप

circumstances npl Your **circumstances** are the conditions of your life, especially the amount of money that you have. परिस्थिति

circus (**circuses**) n A **circus** is a travelling show performed in a large tent, with performers such as clowns and trained animals. सर्कस

citizen (**citizens**) n If someone is a **citizen** of a country, they are legally accepted as belonging to that country. नागरिक

citizenship n If you have **citizenship** of a country, you are legally accepted as belonging to it. नागरिकत्व

city (**cities**) n A **city** is a large town. मोठे शहर

city centre (**city centres**) n The **city centre** is the busiest part of a city, where most of the shops and businesses are. शहराचा मध्यवर्ती भाग

civilian (**civilians**) adj In a military situation, **civilian** is used to describe people or things that are not military. नागरिक ▷ n A **civilian** is anyone who is not a member of the armed forces. नागरिक

civilization (**civilizations**) n A **civilization** is a human society with its own social organization and culture. नागरी संस्कृती

civil rights npl **Civil rights** are the rights that people have to equal treatment and equal opportunities, whatever their race, sex, or religion. नागरी हक्क

civil servant (**civil servants**) n A **civil servant** is a person who works in a government department. नागरी सेवेतील व्यक्ती

civil war (**civil wars**) n A **civil war** is a war which is fought between different groups of people living in the same country. यादवी युद्ध

claim (**claims, claiming, claimed**) n A **claim** is something which someone says which they cannot prove and which may be false. दावा ▷ vt If you say that someone **claims** that something is true, you mean they say that it is true but you are not sure whether or not they are telling the truth. दावा करणे

claim form (**claim forms**) n A **claim form** is a formal written request to the government, an insurance company, or another organization for money that you think you are entitled to according to their rules. दावा प्रपत्र

clap (claps, clapping, clapped) v When you **clap**, you hit your hands together to show appreciation or attract attention. टाळ्या वाजवणे

clarify (clarifies, clarifying, clarified) vt To **clarify** something means to make it easier to understand. *(formal)* स्पष्टीकरण देणे

clarinet (clarinets) n A **clarinet** is a wind instrument with a single reed in its mouthpiece. क्लॅरिनेट

clash (clashes, clashing, clashed) vi When people **clash**, they fight, argue, or disagree with each other. संघर्ष करणे

clasp (clasps) n A **clasp** is a small metal fastening. फासा, चाप

class (classes) n A **class** is a group of pupils or students who are taught together. वर्ग

classic (classics) adj A **classic** example of something has all the features which you expect that kind of thing to have. नमुनेदार ▷ n A **classic** is a piece of writing, film, or piece of music of high quality that has become a standard against which similar things are judged. दर्जेदार

classical adj You use **classical** to describe something that is traditional in form, style, or content. शास्त्रीय

classmate (classmates) n Your **classmates** are students in the same class as you at school or college. वर्गमित्र

classroom (classrooms) n A **classroom** is a room in a school where lessons take place. वर्गखोली

classroom assistant (classroom assistants) n A **classroom assistant** is a person whose job is to help a schoolteacher in the classroom. वर्गखोली सहायक

clause (clauses) n A **clause** is a section of a legal document. कलम

claustrophobic adj You describe a place or situation as **claustrophobic** when it makes you feel uncomfortable and unhappy because you are enclosed or restricted. घुसमट करणारी बंदिस्त जागा

claw (claws) n The **claws** of a bird or animal are the thin curved nails on its feet. पक्षी किंवा प्राण्यांची अणकुचीदार बाकदार नखे

clay n **Clay** is a type of earth that is soft when it is wet and hard when it is baked dry. चिकणमाती

clean (cleaner, cleanest, cleans, cleaning, cleaned) adj Something that is **clean** does not have any dirt or marks on it. स्वच्छ ▷ vt When you **clean** something, you take all the dirt off it. साफ करणे

cleaner (cleaners) n A **cleaner** is someone who is employed to clean the rooms and furniture inside a building or someone whose job is to clean a particular type of thing. सफाई करणारा

cleaning n **Cleaning** is the action of making something clean. साफसफाई

cleaning lady (cleaning ladies) n A **cleaning lady** is a woman who is employed to clean the rooms and furniture inside a building. सफाई करणारी स्त्री

cleanser (cleansers) n A **cleanser** is a liquid or cream that you use for cleaning something, especially your skin. क्लिन्झर

cleansing lotion (cleansing lotions) n **Cleansing lotion** is a liquid or cream that you use for cleaning your skin. क्लिन्झिंग लोशन

clear (clearer, clearest, clears, clearing, cleared) adj If something is **clear**, it is easy to understand, to see, or to hear. स्पष्ट ▷ adj If something like glass or plastic is **clear**, you can see through it. स्वच्छ ▷ adj If a place is **clear**, it does not have anything there that you do not want. साफ ▷ vt When you **clear** a place, you take away all the things you do not want there. साफ करणे

clearly adv **Clearly** means in a manner that is easy to understand, see, or hear. स्पष्टपणे

clear off (clears off, clearing off, cleared off) v If you tell someone to **clear off**, you are telling them in a rude way to go away.

(informal) "चालते व्हा" असे सांगणे *The boys told me to clear off.*

clear up (clears up, clearing up, cleared up) *v* When you **clear up**, or when you **clear** a place **up**, you tidy a place and put things away. साफ करणे *I cleared up my room.*

clementine (clementines) *n* A **clementine** is a fruit that looks like a small orange. क्लिमेंटाईन

clever (cleverer, cleverest) *adj* A **clever** person is intelligent and able to understand things easily or to plan things well. हुशार

click (clicks, clicking, clicked) *n* A **click** is a short, light, often metallic sound. क्लिक असा आवाज ▷ *v* If something **clicks** or if you **click** it, it makes a short, sharp sound. क्लिक असा आवाज करणे

client (clients) *n* A **client** is someone for whom a professional person or organization is providing a service or doing some work. ग्राहक

cliff (cliffs) *n* A **cliff** is a high area of land with a very steep side, especially one next to the sea. सुळका

climate (climates) *n* The **climate** of a place is the general weather conditions that are typical of it. हवामान

climate change *n* **Climate change** is change that is taking place in the Earth's climate that is believed to be the result of human activity. हवामानातील बदल

climb (climbs, climbing, climbed) *v* If you **climb** something such as a tree, mountain, or ladder, or **climb** up it, you move towards the top of it. If you **climb** down it, you move towards the bottom of it. चढणे

climber (climbers) *n* A **climber** is someone who climbs rocks or mountains as a sport. चढणारा

climbing *n* **Climbing** is the activity of climbing rocks or mountains. आरोहण

clinic (clinics) *n* A **clinic** is a building where people receive medical advice or treatment. दवाखाना

clip (clips) *n* A **clip** is a small metal or plastic device that is used for holding things together. चाप

clippers *npl* **Clippers** are a tool used for cutting small amounts from something, especially from someone's hair or nails. क्लीपर्स

cloakroom (cloakrooms) *n* A **cloakroom** is a small room in a public building where people can leave their coats. क्लोकरूम

clock (clocks) *n* A **clock** is an instrument, for example in a room or on the outside of a building, that shows you what the time is. घड्याळ

clockwise *adv* When something is moving **clockwise**, it is moving in a circle in the same direction as the hands on a clock. सव्य

clog (clogs) *n* **Clogs** are heavy leather or wooden shoes with thick wooden soles. चामड्याचे किंवा लाकडाचे जाडजूड बूट

clone (clones, cloning, cloned) *n* If someone or something is a **clone** of another person or thing, they are so similar to this person or thing that they seem to be exactly the same as them. क्लोन ▷ *vt* If you **clone** an animal or plant, you produce it artificially from a cell of another animal or plant, so that it is exactly the same as the original. क्लोन (प्रतिरूप) तयार करणे

close (closer, closest, closes, closing, closed) *adj* If something is **close** to another thing, it is near it. जवळ ▷ *adv* **Close** means near to something else. जवळ ▷ *vt* When you **close** something, you shut it. बंद करणे

close by *adj* Something that is **close by** is near to you. जवळपास

closed *adj* A **closed** group of people does not welcome new people or ideas from outside. प्रतिगामी

closely *adv* **Closely** means near to something else. जवळून

closing time (closing times) *n* **Closing time** is the time when something such as a shop, library, or pub closes and people have to leave. बंद करण्याची वेळ

closure (closures) n The **closure** of a business or factory is the permanent shutting of it. व्यवसाय बंद करणे

cloth (cloths) n Cloth is material that is used to make things like clothes and curtains. कापड ▷ n A **cloth** is a piece of material that you use to clean something. कपडा

clothes npl Clothes are the things that people wear, such as shirts, coats, trousers, and dresses. कपडे

clothes line (clothes lines) n A **clothes line** is a thin rope on which you hang washing so that it can dry. कपडे सुकत घालण्याची दोरी

clothes peg (clothes pegs) n A **clothes peg** is a small device which you use to fasten clothes to a washing line. चिमटा

clothing n Clothing is the clothes people wear. कपडे

cloud (clouds) n A **cloud** is a mass of water vapour that is seen as a white or grey mass in the sky. ढग

cloudy (cloudier, cloudiest) adj If it is **cloudy**, there are a lot of clouds in the sky. ढगाळ

clove (cloves) n Cloves are small dried flower buds used as a spice. लवंग

clown (clowns) n A **clown** is a performer who wears funny clothes and bright make-up, and does silly things to make people laugh. विदूषक

club (clubs) n A **club** is an organization of people who are all interested in a particular activity. क्लब ▷ n A **club** is a thick, heavy stick that can be used as a weapon. सोटा

club together (clubs together, clubbed together, clubbing together) v If people **club together** to do something, they all give money towards the cost of it. पैसे जमवणे For my thirtieth birthday, my friends clubbed together and bought me a watch.

clue (clues) n A **clue** to a problem, mystery, or puzzle is something that helps you find the answer. सूचक गोष्ट, धागादोरा

clumsy (clumsier, clumsiest) adj A **clumsy** person moves or handles things in an awkward way. अकुशल, वेंधळा

clutch (clutches) n If you are in another person's **clutches**, that person has control over you. बंधन, नियंत्रण

clutter n Clutter is a lot of unnecessary or useless things in an untidy state. कुचकामी वस्तूंचा पसारा

coach (coaches) n A **coach** is someone who trains a person or team of people in a particular sport. प्रशिक्षक ▷ n A **coach** is a large comfortable bus that carries passengers on long journeys. कोच

coal n Coal is a hard black substance taken from underground and burned as fuel. दगडी कोळसा

coarse (coarser, coarsest) adj Coarse things have a rough texture. खडबडीत

coast (coasts) n The **coast** is an area of land next to the sea. समुद्रकिनारा

coastguard (coastguards) n A **coastguard** is an official who watches the sea near a coast, in order to get help when it is needed and to prevent smuggling. तटरक्षक

coat (coats) n A **coat** is a piece of clothing with long sleeves worn over your other clothes when you go outside. कोट

coathanger (coathangers) n A **coathanger** is a curved piece of wood, metal, or plastic that you hang a piece of clothing on. कोटाचा हँगर

cobweb (cobwebs) n A **cobweb** is the fine net that a spider makes in order to catch insects. कोळ्याचे जाळे

cock (cocks) n A **cock** is an adult male chicken. कोंबडा

cockerel (cockerels) n A **cockerel** is a young male chicken. लहान वयाचा कोंबडा

cockpit (cockpits) n The **cockpit** in a small plane or racing car is the part where the pilot or driver sits. कॉकपिट

cockroach (cockroaches) n A **cockroach** is a large brown insect that is often found in dirty or damp places. झुरळ

cocktail (cocktails) n A **cocktail** is an alcoholic drink containing several ingredients. कॉकटेल

cocoa n **Cocoa** is a brown powder used in making chocolate. कोको

coconut (coconuts) n A **coconut** is a very large nut with a hairy shell, white flesh, and milky juice inside. नारळ

cod (cods, cod) n A **cod** is a large sea fish with white flesh. कॉड नावाचा मासा

code (codes) n A **code** is a set of rules about how people should behave. संहिता

coeliac adj **Coeliac** means of or relating to the abdomen. पोटातला

coffee (coffees) n **Coffee** is a drink made from the roasted beans of the coffee plant. कॉफी

coffee bean (coffee beans) n **Coffee beans** are small dark-brown beans that are roasted and ground to make coffee. They are the seeds of the coffee plant. कॉफीच्या झाडाच्या शेंगा

coffeepot (coffeepots) n A **coffeepot** is a tall narrow pot with a spout and a lid, in which coffee is made or served. कॉफीचे भांडे

coffee table (coffee tables) n A **coffee table** is a small low table in a living room. दिवाणखान्यातले छोटे टेबल

coffin (coffins) n A **coffin** is a box in which a dead body is buried or cremated. शवपेटी

coin (coins) n A **coin** is a small piece of metal used as money. नाणे

coincide (coincides, coinciding, coincided) vi If one event **coincides** with another, they happen at the same time. योगायोगाने होणे

coincidence (coincidences) n A **coincidence** happens when two or more things occur at the same time by chance. योगायोग

Coke® (Cokes) n **Coke** is a sweet, brown, non-alcoholic fizzy drink. कोक

colander (colanders) n A **colander** is a container in the shape of a bowl with holes in it which you wash or drain food in. गाळणी

cold (colder, coldest, colds) adj If something is **cold**, it is not hot. थंड ▷ n When you have a **cold**, you sneeze and cough a lot, and you have a sore throat. सर्दी ▷ adj If you are **cold**, you do not feel comfortable because you are not warm enough. थंड

cold sore (cold sores) n **Cold sores** are small sore spots that sometimes appear on or near someone's lips and nose when they have a cold. सर्दीपडशामुळे तोंडाजवळ उठणारे पुरळ

coleslaw n **Coleslaw** is a salad of chopped raw cabbage, carrots, onions, and sometimes other vegetables, usually with mayonnaise. कोलस्लॉ

collaborate (collaborates, collaborating, collaborated) vi When people **collaborate**, they work together on a particular project. जोडीने/एकत्र काम करणे

collapse (collapses, collapsing, collapsed) vi If a building or other structure **collapses**, it falls down very suddenly. कोसळणे

collar (collars) n The **collar** of a shirt or jacket is the part that goes around your neck. कॉलर ▷ n A **collar** is a band that goes around the neck of a dog or cat. गळपट्टा

collarbone (collarbones) n Your **collarbones** are the two long bones which run from your throat to your shoulders. कॉलरबोन (सरीचे हाड)

colleague (colleagues) n Your **colleagues** are the people you work with, especially in a professional job. सहकारी

collect (collects, collecting, collected) vt If you **collect** things, you bring them together. जमा करणे ▷ vt If you **collect** someone from a place, you go there and take them away. सोबत घेऊन जाणे

collection (collections) n A **collection** of things is a group of similar things that you have deliberately acquired, usually over a period of time. संग्रह

collective (**collectives**) *adj* **Collective** means shared by or involving every member of a group of people. सामूहिक ▷ *n* A **collective** is a business or farm whose employees share the decision-making and the profits. सामुदायिक

collector (**collectors**) *n* A **collector** is a person who collects things of a particular type as a hobby. संग्राहक

college (**colleges**) *n* A **college** is an institution where students study after they have left school. महाविद्यालय

collide (**collides, colliding, collided**) *vi* If people or vehicles **collide**, they bump into each other. टक्कर होणे

collie (**collies**) *n* A **collie** or a **collie dog** is a dog with long hair and a long, narrow nose. कोली जातीचा कुत्रा

colliery (**collieries**) *n* A **colliery** is a coal mine. कोळशाची खाण

collision (**collisions**) *n* A **collision** occurs when a moving object hits something. टक्कर

Colombia *n* **Colombia** is a republic in north-west South America. कोलंबिया

Colombian (**Colombians**) *adj* **Colombian** means belonging or relating to Colombia or its people or culture. कोलंबियन ▷ *n* A **Colombian** is a Colombian citizen, or a person of Colombian origin. कोलंबियन

colon (**colons**) *n* A **colon** is the punctuation mark (:). द्विबिंदुचिन्ह

colonel (**colonels**) *n* A **colonel** is a senior officer in an army, air force, or the marines. कर्नल

colour (**colours**) *n* The **colour** of something is the appearance that it has as a result of reflecting light. Red, blue, and green are colours. रंग

colour-blind *adj* Someone who is **colour-blind** cannot see the difference between colours, especially between red and green. रंगांधळा

colourful *adj* Something that is **colourful** has bright colours. रंगीबेरंगी

colouring *n* Someone's **colouring** is the colour of their hair, skin, and eyes. रंगछटा, वर्ण

column (**columns**) *n* A **column** is a tall solid cylinder, especially one supporting part of a building. स्तंभ, खांब

coma (**comas**) *n* If someone is in a **coma**, they are deeply unconscious. बेशुद्धी, कोमा

comb (**combs, combing, combed**) *n* A **comb** is a flat piece of plastic or metal with narrow pointed teeth along one side, which you use to tidy your hair. कंगवा ▷ *vt* When you **comb** your hair, you tidy it using a comb. विंचरणे

combination (**combinations**) *n* A **combination** is a mixture of things. एकत्रीकरण

combine (**combines, combining, combined**) *v* If you **combine** two or more things, or if they **combine**, they exist or join together. एकत्र करणे

come (**comes, coming, came**) *vi* When you **come** to a place, you move towards it or arrive there. येणे

come back (**comes back, coming back, came back**) *v* If someone **comes back** to a place, they return to it. परत येणे *I came back to my hometown and decided to be a photographer.*

comedian (**comedians**) *n* A **comedian** is an entertainer whose job is to make people laugh by telling jokes. विनोद करणारा

come down (**comes down, coming down, came down**) *v* If the cost, level, or amount of something **comes down**, it becomes less than it was before. कमी होणे *The price of petrol is coming down.*

comedy n **Comedy** consists of types of entertainment that are intended to make people laugh. मनोरंजक विनोदी कार्यक्रम

come from (comes from, coming from, came from) v If someone or something **comes from** a particular place or thing, that place or thing is their origin or source. .चे रहिवासी असणे *Half the students come from abroad.*

come in (comes in, coming in, came in) v If information or a report **comes in**, you receive it. प्राप्त होणे *Reports are now coming in of trouble at the event.*

come out (comes out, coming out, came out) v When a new product **comes out**, it becomes available to the public. उपलब्ध होणे *The actor has a new movie coming out.*

come round (comes round, coming round, came round) v When someone who is unconscious **comes round** or **comes around**, they recover consciousness. शुद्धीवर येणे *When I came round I was on the kitchen floor.*

comet (comets) n A **comet** is an object that travels around the sun leaving a bright trail behind it. धूमकेतू

come up (comes up, coming up, came up) v If someone **comes up** to you, they walk over to you. कडे चालत येणे *Her cat came up and rubbed itself against their legs.*

comfortable adj You describe things such as furniture as **comfortable** when they make you feel physically relaxed. आरामशीर

comic (comics) n A **comic** is an entertainer who tells jokes in order to make people laugh. विनोद सांगून मनोरंजन करणारा नट

comic book (comic books) n A **comic book** is a magazine that contains stories told in pictures. कॉमिक पुस्तक

comic strip (comic strips) n A **comic strip** is a series of drawings that tell a story, especially in a newspaper or magazine. कॉमिक स्ट्रीप

coming adj A **coming** event or time will happen soon. येणारा

comma (commas) n A **comma** is the punctuation mark (,). स्वल्पविराम

command (commands) n If you give someone a **command** to do something, you order them to do it. *(written)* आज्ञा

comment (comments, commenting, commented) n A **comment** is something that you say which expresses your opinion of something or which gives an explanation of it. मत ▷ vi If you **comment** on something, you give your opinion about it or you give an explanation for it. भाष्य करणे

commentary (commentaries) n A **commentary** is a spoken description of an event that is broadcast on radio or television while it is taking place. समालोचन

commentator (commentators) n A **commentator** is a broadcaster who gives a commentary on an event. समालोचक

commercial (commercials) n A **commercial** is an advertisement broadcast on television or radio. जाहिरात

commercial break (commercial breaks) n A **commercial break** is the interval during a commercial television programme, or between programmes, during which advertisements are shown. व्यावसायिक विश्रांती

commission (commissions) n A **commission** is a piece of work that someone is asked to do and is paid for. दलाली

commit (commits, committing, committed) vt If someone **commits** a crime or a sin, they do something illegal or bad. वाईट कृत्य करणे

committee (committees) n A **committee** is a group of people who represent a larger group or organization and make decisions for them. समिती

common (commoner, commonest) adj If something is **common**, it is found in large numbers or it happens often. सर्वसाधारण

common sense n **Common sense** is the natural ability to make good judgements and behave sensibly. व्यवहारज्ञान, शहाणपण

communicate (communicates, communicating, communicated) vi If you

communicate with someone, you give them information, for example by speaking, writing, or sending radio signals. संवाद साधणे

communication n **Communication** is the act of sharing or exchanging information with someone, for example by speaking, writing, or sending radio signals. संवाद, दळणवळण

communion n **Communion** with nature or with a person is the feeling that you are sharing thoughts or feelings with them. सख्य

communism n **Communism** is the political belief that all people are equal and that workers should control the means of producing things. साम्यवाद

communist (**communists**) adj **Communist** means relating to communism. कम्युनिस्ट पक्ष ▷ n A **communist** is someone who believes in communism. साम्यवादी

community (**communities**) n The **community** is all the people who live in a particular area or place. समाज

commute (**commutes, commuting, commuted**) vi If you **commute**, you travel a long distance to work every day. दररोज प्रवास करणे

commuter (**commuters**) n A **commuter** is a person who travels a long distance to work every day. दैनंदिन प्रवासी

compact adj Something that is **compact** is small or takes up very little space. सुटसुटीत, आटोपशीर

compact disc (**compact discs**) n **Compact discs** are small discs on which sound, especially music, is recorded. The abbreviation 'CD' is also used. कॉंपॅक्ट डिस्क

companion (**companions**) n A **companion** is someone who you spend time with or travel with. सहचारी

company (**companies**) n A **company** is a business organization that makes money by selling goods or services. कंपनी

company car (**company cars**) n A **company car** is a car which an employer gives to an employee to use as their own. कंपनी कार

comparable adj Something that is **comparable** to something is roughly similar, for example in amount or importance. तुलना करण्याजोगा

comparatively adv **Comparatively** means compared to something else. तुलनात्मकरीत्या

compare (**compares, comparing, compared**) vt If you **compare** things, you consider them and discover the differences or similarities between them. तुलना करणे

comparison (**comparisons**) n When you make a **comparison** between two or more things, you discover the differences or similarities between them. तुलना

compartment (**compartments**) n A **compartment** is one of the separate sections of a railway carriage. कप्पा

compass (**compasses**) n A **compass** is an instrument that you use for finding directions. It has a dial and a magnetic needle that always points to the north. होकायंत्र

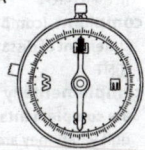

compatible adj If things, systems, or ideas are **compatible**, they work well together or can exist together successfully. अनुरूप

compensate (**compensates, compensating, compensated**) vt If someone is **compensated** for something unpleasant which has happened to them, they receive compensation for it. नुकसानभरपाई देणे

compensation n **Compensation** is money that someone who has undergone loss or suffering claims from the person or organization responsible. नुकसानभरपाई

compere (**comperes**) n A **compere** is the person who introduces the people taking part in a radio or television show or a live show. सूत्रधार

compete (**competes, competing, competed**) vi If one person or organization **competes** with another for something, they try to get that thing for themselves and stop the other getting it. स्पर्धा करणे

competent *adj* Someone who is **competent** is efficient and effective. सक्षम

competition (competitions) *n* Competition is a situation in which two or more people or groups are trying to get something which not everyone can have. स्पर्धा

competitive *adj* **Competitive** situations or activities are ones in which people compete with each other. स्पर्धात्मक

competitor (competitors) *n* A company's **competitors** are other companies that sell similar kinds of goods or services. स्पर्धक

complain (complains, complaining, complained) *v* If you **complain** about something, you say you are not satisfied with it. तक्रार करणे

complaint (complaints) *n* A **complaint** is a statement of dissatisfaction about a situation. तक्रार

complementary *adj* If two different things are **complementary**, they form a complete unit when they are brought together, or they combine well with each other. *(formal)* पूरक

complete *adj* You use **complete** to emphasize that something is as great in extent, degree, or amount as it possibly can be. परिपूर्ण

completely *adv* **Completely** means as much in extent, degree, or amount as possible. संपूर्णपणे

complex (complexes) *adj* **Complex** things have many different parts and are hard to understand. गुंतागुंतीचे ▷ *n* A **complex** is a group of buildings used for a particular purpose. संकुल

complexion (complexions) *n* Your **complexion** is the natural colour or condition of the skin on your face. वर्ण, कांति

complicated *adj* Something that is **complicated** has many parts and is therefore difficult to understand. गुंतागुंतीचे

complication (complications) *n* A **complication** is a problem or difficulty. गुंतागुंत

compliment (compliments, complimenting, complimented) *n* A **compliment** is a polite remark that you say to someone to show that you like their appearance, appreciate their qualities, or approve of what they have done. प्रशंसा ▷ *vt* If you **compliment** someone, you say something nice about them. प्रशंसा करणे

complimentary *adj* If you are **complimentary** about something, you express admiration for it. स्तुतीपर

component (components) *n* The **components** of something are its parts. घटक

composer (composers) *n* A **composer** is a person who writes music. संगीतकार

composition (compositions) *n* The **composition** of something is the things that it consists of and the way that they are arranged. रचना

comprehension *n* **Comprehension** is the ability to understand something or the process of understanding something. *(formal)* आकलन

comprehensive *adj* Something that is **comprehensive** includes everything necessary or relevant. व्यापक

compromise (compromises, compromising, compromised) *n* A **compromise** is a situation in which people accept something slightly different from what they really want. तडजोड ▷ *vi* If you **compromise** with someone, you reach an agreement with them in which you both give up something that you originally wanted. You can also say that two people or groups **compromise**. समझोता करणे

compulsory *adj* If something is **compulsory**, you must do it because a law or someone in authority says you must. अनिवार्य

computer (computers) *n* A **computer** is an electronic machine which makes quick calculations and deals with large amounts of information. संगणक

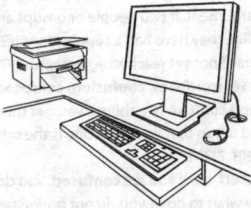

computer game (computer games) n A **computer game** is a game that you play on a computer or on a small portable piece of electronic equipment. संगणकावरील खेळ

computer science n **Computer science** is the study of computers and their application. संगणक विज्ञान

computing n **Computing** is the activity of using a computer and writing programs for it. संगणकाचा वापर करणे

concentrate (concentrates, concentrating, concentrated) vi If you **concentrate** on something, you give it all your attention. एकाग्र होणे

concentration n **Concentration** on something involves giving all your attention to it. एकाग्रता

concern (concerns) n **Concern** is worry about a situation. काळजी

concerned adj If you are **concerned** about something, you are worried about it. काळजीत पडलेला

concerning prep You use **concerning** to show what a piece of information is about. (formal) संबंधी Contact the teacher for more information concerning the class.

concert (concerts) n A **concert** is a performance of music. जलसा

concerto (concerti, concertos) n A **concerto** is a piece of music for a solo instrument and an orchestra. इतर वाद्यवृंद फक्त साथीला घेऊन मुख्यतः एकाच वाद्यावर वाजवायची संगीतरचना

concession (concessions) n If you make a **concession** to someone, you agree to let them do or have something, especially in order to end an argument or conflict. सवलत

concise adj Something that is **concise** gives all the necessary information in a very brief form. संक्षिप्त

conclude (concludes, concluding, concluded) vt If you **conclude** that something is true, you decide that it is true using the facts you know. निष्कर्ष काढणे

conclusion (conclusions) n When you come to a **conclusion**, you decide that something is true after you have thought about it carefully. निष्कर्ष

concrete n **Concrete** is a substance used for building. It is made from cement, sand, small stones, and water. कॉंक्रीट

concussion n If you suffer **concussion** after you hit your head, you lose consciousness or feel sick or confused. मेंदूला झालेली इजा

condemn (condemns, condemning, condemned) vt If you **condemn** something, you say that it is bad and unacceptable. धिक्कार करणे

condensation n **Condensation** consists of small drops of water which form when warm water vapour or steam touches a cold surface such as a window. द्रवीभवन, गोठण्याची स्थिती

condition (conditions) n The **condition** of someone or something is the state they are in. स्थिती

conditional adj If a situation or agreement is **conditional** on something, it will only happen if this thing happens. सशर्त

conditioner (conditioners) n A **conditioner** is a substance which you can put on your hair after you have washed it to make it softer. कंडिशनर

condom (condoms) n A **condom** is a rubber covering which a man wears on his penis as a contraceptive. निरोध

conduct (**conducts, conducting, conducted**) vt When you **conduct** an activity or task, you organize it and carry it out. आयोजित करणे

conductor (**conductors**) n A **conductor** is a person who stands in front of an orchestra or choir and directs its performance. संयोजक

cone (**cones**) n A **cone** is a shape with a circular base and smooth curved sides ending in a point at the top. शंकु

conference (**conferences**) n A **conference** is a meeting, often lasting a few days, which is organized on a particular subject. परिषद

confess (**confesses, confessing, confessed**) v If you **confess** to doing something wrong or something that you are ashamed of, you admit that you did it. कबुली देणे

confession (**confessions**) n A **confession** is a signed statement by someone in which they admit that they have committed a particular crime. कबुली

confetti npl **Confetti** is small pieces of coloured paper that people throw over the bride and bridegroom at a wedding. कॉनफेट्टी

confidence n If you have **confidence** in someone, you feel you can trust them. विश्वास ▷ n If you have **confidence**, you feel sure about your abilities, qualities, or ideas. आत्मविश्वास ▷ n If you tell someone something in **confidence**, you tell them a secret. गुस

confident adj If you are **confident** about something, you are certain that it will happen in the way you want it to. खात्री असलेला

confidential adj Information that is **confidential** is meant to be kept secret. गोपनीय

confirm (**confirms, confirming, confirmed**) vt If something **confirms** what you believe, it shows that it is definitely true. पुष्टी करणे

confirmation n **Confirmation** is the act of showing that something you believe is definitely true, or something that shows this. पुष्टी

confiscate (**confiscates, confiscating, confiscated**) vt If you **confiscate** something

from someone, you take it away from them, often as a punishment. जप्त करणे

conflict n **Conflict** is serious disagreement and argument. If two people or groups are in **conflict**, they have had a serious disagreement and have not yet reached agreement. संघर्ष

confuse (**confuses, confusing, confused**) vt If you **confuse** two things, you get them mixed up, so that you think one is the other. गोंधळात टाकणे

confused adj If you are **confused**, you do not know what to do or you do not understand what is happening. गोंधळलेला

confusing adj Something that is **confusing** makes it difficult for people to know what to do or what is happening. गोंधळात टाकणारा

confusion n If there is **confusion** about something, the facts are not clear. गोंधळ

congestion n If there is **congestion** in a place, the place is extremely crowded and blocked with traffic or people. दाटीवाटी

Congo n The **Congo** is a republic in south central Africa. काँगो

congratulate (**congratulates, congratulating, congratulated**) vt If you **congratulate** someone, you express pleasure for something good that has happened to them, or you praise them for something they have achieved. अभिनंदन करणे

congratulations npl You say '**congratulations**' to someone in order to congratulate them. अभिनंदन

conifer (**conifers**) n **Conifers** are a group of trees and shrubs, for example pine trees and fir trees, that grow in cooler areas of the world. They have fruit called cones, and very thin leaves called needles which they do not normally lose in winter. शंकूच्या आकाराची फळे येणारे हिमप्रदेशातील झाड

conjugation n In grammar, **conjugation** is the act of giving the different forms of a verb according to the number of people it refers to, or according to whether it refers to the past, present, or future. व्याकरणातील धातूंचा गण

conjunction (conjunctions) n A **conjunction** of two or more things is the occurrence of them at the same time or place. *(formal)* संयोग

conjurer (conjurers) n A **conjurer** is a person who entertains people by doing magic tricks. जादूगर

connection (connections) n A **connection** is a relationship between two people, groups, or things. संबंध

conquer (conquers, conquering, conquered) vt If one country or group of people **conquers** another, they take complete control of their land. जिंकणे

conscience (consciences) n Your **conscience** is the part of your mind that tells you if what you are doing is wrong. If you have a guilty **conscience**, or if you have something on your **conscience**, you feel guilty because you know you have done something wrong. सद्सद्विवेकबुद्धि

conscientious adj Someone who is **conscientious** is very careful to do their work properly. प्रामाणिक

conscious adj If you are **conscious** of something, you notice it or are aware of it. जाणीव असलेला

consciousness n Your **consciousness** consists of your mind, thoughts, beliefs, and attitudes. जाणीव

consecutive adj **Consecutive** periods of time or events happen one after the other without interruption. सलगचा, लागोपाठचा

consensus n A **consensus** is general agreement amongst a group of people. एकमत

consequence (consequences) n The **consequences** of something are the results or effects of it. परिणाम

consequently adv **Consequently** means as a result. *(formal)* परिणामतः

conservation n **Conservation** is the preservation and protection of the environment. संरक्षण

conservative adj Someone who is **conservative** has right-wing views. पुराणमतवादी

conservatory (conservatories) n A **conservatory** is a glass room built onto a house. देखरेखीसाठी बनवलेली काचेची खोली

consider (considers, considering, considered) vt If you **consider** a person or thing to be something, this is your opinion of them. विचार करणे

considerate adj A **considerate** person pays attention to the needs, wishes, or feelings of other people. समजूतदार

considering prep You use **considering** to show that you haven't forgotten an important fact. चा विचार करता *Considering the time, I think we'll have to wait until tomorrow.*

consistent adj A **consistent** person always behaves or responds in the same way. सातत्यपूर्ण

consist of (consists of, consisting of, consisted of) v Something that **consists of** particular things or people is formed from them. चे बनलेले असणे *The cabin consisted of two small rooms.*

consonant (consonants) n A **consonant** is a sound such as /p/ or /f/ which you pronounce by stopping the air flowing freely through your mouth. व्यंजन

conspiracy (conspiracies) n **Conspiracy** is the secret planning by a group of people to do something wrong or illegal. कट, कारस्थान

constant adj Something that is **constant** happens all the time or is always there. सतत

constantly adv If something happens **constantly**, it happens all the time. सातत्याने

constipated adj Someone who is **constipated** has difficulty in getting rid of solid waste from their body. बद्धकोष्ठता असलेली व्यक्ती

constituency (constituencies) n A **constituency** is an area, and the people who live in it. In an election, the people in the constituency choose one person for the government. मतदारसंघ

constitution (constitutions) n The **constitution** is the laws of a country or organization. राज्यघटना

construct (constructs, constructing, constructed) vt If you **construct** something, you build, make, or create it. बांधणे

construction (constructions) n **Construction** is the building or creating of something. बांधकाम

constructive adj A **constructive** discussion, comment, or approach is useful and helpful. रचनात्मक

consul (consuls) n A **consul** is a government official who lives in a foreign city and looks after all the people there who are from his or her own country. राजदूत

consulate (consulates) n A **consulate** is the place in a city where a foreign government official works and looks after all the people there who are from his or her own country. राजदूतावास

consult (consults, consulting, consulted) v If you **consult** someone or something, you refer to them for advice or information. You can also **consult with** someone. सल्ला घेणे

consultant (consultants) n A **consultant** is an experienced doctor specializing in one area of medicine. सल्ला देणारा डॉक्टर

consumer (consumers) n A **consumer** is a person who buys things or uses services. ग्राहक

contact (contacts, contacting, contacted) n **Contact** involves meeting or communicating with someone. संपर्क ▷ vt If you **contact** someone, you telephone them or write to them. संपर्क करणे

contact lenses npl **Contact lenses** are small lenses that you put on your eyes to help you to see better. कॉंटॅक्ट लेन्सेस

contagious adj A **contagious** disease can be caught by touching people or things that are infected with it. संसर्गजन्य

contain (contains, containing, contained) vt If something such as a box or a room **contains** things, those things are in it. सामावलेले असणे

container (containers) n A **container** is something such as a box or bottle that is used to hold things. साठवणुकीचे डबे किंवा खोके

contemporary adj **Contemporary** means existing now or at the time you are talking about. समकालीन

contempt n If you have **contempt** for someone or something, you have no respect for them. अनादर, अवहेलना

content (contents) n The **content** of a piece of writing, speech, or television programme is its subject and the ideas expressed in it. मजकूर, अंतर्भूत गोष्ट ▷ adj If you are **content**, you are happy. समाधानी

contents npl The **contents** of a container such as a bottle, box, or room are the things inside it. आत ठेवलेले सामानसुमान

contest (contests) n A **contest** is a competition or game. स्पर्धा

contestant (contestants) n A **contestant** in a competition or quiz is a person who takes part in it. स्पर्धक

context (contexts) n The **context** of an idea or event is the general situation in which it occurs. मागचा पुढचा संदर्भ

continent (continents) n A **continent** is a very large area of land, such as Africa or Asia, that consists of several countries. खंड

continual adj **Continual** means happening without stopping, or happening again and again. सततचा

continually adv If something happens **continually**, it happens without stopping, or happens again and again. निरंतर

continue (continues, continuing, continued) vt If you **continue** to do something, you do not stop doing it. चालू ठेवणे ▷ vi If something **continues**, it does not stop. चालू राहणे

continuous adj A **continuous** process or event continues for a period of time without stopping. निरंतर

contraception n Methods of preventing pregnancy are called **contraception**. गर्भरोध

contraceptive (contraceptives) n A **contraceptive** is a device or pill used to prevent pregnancy. गर्भनिरोधनाचे साधन

contract (contracts) n A **contract** is a legal agreement, usually between two companies or between an employer and employee, which involves doing work for a stated sum of money. करार

contractor (contractors) n A **contractor** is a person or company that works for other people or companies. ठेकेदार

contradict (contradicts, contradicting, contradicted) vt If you **contradict** someone, you say or suggest that what they have just said is wrong. असहमती दर्शवणे

contradiction (contradictions) n A **contradiction** is an aspect of a situation which appears to conflict with other aspects, so that they cannot all exist or be successful. विरोधाभास

contrary n You use **on the contrary** when you are contradicting what has just been said. उलटपक्षी

contrast (contrasts) n A **contrast** is a great difference between two or more things. तफावत

contribute (contributes, contributing, contributed) vi If you **contribute** to something, you say or do something to help make it successful. हातभार लावणे

contribution (contributions) n If you make a **contribution** to something, you do something to help make it successful or to produce it. योगदान

control (controls, controlling, controlled) n **Control** of an organization, place, or system is the power to make all the important decisions about the way that it is run. नियंत्रण ▷ vt The people who **control** an organization or place have the power to take all the important decisions about the way that it is run. नियंत्रित करणे

controversial adj Someone or something that is **controversial** causes intense public argument, disagreement, or disapproval. विवादास्पद

convenient adj Something that is **convenient** is easy, useful, or suitable for a particular purpose. सुविधाजनक

conventional adj **Conventional** people behave in a way that is accepted as normal in their society. परंपरावादी

conversation (conversations) n If you have a **conversation** with someone, you talk to each other, usually in an informal situation. संभाषण

convert (converts, converting, converted) v To **convert** one thing into another means to change it into a different shape or form. परिवर्तन करणे

convertible (convertibles) adj **Convertible** money can be easily exchanged for other forms of money. परिवर्तनशील ▷ n A **convertible** is a car with a soft roof that can be folded down or removed. जिचे छत कापडी आहे व जे काढता येऊ शकते अशी गाडी

conveyor belt (conveyor belts) n A **conveyor belt** or a **conveyor** is a continuously moving strip which is used in factories to move objects along. फिरता पट्टा

convict (convicts, convicting, convicted) vt If someone **is convicted** of a crime, they are found guilty of it in a law court. आरोप सिद्ध होऊन दोषी ठरवणे

convince (convinces, convincing, convinced) vt If someone or something **convinces** you of something, they make you believe that it is true or that it exists. पटवून देणे

convincing adj If someone or something is **convincing**, you believe them. पटणारा

convoy (convoys) n A **convoy** is a group of vehicles or ships travelling together. ताफा

cook (cooks, cooking, cooked) n A **cook** is a person whose job is to prepare and cook food. स्वयंपाकी ▷ v When you **cook**, or **cook** a meal, you prepare and heat food so it can be eaten. स्वयंपाक करणे

cookbook (cookbooks) n A **cookbook** is a book that contains recipes for preparing food. पाककृतीवरील पुस्तक

cooker (cookers) n A **cooker** is a large metal device used for cooking food using gas or electricity. कूकर

cookery n **Cookery** is the activity of preparing and cooking food. स्वयंपाकाची क्रिया

cookery book (**cookery books**) n A **cookery book** is a book that contains recipes for preparing food. पाककियेवरील पुस्तक

cooking n **Cooking** is the act of preparing and heating food so it can be eaten. स्वयंपाक

cool (**cooler, coolest**) adj Something that is **cool** has a low temperature but is not cold. थंड ▷ adj If you say that someone is **cool**, you mean that they are fashionable and attractive. (informal) ऐटबाज

cooperation n **Cooperation** is the action of working together with or helping someone. सहकार्य

cop (**cops**) n A **cop** is a policeman or policewoman. (informal) पोलीस

cope (**copes, coping, coped**) vi If you **cope** with a problem, task, or difficult situation, you deal with it successfully. यशस्वीपणे हाताळणे

copper n **Copper** is a soft reddish-brown metal. तांबे

copy (**copies, copying, copied**) n If you make a **copy** of something, you produce something that looks like the original thing. नक्कल करणे ▷ n A **copy** of a book, newspaper, or record is one of many identical ones that have been printed or produced. प्रत ▷ vt If you **copy** something, you produce something that looks like the original thing. नक्कल तयार करणे

copyright (**copyrights**) n If someone has the **copyright** on a piece of writing or music, it is illegal to reproduce or perform it without their permission. लेखाधिकार

coral (**corals**) n **Coral** is a hard substance formed from the skeletons of very small sea animals. पोवळे

cordless adj A **cordless** telephone or piece of electric equipment is operated by a battery fitted inside it and is not connected to the electricity mains. कॉर्डलेस

corduroy n **Corduroy** is thick cotton cloth with parallel raised lines on the outside. कॉर्डुरॉय

core (**cores**) n The **core** of a fruit is the central part containing seeds or pips. गर, गाभा

coriander n **Coriander** is a plant with leaves that are used as a spice and leaves that are used as a herb. धणे, कोथिंबीर

cork n **Cork** is a soft light substance which forms the bark of a Mediterranean tree. बुचाच्या झाडाची साल

corkscrew (**corkscrews**) n A **corkscrew** is a device for pulling corks out of bottles. बूच खेचून काढण्याचे साधन

corn n **Corn** refers to crops such as wheat and barley, or their seeds. कणीस येणारे पीक (मका, गहू इ.)

corner (**corners**) n A **corner** is a place where two sides or edges of something meet, or where a road meets another road. कोपरा

cornet (**cornets**) n A **cornet** is a musical instrument of the brass family that looks like a small trumpet. शिंग (वाजवायचे)

cornflakes npl **Cornflakes** are small flat pieces of maize that are eaten with milk as a breakfast cereal. कॉर्नफ्लेक्स

cornflour n **Cornflour** is a fine white powder made from maize and used to make sauces thicker. मक्याचे पीठ

corporal (**corporals**) *n* A **corporal** is a non-commissioned officer in the army. कॉर्पोरल

corporal punishment *n* **Corporal punishment** is the punishment of people by hitting them. शारीरिक शिक्षा

corpse (**corpses**) *n* A **corpse** is a dead body. प्रेत

correct (**corrects, correcting, corrected**) *adj* Something that is **correct** is accurate and has no mistakes. *(formal)* बरोबर ▷ *vt* If you **correct** a mistake, problem, or fault, you put it right. सुधारणे

correction (**corrections**) *n* A **correction** is something which puts right something that is wrong. दुरुस्ती

correctly *adv* If you do something **correctly**, you do it in the correct way. योग्यपणे

correspondence *n* **Correspondence** is the act of writing letters to someone. पत्रव्यवहार

correspondent (**correspondents**) *n* A **correspondent** is a television or newspaper reporter. वार्ताहर

corridor (**corridors**) *n* A **corridor** is a long passage in a building or train, with rooms on one or both sides. दोन्ही वा एका बाजूला खोल्या असलेली इमारतीमधील वा रेल्वेमधील लांब वाट

corrupt *adj* A **corrupt** person behaves in a way that is morally wrong, especially by doing illegal things for money. भ्रष्ट

corruption *n* **Corruption** is dishonesty and illegal behaviour by people in positions of power. भ्रष्टाचार

cosmetics *npl* **Cosmetics** are substances such as lipstick or face powder. सौंदर्यप्रसाधन

cosmetic surgery *n* **Cosmetic surgery** is surgery done to make a person look more attractive. सौंदर्यवर्धक शस्त्रक्रिया

cost (**costs, costing**) *n* The **cost** of something is the amount of money needed to buy, do, or make it. किंमत ▷ *vt* If something **costs** a particular amount of money, you can buy, do, or make it for that amount. किंमत मोजणे

Costa Rica *n* **Costa Rica** is a republic in Central America. कोस्टा रिका

cost of living *n* The **cost of living** is the average amount of money that people need to spend on food, housing, and clothing. राहणीमानाचा खर्च

costume (**costumes**) *n* An actor's or performer's **costume** is the set of clothes they wear while they are performing. वेषभूषा

cosy (**cosier, cosiest**) *adj* A **cosy** house or room is comfortable and warm. उबदार

cot (**cots**) *n* A **cot** is a bed for a baby, with bars or panels round it so that the baby cannot fall out. पलंग

cottage (**cottages**) *n* A **cottage** is a small house, usually in the country. लहान घर

cottage cheese *n* **Cottage cheese** is a soft, white, lumpy cheese made from sour milk. नासक्या दुधापासून बनवलेले चीज

cotton (**cottons**) *n* **Cotton** is a kind of cloth that is made from the **cotton** plant. सुती कापड ▷ *n* **Cotton** is thread that you use to sew with. सुती धागा

cotton bud (**cotton buds**) *n* A **cotton bud** is a small stick with a ball of cotton wool at each end, which people use, for example, for applying make-up. कॉटन बड

cotton wool *n* **Cotton wool** is soft fluffy cotton, often used for applying creams to your skin. कॉटन वूल

couch (**couches**) *n* A **couch** is a long soft piece of furniture for sitting or lying on. कोच

couchette (**couchettes**) *n* A **couchette** is a bed on a train or a boat which is either folded against the wall or used as an ordinary seat during the day. कोचेट

cough (**coughs, coughing, coughed**) *n* A **cough** is an act, instance, or sound of coughing. खोकला ▷ *vi* When you **cough**, you force air out of your throat with a sudden, harsh noise. You often cough when you are ill, or when you are nervous or want to attract someone's attention. खोकणे

cough mixture (**cough mixtures**) *n* **Cough mixture** is a liquid medicine that you take when you have a cough. खोकल्याचे औषध

could v If you say you **could** do something, you mean that you were able to do it. शकलो / I could see through the window.

council (councils) n A **council** is a group of people elected to govern a town or other area. परिषद

council house (council houses) n A **council house** is a house that is owned by a local council and that people can rent at a low cost. काउंसिल हाऊस

councillor (councillors) n A **councillor** is a member of a local council. नगरसेवक

count (counts, counting, counted) vi When you **count**, you say numbers in order, one after the other. मोजणे ▷ vt When you **count** all the things in a group, you add them up to see how many there are. मोजणे

counter (counters) n In a shop, a **counter** is a long flat surface at which customers are served. काऊंटर

count on (counts on, counting on, counted on) v If you **count on** someone or something, you rely on them to support you. अवलंबून असणे / I can always count on you to cheer me up.

country (countries) n A **country** is a part of the world with its own people and laws. देश ▷ n The **country** is land that is away from towns and cities. There are farms and woods in the **country**. खेडेगाव

countryside n The **countryside** is land away from towns and cities. ग्रामीण भाग

couple (couples) n A couple is two people who are married or who are having a romantic relationship. जोडी, जोडपे ▷ det A **couple** of people or things means two or around two of them. एकदोन, काही Things should get better in a couple of days.

courage n **Courage** is the quality shown by someone who does something difficult or dangerous, even though they may be afraid. साहस, धैर्य

courageous adj Someone who is **courageous** does something difficult or dangerous, even though they may be afraid. धीट

courgette (courgettes) n **Courgettes** are long thin green vegetables. कोरगेटस्

courier (couriers) n A **courier** is a person who is paid to take letters and parcels direct from one place to another. कुरिअर

course (courses) n The **course** of a vehicle is the route along which it is travelling. मार्ग

court (courts) n A **court** is a place where a judge and a jury decide if someone has done something wrong. न्यायालय ▷ n A **court** is an area for playing a game such as tennis. कोर्ट, खेळण्याची बंदिस्त जागा

courtyard (courtyards) n A **courtyard** is a flat open area of ground surrounded by buildings or walls. अंगण

cousin (cousins) n Your **cousin** is the child of your uncle or aunt. चुलत भाऊ/बहीण, मामे भाऊ/बहीण

cover (covers, covering, covered) n A **cover** is something that you put over another thing. झाकण ▷ vt If you **cover** something, you put another thing over it. झाकणे

cover charge (cover charges) n A **cover charge** is a sum of money that you must pay in some restaurants and nightclubs in addition to the money that you pay there for your food and drink. झाकण

cow (cows) n A **cow** is a large female animal kept on farms for its milk. गाय

coward (cowards) n A **coward** is someone who is easily frightened and avoids dangerous or difficult situations. भ्याड

cowardly adj Someone who is **cowardly** is easily frightened and avoids doing dangerous or difficult things. भ्याड

cowboy (cowboys) n A **cowboy** is a male character in a western. काऊबॉय

crab (crabs) n A **crab** is a sea creature with a flat round body covered by a shell, and five pairs of legs with claws on the front pair. खेकडा

crack (cracks, cracking, cracked) n A **crack** is a very narrow gap between two things. तडा ▷ n A **crack** is a line on the surface of something when it is slightly damaged. भेग ▷ v If something **cracks** or if you **crack** it, it becomes damaged, and lines appear on the surface where it has broken. तडा जाणे

crack down on (cracks down on, cracking down on, cracked down on) v If people in authority **crack down on** a group of people, they become stricter in making the group obey rules or laws. कडक कारवाई करणे *The police are cracking down on motorists who drive too fast.*

cracked adj An object that is **cracked** has lines on its surface because it is damaged. तडा गेलेला

cracker (crackers) n A **cracker** is a thin crisp savoury biscuit. क्रॅकर बिस्किट

cradle (cradles) n A **cradle** is a baby's bed with high sides. पाळणा

craft (craft) n You can refer to a boat, a spacecraft, or an aircraft as a **craft**. यान

craftsman (craftsmen) n A **craftsman** is a man who makes things skilfully with his hands. कारागीर

cram (crams, cramming, crammed) v If you **cram** things or people into a place, or if they **cram** it, there are so many of them in it at one time that it is completely full. कोंबणे

crammed adj If a place is **crammed** with things or people, it is very full of them. खच्चून भरलेला

cranberry (cranberries) n **Cranberries** are red berries with a sour taste. They are often used to make a sauce or jelly that you eat with meat. कॅनबेरी

crane (cranes) n A **crane** is a large bird with a long neck and long legs. **Cranes** live near water. सारस ▷ n A **crane** is a tall machine that can lift very heavy things. क्रेन

crash (crashes, crashing, crashed) n A **crash** is an accident when a vehicle hits something. टक्कर ▷ vi If a computer or a computer program **crashes**, it suddenly stops working. अचानक बिघडणे ▷ v If a moving vehicle **crashes**, or if you **crash** it, it hits something.

धडकणे ▷ n A **crash** is a sudden, loud noise. मोठा आवाज

crawl (crawls, crawling, crawled) vi When you **crawl**, you move forward on your hands and knees. रांगणे

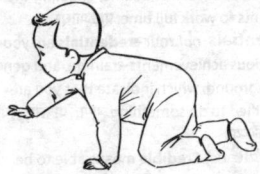

crayfish (crayfish) n A **crayfish** is a small shellfish with five pairs of legs which lives in rivers and streams. You can eat some types of crayfish. क्रेफीश

crayon (crayons) n A **crayon** is a rod of coloured wax used for drawing. मेणयुक्त रंगखडू

crazy (crazier, craziest) adj If you describe someone or something as **crazy**, you think they are very foolish or strange. *(informal)* वेडसर

cream adj Something that is **cream** in colour is yellowish-white. पिवळसर पांढरा रंग ▷ n **Cream** is a thick liquid that is produced from milk. You can use it in cooking or put it on fruit or puddings. मलई, साय

crease (creases) n **Creases** are lines that are made in cloth or paper when it is crushed or folded. सुरकुती

creased adj If something such as cloth or paper is **creased**, there are lines in it because it has been crushed or folded. सुरकुतलेला

create (creates, creating, created) vt To **create** something means to cause it to happen or exist. निर्माण करणे

creation (creations) n The **creation** of something is the act of bringing it into existence. निर्मिती

creative adj A **creative** person has the ability to invent and develop original ideas, especially in art. सर्जनशील, कल्पक

creature (**creatures**) *n* You can refer to any living thing that is not a plant as a **creature**. जीवजंतु

crèche (**crèches**) *n* A **crèche** is an establishment where very young children are looked after in the daytime, enabling their parents to work full time. पाळणाघर

credentials *npl* Your **credentials** are your previous achievements, training, and general background, which indicate that you are qualified to do something. गुण, पात्रता, पूर्वीच्या कामगिऱ्या

credible *adj* **Credible** means able to be trusted or believed. विश्वसनीय

credit *n* **Credit** is a system where you pay for goods or services several weeks or months after you have received them. उधार

credit card (**credit cards**) *n* A **credit card** is a plastic card that you use to buy goods on credit. क्रेडिट कार्ड

creep (**creeps, creeping, crept**) *vi* If you **creep** somewhere, you move in a very slow and quiet way. हळुवारपणे चालणे ▷ *vi* If an animal **creeps**, it moves along close to the ground. सरपटणे

crematorium (**crematoria, crematoriums**) *n* A **crematorium** is a building in which the bodies of dead people are burned. स्मशान

cress *n* **Cress** is a plant with small green leaves that are used in salads or to decorate food. आळीव

crew (**crews**) *n* The **crew** of a ship, an aircraft, or a spacecraft consists of the people who work on it and operate it. **Crew** can take the singular or plural form of the verb. जहाजावरील/ विमानावरील सर्व अधिकारी व कर्मचारी

crew cut (**crew cuts**) *n* A **crew cut** is a man's hairstyle in which his hair is cut very short. क्र्यू कट

cricket (**crickets**) *n* **Cricket** is a game where two teams take turns to hit a ball with a bat and run up and down. क्रिकेट ▷ *n* A **cricket** is a small jumping insect that rubs its wings together to make a high sound. टोळासारखा एक कीटक

crime (**crimes**) *n* A **crime** is an illegal action or activity for which a person can be punished by law. गुन्हा

criminal (**criminals**) *adj* **Criminal** means connected with crime. गुन्हेगारी ▷ *n* A **criminal** is a person who has committed a crime. गुन्हेगार

crisis (**crises**) *n* A **crisis** is a situation in which something or someone is affected by one or more very serious problems. पेचप्रसंग

crisp (**crisper, crispest**) *adj* **Crisp** food is pleasantly hard and crunchy. खुसखुशीत

crisps *npl* **Crisps** are very thin slices of fried potato that are eaten cold as a snack. क्रिस्प्स

crispy (**crispier, crispiest**) *adj* Food that is **crispy** is pleasantly hard, or has a pleasantly hard surface. खुसखुशीत

criterion (**criteria**) *n* A **criterion** is a factor on which you judge or decide something. निकष

critic (**critics**) *n* A **critic** is a person who writes reviews and expresses opinions about books, films, music, and art. समीक्षक

critical *adj* A **critical** time or situation is extremely important. महत्त्वाचा क्षण

criticism (**criticisms**) *n* **Criticism** is the action of expressing disapproval of something or someone. टीका

criticize (**criticizes, criticizing, criticized**) *vt* If you **criticize** someone or something, you express your disapproval of them by saying what you think is wrong with them. टीका करणे

Croatia *n* **Croatia** is a republic in south-east Europe. क्रोएशिया

Croatian (**Croatians**) *adj* **Croatian** means of, relating to, or characteristic of Croatia, its people, or their language. क्रोएशियन ▷ *n* A **Croatian** is a native or inhabitant of Croatia. क्रोएशियन ▷ *n* **Croatian** is the language that is spoken in Croatia. क्रोएशियन

crochet (**crochets, crocheting, crocheted**) *v* If you **crochet**, you make cloth by using a needle with a small hook at the end. विणकाम करणे

crocodile (**crocodiles**) *n* A **crocodile** is a large reptile with a long body. Crocodiles live in rivers. मगर

crocus (**crocuses**) n **Crocuses** are small white, yellow, or purple flowers that grow in the early spring. क्रॉकस

crook (**crooks**) n A **crook** is a criminal or a dishonest person. (*informal*) लुच्चा

crop (**crops**) n **Crops** are plants such as wheat and potatoes that are grown in large quantities for food. पीक

cross (**crosser, crossest, crosses, crossing, crossed**) adj If you are **cross**, you feel angry about something. रागावणे ▷ n A **cross** is a mark that you write. It looks like X or +. क्रॉस ▷ vt If you **cross** something, you go from one side of it to the other. ओलांडणे

cross-country n **Cross-country** is the sport of running, riding, or skiing across open countryside. क्रॉस-कंट्री

crossing (**crossings**) n A **crossing** is a boat journey to the other side of a sea. नावेने पैलतीरी जाणे

cross out (**crosses out, crossing out, crossed out**) v If you **cross out** words, you draw a line through them. खोडणे *He crossed out her name and added his own.*

crossroads (**crossroads**) n A **crossroads** is a place where two roads meet and cross. चौक

crossword (**crosswords**) n A **crossword** or a **crossword puzzle** is a word game in which you work out answers to clues, and write the answers in the white squares of a pattern of black and white squares. शब्दकोडे

crouch down (**crouches down, crouching down, crouched down**) v If you **are crouching down**, your legs are bent under you so that you are close to the ground and leaning forward slightly. खाली वाकणे *He crouched down and reached under the mattress.*

crow (**crows**) n A **crow** is a large black bird which makes a loud harsh noise. कावळा

crowd (**crowds**) n A **crowd** is a large group of people who have gathered together. जमाव

crowded adj A **crowded** place is full of people or things. गजबजलेला

crown (**crowns**) n A **crown** is a circular ornament, usually made of gold and jewels, which a king or queen wears on their head at official ceremonies. मुकुट

crucial adj Something that is **crucial** is extremely important. महत्त्वपूर्ण

crucifix (**crucifixes**) n A **crucifix** is a cross with a figure of Christ on it. क्रूसिफिक्स

crude (**cruder, crudest**) adj Something that is **crude** is simple and not sophisticated. ओबडधोबड

cruel (**crueller, cruellest**) adj Someone who is **cruel** deliberately causes pain or distress. क्रूर

cruelty (**cruelties**) n **Cruelty** is behaviour that deliberately causes pain or distress to people or animals. क्रूरता

cruise (**cruises**) n A **cruise** is a holiday spent on a ship or boat which visits a number of places. जलपर्यटन

crumb (**crumbs**) n **Crumbs** are tiny pieces that fall from bread, biscuits, or cake when you cut or eat them. चुरा

crush (**crushes, crushing, crushed**) vt To **crush** something means to press it very hard so that its shape is destroyed or so that it breaks into pieces. चिरडणे

crutch (**crutches**) n A **crutch** is a stick which someone with an injured foot or leg uses to support them when walking. कुबडी

cry (**cries, crying, cried**) n A **cry** is a loud sound that you make with your voice. ओरडणे ▷ vi When you **cry**, tears come from your eyes. People **cry** when they are sad or hurt. रडणे

crystal (**crystals**) n A **crystal** is a piece of a mineral that has formed naturally into a regular symmetrical shape. स्फटिक

cub (**cubs**) n A **cub** is a young wild animal such as a lion, wolf, or bear. छावा, बछडा

Cuba n Cuba is a republic and the largest island in the Caribbean, at the entrance to the Gulf of Mexico. क्युबा

Cuban (**Cubans**) adj **Cuban** means belonging or relating to Cuba, or to its people or culture. क्युबन ▷ n A **Cuban** is a Cuban citizen, or a person of Cuban origin. क्युबन

cube (cubes) *n* A **cube** is a solid shape with six square surfaces which are all the same size. घन

cubic *adj* **Cubic** is used to describe units of volume. घन (परिमाण)

cuckoo (cuckoos) *n* A **cuckoo** is a grey bird which makes an easily recognizable sound consisting of two quick notes. कोकीळ

cucumber (cucumbers) *n* A **cucumber** is a long dark green vegetable. काकडी

cuddle (cuddles, cuddling, cuddled) *n* A **cuddle** is a close embrace, especially when prolonged. दीर्घ मिठी ▷ *vt* If you **cuddle** someone, you put your arms round them and hold them close as a way of showing your affection. मिठी मारणे

cue (cues) *n* A **cue** is something said or done by a performer that is a signal for another performer to begin speaking or to begin doing something. सूचक इशारा

cufflinks *npl* **Cufflinks** are small decorative objects used for holding together shirt cuffs around the wrist. कफलिंक्स

culprit (culprits) *n* The person who committed a crime or did something wrong can be referred to as the **culprit**. गुन्हेगार

cultural *adj* **Cultural** means relating to the arts generally, or to the arts and customs of a particular society. सांस्कृतिक

culture *n* **Culture** consists of activities such as art, music, literature, and theatre. संस्कृती

cumin *n* **Cumin** is a sweet-smelling spice, and is popular in cooking. जिरे

cunning *adj* A **cunning** person is clever and deceitful. धूर्त

cup (cups) *n* A **cup** is a small round container with a handle, which you drink from. पेला

cupboard (cupboards) *n* A **cupboard** is a piece of furniture with doors at the front and usually shelves inside. कपाट

curb (curbs) *n* A **curb** is something that restrains or holds something else back. बंधन

cure (cures, curing, cured) *n* A **cure** for an illness is a medicine or other treatment that cures the illness. उपचार ▷ *vt* If a doctor or a medical treatment **cures** someone, or **cures** their illness, they make the person well again. आजारातून बरे करणे

curfew (curfews) *n* A **curfew** is a law stating that people must stay inside their houses after a particular time at night. संचारबंदी

curious *adj* If you are **curious** about something, you are interested in it and want to learn more about it. जिज्ञासू

curl (curls) *n* **Curls** are lengths of hair shaped in curves and circles. केसांच्या कुरळ्या बटा

curler (curlers) *n* **Curlers** are small plastic or metal tubes that women roll their hair round in order to make it curly. कर्लर

curly (curlier, curliest) *adj* **Curly** hair is full of curls. कुरळे

currant (currants) *n* **Currants** are small dried black grapes, used especially in cakes. काळ्या मनुका

currency (currencies) *n* The money used in a country is referred to as its **currency**. चलन

current (currents) *adj* Something that is **current** is happening, being done, or being used at the present time. सध्याचा ▷ *n* A

current is a steady, continuous, flowing movement of water or air. प्रवाह ▷ n An electric **current** is electricity flowing through a wire or circuit. प्रवाह

current account (**current accounts**) n A **current account** is a bank account which you can take money out of at any time. चालू खाते

current affairs npl **Current affairs** are political events and problems which are discussed in the media. चालू घडामोडी

currently adv **Currently** means at the present time. सध्या

curriculum (**curriculums, curricula**) n A **curriculum** is all the different courses of study that are taught in a school, college, or university. अभ्यासक्रम

curriculum vitae n A **curriculum vitae** is a brief written account of your personal details, your education, and jobs you have had, which you send when you are applying for a job. The abbreviation 'CV' is also used. शैक्षणिक पात्रता व अनुभव यांची माहिती

curry (**curries**) n **Curry** is an Asian dish made with hot spices. कढी, आमटी

curry powder (**curry powders**) n **Curry powder** is a powder made from a mixture of spices. It is used in cooking, especially when making curry. कढी मसाला

curse (**curses**) n A **curse** is rude or offensive language which someone uses, usually because they are angry. (written) शिव्याशाप

cursor (**cursors**) n On a computer screen, the **cursor** is a small, movable shape which indicates where anything typed by the user will appear. कर्सर

curtain (**curtains**) n **Curtains** are hanging pieces of material which you can pull across a window to keep light out or prevent people from looking in. पडदा

cushion (**cushions**) n A **cushion** is a fabric case filled with soft material, which you put on a seat to make it more comfortable. उशी

custard n **Custard** is a sweet yellow sauce made from milk and eggs or from milk and a powder. It is eaten with puddings. कस्टर्ड

custody n **Custody** is the legal right to look after a child, especially the right given to a child's father or mother when they get divorced. ताबा

custom (**customs**) n A **custom** is an activity, a way of behaving, or an event which is usual or traditional in a particular society or in particular circumstances. रूढी

customer (**customers**) n A **customer** is someone who buys goods or services, especially from a shop. ग्राहक

customized adj Something that is **customized** has had its appearance or features changed to suit someone's tastes or needs. आपल्या गरजेनुसार बनवलेली वस्तू

customs npl **Customs** is the official organization responsible for collecting taxes on goods coming into a country and preventing illegal goods from being brought in. कस्टम्स

customs officer (**customs officers**) n A **customs officer** is a person who works for the official organization responsible for collecting taxes on goods coming into a country and preventing illegal goods from being brought in. कस्टम्स अधिकारी

cut (**cuts, cutting**) n A **cut** is a place on your skin where something sharp has gone through it. कापल्याने झालेली जखम ▷ v If you **cut** something, you use a knife or scissors to divide it into pieces. कापणे ▷ vt If you **cut** yourself, something sharp goes through your skin and blood comes out. कापणे

cutback (**cutbacks**) n A **cutback** is a reduction in something. कमी करणे

cut down (**cuts down, cutting down**) v If you **cut down** on something, you use or do less of it. कमी करणे He cut down on coffee.

cute (**cuter, cutest**) adj **Cute** means pretty or attractive. (informal) आकर्षक

cutlery *n* The knives, forks, and spoons that you eat with are referred to as **cutlery**. कटलरी

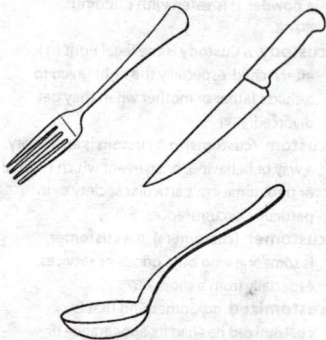

cutlet (**cutlets**) *n* A **cutlet** is a small piece of meat which is usually fried or grilled. कटलेट

cut off (**cuts off, cutting off**) *v* If you **cut** something **off**, you remove it with a knife or a similar tool. काढून टाकणे *She cut off a large piece of meat.*

cutting (**cuttings**) *n* A **cutting** is a piece of writing cut from a newspaper or magazine. कात्रण

cut up (**cuts up, cutting up**) *v* If you **cut** something **up**, you cut it into several pieces. तुकडे करणे *Halve the tomatoes, then cut them up.*

CV (**CVs**) *abbr* Your **CV** is a brief written account of your personal details, your education, and jobs you have had, which you send when you are applying for a job. **CV** is an abbreviation for 'curriculum vitae'. सीव्ही

cybercafé (**cybercafés**) *n* A **cybercafé** is a café where people can pay to use the Internet. सायबरकॅफे

cybercrime *n* **Cybercrime** is the illegal use of computers and the Internet. इंटरनेटसंबंधी गुन्हे

cycle (**cycles, cycling, cycled**) *n* A **cycle** is a bicycle. सायकल ▷ *n* A **cycle** is a series

of events or processes that is continually repeated, always in the same order. चक्र ▷ *vi* If you **cycle**, you ride a bicycle. सायकल चालवणे

cycle lane (**cycle lanes**) *n* A **cycle lane** is a part of a road or path that only bicycles are allowed to use. सायकल लेन

cycle path (**cycle paths**) *n* A **cycle path** is a special path on which people can travel by bicycle separately from motor vehicles. सायकलसाठी राखून ठेवलेला रस्ता

cycling *n* **Cycling** is the action of riding a cycle. सायकलस्वारी

cyclist (**cyclists**) *n* A **cyclist** is someone who rides a bicycle. सायकलचालक

cyclone (**cyclones**) *n* A **cyclone** is a violent tropical storm. चक्रीवादळ

cylinder (**cylinders**) *n* A **cylinder** is a shape or container with flat circular ends and long straight sides. दंडगोल

cymbals (**cymbals**) *npl* **Cymbals** are flat circular brass objects that are used as musical instruments. You hit two cymbals together to make a loud noise. झांजा

Cypriot (**Cypriots**) *adj* **Cypriot** means belonging or relating to Cyprus, or to its people or culture. सायप्रिअट ▷ *n* A **Cypriot** is a Cypriot citizen, or a person of Cypriot origin. सायप्रिअट

Cyprus *n* **Cyprus** is an island in the East Mediterranean. सायप्रस

cyst (**cysts**) *n* A **cyst** is a growth containing liquid that appears inside your body or under your skin. गाठ

cystitis *n* **Cystitis** is a bladder infection. सिस्टीटिस

Czech (**Czechs**) *adj* **Czech** means belonging or relating to the Czech Republic, or to its people, language, or culture. झेक ▷ *n* A **Czech** is a person who comes from the Czech Republic. झेक ▷ *n* **Czech** is the language spoken in the Czech Republic. झेक

Czech Republic *n* The **Czech Republic** is a country in central Europe. झेक प्रजासत्ताक

d

dad (dads) n Your **dad** is your father. You can call your dad 'Dad'. (informal) वडील

daddy (daddies) n Children often call their father **daddy**. (informal) बाबा

daffodil (daffodils) n A **daffodil** is a yellow flower that blooms in the spring. डॅफडिल

daft (dafter, daftest) adj **Daft** means stupid and not sensible. मूर्खपणाचा

daily adj **Daily** means of or occurring every day or every weekday. दररोज ▷ adv If something happens **daily**, it happens every day. दैनंदिन दररोज

dairy (dairies) n A **dairy** is a shop or company that sells milk, butter, and cheese. दुग्धालय

dairy produce n **Dairy produce** is foods such as butter and cheese that are made from milk. दुग्धोत्पादने

dairy products npl **Dairy products** are foods such as butter and cheese that are made from milk. दुग्धोत्पादने

daisy (daisies) n A **daisy** is a small wild flower with a yellow centre and white petals. डेझी

dam (dams) n A **dam** is a wall built across a river to stop the flow of the water and make a lake. धरण

damage (damages, damaging, damaged) n **Damage** is injury or harm that is caused to something. हानी ▷ vt If you **damage** something, you injure or harm it. हानी पोहोचविणे

damp (damper, dampest) adj **Damp** means slightly wet. ओलसर

dance (dances, dancing, danced) n A **dance** is a series of steps and rhythmic movements which you do to music. It is also a piece of music which people can dance to. नृत्य ▷ vi When you **dance**, you move around in time to music. नाचणे

dancer (dancers) n A **dancer** is a person who is dancing, or who earns money by dancing. नर्तक

dancing n When people dance for enjoyment or to entertain others, you can refer to this activity as **dancing**. नृत्य

dandelion (dandelions) n A **dandelion** is a wild plant which has yellow flowers first, then a fluffy ball of seeds. डॅडिलिअन

dandruff n **Dandruff** is small white pieces of dead skin in someone's hair, or fallen from someone's hair. केसातील कोंडा

Dane (Danes) n A **Dane** is a person who comes from Denmark. डेन

danger n **Danger** is the possibility that someone may be harmed or killed. धोका

dangerous adj If something is **dangerous**, it may hurt or harm you. धोकादायक

Danish adj **Danish** means relating to or belonging to Denmark, or to its people, language, or culture. डॅनिश ▷ n **Danish** is the language spoken in Denmark. डॅनिश

dare (dares, daring, dared) vt If you **dare** to do something, you are brave enough to do it. हिंमत करणे Most people don't dare to argue with him.

daring adj A **daring** person does things which might be dangerous or shocking. धाडसी

dark (darker, darkest) n When it is **dark**, there is no light or not much light. अंधार ▷ n The **dark** is the lack of light in a place. अंधार ▷ n A **dark** colour is not pale. गडद

darkness n **Darkness** is the lack of light in a place. अंधार

darling (darlings) n You call someone **darling** if you love them or like them very much. प्रिय

dart (darts) n A **dart** is a small, narrow object with a sharp point which you can throw or shoot. लहान तीक्ष्ण तीर

darts npl **Darts** is a game in which you throw darts at a round board with numbers on it. डार्टस नावाचा खेळ

dash (dashes, dashing, dashed) vi If you **dash** somewhere, you run or go there quickly and suddenly. धडक, मुसंडी

dashboard (dashboards) n The **dashboard** in a car is the panel facing the driver's seat where most of the instruments and switches are. डॅशबोर्ड

data npl You can talk about information as **data**, especially when it is in the form of facts or numbers. माहिती

database (databases) n A **database** is a collection of data stored in a computer in a way that makes it easy to obtain. डेटाबेस

date (dates) n A **date** is a particular day or year, for example 7th June 2010, or 1066. तारीख

daughter (daughters) n Your **daughter** is your female child. स्वत:ची मुलगी

daughter-in-law (daughters-in-law) n Your **daughter-in-law** is the wife of your son. सून

dawn (dawns) n **Dawn** is the time of day when light first appears in the sky, before the sun rises. पहाट

day (days) n A **day** is the length of time between one midnight and the next. There are twenty-four hours in a day, and seven **days** in a week. दिवस ▷ n **Day** is the time when there is light outside. दिवस

day return (day returns) n A **day return** is a train or bus ticket which allows you to go somewhere and come back on the same day for a lower price than an ordinary return ticket. परतीचे तिकीट

daytime n **Daytime** is the part of a day when it is light. दिवसाची वेळ

dead adj A person, animal, or plant that is **dead** is no longer living. मृत ▷ adv **Dead** means 'precisely' or 'exactly'. अगदी, पूर्णपणे

dead end (dead ends) n If a street is a **dead end**, there is no way out at one end of it. रस्त्याचे शेवटचे टोक

deadline (deadlines) n A **deadline** is a time or date before which a particular task must be finished or a particular thing must be done. अंतिम तारीख

deaf (deafer, deafest) adj Someone who is **deaf** is unable to hear anything or is unable to hear very well. बहिरा

deafening adj A **deafening** noise is a very loud noise. कानठळ्या बसविणारा आवाज

deal (deals, dealing, dealt) n If you make a **deal**, you agree to do something with somebody. व्यवहार ▷ v If you **deal** playing cards, you give them out to the players in a game of cards. पत्ते पिसून वाटण्याची क्रिया, पिशी

dealer (dealers) n A **dealer** is a person whose business involves buying and selling things. व्यापारी

deal with (deals with, dealing with, dealt with) v When you **deal with** a situation or problem, you do what is necessary to achieve the result you want. व्यवहार करणे How do you deal with an uninvited guest?

dear (dearer, dearest) adj You use **dear** to describe someone or something that you feel affection for. प्रिय ▷ adj Something that is **dear** costs a lot of money. (informal) महाग

death (deaths) n **Death** is the end of the life of a person or animal. मृत्यू

debate (debates, debating, debated) n A **debate** is a discussion about a subject on which people have different views. चर्चा ▷ vt When people **debate** a topic, they discuss it fairly formally, putting forward different views. You can also say that one person **debates** a topic with another person. चर्चा करणे

debit (debits, debiting, debited) n A **debit** is a record of the money taken from your bank account. खात्यातून काढलेल्या पैशांची नोंद ▷ vt When your bank **debits** your account, money is taken from it and paid to someone else. देण्यासाठी पैसे काढणे

debit card (debit cards) n A **debit card** is a bank card that you can use to pay for things. When you use it, the money is taken out of your bank account immediately. डेबिट कार्ड

debt (debts) n A **debt** is a sum of money that you owe someone. कर्ज

decade (decades) n A **decade** is a period of ten years, especially one that begins with a year ending in 0, for example 2000 to 2009. दशक

decaffeinated coffee (decaffeinated coffees) n Decaffeinated coffee has had most of the caffeine removed from it. कॅफिन काढलेली कॉफी

decay (decays, decaying, decayed) vi When something such as a dead body, a dead plant, or a tooth **decays**, it is gradually destroyed by a natural process. कुजणे

deceive (deceives, deceiving, deceived) vt If you **deceive** someone, you make them believe something that is not true. फसविणे

December (Decembers) n **December** is the twelfth and last month of the year in the Western calendar. डिसेंबर

decent adj Decent means acceptable in standard or quality. नीटनेटका, योग्य

decide (decides, deciding, decided) vt If you **decide** to do something, you choose to do it. ठरविणे

decimal adj A **decimal** system involves counting in units of ten. दशमान

decision (decisions) n When you make a **decision**, you choose what should be done or which is the best of various alternatives. निर्णय

decisive adj If a fact, action, or event is **decisive**, it makes it certain that there will be a particular result. निर्णायक

deck (decks) n A **deck** on a bus or ship is a downstairs or upstairs area. बसचा किंवा जहाजाचा वरचा माळा

deckchair (deckchairs) n A **deckchair** is a simple chair with a folding frame, and a piece of canvas as the seat and back. Deckchairs are usually used on the beach, on a ship, or in the garden. डेकचेअर

declare (declares, declaring, declared) vt If you **declare** that something is the case, you say that it is true in a firm, deliberate way. (written) जाहीर करणे

decorate (decorates, decorating, decorated) vt If you **decorate** something, you make it more attractive by adding things to it. सजवणे

decorator (decorators) n A **decorator** is a person whose job is to paint houses or put wallpaper up. सजावटकार

decrease (decreases, decreasing, decreased) n A **decrease** is a reduction in the quantity or size of something. घट ▷ v When something **decreases**, or when you **decrease** it, it becomes less in quantity, size, or intensity. घट होणे

dedicated adj If you describe a person as **dedicated**, you mean that they are devoted to a particular purpose or cause. एखाद्या कार्याला वाहून घेतलेली व्यक्ती

dedication n **Dedication** is the state of being devoted to a particular purpose or cause. समर्पण

deduct (deducts, deducting, deducted) vt When you **deduct** an amount from a total, you subtract it from the total. वजा करणे

deep (deeper, deepest) adj If something is **deep**, it extends a long way down from the ground or from the top surface of something. खोल

deep-fry (deep-fries, deep-frying, deep-fried) vt If you **deep-fry** food, you fry it in a large amount of fat or oil. भरपूर तेलात तळून काढणे

deeply adv **Deeply** means seriously, strongly, or to a great degree. खोलवर

deer (deer) n A **deer** is a large wild animal. Male deer usually have large, branching horns. हरिण

defeat (defeats, defeating, defeated) n **Defeat** is the state of being beaten in a battle, game, or contest, or of failing to achieve what you wanted to. पराभव ▷ *vt* If you **defeat** someone, you win a victory over them in a battle or contest. पराभव करणे

defect (**defects**) *n* A **defect** is a fault or imperfection in a person or thing. दोष

defence *n* **Defence** is action taken to protect someone or something from attack. संरक्षण

defend (**defends, defending, defended**) *vt* If you **defend** someone or something, you take action to protect them. संरक्षण करणे

defendant (**defendants**) *n* The **defendant** in a trial is the person accused of a crime. प्रतिवादी

defender (**defenders**) *n* If you are a **defender** of a particular thing or person that has been criticized or attacked, you support that thing or person in public. पाठीराखा

deficit (**deficits**) *n* A **deficit** is the amount by which something is less than the amount that is needed. तूट

define (**defines, defining, defined**) *vt* If you **define** something, you say exactly what it is or exactly what it means. स्पष्ट करणे

definite *adj* If something is **definite**, it is firm and clear, and unlikely to be changed. निश्चित

definitely *adv* You use **definitely** to emphasize that something is the case and will not change. निश्चितपणे

definition (**definitions**) *n* A **definition** of a word or term is a statement giving its meaning, especially in a dictionary. व्याख्या

degree (**degrees**) *n* You use **degree** to indicate the extent to which something happens or is the case. तीव्रता, प्रमाण

degree Celsius (**degrees Celsius**) *n* A **degree Celsius** is a unit of measurement on the Celsius scale that is used to measure temperatures. अंश सेल्सिअस

degree centigrade (**degrees centigrade**) *n* A **degree centigrade** is a unit of measurement on the centigrade scale that is used to measure temperatures. डिग्री सेंटिग्रेड

degree Fahrenheit (**degrees Fahrenheit**) *n* A **degree Fahrenheit** is a unit of measurement on the Fahrenheit scale that is used to measure temperatures. डिग्री फॅरेनहीट

dehydrated *adj* When something such as food is **dehydrated**, all the water is removed from it, often in order to preserve it. निर्जलीकरण केलेले

delay (**delays, delaying, delayed**) *n* If there is a **delay**, something does not happen until later than planned or expected. उशीर ▷ *vt* If you **delay** doing something, you do not do it until a later time. उशीर करणे

delayed *adj* If a person or thing is **delayed**, they are made late. विलंबित

delegate (**delegates, delegating, delegated**) *n* A **delegate** is a person chosen to vote or make decisions on behalf of a group of people, especially at a conference or meeting. जबाबदारी वा कामगिरी सोपविणे ▷ *vt* If you **delegate** duties, responsibilities, or power to someone, you give them those duties or responsibilities or that power, so that they can act on your behalf. जबाबदारी वा कामगिरी सेपविणे

delete (**deletes, deleting, deleted**) *vt* If you **delete** something that has been written down or stored in a computer, you cross it out or remove it. डिलीट करणे

deliberate *adj* If something that you do is **deliberate**, you intended to do it. जाणूनबुजून केलेले

deliberately *adv* If you do something **deliberately**, you intended to do it. मुद्दाम

delicate *adj* Something that is **delicate** is small and beautifully shaped. नाजूक

delicatessen (**delicatessens**) *n* A **delicatessen** is a shop that sells unusual or foreign foods. डेलिकेटसन

delicious *adj* **Delicious** food or drink has an extremely pleasant taste. स्वादिष्ट

delight *n* **Delight** is a feeling of very great pleasure. आनंद

delighted *adj* If you are **delighted**, you are extremely pleased and excited about something. आनंदित

delightful *adj* Someone or something that is **delightful** is very pleasant. आनंदी

deliver (delivers, delivering, delivered) vt If you **deliver** something somewhere, you take it there. नेऊन देणे

delivery (deliveries) n **Delivery** is the act of bringing of letters, parcels, or goods to someone's house or office. बटवडा

demand (demands, demanding, demanded) n A **demand** is a firm request for something. मागणी ▷ vt If you **demand** something such as information or action, you ask for it in a very forceful way. मागणी करणे

demanding adj A **demanding** job requires a lot of time, energy, or attention. आव्हानात्मक

demo (demos) n A **demo** is a march or gathering by a group of people to show their opposition to something or their support for something. (informal) निदर्शन

democracy n **Democracy** is a political system in which people choose their government by voting for them in elections. लोकशाही

democratic adj A **democratic** country, organization, or system is governed by representatives who are elected by the people. लोकशाही राज्यपद्धती

demolish (demolishes, demolishing, demolished) vt When a building **is demolished**, it is knocked down, often because it is old or dangerous. बांधकाम पाडून टाकणे

demonstrate (demonstrates, demonstrating, demonstrated) vt To **demonstrate** a fact or theory means to make it clear to people. सिद्ध करणे

demonstration (demonstrations) n A **demonstration** of something is the act of making it clear to people. प्रात्यक्षिक

demonstrator (demonstrators) n **Demonstrators** are people who are marching or gathering somewhere to show their opposition to something or their support for something. निदर्शक

denim n **Denim** is a thick cotton cloth used to make clothes. Jeans are made from denim. डेनिम

denims npl **Denims** are casual trousers made of denim. डेनिमपासून बनवलेले कपडे

Denmark n **Denmark** is a kingdom in north Europe, between the Baltic and the North Sea. डेन्मार्क

dense (denser, densest) adj Something that is **dense** contains a lot of things or people in relation to its size. घनदाट

density (densities) n The **density** of something is the extent to which it fills a place. घनता

dent (dents, denting, dented) n A **dent** is a hollow in the surface of something which has been caused by hitting or pressing it. पोचा ▷ vt If you **dent** something, you damage it by hitting or pressing it, causing a hollow dip to form in it. पोचा पाडणे

dental adj **Dental** is used to describe things relating to teeth. दंतविषयक

dental floss n **Dental floss** is a type of thread that is used to clean the gaps between your teeth. डेंटल फ्लॉस

dentist (dentists) n A **dentist** is a person qualified to treat people's teeth. दंतवैद्य

dentures npl **Dentures** are artificial teeth. कवळी

deny (denies, denying, denied) vt If you **deny** something, you say that it is not true. नाकारणे

deodorant (deodorants) n **Deodorant** is a substance that you put on your body to reduce or hide the smell of perspiration. डिओडरन्ट (दुर्गंधीनाशक)

depart (departs, departing, departed) vi
To **depart** from a place means to leave it and
start a journey to another place. प्रवासास निघणे

department (departments) n A
department is one of the sections of a large
shop or organization such as a university.
विभाग

department store (department stores) n A
department store is a large shop which sells
many different kinds of goods. डिपार्टमेंट स्टोअर

departure (departures) n **Departure** is the
act of leaving a place or a job. प्रस्थान

departure lounge (departure lounges) n
In an airport, the **departure lounge** is the
place where passengers wait before they get
onto their plane. प्रस्थान कक्ष

depend (depends, depending, depended)
vi If you say that one thing **depends** on
another, you mean that the first thing will be
affected or decided by the second. अवलंबून
असणे

deport (deports, deporting, deported) vt
If a government **deports** someone, it sends
them out of the country. देशाबाहेर घालवून देणे

deposit (deposits) n A **deposit** is a sum of
money given as part payment for something,
or as security when you rent something. ठेव

depressed adj If you are **depressed**, you
are sad and feel you cannot enjoy anything,
because your situation is difficult and
unpleasant. खिन्न

depressing adj Something that is **depressing**
makes you feel sad and disappointed. उदास

depression n **Depression** is a mental state
in which someone feels unhappy and has no
energy or enthusiasm. नैराश्य

depth (depths) n The **depth** of something
such as a hole is the distance between its top
and bottom surfaces. खोली

deputy head (deputy heads) n The **deputy
head** of a school is the second most important
person after the head teacher. उप मुख्याध्यापक

descend (descends, descending,
descended) v If you **descend**, or if you

descend something, you move downwards.
(formal) खाली उतरणे

describe (describes, describing, described)
vt If you **describe** someone or something, you
say what they are like. वर्णन करणे

description (descriptions) n A **description**
of someone or something is a statement
which explains what they are or what they
look like. वर्णन

desert (deserts) n A **desert** is a large area of
land, usually in a hot region, which has almost
no water, rain, trees, or plants. वाळवंट

desert island (desert islands) n A **desert
island** is a small tropical island, where nobody
lives. निर्वासित बेट

deserve (deserves, deserving, deserved) vt
If you say that someone **deserves** something,
you mean that they should have it or do it
because of their qualities or actions. पात्र/
लायक/योग्य असणे

design (designs, designing, designed) n
Design is the process and art of planning
and making detailed drawings of something.
आराखडा ▷ vt When someone **designs** a
garment, building, machine, or other object,
they plan it and make a detailed drawing of
it from which it can be built or made. आराखडा
तयार करणे

designer (designers) n A **designer** is a
person whose job involves planning the form
of a new object. डिझायनर

desire (desires, desiring, desired) n A **desire**
is a strong wish to do or have something.
इच्छा ▷ vt If you **desire** something, you want
it. इच्छा असणे

desk (desks) n A **desk** is a table which you sit
at in order to write or work. डेस्क

despair n **Despair** is the feeling that
everything is wrong and that nothing will
improve. नैराश्य

desperate adj If you are **desperate**, you are in
such a bad situation that you will try anything
to change it. बेताल, वाट्टेल ते करायला तयार
असणारा

desperately *adv* If you do something **desperately**, you are in such a bad situation that you are willing to try anything to achieve it. जिवावर उदार होऊन,

despise (despises, despising, despised) *vt* If you **despise** someone or something, you hate them very much. तिरस्कार करणे

despite *prep* If you say that one thing is true **despite** another thing, it's a surprise to you that the first thing is true. असे असूनसुद्धा *The party was fun, despite the rain.*

dessert (desserts) *n* **Dessert** is something sweet, such as fruit or a pudding, that you eat at the end of a meal. डेझर्ट

dessert spoon (dessert spoons) *n* A **dessert spoon** is a spoon which is midway between the size of a teaspoon and a tablespoon. You use it to eat desserts. डेझर्ट स्पून

destination (destinations) *n* Your **destination** is the place you are going to. पोहोचण्याचे ठिकाण

destiny (destinies) *n* A person's **destiny** is everything that happens to them during their life, including what will happen in the future. नियती

destroy (destroys, destroying, destroyed) *vt* To **destroy** something means to cause so much damage to it that it is completely ruined or does not exist any more. नष्ट करणे

destruction *n* **Destruction** is the act of destroying something, or the state of being destroyed. विध्वंस

detached house (detached houses) *n* A **detached house** is one that is not joined to any other house. सुटे घर

detail (details) *n* The **details** of something are its small, individual features or elements. If you examine or discuss something **in detail**, you examine all these features. तपशील

detailed *adj* A **detailed** report or plan contains a lot of details. तपशीलवार

detective (detectives) *n* A **detective** is someone whose job is to discover the facts about a crime or other situation. गुप्तहेर

detention (detentions) *n* **Detention** is the arrest or imprisonment of someone, especially for political reasons. तुरुंगात अडकवून ठेवणे

detergent (detergents) *n* **Detergent** is a chemical substance used for washing things such as clothes or dishes. डिटर्जंट, प्रक्षालक

deteriorate (deteriorates, deteriorating, deteriorated) *vi* If something **deteriorates**, it becomes worse. ऱ्हास होणे

determined *adj* If you are **determined** to do something, you have made a firm decision to do it and will not let anything stop you. दृढनिश्चयी

detour (detours) *n* If you make a **detour** on a journey, you go by a route which is not the shortest way. लांबच्या रस्त्याने जाणे

devaluation (devaluations) *n* **Devaluation** is an official reduction in the value of a currency. अवमूल्यन

devastated *adj* If you are **devastated** by something, you are very shocked and upset by it. उध्वस्त होणे

devastating *adj* You describe something as **devastating** when it is very damaging or upsetting. नासधूस करणारा

develop (develops, developing, developed) *vt* When someone **develops** something, the thing grows or changes over a period of time and usually becomes more advanced or complete. विकसीत करणे ▷ *vi* When someone or something **develops**, the person or thing grows or changes over a period of time and usually becomes more advanced or complete. प्रगत होणे

developing country (developing countries) *n* A **developing country** is a poor country that does not have many industries. विकसनशील देश

development *n* **Development** is the gradual growth or formation of something. विकास

device (devices) *n* A **device** is an object that has been made for a particular purpose. उपकरण

Devil *n* In Christianity, Judaism, and Islam, **the Devil** is the most powerful evil spirit. राक्षस

devise (**devises, devising, devised**) *vt* If you **devise** something, you have the idea for it and design it. युक्ती शोधणे

devoted *adj* If you are **devoted** to someone or something, you care about them or love them very much. समर्पित

diabetes *n* **Diabetes** is a condition in which someone's body is unable to control the level of sugar in their blood. मधुमेह

diabetic (**diabetics**) *adj* **Diabetic** means of, relating to, or having diabetes. मधुमेहसंबंधी ▷ *n* A **diabetic** is a person who suffers from diabetes. मधुमेही

diagnosis (**diagnoses**) *n* **Diagnosis** is identifying what is wrong with someone who is ill or with something that is not working properly. निदान

diagonal *adj* A **diagonal** line or movement goes in a slanting direction. तिरपा

diagram (**diagrams**) *n* A **diagram** is a drawing which is used to explain something. आकृती

dial (**dials, dialling, dialled**) *v* If you **dial**, or if you **dial** a number, you turn the dial or press the buttons on a telephone. फोनचा नंबर फिरवणे

dialect (**dialects**) *n* A **dialect** is a form of a language spoken in a particular area. बोली भाषा

dialling code (**dialling codes**) *n* A **dialling code** for a particular city or region is the series of numbers that you have to dial before a particular telephone number if you are making a call to that place from a different area. डायलिंग कोड

dialling tone (**dialling tones**) *n* The **dialling tone** is the noise which you hear when you pick up a telephone receiver and which means that you can dial the number you want. डायलिंग टोन

dialogue (**dialogues**) *n* **Dialogue** is communication or discussion between people or groups. संवाद

diameter (**diameters**) *n* The **diameter** of a circle or sphere is the length of a straight line through the middle of it. व्यास

diamond (**diamonds**) *n* A **diamond** is a kind of jewel that is hard, clear, and shiny. हिरा ▷ *n* A **diamond** is a shape with four straight sides. चौकोन, चौकट

diarrhoea *n* When someone has **diarrhoea**, a lot of liquid waste material comes out of their bowels because they are ill. अतिसार

diary (**diaries**) *n* A **diary** is a notebook with a separate space for each day of the year. दैनंदिनी

dice (**dice**) *npl* **Dice** are small cubes with one to six spots on each face, used in games. फासा

dictation *n* **Dictation** is the speaking or reading aloud of words for someone else to write down. लेखनार्थ मोठ्याने सांगितलेला मजकूर

dictator (**dictators**) *n* A **dictator** is a ruler who has complete power in a country; used showing disapproval. हुकूमशहा

dictionary (**dictionaries**) *n* A **dictionary** is a book in which the words and phrases of a language are listed, usually in alphabetical order, together with their meanings or their translations in another language. शब्दकोश

die (**dies, dying, died**) *vi* When people, animals, or plants **die**, they stop living. मरणे

diet (**diets, dieting, dieted**) *n* Your **diet** is the type and range of food that you regularly eat. आहार ▷ *vi* If you **are dieting**, you eat special kinds of food or you eat less food than usual because you are trying to lose weight. आहारनियंत्रण करणे

difference (**differences**) *n* The **difference** between things is the way in which they are different from each other. फरक

different *adj* If two things are **different**, they are not like each other. वेगळा

difficult *adj* If something is **difficult**, it is not easy to do or to understand. कठीण

difficulty (**difficulties**) *n* A **difficulty** is a problem. समस्या

dig (**digs, digging, dug**) *v* When people or animals **dig**, they make a hole in the ground or in a pile of stones or debris. खड्डा खणणे

digest (**digests, digesting, digested**) *v* When food **digests** or when you **digest** it, it passes through your body to your stomach. Your stomach removes the substances that your body needs and gets rid of the rest. अन्न पचणे

digestion *n* **Digestion** is the process of digesting food. अन्नाचे पचन

digger (**diggers**) *n* A **digger** is a machine that is used for digging. खणणारे यंत्र

digital *adj* **Digital** systems record or transmit information in the form of thousands of very small signals. डिजिटल

digital camera (**digital cameras**) *n* A **digital camera** is a camera that produces digital images that can be stored on a computer. डिजिटल कॅमेरा

digital radio *n* **Digital radio** is radio in which the signals are transmitted in digital form and received by the radio receiver. डिजिटल रेडिओ

digital television *n* **Digital television** is television in which the signals are transmitted in digital form and received by the television receiver. डिजिटल टेलिव्हिजन

digital watch (**digital watches**) *n* A **digital watch** gives information by displaying numbers rather than by having a pointer which moves round a dial. डिजिटल घड्याळ

dignity *n* If someone behaves with **dignity**, they are serious, calm, and controlled. प्रतिष्ठा

dilemma (**dilemmas**) *n* A **dilemma** is a difficult situation in which you have to choose between two or more alternatives. द्विधा मनःस्थिती

dilute (**dilutes, diluting, diluted**) *v* If a liquid **is diluted**, it is mixed with water or another liquid, and becomes weaker. सौम्य करणे ▷ *adj* A **dilute** liquid is very thin and weak, usually because it has had water added to it. सौम्य

dim (**dimmer, dimmest**) *adj* **Dim** light is not bright. You can also say that something is **dim** when the light is not bright enough to see very well. अंधूक

dimension (**dimensions**) *n* A particular **dimension** of something is a particular aspect of it. पैलू

diminish (**diminishes, diminishing, diminished**) *v* When something **diminishes**, its importance, size, or intensity is reduced. कमी होणे

din *n* A **din** is a very loud and unpleasant noise that lasts for some time. खूप मोठा गोंगाट

diner (**diners**) *n* A **diner** is a small cheap restaurant that is open all day. डायनर

dinghy (**dinghies**) *n* A **dinghy** is a small boat that you sail or row. छोटा मचवा

dining car (**dining cars**) *n* A **dining car** is a carriage on a train where passengers can have a meal. डायनिंग कार

dining room (**dining rooms**) *n* The **dining room** is the room in a house or hotel where people have their meals. डायनिंग रूम

dinner (**dinners**) *n* **Dinner** is the main meal of the day, eaten in the evening. रात्रीचे जेवण

dinner jacket (**dinner jackets**) *n* A **dinner jacket** is a jacket, usually black, worn by men for formal social events. डिनर जॅकेट

dinner party (**dinner parties**) *n* A **dinner party** is a social event where a small group of people are invited to have dinner and spend the evening at someone's house. रात्रीची मेजवानी

dinner time n **Dinner time** is the period of the day when most people have their main meal, usually in the evening. रात्रीच्या जेवणाची वेळ

dinosaur (**dinosaurs**) n **Dinosaurs** were large reptiles which lived in prehistoric times. डायनोसोर

dip (**dips, dipping, dipped**) n A **dip** is a thick creamy sauce. You dip pieces of raw vegetable or biscuits into the sauce and then eat them. गोड दाट चटणी ▷ vt If you **dip** something into a liquid, you put it in and then quickly take it out again. बुडविणे

diploma (**diplomas**) n A **diploma** is a qualification which may be awarded to a student by a university, college, or high school. पदविका

diplomat (**diplomats**) n A **diplomat** is a senior official, usually based at an embassy, who negotiates with another country on behalf of his or her own country. परराष्ट्रनीतीमध्ये निपुण अधिकारी

diplomatic adj **Diplomatic** means relating to diplomacy and diplomats. परराष्ट्रनीतीसंबंधी

dipstick (**dipsticks**) n A **dipstick** is a metal rod with marks along one end. It is used to measure the amount of liquid in a container, especially the amount of oil in a car engine. डिपस्टिक

direct (**directs, directing, directed**) adj **Direct** means moving towards a place or object, without changing direction and without stopping, for example in a journey. थेट ▷ vt If you **direct** something at a particular thing, you aim or point it at that thing. निर्देश करणे

direct debit (**direct debits**) n If you pay a bill by **direct debit**, you give permission for the company who is owed money to transfer the correct amount from your bank account into theirs, usually every month. डायरेक्ट डेबिट

direction (**directions**) n A **direction** is the way that you go to get to a place. दिशा

directions npl **Directions** are words or pictures that show you how to do something, or how to get somewhere. सूचना, मार्गदर्शन

directly adv If you go somewhere **directly**, you go there without changing direction and without stopping. थेट

director (**directors**) n The **director** of a play, film, or television programme is the person who decides how it will appear on stage or screen, and who tells the actors and technical staff what to do. दिग्दर्शक

directory (**directories**) n A **directory** is a book which gives lists of information such as people's names, addresses, and telephone numbers. मार्गदर्शिका

directory enquiries npl **Directory enquiries** is a service which you can telephone to find out someone's telephone number. डिरेक्टरी एन्क्वायरिज

dirt n If there is **dirt** on something, there is dust, mud, or a stain on it. डाग

dirty (**dirtier, dirtiest**) adj If something is **dirty**, it is marked or covered with stains, spots, or mud, and needs to be cleaned. मळलेला

disability (**disabilities**) n A **disability** is a physical or mental condition that restricts the way someone can live their life. अपंगत्व

disabled adj Someone who is **disabled** has an illness, injury, or condition that tends to restrict the way that they can live their life, especially by making it difficult for them to move about. अपंग

disadvantage (**disadvantages**) n A **disadvantage** is a part of a situation which causes problems. तोटा

disagree (**disagrees, disagreeing, disagreed**) vi If you **disagree** with someone, you have a different opinion to them about something. सहमत न होणे

disagreement (**disagreements**) n **Disagreement** means objecting to something. असहमती

disappear (**disappears, disappearing, disappeared**) vi If someone or something

disappears, they go where they cannot be seen or found. नाहीसे होणे

disappearance (**disappearances**) *n* If you refer to someone's **disappearance**, you are referring to the fact that nobody knows where they have gone. अदृश्य होणे

disappoint (**disappoints, disappointing, disappointed**) *vt* If things or people **disappoint** you, they are not as good as you had hoped, or do not do what you hoped they would do. निराश करणे

disappointed *adj* If you are **disappointed**, you are sad because something has not happened or because something is not as good as you hoped it would be. निराश

disappointing *adj* Something that is **disappointing** is not as good or as large as you hoped it would be. निराश करणारे

disappointment *n* **Disappointment** is the state of feeling sad because something has not happened or because something is not as good as you hoped it would be. नैराश्य

disaster (**disasters**) *n* A **disaster** is a very bad accident such as an earthquake or a plane crash. आपत्ती

disastrous *adj* Something that is **disastrous** has extremely bad consequences and effects or is very unsuccessful. आपत्तीजनक

disc (**discs**) *n* A **disc** is a flat, circular shape or object. तबकडी

discipline *n* **Discipline** is the practice of making people obey rules or standards of behaviour, and punishing them when they do not. शिस्त

disc jockey (**disc jockeys**) *n* A **disc jockey** is someone who plays and introduces pop records on the radio or at a club. डिस्क जॉकी

disclose (**discloses, disclosing, disclosed**) *vt* If you **disclose** new or secret information, you tell it to someone. उघड करणे

disco (**discos**) *n* A **disco** is a place or event where people dance to pop music. डिस्को

disconnect (**disconnects, disconnecting, disconnected**) *vt* To **disconnect** a piece

of equipment means to separate it from its source of power. संपर्क तोडणे

discount (**discounts**) *n* A **discount** is a reduction in the price of something. सवलत

discourage (**discourages, discouraging, discouraged**) *vt* If someone or something **discourages** you, they cause you to lose your enthusiasm about doing something. नाउमेद करणे

discover (**discovers, discovering, discovered**) *vt* If you **discover** something that you did not know about before, you become aware of it or learn of it. शोध लावणे

discretion *n* **Discretion** is the quality of behaving in a quiet and controlled way without attracting attention or giving away private information. *(formal)* विवेक, शांतता

discrimination *n* **Discrimination** is the practice of treating one person or group of people less fairly or less well than other people or groups. भेदाभेद

discuss (**discusses, discussing, discussed**) *vt* If people **discuss** something, they talk about it, often in order to reach a decision. चर्चा करणे

discussion (**discussions**) *n* If there is **discussion** about something, people talk about it, often in order to reach a decision. चर्चा

disease (**diseases**) *n* A **disease** is an illness which affects people, animals, or plants. रोग

disgraceful *adj* If you say that something is **disgraceful**, you disapprove of it strongly. लज्जास्पद

disguise (**disguises, disguising, disguised**) *vt* If you **disguise** yourself , you put on clothes which make you look like someone else or alter your appearance in other ways, so that people will not recognize you. वेषांतर करणे

disgusted *adj* If you are **disgusted**, you have a strong feeling of dislike or disapproval. किळस आलेला

disgusting *adj* If you say that something is **disgusting**, you think it is extremely unpleasant or unacceptable. किळसवाणा

d

dish (dishes) n A **dish** is a shallow container used for cooking or serving food. थाळी

dishcloth (dishcloths) n A **dishcloth** is a cloth used to dry dishes after they have been washed. डिश क्लॉथ

dishonest adj If you say someone is **dishonest**, you mean that they are not honest and you cannot trust them. अप्रामाणिक

dish towel (dish towels) n A **dish towel** is a cloth used to dry dishes after they have been washed. डिश टॉवेल

dishwasher (dishwashers) n A **dishwasher** is an electrically operated machine that washes and dries plates, saucepans, and cutlery. डिशवॉशर

disinfectant (disinfectants) n Disinfectant is a substance that kills germs. जंतुनाशक

disk (disks) n In a computer, the **disk** is the part where information is stored. डिस्क

disk drive (disk drives) n The **disk drive** on a computer is the part that contains the hard disk or into which a disk can be inserted. डिस्क ड्राईव्ह

diskette (diskettes) n A **diskette** is a small magnetic disk that used to be used for storing computer data and programs. डिस्केट

dislike (dislikes, disliking, disliked) vt If you **dislike** someone or something, you consider them to be unpleasant and do not like them. नावड असणे

dismal adj Something that is **dismal** is depressingly bad. उद्वेगजनक

dismiss (dismisses, dismissing, dismissed) vt If you **dismiss** something, you decide that it is not important enough for you to think about. फेटाळणे, काढून टाकणे

disobedient adj If you are **disobedient**, you deliberately do not do what someone in authority tells you to do, or what a rule or law says that you should do. अवज्ञा करणारा

disobey (disobeys, disobeying, disobeyed) v When someone **disobeys** a person or an order, they deliberately do not do what they have been told to do. अवज्ञा करणे

dispenser (dispensers) n A **dispenser** is a machine or container from which you can get things. डिस्पेन्सर

display (displays, displaying, displayed) n **Display** is the act of exhibiting or showing something. प्रदर्शन ▷ vt If you **display** something that you want people to see, you put it in a particular place, so that people can see it easily. प्रदर्शन करणे

disposable adj Disposable things are designed to be thrown away after use. वापर करून टाकून देण्याजोगे

disqualify (disqualifies, disqualifying, disqualified) vt When someone **is disqualified** from an event or an activity, they are officially stopped from taking part in it. अपात्र ठरविणे

disrupt (disrupts, disrupting, disrupted) vt If someone or something **disrupts** an event or process, they cause problems that prevent it from continuing normally. अडथळा आणणे

dissatisfied adj If you are **dissatisfied** with something, you are not content or pleased with it. असमाधानी

dissolve (dissolves, dissolving, dissolved) v If a substance **dissolves** in liquid, or if you **dissolve** a substance, it mixes with the liquid, becoming weaker until it finally disappears. विरघळणे

distance (distances) n The **distance** between two places is the amount of space between them. अंतर

distant adj Distant means far away. दूर अंतरावरील

distillery (distilleries) *n* A **distillery** is a place where whisky or a similar strong alcoholic drink is made. मद्याकनिर्मिती कारखाना

distinction (distinctions) *n* A **distinction** is a difference between similar things. फरक

distinctive *adj* Something that is **distinctive** has special qualities that make it easily recognizable. वेगळा

distinguish (distinguishes, distinguishing, distinguished) *v* If you can **distinguish** one thing from another, you can see or understand the difference between them. फरक करणे

distract (distracts, distracting, distracted) *vt* If something **distracts** you, or if it **distracts** your attention, it stops you concentrating. लक्ष दुसरीकडे वळविणे

distribute (distributes, distributing, distributed) *vt* If you **distribute** things, you hand them or deliver them to a number of people. वाटप करणे

distributor (distributors) *n* A **distributor** is a company that supplies goods to shops or other businesses. वितरक

district (districts) *n* A **district** is an area of a town or country. जिल्हा

disturb (disturbs, disturbing, disturbed) *vt* If you **disturb** someone, you interrupt what they are doing and cause them inconvenience. त्रास देणे

ditch (ditches, ditching, ditched) *n* A **ditch** is a long narrow channel cut into the ground at the side of a road or field. लांब अरुंद खड्डा ▷ *vt* If you **ditch** something, you get rid of it. त्याग करणे

dive (dives, diving, dived) *n* A **dive** is a headlong plunge into water, especially one of several formalized movements made as a sport. सूर (पाण्यातला) ▷ *vi* If you **dive** into some water, you jump in head-first with your arms held straight above your head. पाण्यात सूर मारणे

diver (divers) *n* A **diver** is a person who swims under water using special breathing equipment. डायव्हर

diversion (diversions) *n* A **diversion** is a special route arranged for traffic when the normal route cannot be used. पर्यायी मार्ग

divide (divides, dividing, divided) *vt* If you **divide** something, you make it into smaller pieces. विभागणे ▷ *vt* When you **divide** numbers, you see how many times one number goes into another number. भाग लावणे

diving *n* **Diving** is the activity of working or looking around underwater, using special breathing equipment. सूर मारण्याची क्रिया

diving board (diving boards) *n* A **diving board** is a board high above a swimming pool from which people can dive into the water. डायव्हिंग बोर्ड

division *n* The **division** of something is the act of separating it into two or more different parts. विभाजन

divorce (divorces) *n* A **divorce** is the formal ending of a marriage by law. घटस्फोट

divorced *adj* Someone who is **divorced** from their former husband or wife has separated from them and is no longer legally married to them. घटस्फोटित

DIY *abbr* **DIY** is the activity of making or repairing things in your home. **DIY** is an abbreviation for 'do-it-yourself'. कोणतीही गोष्ट स्वतःच करणे

dizzy (dizzier, dizziest) *adj* If you feel **dizzy**, you feel that you are losing your balance and are about to fall. भोवळ आल्यासारखे वाटणे

DJ (DJs) *abbr* A **DJ** is someone who plays and introduces pop records on the radio or at a club. डीजे

DNA *n* **DNA** is a chemical that is found in all living cells. It contains genetic information. **DNA** is an abbreviation for 'deoxyribonucleic acid'. डीएनए

do (does, doing, did, done) *vt* If you **do** something, you spend some time on it or finish it. करणे *I tried to do some work.*

dock (docks) *n* A **dock** is an enclosed area of water where ships are loaded, unloaded, or repaired. गोदी, बंदर

doctor (doctors) *n* A **doctor** is someone who is qualified in medicine and treats people who are ill. डॉक्टर

document (documents) *n* A **document** is an official piece of paper with writing on it. कागदपत्र

documentary (documentaries) *n* A **documentary** is a radio or television programme or a film which provides factual information about a particular subject. माहितीपट

documentation *n* **Documentation** consists of documents which provide a record of something. कागदपत्रे बनविणे

documents *npl* **Documents** are official pieces of paper with writing on them. कागदपत्रे

dodge (dodges, dodging, dodged) *vi* If you **dodge** somewhere, you move there suddenly to avoid being hit, caught, or seen. सटकणे

dog (dogs) *n* A **dog** is an animal that is often kept as a pet or used to guard or hunt things. कुत्रा

dole *n* The **dole** is money that is given regularly by the government to people who are unemployed. बेकारीभत्ता

doll (dolls) *n* A **doll** is a child's toy which looks like a small person or baby. बाहुली

dollar (dollars) *n* The **dollar** is a unit of money in the USA, Canada, and some other countries. It is represented by the symbol $. डॉलर

dolphin (dolphins) *n* A **dolphin** is a mammal with fins and a pointed nose which lives in the sea. डॉल्फिन

domestic *adj* **Domestic** political activities and situations happen or exist within one particular country. स्वदेशी

Dominican Republic *n* The **Dominican Republic** is a republic in the Caribbean, on the eastern side of the island of Hispaniola. डॉमिनिकन प्रजासत्ताक

domino (dominoes) *n* A **domino** is a small rectangular block marked with two groups of spots on one side. **Dominoes** are used for playing various games. डॉमिनो

dominoes *npl* **Dominoes** is a game played using small rectangular blocks, called **dominoes**, which are marked with two groups of spots on one side. डॉमिनोज

donate (donates, donating, donated) *vt* If you **donate** something to a charity or other organization, you give it to them. दान करणे

done *adj* A task that is **done** has been completed. पूर्ण केलेले

donkey (donkeys) *n* A **donkey** is an animal like a small horse with long ears. गाढव

donor (donors) *n* A **donor** is someone who gives a part of their body or some of their blood to be used by doctors to help a person who is ill. दाता

door (doors) *n* A **door** is a swinging or sliding piece of wood, glass, or metal, which is used to open and close the entrance to a building, room, cupboard, or vehicle. दरवाजा

doorbell (doorbells) n A **doorbell** is a bell on the outside of a house which you can ring so that the people inside know that you want to see them. दरवाजाची घंटा

door handle (door handles) n A **door handle** is a small round object or a lever that is attached to a door and is used for opening and closing it. दरवाजाची मूठ

doorman (doormen) n A **doorman** is a man who stands at the door of a club, prevents unwanted people from coming in, and makes people leave if they cause trouble. रखवालदार

doorstep (doorsteps) n A **doorstep** is a step on the outside of a building, in front of a door. पायरी

dormitory (dormitories) n A **dormitory** is a large bedroom where several people sleep. अनेक लोकांसाठी असलेली झोपण्याची मोठी खोली

dose (doses) n A **dose** of a medicine or drug is a measured amount of it. औषधाची मात्रा

dot (dots) n A **dot** is a very small round mark. बिंदू

double (doubles, doubling, doubled) adj You use **double** to describe a pair of similar things. दुहेरी ▷ v When something **doubles** or when you **double** it, it becomes twice as great in number, amount, or size. दुप्पट होणे

double bass (double basses) n A **double bass** is the largest instrument in the violin family. You play it standing up. उभ्याने वाजवायचे व्हायोलिनसारखे मोठे वाद्य

double glazing n If someone has **double glazing** in their house, their windows are fitted with two layers of glass. People put in double glazing in order to keep buildings warmer or to keep out noise. डबल ग्लेझिंग

doubt (doubts, doubting, doubted) n If you feel **doubt** or **doubts** about something, you feel uncertain about it. शंका ▷ vt If you **doubt** something, or if you **doubt** whether something is true or possible, you believe that it is probably not true, genuine, or possible. शंका घेणे

doubtful adj Something that is **doubtful** seems unlikely or uncertain. संशयास्पद

dough n **Dough** is a mixture of flour and water, and sometimes also sugar and fat, which can be cooked to make bread, pastry, and biscuits. कणीक

doughnut (doughnuts) n A **doughnut** is a lump or ring of sweet dough cooked in hot fat. डोनट

do up (does up, doing up, did up, done up) v If you **do** something **up**, you fasten it. घट्ट लावणे She did up the buttons.

dove (doves) n A **dove** is a white bird that looks like a pigeon. पारवा

do without (does without, doing without, did without, done without) v If you **do without** something, you manage or survive in spite of not having it. एखाद्या गोष्टीशिवाय काम चालवणे We can't do without the help of your organisation.

down adv When something moves **down**, it goes from a higher place to a lower place. खाली

download (downloads, downloaded, downloading) vt To **download** data means to transfer it to or from a computer along a line such as a telephone line, a radio link, or a computer network. डाऊनलोड करणे

downpour (downpours) n A **downpour** is a heavy fall of rain. मुसळधार पाऊस

Down's syndrome n **Down's syndrome** is a condition that some people are born with. People who have Down's syndrome have a flat forehead and sloping eyes and lower than average intelligence. डाऊन्स सिंड्रोम

downstairs adj **Downstairs** means situated on the ground floor of a building or on a lower floor than you are. खालचा मजला ▷ adv If you go **downstairs** in a building, you go down a staircase towards the ground floor. खालच्या मजल्यावर

doze (dozes, dozing, dozed) vi When you **doze**, you sleep lightly or for a short period, especially during the daytime. डुलकी घेणे

dozen (dozens) num A **dozen** means twelve. डझन

doze off (dozes off, dozing off, dozed off) v
If you **doze off**, you fall into a light sleep. डुलकी
लागणे *She dozed off for a few moments.*

drab (drabber, drabbest) adj Something that
is **drab** is dull and not attractive or exciting.
अनाकर्षक

draft (drafts) n A **draft** is an early version of a
letter, book, or speech. मसुदा

drag (drags, dragging, dragged) vt If you
drag something or someone somewhere, you
pull them there with difficulty. खेचणे

dragon (dragons) n In stories and legends,
a **dragon** is an animal like a big lizard. It has
wings and claws, and breathes out fire. ड्रॅगन

dragonfly (dragonflies) n A **dragonfly** is a
brightly coloured insect with a long thin body
and two sets of wings. पतंग (कीटक)

drain (drains, draining, drained) n A **drain**
is a pipe that carries water or sewage away
from a place, or an opening in a surface that
leads to the pipe. गटार ▷ v If you **drain** a
liquid from a place or object, you remove the
liquid by causing it to flow somewhere else. If
a liquid **drains** somewhere, it flows there. पाणी
काढून टाकणे

draining board (draining boards) n The
draining board is the place on a sink unit
where things such as cups, plates, and cutlery
are put to drain after they have been washed.
भांडी सुकविण्याचा बोर्ड

drainpipe (drainpipes) n A **drainpipe** is
a pipe attached to the side of a building,
through which rainwater flows from the roof
into a drain. ड्रेन पाईप

drama (dramas) n A **drama** is a serious play
for the theatre, television, or radio. नाटक

dramatic adj A **dramatic** change is sudden
and noticeable. नाट्यमय

drastic adj A **drastic** course of action is
extreme and is usually taken urgently. आमूलाग्र

draught (draughts) n A **draught** is an
unwelcome current of air coming into a room
or vehicle. वाऱ्याचा झोत

draughts npl **Draughts** is a game for two
people, played with 24 round pieces on a
board. ड्रॉट्स नावाचा एक खेळ

draw (draws, drawing, drew, drawn) v When
you **draw**, or when you **draw** something, you
use pens, pencils, or crayons to make a picture.
चित्र काढणे ▷ vi In a game, if one person or team
draws with another one, or if two people or
teams **draw**, they finish with the same number
of points. सामना अनिर्णित राहणे ▷ v You can use
draw to indicate that someone or something
moves somewhere or is moved there. ओढणे

drawback (drawbacks) n A **drawback** is
an aspect of something that makes it less
acceptable. दोष

drawer (drawers) n A **drawer** is a part of a
desk or other piece of furniture that is shaped
like a rectangular box. You pull it towards you
to open it. कप्पा

drawing (drawings) n A **drawing** is a picture
or plan made by means of lines on a surface,
especially one made with a pencil or pen
without the use of colour. चित्र

drawing pin (drawing pins) n A **drawing
pin** is a short pin with a broad, flat top which
is used for fastening papers or pictures to a
board, wall, or other surface. ड्रॉईंग पिन

dreadful adj If you say that something is
dreadful, you mean that it is very unpleasant
or very poor in quality. वाईट

dream (**dreams, dreaming, dreamed, dreamt**) *n* A **dream** is an imaginary series of events that you experience in your mind while you are asleep. स्वप्न ▷ *v* When you **dream**, you experience imaginary events in your mind while you are asleep. स्वप्न पाहणे

drench (**drenches, drenching, drenched**) *vt* To **drench** something or someone means to make them completely wet. भिजून चिंब होणे

dress (**dresses, dressing, dressed**) *n* A **dress** is something a girl or a woman can wear. It covers the body and part of the legs. पोशाख ▷ *vi* When you **dress**, you put on clothes. कपडे अंगावर चढणे

dressed *adj* If you are **dressed**, you are wearing clothes rather than being naked. कपडे घातलेली व्यक्ती

dresser (**dressers**) *n* A **dresser** is a chest of drawers, sometimes with a mirror on the top. ड्रेसर

dressing gown (**dressing gowns**) *n* A **dressing gown** is a loose-fitting coat worn over pyjamas or other night clothes. ड्रेसिंग गाऊन

dressing table (**dressing tables**) *n* A **dressing table** is a small table in a bedroom with drawers and a mirror. ड्रेसिंग टेबल

dress up (**dresses up, dressing up, dressed up**) *v* If you **dress up**, you put on different clothes, in order to look smarter or to disguise yourself. चांगले कपडे घालणे *You do not need to dress up for dinner.*

dried *adj* **Dried** food or milk has had all the water removed from it so that it will last for a long time. सुका

drift (**drifts, drifting, drifted**) *n* A **drift** is a movement away from somewhere or something, or a movement towards somewhere or something different. प्रवाहाबरोबर वहावत जाण्याची क्रिया ▷ *vi* When something **drifts** somewhere, it is carried there by the wind or by water. वारा वा पाण्याच्या प्रवाहाबरोबर वाहून जाणे

drill (**drills, drilling, drilled**) *n* A **drill** is a tool for making holes. ड्रिल ▷ *v* When you **drill** into something or **drill** a hole in it, you make a hole using a drill. भोक पाडणे

drink (**drinks, drinking, drank, drunk**) *n* A **drink** is an amount of a liquid which you drink. पेय ▷ *v* When you **drink**, or **drink** a liquid, you take it into your mouth and swallow it. पिणे

drink-driving *n* **Drink-driving** is the offence of driving a car after drinking more than the amount of alcohol that is legally allowed. मद्यपान करून गाडी चालविणे

drinking water *n* **Drinking water** is water which it is safe to drink. पिण्याचे पाणी

drip (**drips, dripping, dripped**) *n* A **drip** is a small individual drop of a liquid. लहान थेंब ▷ *vi* When liquid **drips** somewhere, it falls in small drops. गळणे, ठिबकणे

drive (**drives, driving, drove, driven**) *n* A **drive** is a journey in a vehicle such as a car. वाहनातला प्रवास ▷ *v* When someone **drives** a vehicle, they make it go where they want. वाहन चालवणे

driver (**drivers**) *n* The **driver** of a vehicle is the person who is driving it. चालक

driveway (**driveways**) *n* A **driveway** is a private road that leads from a public road to a house or garage. वाहनासाठीचा खाजगी रस्ता

driving instructor (**driving instructors**) *n* A **driving instructor** is someone who teaches people to drive a vehicle. वाहनचालक प्रशिक्षक

driving lesson (**driving lessons**) *n* A **driving lesson** is a one of a course of lessons during which a person is taught how to drive a vehicle. वाहन चालविण्याचा धडा

driving licence (**driving licences**) *n* A **driving licence** is a card showing that you are qualified to drive. चालक परवाना

driving test (**driving tests**) *n* A **driving test** is a test that must be passed before you are qualified to drive a vehicle. वाहन चालविण्याची चाचणी

drizzle n **Drizzle** is light rain falling in fine drops. रिमझिम पाऊस

drop (drops, dropping, dropped) n If there is a **drop** in something, it quickly becomes less. घट ▷ v If a level or amount **drops** or if someone or something **drops** it, it quickly becomes less. घट होणे

drought (droughts) n A **drought** is a long period of time during which no rain falls. दुष्काळ

drown (drowns, drowning, drowned) v When someone **drowns**, or when they **are drowned**, they die because they have gone under water and cannot breathe. बुडणे

drowsy (drowsier, drowsiest) adj If you are **drowsy**, you feel sleepy and cannot think clearly. पेंगणारा

drug (drugs) n A **drug** is a chemical substance given to people to treat or prevent an illness or disease. औषध

drum (drums) n A **drum** is a musical instrument consisting of a skin stretched tightly over a round frame. ड्रम

drummer (drummers) n A **drummer** is a person who plays a drum or drums in a band or group. ड्रम वाजविणारा

drunk (drunks) adj If someone is **drunk**, they have consumed too much alcohol. मद्यपान केलेली व्यक्ती ▷ n A **drunk** is someone who is drunk or who often gets drunk. मद्यपान केलेली व्यक्ती

dry (drier, dryer, driest, dries, drying, dried) adj If something is **dry**, it has no water or other liquid on it or in it. कोरडा ▷ v When you **dry** something, or when it **dries**, it becomes dry. कोरडे करणे

dry cleaner (dry cleaners) n A **dry cleaner** or a **dry cleaner's** is a shop where dry-cleaning is done. ड्राय क्लिनर

dry-cleaning n **Dry-cleaning** is the action or work of cleaning things such as clothes using chemicals rather than water. ड्राय क्लिनिंग

dryer (dryers) n A **dryer** is a machine for drying things, for example clothes or people's hair. ड्रायर

dual carriageway (dual carriageways) n A **dual carriageway** is a road which has two lanes of traffic travelling in each direction with a strip of grass or concrete down the middle to separate the two lots of traffic. दुपदरी रस्ता

dubbed adj If a film or soundtrack in a foreign language is **dubbed**, a new soundtrack is added with actors giving a translation. चित्रपटासाठी वापरलेला भाषांतरित आवाज

dubious adj You describe something as **dubious** when you think it is not completely honest, safe, or reliable. संदिग्ध

duck (ducks) n A **duck** is a common water bird with short legs and a large flat beak. बदक

due adj If something is **due** at a particular time, it is expected to happen or to arrive at that time. घडणे अपेक्षित

due to prep If something is **due to** another thing, it is a result of that thing. च्या कारणाने *He couldn't do the job, due to pain in his hands.*

dull (duller, dullest) adj Something that is **dull** is not interesting. नीरस ▷ adj A **dull** colour is not bright. फिकट

dumb adj Someone who is **dumb** is completely unable to speak. मुका

dummy (dummies) n A **dummy** is a model of a person, often used to display clothes. हुबेहूब प्रतिकृती

dump (dumps, dumping, dumped) n A **dump** is a site provided for people to leave their rubbish. कचरा टाकण्याची जागा ▷ vt If something **is dumped** somewhere, it is

d

put there because it is no longer wanted or needed. (informal) अडगळीत टाकणे

dumpling (**dumplings**) n **Dumplings** are small lumps of dough that are cooked and eaten, either with meat and vegetables or as part of a sweet pudding. डम्प्लिंगस्

dungarees npl **Dungarees** are a one-piece garment consisting of trousers, a piece of cloth which covers your chest, and straps which go over your shoulders. डंगरिस

dungeon (**dungeons**) n A **dungeon** is a dark underground prison in a castle. अंधारकोठडी

duration n The **duration** of an event or state is the time that it lasts. कालावधी

during prep If something happens **during** a period of time, it happens between the beginning and the end of that period. दरम्यान Storms are common during the winter.

dusk n **Dusk** is the time just before night when it is not yet completely dark. सांजवेळ

dust (**dusts, dusting, dusted**) n **Dust** consists of very small dry particles of earth, sand, or dirt. धूळ ▷ v When you **dust** or **dust** furniture or other objects, you remove dust from them using a dry cloth. धूळ झटकणे

dustbin (**dustbins**) n A **dustbin** is a large container for rubbish. कचरापेटी

dustman (**dustmen**) n A **dustman** is a person whose job is to empty the rubbish from people's dustbins and take it away to be disposed of. कचरा वाहून नेणारी व्यक्ती

dustpan (**dustpans**) n A **dustpan** is a small flat container made of metal or plastic. You hold it flat on the floor and put dirt and dust into it using a brush. केर भरण्याची सुपळी

dusty (**dustier, dustiest**) adj Something that is **dusty** is covered with dust. धूळ साचलेला

Dutch adj **Dutch** means relating to or belonging to the Netherlands, or to its people, language, or culture. डच ▷ n **Dutch** is the language spoken in the Netherlands. डच

Dutchman (**Dutchmen**) n A **Dutchman** is a man who is a native of the Netherlands. डचमेन

Dutchwoman (**Dutchwomen**) n A **Dutchwoman** is a woman who is a native of the Netherlands. डचवूमन

duty (**duties**) n **Duty** is the work that you have to do as your job. नोकरी

duty-free adj **Duty-free** goods are sold at airports or on planes or ships at a cheaper price than usual because they are not taxed. करमुक्त ▷ n **Duty-free** is goods sold at airports or on planes or ships at a cheaper price than usual because they are not taxed. करमुक्त

duvet (**duvets**) n A **duvet** is a large cover filled with feathers or similar material, which you use to cover yourself in bed. रजई

DVD (**DVDs**) n A **DVD** is a disc similar to a compact disc on which a film or music is recorded. **DVD** is an abbreviation for 'digital video disc' or 'digital versatile disc'. डीव्हीडी

DVD burner (**DVD burners**) n A **DVD burner** is a piece of computer equipment that you use for copying data from a computer onto a DVD. डीव्हीडी बर्नर

DVD player (**DVD players**) n A **DVD player** is a machine for playing DVDs. डीव्हीडी प्लेअर

dwarf (**dwarfs, dwarves**) n In children's stories, a **dwarf** is an imaginary creature that is like a small man. Dwarves often have magical powers. बुटका

dye (**dyes, dyeing, dyed**) n **Dye** is a substance which is used to dye something. रंगद्रव्य ▷ vt If you **dye** something, you change its colour by soaking it in a special liquid. रंगविणे

dynamic adj A **dynamic** person is full of energy; used showing approval. चैतन्यशील

dyslexia n If someone suffers from **dyslexia**, they have difficulty with reading because of a slight disorder of their brain. डिस्लेक्सिया

dyslexic adj If someone is **dyslexic**, they have difficulty with reading because of a slight disorder of their brain. डिस्लेक्सिक

e

each det **Each** thing or person in a group means every member as an individual. प्रत्येक *Each book is beautifully illustrated.* ▷ pron **Each** means every one. प्रत्येक *He gave each of us a book.*

eagle (eagles) n An **eagle** is a large bird that hunts and kills small animals for food. गरुड

ear (ears) n Your **ears** are the two parts of your body with which you hear sounds. कान

earache (earaches) n **Earache** is a pain in the inside part of your ear. कर्णशूळ

eardrum (eardrums) n Your **eardrums** are the thin pieces of tightly stretched skin inside each ear, which vibrate when sound waves reach them. कानाचा पडदा

earlier adv **Earlier** is used to refer to a point or period in time before the present or before the one you are talking about. अगोदर

early (earlier, earliest) adj If you are **early**, you arrive before the time that you were expected to come. लवकर ▷ adv **Early** means before the usual time that a particular event or activity happens. लवकर ▷ adj **Early** means near the first part of something. आधी

earn (earns, earning, earned) vt If you **earn** money, you receive it in return for work that you do. कमावणे

earnings npl Your **earnings** are the money that you earn by working. कमाई

earphones npl **Earphones** are a small piece of equipment which you wear over or inside your ears so that you can listen to a radio or MP3 player without anyone else hearing. इअरफोन

earplugs npl **Earplugs** are small pieces of a soft material which you put into your ears to keep out noise, water, or cold air. इअरप्लग

earring (earrings) n **Earrings** are pieces of jewellery which you attach to your ears. कर्णभूषण

earth n The **earth** is the planet that we live on. पृथ्वी ▷ n **Earth** is the soil that plants grow in. माती

earthquake (earthquakes) n An **earthquake** is a shaking of the ground caused by movement of the earth's surface. भूकंप

easily adv You use **easily** to emphasize that something is very likely to happen, or is certainly true. सहज

east n The **east** edge, corner, or part of a place or country is the part which is towards the east. पूर्वेकडील ▷ n If you go **east**, you travel towards the east. पूर्वेकडे ▷ n The **east** is the direction in which you look to see the sun rise. पूर्व दिशा

eastbound adj **Eastbound** roads or vehicles lead to or are travelling towards the east. *(formal)* पूर्वकडे जाणारा

Easter (Easters) n **Easter** is a Christian festival and holiday, when the resurrection of Jesus Christ is celebrated. ईस्टर

Easter egg (Easter eggs) n An **Easter egg** is an egg made of chocolate that is given as a present at Easter. In some countries, Easter eggs are hidden and children then look for them. ईस्टर एग

eastern adj **Eastern** means in or from the east of a region or country. पूर्वेकडील, पौर्वात्य

easy (easier, easiest) adj If a job or action is **easy**, you can do it without difficulty. सोपे

easy chair (easy chairs) n An **easy chair** is a large, comfortable padded chair. आरामखुर्ची

easy-going adj If you describe someone as **easy-going**, you approve of the fact that that they are not easily worried or upset. निश्चिंत, शांत

eat (eats, eating, ate, eaten) v When you **eat**, you chew and swallow food. खाणे

e-book (e-books) n An **e-book** is a book which is produced for reading on a computer screen. **E-book** is an abbreviation for 'electronic book'. ई-बुक

eccentric adj If you say that someone is **eccentric**, you mean that they behave in a strange way, and have habits or opinions that are different from those of most people. विक्षिप्त

echo (echoes) n An **echo** is a sound caused by a noise being reflected off a surface such as a wall. प्रतिध्वनि

ecofriendly adj **Ecofriendly** products or services are less harmful to the environment than other similar products or services. पर्यावरणस्नेही

ecological adj **Ecological** means involved with or concerning ecology. पर्यावरणीय

ecology n **Ecology** is the study of the relationship between living things and their environment. पर्यावरणशास्त्र

e-commerce n **E-commerce** is the buying, selling, and ordering of goods and services using the Internet. ई-कॉमर्स

economic adj **Economic** means concerned with the organization of the money, industry, and trade of a country, region, or society. अर्थशास्त्रसंबंधी

economical adj Something that is **economical** does not require a lot of money to operate. मितव्ययी, काटकसरीचा

economics npl **Economics** is the study of the way in which money, industry, and trade are organized in a society. अर्थशास्त्र

economist (economists) n An **economist** is a person who studies, teaches, or writes about economics. अर्थशास्त्रज्ञ

economize (economizes, economizing, economized) vi If you **economize**, you save money by spending it very carefully. काटकसर करणे

economy (economies) n The **economy** of a country or region is the system by which money, industry, and trade are organized. अर्थव्यवस्था

economy class n **Economy class** is a class of travel in aircraft, providing less luxurious accommodation than first class at a lower fare. इकॉनॉमी क्लास

ecstasy (ecstasies) n **Ecstasy** is a feeling of great happiness. परमानंद

Ecuador n **Ecuador** is a republic in South America, on the Pacific. इक्वाडोर

eczema n **Eczema** is a skin condition which makes your skin itch and become sore and broken. गजकर्ण

edge (edges) n The **edge** of something is the place or line where it stops, or the part of it that is furthest from the middle. काठ, कड

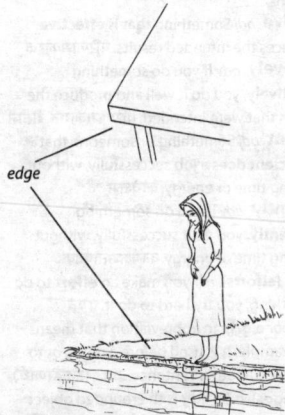

edge

edgy (edgier, edgiest) adj If you feel **edgy**, you are nervous and anxious. *(informal)* दडपणाखाली असलेली व्यक्ती

edible adj If something is **edible**, it is safe to eat. खाण्यायोग्य

edition (editions) n An **edition** is a particular version of a book, magazine, or newspaper that is printed at one time. आवृत्ती

editor (editors) n An **editor** is a person in charge of a newspaper or magazine, or a section of a newspaper or magazine, who makes decisions concerning the contents. संपादक

educated adj **Educated** people have reached a high standard of learning. सुशिक्षित

education (**educations**) n **Education** means learning and teaching. शिक्षण

educational adj **Educational** matters or institutions are concerned with or relate to education. शैक्षणिक

eel (**eels**) n An **eel** is a fish with a long, thin body. ईल मासा

effect (**effects**) n An **effect** is a change, reaction, or impression that is caused by something or is the result of something. परिणाम

effective adj Something that is **effective** produces the intended results. परिणामकारक

effectively adv If you do something **effectively**, you do it well and produce the results that were intended. परिणामकारक रीतीने

efficient adj Something or someone that is **efficient** does a job successfully, without wasting time or energy. कार्यक्षम

efficiently adv If you do something **efficiently**, you do it successfully, without wasting time or energy. कार्यक्षमतापूर्वक

effort (**efforts**) n If you make an **effort** to do something, you try hard to do it. प्रयत्न

e.g. abbr **e.g.** is an abbreviation that means 'for example'. It is used before a noun, or to introduce another sentence. उदा. (उदाहरणार्थ)

egg (**eggs**) n An **egg** is the rounded object produced by a female bird from which a baby bird later emerges. Reptiles, fish, and insects also produce eggs. अंडे

eggcup (**eggcups**) n An **eggcup** is a small container in which you put a boiled egg while you eat it. एग कप

egg white (**egg whites**) n An **egg white** is the clear liquid part of an egg, which becomes white when you cook it. अंड्यातील पांढरा भाग

egg yolk (**egg yolks**) n An **egg yolk** is the yellow part in the middle of the egg. अंड्यातील पिवळा बलक

Egypt n **Egypt** is a republic in north-east Africa, on the Mediterranean and Red Sea. इजिप्त

Egyptian (**Egyptians**) adj **Egyptian** means belonging or relating to Egypt or to its people, language, or culture. इजिप्शियन ▷ n The **Egyptians** are the people who come from Egypt. इजिप्शियन

eight num **Eight** is the number 8. आठ

eighteen (**eighteens**) num **Eighteen** is the number 18. अठरा

eighteenth adj The **eighteenth** item in a series is the one that you count as number eighteen. अठरावा

eighth (**eighths**) adj The **eighth** item in a series is the one that you count as number eight. आठवा ▷ n An **eighth** is one of eight equal parts of something. एक अष्टमांश

eighty num **Eighty** is the number 80. ऐंशी

Eire n **Eire** is the Irish name for Ireland. ऐर

either adv You use **either** in negative sentences to mean also. (दोन नकारार्थी क्रियापदांनंतर वापर) det **Either** means each. दोहोंपैकी कोणताही एक The teams waited at either end of the gym. ▷ pron You can use **either** when there are two things to choose from. दोहोंपैकी कोणताही She wants a husband and children. I don't want either. ▷ det **Either** means one of two things or people. दोहोंपैकी एक You can choose either date.

either ... or conj You use **either** in front of the first of two or more alternatives, when you are stating the only possibilities or choices that there are. The other alternatives are introduced by **or**. एकतर... नाहीतर (पर्याय दाखवताना वापर) Sightseeing is best done either by tour bus or by bicycles.

elastic n **Elastic** is a rubber material that stretches when you pull it and returns to its original size when you let it go. इलॅस्टिक

elastic band (**elastic bands**) n An **elastic band** is a thin circle of very stretchy rubber that you can put around things in order to hold them together. इलेस्टिक बँड

Elastoplast® (**Elastoplasts**) n **Elastoplast** is a type of sticky tape that you use to cover small cuts on your body. इलेस्टोप्लास्ट

elbow (**elbows**) n Your **elbow** is the joint where your arm bends in the middle. कोपर

elder adj The **elder** of two people is the one who was born first. वयाने मोठा

elderly adj You use **elderly** as a polite way of saying that someone is old. वयस्क

eldest adj The **eldest** person in a group is the one who was born before all the others. ज्येष्ठ

elect (**elects, electing, elected**) vt When people **elect** someone, they choose that person to represent them, by voting. निवडून देणे

election (**elections**) n An **election** is a process in which people vote to choose a person or group of people to hold an official position. निवडणूक

electorate (**electorates**) n The **electorate** of a country is the people there who have the right to vote in an election. मतदारसंघ

electric adj An **electric** device works by means of electricity. विद्युत

electrical adj **Electrical** devices work by means of electricity. विजेचा

electric blanket (**electric blankets**) n An **electric blanket** is a blanket with wires inside it which carry an electric current that keeps the blanket warm. इलेक्ट्रिक ब्लँकेट

electrician (**electricians**) n An **electrician** is a person whose job is to install and repair electrical equipment. विजेचे काम करणारा

electricity n **Electricity** is a form of energy used for heating and lighting, and to provide power for machines. विद्युतशक्ती

electric shock (**electric shocks**) n If you get an **electric shock**, you get a sudden painful feeling when you touch something which is connected to a supply of electricity. विजेचा झटका

electronic adj An **electronic** device has transistors and silicon chips which control and change the electric current passing through it. इलेक्ट्रॉनिक

electronics npl You can refer to electronic devices, or the part of a piece of equipment that consists of electronic devices, as the **electronics**. इलेक्ट्रॉनिक्स

elegant adj If you describe a person or thing as **elegant**, you think they are pleasing and graceful in appearance or style. शानदार

element (**elements**) n An **element** of something is one of the parts which make up the whole thing. घटक

elephant (**elephants**) n An **elephant** is a very large animal with a long trunk. हत्ती

eleven num **Eleven** is the number 11. अकरा

eleventh adj The **eleventh** item in a series is the one that you count as number eleven. अकरावा

eliminate (**eliminates, eliminating, eliminated**) vt To **eliminate** something means to remove it completely. (formal) काढून टाकणे

elm (**elms**) n An **elm** is a tree with broad leaves which it loses in autumn. एल्म नावाचं झाड

else adv You use **else** after words such as 'someone' and 'everyone', and after question words like 'what', to talk about another person, place, or thing. आणखी काही/कुठे/काय

elsewhere adv **Elsewhere** means in other places or to another place. अन्यत्र

email (**emails, emailing, emailed**) n **Email** is a system of sending written messages electronically from one computer to another. **Email** is an abbreviation of 'electronic mail'. ईमेल ▷ vt If you **email** a person, you contact them by electronic mail. ईमेल करणे

email address (**email addresses**) n Your **email address** is the combination of letters, numbers, and symbols that people use for sending email to you. ईमेल ऍड्रेस

embankment (**embankments**) n An **embankment** is a thick wall built of earth, often supporting a railway line or road. बांध

embarrassed adj A person who is **embarrassed** feels shy, ashamed, or guilty about something. लज्जित/पंचाईत होणे

e

embarrassing adj Something that is **embarrassing** makes you feel shy or ashamed. अडचणीत टाकणारी/लज्जास्पद परिस्थिती

embassy (**embassies**) n An **embassy** is a group of officials, headed by an ambassador, who represent their government in a foreign country. वकिलात

embroider (**embroiders, embroidering, embroidered**) vt If cloth **is embroidered** with a design, the design is stitched into it. कशिदाकाम करणे

embroidery n **Embroidery** consists of designs sewn onto cloth. कशिदाकाम

emergency (**emergencies**) n An **emergency** is an unexpected and serious situation such as an accident, which must be dealt with quickly. आणीबाणी

emergency exit (**emergency exits**) n The **emergency exit** in a building or on a vehicle is a special doorway that is to be used only in an emergency. आणीबाणीच्या प्रसंगी बाहेर पडण्याचा मार्ग

emergency landing (**emergency landings**) n An **emergency landing** is an occasion when a plane is forced to land, for example, because of a technical problem or bad weather. आणीबाणीच्या प्रसंगी खाली उतरणे

emigrate (**emigrates, emigrating, emigrated**) vi If you **emigrate**, you leave your own country to live in another. दुसऱ्या देशात स्थलांतरित होणे

emotion (**emotions**) n An **emotion** is a feeling such as happiness, love, fear, anger, or hatred, which can be caused by the situation that you are in or the people you are with. भावना

emotional adj **Emotional** means relating to emotions and feelings. भावनिक

emperor (**emperors**) n An **emperor** is a man who rules an empire. सम्राट

emphasize (**emphasizes, emphasizing, emphasized**) vt To **emphasize** something means to indicate that it is particularly important or true, or to draw special attention to it. ला महत्त्व देणे

empire (**empires**) n An **empire** is a group of countries controlled by one powerful country. साम्राज्य

employ (**employs, employing, employed**) vt If a person or company **employs** you, they pay you to work for them. नोकरीवर ठेवणे

employee (**employees**) n An **employee** is a person who is paid to work for a company or organization. कर्मचारी

employer (**employers**) n Your **employer** is the organization or person that you work for. नोकरी देणारी व्यक्ती (किंवा संस्था)

employment n If you are in **employment**, you have a paid job. नोकरी

empty (**emptier, emptiest, empties, emptying, emptied**) adj An **empty** place, vehicle, or container has no people or things in it. रिकामे ▷ vt If you **empty** a container, or if you **empty** something out of it, you remove its contents. रिकामे करणे

enamel n **Enamel** is a substance which can be heated and put onto metal in order to decorate or protect it. इनेमल

encourage (**encourages, encouraging, encouraged**) vt If you **encourage** someone, you give them confidence, for example by letting them know that what they are doing is good. उत्तेजन देणे

encouragement (**encouragements**) n **Encouragement** is the activity of encouraging someone. उत्तेजन

encouraging adj Something that is **encouraging** gives you hope or confidence. उत्तेजन देणारा

encyclopaedia (**encyclopaedias**) n An **encyclopaedia** is a book, set of books, or CD-ROM in which many facts are arranged for reference. ज्ञानकोश

end (**ends, ending, ended**) n The **end** of something is the last part of it. शेवट ▷ vi When a situation or activity **ends**, or when something or someone **ends**, it stops. शेवट होणे

endanger (endangers, endangering, endangered) vt To **endanger** something or someone means to put them in a situation where they might be harmed or destroyed. संकटात लोटणे

ending (endings) n An **ending** is an act of bringing to or reaching an end. शेवट

endless adj If you describe something as **endless**, you mean that it lasts so long that it seems as if it will never end. न संपणारा

enemy (enemies) n Your **enemy** is someone who intends to harm you. शत्रू

energetic adj An **energetic** person has a lot of energy. उत्साहपूर्ण

energy n If you have **energy**, you have the strength to move around a lot and do things. शक्ती ▷ n **Energy** is the power that makes machines work. ऊर्जा

engaged adj Someone who is **engaged in** or **on** a particular activity is doing it or involved with it. (formal) गुंतलेला

engaged tone (engaged tones) n An **engaged tone** is a repeated single note heard on a telephone when the number called is already in use. एंगेज्ड टोन

engagement (engagements) n An **engagement** is an arrangement that you have made to do something at a particular time. अगोदर ठरवलेले काम किंवा भेट

engagement ring (engagement rings) n An **engagement ring** is a ring worn by a woman when she has agreed to marry someone. वाङ्‌निश्चयाची अंगठी

engine (engines) n An **engine** is a machine that makes things like cars and planes move. इंजिन ▷ n An **engine** is the front part of a train that pulls it along. इंजिन

engineer (engineers) n An **engineer** is a person who designs, builds, and repairs machines, or structures such as roads, railways, and bridges. अभियंता

engineering n **Engineering** is the work of designing and constructing machines or structures such as roads and bridges. अभियांत्रिकी

England n **England** is the largest division of Great Britain, bordering on Scotland and Wales. इंग्लंड

English adj **English** means belonging or relating to England. इंग्रज ▷ n **English** is the language spoken in Great Britain and Ireland, the United States, Canada, Australia, and many other countries. इंग्रजी

Englishman (Englishmen) n An **Englishman** is a man who comes from England. इंग्रज

Englishwoman (Englishwomen) n An **Englishwoman** is a woman who comes from England. इंग्रज स्त्री

engrave (engraves, engraving, engraved) vt If you **engrave** something with a design or words, you cut the design or words into its surface. कोरणे

enjoy (enjoys, enjoying, enjoyed) vt If you **enjoy** something, it gives you pleasure and satisfaction. आनंद लुटणे

enjoyable adj Something that is **enjoyable** gives you pleasure. आनंददायक

enlargement n The **enlargement** of something is the process or result of making it bigger. आकाराने मोठे करण्याची क्रिया

enormous adj **Enormous** means extremely large in size, amount, or degree. प्रचंड

enough det If you have **enough** of something, you have as much as you need. पुरेसा I don't have enough money to buy both books. ▷ pron **Enough** means as much as is needed or required. पुरेसा Although they are trying hard, they are not doing enough.

enquire (enquired, enquiring, enquires) v If you **enquire** about something, you ask for information about it. (formal) चौकशी करणे

enquiry (enquiries) n An **enquiry** is a question which you ask in order to get information. चौकशी

ensure (ensures, ensuring, ensured) vt To **ensure** that something happens means to make certain that it happens. (formal) खात्री करणे

enter (enters, entering, entered) _v_ When you **enter** a place, you come or go into it. (formal) प्रवेश करणे

entertain (entertains, entertaining, entertained) _v_ If you **entertain**, or **entertain** people, you do something that amuses or interests them. करमणूक करणे

entertainer (entertainers) _n_ An **entertainer** is a person whose job is to entertain audiences, for example by telling jokes, singing, or dancing. करमणूक करणारा

entertaining _adj_ Something that is **entertaining** is amusing or interesting. मनोरंजक

enthusiasm _n_ **Enthusiasm** is great eagerness to do something or to be involved in something. उत्साह

enthusiastic _adj_ If you are **enthusiastic** about something, you show how much you like or enjoy it by the way that you behave and talk. उत्साही

entire _adj_ You use **entire** when you want to emphasize that you are referring to the whole of something. पूर्ण

entirely _adv_ **Entirely** means completely. पूर्णपणे

entrance (entrances) _n_ The **entrance** of a place is the way you get into it. प्रवेशद्वार

entrance fee (entrance fees) _n_ An **entrance fee** is a sum of money which you pay before you go into somewhere such as a cinema or museum, or which you have to pay in order to join an organization or institution. प्रवेश शुल्क

entry (entries) _n_ An **entry** is something that you complete in order to take part in a competition, for example the answers to a set of questions. प्रवेशिका

entry phone (entry phones) _n_ An **entry phone** is a type of telephone on the wall next to the entrance to a building enabling a person inside the building to speak to a person outside before opening the door. प्रवेशद्वारावरील फोन

envelope (envelopes) _n_ An **envelope** is the rectangular paper cover in which you send a letter through the post. लिफाफा

envious _adj_ If you are **envious** of someone else, you envy them. मत्सरी

environment (environments) _n_ Someone's **environment** is their surroundings, especially the conditions in which they grow up, live, or work. पर्यावरण

environmental _adj_ **Environmental** means concerned with the protection of the natural world of land, sea, air, plants, and animals. पर्यावरणविषयक

environmentally friendly _adj_ **Environmentally friendly** products do not harm the environment. पर्यावरणस्नेही

envy (envies, envying, envied) _n_ **Envy** is the feeling you have when you wish you could have the same thing or quality that someone else has. हेवा ▷ _vt_ If you **envy** someone, you wish that you had the same things or qualities that they have. हेवा वाटणे

epidemic (epidemics) _n_ If there is an **epidemic** of a particular disease somewhere, it spreads quickly to a very large number of people there. रोगाची साथ

episode (episodes) _n_ You can refer to an event or a short period of time as an **episode** if you want to suggest that it is important or unusual, or has some particular quality. घटनेचा एक भाग, प्रकरण

equal (equals, equalling, equalled) _adj_ If two things are **equal**, or if one thing is **equal** to another, they are the same in size, number, or value. समान ▷ _vt_ To **equal** something or someone means to be as good or as great as them. बरोबरी करणे

equality n **Equality** is a situation or state where all the members of a society or group have the same status, rights, and opportunities. समानता

equalize (equalizes, equalizing, equalized) vt To **equalize** a situation means to give everyone the same rights or opportunities. बरोबरीच्या पातळीवर आणणे

equation (equations) n An **equation** is a mathematical statement saying that two amounts or values are the same, for example 6x4=12x2. समीकरण

equator n **The equator** is an imaginary line round the middle of the earth, halfway between the North and South poles. विषुववृत्त

Equatorial Guinea n **Equatorial Guinea** is a republic of West Africa. विषुववृत्तीय गिनी

equipment n **Equipment** consists of the things such as tools or machines which are used for a particular purpose. उपकरण

equipped adj If someone or something is **equipped**, they are provided with the tools or equipment that is needed. सुसज्ज

equivalent n If one amount or value is the **equivalent** of another, they are the same. समान

erase (erases, erasing, erased) vt If you **erase** a thought or feeling, you destroy it completely so that you can no longer remember it or feel it. खोडून टाकणे

Eritrea n **Eritrea** is a small country in north-east Africa, on the Red Sea. एरिट्रिया

error (errors) n An **error** is a mistake. चूक

escalator (escalators) n An **escalator** is a moving staircase. फिरता जिना

escape (escapes, escaping, escaped) n Someone's **escape** is the act of getting away from a particular place or situation. सुटका ▷ vi If you **escape** from a place, you succeed in getting away from it. निसटणे

escort (escorts, escorting, escorted) vt If you **escort** someone somewhere, you accompany them there, usually in order to make sure that they leave a place or get to their destination. संरक्षक म्हणून सोबत जाणे

especially adv You use **especially** to emphasize that what you are saying applies more to one person or thing than to any others. विशेषतः

espionage n **Espionage** is the activity of finding out the political, military, or industrial secrets of your enemies or rivals by using spies. *(formal)* हेरगिरी

essay (essays) n An **essay** is a piece of writing on a particular subject. निबंध

essential adj Something that is **essential** is absolutely necessary. अत्यावश्यक

estate (estates) n An **estate** is a large area of land in the country owned by one person or organization. संपदा

estate agent (estate agents) n An **estate agent** is someone who works for a company selling houses and land. मालमत्तेचे व्यवहार करणारा दलाल

estate car (**estate cars**) *n* An **estate car** is a car with a long body, a door at the rear, and space behind the back seats. इस्टेट कार

estimate (**estimates, estimating, estimated**) *n* An **estimate** is an approximate calculation of a quantity or value. अंदाजित मूल्य ▷ *vt* If you **estimate** a quantity or value, you make an approximate judgment or calculation of it. अंदाज करणे

Estonia *n* **Estonia** is a republic in north-east Europe, on the Gulf of Finland and the Baltic. एस्टोनिया

Estonian (**Estonians**) *adj* **Estonian** means of, relating to, or characteristic of Estonia, its people, or their language. एस्टोनियन ▷ *n* An **Estonian** is a native or inhabitant of Estonia. एस्टोनियन ▷ *n* **Estonian** is the official language of Estonia. एस्टोनियन

etc *abbr* **etc** is used at the end of a list to show that you have not given a full list. **etc** is a written abbreviation for 'etcetera'. इत्यादी

eternal *adj* Something that is **eternal** lasts for ever. निरंतर, अक्षय

eternity *n* **Eternity** is time without an end, or a state of existence outside time, especially the state which some people believe they will pass into after they have died. अनंत काल

ethical *adj* **Ethical** means relating to beliefs about right and wrong. नैतिक

Ethiopia *n* **Ethiopia** is a state in north-east Africa, on the Red Sea. इथिओपिआ

Ethiopian (**Ethiopians**) *adj* **Ethiopian** means belonging or relating to Ethiopia, or to its people, language, or culture. इथिओपिअन ▷ *n* An **Ethiopian** is an Ethiopian citizen, or a person of Ethiopian origin. इथिओपिअन

ethnic *adj* **Ethnic** means relating to different racial or cultural groups of people. मानववंशविषयक

EU *n* **The EU** is an organization of European countries which have joint policies on matters such as trade, agriculture, and finance. **EU** is an abbreviation of 'European Union'. युरोपियन युनियन

euro (**euros**) *n* The **euro** is a unit of currency that is used by the member countries of the European Union which have joined the European Monetary union. युरो (युरोपमधील चलन)

Europe *n* **Europe** is the second smallest continent in the world, situated between western Asia and the Atlantic Ocean. युरोप

European (**Europeans**) *adj* **European** means coming from or relating to Europe. युरोपियन ▷ *n* A **European** is a person who comes from Europe. युरोपियन

European Union *n* The **European Union** is an organization of European countries which have joint policies on matters such as trade, agriculture, and finance. युरोपियन युनियन

evacuate (**evacuates, evacuating, evacuated**) *v* If people **are evacuated** from a place, they move out of it because it has become dangerous. सुरक्षित स्थळी हलविणे

eve (**eves**) *n* The **eve** of an event is the day before it, or the period of time just before it. पूर्वसंध्या

even *adj* Something that is **even** is flat and smooth. सपाट ▷ *adv* You use **even** to suggest that what comes just after or just before it in the sentence is surprising. अगदी ▷ *adj* An **even** number is a number that you can divide by two, with nothing left over. सम

evening (**evenings**) *n* The **evening** is the part of each day between the end of the afternoon and the time when you go to bed. संध्याकाळ

evening class (**evening classes**) *n* An **evening class** is a course for adults that is taught in the evening rather than during the day. संध्याशाळा

evening dress *n* **Evening dress** consists of the formal clothes that people wear to formal occasions in the evening. औपचारिक पेहराव

event (**events**) *n* An **event** is something that happens. प्रसंग

eventful *adj* If you describe an event or a period of time as **eventful**, you mean that a lot of interesting, exciting, or important things have happened during it. घटनापूर्ण

eventually *adv* **Eventually** means in the end, especially after a lot of delays, problems, or arguments. अखेरीस

ever *adv* **Ever** means at any time. कधीही

every *adj* You use **every** to mean all the people or things in a group. सर्व

everybody *pron* **Everybody** means all the people in a group, or all the people in the world. प्रत्येकजण *Everybody likes him.*

everyone *pron* **Everyone** means all the people in a group, or all the people in the world. प्रत्येकजण *Everyone knows who she is.*

everything *pron* **Everything** means all of something. प्रत्येक गोष्ट *He told me everything that happened.*

everywhere *adv* **Everywhere** means in every place. सगळीकडे

evidence *n* **Evidence** is anything that makes you believe that something is true or exists. पुरावा

evil *adj* If an act or a person is **evil**, they are morally very bad. दुष्ट

evolution *n* **Evolution** is a process in which animals and plants slowly change over many years. उत्क्रांती

ewe (**ewes**) *n* A **ewe** is an adult female sheep. मेंढी

exact *adj* Something that is **exact** is correct, accurate, and complete in every way. अचूक

exactly *adv* **Exactly** means in an exact manner, accurately or precisely. अचूकपणे, अगदी

exaggerate (**exaggerates, exaggerating, exaggerated**) *v* If you **exaggerate**, or **exaggerate** something, you make the thing that you are talking about seem bigger or more important than it actually is. अतिशयोक्ति करणे

exaggeration *n* **Exaggeration**, or an **exaggeration**, is the act of saying that something is bigger, worse, or more important than it really is. अतिशयोक्ति

exam (**exams**) *n* An **exam** is a formal test taken to show your knowledge of a subject. परीक्षा

examination (**examinations**) *n* An **examination** is a formal test taken to show your knowledge of a subject. *(formal)* परीक्षा

examine (**examines, examining, examined**) *vt* If you **examine** something, you look at it or consider it carefully. तपासणे

examiner (**examiners**) *n* An **examiner** is a person who sets or marks an exam. परीक्षक

example (**examples**) *n* An **example** is something which represents or is typical of a particular group of things. उदाहरण, नमुना

excellent *adj* Something that is **excellent** is very good indeed. उत्कृष्ट

except *prep* You use **except** or **except for** to show that you are not counting something or somebody. व्यतिरिक्त *The shops are open every day except Sunday.*

exception (**exceptions**) *n* An **exception** is a situation, thing, or person that is not included in a general statement. अपवाद

exceptional *adj* You use **exceptional** to describe someone or something that has a particular quality to an unusually high degree. अपवादात्मक

excess baggage *n* On a plane journey, **excess baggage** is luggage that is larger or weighs more than your ticket allows, so that you have to pay extra to take it on board. तिकिटावर नेण्यास परवानगी असलेल्या सामानापेक्षा जास्त सामान

excessive *adj* If something is **excessive**, it is too great in amount or degree. अतिशय

exchange (**exchanges, exchanging, exchanged**) *vt* If two or more people **exchange** things of a particular kind, they give them to each other at the same time. अदलाबदल करणे

exchange rate (**exchange rates**) *n* The **exchange rate** of a country's unit of currency is the amount of another country's currency that you get in exchange for it. परकीय चलनदर

excited *adj* If you are **excited**, you are looking forward to something eagerly. उत्सुक

exciting *adj* Something that is **exciting** makes you feel very happy or enthusiastic. उतेजित करणारे

exclamation mark (**exclamation marks**) *n* An **exclamation mark** is the punctuation mark (!). उद्गारचिन्ह

exclude (**excludes, excluding, excluded**) *vt* If you **exclude** someone from a place or activity, you prevent them from entering it or taking part in it. दूर/बाजूला ठेवणे

excluding *prep* You use **excluding** before mentioning a person or thing to show that you are not including them in your statement. वगळून *This applies to most vertebrates (excluding mammals).*

exclusively *adv* **Exclusively** is used to refer to situations or activities that involve only the thing or things mentioned, and nothing else. केवळ

excuse (**excuses, excusing, excused**) *n* An **excuse** is a reason which you give in order to explain why something has been done or has not been done, or to avoid doing something. सबब ▷ *vt* To **excuse** someone or to **excuse** their behaviour means to provide reasons for their actions, especially when other people disapprove of these actions. समर्थन करणे

execute (**executes, executing, executed**) *vt* To **execute** someone means to kill them as a punishment. देहांत शासन करणे

execution (**executions**) *n* **Execution** is the act or process of killing someone as a punishment. देहदंड

executive (**executives**) *n* An **executive** is someone employed by a company at a senior level. अधिकारी

exercise (**exercises**) *n* When you do **exercise**, you move your body so that you can keep healthy and strong. *(formal)* व्यायाम ▷ *n* An **exercise** is something you do to practise what you have learnt. अभ्यास

exhaust (**exhausts**) *n* The **exhaust** or the **exhaust pipe** is the pipe which carries the gas out of the engine of a vehicle. धुराडे

exhausted *adj* If you are **exhausted**, you are very tired. दमलेला

exhaust fumes *npl* **Exhaust fumes** are the gas or steam that is produced when the engine of a vehicle is running. एक्झॉस्ट फ्यूम्स

exhibition (**exhibitions**) *n* An **exhibition** is a public display of art, products, skills, activities, etc. प्रदर्शन

ex-husband (**ex-husbands**) *n* A woman's **ex-husband** was once her husband but is no longer her husband. माजी पती

exile *n* If someone is living in **exile**, they are living in a foreign country because they cannot live in their own country, usually for political reasons. हद्दपारी

exist (**exists, existing, existed**) *vi* If something **exists**, it is present in the world as a real thing. अस्तित्वात असणे

exit (**exits**) *n* An **exit** is a doorway through which you can leave a public building. बाहेर पडण्याचा मार्ग

exotic *adj* Something that is **exotic** is unusual and interesting, usually because it comes from another country. विदेशी

expect (**expects, expecting, expected**) *vt* If you **expect** something to happen, you believe that it will happen. अपेक्षा करणे

expedition (**expeditions**) *n* An **expedition** is a journey made for a particular purpose such as exploration. मोहीम

expel (expels, expelling, expelled) vt
If someone **is expelled** from a school or
organization, they are officially told to leave
because they have behaved badly. बाहेर
घालवणे

expenditure (expenditures) n **Expenditure**
is the spending of money on something,
or the money that is spent on something.
(formal) खर्च

expenses npl Your **expenses** are the money
you spend while doing something in the
course of your work, which will be paid back
to you afterwards. खर्च

expensive adj If something is **expensive**, it
costs a lot of money. खर्चिक

experience (experiences) n **Experience**
is knowledge or skill in a particular job or
activity, which you have gained from doing
that job or activity. अनुभव

experienced adj If you describe someone as
experienced, you mean that they have been
doing a particular job or activity for a long
time, and therefore know a lot about it or are
very skilful at it. अनुभवी

experiment (experiments) n An
experiment is a scientific test which is done
to discover what happens to something in
particular conditions. प्रयोग

expert (experts) n An **expert** is a person
who is very skilled at doing something or who
knows a lot about a particular subject. तज्ज्ञ

expire (expires, expiring, expired) vi When
something such as a contract or a visa **expires**,
it comes to an end or is no longer valid. संपणे

expiry date (expiry dates) n The **expiry
date** of an official document or agreement is
the date after which it is no longer valid. मुदत
संपण्याची तारीख

explain (explains, explaining, explained)
vt If you **explain** something, you give details
about it or describe it so that it can be
understood. समजावून सांगणे

explanation (explanations) n If you give an
explanation, you give reasons why something

happened, or describe something in detail.
स्पष्टीकरण

explode (explodes, exploding, exploded)
vi If something such as a bomb **explodes**, it
bursts with great force. स्फोट होणे

exploit (exploits, exploiting, exploited) vt
If someone **exploits** you, they unfairly use
your work or ideas and give you little in
return. शोषण करणे

exploitation n **Exploitation** is the act of
treating someone unfairly by using their work
or ideas and giving them little in return. शोषण

explore (explores, exploring, explored) v
If you **explore**, or **explore** a place, you travel
around it to find out what it is like. शोध घेणे

explorer (explorers) n An **explorer** is
someone who travels to places about which
very little is known, in order to discover what
is there. शोध घेणारा

explosion (explosions) n An **explosion** is a
sudden violent burst of energy, for example
one caused by a bomb. स्फोट

explosive (explosives) n An **explosive**
is a substance or device that can cause an
explosion. स्फोटक पदार्थ

export (exports, exporting, exported) n
Export is the selling of products or raw
materials to another country. निर्यात ▷ v To
export products or raw materials means to
sell them to another country. निर्यात करणे

express (expresses, expressing, expressed)
vt When you **express** an idea or feeling, you
show what you think or feel. व्यक्त करणे

expression (expressions) n The **expression**
of ideas or feelings is the showing of them
through words, actions, or art. हावभाव

extension (extensions) n An **extension** is
a new room or building which is added to an
existing building. विस्तारित कक्ष

extension cable (extension cables) n
An **extension cable** is an electrical cable
that is connected to the cable on a piece of
equipment in order to make it reach further.
एक्सटेन्शन केबल

extensive *adj* Something that is **extensive** covers a large area. प्रशस्त

extensively *adv* If you travel **extensively**, you cover a large physical area. मोठ्या प्रमाणावर

extent *n* The **extent** of a situation is how great, important, or serious it is. प्रमाण

exterior *adj* You use **exterior** to refer to the outside parts of something, or to things that are outside something. बाह्य

external *adj* **External** means happening, coming from, or existing outside a place, person, or area of activity. बाह्य

extinct *adj* If a species of animals is **extinct**, it no longer has any living members. अस्तित्वात नसलेला

extinguisher (**extinguishers**) *n* An **extinguisher** is a metal cylinder which contains water or chemicals at high pressure which can put out fires. अग्निशामक

extortionate *adj* If you describe something such as a price as **extortionate**, you are emphasizing that it is much greater than it should be. प्रमाणापेक्षा मोठा

extra *adj* You use **extra** to describe an amount, person, or thing that is added to others of the same kind, or that can be added to others of the same kind. जादा ▷ *adv* You can use **extra** in front of adjectives and adverbs to emphasize the quality that they are describing. जादा

extraordinary *adj* An **extraordinary** person or thing has some extremely good or special quality. असामान्य

extravagant *adj* Someone who is **extravagant** spends more money than they can afford or uses more of something than is reasonable. उधळ्या

extreme *adj* **Extreme** means very great in degree or intensity. अतिशय

extremely *adv* You use **extremely** in front of adjectives and adverbs to emphasize that the specified quality is present to a very great degree. अतिशय

extremism *n* **Extremism** is the behaviour or beliefs of people who try to bring about political change by using violent or extreme methods. जहालमतवाद

extremist (**extremists**) *n* If you describe someone as an **extremist**, you disapprove of them because they try to bring about political change by using violent or extreme methods. जहालमतवादी

ex-wife (**ex-wives**) *n* A man's **ex-wife** was once his wife but is no longer his wife. माजी पत्नी

eye (**eyes**) *n* Your **eyes** are the parts of your body with which you see. डोळा

eyebrow (**eyebrows**) *n* Your **eyebrows** are the lines of hair which grow above your eyes. भुवई

eye drops *npl* **Eye drops** are a kind of medicine that you put in your eyes one drop at a time. आय ड्रॉप्स

eyelash (**eyelashes**) *n* Your **eyelashes** are the hairs which grow on the edges of your eyelids. पापणीचा केस

eyelid (**eyelids**) *n* Your **eyelids** are the two flaps of skin which cover your eyes when they are closed. पापणी

eyeliner (**eyeliners**) *n* **Eyeliner** is a special kind of pencil which some women use on the edges of their eyelids next to their eyelashes in order to look more attractive. आय लायनर

eye shadow (**eye shadows**) *n* **Eye shadow** is a substance which you can paint on your eyelids in order to make them a different colour. आय शेंडो

eyesight *n* Your **eyesight** is your ability to see. दृष्टी

f

fabric (fabrics) n **Fabric** is cloth. कापड

fabulous adj You use **fabulous** to emphasize how wonderful or impressive you think something is. (informal) अद्भुत, विस्मयकारक

face (faces, facing, faced) n Your **face** is the front part of your head. चेहरा ▷ vt To **face** a particular direction means to look directly in that direction. कडे तोंड करून उभे राहणे

face cloth (face cloths) n A **face cloth** is a small cloth made of towelling which you use for washing yourself. फेस क्लॉथ

facial (facials) adj **Facial** is used to describe things that relate to your face. चेहऱ्याशी संबंधित ▷ n A **facial** is a sort of beauty treatment in which someone's face is massaged, and creams and other substances are rubbed into it. फेशीअल

facilities npl **Facilities** are buildings, equipment, or services that are provided for a particular purpose. सुविधा

fact (facts) n **Facts** are pieces of information which can be proved to be true. वस्तुस्थिती

factory (factories) n A **factory** is a large building where machines are used to make goods in large quantities. कारखाना

fade (fades, fading, faded) v When something **fades**, or when something **fades** it, it slowly becomes less intense in brightness, colour, or sound. निस्तेज, फिकट होणे

fail (fails, failing, failed) v If you **fail** or **fail** to do something that you were trying to do, you do not succeed in doing it. अयशस्वी होणे

failure (failures) n **Failure** is a lack of success in doing or achieving something. अपयश

faint (fainter, faintest, faints, fainting, fainted) adj Something that is **faint** is not strong or intense. निस्तेज, हलका ▷ vi If you **faint**, you lose consciousness for a short time, especially because you are hungry, or because of pain, heat, or shock. चक्कर येणे

fair (fairer, fairest, fairs) adj If something is **fair**, it seems right because it is the same for everyone. योग्य ▷ adj **Fair** hair is pale yellow in colour. पिंगट केस ▷ n A **fair** is a place where you can play games to win prizes, and you can ride on special, big machines for fun. जत्रा

fairground (fairgrounds) n A **fairground** is a part of a park or field where people pay to ride on various machines for amusement or try to win prizes in games. जत्रेचे मैदान

fairly adv **Fairly** means to quite a large degree. मोठ्या प्रमाणावर

fairness n **Fairness** is the quality of being reasonable, right, and just. रास्तपणा

fairy (fairies) n A **fairy** is an imaginary creature with magical powers. परी

fairytale (fairytales) n A **fairytale** is a story for children involving magical events and imaginary creatures. परिकथा

faith n If you have **faith** in someone or something, you feel confident about their ability or goodness. विश्वास

faithful adj If you are **faithful** to a person, organization, or idea, you remain firm in your support for them. एकनिष्ठ

faithfully adv If you do something **faithfully**, you remain firm in your support for a person, organization, or idea. एकनिष्ठेने

fake (fakes) adj A **fake** fur or a **fake** painting, for example, is a fur or painting that has been made to look valuable or genuine, usually in order to deceive people. खोटा ▷ n A **fake** is an object, person, or act that is not genuine. नकली

fall (falls, falling, fell, fallen) n A **fall** is an act of falling. पडण्याची क्रिया ▷ vi If a person or thing **falls**, they move towards the ground suddenly by accident. खाली पडणे

fall down (falls down, falling down, fell down, fallen down) v If a person or thing **falls down**, they move from an upright position, so that they are lying on the ground. खाली पडणे *He fell down the stairs.*

fall for (falls for, falling for, fell for, fallen for) v If you **fall for** someone, you are strongly attracted to them and start loving them. प्रेमात पडणे *I fell for him right away.*

fall out (falls out, falling out, fell out, fallen out) v If a person's hair or a tooth **falls out**, it becomes loose and separates from their body. पडून जाणे

false adj If something is **false**, it is incorrect, untrue, or mistaken. चुकीचा

false alarm (false alarms) n When you think something dangerous is about to happen, but then discover that you were mistaken, you can say that it was a **false alarm**. खोटी भीती

fame n If you achieve **fame**, you become very well known. प्रसिद्धी

familiar adj If someone or something is **familiar** to you, you recognize them or know them well. परिचित

family (families) n A **family** is a group of people who are related to each other, especially parents and their children. कुटुंब

famine (famines) n A **famine** is a serious shortage of food in a country, which may cause many deaths. दुष्काळ

famous adj Someone or something that is **famous** is very well known. सुप्रसिद्ध

fan (fans) n If you are a **fan** of someone or something, you admire them and are very interested in them. चाहता

fanatic (fanatics) n If you describe someone as a **fanatic**, you disapprove of them because you consider their behaviour or opinions to be very extreme. दुराग्रही

fan belt (fan belts) n In a car engine, the **fan belt** is the belt that drives the fan which keeps the engine cool. फॅन बेल्ट

fancy (fancies, fancying, fancied, fancier, fanciest) vt If you **fancy** something, you want to have it or do it. *(informal)* काही करण्याची कल्पना/इच्छा करणे ▷ adj Something that is **fancy** is special and not ordinary. असामान्य, भपकेदार

fancy dress n **Fancy dress** is clothing that you wear for a party at which everyone tries to look like a famous person or a person from a story, from history, or from a particular profession. भपकेदार पोषाख

fantastic adj If you say that something is **fantastic**, you are emphasizing that you think it is very good. *(informal)* विलक्षण

FAQ (FAQs) abbr **FAQ** is used especially on websites to refer to questions about a particular topic. **FAQ** is an abbreviation for 'frequently asked questions'. नेहमी विचारले जाणारे प्रश्न

far (farther, farthest) adj You use **far** to refer to the part that is the greatest distance from the centre. खूप दूर ▷ adv If something is **far** away, it is a long way away. दूर

fare (fares) n The **fare** is the money that you pay for a journey by bus, taxi, train, boat, or aeroplane. प्रवासाचे भाडे

Far East n In the West, the expression '**The Far East**' is used to refer to all the countries of Eastern Asia, including China and Japan. पौर्वात्य

farewell! excl **Farewell!** means the same as goodbye! बरे आहे, नमस्कार!

farm (farms) n A **farm** is an area of land consisting of fields and buildings, where crops are grown or animals are raised. शेत

farmer (farmers) n A **farmer** is a person who owns or manages a farm. शेतकरी

farmhouse (farmhouses) n A **farmhouse** is the main house on a farm, usually where the farmer lives. शेतावरील शेतकऱ्याचे घर

farming n **Farming** is the activity of growing crops or keeping animals on a farm. शेती

Faroe Islands n The **Faroe Islands** are a group of 21 islands in the North Atlantic, between Iceland and the Shetland Islands. फरो बेटे

fascinating *adj* If you find something **fascinating**, you find it extremely interesting. मोहिनी घालणारा

fashion *n* **Fashion** is the area of activity that involves styles of clothing and appearance. लोकप्रिय झालेले अद्ययावत कपडे, शैली इत्यादी

fashionable *adj* Something that is **fashionable** is popular or approved of at a particular time. लोकप्रिय

fast (faster, fastest) *adj* **Fast** means happening, moving, or doing something at great speed. You also use **fast** in questions or statements about speed. जलद ▷ *adv* You use **fast** to say that something happens without any delay. जलद, लवकर

fat (fatter, fattest, fats) *n* A **fat** person has a lot of flesh on their body and weighs too much. लठ्ठ ▷ *n* **Fat** is a substance in many foods which your body uses to produce energy. मेद

fatal *adj* A **fatal** action has undesirable results. प्राणघातक

fate *n* **Fate** is a power that some people believe controls everything that happens. दैव

father (fathers) *n* Your **father** is your male parent. वडील

father-in-law (fathers-in-law) *n* Your **father-in-law** is the father of your husband or wife. सासरा

fault *n* If a bad or undesirable situation is your **fault**, you caused it or are responsible for it. चूक

faulty *adj* A **faulty** machine or piece of equipment is not working properly. सदोष

fauna *npl* Animals, especially those in a particular area, can be referred to as **fauna**. विशिष्ट प्रदेशातील प्राणिजात

favour *n* If you regard something or someone with **favour**, you like or support them. पसंती

favourite (favourites) *adj* Your **favourite** thing or person of a particular type is the one you like most. आवडता ▷ *n* A **favourite** is a person or thing regarded with especial preference or liking. आवडता

fax (faxes, faxing, faxed) *n* A **fax** or a **fax machine** is a piece of equipment used to send and receive documents electronically along a telephone line. फॅक्स ▷ *vt* If you **fax** a document, you send a document from one fax machine to another. फॅक्स करणे

fear (fears, fearing, feared) *n* **Fear** is the unpleasant feeling of worry that you get when you think that you are in danger or that something horrible is going to happen. भीती ▷ *vt* If you **fear** something unpleasant, you are worried that it might happen, or might have happened. भीती वाटणे

feasible *adj* If something is **feasible**, it can be done, made, or achieved. व्यवहार्य

feather (feathers) *n* A bird's **feathers** are the light soft things covering its body. पीस

feature (features) *n* A particular **feature** of something is an interesting or important part or characteristic of it. खास वैशिष्ट्य

February (Februaries) *n* **February** is the second month of the year in the Western calendar. फेब्रुवारी महिना

fed up *adj* Someone who is **fed up** is bored or annoyed. *(informal)* विटलेला

fee (fees) *n* A **fee** is a sum of money that you pay to be allowed to do something. शुल्क

feed (feeds, feeding, fed) *vt* If you **feed** a person or animal, you give them food. भरवणे

feedback *n* When you get **feedback** on your work or progress, someone tells you how well or badly you are doing. प्रतिसाद

feel (feels, feeling, felt) v The way you **feel**, for example happy or sad, or cold or tired, is how you are at the time. वाटणे ▷ vt If you **feel** something, you touch it with your hand to see what it is like. जाणवणे

feeling (feelings) n A **feeling** is an emotion. भावना

feet npl Your **feet** are the parts of your body that are at the ends of your legs, and that you stand on. पावले

felt n **Felt** is a type of thick cloth made from wool or other fibres packed tightly together. फेल्ट जातीचे लोकरीचे कापड

felt-tip (felt-tips) n A **felt-tip** or a **felt-tip pen** is a pen which has a piece of fibre at the end that the ink comes through. फेल्ट-टिप पेन

female (females) adj Someone who is **female** is a woman or a girl. स्त्री ▷ n Women and girls are sometimes referred to as **females** when they are being considered as a type. महिला वर्ग

feminine adj **Feminine** means relating to women or considered typical of or suitable for them. स्त्रियांसाठी, स्त्रियांसंबंधित

feminist (feminists) n A **feminist** is a person who believes that women should have the same rights and opportunities as men. स्त्रीवादी

fence (fences) n A **fence** is a barrier made of wood or wire supported by posts. कुंपण

fennel n **Fennel** is a plant with a crisp rounded base and feathery leaves. It can be eaten as a vegetable or the leaves can be used as a herb. एक प्रकारची बडीशेप

fern (ferns) n A **fern** is a plant with long stems, thin leaves, and no flowers. नेचे

ferret (ferrets) n A **ferret** is a small, fierce animal which hunts rabbits and rats. फेरिट/ शिकार शोधून काढणारे जनावर

ferry (ferries) n A **ferry** is a boat that carries passengers or vehicles across a river or a narrow stretch of sea. नौका

fertile adj Land or soil that is **fertile** is able to support a large number of strong healthy plants. सुपीक

fertilizer (fertilizers) n **Fertilizer** is a substance that you spread on the ground to make plants grow more successfully. खत

festival (festivals) n A **festival** is an organized series of events and performances. उत्सव

fetch (fetches, fetching, fetched) vt If you **fetch** something or someone, you go and get them from where they are. जाऊन आणणे

fever (fevers) n If you have a **fever**, your temperature is higher than usual because you are ill. ताप

few det A **few** means some, but not many. काही *She gave me a few sweets.* ▷ pron You use a **few** to refer to a small number of things or people. काही *The doctors are all busy and a few work more than 100 hours a week.*

fewer (fewest) adj You use **fewer** to indicate that you are talking about a number of people or things that is smaller than another number. कमी

fiancé (fiancés) n A woman's **fiancé** is the man she has agreed to marry. वाग्दत्त वर

fiancée (fiancées) n A man's **fiancée** is the woman he has agreed to marry. वाग्दत्त वधू

fibre (fibres) n A **fibre** is a thin thread of a natural or artificial substance, especially one used to make cloth or rope. तंतू

fibreglass n **Fibreglass** is plastic strengthened with short, thin threads of glass. तंतुमय काच

fiction n **Fiction** is stories about imaginary people and events. काल्पनिक कथा

field (fields) n A **field** is an enclosed area of land where crops are grown or animals are kept. शेत

fierce (fiercer, fiercest) adj A **fierce** animal or person is very aggressive or angry. भयंकर

fifteen num **Fifteen** is the number 15. पंधरा

fifteenth adj The **fifteenth** item in a series is the one that you count as number fifteen. पंधरावा

fifth adj The **fifth** item in a series is the one that you count as number five. पाचवा

fifty num **Fifty** is the number 50. पन्नास

fifty-fifty *adj* If a division or sharing of something such as money or property between two people is **fifty-fifty**, each person gets half of it. *(informal)* अर्ध-अर्ध समान वाटप ▷ *adv* If something such as money or property is divided or shared **fifty-fifty** between two people, each person gets half of it. *(informal)* अर्ध-अर्ध समान वाटप

fig (**figs**) *n* A **fig** is a soft sweet fruit full of tiny seeds. Figs grow on trees in hot countries. अंजीर

fight (**fights, fighting, fought**) *n* A **fight** against something is an attempt to stop it. लढा ▷ *v* If you **fight** something unpleasant, you try in a determined way to prevent it or stop it happening. विरोध करणे

fighting *n* **Fighting** is a battle, struggle, or physical combat. लढाई

figure (**figures**) *n* A **figure** is a particular amount expressed as a number, especially a statistic. आकडेवारी

figure out (**figures out, figuring out, figured out**) *v* If you **figure out** a solution to a problem or the reason for something, you succeed in solving it or understanding it. *(informal)* उपाय शोधून काढणे *His parents could not figure out how to start their new computer.*

Fiji *n* **Fiji** is an independent republic, consisting of 844 islands in the south-west Pacific. फिजी

file (**files, filing, filed**) *n* A **file** is a box or folder in which documents are kept. फाईल ▷ *n* A **file** is a tool with rough surfaces, used for smoothing and shaping hard materials. कानस ▷ *vt* If you **file** a document, you put it in the correct file. फाईलमध्ये ठेवणे ▷ *vt* If you **file** an object, you smooth or shape it with a file. कानसीने घासणे

Filipino (**Filipinos**) *adj* **Filipino** means belonging or relating to the Philippines, or to its people or culture. फिलिपिनो ▷ *n* A **Filipino** is a person who comes from the Philippines. फिलिपिनो

fill (**fills, filling, filled**) *v* If you **fill** a container or area, or if it **fills**, an amount of something enters it that is enough to make it full. भरणे

fillet (**fillets, filleting, filleted**) *n* A **fillet** of fish or meat is a piece that has no bones in it. बिनहाडाचा मांसाचा तुकडा ▷ *vt* When you **fillet** fish or meat, you prepare it by taking the bones out. हाडविरहित करणे

fill in (**fills in, filling in, filled in**) *v* When you **fill in** a form, you write information in the spaces on it. भरणे *Fill in the coupon and send it to the address shown.*

fill up (**fills up, filling up, filled up**) *v* If you **fill up** a container **up**, you keep putting or pouring something into it until it is full. काठोकाठ भरणे *Filling up your car's petrol tank these days is very expensive.*

film (**films**) *n* A **film** consists of moving pictures that have been recorded so that they can be shown in a cinema or on television. चित्रपट

film star (**film stars**) *n* A **film star** is a famous actor or actress who appears in films. चित्रपट अभिनेता/अभिनेत्री

filter (**filters, filtering, filtered**) *n* A **filter** is a device through which a substance is passed when it is being filtered. गाळणी ▷ *vt* To **filter** a substance, or to **filter** particles out of a substance, means to pass it through a device which removes the particles from it. गाळणे

filthy (**filthier, filthiest**) *adj* Something that is **filthy** is very dirty indeed. घाणेरडा

final (**finals**) *adj* In a series of events, things, or people, the **final** one is the last one, or the one that happens at the end. अंतिम ▷ *n* A **final**

is the last game or contest in a series, which decides the overall winner. अंतिम सामना

finalize (finalizes, finalizing, finalized) *vt* If you **finalize** something that you are arranging, you complete the arrangements for it. शेवट करणे

finally *adv* If something **finally** happens, it happens after a long delay. शेवटी

finance (finances, financing, financed) *n* **Finance** is funds provided to pay for a project or a purchase, or the provision of these funds. अर्थसहाय्य ▷ *vt* When someone **finances** something such as a project or a purchase, they provide the money that is needed to pay for them. अर्थसहाय्य करणे

financial *adj* **Financial** means relating to or involving money. आर्थिक

financial year (financial years) *n* A **financial year** is a period of twelve months, used by government, business, and other organizations in order to calculate their budgets, profits, and losses. आर्थिक वर्ष

find (finds, finding, found) *vt* If you **find** someone or something, you see them or learn where they are. सापडणे

find out (finds out, finding out, found out) *v* If you **find** something **out**, you learn it, often by making an effort to do so. शोधणे *They wanted to find out the truth.*

fine (finer, finest, fines) *adj* When the weather is **fine**, it is dry and sunny. चांगला ▷ *adj* If you say that you are **fine**, you mean that you are well or happy. चांगला ▷ *n* A **fine** is money that a person is ordered to pay because they have done something wrong. दंड ▷ *adj* Something that is **fine** is very thin. बारीक

finger (fingers) *n* Your **fingers** are the four long moveable parts at the end of your hands. बोट

fingernail (fingernails) *n* Your **fingernails** are the hard areas on the ends of your fingers. नख

fingerprint (fingerprints) *n* **Fingerprints** are marks made by a person's fingers which show

the lines on the skin. Everyone's fingerprints are different, so they can be used to identify criminals. बोटाचा ठसा

finish (finishes, finishing, finished) *n* The **finish** of something is the end of it or the last part of it. शेवट ▷ *vi* When you **finish** doing or dealing with something, you do or deal with the last part of it, so that there is no more for you to do or deal with. संपवणे

finished *adj* If you are **finished with** something, you are no longer doing it or interested in it. संपलेले

Finland *n* **Finland** is a republic in north Europe, on the Baltic Sea. फिनलंड

Finn (Finns) *n* The **Finns** are the people of Finland. फिन

Finnish *adj* **Finnish** means belonging or relating to Finland or to its people, language, or culture. फिनिश ▷ *n* **Finnish** is the language spoken in Finland. फिनिश

fire *n* **Fire** is the hot, bright flames that come from something that is burning. आग

fire alarm (fire alarms) *n* A **fire alarm** is a device that makes a noise, for example with a bell, to warn people when there is a fire. आगीचा इशारा

fire brigade (fire brigades) *n* The **fire brigade** is an organization which has the job of putting out fires. अग्निशामक दल

fire escape (fire escapes) *n* A **fire escape** is a metal staircase on the outside of a building, which can be used to escape from the building if there is a fire. आग लागल्यास उतरून जाण्याची शिडी

fire extinguisher (fire extinguishers) *n* A **fire extinguisher** is a metal cylinder which contains water or chemicals at high pressure which can put out fires. अग्निशामक

fireman (firemen) *n* A **fireman** is a person whose job is to put out fires. अग्निशमन दलातील जवान

fireplace (fireplaces) *n* In a room, the **fireplace** is the place where a fire can be lit. शेकोटी

firewall (firewalls) *n* A **firewall** is a computer system or program that automatically prevents an unauthorized person from gaining access to a computer when it is connected to a network such as the Internet. फायरवॉल

fireworks *npl* **Fireworks** are small objects that are lit to entertain people on special occasions. They burn in a bright, attractive, and often noisy way. फटाके

firm (firmer, firmest, firms) *adj* Something that is **firm** is fairly hard and does not change much in shape when it is pressed. भक्कम ▷ *n* A **firm** is a business selling or producing something. फर्म

first (firsts) *adj* If a person or thing is **first**, they come before all the others. प्रथम ▷ *adv* If you do something **first**, you do it before anyone else does, or before you do anything else. प्रथम ▷ *n* An event that is described as a **first** has never happened before. प्रथम

first aid *n* **First aid** is medical treatment given as soon as possible to a sick or injured person. प्रथमोपचार

first-aid kit (first-aid kits) *n* A **first-aid kit** is a bag or case containing basic medical supplies that are designed to be used on someone who is injured or who suddenly becomes ill. प्रथमोपचार पेटी

first-class *adj* Something or someone that is **first-class** is of the highest quality or standard. प्रथम श्रेणी

firstly *adv* You use **firstly** when you are about to mention the first in a series of items. प्रथमत:

first name (first names) *n* Your **first name** is the first of the names that you were given when you were born, as opposed to your family name. प्रथम नाम

fir tree (fir trees) *n* A **fir** or a **fir tree** is a tall pointed tree. फर वृक्ष

fiscal *adj* **Fiscal** means related to government money or public money, especially taxes. आर्थिक

fiscal year (fiscal years) *n* The **fiscal year** is a twelve-month period beginning and ending in April, which governments and businesses use to plan their finances. आर्थिक वर्ष

fish (fish, fishes, fishing, fished) *n* A **fish** is a creature with a tail and fins that lives in water. मासा ▷ *vi* If you **fish**, you try to catch fish. मासेमारी करणे

fisherman (fishermen) *n* A **fisherman** is a person who catches fish as a job or for sport. मच्छिमार

fishing *n* **Fishing** is the sport or business of catching fish. मासेमारी

fishing boat (fishing boats) *n* A **fishing boat** is a boat that is used in the business of catching fish. मच्छिमार होडी

fishing rod (fishing rods) *n* A **fishing rod** is a long, thin pole which has a line and hook attached to it and which is used for catching fish. मासेमारीचा गळ

fishing tackle *n* **Fishing tackle** consists of all the equipment that is used in the sport of fishing, such as fishing rods, lines, hooks, and bait. मासेमारीची साधनसामग्री

fishmonger (fishmongers) *n* A **fishmonger** is a shopkeeper who sells fish. मासेविक्रेता

fist (fists) *n* You refer to someone's hand as their **fist** when they have bent their fingers towards their palm. मूठ

fit (fitter, fittest, fits, fitting, fitted) *adj* If something is **fit** for a particular purpose, it is suitable for that purpose. योग्य ▷ *n* If something is a good **fit**, it fits well. घट्ट ▷ *vt* If something **fits** you, it is the right size and shape for you. मापाचे असणे

fit in (fits in, fitting in, fitted in) *v* If you manage to **fit** a person or task **in**, you manage to find time to deal with them. जुळणे *I find that I just can't fit in the housework.*

fitted carpet (fitted carpets) *n* A **fitted carpet** is cut to the same shape as a room so that it covers the floor completely. योग्य आकाराचा गालिचा

fitted kitchen (fitted kitchens) *n* A **fitted kitchen** is a kitchen with units that are attached to the wall. मांडण्या भिंतीला लावलेले स्वयंपाकघर

fitted sheet (fitted sheets) *n* A **fitted sheet** is a bedsheet with the corners sewn so that they fit over the corners of the mattress and do not have to be folded. जोडून ठेवलेली चादर

fitting room (fitting rooms) *n* A **fitting room** is a room or cubicle in a shop where you can put on clothes to see how they look. कपडे घालून पहाण्याची खोली

five *num* **Five** is the number 5. पाच

fix (fixes, fixing, fixed) *vt* If you **fix** something to another thing, you join them together. घट्ट बसवणे ▷ *vt* If you **fix** something that is broken, you mend it. जोडणे

fixed *adj* You use **fixed** to describe something which stays the same and does not vary. स्थिर

fizzy (fizzier, fizziest) *adj* **Fizzy** drinks are full of little bubbles of gas. बुडबुडेयुक्त

flabby (flabbier, flabbiest) *adj* **Flabby** people are rather fat, with loose flesh over their bodies. थुलथुलीत

flag (flags) *n* A **flag** is a piece of coloured cloth used as a sign for something or as a signal. झेंडा

flame (flames) *n* A **flame** is a hot bright stream of burning gas that comes from something that is burning. ज्वाला

flamingo (flamingos, flamingoes) *n* A **flamingo** is a bird with pink feathers, long thin legs, a long neck, and a curved beak. Flamingos live near water in warm countries. रोहित पक्षी

flammable *adj* **Flammable** chemicals, gases, cloth, or other things catch fire and burn easily. ज्वालाग्राही

flan (flans) *n* A **flan** is a food that has a base and sides of pastry or sponge cake. The base is filled with fruit or savoury food. फ्लॅन

flannel (flannels) *n* A **flannel** is a small cloth that you use for washing yourself. लोकरीचे मऊ कापड

flap (flaps, flapping, flapped) *v* If something that is attached at one end **flaps**, or if you **flap** it, it moves quickly up and down or from side to side. फडफडणे

flash (flashes, flashing, flashed) *n* A **flash** of light is a sudden, short burst of it. चमक, लखलखबाट ▷ *v* If a light **flashes**, or if you **flash** a light, it shines brightly and suddenly. प्रकाशझोत/लखख प्रकाश टाकणे

flask (flasks) *n* A **flask** is a bottle used for carrying alcoholic or hot drinks around with you. थर्मास

flat (flatter, flattest, flats) *adj* Something that is **flat** is level and smooth. सपाट ▷ *n* A **flat** is a set of rooms for living in, that is part of a larger building. सदनिका

flat-screen *adj* A **flat-screen** television set or computer monitor has a slim flat screen. फ्लॅट स्क्रीन असलेला

flatter (flatters, flattering, flattered) *vt* If someone **flatters** you, they praise you in an exaggerated way that is not sincere. खुशामत करणे

flattered *adj* If you are **flattered** by something that has happened, you are pleased about it because it makes you feel important. आनंदित होणे

flavour (flavours) *n* The **flavour** of a food or drink is its taste. चव

flavouring (flavourings) n Flavourings are substances that are added to food or drink to give it a particular taste. स्वाद

flaw (flaws) n A **flaw** in something such as a theory is a mistake in it. त्रुटी

flea (fleas) n A **flea** is a small jumping insect that sucks human or animal blood. पिसू

flea market (flea markets) n A **flea market** is an outdoor market which sells cheap used goods and sometimes also very old furniture. स्वस्त व जुन्या वस्तू मिळण्याचे दुकान

flee (flees, fleeing, fled) v If you **flee**, you escape from something or someone by running away. (written) पळून जाणे

fleece (fleeces) n A sheep's **fleece** is its coat of wool. मेंढीची लोकर

fleet (fleets) n A **fleet** is an organized group of ships. जहाजांचा ताफा

flex (flexes) n A **flex** is an electric cable containing wires that is connected to an electrical appliance. विद्युत उपकरणाला जोडलेली केबल

flexible adj A **flexible** object or material can be bent easily without breaking. लवचिक

flexitime n **Flexitime** is a system that allows employees to vary the time that they start or finish work, provided that an agreed total number of hours are spent at work. सोयीनुसार नोकरीचे तास

flight (flights) n A **flight** is a journey made by flying, usually in an aeroplane. विमानोड्डाण

flight attendant (flight attendants) n On an aeroplane, the **flight attendants** are the people whose job is to look after the passengers and serve their meals. विमानातील प्रवाशांची काळजी घेणारा कर्मचारी

fling (flings, flinging, flung) vt If you **fling** something or someone somewhere, you throw them there suddenly, using a lot of force. जोराने फेकणे

flip-flops npl **Flip-flops** are open shoes which are held on your feet by a strap that goes between your toes. चप्पल

flippers npl **Flippers** are flat pieces of rubber that you can wear on your feet to help you swim more quickly, especially underwater. फ्लिपर्स

flirt (flirts, flirting, flirted) n A **flirt** is someone who flirts a lot. प्रेमाचे ढोंग करणारी व्यक्ती ▷ vi If you **flirt** with someone, you behave as if you are sexually attracted to them, in a playful or not very serious way. प्रेमाचे ढोंग करणे

float (floats, floating, floated) n A **float** is a light object that is used to help someone or something float in water. तराफा ▷ vi If something **floats** in a liquid, it stays on top of it. तरंगणे ▷ vi If something **floats** in the air, it moves slowly through it. तरंगणे

flock (flocks) n A **flock** of birds, sheep, or goats is a group of them. **Flock** can take the singular or plural form of the verb. थवा, कळप

flood (floods, flooding, flooded) n If there is a **flood**, a large amount of water covers an area which is usually dry. पूर ▷ vt If something such as a river or a burst pipe **floods** an area that is usually dry, it becomes covered with water. पूर आणणे ▷ vi If an area that is usually dry **floods**, it becomes covered with water. पूर येणे

flooding n If **flooding** occurs, an area of land that is usually dry is covered with water after heavy rain or after a river or lake flows over its banks. पूर

floodlight (floodlights) n **Floodlights** are powerful lamps which are used to light sports grounds and the outsides of public buildings. मोठ्या प्रकाशझोताचे दिवे

floor (floors) n A **floor** is the part of a room that you walk on. जमीन ▷ n A **floor** of a building is all the rooms in it that are at the same height. मजला

flop (**flops**) n If something is a **flop**, it is completely unsuccessful. अपयशी

floppy disk (**floppy disks**) n A **floppy disk** is a small magnetic disk that used to be used for storing computer data and programs. फ्लॉपी डिस्क

flora npl You can refer to plants as **flora**, especially the plants growing in a particular area. (formal) विशिष्ट प्रदेशातील वनस्पतीजात

florist (**florists**) n A **florist** is a shopkeeper who sells flowers and indoor plants. फुले विकणारा

flour (**flours**) n Flour is a white or brown powder that is made by grinding grain. It is used to make bread, cakes, and pastry. पीठ

flow (**flows, flowing, flowed**) vi If a liquid, gas, or electrical current **flows** somewhere, it moves there steadily and continuously. वाहणे

flower (**flowers, flowering, flowered**) n A **flower** is the brightly coloured part of a plant which grows at the end of a stem. फूल ▷ vi When a plant or tree **flowers**, its flowers appear and open. फुलणे

flu n Flu is an illness caused by a virus. The symptoms are like those of a bad cold, but more serious. सर्दी-पडसे

fluent adj Someone who is **fluent** in a particular language can speak it easily and correctly. अस्खलित

fluorescent adj A **fluorescent** surface or colour has a very bright appearance when light is directed onto it. चमकदार

flush (**flushes, flushing, flushed**) n A **flush** is a rosy colour, especially in the cheeks. लाली ▷ vi If you **flush**, your face goes red because you are hot or ill, or because you are feeling a strong emotion such as embarrassment or anger. लालबुंद होणे

flute (**flutes**) n A **flute** is a musical wind instrument consisting of a long tube with holes in it. You play it by blowing over a hole at one end while holding it sideways. बासरी

fly (**flies, flying, flew, flown**) n A **fly** is a small insect with two thin, clear wings. माशी ▷ vi When a bird or plane **flies**, it moves through the air. उडणे

fly away (**flies away, flying away, flew away, flown away**) v When something such as a bird, insect, or aircraft **flies away**, it leaves a place by moving through the air. उडून जाणे
With a flap and a screech, the falcon flew away.

foal (**foals**) n A **foal** is a very young horse. शिंगरू

focus (**foci, focuses, focusing, focused**) n The **focus** of something is the main topic or main thing that it is concerned with. मुख्य विषय ▷ v If you **focus** on a particular topic, or if your attention **is focused** on it, you concentrate on it and deal with it. लक्ष केंद्रित करणे

foetus (**foetuses**) n A **foetus** is an unborn animal or human being in its later stages of development. गर्भ

fog (**fogs**) n When there is **fog**, there are tiny drops of water in the air which form a thick cloud and make it difficult to see things. धुके

foggy (**foggier, foggiest**) adj When it is **foggy**, there is fog. धुके भरलेले

fog light (**fog lights**) n A **fog light** is a very bright light on the front or back of a car to help the driver to see or be seen in fog. फॉग लाईट

foil n Foil is metal that is as thin as paper. It is used to wrap food in. फॉईल

fold (**folds, folding, folded**) n A **fold** in a piece of paper or cloth is a bend that you make in it when you put one part of it over another part and press the edge. घडी ▷ vt If you **fold** something such as a piece of paper or cloth, you bend it so that one part covers another part, often pressing the edge so that it stays in place. घडी घालणे

folder (**folders**) n A **folder** is a thin piece of cardboard in which you can keep loose papers. फोल्डर

folding adj A **folding** piece of furniture, bicycle, etc. can be folded, so that it can be carried or stored in a small space. घडी घालता येण्याजोगी वस्तू

folklore n **Folklore** consists of the traditional stories, customs, and habits of a particular community or nation. लोककला

folk music n **Folk music** is music which is traditional or typical of a particular community or nation. लोकसंगीत

follow (**follows, following, followed**) v If you **follow** someone who is going somewhere, you move along behind them. कुणाच्यातरी मागे जाणे

following adj The **following** day, week, or year is the day, week, or year after the one you have just talked about. येणारा

food (**foods**) n **Food** is what people and animals eat. अन्न

food poisoning n If you get **food poisoning**, you become ill because you have eaten food that has gone bad. अन्नातून झालेली विषबाधा

food processor (**food processors**) n A **food processor** is a piece of electrical equipment that is used to mix, chop, or beat food, or to make it into a liquid. फूड प्रोसेसर

fool (**fools, fooling, fooled**) n If you call someone a **fool**, you are indicating that you think they are not sensible and show a lack of good judgement. मूर्ख ▷ vt If someone **fools** you, they deceive or trick you. मूर्ख बनविणे

foot (**feet**) n Your **feet** are the parts of your body that are at the ends of your legs, and that you stand on. पाऊल

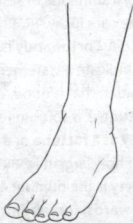

football (**footballs**) n **Football** is a game played by two teams of eleven people who kick a ball and try to score goals by getting the ball into a net. फूटबॉल ▷ n A **football** is the ball that you use to play football. फूटबॉल

footballer (**footballers**) n A **footballer** is a person who plays football. फूटबॉलपटू

football match (**football matches**) n A **football match** is an organized game that is played between two football teams. फूटबॉलचा सामना

football player (**football players**) n A **football player** is a person who plays football, especially as a profession. फूटबॉलपटू

footpath (**footpaths**) n A **footpath** is a path for people to walk on. पदपथ

footprint (**footprints**) n A **footprint** is the mark of a person's foot or shoe left on a surface. पावलाचा ठसा

footstep (**footsteps**) n A **footstep** is the sound made by someone's feet touching the ground when they are walking or running. पावलांचा आवाज

for prep If something is **for** someone, they will have it or use it. साठी, करिता These flowers are for you. ▷ prep You use **for** when you are talking about the way in which you use something. -साठी This knife is for cutting bread. ▷ prep If someone does something **for** you, they do it so that you do not have to do it. साठी I held the door open for the next person.

forbid (**forbids, forbidding, forbade, forbidden**) vt If you **forbid** someone to do something, or if you **forbid** an activity, you order that it must not be done. बंदी घालणे

forbidden adj If something is **forbidden**, you are not allowed to do it or have it. बंदी घातलेला

force (**forces, forcing, forced**) n **Force** is power or strength. बळ ▷ vt If something or someone **forces** you to do something, they make you do it, even though you do not want to. जबरदस्ती करणे

forecast (**forecasts**) n A **forecast** is a statement of what is expected to happen in the future, especially in relation to a particular event or situation. अंदाज

foreground n The **foreground** of a picture is the part that seems nearest to you. चित्रातील जवळ वाटणारा भाग

forehead (**foreheads**) n Your **forehead** is the flat area at the front of your head above your eyebrows and below where your hair grows. कपाळ

foreign adj Something that is **foreign** comes from or relates to a country that is not your own. परदेशी

foreigner (**foreigners**) n A **foreigner** is someone who belongs to a country that is not your own. परदेशी

foresee (**foresees, foreseeing, foresaw, foreseen**) vt If you **foresee** something, you expect and believe that it will happen. आगाऊ समजणे

forest (**forests**) n A **forest** is a large area where trees grow close together. जंगल

forever adv Something that will happen or continue **forever** will always happen or continue. सदैव

forge (**forges, forging, forged**) vt If someone **forges** banknotes, documents, or paintings, they make false copies of them in order to deceive people. खोटी कागदपत्रे बनविणे वा खोटी सही करणे

forgery n **Forgery** is the crime of making fake banknotes, documents, or paintings. खोटी कागदपत्रे किंवा सही करण्याची कृती

forget (**forgets, forgetting, forgot, forgotten**) vt If you **forget** something, or if you **forget** how to do something, you cannot think of it or think of how to do it, although you knew it in the past. विसरणे

forgive (**forgives, forgiving, forgave, forgiven**) vt If you **forgive** someone who has done something wrong, you stop being angry with them. क्षमा करणे

forgotten adj Something that is **forgotten** is no longer remembered or thought about by people. विस्मृतीत गेलेला

fork (**forks**) n A **fork** is an implement that you use when you are eating food. It consists of three or four long thin points on the end of a handle. काटा

form (**forms**) n A **form** of something is a type or kind of it. प्रकार

formal adj **Formal** speech or behaviour is very correct and serious rather than relaxed and friendly, and is used especially in official situations. औपचारिक

formality n **Formality** is speech or behaviour which is correct and serious, rather than relaxed and friendly, and is used especially in official situations. औपचारिकता

format (**formats, formatting, formatted**) n The **format** of something is the way it is arranged and presented. नमुना ▷ vt To **format** a computer disk means to run a program so that the disk can be written on. फॉरमॅट करणे

former adj You use **former** when you are talking about someone or something in the past. पूर्वीचा

formerly adv If something happened or was **formerly** true, it happened or was true in the past. अगोदर

formula (**formulae, formulas**) n A **formula** is a plan that is made as a way of dealing with a problem. सूत्र

fort (**forts**) n A **fort** is a strong building that is used as a military base. किल्ला

fortnight (**fortnights**) n A **fortnight** is a period of two weeks. पंधरवडा

fortunate adj If someone or something is **fortunate**, they are lucky. सुदैवी

fortunately adv **Fortunately** is used to introduce or indicate a statement about an event or situation that is good. सुदैवाने

fortune (**fortunes**) n You can refer to a large sum of money as a **fortune** or a small **fortune** to emphasize how large it is. संपत्ती

forty num **Forty** is the number 40. चाळीस

forward (**forwards, forwarding, forwarded**) adv If you move or look **forward**, you move or look in a direction that is in front of you. पुढे ▷ vt If a letter or message **is forwarded** to someone, it is sent to the place where they are, after having been sent to a different place earlier. पुढे पाठवणे

forward slash (**forward slashes**) _n_ A **forward slash** is the sloping line (/) that separates letters, words, or numbers. फॉरवर्ड स्लेश

foster (**fosters, fostering, fostered**) _vt_ If you **foster** a child, you take him or her into your family as a foster child. मूल वाढवणे

foster child (**foster children**) _n_ A **foster child** is a child looked after temporarily or brought up by people other than its parents. वाढवलेले मूल

foul (**fouler, foulest, fouls**) _adj_ If you describe something as **foul**, you mean it is dirty and smells or tastes unpleasant. ओंगळ ▷ _n_ In sports such as football, a **foul** is an action that is against the rules. खेळातील नियमांविरुद्ध केलेली कृती

foundations _npl_ The **foundations** of a building or other structure are the layer of bricks or concrete below the ground that it is built on. पाया

fountain (**fountains**) _n_ A **fountain** is an ornamental feature in a pool which consists of a jet of water that is forced up into the air by a pump. कारंजे

fountain pen (**fountain pens**) _n_ A **fountain pen** is a pen which uses ink that you have drawn up inside it from a bottle. फाऊंटन पेन

four _num_ **Four** is the number 4. चार

fourteen _num_ **Fourteen** is the number 14. चौदा

fourteenth _adj_ The **fourteenth** item in a series is the one that you count as number fourteen. चौदावा

fourth _adj_ The **fourth** item in a series is the one that you count as number four. चौथा

four-wheel drive (**four-wheel drives**) _n_ A **four-wheel drive** is a vehicle in which all four wheels receive power from the engine. फोर व्हिल ड्राईव्ह

fox (**foxes**) _n_ A **fox** is a wild animal which looks like a dog and has reddish-brown fur and a thick tail. कोल्हा

fracture (**fractures**) _n_ A **fracture** is a crack or break in something. तडा, मोडलेले हाड

fragile _adj_ If you describe a situation as **fragile**, you mean that it is weak or uncertain, and unlikely to be able to resist strong pressure or attack. तकलादू, नाजूक

frail (**frailer, frailest**) _adj_ Someone who is **frail** is not very strong or healthy. अशक्त

frame (**frames**) _n_ The **frame** of a picture or mirror is the part around its edges. चौकट

France _n_ **France** is a republic in western Europe, between the English Channel, the Mediterranean, and the Atlantic. फ्रान्स

frankly _adv_ You use **frankly** when you are expressing an opinion or feeling to emphasize that you mean what you are saying. मोकळेपणाने, स्पष्टपणे

frantic _adj_ If someone is **frantic**, they are behaving in a desperate, wild, and disorganized way, because they are frightened, worried, or in a hurry. वेडपिसा

fraud (**frauds**) _n_ **Fraud** is the crime of gaining money by a trick or lying. बनवाबनवी

freckles _npl_ If someone has **freckles**, they have small light brown spots on their skin. अंगावरील तपकिरी रंगाचे ठिपके

free (**freer, freest, frees, freeing, freed**) _adj_ If you are **free**, you can do what you like or go where you like. स्वतंत्र ▷ _adj_ If something is **free**, you can have it without paying any money for it. मोफत ▷ _vt_ If you **free** someone of something unpleasant, you remove it from them. मुक्त करणे

freedom (**freedoms**) _n_ **Freedom** is the state of being allowed to do what you want. स्वातंत्र्य

free kick (**free kicks**) _n_ In a game of football, when there is a **free kick**, the ball is given to a member of one side to kick because a member of the other side has broken a rule. फ्री किक

freelance _adj_ Someone who does **freelance** work or who is, for example, a **freelance** journalist or photographer is not employed by one organization, but is paid for each piece of work they do by the organization they do it for. मुक्त(एका संस्थेशी बांधील नसलेला) *adv* If someone works **freelance**, they are not employed by one organization, but are paid for each piece of work they do by the organization they do it for. मुक्त(एका संस्थेशी बांधील नसलेला)

freeze (freezes, freezing, froze, frozen) *vi* When water **freezes**, it is so cold that it becomes ice. गोठणे ▷ *vt* If you **freeze** food, you make it very cold so that it will not go bad. गोठवणे

freezer (freezers) *n* A **freezer** is a fridge in which the temperature is kept below freezing point so that you can store food inside it for long periods. फ्रीझर

freezing *adj* Something that is **freezing** is very cold. गोठविणारा

freight *n* **Freight** is the movement of goods by lorries, trains, ships, or aeroplanes. मालाची वाहतूक

French *adj* **French** means belonging or relating to France, or to its people, language, or culture. फ्रेंच ▷ *n* **French** is the language spoken by people who live in France and in parts of some other countries, including Belgium, Canada, and Switzerland. फ्रेंच

French beans *npl* **French beans** are narrow green beans that are eaten as a vegetable. They grow on a tall climbing plant and are the cases that contain the seeds of the plant. श्रावण घेवडा

French horn (French horns) *n* A **French horn** is a musical instrument shaped like a long round metal tube with one wide end, which is played by blowing into it. फ्रेंच हॉर्न

Frenchman (Frenchmen) *n* A **Frenchman** is a man who comes from France. फ्रान्सचा रहिवासी पुरुष

Frenchwoman (Frenchwomen) *n* A **Frenchwoman** is a woman who comes from France. फ्रान्सची रहिवासी स्त्री

frequency *n* The **frequency** of an event is the number of times it happens. वारंवारता

frequent *adj* If something is **frequent**, it happens often. वारंवार घडणारा

fresh (fresher, freshest) *adj* A **fresh** thing or amount replaces or is added to an existing thing or amount. ताजा ▷ *adj* If food is **fresh**, it has been picked or made a short time ago. ताजा ▷ *adj* **Fresh** water has no salt in it. The water in rivers is **fresh**. गोडे ▷ *adj* **Fresh** air is clean and cool. ताजा

freshen up (freshens up, freshening up, freshened up) *v* If you **freshen** something **up**, you make it clean and pleasant in appearance or smell. ताजेतवाने करणे *A thorough brushing helps to freshen up your mouth.*

freshwater fish (freshwater fish, freshwater fishes) *n* A **freshwater fish** lives in water that is not salty. गोड्या पाण्यातील मासा

fret (frets, fretting, fretted) *vi* If you **fret** about something, you worry about it. काळजी करणे

Friday (Fridays) *n* **Friday** is the day after Thursday and before Saturday. शुक्रवार

fridge (fridges) *n* A **fridge** is a large metal container for storing food at low temperatures to keep it fresh. फ्रीज

fried *adj* If food is **fried**, it is cooked in a pan containing hot fat. तळलेले

friend (friends) *n* A **friend** is someone who you know well and like, but who is not related to you. मित्र

friendly (friendlier, friendliest) *adj* A **friendly** person is kind and pleasant. मित्रत्वाचा

friendship (friendships) *n* A **friendship** is a relationship or state of being friends between two people who like each other. मैत्री

fright *n* **Fright** is a sudden feeling of fear. भीती

frighten (frightens, frightening, frightened) *vt* If something or someone **frightens** you, they cause you to suddenly feel afraid or anxious. घाबरविणे

frightened *adj* If you are **frightened**, you feel anxious or afraid. घाबरलेला

frightening *adj* If something is **frightening**, it makes you feel afraid or anxious. घाबरवणारा

fringe (fringes) n A **fringe** is hair which is cut so that it hangs over your forehead. केसांची झुलपे

frog (frogs) n A **frog** is a small creature with smooth skin, big eyes, and long back legs which it uses for jumping. बेडूक

from prep If something comes **from** a person, they give it to you or send it to you. कडून / *I received a letter from him yesterday.* ▷ prep If someone or something moves **from** a place, they leave it. पासून, मधून *Everyone watched as she ran from the room.* ▷ prep You use **from** to say what somebody used to make something. पासून *This bread is made from white flour.*

front (fronts) adj **Front** is used to refer to the side or part of something that is towards the front or nearest to the front. पुढची बाजू ▷ n The **front** of something is the part of it that faces you, or that faces forward, or that you normally see or use. पुढची बाजू

frontier (frontiers) n A **frontier** is a border between two countries. आघाडी

frost (frosts) n When there is **frost** or a **frost**, the temperature outside falls below freezing point and the ground becomes covered in ice crystals. गोठलेले दव

frosty (frostier, frostiest) adj If the weather is **frosty**, the temperature is below freezing. गोठलेले

frown (frowns, frowning, frowned) vi When someone **frowns**, their eyebrows become drawn together, because they are annoyed, worried, or puzzled, or because they are concentrating. कपाळावर आठ्या घालणे

frozen adj If the ground is **frozen**, it has become very hard because the weather is very cold. गोठलेले

fruit (fruit, fruits) n **Fruit** is something which grows on a tree or bush and which contains seeds or a stone covered by edible flesh. Apples, oranges, and bananas are all fruit. फळ

fruit juice n **Fruit juice** is the liquid that can be obtained from a fruit and drunk. फळाचा रस

fruit salad (fruit salads) n **Fruit salad** is a mixture of pieces of different kinds of fruit. It is usually eaten as a dessert. फ्रूट सॅलाड

frustrated adj If you are **frustrated**, you are upset or angry because you are unable to do anything about a situation. उद्विग्न झालेला

fry (fries, frying, fried) vt When you **fry** food, you cook it in a pan containing hot fat. तळणे

frying pan (frying pans) n A **frying pan** is a flat metal pan with a long handle, in which you fry food. तळण्याचा तवा

fuel (fuels) n **Fuel** is a substance such as coal, oil, or petrol that is burned to provide heat or power. इंधन

fulfil (fulfils, fulfills, fulfilling, fulfilled) vt If you **fulfil** a promise, dream, or ambition, you do what you said or hoped you would do. पूर्ण करणे

full (fuller, fullest) adj Something that is **full** contains as much of a substance or as many objects as it can. भरलेला

full moon n You use **full moon** to describe one of the four phases of the moon, occurring when the earth lies between the sun and the moon so that the moon is visible as a fully illuminated disc. पौर्णिमा

full stop (full stops) n A **full stop** is the punctuation mark (.) which you use at the end of a sentence when it is not a question or exclamation. पूर्ण विराम

full-time adj **Full-time** work or study involves working or studying for the whole of each normal working week rather than for part of it. पूर्ण वेळ ▷ adv If you do something **full-time**, you do it for the whole of each normal working week. पूर्ण वेळ

fully adv **Fully** means to the greatest degree or extent possible. पूर्णतः

fumes npl **Fumes** are unpleasantly strong or harmful gases or smells. धुराचा लोट

fun adj If someone is **fun**, you enjoy their company. If something is **fun**, you enjoy doing it. गंमत ▷ n You refer to an activity or situation as **fun** if you think it is pleasant and enjoyable. गंमत

funds npl **Funds** are amounts of money that are available to be spent. निधी

funeral (funerals) n A **funeral** is a ceremony for the burial or cremation of someone who has died. अंत्यसंस्कार

funeral parlour (funeral parlours) n A **funeral parlour** is a place where dead people are prepared for burial or cremation. फ्युनरल पार्लर

funfair (funfairs) n A **funfair** is an event held in a park or field at which people pay to ride on various machines for amusement or try to win prizes in games. फनफेअर

funnel (funnels) n A **funnel** is an object with a wide top and a tube at the bottom, which is used to pour substances into a container. नरसाळे

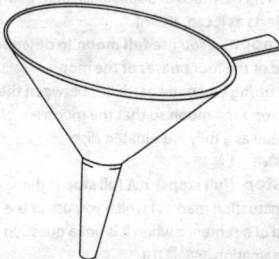

funny (funnier, funniest) adj If something is **funny**, it makes you laugh. मजेशीर ▷ adj **Funny** means strange. चमत्कारिक

fur n **Fur** is the thick hair that grows on the bodies of many animals, such as rabbits and bears, and is sometimes used to make clothes or rugs. फरचा

fur coat (fur coats) n A **fur coat** is a coat made from real or artificial fur. फरचा कोट

furious adj If someone is **furious**, they are extremely angry. संतापलेला

furnished adj A **furnished** room or house is available to be rented together with the furniture in it. सामानसुमानाने सज्ज

furniture n **Furniture** consists of large movable objects such as tables, chairs, or beds that are used in a room for sitting or lying on, or for putting things on or in. फर्निचर

further (furthest) adj A **further** thing or amount is an additional one. पुढील ▷ adv **Further** means to a greater degree or extent. पुढे

further education n **Further education** is the education of people who have left school but who are not at a university or a college of education. महाविद्यालयीन शिक्षण

fuse (fuses) n In an electrical appliance, a **fuse** is a wire safety device which melts and stops the electric current if there is a fault. फ्युज

fuse box (fuse boxes) n The **fuse box** is the box that contains the fuses for all the electric circuits in a building. It is usually fixed to a wall. फ्यूज बॉक्स

fuss n **Fuss** is anxious or excited behaviour which serves no useful purpose. अकारण चिंता

fussy (fussier, fussiest) adj Someone who is **fussy** is very concerned with unimportant details and is difficult to please. क्षुल्लक गोष्टीवरून गडबड करणारी व्यक्ती

future adj **Future** things will happen or exist after the present time. भविष्यातील ▷ n The **future** is the period of time after the present. पुढचा / निकटचा/भविष्य काळ

g

Gabon *n* **Gabon** is a republic in west central Africa, on the Atlantic. गॅबन

gain (**gains, gaining, gained**) *n* A **gain** is an improvement or increase. वाढ ▷ *vt* If you **gain** something, you get it. मिळवणे

gale (**gales**) *n* A **gale** is a very strong wind. वादळी वारा

gall bladder (**gall bladders**) *n* Your **gall bladder** is the organ in your body which helps digestion and is next to your liver. पित्ताशय

gallery (**galleries**) *n* A **gallery** is a place that has permanent exhibitions of works of art in it. कलादालन

gallop (**gallops, galloping, galloped**) *n* A **gallop** is a ride on a horse that is galloping. घोड्याची चौखूर धाव ▷ *vi* When a horse **gallops**, it runs very fast. चौखूर धावणे

gallstone (**gallstones**) *n* A **gallstone** is a small, painful lump which can develop in your gall bladder. पित्ताशयातील खडा

Gambia *n* **Gambia** is a republic in West Africa. गांबिया

gamble (**gambles, gambling, gambled**) *v* If you **gamble** on something, you take a risk because you hope that something good will happen. जुगार खेळणे

gambler (**gamblers**) *n* A **gambler** is someone who bets money regularly, for example in card games or horse racing. जुगारी

gambling *n* **Gambling** is the act or activity of betting money, for example in card games or on horse racing. जुगार

game (**games**) *n* A **game** is something you play that has rules, for example football. खेळ ▷ *n* Children play a **game** when they pretend to be other people. खेळ

games console (**games consoles**) *n* A **games console** is an electronic device used for playing computer games on a television screen. गेम्स कन्सोल

gang (**gangs**) *n* A **gang** is a group of people who join together for some purpose, often criminal. टोळी

gangster (**gangsters**) *n* A **gangster** is a member of a group of violent criminals. गुंडांच्या टोळीतील माणूस

gap (**gaps**) *n* A **gap** is a space between two things or a hole in something solid. फट

garage (**garages**) *n* A **garage** is a building where you keep a car. गॅरेज ▷ *n* A **garage** is a place where you can get your car repaired. गॅरेज

garden (**gardens**) *n* A **garden** is an area of land next to a house, with plants, trees, and grass. बाग

garden centre (**garden centres**) *n* A **garden centre** is a large shop, usually with an outdoor area, where you can buy things for your garden such as plants and gardening tools. गार्डन सेंटर

gardener (**gardeners**) *n* A **gardener** is a person who is paid to work in someone else's garden. माळी

gardening *n* **Gardening** is the activity of planning and cultivating a garden. बागकाम

garlic *n* **Garlic** is a plant like a small onion, with a strong flavour, which you use in cooking. लसूण

garment (garments) n A **garment** is a piece of clothing.

gas (gases) n A **gas** is any substance that is neither liquid nor solid. वायू

gas cooker (gas cookers) n A **gas cooker** is a large metal device for cooking food using gas. गॅस कूकर

gasket (gaskets) n A **gasket** is a flat piece of soft material that you put between two joined surfaces in a pipe or engine in order to make sure that gas and oil cannot escape. गास्केट

gate (gates) n A **gate** is a structure like a door that you use to enter a field, a garden, or the area around a building. फाटक

gateau (gateaux) n A **gateau** is a very rich, fancy cake, especially one with cream in it. क्रिम असलेला मोठा केक

gather (gathers, gathering, gathered) v When people **gather** somewhere, or if someone **gathers** them there, they come together in a group. एकत्र गोळा होणे

gauge (gauges, gauging, gauged) n A **gauge** is a device that measures the amount or quantity of something and shows the amount measured. परिमाण ▷ vt If you **gauge** something, you measure it or judge it. मोजणे

gaze (gazes, gazing, gazed) vi If you **gaze** at someone or something, you look steadily at them for a long time. टक लावून पाहणे

gear (gears) n A **gear** is a piece of machinery, for example in a car or on a bicycle, which helps to control its movement. गिअर ▷ n The **gear** for a particular activity is the equipment and special clothes that you use. गिअर (कळ, चक्रे वगैरेंनी युक्त असे उपकरण)

gearbox (gearboxes) n A **gearbox** is the system of gears in an engine or vehicle. गिअरबॉक्स

gear lever (gear levers) n A **gear lever** or a **gear stick** is the lever that you use to change gear in a car or other vehicle. गिअर लिव्हर

gel (gels) n Gel is a smooth, soft, jelly-like substance, especially one used to keep your hair in a particular style. जेल

gem (gems) n A **gem** is a jewel. रत्न

Gemini n **Gemini** is one of the twelve signs of the zodiac. Its symbol is a pair of twins. People who are born between 21st May and 20th June come under this sign. मिथुन राश

gender (genders) n A person's **gender** is the fact that they are male or female. लिंग

gene (genes) n A **gene** is the part of a cell in a living thing which controls its physical characteristics, growth, and development. जनुक

general (generals) adj If you talk about the **general** situation somewhere or talk about something in **general** terms, you are describing the situation as a whole rather than part of it. सर्वसामान्य ▷ n A **general** is a senior officer in the armed forces, usually in the army. सेनापती

general anaesthetic (general anaesthetics) n A **general anaesthetic** is a substance that doctors use to stop you feeling pain during an operation. It causes you to lose consciousness. सर्व शरीरावर परिणाम घडवणारे बधिरीकरण

general election (general elections) n A **general election** is a time when people choose a new government. सार्वत्रिक निवडणूक

generalize (generalizes, generalizing, generalized) v If you **generalize**, you say something that is usually, but not always, true. सर्वसाधारण विधान

general knowledge n **General knowledge** is knowledge about many different things, as opposed to detailed knowledge about one particular subject. सामान्य ज्ञान

generally adv You use **generally** to summarize a situation, activity, or idea without referring to the particular details of it. सामान्यत:

generation (generations) n A **generation** is all the people in a group or country who are of a similar age, especially when they are considered as having the same experiences or attitudes. पिढी

generator (**generators**) *n* A **generator** is a machine which produces electricity. विद्युतजनित्र

generosity *n* If you refer to someone's **generosity**, you mean that they are generous, especially in doing or giving more than is usual or expected. औदार्य

generous *adj* A **generous** person gives more of something, especially money, than is usual or expected. दानशूर

genetic *adj* You use **genetic** to describe something that is related to genetics or genes. आनुवंशिक

genetically-modified *adj* **Genetically-modified** plants and animals have had one or more genes changed. The abbreviation **GM** is often used. जनुकीयदृष्ट्या सुधारित

genetics *n* **Genetics** is the study of how characteristics are passed from one generation to another by means of genes. आनुवंशिकतेचा अभ्यास

genius *n* **Genius** is very great ability or skill in something. अलौकिक बुद्धिमता

gentle (**gentler**, **gentlest**) *adj* A **gentle** person is kind, mild, and calm. सभ्य

gentleman (**gentlemen**) *n* A **gentleman** is a man from a family of high social standing. सभ्यगृहस्थ गृहस्थ

gently *adv* If you do something **gently** you do it in a kind, mild, and calm manner. हळुवारपणे

gents *n* The **gents** is a public toilet for men. पुरुषांसाठीचे सार्वजनिक प्रसाधनगृह

genuine *adj* Something that is **genuine** is real and exactly what it appears to be. अस्सल

geography *n* **Geography** is the study of the countries of the world and things such as the land, oceans, weather, towns, and population. भूगोलशास्त्र

geology *n* **Geology** is the study of the earth's structure, surface, and origins. भूगर्भशास्त्र

Georgia *n* **Georgia** is a state of the southeastern United States, on the Atlantic. जॉर्जिया ▷ *n* **Georgia** is a republic in north-west Asia, on the Black Sea. जॉर्जिया

Georgian (**Georgians**) *adj* **Georgian** means belonging to or connected with the republic of Georgia, in north-west Asia, or to its people, language, or culture. जॉर्जियन ▷ *n* A **Georgian** is a person who comes from the republic of Georgia, in north-west Asia. जॉर्जियन

geranium (**geraniums**) *n* A **geranium** is a plant with red, pink, or white flowers. जिरेनिअम

gerbil (**gerbils**) *n* A **gerbil** is a small, furry animal. जर्बिल

geriatric *adj* **Geriatric** is used to describe things relating to the illnesses and medical care of old people. वृद्ध माणसांच्या आजार व उपचारासंबंधी

germ (**germs**) *n* A **germ** is a very small organism that causes disease. रोगजंतू

German (**Germans**) *adj* **German** means belonging or relating to Germany, or to its people, language, or culture. जर्मन ▷ *n* A **German** is a person who comes from Germany. जर्मन ▷ *n* **German** is the language spoken in Germany, Austria, and parts of Switzerland. जर्मन

German measles *n* **German measles** is a disease which causes you to have a cough, a sore throat, and red spots on your skin. गोवर

Germany *n* **Germany** is a country in central Europe. जर्मनी

gesture (**gestures**) *n* A **gesture** is a movement that you make with a part of your body, especially your hands, to express emotion or information. हावभाव

get (**gets**, **getting**, **got**) *v* You can use **get** to mean the same as 'become'. होणे *We should go before it gets dark.* ▷ *vi* If you **get** somewhere, you arrive there. पोहोचणे ▷ *vt* If you **get** something, someone gives it to you. मिळणे ▷ *vt* If you **get** something, you go to where it is and bring it back. आणणे

get away (**gets away**, **getting away**, **got away**) *v* If you **get away**, you succeed in leaving a place or situation that you do not want to be in. बाहेर पडणे, निसटणे *The thieves got away through an upstairs window.*

get back (gets back, getting back, got back)
v If you **get** something **back** after you have
lost it or after it has been taken from you, you
have it again. परत मिळणे *You can cancel the
contract and get your money back.*

get in (gets in, getting in, got in) *v* When a
train, bus, or plane **gets in**, it arrives. पोहोचणे
Her train gets in at about ten to two.

get into (gets into, getting into, got into) *v*
If you **get into** an activity, you start doing it or
being involved in it. सहभागी होणे *He was eager
to get into politics.*

get off (gets off, getting off, got off) *v* If
someone who has broken a law or rule **gets
off**, they are not punished, or only slightly
punished. विशेष शिक्षा न होता सुटणे *He is likely
to get off with a small fine.*

get on (gets on, getting on, got on) *v* If you
get on with someone, you have a friendly
relationship with them. सूर जुळणे *I get on very
well with his wife.*

get out (gets out, getting out, got out) *v* If
you **get out**, you leave a place because you
want to escape from it, or because you are
made to leave it. निघून जाणे *I told him to leave
and get out.*

get over (gets over, getting over, got over)
v If you **get over** an unpleasant experience or
an illness, you recover from it. सावरणे *It took
me a long time to get over the illness.*

get together (gets together, getting
together, got together) *v* When people
get together, they meet in order to discuss
something or to spend time together. एकत्र
जमणे *This is a time for families to get together
and enjoy themselves.*

get up (gets up, getting up, got up) *v* If you
are sitting or lying and then **get up**, you rise
to a standing position. उभे राहणे *I got up and
walked over to where he was.*

Ghana *n* **Ghana** is a republic in West Africa, on
the Gulf of Guinea. घाना

Ghanaian (Ghanaians) *adj* **Ghanaian**
means belonging or relating to Ghana, or to

its people, language or culture. घानियन ▷ *n*
Ghanaians are people who are Ghanaian.
घानियन

ghost (ghosts) *n* A **ghost** is the spirit of a
dead person that someone believes they can
see or feel. भूत

giant (giants) *adj* You use **giant** to describe
something that is much larger or more
important than most other things of its kind.
महाकाय ▷ *n* A large successful organization
or country can be referred to as a **giant**. प्रचंड
उलाढाल असलेली कंपनी

gift (gifts) *n* A **gift** is something that you give
someone as a present. भेटवस्तू

gifted *adj* A **gifted** person has a natural ability
for doing most things or for doing a particular
activity. नैसर्गिक देणगी लाभलेले

gift voucher (gift vouchers) *n* A **gift
voucher** is a card or piece of paper that you
buy at a shop and give to someone, which
entitles the person to exchange it for goods
worth the same amount. भेटवस्तूंचे कूपन

gigantic *adj* If you describe something as
gigantic, you are emphasizing that it is
extremely large in size, amount, or degree.
अवाढव्य

giggle (giggles, giggling, giggled) *vi* If
someone **giggles**, they laugh in a childlike
way, because they are amused, nervous, or
embarrassed. फिदीफिदी हसणे

gin (gins) *n* **Gin** is a colourless alcoholic drink.
जिन

ginger *adj* **Ginger** is used to describe things
that are orangey-brown in colour. लालसर
तेजस्वी ▷ *n* **Ginger** is the root of a plant that
is used to flavour food. It has a sweet spicy
flavour. आले

giraffe (giraffes) *n* A **giraffe** is a large African
animal with a very long neck, long legs, and
dark patches on its body. जिराफ

girl (girls) *n* A **girl** is a female child. मुलगी

girlfriend (girlfriends) *n* Someone's
girlfriend is a girl or woman with whom they
are having a romantic relationship. प्रेयसी

give (**gives, giving, gave, given**) *vt* If you **give** someone something, you let them have it to keep. देणे

give back (**gives back, giving back, gave back, given back**) *v* If you **give** something **back**, you return it to the person who gave it to you. परत देणे *I gave the textbook back to him.*

give in (**gives in, giving in, gave in, given in**) *v* If you **give in**, you admit that you are defeated or that you cannot do something. पराभव मान्य करणे *All right. I give in. What did you do with it?*

give out (**gives out, giving out, gave out, given out**) *v* If you **give out** a number of things, you distribute them among a group of people. वाटप करणे *They were giving out leaflets.*

give up (**gives up, giving up, gave up, given up**) *v* If you **give up** something, you stop doing it or having it. सोडून देणे *We almost gave up hope.*

glacier (**glaciers**) *n* A **glacier** is a huge mass of ice which moves very slowly, often down a mountain. हिमनग

glad *adj* If you are **glad** about something, you are happy and pleased about it. आनंदी

glamorous *adj* If you describe someone or something as **glamorous**, you mean that they are more attractive, exciting, or interesting than ordinary people or things. मनमोहक

glance (**glances, glancing, glanced**) *n* A **glance** is a quick look at someone or something. दृष्टिक्षेप ▷ *vi* If you **glance** at something or someone, you look at them very quickly and then look away again immediately. दृष्टिक्षेप टाकणे

gland (**glands**) *n* **Glands** are organs in your body that produce chemical substances which your body needs. ग्रंथी

glare (**glares, glaring, glared**) *vi* If you **glare** at someone, you look at them with an angry expression on your face. रागाने पाहणे

glaring *adj* If you describe something bad as **glaring**, you mean that it is very obvious. सुस्पष्ट

glass (**glasses**) *n* **Glass** is a hard, clear material that is used to make things like windows and bottles. It is quite easy to break **glass**. काच ▷ *n* A **glass** is a container made from **glass** that you can drink out of. ग्लास, काचेचा पेला

glasses *npl* **Glasses** are two lenses in a frame that some people wear in front of their eyes in order to see better. चष्मा

glider (**gliders**) *n* A **glider** is an aircraft without an engine which flies by floating on the air. इंजिनाशिवाय तरंगणारे आकाशयान

gliding *n* **Gliding** is the sport or activity of flying in a glider. ग्लायडिंग

global *adj* **Global** means concerning or including the whole world. जागतिक

globalization *n* **Globalization** is the idea that the world is developing a single economy as a result of improved technology and communications. जागतिकीकरण

global warming *n* The problem of the gradual rise in the earth's temperature is referred to as **global warming**. जागतिक तापमानवाढ

globe (**globes**) *n* You can refer to the earth as the **globe**. पृथ्वी

gloomy (**gloomier, gloomiest**) *adj* If a place is **gloomy**, it is almost dark so that you cannot see very well. अंधारी

glorious *adj* If you describe something as **glorious**, you are emphasizing that it is very beautiful or wonderful. अत्यंत सुंदर

glory n **Glory** is fame and admiration that you get for an achievement. मानसन्मान

glove (gloves) n **Gloves** are pieces of clothing which cover your hand and wrist and have individual sections for each finger. हातमोजे

glove compartment (glove compartments) n The **glove compartment** in a car is a small cupboard or shelf below the front windscreen. हातमोजे ठेवण्याचा कप्पा

glucose n **Glucose** is a type of sugar. शर्करा

glue (glues, glueing, gluing, glued) n **Glue** is a sticky substance used for joining things together. गोंद ▷ vt If you **glue** one object to another, you stick them together, using glue. चिकटवणे

gluten n **Gluten** is a substance found in cereal grains such as wheat. पिष्टमय पदार्थ काढून घेतल्यानंतर उरणारा चिकट पदार्थ

GM abbr **GM** crops have had one or more genes changed, for example in order to make them resist pests better. **GM** is an abbreviation for 'genetically modified'. जनुकीयदृष्ट्या सुधारित

go (goes, going, went, gone) vi If you **go** somewhere, you move there from another place. जाणे ▷ v If you say that something is **going** to happen, you mean that it will happen. घडणे

go after (goes after, going after, went after, gone after) v If you **go after** something, you try to get it, catch it, or hit it. पाठपुरावा करणे *The company is going after the Asia Pacific market.*

go ahead (goes ahead, going ahead, went ahead, gone ahead) v If someone **goes ahead** with something, they begin to do it or make it. पुढे जाणे *The board will vote on whether to go ahead with the plan.*

goal (goals) n In games such as football or hockey, the **goal** is the space into which the players try to get the ball in order to score. फूटबॉल, हॉकी, इ. खेळातला गोल

goalkeeper (goalkeepers) n A **goalkeeper** is the player in a sports team whose job is to guard the goal. गोलकीपर

goat (goats) n A **goat** is an animal which is a bit bigger than a sheep and has horns. बकरा (m) बकरी(f)

go away (goes away, going away, went away, gone away) v If you **go away**, you leave a place or a person's company. दूर जाणे *I think we need to go away and think about this.*

go back (goes back, going back, went back, gone back) v If something **goes back** to a particular time in the past, it was made or started at that time. पूर्वीपासून चालू असणे, मागे जाणे (काळ) *The feud goes back to the 11th century.*

go by (goes by, going by, went by, gone by) v If you say that time **goes by**, you mean that it passes. सरणे *I gradually forgot about him as the years went by.*

God n The name **God** is given to the spirit or being who is worshipped as the creator and ruler of the world, especially by Christians, Jews, and Muslims. देव

go down (goes down, going down, went down, gone down) v If a price, level, or amount **goes down**, it becomes lower than it was. कमी होणे *Crime has gone down 70%.*

goggles npl **Goggles** are large glasses that fit closely to your face around your eyes to protect them, for example in a laboratory. संरक्षक चष्मा

go in (goes in, going in, went in, gone in) v If the sun **goes in**, it becomes covered by a cloud. झाकले जाणे *The sun went in, and it felt cold.*

gold (golds) n **Gold** is a valuable yellow-coloured metal used for making jewellery, and as an international currency. सोने

golden adj Something that is **golden** is bright yellow. सोनेरी

goldfish (goldfish, goldfishes) n A **goldfish** is a small orange-coloured fish. सोनेरी मासा

gold-plated adj Something that is **gold-plated** is covered with a very thin layer of gold. सोन्याचा मुलामा दिलेले

golf *n* Golf is a game in which you use long sticks called clubs to hit a ball into holes that are spread out over a large area of grassy land. गोल्फ नावाचा खेळ

golf club (golf clubs) *n* A **golf club** is a long, thin, metal stick with a piece of wood or metal at one end that you use to hit the ball in golf. गोल्फची काठी ▷ *n* A **golf club** is a social organization which provides a golf course and a clubhouse for its members. गोल्फ क्लब

golf course (golf courses) *n* A **golf course** is an area of land where people play golf. गोल्फचे मैदान

gone *adj* Someone or something that is **gone** is no longer present or no longer exists. गेलेला

good (better, best) *adj* If you say that something is **good**, you like it. चांगला ▷ *adj* If you are **good**, you behave well. चांगला ▷ *adj* If you are **good** at something, you do it well. प्रवीण

goodbye! *excl* You say 'goodbye!' to someone when you or they are leaving, or at the end of a telephone conversation. बरंय... येतो आता

good-looking (better-looking, best-looking) *adj* A **good-looking** person has an attractive face. सुस्वरूप

good-natured *adj* A **good-natured** person or animal is naturally friendly and does not get angry easily. सुस्वभावी

goods *npl* **Goods** are things that are made to be sold. वस्तू

go off (goes off, going off, went off, gone off) *v* If an explosive device or a gun **goes off**, it explodes or fires. फुटणे *A few minutes later the bomb went off, destroying the vehicle.*

google (googles, googling, googled) *v* If you **google** someone or something, you search the Internet for information about them, especially using the website Google®. गूगलच्या सहाय्याने शोध घेणे

go on (goes on, going on, went on, gone on) *v* If you **go on** doing something, or **go on with**

an activity, you continue to do it. चालू ठेवणे *She just went on laughing.*

goose (geese) *n* A **goose** is a large bird similar to a duck, with a long neck. हंसाच्या जातीचा पक्षी

gooseberry (gooseberries) *n* A **gooseberry** is a small green fruit that has a sharp taste and is covered with tiny hairs. गूजबेरी

goose pimples *npl* If you get **goose pimples**, the hairs on your skin stand up so that it is covered with tiny bumps. रोमांच

go out (goes out, going out, went out, gone out) *v* When you **go out**, you do something enjoyable away from your home, for example you go to a restaurant or the cinema. मौजमजा करण्यासाठी बाहेर पडणे *I'm going out to dinner tonight.*

go past (goes past, going past, went past, gone past) *v* If you **go past** someone or something, you go near them and keep moving, so that they are then behind you. जवळून जाणे *He went past me and into the hall.*

gorgeous *adj* Someone or something that is **gorgeous** is extremely pleasant or attractive. *(informal)* आकर्षक

gorilla (gorillas) *n* A **gorilla** is a very large ape. गोरिला

go round (goes round, going round, went round, gone round) *v* If you **go round** to someone's house, you visit them at their house. भेट देणे *I went round to his house last night.*

gossip (gossips, gossiping, gossiped) *n* **Gossip** is informal conversation, often about other people's private affairs. कुटाळक्या, दुसऱ्यांच्या खासगी जीवनाबाबत केलेल्या गप्पाटप्पा ▷ *vi* If you **gossip** with someone, you talk informally with them, especially about other people or local events. चकाट्या पिटणे

go through (goes through, going through, went through, gone through) *v* If you **go through** a difficult experience or period of time, it happens to you. मधून जाणे *He was going through a very difficult time.*

go up (goes up, going up, went up, gone up) v If a price, amount, or level **goes up**, it becomes higher or greater than it was. वाढणे *Interest rates went up.*

government (governments) n The **government** of a country is the group of people who are responsible for running it. सरकार

GP (GPs) abbr A **GP** is a doctor who treats all types of illness, instead of specializing in one area of medicine. **GP** is an abbreviation for 'general practitioner'. जनरल प्रॅक्टिशनर

GPS (GPSs) abbr **GPS** is a system that uses signals from satellites to find out the position of an object. **GPS** is an abbreviation for 'global positioning system'. जीपीएस

grab (grabs, grabbing, grabbed) vt If you **grab** something, you take it or pick it up roughly. पकडणे

graceful adj Someone or something that is **graceful** moves in a smooth and elegant way that is attractive to watch. डौलदार

grade (grades) n The **grade** of a product is its quality. दर्जा

gradual adj A **gradual** change or process happens in small stages over a long period of time, rather than suddenly. हळूहळू

gradually adv If something changes or is done **gradually**, it changes or is done in small stages over a long period of time, rather than suddenly. हळूहळू

graduate (graduates) n A **graduate** is a student who has completed a course at a college or university. पदवीधर

graduation n **Graduation** is the successful completion of a course of study at a university, college, or school, for which you receive a degree or diploma. पदवी

graffiti npl **Graffiti** is words or pictures that are written or drawn in public places, for example on walls or trains. सार्वजनिक भिंतीवरील लिखाण किंवा चित्रे

grain (grains) n A **grain** is the seed of a cereal plant, for example rice or wheat. धान्य ▷ n A

grain of something, for example sand or salt, is a tiny piece of it. दाणे

gram (grams) n A **gram** or **gramme** is a unit of weight equal to one thousandth of a kilogram. ग्रॅम

grammar n **Grammar** is the ways that words can be put together in order to make sentences. व्याकरण

grammatical adj **Grammatical** is used to describe something relating to grammar. व्याकरणविषयक

grand (grander, grandest) adj If you describe a building or landscape as **grand**, you mean that it is splendid or impressive. भव्य

grandchild (grandchildren) n Someone's **grandchild** is the child of their son or daughter. नातवंड

granddad (granddads) n Your **granddad** is your grandfather. You can call your granddad 'Granddad'. *(informal)* आजोबा

granddaughter (granddaughters) n Someone's **granddaughter** is the daughter of their son or daughter. नात

grandfather (grandfathers) n Your **grandfather** is the father of your father or mother. You can call your grandfather 'Grandfather'. आजोबा

grandma (grandmas) n Your **grandma** is your grandmother. You can call your grandma 'Grandma'. *(informal)* आजी

grandmother (grandmothers) n Your **grandmother** is the mother of your father or mother. You can call your grandmother 'Grandmother'. आजी

grandpa (grandpas) n Your **grandpa** is your grandfather. You can call your grandpa 'Grandpa'. *(informal)* आजोबा

grandparents npl Your **grandparents** are the parents of your father or mother. आजी-आजोबा

grandson (grandsons) n Someone's **grandson** is the son of their son or daughter. नातू

granite n **Granite** is a very hard rock used in building. ग्रॅनाईट

granny (grannies) n Some people refer to or address their grandmother as **granny**. (informal) आजी

grant (grants) n A **grant** is an amount of money that the government or other institution gives to a person or an organization for a particular purpose. अनुदान

grape (grapes) n **Grapes** are small green or purple fruit that grow in bunches. द्राक्षे

grapefruit (grapefruit, grapefruits) n A **grapefruit** is a large, round, yellow fruit that has a sharp taste. ग्रेप फ्रूट

graph (graphs) n A **graph** is a mathematical diagram which shows the relationship between two or more sets of numbers or measurements. आलेख

graphics npl **Graphics** are drawings and pictures that are composed using simple lines and sometimes strong colours. चित्रलेख

grasp (grasps, grasping, grasped) vt If you **grasp** something, you take it in your hand and hold it very firmly. पकडणे

grass (grasses) n **Grass** is a very common green plant with narrow leaves that forms a layer covering an area of ground. गवत ▷ n A **grass** is someone who tells the police or other authorities about criminal activities they know about. (informal) खबऱ्या

grasshopper (grasshoppers) n A **grasshopper** is an insect with long back legs that jumps high into the air and makes a high, vibrating sound. नाकतोडा

grate (grates, grating, grated) vt When you **grate** food, you shred it into very small pieces using a tool called a grater. किसणे

grateful adj If you are **grateful** for something that someone has given you or done for you, you are pleased and wish to thank them. कृतज्ञ

grave (graves) n A **grave** is a place where a dead person is buried. थडगे

gravel n **Gravel** consists of very small stones. खडबडीत वाळू

gravestone (gravestones) n A **gravestone** is a large stone with words carved into it, which is placed on a grave. थडग्यावरील चिरा

graveyard (graveyards) n A **graveyard** is an area of land where dead people are buried. दफनभूमी

gravy n **Gravy** is a sauce made from the juices that come from meat when it cooks. रस्सा

grease n **Grease** is a thick substance used to oil the moving parts of machines. वंगण

greasy (greasier, greasiest) adj Something that is **greasy** is covered with grease or contains a lot of grease. वंगण लावलेली वस्तू

great (greater, greatest) adj **Great** means very large. मोठा ▷ adj **Great** means very important. महान ▷ adj If you say that something is **great**, you mean that it is very good. मजेशीर

Great Britain n **Great Britain** is the island consisting of England, Scotland, and Wales, which together with Northern Ireland makes up the United Kingdom. ग्रेट ब्रिटन

great-grandfather (great-grandfathers) n Your **great-grandfather** is the father of your grandmother or grandfather. पणजोबा

great-grandmother (great-grandmothers) n Your **great-grandmother** is the mother of your grandmother or grandfather. पणजी

Greece n **Greece** is a republic in south-east Europe. ग्रीस

greedy (greedier, greediest) adj Someone who is **greedy** wants more of something than is necessary or fair. लोभी

Greek (Greeks) adj **Greek** means belonging or relating to Greece, or to its people, language, or culture. ग्रीक ▷ n A **Greek** is a person who comes from Greece. ग्रीक ▷ n **Greek** is the language spoken in Greece. ग्रीक

green (greener, greenest) adj Something that is **green** is the colour of grass or leaves. हिरवा ▷ adj If you say that someone is **green**, you mean that they have had very little experience of life or a particular job. नवखा, अननुभवी

Green (Greens) n **Greens** are members of political movements concerned with the protection of the environment. ग्रीन चळवळीचा सभासद

greengrocer n A **greengrocer** or a **greengrocer's** is a shop that sells fruit and vegetables. भाजी विक्रेता

greenhouse (greenhouses) n A **greenhouse** is a glass building in which you grow plants that need to be protected from bad weather. हरितगृह

Greenland n **Greenland** is a large island, lying mostly within the Arctic Circle. ग्रीनलँड

green salad (green salads) n A **green salad** is a salad made mainly with lettuce and other green vegetables. हिरव्या भाज्यांचे सेलड

greet (greets, greeting, greeted) vt When you **greet** someone, you say something friendly such as 'hello' when you meet them. स्वागत/अभिवादन करणे

greeting (greetings) n A **greeting** is something friendly that you say or do when you meet someone. स्वागतपर

greetings card (greetings cards) n A **greetings card** is a folded card with a picture on the front and greetings inside that you give or send to someone, for example on their birthday. भेटकार्ड

grey (greyer, greyest) adj Something that is **grey** is the colour of ashes or of clouds on a rainy day. करडा रंग

grey-haired adj A **grey-haired** person has grey hair. करडे केस असलेली व्यक्ती

grid (grids) n A **grid** is a pattern of straight lines that cross over each other to form squares. चौकटीची जाळी

grief n **Grief** is extreme sadness. तीव्र दुःख

grill (grills, grilling, grilled) n A **grill** is a part of a cooker where food is grilled. ग्रील ▷ vt If you **grill** food, you cook it using strong heat directly above or below it. भाजणे

grilled adj If food is **grilled**, it is cooked using strong heat directly above or below it. भाजलेला

grim (grimmer, grimmest) adj A situation or news that is **grim** is unpleasant. दुःखद

grin (grins, grinning, grinned) n A **grin** is a broad smile. मोठे हसू/स्मित ▷ vi When you **grin**, you smile broadly. मोठे स्मित करणे

grind (grinds, grinding, ground) vt When something such as corn or coffee **is ground**, it is crushed until it becomes a fine powder. दळणे

grip (grips, gripping, gripped) vt If you **grip** something, you take hold of it with your hand and continue to hold it firmly. पकडून ठेवणे

gripping adj If something is **gripping**, it holds your interest or attention. खिळवून ठेवणारे

grit n **Grit** consists of tiny pieces of stone, often put on roads in winter to make them less slippery. वाळूचे खडे

groan (groans, groaning, groaned) vi If you **groan**, you make a long, low sound because you are in pain, or because you are upset or unhappy about something. विव्हळणे

grocer (grocers) n A **grocer** is a shopkeeper who sells foods such as flour, sugar, and tinned foods. किराणा दुकानदार ▷ n A **grocer** or a **grocer's** is a small shop that sells foods such as flour, sugar, and canned goods. किराणा सामानाचे दुकान

groceries npl **Groceries** are foods you buy at a grocer's or at a supermarket. किराणा सामान

groom (grooms) n A **groom** is a man who is getting married. नवरदेव

grope (gropes, groping, groped) vi If you **grope** for something that you cannot see, you search for it with your hands. चाचपडणे

gross (grosser, grossest) adj You use **gross** to emphasize the degree to which something is unacceptable or unpleasant. असभ्य, धडधडीत, एकूण

grossly adv **Grossly** means in a manner that is unacceptable or unpleasant to a very great degree. उघडउघड, असभ्यपणे

ground (grounds, grounding, grounded) n **The ground** is the surface of the earth or the floor of a room. जमीन ▷ vt If an argument, belief, or opinion **is grounded** in something, that thing is used to justify it. आधार

ground floor (ground floors) *n* The **ground floor** of a building is the floor that is level or almost level with the ground outside. तळमजला

group (groups) *n* A **group** of people or things is a number of them together in one place at one time. गट

grouse (grouses, grouse) *n* A **grouse** is a complaint. तक्रार ▷ *n* **Grouse** are small fat birds which are often shot for sport and can be eaten. ग्राऊस पक्षी

grow (grows, growing, grew, grown) *vt* When you **grow** something, you cause it to develop or increase in size or length. वाढविणे ▷ *vi* When something or someone **grows**, they develop and increase in size or intensity. वाढणे

growl (growls, growling, growled) *vi* When a dog or other animal **growls**, it makes a low noise in its throat, usually because it is angry. गुरगुरणे

grown-up (grown-ups) *n* Children, or people talking to children, often refer to adults as **grown-ups**. प्रौढ

growth *n* The **growth** of something such as an industry, organization, or idea is its development in size, wealth, or importance. वाढ

grow up (grows up, growing up, grew up, grown up) *v* When someone **grows up**, they gradually change from being a child into being an adult. मोठे होणे *She grew up in this city.*

grub (grubs) *n* A **grub** is an insect which has just hatched from its egg. अंड्यातून नुकताच बाहेर पडलेला कीटक

grudge (grudges) *n* If you have a **grudge** against someone, you have unfriendly feelings towards them because they have harmed you in the past. अढी

gruesome *adj* Something that is **gruesome** is horrible and shocking. भयंकर

grumpy (grumpier, grumpiest) *adj* If you say that someone is **grumpy**, you think they are bad-tempered and miserable. चिडखोर

guarantee (guarantees, guaranteeing, guaranteed) *n* Something that is a **guarantee** of something else makes it certain that it will happen or that it is true. हमी ▷ *vt* If one thing **guarantees** another, the first is certain to cause the second to happen. हमी देणे

guard (guards, guarding, guarded) *n* A **guard** is someone such as a soldier, police officer, or prison officer who is guarding a particular place or person. रक्षक ▷ *vt* If you **guard** a place, person, or object, you watch them carefully, either to protect them or to stop them from escaping. रक्षण करणे

Guatemala *n* **Guatemala** is a republic in Central America. ग्वाटेमाला

guess (guesses, guessing, guessed) *n* A **guess** is an attempt to give an answer or provide an opinion when you do not know if it is true. अंदाज ▷ *v* If you **guess** something, you give an answer or provide an opinion when you do not know if it is true. अंदाज वर्तवणे

guest (guests) *n* A **guest** is someone who has been invited to stay in your home, attend an event, or appear on a radio or television show. पाहुणा

guesthouse (guesthouses) *n* A **guesthouse** is a small hotel. अतिथीगृह

guide (guides) *n* A **guide** is a book hat gives you information or instructions to help you do or understand something. मार्गदर्शक

guidebook (guidebooks) *n* A **guidebook** is a book that gives tourists information about a town, area, or country. मार्गदर्शक पुस्तक

guide dog (guide dogs) *n* A **guide dog** is a dog that has been trained to lead a blind person. मार्गदर्शक कुत्रा

guided tour (guided tours) *n* If someone takes you on a **guided tour** of a place, they show you the place and tell you about it. मार्गदर्शक सोबत असलेला प्रवास

g

guilt *n* Guilt is an unhappy feeling that you have because you have done something bad. अपराधीपणाची भावना

guilty (**guiltier, guiltiest**) *adj* If you feel **guilty**, you feel unhappy because you have done something bad or have failed to do something which you should have done. अपराधी

Guinea *n* Guinea is a republic in West Africa, on the Atlantic. गिनी

guinea pig (**guinea pigs**) *n* If someone is used as a **guinea pig** in an experiment, a drug or other treatment is tested for the first time on them. प्रयोगासाठी वापरण्यात येणारा प्राणी किंवा मनुष्य ▷ *n* A **guinea pig** is a small furry animal without a tail. गिनी पिग

guitar (**guitars**) *n* A **guitar** is a wooden musical instrument with six strings which are plucked or strummed. गिटार

Gulf States *npl* The **Gulf States** are the oil-producing states around the Persian Gulf: Iran, Iraq, Kuwait, Saudi Arabia, Bahrain, Qatar, the United Arab Emirates, and Oman. आखाती देश

gum *n* Gum is a substance, often mint-flavoured, which you chew for a long time but do not swallow. गम

gun (**guns**) *n* A **gun** is a weapon from which bullets or pellets are fired. बंदूक

gust (**gusts**) *n* A **gust** is a short, strong, sudden rush of wind. वाऱ्याचा जोरदार झोत

gut (**guts**) *n* A person's or animal's **guts** are all their internal organs. आतडे

guy (**guys**) *n* A **guy** is a man. (*informal*) पुरुष

Guyana *n* Guyana is a republic in north-east South America, on the Atlantic. गुयाना

gym (**gyms**) *n* A **gym** is a club or room, usually containing special equipment, where people can exercise. व्यायामशाळा

gymnast (**gymnasts**) *n* A **gymnast** is someone who is trained in gymnastics. कसरतपटू

gymnastics *npl* Gymnastics consists of physical exercises that develop your strength, co-ordination, and agility. कसरतीचे व्यायामप्रकार

gynaecologist (**gynaecologists**) *n* A **gynaecologist** is a doctor who specialises in women's diseases and medical conditions. स्त्रीरोग विशेषज्ञ

gypsy (**gypsies**) *n* A **gypsy** is a member of a race of people who travel from place to place in caravans, rather than living in one place. जिप्सी

h

habit (**habits**) *n* A **habit** is something that you do often or regularly. सवय

hack (**hacks, hacking, hacked**) *v* If you **hack** something or **hack** at it, you cut it with strong, rough strokes using a sharp tool such as an axe or knife. घाव घालणे

hacker (**hackers**) *n* A computer **hacker** is someone who tries to break into computer systems, especially in order to get secret information. हॅकर

haddock (**haddock**) *n* A **haddock** is a type of sea fish. हॅडॉक (एक प्रकारचा मासा)

haemorrhoids *npl* Haemorrhoids are painful swellings that can appear in the veins inside the anus. मूळव्याध

haggle (**haggles, haggling, haggled**) *vi* If you **haggle**, you argue about something before reaching an agreement, especially about the cost of something. घासाघीस करणे

hail (hails, hailing, hailed) n Hail consists of tiny balls of ice that fall like rain from the sky. गारा ▷ vt If a person or event **is hailed** as important or successful, they are praised publicly. स्तुती करणे

hair (hairs) n Your **hair** is the mass of fine thread-like strands that grow on your head. केस

hairband (hairbands) n A **hairband** is a strip of fabric or curved plastic worn by women in their hair, that fits closely over the top of the head and behind the ears. हेअर बँड

hairbrush (hairbrushes) n A **hairbrush** is a brush that you use to brush your hair. हेअर ब्रश

haircut (haircuts) n If you have a **haircut**, someone cuts your hair for you. हेअरकट

hairdo (hairdos) n A **hairdo** is the style in which your hair has been cut and arranged. (informal) केशरचना

hairdresser (hairdressers) n A **hairdresser** is a person who cuts, washes, and styles people's hair. केशरचनाकार ▷ n A **hairdresser** or a **hairdresser's** is a place where you can get your hair cut, washed, and shaped. केशरचनेचे दुकान

hairdryer (hairdryers) n A **hairdryer** is a machine that you use to dry your hair. हेअर ड्रायर

hair gel (hair gels) n Hair gel is a thick substance like jelly that you use to keep your hair in a particular style. हेअर जेल

hairgrip (hairgrips) n A **hairgrip** is a small piece of metal or plastic bent back on itself, which you use to hold your hair in position. हेअर ग्रीप

hairspray n Hairspray is a sticky substance that you spray out of a can onto your hair in order to hold it in place. हेअर स्प्रे

hairstyle (hairstyles) n Your **hairstyle** is the style in which your hair has been cut or arranged. केशरचना

hairy (hairier, hairiest) adj Someone or something that is **hairy** is covered with a lot of hair. केसाळ

Haiti n Haiti is a republic in the Caribbean, on the western side of the island of Hispaniola. हैती

half (halves) adj Half means being a half or approximately a half. अर्धा ▷ adv You use **half** to say that something is only partly the case. अर्धा ▷ n A **half** is one of two equal parts that make up a whole thing. अर्धा

half board n If you stay at a hotel and have **half board**, your breakfast and evening meal are included in the price of your stay at the hotel, but not your lunch. हाफ बोर्ड

half-hour (half-hours) n A **half-hour** is a period of 30 minutes. अर्धा तास

half-price adj If something is **half-price**, it costs only half what it usually costs. अर्ध्या किमतीत ▷ adv If you do something **half-price** or if you buy or sell something **half-price**, it costs only half what it usually costs. अर्ध्या किमतीत

half-term (half-terms) n Half-term is a short holiday in the middle of a school term. कमी कालावधीची सुट्टी

half-time n In sport, **half-time** is the short rest period between the two parts of a game. खेळातील विश्रांतीची वेळ, मध्यान्तर

halfway adv Halfway means in the middle of a place or in between two points, at an equal distance from each of them. मध्यावर

hall (halls) n In a house or flat, the **hall** is the area just inside the front door. दिवाणखाना

hallway (hallways) n A **hallway** is the entrance hall of a house or other building. दर्शनी भाग

halt (halts) n A **halt** is an interruption or end to activity, movement, or progress. थांबा

hamburger (hamburgers) n A **hamburger** is a flat round mass of minced beef, fried and eaten in a bread roll. हॅंबर्गर

hammer (**hammers**) n A **hammer** is a tool used for hitting things. It consists of a heavy piece of metal at the end of a handle. हातोडा

hammock (**hammocks**) n A **hammock** is a piece of strong cloth or netting which is hung between two supports and used as a bed. टांगलेला कापडी बिछाना

hamster (**hamsters**) n A **hamster** is a small furry animal which is similar to a mouse. हॅम्स्टर

hand (**hands, handing, handed**) n Your **hands** are the parts of your body that are at the ends of your arms, and that you use to hold things. A **hand** has four fingers and a thumb. हात ▷ vt If you **hand** something to someone, you pass it to them. देणे

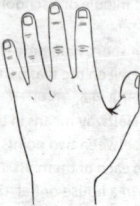

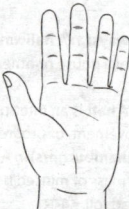

handbag (**handbags**) n A **handbag** is a small bag used by women to carry things such as money and keys. हॅंडबॅग

handball n **Handball** is a team sport in which the players try to score goals by throwing or hitting a large ball with their hand. हॅंडबॉल

handbook (**handbooks**) n A **handbook** is a book giving advice or instructions on how to do a practical task. माहितीपुस्तिका

handbrake (**handbrakes**) n In a vehicle, the **handbrake** is a brake which the driver operates with his or her hand, for example when parking. हॅंडब्रेक

handcuffs npl **Handcuffs** are two metal rings linked by a short chain which are locked round a prisoner's wrists. बेड्या

handkerchief (**handkerchiefs**) n A **handkerchief** is a small square of fabric which you use for blowing your nose. हातरुमाल

handle (**handles, handling, handled**) n A **handle** is the part of something, for example a tool or a bag, that you use to hold it. मूठ ▷ vt If you **handle** a situation, you deal with it. हाताळणे ▷ n A **handle** is something that is joined to a door, a window, or a drawer, that you use to open and close it. हॅंडल, मूठ

handlebars npl The **handlebars** of a bicycle consist of a curved metal bar with handles at each end which are used for steering. सायकलचा हॅंडल

hand luggage n When you travel by air, your **hand luggage** is the luggage you have with you in the plane, rather than the luggage that is carried elsewhere in the plane. विमानातून हाती वाहून नेण्याचे सामान

handmade adj If something is **handmade**, it is made without using machines. हाताने बनविलेली वस्तू

hands-free adj A **hands-free** phone or other device can be used without being held in your hand. हॅंड्स फ्री

hands-free kit (**hands-free kits**) n A **hands-free kit** is equipment that enables you to use your mobile phone, for example

handsome *adj* A **handsome** man has an attractive face. देखणा

handwriting *n* Your **handwriting** is your style of writing with a pen or pencil. हस्ताक्षर

handy (**handier, handiest**) *adj* Something that is **handy** is useful. उपयुक्त

hang (**hangs, hanging, hung**) *vt* If you **hang** something somewhere, you fix the top of it to something so that it does not touch the ground. लटकावणे ▷ *vi* If something **hangs** somewhere, it is attached at the top so it does not touch the ground. लटकणे

hanger (**hangers**) *n* A **hanger** is a curved piece of metal, plastic or wood used for hanging clothes on. हँगर

hang-gliding *n* **Hang-gliding** is the activity of flying from high places in a type of glider made from a large piece of cloth fixed to a frame. The pilot hangs underneath the glider. हँग ग्लायडिंग

hang on (**hangs on, hanging on, hung on**) *v* If you ask someone to **hang on**, you mean you want them to wait for a moment. *(informal)* थोडा वेळ वाट पहाणे *Hang on a second. I'll come with you.*

hangover (**hangovers**) *n* A **hangover** is a headache and feeling of sickness that you have after drinking too much alcohol. हँगओव्हर

hang up (**hangs up, hanging up, hung up**) *v* If you **hang up** or you **hang up** the phone, you end a phone call. फोन ठेऊन देणे *Don't hang up!*

hankie (**hankies**) *n* A **hankie** is a small square of fabric which you use for blowing your nose. *(informal)* हातरुमाल

happen (**happens, happening, happened**) *vi* When something **happens**, it occurs or is done without being planned. घडणे

happily *adv* You can add **happily** to a statement to show that you are glad that something happened or is true. आनंदाने

happiness *n* **Happiness** is feelings of joy or contentment. आनंद

happy (**happier, happiest**) *adj* Someone who is **happy** has feelings of joy or contentment. आनंदी

harassment *n* **Harassment** is behaviour which is intended to trouble or annoy someone, for example repeated attacks on them or attempts to cause them problems. छळ

harbour (**harbours**) *n* A **harbour** is an area of deep water which is protected from the sea by land or walls, so that boats can be left there safely. बंदर

hard (**harder, hardest**) *adj* If something is **hard**, you have to try a lot to do it or to understand it. अवघड ▷ *adj* Something that is **hard** is solid, and it is not easy to bend it or break it. कठीण ▷ *adv* If you work **hard**, you work with a lot of effort. मेहनतीचा

hardboard *n* **Hardboard** is a material which is made by pressing very small pieces of wood very closely together to form a thin, slightly flexible sheet. हार्ड बोर्ड

hard disk (**hard disks**) *n* A **hard disk** is a hard plastic disk inside a computer on which data and programs are stored. हार्ड डिस्क

hardly *adv* You use **hardly** to say that something is almost, or only just, true. क्वचित ▷ *adv* When you say things like **hardly ever** and **hardly any**, you mean almost never or almost none. क्वचित

hard shoulder (**hard shoulders**) *n* The **hard shoulder** is the area at the side of a motorway or other road where you are allowed to stop if your car breaks down. बंद पडलेल्या मोटारी रोडवर उभ्या करण्याची जागा

hard up (**harder up, hardest up**) *adj* If you are **hard up**, you have very little money. *(informal)* कंगाल

hardware *n* Computer **hardware** is computer equipment as opposed to the programs that are written for it. Printers and monitors are computer hardware. हार्डवेअर

hare (**hares**) n A **hare** is an animal like a large rabbit, but with longer ears and legs. मोठा ससा

harm (**harms**, **harming**, **harmed**) vt To **harm** a person or animal means to cause them physical injury, usually on purpose. हानी पोहोचविणे

harmful adj Something that is **harmful** has a bad effect on someone or something else. हानिकारक

harmless adj Something that is **harmless** does not have any bad effects. निरुपद्रवी

harp (**harps**) n A **harp** is a large musical instrument consisting of a triangular frame with vertical strings which you pluck with your fingers. हार्प

harsh (**harsher**, **harshest**) adj **Harsh** climates or living conditions are very difficult for people, animals, and plants to exist in. प्रतिकूल, कठोर

harvest (**harvests**, **harvesting**, **harvested**) n The **harvest** is the gathering of a crop. सुगी ▷ vt When you **harvest** a crop, you gather it in. कापणी करणे

hastily adv If you do something **hastily**, you do it in a hurry, without planning or preparation. घाईघाईने

hat (**hats**) n A **hat** is a covering that you wear on your head. हॅट

hatchback (**hatchbacks**) n A **hatchback** is a car with an extra door at the back which opens upwards. हॅचबॅक

hate (**hates**, **hating**, **hated**) vt If you **hate** someone or something, you have an extremely strong feeling of dislike for them. द्वेष करणे

hatred n **Hatred** is an extremely strong feeling of dislike for someone or something. द्वेष

haunted adj A **haunted** building or other place is one where a ghost regularly appears. भुतांनी झपाटलेले

have (**has**, **having**, **had**) v You use **have** and **has** with another verb to form the present perfect. वर्तमानकाळाचे पूर्णकाळदर्शक सहाय्यकारी रूप Alex hasn't left yet. ▷ v When you **have**

something, you feel it, or it happens to you. लागण होणे I have a bad cold.

have to (**has to**, **having to**, **had to**) v You use **have to** when you are saying that something is necessary, obligatory, or must happen. If you do not **have to** do something, it is not necessary or obligatory for you to do it. एखादी गोष्ट करावीच लागणे He had to go to Germany.

hawthorn (**hawthorns**) n A **hawthorn** is a small tree which has sharp thorns and produces white or pink flowers. एक काटेरी झुडूप

hay n **Hay** is grass which has been cut and dried so that it can be used to feed animals. वाळलेले गवत, कडबा

hay fever n If someone suffers from **hay fever**, they have an allergy to pollen which makes their nose, throat, and eyes become red and swollen. विशिष्ट गवताच्या तुसापासून होणारी बाधा

haystack (**haystacks**) n A **haystack** is a large, solid pile of hay, often covered with a straw roof to protect it, which is left in the field until it is needed. गवताची गंजी

hazard warning lights npl The **hazard warning lights** on a motor vehicle are small lights set to flash all at the same time to indicate that the vehicle is stopped and blocking the traffic. धोक्याची सूचना देणारा दिवा

hazelnut (**hazelnuts**) n **Hazelnuts** are nuts from a hazel tree, which can be eaten. हेझलनट

he pron You use **he** to talk about a man, a boy, or a male animal. तो He could never remember all our names.

head (**heads**, **heading**, **headed**) n The **head** of something is the person who is its leader. प्रमुख ▷ n Your **head** is the part of your body at the top that has your eyes, ears, nose, mouth, and brain in it. डोके ▷ vt If someone or something **heads** a line, they are at the front of it. नेतृत्व करणे

headache (**headaches**) n If you have a **headache**, you have a pain in your head. डोकेदुखी

headlight (headlights) n A vehicle's **headlights** are the large bright lights at the front of it. वाहनाचे पुढील दिवे

headline (headlines) n A **headline** is the title of a newspaper story, printed in large letters at the top of it. मथळा

head office (head offices) n The **head office** of a company is its main office. मुख्य कार्यालय

headphones npl **Headphones** are small speakers which you wear over your ears in order to listen to music or other sounds without other people hearing. हेडफोन्स

headquarters npl The **headquarters** of an organization are its main offices. **Headquarters** can take the singular or plural form of the verb. मुख्यालय

headroom n **Headroom** is the amount of space below a roof or bridge. छताखालची किंवा पुलाखालची मोकळी जागा

headscarf (headscarves) n A **headscarf** is a piece of cloth which some women wear around their heads, for example to keep their hair neat, or as part of their religious beliefs. डोक्याला बांधण्याचा रुमाल

headteacher (headteachers) n A **headteacher** is a teacher who is in charge of a school. मुख्याध्यापक

heal (heals, healing, healed) vi When an injury such as a broken bone **heals**, it becomes healthy and normal again. जखम बरी होणे

health n Your **health** is the condition of your body. आरोग्य

healthy (healthier, healthiest) adj Someone who is **healthy** is well and strong and is not often ill. निरोगी ▷ adj Something that is **healthy** is good for you. आरोग्यदायी

heap (heaps) n A **heap** of things is a messy pile of them. ढीग

hear (hears, hearing, heard) v When you **hear** sounds, you are aware of them because they reach your ears. ऐकणे

hearing n **Hearing** is the sense which makes it possible for you to be aware of sounds. श्रवण

hearing aid (hearing aids) n A **hearing aid** is a device which people with hearing difficulties wear in their ear to enable them to hear better. श्रवणयंत्र

heart (hearts) n Your **heart** is the organ in your chest that pumps the blood around your body. हृदय

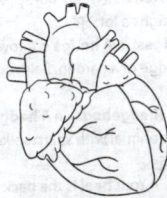

heart attack (heart attacks) n If someone has a **heart attack**, their heart begins to beat irregularly or stops completely. हृदय विकाराचा झटका

heartbroken adj Someone who is **heartbroken** is extremely sad and upset. दु:खी

heartburn n **Heartburn** is a painful burning sensation in your chest, caused by indigestion. हृदयदाह

heat (heats, heating, heated) n **Heat** is warmth or the quality of being hot. उष्णता ▷ vt When you **heat** something, you raise its temperature, for example by using a flame or a special piece of equipment. उष्णता देणे

heater (heaters) n A **heater** is a piece of equipment which is used to warm a place or to heat water. हीटर

heather n **Heather** is a low spreading plant with small purple, pink, or white flowers that grows wild on hills or moorland. हीथर

heating n **Heating** is the process or equipment involved in keeping a building warm. गरम करण्याची क्रिया

heat up (**heats up, heating up, heated up**) v When you **heat** something **up**, especially food which has already been cooked and allowed to go cold, you make it hot. गरम करणे *She heated up some soup for me.*

heaven n In some religions, **heaven** is said to be the place where God lives and where good people go when they die. स्वर्ग

heavily adv You can use **heavily** to indicate that something is great in amount, degree, or intensity. जोराने

heavy (**heavier, heaviest**) adj Something that is **heavy** weighs a lot. जड

hedge (**hedges**) n A **hedge** is a row of bushes along the edge of a garden, field, or road. झुडपांचे कुंपण

hedgehog (**hedgehogs**) n A **hedgehog** is a small brown animal with sharp spikes covering its back. साळू

heel (**heels**) n Your **heel** is the back part of your foot, just below your ankle. टाच

height (**heights**) n The **height** of a person or thing is their measurement from bottom to top. उंची

heir (**heirs**) n Someone's **heir** is the person who will inherit their money, property, or title when they die. वारस

heiress (**heiresses**) n An **heiress** is a woman who will inherit property, money, or a title. स्त्री वारसदार

helicopter (**helicopters**) n A **helicopter** is an aircraft with no wings. It hovers or moves vertically and horizontally by means of large overhead blades which rotate. हेलिकॉप्टर

hell n According to some religions, **hell** is the place where the Devil lives, and where wicked people are sent to be punished when they die. नरक

hello! excl You say '**hello!**' to someone when you meet them. नमस्कार

helmet (**helmets**) n A **helmet** is a hard hat which you wear to protect your head. हेल्मेट

help (**helps, helping, helped**) excl You shout '**help!**' when you are in danger in order to attract someone's attention so that they can come and rescue you. धावा! मदत करा! ▷ n **Help** is the act of helping. मदत ▷ v If you **help** someone, you make something easier for them to do, for example by doing part of their work or by giving them advice or money. मदत करणे

helpful adj If someone is **helpful**, they help you by doing work for you or by giving you advice or information. मदत करण्यात तत्पर

helpline (**helplines**) n A **helpline** is a special telephone service that people can call to get advice about a particular subject. हेल्पलाईन

hen (**hens**) n A **hen** is a female chicken. कोंबडी

hen night (**hen nights**) n A **hen night** is a party for a woman who is getting married very soon, to which only women are invited. हेन नाईट

hepatitis n **Hepatitis** is a serious disease which affects the liver. कावीळ

her det You use **her** to say that something belongs to a woman or a girl. तिचा *I borrowed her pen.* ▷ pron You use **her** to talk about a woman or a girl. तिला *I had something to say to her.*

herbal tea (**herbal teas**) n Herbal tea is tea made from or using herbs. हर्बल टी/ वनौषधींपासून बनवलेला चहा

herbs npl **Herbs** are plants whose leaves are used in cookery to add flavour to food, or as a medicine. वनौषधी

here adv **Here** means the place where you are. येथे

hereditary adj A **hereditary** characteristic or illness is passed on to a child from its parents before it is born. आनुवंशिक

heritage (**heritages**) n A country's **heritage** consists of all the qualities and traditions that have continued over many years, especially when they are considered to be of historical importance. परंपरा

hernia (hernias) *n* A **hernia** is a medical condition in which one of your internal organs sticks through a weak point in the surrounding tissue. हर्निया/अंतर्गळ

hero (heroes) *n* The **hero** of a book, play, or film is the main male character, who usually has good qualities. नायक

heroine (heroines) *n* The **heroine** of a book, play, or film is its main female character, who usually has good qualities. नायिका

heron (herons) *n* A **heron** is a large bird which has long legs and a long beak, and which eats fish. बगळा

herring (herring, herrings) *n* A **herring** is a long silver-coloured fish. हेरिंग नावाचा मासा

hers *pron* You use **hers** to say that something belongs to a woman or a girl. तिचा *She said that the bag was hers.*

herself *pron* You use **herself** when you want to say that something a woman or a girl does has an effect on her. तिने स्वत: *She pulled herself out of the water.*

hesitate (hesitates, hesitating, hesitated) *vi* If you **hesitate**, you pause slightly while you are doing something or just before you do it, usually because you are uncertain, embarrassed, or worried. काही करण्यापूर्वी विचार वा काचकूच करणे

HGV *abbr* An **HGV** is a large vehicle such as a lorry. **HGV** is an abbreviation for 'heavy goods vehicle'. अवजड वाहन

hi! *excl* In informal situations, you say '**hi!**' to greet someone. हाय! (अभिवादन)

hiccups *npl* When you have **hiccups**, you make repeated sharp sounds in your throat, often because you have been eating or drinking too quickly. उचकी

hidden *adj* Something that is **hidden** is not easily noticed. लपलेला

hide (hides, hiding, hid, hidden) *vt* If you **hide** something, you put it where no one can see it or find it. लपविणे ▷ *vi* If you **hide**, you go

somewhere where people cannot easily find you. लपणे ▷ *vt* If you **hide** what you feel, you do not let people know about it. लपविणे

hide-and-seek *n* **Hide-and-seek** is a children's game in which one player covers his or her eyes until the other players have hidden themselves, and then he or she tries to find them. लपंडाव

hideous *adj* If you say that someone or something is **hideous**, you mean that they are extremely unpleasant or ugly. विद्रूप

hifi (hifis) *n* A **hifi** is a set of equipment on which you play CDs and tapes, and which produces stereo sound of very good quality. हायफाय

high (higher, highest) *adj* Something that is **high** is tall or is a long way above the ground. उंच ▷ *adv* If items are piled **high**, they are arranged in a tall pile. उंच ▷ *adj* **High** means great in amount or strength. खूप ▷ *adj* A **high** sound or voice goes up a long way. मोठा

highchair (highchairs) *n* A **highchair** is a chair with long legs for a small child to sit in while they are eating. उंच खुर्ची

higher education *n* **Higher education** is education at universities and colleges. उच्चशिक्षण

high-heeled *adj* **High-heeled** shoes are women's shoes that have high heels. उंच टाचांचे

high heels *npl* You can refer to women's shoes that have high heels as **high heels**. उंच टाचांचे

high jump *n* The **high jump** is an athletics event which involves jumping over a raised bar. उंच उडी

highlight (**highlights, highlighting, highlighted**) *n* The **highlights** of an event, activity, or period of time are the most interesting or exciting parts of it. क्षणचित्रे ▷ *vt* If you **highlight** a point or problem, you draw attention to it. एखाद्या मुद्द्यावर प्रकाश टाकणे

highlighter (**highlighters**) *n* A **highlighter** is a pen with brightly coloured ink that is used to mark parts of a document. कागदावरील महत्त्वाच्या ओळीना रंग देणारे पेन

high-rise (**high-rises**) *n* A **high-rise** is a modern building which is very tall and has many levels or floors. खूप उंच इमारत

high season *n* The **high season** is the time of year when a place has most tourists or visitors. गर्दीचा हंगाम

Highway Code *n* The **Highway Code** is an official book which contains the rules which tell people how to use public roads safely. रस्त्यावर कसे वागावे याचे नियम

hijack (**hijacks, hijacking, hijacked**) *vt* If someone **hijacks** a plane or other vehicle, they illegally take control of it by force while it is travelling from one place to another. वाहनाचे अपहरण करणे

hijacker (**hijackers**) *n* A **hijacker** is a person who hijacks a plane or other vehicle. अपहरणकर्ता

hike (**hikes**) *n* A **hike** is a long walk in the country, especially one that you go on for pleasure. शहराबाहेरची दूरवरची रपेट

hiking *n* **Hiking** is the activity of going on long walks in the country, especially for pleasure. शहराबाहेरची दूरवरची रपेट करणे

hilarious *adj* If something is **hilarious**, it is extremely funny. विनोदी

hill (**hills**) *n* A **hill** is an area of land that is higher than the land that surrounds it, but not as high as a mountain. टेकडी

hill-walking *n* **Hill-walking** is the activity of walking through hilly country for pleasure. टेकड्यांवरून भटकणे

him *pron* You use **him** to talk about a man or a boy. त्याला *We met him at the station.*

himself *pron* You use **himself** when you want to say that something a man or a boy does has an effect on him. तो स्वत: *He fell and hurt himself.*

Hindu (**Hindus**) *adj* **Hindu** is used to describe things that belong or relate to Hinduism. हिंदू ▷ *n* A **Hindu** is a person who believes in Hinduism. हिंदू

Hinduism *n* **Hinduism** is an Indian religion, which has many gods and teaches that people have another life on earth after they die. हिंदू धर्म

hinge (**hinges**) *n* A **hinge** is a moveable joint made of metal, wood, or plastic that joins two things so that one of them can swing freely. बिजागरे

hint (**hints, hinting, hinted**) *n* A **hint** is a suggestion about something that is made in an indirect way. सूचक गोष्ट ▷ *vi* If you **hint** at something, you suggest it in an indirect way. अप्रत्यक्षपणे सुचवणे

hip (**hips**) *n* Your **hips** are the two areas or bones at the sides of your body between the tops of your legs and your waist. नितंब

hippie (**hippies**) *n* In the 1960s and 1970s, **hippies** were people who rejected conventional society and tried to live a life based on peace and love. हिप्पी

hippo (**hippos**) *n* A **hippo** is a hippopotamus. *(informal)* पाणघोडा

hippopotamus (**hippopotami, hippopotamuses**) *n* A **hippopotamus** is a very large African animal with short legs and thick, hairless skin. Hippopotamuses live in and near rivers. पाणघोडा

hire (**hires, hiring, hired**) *n* You use **hire** to refer to the activity or business of hiring something. भाडे ▷ *vt* If you **hire** someone, you employ them or pay them to do a particular job for you. भाड्याने देणे

his *det* You use **his** to say that something belongs to a man or a boy. त्याचा *He showed* me his new football. ▷ *pron* You use **his** to say that something belongs to a man or a boy. त्याचा *He listened to the advice, but the decision was his.*

historian (**historians**) *n* A **historian** is a person who specializes in the study of history and who writes about it. इतिहासतज्ज्ञ

historical *adj* **Historical** people, situations, or things existed in the past and are considered to be a part of history. ऐतिहासिक

history (**histories**) *n* You can refer to the events of the past as **history**. You can also refer to the past events which concern a particular topic or place as its **history**. इतिहास

hit (**hits, hitting**) *n* A **hit** is the act of a moving object touching another object very quickly or hard. फटका ▷ *vt* If you **hit** something, you touch it with a lot of strength. फटका मारणे

hitch (**hitches**) *n* A **hitch** is a slight problem. छोटी समस्या

hitchhike (**hitchhikes, hitchhiking, hitchhiked**) *vi* If you **hitchhike**, you travel by getting free lifts from passing vehicles. लिफ्ट मागणे

hitchhiker (**hitchhikers**) *n* A **hitchhiker** is someone who travels somewhere by getting free lifts from passing vehicles. लिफ्ट मागणारा

hitchhiking *n* **Hitchhiking** is the activity or process of travelling by getting lifts from passing vehicles without paying. लिफ्ट

HIV-negative *adj* If someone is **HIV-negative**, they are not infected with the HIV virus, which reduces the ability of people's bodies to fight illness and which can cause AIDS. एचआयव्हीची बाधा न झालेले

HIV-positive *adj* If someone is **HIV-positive**, they are infected with the HIV virus, which reduces the ability of people's bodies to fight illness, and they may develop AIDS. एचआयव्हीची बाधा झालेले

hobby (**hobbies**) *n* A **hobby** is something that you enjoy doing in your spare time, for example reading or playing tennis. छंद

hockey *n* **Hockey** is a sport played between two teams of 11 players who use long curved sticks to hit a small ball and try to score goals. हॉकी

hold (**holds, holding, held**) *vt* When you **hold** something, you have it in your hands or your arms. पकडणे ▷ *vt* If something **holds** an amount of something, then that is how much it has room for inside. सामावण्याची क्षमता असणे

holdall (**holdalls**) *n* A **holdall** is a strong bag which you use to carry your clothes and other things, for example when you are travelling. प्रवासाला जाताना सामान ठेवण्याची बॅग

hold on (**holds on, holding on, held on**) *v* If you **hold on** or **hold onto** something, you keep your hand firmly round something. पकडून ठेवणे *He held on to a coffee cup.*

hold up (**holds up, holding up, held up, hold-ups**) *v* If someone or something **holds you up**, they delay you. अडवून धरणे *Why were you holding everyone up?* ▷ *n* A **hold-up** is a situation in which someone is threatened with a weapon in order to make them hand over money or valuables. शस्त्राचा धाक दाखवून लुटणे

hole (**holes**) *n* A **hole** is an opening or hollow space in something. भोक

holiday (**holidays**) *n* A **holiday** is a period of time during which you relax and enjoy yourself away from home. सुट्टी

Holland *n* **Holland** is another name for the Netherlands. हॉलंड

hollow *adj* Something that is **hollow** has a hole or space inside it. पोकळ

holly (hollies) n **Hollies** are a group of evergreen trees and shrubs which have hard, shiny, prickly leaves, and also have bright red berries in winter. होली या सदाहरित वृक्षांचा समूह

holy (holier, holiest) adj Something that is **holy** is considered to be special because it relates to God or to a particular religion. पवित्र

home (homes) adv **Home** means to or at the place where you live. ▷ n Your **home** is the place where you live. घर

home address (home addresses) n Your **home address** is the address of your house or flat. घरचा पत्ता

homeland (homelands) n Your **homeland** is your native country. (written) स्वदेश

homeless adj **Homeless** people have nowhere to live. बेघर

home-made adj **Home-made** things are made in someone's home, rather than in a shop or factory. घरी बनवलेला

home match (home matches) n When a sports team plays a **home match**, they play a game on their own ground, rather than on the opposing team's ground. (खेळासंबंधी) यजमान संघाचे मैदान

homeopathic adj **Homeopathic** means relating to or used in homeopathy. होमिओपॅथिक

homeopathy n **Homeopathy** is a way of treating illness in which the patient is given very small amounts of a drug which would produce symptoms of the illness if taken in large quantities. होमिओपथी

home page (home pages) n On the Internet, a person's or organization's **home page** is the main page of information about them. होम पेज

homesick adj If you are **homesick**, you feel unhappy because you are away from home and are missing your family and friends. घरची आठवण येणारी व्यक्ति

homework n **Homework** is school work given to pupils to do at home. गृहपाठ

Honduras n **Honduras** is a republic in Central America. होंडुरास

honest adj If you describe someone as **honest**, you mean that they always tell the truth, and do not try to deceive people or break the law. प्रामाणिक

honestly adv If you do something **honestly**, you are truthful, and do not try to deceive people or break the law. प्रामाणिकपणे

honesty n **Honesty** is honest behaviour. प्रामाणिकपणा

honey (honeys) n **Honey** is a sweet, sticky, edible substance made by bees. मध

honeymoon (honeymoons) n A **honeymoon** is a holiday taken by a couple who have just married. मधुचंद्र

honeysuckle (honeysuckles) n **Honeysuckle** is a climbing plant with sweet-smelling yellow, pink, or white flowers. हनिसकल नावाची वेल

honour n **Honour** means doing what you believe to be right and being confident that you have done what is right. सन्मान

hood (hoods) n A **hood** is a part of some pieces of clothing which covers your head. हूड (टोपडे)

hook (hooks) n A **hook** is a bent piece of metal or plastic that is used for catching or holding things, or for hanging things up. हूक

hooray! excl People sometimes shout '**hooray!**' when they are very happy and excited about something. उत्साहाच्या भरात हुर्रे असा केलेला चित्कार

hoover (hoovers, hoovering, hoovered) v If you **hoover** a carpet, you clean it using a vacuum cleaner. व्हॅक्यूम क्लिनरच्या सहाय्याने गालिचा साफ करणे

Hoover® (hoovers) n A **Hoover** is an electric machine which sucks up dust and dirt from carpets. हूवर

hop (hops, hopping, hopped) vi If you **hop**, you jump on one foot. एका पायावर उड्या मारणे ▷ vi When animals or birds **hop**, they jump with two feet together. दोन पायांवर उड्या मारणे

hope (hopes, hoping, hoped) n **Hope** is a feeling of desire and expectation that things will go well in the future. आशा ▷ v If you **hope** that something is true, or if you **hope** for something, you want it to be true or to happen, and you usually believe that it is possible or likely. आशा व्यक्त करणे

hopeful adj If you are **hopeful**, you are fairly confident that something that you want to happen will happen. आशावादी

hopefully adv **Hopefully** is often used when mentioning something that you hope and are fairly confident will happen. अशी आशा करू या की...

hopeless adj If you feel **hopeless**, you feel desperate because there seems to be no possibility of success. निराश

horizon n The **horizon** is the distant line where the sky seems to touch the land or the sea. क्षितिज

horizontal adj Something that is **horizontal** is flat and parallel with the ground. क्षितिजासमांतर आडवी

hormone (hormones) n A **hormone** is a chemical, usually occurring naturally in your body, that stimulates certain organs of your body. संप्रेरक

horn (horns) n On a vehicle such as a car, the **horn** is the device that makes a loud noise. भोंगा, हॉर्न ▷ n A **horn** is one of the hard bones with sharp points that grow out of some animals' heads. Goats and bulls have **horns**. शिंग ▷ n A **horn** is an instrument that you blow into to make music. कर्णा, फुंकायचे शिंग

horoscope (horoscopes) n Your **horoscope** is a forecast of events which some people believe will happen to you in the future, based on the position of the stars when you were born. कुंडली

horrendous adj Something that is **horrendous** is very bad or unpleasant. भयानक

horrible adj If you say that someone or something is **horrible**, you mean that they are very unpleasant. *(informal)* भयंकर

horrifying adj If you describe something as **horrifying**, you mean that it is shocking or disgusting. भयंकर

horror n **Horror** is a strong feeling of alarm caused by something extremely unpleasant. भीती

horror film (horror films) n A **horror film** is a film that is intended to be very frightening. भयपट

horse (horses) n A **horse** is a large animal which people can ride. घोडा

horse racing n **Horse racing** is a sport in which horses ridden by people called jockeys run in races, sometimes jumping over fences. घोड्यांची शर्यत

horseradish n **Horseradish** is a small white vegetable that is the root of a crop. It has a very strong sharp taste and is often made into a sauce. एक प्रकारचा मुळा

horse riding n **Horse riding** is the activity of riding a horse, especially for enjoyment or as a form of exercise. घोड्यावर केलेली रपेट

horseshoe (horseshoes) n A **horseshoe** is a piece of metal shaped like a U which is fixed to a horse's hoof. घोड्याचा नाल

hose (hoses) n A **hose** is a long, flexible pipe through which water is carried in order to do things such as put out fires or water gardens. पाण्याचा लवचिक लांबलचक पाईप

hosepipe (hosepipes) n A **hosepipe** is a hose that people use to water their gardens or wash their cars. बागेला पाणी देण्याचा लवचिक लांबलचक पाईप

hospital (hospitals) n A **hospital** is a place where people who are ill are looked after by doctors and nurses. रुग्णालय

hospitality n **Hospitality** is friendly, welcoming behaviour towards guests or strangers. आदरातिथ्य

host (hosts) n The **host** at a party is the person who has invited everybody. यजमान ▷ n A **host** of things is a lot of them. मोठी संख्या, समुदाय

hostage (hostages) n A **hostage** is someone who has been captured by a person or organization and who may be killed or injured if people do not do what that person or organization demands. ओलीस ठेवलेली व्यक्ती

hostel (hostels) n A **hostel** is a large house where people can stay cheaply for a short time. वसतिगृह

hostile adj If someone is **hostile** to another person or to an idea or suggestion, they show their dislike for them in an aggressive way. आक्रमक, प्रतिकूल

hot (hotter, hottest) adj If something is **hot**, it has a high temperature. गरम

hot dog (hot dogs) n A **hot dog** is a long bread roll with a sausage in it. हॉट डॉग

hotel (hotels) n A **hotel** is a building where people stay, paying for their rooms and meals. हॉटेल

hot-water bottle (hot-water bottles) n A **hot-water bottle** is a rubber container that you fill with hot water and put in a bed to make it warm. गरम पाण्याची बाटली

hour (hours) n An **hour** is a period of sixty minutes. तास

hourly adj An **hourly** event happens once every hour. तासागणिक ▷ adv If something happens **hourly**, it happens once every hour. तासागणिक

house (houses) n A **house** is a building in which people live. घर

household (households) n A **household** is all the people in a family or group who live together in a house. कुटुंब

housewife (housewives) n A **housewife** is a married woman who does not have a paid job, but instead looks after her home and children. गृहिणी

house wine (house wines) n A restaurant's **house wine** is the cheapest wine it sells, which is not listed by name on the wine list. हाउस वाइन

housework n **Housework** is the work such as cleaning and cooking that you do in your home. घरकाम

hovercraft (hovercraft) n A **hovercraft** is a vehicle that can travel across land and water. It floats above the land or water on a cushion of air. हॉवरक्राफ्ट

how adv You use the word **how** when you ask about the way that something happens or the way that you do something. कसा ▷ adv You use **how** when you ask about an amount. किती

however adv You use **however** when you are saying something that somebody might not expect because of what you have just said. तथापि

howl (howls, howling, howled) vi If an animal such as a wolf or a dog **howls**, it makes a long, loud, crying sound. केकाटणे, गळा काढणे

HQ (HQs) abbr The **HQ** of an organization is the centre or building from which its operations are directed. **HQ** is an abbreviation for 'headquarters'. मुख्यालय

hubcap (hubcaps) n A **hubcap** is a metal or plastic disc that covers and protects the centre of a wheel on a car, truck, or other vehicle. हबकॅप

hug (hugs, hugging, hugged) n If you give someone a **hug**, you put your arms around them and hold them tightly, for example because you like them or are pleased to see them. मिठी ▷ vt When you **hug** someone, you put your arms around them and hold them tightly, for example because you like them or are pleased to see them. You can also say that two people hug each other or that they **hug**. प्रेमाने मिठी मारणे

huge (huger, hugest) adj Something that is **huge** is extremely large in size, amount, or degree. प्रचंड

hull (hulls) n The **hull** of a boat is the main part of its body. गलबताचा मुख्य भाग वा सांगाडा

hum (hums, humming, hummed) vi If something **hums**, it makes a low continuous noise. गुंजन करणे, घोंगावणे

human adj **Human** means relating to or concerning people. मानवी

human being (human beings) n A **human being** is a man, woman, or child. मानव

humanitarian adj If a person or society has **humanitarian** ideas or behaviour, they try to avoid making people suffer or they help people who are suffering. माणुसकीच्या नात्याने

human rights npl **Human rights** are basic rights which many societies believe that all people should have. मानवी हक्क

humble (humbler, humblest) adj A **humble** person is not proud and does not believe that they are better than other people. नम्र

humid adj You use **humid** to describe an atmosphere or climate that is very damp, and usually very hot. दमट

humidity n **Humidity** is dampness in the air. आर्द्रता

humorous adj If someone or something is **humorous**, they are amusing, especially in a clever or witty way. विनोदी

humour n You can refer to the amusing things that people say as their **humour**. विनोद

hundred num A **hundred** is the number 100. शंभर

Hungarian (Hungarians) adj **Hungarian** means belonging or relating to Hungary, or to its people, language, or culture. हंगेरियन ▷ n A **Hungarian** is a person who comes from Hungary. हंगेरियन

Hungary n **Hungary** is a republic in central Europe. हंगेरी

hunger n **Hunger** is the feeling of weakness or discomfort that you get when you need something to eat. भूक

hungry (hungrier, hungriest) adj When you are **hungry**, you want food. भुकेला

hunt (hunts, hunting, hunted) vi If you **hunt** for something, you try to find it. शोधणे ▷ v

When animals **hunt**, they chase another animal to kill it for food. शिकार करणे

hunter (hunters) n A **hunter** is a person who hunts wild animals for food or as a sport. शिकारी

hunting n **Hunting** is the chasing and killing of wild animals by people or other animals, for food or as a sport. शिकार

hurdle (hurdles) n A **hurdle** is a difficulty that you must overcome in order to achieve something. अडथळा

hurricane (hurricanes) n A **hurricane** is a very violent storm with strong winds. मोठे वादळ

hurry (hurries, hurrying, hurried) n If you are in a **hurry** to do something, you need or want to do something quickly. If you do something in a **hurry**, you do it quickly or suddenly. घाई ▷ vi If you **hurry** somewhere, you go there quickly. घाईघाईने जाणे

hurry up (hurries up, hurrying up, hurried up) v If you tell someone to **hurry up**, you are telling them to do something more quickly. घाई करणे *Hurry up with that coffee, will you.*

hurt (hurts, hurting, hurt) adj If you are **hurt**, you have been injured. जखमी ▷ vt If you **hurt** yourself or **hurt** a part of your body, you feel pain because you have injured yourself. जखमी करणे

husband (husbands) n A woman's **husband** is the man she is married to. पती

hut (huts) n A **hut** is a small, simple building, often made of wood, mud, or grass. झोपडी

hyacinth (hyacinths) n A **hyacinth** is a plant with a lot of small, sweet-smelling flowers growing closely around a single stem. It grows from a bulb and the flowers are usually blue, pink, or white. हायसिंथ नावाची वनस्पती

hydrogen n **Hydrogen** is a colourless gas that is very light. हायड्रोजन

hygiene n **Hygiene** is the practice of keeping yourself and your surroundings clean, especially in order to prevent the spread of disease. आरोग्य

hypermarket (hypermarkets) n A
hypermarket is a very large supermarket.
हायपर मार्केट

hyphen (hyphens) n A **hyphen** is the
punctuation sign (-) used to join words
together. संयोचिन्ह, जोडरेघ

i

I pron You use **I** to talk about yourself. मी I like
cats.

ice n **Ice** is frozen water. बर्फ

iceberg (icebergs) n An **iceberg** is a large, tall
piece of ice floating in the sea. हिमनग

icebox (iceboxes) n An **icebox** is a container
which is kept cool so that the food and drink
inside stays fresh. (old-fashioned) बर्फाची पेटी

ice cream (ice creams) n **Ice cream** is a very
cold sweet food made from frozen milk, fats,
and sugar. आईस्क्रिम

ice cube (ice cubes) n An **ice cube** is a small
square block of ice that you put into a drink in
order to make it cold. बर्फाचे केलेले चौकोनी तुकडे

ice hockey n **Ice hockey** is a game like hockey
played on ice. आईस हॉकी

Iceland n **Iceland** is an island republic in the
North Atlantic, regarded as part of Europe.
आईसलंड

Icelandic adj **Icelandic** means belonging or
relating to Iceland, or to its people, language,

or culture. आईसलँडिक ▷ n **Icelandic** is the
official language of Iceland. आईसलँडिक

ice lolly (ice lollies) n An **ice lolly** is a piece
of flavoured ice or ice cream on a stick. आईस
लॉली

ice rink (ice rinks) n An **ice rink** is a level
area of ice, usually inside a building, that has
been made artificially and kept frozen so that
people can skate on it. आईस रिंक

ice-skating n **Ice-skating** is a sport or leisure
activity which involves people moving about
on ice wearing ice-skates. बर्फावरील स्केटिंग

icing n **Icing** is a sweet substance made from
powdered sugar that is used to cover and
decorate cakes. आयसिंग

icing sugar n **Icing sugar** is very fine white
sugar that is used for making icing and sweets.
आयसिंग शुगर

icon (icons) n If you describe something or
someone as an **icon**, you mean that they
are important as a symbol of something.
अनुकरणीय व्यक्ती

icy (icier, iciest) adj **Icy** air or water is
extremely cold. अति थंड

ID card (ID cards) n An **ID card** is a card with
a person's name, photograph, date of birth,
and other information on it. ओळखपत्र

idea (ideas) n An **idea** is a plan or suggestion.
कल्पना

ideal adj The **ideal** person or thing for a
particular purpose is the best one for it. आदर्श

ideally adv If you say that **ideally** a particular
thing should happen or be done, you mean
that this is what you would like to happen or
be done, but you know that this may not be
possible or practical. आदर्श रीतीने

identical adj Things that are **identical** are
exactly the same. एकसारखा

identification n When someone asks you
for **identification**, they are asking to see
something such as a passport which proves
who you are. ओळख

identify (identifies, identifying, identified)
vt If you can **identify** someone or something,

you can recognize them and say who or what they are. ओळखणे

identity (**identities**) n Your **identity** is who you are. ओळख

identity card (**identity cards**) n An **identity card** is a card with a person's name, photograph, date of birth, and other information about them on it. ओळखपत्र

identity theft n **Identity theft** is the crime of getting personal information about another person without their knowledge, for example in order to gain access to their bank account. चोरून प्राप्त केलेली गुप्त माहिती

ideology (**ideologies**) n An **ideology** is a set of beliefs, especially the political beliefs on which people, parties, or countries base their actions. विचारधारा, मतप्रणाली

idiot (**idiots**) n If you call someone an **idiot**, you mean that they are very stupid. मूर्ख

idiotic adj If you call someone or something **idiotic**, you mean that they are very stupid or silly. मूर्खपणाचे

idle adj If you describe someone as **idle** you disapprove of them not doing anything when they should be doing something. बिनकामाचा

i.e. abbr **i.e.** is used to introduce a word or sentence which makes what you have just said clearer or gives details. म्हणजेच

if conj You use **if** to talk about things that might happen, or that might have happened. जर *You can go if you want.* ❑ *If he was there, I didn't see him.*

ignition (**ignitions**) n In a car, the **ignition** is the mechanism which lights the fuel and starts the engine, usually operated by turning a key. इग्निशन

ignorance n **Ignorance** of something is lack of knowledge about it. अज्ञान

ignorant adj If you refer to someone as **ignorant**, you mean that they do not know much because they are not well educated. If someone is **ignorant** of a fact, they do not know it. अज्ञानी

ignore (**ignores**, **ignoring**, **ignored**) vt If you **ignore** someone or something, you deliberately take no notice of them. दुर्लक्ष करणे

ill adj Someone who is **ill** is suffering from a disease or a health problem. आजारी

illegal adj If something is **illegal**, the law says that it is not allowed. बेकायदेशीर

illegible adj Writing that is **illegible** is so unclear that you cannot read it. वाचता न येण्याजोगे

illiterate adj Someone who is **illiterate** cannot read or write. निरक्षर

illness (**illnesses**) n **Illness** is the fact or experience of being ill. आजारपण

ill-treat (**ill-treats**, **ill-treating**, **ill-treated**) vt If someone **ill-treats** you, they treat you badly or cruelly. क्रूरपणे वागणे

illusion (**illusions**) n An **illusion** is something that appears to exist or to be a particular thing but in reality does not exist or is something else. आभास

illustration (**illustrations**) n An **illustration** of something is a clear example of it. उदाहरण

image (**images**) n If you have an **image** of someone or something, you have a picture or idea of them in your mind. प्रतिमा

imaginary adj An **imaginary** person, place, or thing exists only in your mind or in a story, and not in real life. काल्पनिक

imagination (**imaginations**) n Your **imagination** is your ability to form pictures or ideas in your mind of new, exciting, or imaginary things. कल्पना

imagine (**imagines**, **imagining**, **imagined**) vt If you **imagine** a situation, your mind forms a picture or idea of it. कल्पना करणे

imitate (**imitates**, **imitating**, **imitated**) vt If you **imitate** someone, you copy what they do or produce. नक्कल करणे

imitation (**imitations**) n An **imitation** of something is a copy of it. नक्कल

immature adj Something that is **immature** is not yet fully developed. अविकसित

immediate adj An **immediate** result, action, or reaction happens or is done without any delay. तात्काळ

immediately adv If something happens **immediately**, it happens without any delay. ताबडतोब

immigrant (**immigrants**) n An **immigrant** is a person who has come to live in a country from another country. स्थलांतरित

immigration n **Immigration** is the fact or process of people coming into a country in order to live and work there. स्थलांतर

immoral adj If you describe someone or their behaviour as **immoral**, you mean that their behaviour is bad or wrong. अनैतिक

immune system (**immune systems**) n Your **immune system** consists of all the cells and processes in your body which protect you from illness and infection. रोगप्रतिकारक शक्ती

impact (**impacts**) n The **impact** that something has on a situation, process, or person is a sudden and powerful effect that it has on them. प्रभाव

impartial adj If you are **impartial**, you are able to act fairly because you are not personally involved in a situation. निःपक्षपाती

impatience n **Impatience** is annoyance caused by having to wait too long for something. उतावीळपणा

impatient adj If you are **impatient**, you are annoyed because you have had to wait too long for something. उतावीळ

impatiently adv If you do something **impatiently**, you do it in an annoyed manner because you have had to wait too long for something. उतावीळपणे

impersonal adj If you describe a place, organization, or activity as **impersonal**, you feel that the people there see you as unimportant or unwanted. व्यक्तिनिरपेक्ष, यांत्रिक

import (**imports**, **importing**, **imported**) n **Imports** are products or raw materials bought from another country for use in your own country. आयात ▷ vt When a country or organization **imports** a product, they buy it from another country for use in their own country. आयात करणे

importance n The **importance** of something is the fact of it being significant, valued, or necessary in a particular situation. महत्त्व

important adj If something is **important**, people care about it and think about it a lot. महत्त्वाचा ▷ adj If someone is **important**, people pay a lot of attention to what they say and do. महत्त्वाचा

impossible adj Something that is **impossible** cannot be done or cannot happen. अशक्य

impractical adj If an idea or course of action is **impractical**, it is not sensible or practical. अव्यवहार्य

impress (**impresses**, **impressing**, **impressed**) v If someone or something **impresses** you, you feel great admiration for them. छाप पाडणे

impressed adj If you are **impressed** by something or someone, you feel great admiration for them. प्रभावित झालेला

impression (**impressions**) n Your **impression** of someone or something is what you think they are like. Your **impression** of a situation is what you think is going on. छाप

impressive adj **Impressive** is used to describe people or things which impress you. छाप पाडणारे

improve (**improves**, **improving**, **improved**) v If something **improves**, or if you **improve** it, it gets better. सुधारणा होणे

improvement (**improvements**) n If there is an **improvement** in something, it becomes better. If you make **improvements** to something, you make it better. सुधारणा

in prep **In** means not outside. आत The juice is in the fridge. ▷ prep You use **in** to say when something happens. मध्ये He was born in winter.

inaccurate adj If a statement or measurement is **inaccurate**, it is not accurate or correct. चुकीचा

inadequate *adj* If something is **inadequate**, there is not enough of it or it is not good enough. अपुरा

inadvertently *adv* If you do something **inadvertently**, you do it without realizing what you are doing. चुकून

inbox (**inboxes**) *n* On a computer, your **inbox** is the part which stores emails that have arrived for you. ई-मेलचा इनबॉक्स

incentive (**incentives**) *n* An **incentive** is something that encourages you to do something. प्रोत्साहन

inch (**inches**) *n* An **inch** is a unit of length, equal to 2.54 centimetres. इंच

incident (**incidents**) *n* An **incident** is an event, especially one involving something unpleasant. *(formal)* प्रसंग

include (**includes, including, included**) *vt* If something **includes** something else, it has it as one of its parts. समाविष्ट असणे

included *adj* You use **included** to emphasize that a person or thing is part of the group of people or things that you are talking about. सहित

including *prep* You use **including** to talk about people or things that are part of a group. सहित *Nine people were hurt, including both drivers.*

inclusive *adj* If a price is **inclusive**, it includes all the charges connected with the goods or services offered. If a price is **inclusive** of postage and packing, it includes the charge for this. समाविष्ट

income (**incomes**) *n* The **income** of a person or organization is the money that they earn or receive. मिळकत

income tax (**income taxes**) *n* **Income tax** is a part of your income that you have to pay regularly to the government. आयकर

incompetent *adj* If you describe someone as **incompetent**, you are criticizing them because they cannot do their job or a task properly. अकार्यक्षम

incomplete *adj* Something that is **incomplete** is not yet finished, or does not

have all the parts or details that it needs. अपूर्ण

inconsistent *adj* If you describe someone as **inconsistent**, you are criticizing them for not behaving in the same way every time a similar situation occurs. सातत्याचा अभाव असलेले

inconvenience (**inconveniences**) *n* If someone or something causes **inconvenience**, they cause problems or difficulties. गैरसोय

inconvenient *adj* Something that is **inconvenient** causes problems or difficulties for someone. गैरसोयीचा

incorrect *adj* Something that is **incorrect** is wrong or untrue. चुकीचा

increase (**increases, increasing, increased**) *n* If there is an **increase** in the number, level, or amount of something, it becomes greater. वाढ ▷ *v* If something **increases** or you **increase** it, it becomes greater in number, level, or amount. वाढ होणे

increasingly *adv* You use **increasingly** to indicate that something is becoming greater, stronger, or more common. वाढत्या प्रमाणावर

incredible *adj* If you describe someone or something as **incredible**, you like them very much or are impressed by them, because they are extremely or unusually good. अतुल्य

indecisive *adj* If you are **indecisive**, you find it difficult to make decisions. निर्णयक्षमतेचा अभाव असलेली व्यक्ती

indeed *adv* You use **indeed** to emphasize your agreement with something that has just been said. खरोखर

independence *n* A person's **independence** is their ability to do things without relying on other people. स्वातंत्र्य

independent *adj* Someone who is **independent** does not rely on other people. स्वतंत्र

index (**indices, indexes**) *n* An **index** is an alphabetical list at the back of a book saying where particular things are mentioned in the book. अनुक्रमणिका ▷ *n* An **index** is a system by which changes in the value of something can be recorded, measured, or interpreted. निर्देशांक

index finger (index fingers) n Your **index finger** is the finger that is next to your thumb. तर्जनी

India n **India** is a republic in south Asia. भारत

Indian (Indians) adj **Indian** means belonging or relating to India, or to its people or culture. भारतीय ▷ n An **Indian** is an Indian citizen, or a person of Indian origin. भारतीय

Indian Ocean n The **Indian Ocean** is an ocean bordered by Africa in the west, Asia in the north, and Australia in the east, and merging with the Antarctic Ocean in the south. भारतीय महासागर

indicate (indicates, indicating, indicated) vt If one thing **indicates** another, the first thing shows that the second is true or exists. दर्शविणे

indicator (indicators) n An **indicator** is a measurement or value which gives you an idea of what something is like. निर्देशक

indigestion n If you have **indigestion**, you have pains in your stomach that are caused by difficulties in digesting food. अपचन

indirect adj An **indirect** result or effect is not caused immediately and obviously by a thing or person, but happens because of something else that they have done. अप्रत्यक्ष

indispensable adj If someone or something is **indispensable**, they are absolutely essential and other people or things cannot function without them. जिच्याशिवाय चालत नाही अशी गोष्ट किंवा व्यक्ती

individual adj **Individual** means relating to one person or thing, rather than to a large group. एखाद्या व्यक्तिसंबंधी

Indonesia n **Indonesia** is a republic in south-east Asia. इंडोनेशिया

Indonesian (Indonesians) adj **Indonesian** means belonging or relating to Indonesia, or to its people or culture. इंडोनेशियन ▷ n An **Indonesian** is an Indonesian citizen, or a person of Indonesian origin. इंडोनेशियन

indoor adj **Indoor** activities or things are ones that happen or are used inside a building, rather than outside. आतील

indoors adv If something happens **indoors**, it happens inside a building. आत

industrial adj **Industrial** means relating to industry. औद्योगिक

industrial estate (industrial estates) n An **industrial estate** is an area which has been specially planned for a lot of factories. औद्योगिक वसाहत

industry n **Industry** is the work and processes involved in making things in factories. उद्योग

inefficient adj A person, organization, system, or machine that is **inefficient** does not work in the most economical way. अकार्यक्षम

inevitable adj If something is **inevitable**, it is certain to happen and cannot be prevented or avoided. अपरिहार्य

inexpensive adj Something that is **inexpensive** does not cost much. कमी खर्चाचे

inexperienced adj If you are **inexperienced**, you have little or no experience of a particular activity. अननुभवी

infantry n The **infantry** are the soldiers in an army who fight on foot. पायदळ

infant school (infant schools) n An **infant school** is a school for children between the ages of five and seven. ब्रिटनमधील चार ते सात वर्षाच्या मुलांसाठी असलेली शाळा

infection (infections) n An **infection** is a disease caused by germs. संसर्ग

infectious adj If you have an **infectious** disease, people near you can catch it from you. संसर्गजन्य

inferior (inferiors) adj Something that is **inferior** is not as good as something else. कनिष्ठ दर्जाचे ▷ n If one person is regarded as another person's **inferior**, they are considered to have less ability, status, or importance. कमी कर्तबगारी असलेली व्यक्ती, कनिष्ठ

infertile adj Someone who is **infertile** is unable to produce babies. वंध्यत्व असलेली व्यक्ती

infinitive (infinitives) n The **infinitive** of a verb is its base form or simplest form, such as 'do', 'take', and 'eat'. The **infinitive** is often used with 'to' in front of it. पुरुषवचनप्रमाणे न बदलणारे इंग्रजी भाषेतील क्रियापद

infirmary (infirmaries) n Some hospitals are called **infirmaries**. रुग्णालय

inflamed adj If part of your body is **inflamed**, it is red or swollen because of an infection or injury. दाहकारक

inflammation (inflammations) n An **inflammation** is a swelling in your body that results from an infection or injury. (formal) दाह

inflatable adj An **inflatable** object is one that you fill with air when you want to use it. फुगवता येण्याजोगी वस्तू

inflation n **Inflation** is a general increase in the prices of goods and services in a country. किंमतीत होणारी वाढ

inflexible adj Something or someone that is **inflexible** cannot or will not change or be altered, even if the situation changes. ताठर

influence (influences, influencing, influenced) n **Influence** is the power to make other people agree with your opinions or make them do what you want. दबाव, प्रभाव ▷ vt If you **influence** someone, you use your power to make them agree with you or do what you want. दबाव टाकणे, प्रभावित करणे

influenza n **Influenza** is an illness caused by a virus. The symptoms are like those of a bad cold, but more serious. (formal) इन्फ्लुएंझा

inform (informs, informing, informed) vt If you **inform** someone of something, you tell them about it. माहिती देणे

informal adj You use **informal** to describe behaviour, speech, or situations that are relaxed and casual rather than correct and serious. अनौपचारिक

information n If you have **information** about a particular thing, you know something about it. माहिती

information office (information offices) n An **information office** is an office where you can go to get information. माहिती कार्यालय

informative adj Something that is **informative** gives you useful information. माहिती देणारे

infrastructure (infrastructures) n The **infrastructure** of a country or society consists of the basic facilities such as transport, communications, power supplies, and buildings, which enable it to work properly. पायाभूत सुविधा

infuriating adj Something that is **infuriating** annoys you very much. संताप आणणारे

ingenious adj Something that is **ingenious** is very clever and involves new ideas or equipment. कल्पकतापूर्ण

ingredient (ingredients) n **Ingredients** are the things that are used to make something, especially all the different foods you use when you are cooking a particular dish. घटक

inhabitant (inhabitants) n The **inhabitants** of a place are the people who live there. रहिवासी

inhaler (inhalers) n An **inhaler** is a small device that helps you to breathe more easily if you have asthma or a bad cold. You put it in your mouth and breathe in deeply, and it sends a small amount of a drug into your lungs. इनहेलर

inherit (inherits, inheriting, inherited) vt If you **inherit** money or property, you receive it from someone who has died. वारसाहक्काने मिळणे

inheritance (inheritances) n An **inheritance** is money or property which you receive from someone who is dead. वारसाहक्क

inhibition (inhibitions) n **Inhibitions** are feelings of embarrassment that make it difficult for you to behave naturally. दाबून ठेवलेल्या भावना, दडपण

initial (initials, initialling, initialled) adj You use **initial** to describe something that happens at the beginning of a process. सुरुवातीचा ▷ vt

If someone **initials** an official document, they write their initials on it, for example to show that they have seen it or that they accept or agree with it. आद्याक्षरांनी सही करणे

initially *adv* **Initially** means in the early stages of a process or situation. सुरुवातीला

initials *npl* **Initials** are the capital letters which begin each word of a name. आद्याक्षरे

initiative (**initiatives**) *n* An **initiative** is an important act intended to solve a problem. पुढाकार

inject (**injects, injecting, injected**) *vt* To **inject** someone with a substance such as a medicine, or to **inject** it into them, means to use a needle and a syringe to put it into their body. इंजेक्शन देणे

injection (**injections**) *n* If you have an **injection**, someone puts a medicine into your body using a needle and a syringe. इंजेक्शन

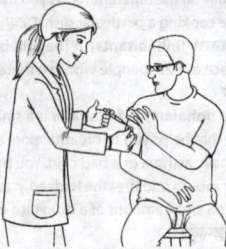

injure (**injures, injuring, injured**) *vt* If you **injure** a person or animal, you damage some part of their body. जखमी करणे

injured *adj* An **injured** person or animal has physical damage to part of their body, usually as a result of an accident or fighting. जखमी

injury (**injuries**) *n* An **injury** is damage done to a person's body. जखम

injury time *n* **Injury time** is the period of time added to the end of a football game because play was stopped during the match when players were injured. फूटबॉलमध्ये खेळाडू जखमी झाल्याने वाढवून दिलेली वेळ

injustice (**injustices**) *n* **Injustice** is unfairness in a situation. अन्याय

ink (**inks**) *n* **Ink** is the coloured liquid used for writing or printing. शाई

in-laws *npl* Your **in-laws** are the parents and close relatives of your husband or wife. सासरची माणसे

inmate (**inmates**) *n* The **inmates** of a prison or a psychiatric hospital are the prisoners or patients who are living there. कैदी, मनोरुग्णालयातील रुग्ण

inn (**inns**) *n* An **inn** is a small hotel or a pub, usually an old one. *(old-fashioned)* खाणावळ

inner *adj* The **inner** parts of something are the parts which are contained or enclosed inside the other parts, and which are closest to the centre. आतील

inner tube (**inner tubes**) *n* An **inner tube** is a rubber tube containing air which is inside a car tyre or a bicycle tyre. टायरच्या आतील ट्यूब

innocent *adj* If someone is **innocent**, they did not commit a crime which they have been accused of. निष्पाप, निर्दोष

innovation (**innovations**) *n* An **innovation** is a new thing or new method of doing something. नवी पद्धत, नवी कल्पना

innovative *adj* Something that is **innovative** is new and original. नावीन्यपूर्ण

inquest (**inquests**) *n* An **inquest** is an official inquiry into the cause of someone's death. मृत्यूच्या कारणांची चौकशी

inquire (**inquires, inquiring, inquired**) *v* If you **inquire** about something, you ask for information about it. *(formal)* चौकशी करणे

inquiries office (**inquiries offices**) *n* An **inquiries office** is an office where you can go or call to get information. चौकशी कार्यालय

inquiry (**inquiries**) *n* An **inquiry** is a question which you ask in order to get information. चौकशी

inquiry desk (**enquiry desks**) *n* The place in a hotel, hospital, airport, or other building where you obtain information is called the **inquiry desk**. चौकशी करण्याची जागा

inquisitive *adj* An **inquisitive** person likes finding out about things, especially secret things. जिज्ञासू

insane *adj* Someone who is **insane** has a mind that does not work in a normal way, with the result that their behaviour is very strange. वेडसर

inscription (**inscriptions**) *n* An **inscription** is a piece of writing carved into a surface, or written on a book or photograph. कोरलेला किंवा लिहिलेला मजकूर

insect (**insects**) *n* An **insect** is a small creature with six legs. Most insects have wings. कीटक

insecure *adj* If you feel **insecure**, you feel that you are not good enough or are not loved. असुरक्षित

insensitive *adj* If you describe someone as **insensitive**, you mean that they are not aware of other people's feelings or problems. असंवेदनशील

inside (**insides**) *adv* **Inside** means indoors. आत ▷ *n* The **inside** of something is the area that its sides surround. आतली बाजू ▷ *prep* If something is **inside** another thing, it is in it. आतमध्ये *There was a letter inside the envelope.*

insincere *adj* If you say that someone is **insincere**, you are being critical of them because they say things they do not really mean, usually pleasant, admiring, or encouraging things. लबाड

insist (**insists, insisting, insisted**) *v* If you **insist** that something should be done, you say very firmly that it must be done. आग्रह धरणे

insomnia *n* Someone who suffers from **insomnia** finds it difficult to sleep. निद्रानाश

inspect (**inspects, inspecting, inspected**) *vt* If you **inspect** something, you examine it or check it carefully. तपासणे

inspector (**inspectors**) *n* An **inspector** is someone whose job is to inspect things. निरीक्षक

instability (**instabilities**) *n* **Instability** is a lack of stability in a place, situation, or person. अस्थिरता

instalment (**instalments**) *n* If you pay for something in **instalments**, you pay small sums of money at regular intervals over a period of time. हप्ता

instance (**instances**) *n* An **instance** is a particular example or occurrence of something. उदाहरण

instant *adj* You use **instant** to describe something that happens immediately. तात्काळ

instantly *adv* If something happens **instantly**, it happens immediately. तात्काळ

instead *adv* If you do not do something, but do something else **instead**, you do the second thing and not the first thing. त्या ऐवजी

instead of *prep* If you do one thing **instead of** another, you do the first thing and not the second thing. त्या ऐवजी *Why don't they walk to work, instead of driving?*

instinct (**instincts**) *n* An **instinct** is the natural tendency that a person has to behave or react in a particular way. नैसर्गिक प्रवृत्ती

institute (**institutes**) *n* An **institute** is an organization or building where a particular type of work is done, especially research or teaching. संस्था

institution (**institutions**) *n* An **institution** is a large organization such as a parliament, a school, or a bank. संस्था

instruct (**instructs, instructing, instructed**) *vt* If you **instruct** someone to do something, you formally tell them to do it. *(formal)* सूचना देणे

instructions *npl* **Instructions** are clear and detailed information on how to do something. सूचना

instructor (**instructors**) *n* An **instructor** is a teacher, especially of driving, skiing, or swimming. प्रशिक्षक

instrument (**instruments**) *n* An **instrument** is a tool that you use to do something. उपकरण ▷ *n* An **instrument** is something, for example a piano or a guitar, that you use to make music. वाद्य

insufficient *adj* Something that is **insufficient** is not enough for a particular purpose. *(formal)* अपुरा

insulation *n* **Insulation** is a thick layer of material used to protect something from cold or noise. वीज वा उष्णता बाहेर जाणार नाही असे आवरण

insulin *n* **Insulin** is a substance that most people produce naturally in their body and which controls the level of sugar in their blood. If your body does not produce enough insulin, then it develops a disease called diabetes. इन्शुलिन

insult **(insults, insulting, insulted)** *n* An **insult** is a rude remark or action which offends someone. अपमान ▷ *vt* If you **insult** someone, you offend them by being rude to them. अपमान करणे

insurance *n* **Insurance** is an arrangement in which you pay money regularly to a company, and they pay money to you if something unpleasant happens to you, for example if your property is stolen. विमा

insurance certificate **(insurance certificates)** *n* An **insurance certificate** is a certificate that shows that a person or organization has insurance. विमा प्रमाणपत्र

insurance policy **(insurance policies)** *n* An **insurance policy** is a written contract between a person and an insurance company. विमा पॉलिसी

insure **(insures, insuring, insured)** *v* If you **insure** yourself or your property, you pay money to an insurance company so that if you become ill or if your property is stolen, the company will pay you a sum of money. विमा उतरवणे

insured *adj* If someone or their property is **insured**, they pay money to an insurance company so that, if they become ill or if their property is damaged or stolen, the company will pay them a sum of money. विमाकृत

intact *adj* Something that is **intact** is complete and has not been damaged or spoilt. जसेच्या तसे

intellectual **(intellectuals)** *adj* **Intellectual** means involving a person's ability to think and to understand ideas and information. बौद्धिक ▷ *n* An **intellectual** is someone who spends a lot of time studying and thinking about complicated ideas. बुद्धिमान व्यक्ती

intelligence *n* Your **intelligence** is your ability to understand and learn things. बुद्धिमता

intelligent *adj* An **intelligent** person has the ability to think, understand, and learn things quickly and well. बुद्धिमान

intend **(intends, intended, intending)** *v* If you **intend** to do something, you have decided or planned to do it. काही करण्याचा हेतू असणे

intense *adj* Something that is **intense** is very great in strength or degree. तीव्र

intensive *adj* An **intensive** activity involves the concentration of energy or people on one particular task. सखोल

intensive care unit **(intensive care units)** *n* The **intensive care unit** is the part of a hospital that provides continuous care and attention, often using special equipment, for people who are very seriously ill or injured. अति दक्षता विभाग

intention **(intentions)** *n* An **intention** is an idea or plan of what you are going to do. हेतू

intentional *adj* Something that is **intentional** is deliberate. जाणून बुजून

intercom **(intercoms)** *n* An **intercom** is a small box with a microphone which is connected to a loudspeaker in another room. You use it to talk to the people in the other room. इंटरकॉम

interest **(interests, interesting, interested)** *n* If you have an **interest** in something, you want to learn or hear more about it. स्वारस्य ▷ *n* **Interest** is extra money that you receive if you have invested a sum of money. व्याज ▷ *vt* If something **interests** you, you want to learn more about it or to continue doing it. आवड निर्माण होणे

interested *adj* If you are **interested** in something, you think it is important and you are keen to learn more about it or spend time doing it. स्वारस्य असलेला

interesting *adj* If you find something **interesting**, it attracts you or holds your attention. आवडीचा

interest rate (**interest rates**) *n* The **interest rate** is the amount of interest that must be paid. It is expressed as a percentage of the amount that is borrowed or gained as profit. व्याजदर

interior (**interiors**) *n* The **interior** of something is the inside or central part of it. आतला भाग

interior designer (**interior designers**) *n* An **interior designer** is a person who is employed to design the decoration for the inside of people's houses. अंतर्गत सजावटकार

intermediate *adj* An **intermediate** stage or level is one that occurs between two other stages or levels. मधला

internal *adj* You use **internal** to describe things that exist or happen inside a place or organization. अंतर्गत

international *adj* **International** means between or involving different countries. आंतरराष्ट्रीय

Internet *n* The **Internet** is the computer network which allows computer users to connect with computers all over the world, and which carries email. इंटरनेट

Internet café (**Internet cafés**) *n* An **Internet café** is a café with computers where people can pay to use the Internet. इंटरनेट कॅफे

Internet user (**Internet users**) *n* An **Internet user** is a person who uses the Internet. इंटरनेटचा वापरकर्ता

interpret (**interprets, interpreting, interpreted**) *vt* If you **interpret** something in a particular way, you decide that this is its meaning or significance. अर्थ लावणे

interpreter (**interpreters**) *n* An **interpreter** is a person whose job is to translate what someone is saying into another language. दुभाषी

interrogate (**interrogates, interrogating, interrogated**) *vt* If someone, especially a police officer, **interrogates** someone, they question him or her for a long time, in order to get information. गुन्ह्यासंबंधीतील चौकशी करणे

interrupt (**interrupts, interrupting, interrupted**) *v* If you **interrupt** someone who is speaking, you say or do something that causes them to stop. अडथळा आणणे

interruption (**interruptions**) *n* An **interruption** is something such as an action, comment, or question, that causes someone or something to stop. अडथळा

interval (**intervals**) *n* The **interval** between two events or dates is the period of time between them. मधला काळ, मध्यंतर

interview (**interviews, interviewing, interviewed**) *n* An **interview** is a formal meeting at which someone is asked questions in order to find out if they are suitable for a job or a course of study. मुलाखत ▷ *vt* If you **are interviewed** for a particular job or course of study, someone asks you questions about yourself to find out if you are suitable for it. मुलाखत घेणे

interviewer (**interviewers**) *n* An **interviewer** is a person who is asking someone questions at an interview. मुलाखतकार

intimate *adj* If two people have an **intimate** friendship, they are very good friends. जिवलग

intimidate (**intimidates, intimidating, intimidated**) *vt* To **intimidate** someone means to frighten them, sometimes as a deliberate way of making them do something. भीती दाखवणे

into *prep* If you put one thing **into** another thing, you put the first thing inside the second thing. आत *Put the apples into a dish.* ▷ *prep* If you go **into** a place or a vehicle, you move from being outside it to being inside it. आत *He got into the car and started the engine.*

intolerant *adj* If you describe someone as **intolerant**, you disapprove of the fact that they do not accept behaviour and opinions that are different from their own. असहिष्णू

intranet (**intranets**) *n* An **intranet** is a network of computers, similar to the Internet, within a company or organization. संस्थेचे अंतर्गत संगणकाचे जाळे (इंट्रानेट)

introduce (**introduces, introducing, introduced**) *vt* To **introduce** something means to cause it to enter a place or exist in a system for the first time. एखादी नवीन बाब सुरू करणे

introduction (**introductions**) *n* The **introduction** of something is the act of causing it to enter a place or exist in a system for the first time. नवीन बाबीची सुरुवात

intruder (**intruders**) *n* An **intruder** is a person who enters a place without permission. घुसखोर

intuition (**intuitions**) *n* Your **intuition** or your **intuitions** are feelings you have that something is true even when you have no evidence or proof of it. अंतर्मनातील भावना

invade (**invades, invading, invaded**) *v* To **invade** a country means to enter it by force with an army. आक्रमण करणे

invalid (**invalids**) *n* An **invalid** is someone who is very ill or disabled and needs to be cared for by someone else. दुसऱ्यावर अवलंबून असलेली अपंग किंवा आजारी व्यक्ती

invent (**invents, inventing, invented**) *vt* If you **invent** something, you are the first person to think of it or make it. शोध लावणे

invention (**inventions**) *n* An **invention** is a machine or system that has been invented by someone. शोध

inventor (**inventors**) *n* An **inventor** is a person who has invented something, or whose job is to invent things. संशोधक

inventory (**inventories**) *n* An **inventory** is a written list of all the objects in a place. सामानाची यादी

inverted commas *npl* **Inverted commas** are the punctuation marks (' ') or (" ") which are used in writing to show where speech or a quotation begins and ends. अवतरण चिन्ह

invest (**invests, investing, invested**) *v* If you **invest** in something, or if you **invest** a sum of money, you use your money in a way that you hope will increase its value, for example by buying shares or property. गुंतवणूक करणे

investigation (**investigations**) *n* An **investigation** is a careful search or examination in order to discover facts, etc. तपास

investment *n* **Investment** is the activity of investing money. गुंतवणूक

investor (**investors**) *n* An **investor** is a person or organization that buys stocks or shares, or pays money into a bank in order to receive a profit. गुंतवणूकदार

invigilator (**invigilators**) *n* An **invigilator** supervises the people who are taking an examination in order to ensure that it starts and finishes at the correct time, and that there is no cheating. पर्यवेक्षक

invisible *adj* If something is **invisible**, you cannot see it, because it is hidden or because it is very small or faint. अदृश्य

invitation (**invitations**) *n* An **invitation** is a written or spoken request to come to an event such as a party or a meeting. आमंत्रण

invite (**invites, inviting, invited**) *vt* If you **invite** someone to something such as a party or a meal, you ask them to come to it. आमंत्रित करणे

invoice (**invoices, invoicing, invoiced**) *n* An **invoice** is an official document that lists goods or services that you have received and says how much money you owe for them. इन्व्हॉईस ▷ *vt* If you **invoice** someone, you send them an invoice. इन्व्हॉईस पाठविणे

involve (**involves, involving, involved**) *vt* If an activity **involves** something, that thing is a necessary part of it. समाविष्ट असणे

iPod® (**iPods**) *n* An **iPod** is a portable MP3 player that can play music downloaded from the Internet. आयपॉड

IQ (**IQs**) *abbr* Your **IQ** is your level of intelligence, as indicated by a special test. **IQ**

is an abbreviation for 'Intelligence Quotient'. बुद्ध्यांक

Iran n **Iran** is a republic in south-west Asia, between the Caspian Sea and the Persian Gulf. इराण

Iranian (**Iranians**) adj **Iranian** means belonging or relating to Iran, or to its people or culture. इराणी ▷ n An **Iranian** is an Iranian citizen, or a person of Iranian origin. इराणी

Iraq n **Iraq** is a republic in south-west Asia, on the Persian Gulf. इराक

Iraqi (**Iraqis**) adj **Iraqi** means belonging or relating to Iraq, or to its people or culture. इराकी ▷ n An **Iraqi** is an Iraqi citizen, or a person of iraqi origin. इराकी

Ireland n **Ireland** is an island off north-west Europe, to the west of Great Britain. आयर्लंड

iris (**irises**) n The **iris** is the round coloured part of a person's eye. डोळ्यातील बुबूळ

Irish adj **Irish** means belonging or relating to Ireland, or to its people, language, or culture. **Irish** sometimes refers to the whole of Ireland, and sometimes only to the Republic of Ireland. आयरिश ▷ n **Irish** is a language spoken in Ireland. आयरिश

Irishman (**Irishmen**) n An **Irishman** is a man who is an Irish citizen or is of Irish origin. आयरिश पुरुष

Irishwoman (**Irishwomen**) n An **Irishwoman** is a woman who is an Irish citizen or is of Irish origin. आयरिश स्त्री

iron (**irons, ironing, ironed**) n **Iron** is a strong, hard, grey metal. लोखंड ▷ v If you **iron** clothes, you make them smooth using an iron. इस्त्री करणे ▷ n An **iron** is a piece of equipment with a flat bottom that gets hot. You move the bottom over clothes to make them smooth. इस्त्री

ironic adj When you make an **ironic** remark, you say something that you do not mean, as a joke. उपरोधिक

ironing n **Ironing** is the act of removing the creases from clothes using an iron. इस्त्री करण्याची क्रिया

ironing board (**ironing boards**) n An **ironing board** is a long narrow board covered with cloth on which you iron clothes. इस्त्री करण्याची फळी

ironmonger (**ironmongers**) n An **ironmonger** or an **ironmonger's** is a shop where articles for the house and garden such as tools, nails, and building supplies are sold. लोखंडी खिळे इत्यादी साहित्य विकणारे दुकान

irony n **Irony** is a form of humour which involves saying things that you do not mean. उपरोध

irregular adj If events or actions occur at **irregular** intervals, the periods of time between them are of different lengths. अनियमित

irrelevant adj If you say that something is **irrelevant**, you mean that it is not important to or not connected with the present situation or discussion. असंबद्ध

irresponsible adj If you describe someone as **irresponsible**, you are criticizing them because they do things without properly considering their possible consequences. बेजबाबदार

irritable adj If you are **irritable**, you are easily annoyed. संतस, चिडखोर

irritating adj Something that is **irritating** keeps annoying you. संतापजनक

Islam n **Islam** is the religion of the Muslims, which teaches that there is only one God and that Mohammed is His prophet. इस्लाम

Islamic adj **Islamic** means belonging or relating to Islam. इस्लामिक

island (**islands**) n An **island** is a piece of land that is completely surrounded by water. बेट

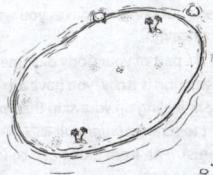

isolated *adj* If someone or something is **isolated** they are separate from other people or things of the same kind, either physically or socially. एकाकी

ISP (ISPs) *abbr* An **ISP** is a company that provides Internet and email services. **ISP** is an abbreviation for 'Internet service provider'. आयएसपी

Israel *n* **Israel** is a republic in south-west Asia, on the Mediterranean Sea. इस्रायल

Israeli (Israelis) *adj* **Israeli** means belonging or relating to Israel, or to its people or culture. इस्रायली ▷ *n* An **Israeli** is a person who comes from Israel. इस्रायली

issue (issues, issuing, issued) *n* An **issue** is an important subject that people are arguing about or discussing. मुद्दा ▷ *vt* If someone **issues** a statement, they make it formally or publicly. जाहीर करणे

it *pron* You use **it** to talk about a thing or an animal. ते (इंग्रजीमधील नपुंसकलिंग सर्वनाम) *This is a good book – have you read it?*

IT *abbr* **IT** is the theory and practice of using computers to store and analyse information. **IT** is an abbreviation for 'information technology'. माहिती तंत्रज्ञान

Italian (Italians) *adj* **Italian** means belonging or relating to Italy, or to its people, language, or culture. इटालियन ▷ *n* An **Italian** is a person who comes from Italy. इटालियन ▷ *n* **Italian** is the language spoken in Italy, and in parts of Switzerland. इटालियन

Italy *n* **Italy** is a republic in southern Europe. इटली

itch (itches, itching, itched) *vi* When a part of your body **itches**, you have an unpleasant feeling on your skin that makes you want to scratch. खाजवणे

itchy *adj* If a part of your body or something you are wearing is **itchy**, you have an unpleasant feeling on your skin that makes you want to scratch. *(informal)* खाज येणारे

item (items) *n* An **item** is one of a collection or list of objects. वस्तू

itinerary (itineraries) *n* An **itinerary** is a plan of a journey, including the route and the places that will be visited. दौऱ्याचा कार्यक्रम

its *det* You use **its** to say that something belongs to a thing or an animal. त्याचा *The lion lifted its head.*

itself *pron* You use **itself** to talk about something that you have just talked about. त्याचे स्वतःचे *The kitten washed itself, then lay down by the fire.*

ivory (ivories) *n* **Ivory** is a valuable type of bone, which forms the tusks of an elephant. हस्तिदंत

ivy *n* **Ivy** is an evergreen plant that grows up walls or along the ground. भिंतीवर आणि मैदानात वाढणारी एक सदाहरित वेल

j

jab (jabs) *n* A **jab** is an injection to prevent illness. प्रतिबंधात्मक इंजेक्शन

jack (jacks) *n* A **jack** is a device for lifting a heavy object such as a car off the ground. जॅक

jacket (jackets) n A **jacket** is a short coat. जॅकेट

jacket potato (jacket potatoes) n A **jacket potato** is a large potato that has been baked with its skin on. भाजलेला मोठा बटाटा

jackpot (jackpots) n A **jackpot** is a large sum of money which is the most valuable prize in a game or lottery. जॅकपॉट

jail (jails, jailing, jailed) n A **jail** is a building where criminals are kept in order to punish them. तुरुंग ▷ vt If someone **is jailed**, they are put in jail. तुरुंगात टाकणे

jam (jams) n **Jam** is a food that you spread on bread, made by cooking fruit with a large amount of sugar. जॅम

Jamaican (Jamaicans) adj **Jamaican** means belonging or relating to Jamaica or to its people or culture. जमैकन ▷ n A **Jamaican** is a person who comes from Jamaica. जमैकन

jam jar (jam jars) n A **jam jar** is a glass container for jam, etc. जॅमची बरणी

jammed adj If a place is **jammed**, a lot of people are packed tightly together there and can hardly move. दाट/खोळंबा झालेला

janitor (janitors) n A **janitor** is a person whose job is to look after a building. इमारतीची देखभाल करणारा

January (Januaries) n **January** is the first month of the year in the Western calendar. जानेवारी

Japan n **Japan** is an archipelago and empire in east Asia, extending between the Sea of Japan and the Pacific. जापान

Japanese (Japanese) adj **Japanese** means belonging or relating to Japan, or to its people, language, or culture. जापानी ▷ n The **Japanese** are the people of Japan. जापानी ▷ n **Japanese** is the language spoken in Japan. जापानी

jar (jars) n A **jar** is a glass container with a lid, used for storing food. बरणी

jaundice n **Jaundice** is an illness that makes your skin and eyes become yellow. कावीळ

javelin (javelins) n A **javelin** is a long spear that is thrown in sports competitions. भाला

jaw (jaws) n Your **jaw** is the part of your face below your mouth and cheeks. जबडा

jazz n **Jazz** is a style of music invented by black American musicians in the early part of the twentieth century. It has very strong rhythms and the musicians often improvise. जाझ

jealous adj If someone is **jealous**, they feel angry because they think that another person is trying to take away someone or something that they love. मत्सरी

jeans npl **Jeans** are casual trousers that are usually made of strong blue denim. जिन्स

Jehovah's Witness (Jehovah's Witnesses) n A **Jehovah's Witness** is a member of a religious organization which accepts some Christian ideas and believes that the world is going to end very soon. जेहोवाज व्हिटनेस

jelly (jellies) n **Jelly** is a transparent food made from gelatine, fruit juice, and sugar, which is eaten as a dessert. जेली

jellyfish (jellyfish) n A **jellyfish** is a sea creature that has a clear soft body and can sting you. जेली फिश

jersey (jerseys) n A **jersey** is a knitted piece of clothing that covers the upper part of your body and your arms. *(old-fashioned)* जर्सी

Jesus n **Jesus** or **Jesus Christ** is the name of the man who Christians believe was the son of God, and whose teachings are the basis of Christianity. येशू ख्रिस्त

jet (jets) n A **jet** is an aeroplane that is powered by jet engines. जेट विमान

jetlag n If you are suffering from **jetlag**, you feel tired and slightly confused after a long journey by aeroplane. विमान लागणे, जेटलाग

jetty (**jetties**) n A **jetty** is a wide stone wall or wooden platform where boats stop to let people get on and off, or to load or unload goods. समुद्रातील धक्का

Jew (**Jews**) n A **Jew** is a person who believes in and practises the religion of Judaism. यहूदी

jewel (**jewels**) n A **jewel** is a valuable stone, like a diamond. रत्न ▷ n **Jewels** are things made with valuable stones, that you wear to decorate your body. दागिने

jeweller (**jewellers**) n A **jeweller** is a person who makes, sells, and repairs jewellery and watches. जवाहिऱ्या ▷ n A **jeweller** or a **jeweller's** is a shop that sells jewellery and watches. दागदागिन्यांचे दुकान

jewellery n **Jewellery** consists of ornaments that people wear such as rings and bracelets. जडजवाहीर, दागदागिने

Jewish adj **Jewish** means belonging or relating to the religion of Judaism or to Jews. यहूदी धर्मीय

jigsaw (**jigsaws**) n A **jigsaw** or **jigsaw puzzle** is a picture on cardboard or wood that has been cut up into odd shapes and which has to be put back together again. जिगसॉ

job (**jobs**) n A **job** is the work that someone does to earn money. कामधंदा

job centre (**job centres**) n A **job centre** is a place where people who are looking for work can go to get advice on finding a job, and to look at advertisements placed by people who are looking for new employees. जॉब सेंटर

jobless adj Someone who is **jobless** does not have a job, but would like one. बेरोजगार

jockey (**jockeys**) n A **jockey** is someone who rides a horse in a race. घोडेस्वार

jog (**jogs, jogging, jogged**) vi If you **jog**, you run slowly, often as a form of exercise. हळूहळू धावणे

jogging n **Jogging** is the act of running at a slow regular pace as part of an exercise routine. हळूहळू धावण्याची क्रिया

join (**joins, joining, joined**) v When things **join**, or you **join** them, they come together. एकत्र येणे ▷ v If you **join** a group of people, you become one of the group. सामील होणे

joiner (**joiners**) n A **joiner** is a person who makes wooden window frames, door frames, doors, and cupboards. सुतार

joint (**joints**) adj **Joint** means shared by or belonging to two or more people. संयुक्त ▷ n A **joint** is a place where two things meet or are fixed together. सांधा ▷ n A **joint** is a fairly large piece of meat which is suitable for roasting. भाजण्यालायक मांसाचा मोठा तुकडा

joint account (**joint accounts**) n A **joint account** is a kind of bank account registered in the name of two or more people. संयुक्त खाते

joke (**jokes, joking, joked**) n A **joke** is something that is said or done to make you laugh, for example a funny story. विनोद ▷ vi If you **joke**, you tell funny stories or say amusing things. विनोद सांगणे

jolly (**jollier, jolliest**) adj A **jolly** person is happy and cheerful. उत्साही, आनंदी

Jordan n **Jordan** is a kingdom in south-west Asia. जॉर्डन

Jordanian (**Jordanians**) adj **Jordanian** means belonging or relating to the country of Jordan, or to its people or culture. जॉर्डनियन ▷ n A **Jordanian** is a Jordanian citizen, or a person of Jordanian origin. जॉर्डनियन

jot down (jots down, jotting down, jotted down) v If you **jot** something **down**, you write it down in the form of a short informal note. लहान-सहान नोंदी ठेवणे *Keep a notebook nearby to jot down queries.*

jotter (jotters) n A **jotter** is a small book for writing notes in. छोटी नोंदवही

journalism n **Journalism** is the job of collecting news and writing about it for newspapers, magazines, television, or radio. पत्रकारिता

journalist (journalists) n A **journalist** is a person whose job is to collect news, and write about it in newspapers or magazines or talk about it on television or radio. पत्रकार

journey (journeys) n When you make a **journey**, you travel from one place to another. प्रवास

joy n **Joy** is a feeling of great happiness. आनंद

joystick (joysticks) n In some computer games, the **joystick** is the lever which the player uses in order to control the direction of the things on the screen. जॉयस्टिक

judge (judges, judging, judged) n A **judge** is the person in a court of law who decides how the law should be applied, for example how criminals should be punished. न्यायाधीश ▷ vt If you **judge** a competition, you decide who or what is the winner. मूल्यांकन करणे, न्याय देणे

judo n **Judo** is a sport or martial art in which two people wrestle and try to throw each other to the ground. ज्युडो

jug (jugs) n A **jug** is a container which is used for holding and pouring liquids. सुरई

juggler (jugglers) n A **juggler** is someone who juggles in order to entertain people. हातचलाखीचे प्रयोग करणारा जादूगार

juice (juices) n **Juice** is the liquid that can be obtained from a fruit. रस

July (Julys) n **July** is the seventh month of the year in the Western calendar. जुलै महिना

jumbo jet (jumbo jets) n A **jumbo jet** or a **jumbo** is a very large plane. जंबो जेट

jump (jumps, jumping, jumped) v If you **jump**, you bend your knees, push against the ground with your feet, and move quickly upwards into the air. उडी मारणे

jumper (jumpers) n A **jumper** is a knitted piece of clothing which covers the upper part of your body and your arms. जंपर

jump leads npl **Jump leads** are two thick wires that can be used to start a car when its battery does not have enough power. The jump leads are used to connect the battery to the battery of another car that is working properly. जंप लीडस्

junction (junctions) n A **junction** is a place where roads or railway lines join. जंक्शन, चौक

June (Junes) n **June** is the sixth month of the year in the Western calendar. जून महिना

jungle (jungles) n A **jungle** is a forest in a tropical country where tall trees and other plants grow very closely together. जंगल

junior adj A **junior** official or employee holds a low-ranking position in an organization or profession. कनिष्ठ

junk n **Junk** is an amount of old or useless things. भंगार

junk mail n **Junk mail** is advertisements and publicity materials that you receive through the post or by email which you have not asked for and which you do not want. नको असलेली पत्रे

jury (juries) n In a court of law, the **jury** is the group of people who have been chosen from the general public to listen to the facts about a crime and to decide whether the person accused is guilty or not. न्यायमंडळ

just adv If you **just** did something, you did it a very short time ago. नुकतेच

justice n **Justice** is fairness in the way that people are treated. न्याय

justify (justifies, justifying, justified) vt If someone or something **justifies** a particular decision, action, or idea, they show or prove that it is reasonable or necessary. समर्थन करणे

k

kangaroo (kangaroos) *n* A **kangaroo** is a large Australian animal. Female kangaroos carry their babies in a pocket on their stomachs. कांगारू

karaoke *n* **Karaoke** is a form of entertainment in which a machine plays the tunes of songs, and people take it in turns to sing the words. कराओके

karate *n* **Karate** is a martial art in which people fight using their hands, elbows, feet, and legs. कराटे

Kazakhstan *n* **Kazakhstan** is a republic in central Asia. कझाकस्तान

kebab (kebabs) *n* A **kebab** is pieces of meat or vegetables grilled on a long thin stick, or slices of grilled meat served in flat bread. कबाब

keen (keener, keenest) *adj* If you are **keen** on doing something, you very much want to do it. If you are **keen** that something should happen, you very much want it to happen. उत्सुक

keep (keeps, keeping, kept) *v* If someone **keeps** still or warm, they stay like that. राहणे ▷ *vi* If someone **keeps** away from a place, they do not go near it. राहणे ▷ *vt* If you **keep** doing something, you do it many times or you do it some more. करीत राहणे ▷ *vt* When you **keep** something, you store it somewhere. ठेवणे

keep-fit *n* **Keep-fit** is the activity of keeping your body in good condition by doing special exercises. व्यायाम करून तंदुरुस्त राहणे

keep out (keeps out, keeping out, kept out) *v* If you **keep out** of something, you avoid

getting involved in it. अलिप्त राहणे *They have kept out of the debate so far.*

keep up (keeps up, keeping up, kept up) *v* If someone or something **keeps up** with another person or thing, the first one moves or progresses as fast as the second. (कामात) एखाद्याच्या बरोबरीने राहणे/मागे न पडणे *She shook her head and started to walk on. He kept up with her.*

kennel (kennels) *n* A **kennel** is a small hut made for a dog to sleep in. कुत्र्याला झोपण्यासाठी बनवलेली छोटी झोपडी

Kenya *n* **Kenya** is a republic in East Africa, on the Indian Ocean. केनिया

Kenyan (Kenyans) *adj* **Kenyan** means belonging or relating to Kenya, or to its people or culture. केनियन ▷ *n* A **Kenyan** is a Kenyan citizen, or a person of Kenyan origin. केनियन

kerb (kerbs) *n* The **kerb** is the raised edge of a pavement which separates it from the road. पदपथाचा कठडा

kerosene *n* **Kerosene** is a strong-smelling liquid which is used as a fuel in heaters, lamps, and engines. रॉकेल

ketchup *n* **Ketchup** is a thick, cold sauce, usually made from tomatoes, that is sold in bottles. केचप

kettle (kettles) *n* A **kettle** is a covered container that you use for boiling water. किटली

key (keys) *n* The **keys** on a computer or instrument are the buttons that you press on it. कळ ▷ *n* A **key** is a piece of metal that opens or closes a lock. किल्ली

keyboard (keyboards) n The **keyboard** of a computer is the set of keys that you press in order to operate it. कीबोर्ड (कळफलक)

keyring (keyrings) n A **keyring** is a metal ring which you use to keep your keys together. You pass the ring through the holes in your keys. चाव्या अडकवायची गोल कडी

kick (kicks, kicking, kicked) n A **kick** is a forceful hit made with your foot. लाथ ▷ v If you **kick** someone or something, you hit them forcefully with your foot. लाथ मारणे

kick off (kicks off, kicking off, kicked off, kick-offs) v If an event, game, series, or discussion **kicks off**, or if someone kicks it **off**, it begins. सुरु होणे The Mayor kicked off the party. ▷ n In football or rugby, **kick-off** is the time at which a particular match starts. सुरुवात

kid (kids, kidding, kidded) n You can refer to a child as a **kid**. (informal) लहान मूल ▷ vi If you **are kidding**, you are saying something that is not really true, as a joke. (informal) मस्करी करणे

kidnap (kidnaps, kidnapping, kidnapped) vt To **kidnap** someone is to take them away illegally and by force, and usually to hold them prisoner in order to demand something from their family, employer, or government. अपहरण करणे

kidney (kidneys) n Your **kidneys** are the two organs in your body that filter unwanted material from your blood and send it out of your body in your urine. मूत्रपिंड

kill (kills, killing, killed) v If a person, animal, or other living thing **is killed**, something or someone causes them to die. ठार मारणे

killer (killers) n A **killer** is a person who has killed someone. खूनी

kilo (kilos) n A **kilo** is a metric unit of weight. One kilogram is a thousand grams, and is equal to 2.2 pounds. किलो

kilometre (kilometres) n A **kilometre** is a metric unit of distance or length. One kilometre is a thousand metres, and is equal to 0.62 miles. किलोमीटर

kilt (kilts) n A **kilt** is a skirt with a lot of vertical folds, traditionally worn by Scottish men. Kilts can also be worn by women and girls. किल्ट

kind (kinder, kindest, kinds) n Someone who is **kind** is friendly and helps you. दयाळू ▷ n A **kind** of thing is a type or sort of that thing. प्रकार

kindly adv If you do something **kindly**, you do it in a gentle, caring, and helpful way. ममतेने

kindness n **Kindness** is the quality of being gentle, caring, and helpful. दयाळूपणा

king (kings) n A **king** is a man who is a member of the royal family of his country, and who is the head of state of that country. राजा

kingdom (kingdoms) n A **kingdom** is a country or region that is ruled by a king or queen. राज्य

kingfisher (kingfishers) n A **kingfisher** is a brightly-coloured bird which lives near rivers and lakes and catches fish. खंड्या पक्षी

kiosk (kiosks) n A **kiosk** is a small shop in a public place such as a street or station. It sells things such as snacks or newspapers which you buy through a window. टपरी

kipper (kippers) n A **kipper** is a fish, usually a herring, which has been preserved by being hung in smoke. किप्पर मासा

kiss (kisses, kissing, kissed) n A **kiss** is the act of touching somebody with your lips to show affection or to greet them. चुंबन ▷ v If you **kiss** someone, you touch them with your lips to show affection, or to say goodbye. चुंबन घेणे

kit (kits) n A **kit** is a group of items that are kept together because they are used for similar purposes. संच

kitchen (kitchens) n A **kitchen** is a room used for cooking and related jobs such as washing dishes. स्वयंपाकघर

kite (kites) n A **kite** is an object consisting of a light frame covered with paper or cloth, which you fly in the air at the end of a long string. पतंग

k

kitten (kittens) n A **kitten** is a very young cat. मांजरीचे पिल्लू

kiwi (kiwis) n A **kiwi**, or **kiwi fruit**, is a fruit with a brown hairy skin and green flesh. किवी नावाचे फळ

km/h abbr **Km/h** is a written abbreviation for 'kilometres per hour'. किमी/तास

knee (knees) n Your **knee** is the place where your leg bends. गुडघा

kneecap (kneecaps) n Your **kneecaps** are the bones at the front of your knees. गुडघ्याची वाटी

kneel (kneels, kneeling, kneeled, knelt) vi When you **kneel**, you bend your legs so that your knees are touching the ground. गुडघे टेकणे

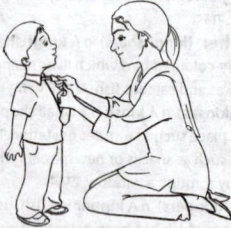

kneel down (kneels down, kneeling down, kneeled down, knelt down) v When you **kneel down**, you bend your legs so that your knees are touching the ground. गुडघे टेकणे She kneeled down beside him.

knickers npl **Knickers** are a piece of underwear worn by women and girls which have holes for the legs and elastic around the top. मुलींची किंवा स्त्रियांची चड्डी

knife (knives) n A **knife** is a tool consisting of a sharp flat piece of metal attached to a handle, used to cut things or as a weapon. सुरी

knit (knits, knitting, knitted) v When someone **knits** something, they make it from wool or a similar thread using knitting needles or a machine. विणणे

knitting n **Knitting** is something, such as an article of clothing, that is being knitted. विणकाम

knitting needle (knitting needles) n **Knitting needles** are thin plastic or metal rods which you use when you are knitting. विणकामाची सुई

knob (knobs) n A **knob** is a round handle or switch. मूठ (दरवाजाची)

knock (knocks, knocking, knocked) n A **knock** is the act or sound of something being hit, such as a door or window, to attract someone's attention. टकटक आवाज ▷ vi If you **knock** on something such as a door or window, you hit it, usually several times, to attract someone's attention. ठोठावणे

knock down (knocks down, knocking down, knocked down) v To **knock down** a building or part of a building means to demolish or destroy it. पाडून टाकणे Why doesn't he just knock the wall down?

knock out (knocks out, knocking out, knocked out) v To **knock** someone **out** means to cause them to become unconscious. बेशुद्ध पाडणे I nearly knocked him out.

knot (knots) n If you tie a **knot** in a piece of string, rope, cloth, or other material, you pass one end or part of it through a loop and pull it tight. गाठ

know (knows, knowing, knew, known) vt If you **know** something, you have that information in your mind. माहीत असणे ▷ vt If you **know** a person, you have met them and spoken to them. माहीत असणे

know-all (know-alls) n If you say that someone is a **know-all**, you are critical of them because they think that they know a lot more than other people. (informal) अति शहाणा

know-how n **Know-how** is knowledge of the methods or techniques of doing something. (informal) तांत्रिक ज्ञान

knowledge *n* **Knowledge** is information and understanding about a subject, which someone has in their mind. ज्ञान

knowledgeable *adj* A **knowledgeable** person knows a lot about many different things or a lot about a particular subject. ज्ञानी

known *adj* You use **known** to describe someone or something that is clearly recognized by or familiar to all people, or to a particular group of people. माहीत असलेला परिचयाचा

Koran *n* The **Koran** is the sacred book on which the religion of Islam is based. कुराण

Korea *n* **Korea** is a former country in East Asia, now divided into two separate countries, North Korea and South Korea. कोरिया

Korean **(Koreans)** *adj* **Korean** means belonging or relating to North or South Korea, or to their people, language, or culture. कोरियन ▷ *n* A **Korean** is a North or South Korean citizen, or a person of North or South Korean origin. कोरियन ▷ *n* **Korean** is the language spoken by people who live in North and South Korea. कोरियन

kosher *adj* Something, especially food, that is **kosher** is approved of or allowed by the laws of the Jews. यहूदी धर्मियाच्या कायद्याने मान्यता असलेले

Kosovo *n* **Kosovo** is a disputed territory in south-east Europe. It is a self-declared independent state, but Serbia considers it to be part of Serbia. कोसोवो

Kuwait *n* **Kuwait** is a state on the north-west coast of the Persian Gulf. कुवेत

Kuwaiti **(Kuwaitis)** *adj* **Kuwaiti** means belonging or relating to Kuwait, or to its people or culture. कुवेती ▷ *n* A **Kuwaiti** is a Kuwaiti citizen, or a person of Kuwaiti origin. कुवेती

Kyrgyzstan *n* **Kyrgyzstan** is a republic in central Asia. किरगिझस्तान

lab **(labs)** *n* A **lab** is a building or room when scientific experiments and research are performed. प्रयोगशाळा

label **(labels)** *n* A **label** is a piece of paper or plastic that is attached to an object in order to give information about it. लेबल

laboratory **(laboratories)** *n* A **laboratory** is a building or room where scientific experiments and research are performed. प्रयोगशाळा

labour *n* **Labour** is very hard work. श्रम

labourer **(labourers)** *n* A **labourer** is a person who does a job which involves a lot of hard physical work. मजूर

lace **(laces)** *n* **Lace** is a pretty cloth that has patterns of holes in it. फीत ▷ *n* **Laces** are like pieces of string for fastening shoes. नाडी

lack *n* If there is a **lack** of something, there is not enough of it, or there is none at all. अभाव

lacquer **(lacquers)** *n* **Lacquer** is a special type of liquid which is put on wood or metal to protect it and make it shiny. लाख

lad (lads) n A **lad** is a boy or young man. *(informal)* मुलगा, तरूण मनुष्य

ladder (ladders) n A **ladder** is a piece of equipment used for climbing up something such as a wall. It consists of two long pieces of wood or metal with steps fixed between them. शिडी

ladies n Some people refer to a public toilet for women as the **ladies**. स्त्रियांसाठी

ladle (ladles) n A **ladle** is a large, round, deep spoon with a long handle, used for serving soup, stew, or sauce. मोठा गोल चमचा

lady (ladies) n You can use **lady** when you are referring to a woman, especially when you are showing politeness or respect. सभ्य स्त्री

ladybird (ladybirds) n A **ladybird** is a small round beetle that is red with black spots. लेडीबर्ड

lag behind (lags behind, lagging behind, lagged behind) vi If you **lag behind** someone or something, you make slower progress than them. मागे राहणे *He now lags 10 points behind the champion.*

lager (lagers) n **Lager** is a kind of pale beer. लागर नावाची बिअर

lagoon (lagoons) n A **lagoon** is an area of calm sea water that is separated from the ocean by sand or rock. खाजण

laid-back adj If you describe someone as **laid-back**, you mean that they behave in a relaxed way as if nothing ever worries them. *(informal)* कसलीही घाई न करता आरामशीरपणे काम करणारा मनुष्य

lake (lakes) n A **lake** is a large area of fresh water, surrounded by land. तलाव

lamb (lambs) n A **lamb** is a young sheep. कोकरू

lame adj A **lame** person or animal cannot walk properly because an injury or illness has damaged one of their legs. लंगडा

lamp (lamps) n A **lamp** is a light that works by using electricity or by burning oil or gas. दिवा

lamppost (lampposts) n A **lamppost** is a tall metal or concrete pole that is fixed beside a road and has a light at the top. रस्त्यावरील दिव्यांचा खांब

lampshade (lampshades) n A **lampshade** is a covering that is fitted round or over an electric light bulb in order to protect it or decorate it, or to make the light less harsh. लॅंपशेड

land (lands, landing, landed) n **Land** is an area of ground. जमीन ▷ v When something **lands**, it comes down to the ground after moving through the air. जमिनीवर उतरणे

landing (landings) n In a house or other building, the **landing** is the area at the top of the staircase which has rooms leading off it. जिना चढून गेल्यानंतरची सपाट जागा

landlady (landladies) n Someone's **landlady** is the woman who allows them to live or work in a building which she owns, in return for rent. भाड्याने घर देणारी मालकीण

landlord (landlords) n Someone's **landlord** is the man who allows them to live or work in a building which he owns, in return for rent. घरमालक

landmark (landmarks) n A **landmark** is a building or feature which is easily noticed and can be used to judge your position or the position of other buildings or features. महत्त्वाची खूण, सीमाचिन्ह

landowner (landowners) n A **landowner** is a person who owns land, especially a large amount of land. जमीनदार

landscape (landscapes) n The **landscape** is everything that you can see when you look across an area of land, including hills, rivers, buildings, and trees. निसर्गदृश्य

landslide (landslides) n If an election is won by a **landslide**, it is won by a large number of votes. निवडणुकीतील प्रचंड विजय

lane (lanes) n A **lane** is a type of road, especially in the country. गल्ली

language (languages) n A **language** is a system of sounds and written symbols used by the people of a particular country, area, or tribe to communicate with each other. भाषा

language laboratory (language laboratories) n A **language laboratory** is a classroom equipped with tape recorders or computers where people can practise listening to and talking foreign languages. विविध भाषा शिकण्यासाठी असलेली भाषा प्रयोगशाळा

language school (language schools) n A **language school** is a private school where a foreign language is taught. परदेशी भाषा शिकविणारी खाजगी शाळा

lanky (lankier, lankiest) adj If you describe someone as **lanky**, you mean that they are tall and thin and move rather awkwardly. काटकुळा व अनाकर्षक

Laos n **Laos** is a republic in south-east Asia. लाओस

lap (laps) n **Your lap** is the flat area formed by your thighs when you are sitting down. मांडी

laptop (laptops) n A **laptop** or a **laptop computer** is a small computer that you can carry around with you. लॅपटॉप

larder (larders) n A **larder** is a room or large cupboard in a house, usually near the kitchen, in which food is kept. स्वयंपाकघराशेजारी असलेली अन्न ठेवण्याची मोठी खोली किंवा कपाट

large (larger, largest) adj A **large** thing or person is big or bigger than usual. मोठा

largely adv You use **largely** to say that a statement is mostly but not completely true. मोठ्या प्रमाणावर

laryngitis n **Laryngitis** is an infection of the throat in which your larynx becomes swollen and painful, making it difficult to speak. घशाची सूज

laser (lasers) n A **laser** is a narrow beam of concentrated light produced by a special machine. लेसर

lass (lasses) n A **lass** is a young woman or girl. तरुणी, मुलगी

last (lasts, lasting, lasted) adj The **last** thing is the one before this one. याआधीचा,

आताचा ▷ adv If something **last** happened on a particular occasion, that is the most recent occasion on which it happened. अगदी अलिकडचा, ताजा ▷ v If an event or situation **lasts** for a particular length of time, it continues for that length of time. टिकणे ▷ adj The **last** thing or person comes after all the others. उशिरा

lastly adv You use **lastly** when you want to make a final point that is connected with the ones you have already mentioned. शेवटी

late (later, latest) adj **Late** means after the usual time that something happens. उशिरा ▷ adj You use **late** when you are talking about someone who is dead. मयत ▷ adv **Late** means after the proper time. उशिरा ▷ adv **Late** means near the end of a period of time. उशिरा

lately adv **Lately** means recently. अलीकडे

later adv You use **later** to refer to a time or situation that is after the one that you have been talking about or after the present one. नंतर

Latin n **Latin** is the language which the ancient Romans used to speak. लॅटिन

Latin America n You can use **Latin America** to refer to the countries of South America, Central America, and Mexico. लॅटिन अमेरिका

Latin American adj **Latin American** means belonging or relating to the countries of South America, Central America, and Mexico. **Latin American** also means belonging or relating to the people or culture of these countries. लॅटिन अमेरिकन

latitude (latitudes) n The **latitude** of a place is its distance from the Equator. अक्षांश

Latvia n **Latvia** is a republic in north-east Europe, on the Gulf of Riga and the Baltic Sea. लॅट्व्हिया

Latvian (Latvians) adj **Latvian** means belonging to or relating to Latvia, its people, or their language. लॅट्व्हियन ▷ n A **Latvian** is a person from Latvia. लॅट्व्हियन ▷ n **Latvian** is the language spoken in Latvia. लॅट्व्हियन

laugh (laughs, laughing, laughed) n A **laugh** is the act of making a sound while smiling and

showing that you are happy or amused. हसू
▷ *vi* When you **laugh**, you smile and make a
sound because something is funny. हसणे

laughter *n* Laughter is the sound of people
laughing. हास्याचा आवाज

launch (launches, launching, launched) *vt*
To **launch** a rocket, missile, or satellite means
to send it into the air or into space. सोडणे
(अवकाशात)

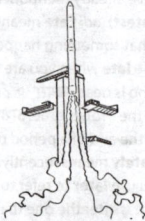

Launderette® (Launderettes) *n* A
Launderette is a place where people can
pay to use machines to wash and dry their
clothes. लॉंड्रेट

laundry *n* Laundry is used to refer to clothes,
sheets, and towels that are about to be
washed, are being washed, or have just been
washed. लॉंड्री

lava *n* Lava is the very hot liquid rock that
comes out of a volcano. लाव्हारस

lavatory (lavatories) *n* A lavatory is a toilet.
शौचालय

lavender *n* Lavender is a garden plant with
sweet-smelling purple flowers. लेव्हेंडर नावाची
वनस्पती

law *n* The law is a system of rules that a society
or government develops to deal with things
like crime. कायदा

lawn (lawns) *n* A lawn is an area of grass that
is kept cut short and is usually part of a garden
or park. हिरवळीचे मैदान

lawnmower (lawnmowers) *n* A lawnmower
is a machine for cutting grass on lawns.
हिरवळीच्या मैदानावरील गवत कापणारे यंत्र

law school (law schools) *n* Law school is
an institution that trains people to become
lawyers. कायद्याचे शिक्षण देणारी शाळा

lawyer (lawyers) *n* A lawyer is a person who
is qualified to advise people about the law and
represent them in court. वकील

laxative (laxatives) *n* A laxative is food or
medicine that you take to make you go to the
toilet. रेचक

lay (lays, laying, laid) *vt* When you **lay**
something somewhere, you put it down so
that it lies there. ठेवणे ▷ *vt* When a bird **lays**
an egg, it pushes an egg out of its body. घालणे

layby (laybys) *n* A layby is a short strip of
road by the side of a main road, where cars can
stop for a while. मुख्य रस्त्याच्या बाजूला असलेला
रस्ता जिथे गाड्या काही वेळ थांबता येऊ शकतात

layer (layers) *n* A layer of a material or
substance is a quantity or flat piece of it that
covers a surface or that is between two other
things. थर

lay off (lays off, laying off, laid off) *v* If
workers **are laid off** by their employers, they
are told to leave their jobs, usually because
there is no more work for them to do. काम
नसल्याने कामगारकपात करणे *They did not sell a
single car for a month and had to lay off workers.*

layout (layouts) *n* The layout of a garden,
building, or piece of writing is the way in
which the parts of it are arranged. आराखडा,
नकाशा

lazy (lazier, laziest) *adj* If someone is **lazy**,
they do not want to work or make an effort.
आळशी

lead (leads, leading, led) *n* Lead is a soft, grey,
heavy metal. शिसे ▷ *n* The **lead** in a play, film,
or show is the most important role in it. मुख्य
भूमिका ▷ *n* If you are in the **lead** in a race or
competition, you are winning. आघाडी ▷ *vt* If
you **lead** someone to a place, you take them
there. घेऊन जाणे

leader (leaders) *n* The leader of an
organization or a group of people is the
person who is in charge of it. नेता

lead-free adj Something such as petrol or paint which is **lead-free** is made without lead, or has no lead added to it. शिसेरहित

lead singer (**lead singers**) n The **lead singer** of a pop group is the person who sings most of the songs. मुख्य गायक

leaf (**leaves**) n A **leaf** is one of the parts of a tree or plant that is flat, thin, and usually green. झाडाचे पान

leaflet (**leaflets**) n The **leaflet** is a little book or a piece of paper containing information about a particular subject. माहितीपुस्तिका

league (**leagues**) n A **league** is a group of people, clubs, or countries that have joined together for a particular purpose. एका विशिष्ट उद्देशाने एकत्र आलेला समूह (कूल)

leak (**leaks, leaking, leaked**) n A **leak** is a crack, hole, or other gap that a substance such as a liquid or gas can pass through. गळती ▷ vi If a container **leaks**, there is a hole or crack in it which lets a substance such as liquid or gas escape. You can also say that a container **leaks** a substance such as liquid or gas. गळणे

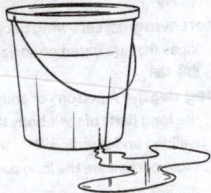

lean (**leans, leaning, leaned, leant**) vi When you **lean** in a particular direction, you bend your body in that direction. झुकणे

lean forward (**leans forward, leaning forward, leaned forward, leant forward**) v When you **lean forward**, you bend your body forwards. पुढे झुकणे He leaned forward to give her a kiss.

lean on (**leans on, leaning on, leaned on, leant on**) v If you **lean on** someone, you depend on them for support and help. अवलंबून असणे You can lean on me.

lean out (**leans out, leaning out, leaned out, leant out**) v When you **lean out**, you bend your body outwards. बाहेरच्या बाजूने झुकणे He opened the window and leaned out.

leap (**leaps, leaping, leaped, leapt**) vi If you **leap**, you jump high in the air or jump a long distance. उडी मारणे

leap year (**leap years**) n A **leap year** is a year which has 366 days. The extra day is 29 February. There is a leap year every four years in the Western calendar. लीप वर्ष

learn (**learns, learning, learned, learnt**) v When you **learn**, you obtain knowledge or a skill through studying or training. शिकणे

learner (**learners**) n A **learner** is someone who is learning about a particular subject or how to do something. शिकणारा

learner driver (**learner drivers**) n A **learner driver** is a person who is learning to drive a car. शिकाऊ चालक

lease (**leases, leasing, leased**) n A **lease** is a legal agreement under which someone pays money to another person in exchange for the use of a building or piece of land for a specified period of time. भाडेपट्टी ▷ vt If you **lease** property or something such as a car, or if someone **leases** it to you, they allow you to use it in return for regular payments of money. भाडेपट्टीने देणे

least adj You use **the least** to mean a smaller amount than any other thing or person, or the smallest amount possible. किमान

leather (**leathers**) n **Leather** is treated animal skin which is used for making shoes, clothes, bags, and furniture. चामडे

leave (leaves, leaving, left) n Leave is a period of time when you are not working at your job, because you are on holiday or vacation. रजा ▷ v When you **leave** a place, you go away from it. सोडणे ▷ vt If you **leave** something somewhere, you do not bring it with you. सोडून येणे

leave out (leaves out, leaving out, left out) v If you **leave** someone or something **out** of something such as an activity or a collection, you do not include them in it. सोडून देणे *I never left him out of my team.*

Lebanese (Lebanese) adj Lebanese means belonging or relating to Lebanon, or to its people or culture. लेबनीज ▷ n A **Lebanese** is a Lebanese citizen, or a person of Lebanese origin. लेबनीज

Lebanon n Lebanon is a republic in west Asia, on the Mediterranean. लेबनन

lecture (lectures, lecturing, lectured) n A **lecture** is a talk that someone gives in order to teach people about a particular subject, usually at a university. व्याख्यान ▷ vi If you **lecture** on a particular subject, you give a lecture or a series of lectures about it. व्याख्यान देणे

lecturer (lecturers) n A **lecturer** is a teacher at university or college. व्याख्याता

leek (leeks) n Leeks are long green and white vegetables which smell like onions. लीक (कांद्यासारखी फळभाजी)

left adj If there is a certain amount of something **left**, it remains when the rest has gone or been used. शिल्लक ▷ adv If you are facing north and you turn **left**, you will be facing west. डावीकडे ▷ n The **left** is one side of something. For example, on a page, English writing begins on the left. डावी बाजू

left-hand adj Left-hand describes the position of something when it is on the left side. डाव्या बाजूचे

left-hand drive (left-hand drives) n A **left-hand drive** is a vehicle which has the steering wheel on the left side, and is designed to be used in countries where people drive on the right-hand side of the road. डाव्या बाजूला चालक बसतो ते वाहन

left-handed adj Someone who is **left-handed** finds it easier to use their left hand rather than their right hand for activities such as writing and throwing a ball. डावखुरी व्यक्ती

left luggage n Left luggage is used to refer to luggage that people leave at a special place in a railway station or an airport, and which they collect later. रेल्वे स्थानक किंवा विमानतळावर ठेऊन दिलेले सामान

left-luggage office (left-luggage offices) n A **left-luggage office** is a special place in a railway station or an airport, where you can leave luggage and collect it later. रेल्वे स्थानक किंवा विमानतळावर सामान ठेऊन जाण्याची जागा

leftovers npl You can refer to food that has not been eaten after a meal as **leftovers**. उच्छिष्ट

left-wing adj Left-wing people have political ideas that are based on socialism. समाजवादी, डावे पक्ष

leg (legs) n A person's or animal's **legs** are the long parts of their body that they use for walking and standing. पाय ▷ n The **legs** of a table or chair are the long parts that it stands on. पाय

legal adj Legal is used to describe things that relate to the law. कायदेशीर

legend (legends) n A **legend** is a very old and popular story that may be based on real events. दंतकथा, आख्यायिका

leggings npl Leggings are tight trousers that are made out of a fabric which stretches easily. लेगिंज

legible adj Legible writing is clear enough to read. सुवाच्य

legislation n Legislation consists of a law or laws passed by a government. *(formal)* सरकारने मंजूर केलेला कायदा

leisure n Leisure is the time when you do not have to work and can do things that you enjoy. फुरसतीचा/मोकळा वेळ

leisure centre (leisure centres) n A **leisure centre** is a large public building containing different facilities for leisure activities, such as a sports hall, a swimming pool, and rooms for meetings. मनोरंजन केंद्र

lemon (lemons) n A **lemon** is a sour yellow citrus fruit. लिंबू

lemonade (lemonades) n **Lemonade** is a clear, sweet, fizzy drink, or a drink that is made from lemons, sugar, and water. लिंबू सरबत

lend (lends, lending, lent) vt When people or organizations such as banks **lend** you money, they give it to you and you agree to pay it back at a future date, often with an extra amount as interest. उसने देणे

length (lengths) n The **length** of something is the amount that it measures from one end to the other. लांबी

lens (lenses) n A **lens** is a thin, curved piece of glass or plastic in something such as a camera or pair of glasses which makes things appear larger or clearer. लेन्स

Lent n **Lent** is the period of forty days before Easter, during which some Christians give up something that they enjoy. ख्रिश्चन धर्मियांचे लेंट

lentils npl **Lentils** are a type of dried seed used in cooking. मसूर

Leo n **Leo** is one of the twelve signs of the zodiac. Its symbol is a lion. People who are born between the 23rd of July and the 22nd of August come under this sign. सिंह रास

leopard (leopards) n A **leopard** is a type of large wild cat from Africa or Asia. Leopards have yellow fur and black spots. चिता

leotard (leotards) n A **leotard** is a tight-fitting piece of clothing, covering the body but not the legs, that some people wear when they practise dancing or do exercise. लिओटार्ड (अंगाच्या वरच्या भागाला घट्ट बसणारा कपडा)

less adv You use **less** to talk about a smaller amount. कमी ▷ pron You use **less** to talk about a smaller amount of something. कमी

Borrowers are spending less and saving more. ▷ adj **Less** means a smaller amount. कमी

lesson (lessons) n A **lesson** is a fixed period of time during which people are taught something. तासिका, धडा

let (lets, letting) vt If you **let** someone do something, you allow them to do it. करू देणे

let down (lets down, letting down) v If you **let** someone **down**, you disappoint them, usually by not doing something that you said you would do. निराश करणे Don't worry, I won't let you down.

let in (lets in, letting in) v If an object **lets in** something such as air or water, it allows air or water to get into it or pass through it. आत येऊ देणे There is no glass in the front door to let in light.

letter (letters) n **Letters** are written symbols that represent the sounds in a language. अक्षर ▷ n A **letter** is a message on paper that you post to someone. पत्र

letterbox (letterboxes) n A **letterbox** is a rectangular hole in a door through which letters are delivered. पत्रपेटी

lettuce (lettuces) n A **lettuce** is a plant with large green leaves that you eat in salads. लेट्यूस नावाची वनस्पती

leukaemia n **Leukaemia** is a serious disease of the blood. ल्यूकेमिया (पंडुरोग)

level (levels) adj If one thing is **level** with another thing, it is at the same height. बरोबरी (उंचीने) n A **level** is a point on a scale, for example a scale of amount, importance, or difficulty. पातळी

level crossing (level crossings) n A **level crossing** is a place where a railway line crosses a road. रेल्वेचे फाटक

lever (levers) n A **lever** is a handle or bar that you pull or push to operate a piece of machinery. यंत्राची मूठ वा दांडा

liar (liars) n A **liar** is someone who tells lies. खोटारडा

liberal adj Someone who has **liberal** views believes people should have a lot of freedom in deciding how to behave and think. मुक्त, मोकळा

liberation n The **liberation** of a place or the people in it means the freeing of them from the political or military control of another country, area, or group of people. मुक्ती

Liberia n Liberia is a republic in West Africa, on the Atlantic. लिबेरिया

Liberian (Liberians) adj Liberian means belonging or relating to Liberia, its people, or its culture. लिबेरियन ▷ n A Liberian is a person who comes from Liberia, or a person of Liberian origin. लिबेरियन

Libra n Libra is one of the twelve signs of the zodiac. Its symbol is a pair of scales. People who are born between the 23rd of September and the 22nd of October come under this sign. तूळ रास

librarian (librarians) n A librarian is a person who works in, or is in charge of a library. ग्रंथपाल

library (libraries) n A public library is a building where things such as books, newspapers, videos, and music are kept for people to read, use, or borrow. ग्रंथालय

Libya n Libya is a republic in North Africa, on the Mediterranean. लिबया

Libyan (Libyans) adj Libyan means belonging or relating to Libya, or to its people or culture. लिबयन ▷ n A Libyan is a Libyan citizen, or a person of Libyan origin. लिबयन

lice npl Lice are small insects that live on the bodies of people or animals. उवा

licence (licences) n A licence is an official document that gives you permission to do, use, or own something. परवाना

lick (licks, licking, licked) vt When people or animals lick something, they move their tongue across its surface. चाटणे

lid (lids) n A lid of a container is the top which you open to reach inside. झाकण

lie (lies, lying, lay, lain) n A lie is something you say that is not true. खोटे ▷ vi When you lie somewhere, your body is flat, and you are not standing or sitting. आडवे होणे

Liechtenstein n Liechtenstein is a small mountainous country in central Europe on the Rhine. लिश्टेंस्टाईन

lie-in (lie-ins) n If you have a lie-in, you rest by staying in bed later than usual in the morning. (informal) सकाळी उशिरापर्यंत लोळत पडणे

lieutenant (lieutenants) n A lieutenant is a junior officer in the army, navy, or air force. लेफ्टनंट

life (lives) n Life is the quality which people, animals, and plants have when they are not dead. जीवन

lifebelt (lifebelts) n A lifebelt is a large ring, usually made of a light substance such as cork, which someone who has fallen into deep water can use to float. लाईफबेल्ट

lifeboat (lifeboats) n A lifeboat is a boat used to rescue people who are in danger at sea. जीवरक्षक नौका

lifeguard (lifeguards) n A lifeguard is a person who works at a beach or swimming pool and rescues people when they are in danger of drowning. जीवरक्षक

life jacket (life jackets) n A life jacket is a sleeveless jacket which keeps you floating in water. लाईफ जॅकेट

life-saving adj A life-saving drug, operation, or action is one that saves someone's life or is likely to save their life. जीवरक्षक, प्राणरक्षक

lifestyle (lifestyles) n Your lifestyle is the way you live, for example the things you normally do. जीवनशैली

lift (lifts, lifting, lifted) n If you give someone a lift, you drive them from one place to another. लिफ्ट देणे ▷ n A lift is a device that carries people or goods up and down inside tall buildings. उद्वाहन (लिफ्ट) vt If you lift something, you move it to another position, especially upwards. उचलणे

light (lighter, lightest, lights, lighting, lit, lighted) adj Something that is light is not heavy. हलका ▷ adj If a place is light, it is bright because of the sun or lamps. प्रकाशित, प्रकाशमान ▷ n Light is the bright energy that comes from the sun, that lets you see things. दिवा ▷ vt When you **light** a fire, it starts burning. पेटवणे ▷ n A **light** is something, like a lamp, that allows you to see. प्रकाश ▷ adj A **light** colour is pale. फिकट

light bulb (light bulbs) n A **light bulb** is the round glass part of an electric light or lamp which light shines from. विजेचा दिवा

lighter (lighters) n A **lighter** is a small device that produces a flame that is used to light cigarettes. लायटर

lighthouse (lighthouses) n A **lighthouse** is a tower near or in the sea which contains a powerful flashing lamp to guide ships or to warn them of danger. दीपस्तंभ

lighting n The **lighting** in a place is the way that it is lit. रोषणाई

lightning n **Lightning** is the bright flashes of light in the sky that you see during a thunderstorm. वीज

like (likes, liking, liked) prep If things or people are **like** each other, they are almost the same. च्या सारखा He's very funny, like my uncle. ▷ vt If you **like** something, you think it is nice or interesting. आवडणे ▷ adj What something or someone is **like** is how they seem to you. सारखा

likely (likelier, likeliest) adj You use **likely** to indicate that something is probably true or will probably happen in a particular situation. काही घडण्याची शक्यता

lilac (lilacs, lilac) n Something that is **lilac** is pale pinkish-purple in colour. फिकट गुलाबी-जांभळ्या रंगाचे ▷ n A **lilac** is a small tree with pleasant-smelling purple, pink, or white flowers. लिलॅक

lily (lilies) n A **lily** is a plant with large sweet-smelling flowers. लिली

lily of the valley (lilies of the valley, lily of the valley) n Lily of the valley are small plants with large leaves and small, white, bell-shaped flowers. घंटेच्या आकाराची फुले येणारी वनस्पती

lime (limes) n A **lime** is a small, round citrus fruit with green skin. एक प्रकारचे लिंबू ▷ n

Lime is a substance containing calcium. It is found in soil and water. चुना

limestone (limestones) n **Limestone** is a white rock which is used for building and making cement. चुनखडी

limit (limits) n A **limit** is the greatest amount, extent, or degree of something that is possible. मर्यादा

limousine (limousines) n A **limousine** is a large and very comfortable car. Limousines are usually driven by a chauffeur and are used by very rich or important people. लिमोझिन

limp (limps, limping, limped) vi If a person or animal **limps**, they walk with difficulty or in an uneven way because one of their legs or feet is hurt. लंगडत चालणे

line (lines) n A **line** is a long, thin mark or shape. रेषा

linen n **Linen** is a kind of cloth that is made from a plant called flax. लिनेन

liner (liners) n A **liner** is a large passenger ship. मोठे प्रवासी जहाज

linguist (linguists) n A **linguist** is someone who is good at speaking or learning foreign languages. बहुभाषाभिज्ञ

linguistic adj **Linguistic** abilities or ideas relate to language. भाषिक

lining (linings) n The **lining** of a piece of clothing or a curtain is a material attached to the inside of it in order to make it thicker or warmer. अस्तर

link (links, linking, linked) n If there is a **link** between two things or situations, there is a relationship between them, for example because one thing causes or affects the other. परस्पर संबंध ▷ vt If someone or something **links** two things or situations, there is a relationship between them, for example because one thing causes or affects the other. जोडणे

lino n **Lino** is a floor covering which is made of cloth covered with a hard shiny substance. लिनो (जाजम)

lion (lions) n A **lion** is a large wild member of the cat family that is found in Africa. Lions have yellowish fur, and male lions have long hair on their head and neck. सिंह

lioness (lionesses) *n* A **lioness** is a female lion. सिंहीण

lip (lips) *n* Your **lips** are the two outer parts of the edge of your mouth. ओठ

lip-read (lip-reads, lip-reading) *vi* If someone can **lip-read**, they are able to understand what someone else is saying by looking at the way the other person's lips move as they speak, without actually hearing any of the words. ओठांच्या हालचालींवरून बोलणे समजून घेणे

lip salve (lip salves) *n* **Lip salve** is an oily substance that is put on cracked or dry lips to help them heal. ओठांना लावायचे मलम

lipstick (lipsticks) *n* **Lipstick** is a coloured substance which women put on their lips. लिपस्टीक

liqueur (liqueurs) *n* A **liqueur** is a strong sweet alcoholic drink. लिक्ग्युअर (मद्यमिश्रित गोड पेय)

liquid (liquids) *n* A **liquid** is a substance such as water which is not solid and which can be poured. द्रवपदार्थ

liquidizer (liquidizers) *n* A **liquidizer** is an electric machine that you use to turn solid food into liquid. लिक्विडायझर

list (lists, listing, listed) *n* A **list** is a set of things which all belong to a particular category, written down one below the other. यादी ▷ *vt* To **list** a set of things means to write them or say them one after another, usually in a particular order. यादी तयार करणे

listen (listens, listening, listened) *vi* If you **listen** to someone who is talking or to a sound, you give your attention to them. लक्ष देणे, ऐकणे ▷ *vi* If you **listen** to someone, you do what they advise you to do, or you believe them. लक्ष देणे, ऐकणे

listener (listeners) *n* People who listen to the radio are often referred to as **listeners**. श्रोता

literally *adv* You can use **literally** to emphasize a statement. अक्षरश:

literature *n* Novels, plays, and poetry are referred to as **literature**. वाङ्मय

Lithuania *n* **Lithuania** is a republic in north-east Europe, on the Baltic Sea. लिथुयाना

Lithuanian (Lithuanians) *adj* **Lithuanian** means belonging or relating to Lithuania, or to its people, language, or culture. लिथुयानियन ▷ *n* A **Lithuanian** is a person who comes from Lithuania. लिथुयानियन ▷ **Lithuanian** is the language spoken in Lithuania. लिथुयानियन

litre (litres) *n* A **litre** is a metric unit of volume. It is equal to approximately 1.76 British pints or 2.11 American pints. लीटर

litter (litters) *n* **Litter** is rubbish which is left lying around outside. कचरा ▷ *n* A **litter** is a group of animals born to the same mother at the same time. एकाच वेळी जन्माला आलेली प्राण्यांची पिल्ले

litter bin (litter bins) *n* A **litter bin** is a container, usually in a street, park, or public building, into which people can put rubbish. कचरा कुंडी

little (littler, littlest) *adj* A person or thing that is **little** is small in size. लहान

live (lives, living, lived) *adj* **Live** animals or plants are alive, rather than being dead or artificial. सजीव ▷ *vi* You **live** in the place where your home is. राहणे ▷ *vi* To **live** means to be alive. जगणे

lively (livelier, liveliest) *adj* You can describe someone as **lively** when they behave in an enthusiastic and cheerful way. उत्साही, जिवंत

live on (lives on, living on, lived on) v If you **live on** a particular amount of money, or if you **live off** it, you have that amount of money to buy things. गुजराण करणे Most students are unable to live on that amount of money.

liver (livers) n Your **liver** is a large organ in your body which cleans your blood. यकृत

living n The work that you do for a **living** is the work that you do to earn the money that you need. उदरनिर्वाह

living room (living rooms) n The **living room** in a house is the room where people sit and relax. दिवाणखाना

lizard (lizards) n A **lizard** is a reptile with short legs and a long tail. पाल

load (loads, loading, loaded) n A **load** is something, usually large or heavy, which is being carried. भार ▷ vt If you **load** a vehicle, you put something on it. सामान भरणे

loaf (loaves) n A **loaf** of bread is bread in a shape that can be cut into slices. पावाची लादी

loan (loans, loaning, loaned) n A **loan** is a sum of money that you borrow. कर्ज ▷ vt If you **loan** something to someone, you lend it to them. कर्जाऊ देणे

loathe (loathes, loathing, loathed) vt If you **loathe** something or someone, you dislike them very much. तिटकारा, किळस

lobster (lobsters) n A **lobster** is a sea creature with a hard shell, two large claws, and eight legs. खेकडा

local adj **Local** means existing in or belonging to the area where you live, or to the area that you are talking about. स्थानिक

local anaesthetic (local anaesthetics) n A **local anaesthetic** is a substance used by a doctor to stop you feeling pain, which affects only a small area of your body. फक्त दुखरी असलेली जागा बधीर करणारे औषध

location (locations) n A **location** is a place, especially the place where something happens or is situated. ठिकाण

lock (locks, locking, locked) n The **lock** on something such as a door is the device which

fastens it when you turn a key in it. कुलूप ▷ n A **lock** of hair is a small bunch of hairs on your head that grow together in the same direction. केसांची बट ▷ vt When you **lock** something, you fasten it by means of a key. कुलूप लावणे

locker (lockers) n A **locker** is a small cupboard for someone's personal belongings, for example in a changing room. छोटी तिजोरी

locket (lockets) n A **locket** is a piece of jewellery containing something such as a picture, which you wear on a chain around your neck. लॉकेट

lock out (locks out, locking out, locked out) v If someone **locks** you **out** of a place, they prevent you entering it by locking the doors. प्रवेशास बंदी करणे They had had a row, and she had locked him out of the apartment.

locksmith (locksmiths) n A **locksmith** is a person whose job is to make or repair locks. कुलूपवाला

lodger (lodgers) n A **lodger** is a person who pays money to live in someone else's house. भाडेकरू

loft (lofts) n A **loft** is the space inside the sloping roof of a building. पोटमाळा

log (logs) n A **log** is a thick piece of wood cut from a branch or trunk of a tree. ओंडका

logical adj In a **logical** argument, each step or point must be true if the step before it is true. तार्किक, तर्कशुद्ध

log in (logs in, logging in, logged in) v If you **log in** or **log on**, you type your name and a password so that you can start using a computer or a website. लॉग इन करणे She turned on her computer and logged in.

logo (logos) n The **logo** of an organization is the special design that it puts on all its products. लोगो

log out (logs out, logging out, logged out) v If you **log out** or **log off**, you stop using a computer or website by clicking on an instruction. लॉग आऊट करणे I logged off and went out for a walk.

lollipop (lollipops) *n* A **lollipop** is a sweet consisting of a hard disc or ball of a sugary substance on the end of a stick. लॉलीपॉप

lolly (lollies) *n* A **lolly** is a sweet consisting of a hard disc or ball of a sugary substance on the end of a stick. लॉली

London *n* **London** is the capital city of the United Kingdom. लंडन

loneliness *n* **Loneliness** is the unhappiness that is felt by someone because they do not have any friends or do not have anyone to talk to. एकाकीपणा

lonely (lonelier, loneliest) *adj* A **lonely** person is unhappy because they are alone, or because they do not have any friends. एकाकी

lonesome *adj* Someone who is **lonesome** is unhappy because they do not have any friends or do not have anyone to talk to. अत्यंत एकाकी

long (longer, longest, longs, longing, longed) *adj* Something that is **long** takes a lot of time. दीर्घ ▷ *adv* **Long** means a great amount of time. खूप वेळ ▷ *v* If you **long** for something, you want it very much. एखादी गोष्ट हवी असणे ▷ *adj* Something that is **long** measures a great distance from one end to the other. लांब

longer *adv* **Longer** means for a greater amount of time. दीर्घकाळपर्यंत

longitude (longitudes) *n* The **longitude** of a place is its distance to the west or east of a line passing through Greenwich in England. रेखांश

long jump *n* The **long jump** is an athletics contest which involves jumping as far as you can from a marker which you run up to. लांब उडी

loo (loos) *n* A **loo** is a toilet. *(informal)* मुतारी

look (looks, looking, looked) *n* A **look** is the act of directing your eyes so that you can see something. नजर ▷ *vi* When you **look** at something, you turn your eyes so that you can see it. पाहणे ▷ *vi* You use **look** when you describe how a person seems. दिसणे

look after (looks after, looking after, looked after) *v* If you **look after** someone or something, you keep them healthy, safe, or in good condition. काळजी घेणे *I love looking after the children.*

look at (looks at, looking at, looked at) *vi* If you **look at** a book, newspaper, or magazine, you read it fairly quickly or read part of it. लगेच नजर फरविणे *You've just got to look at the last bit of Act Three.*

look for (looks for, looking for, looked for) *v* If you **look for** something, for example something that you have lost, you try to find it. शोधणे *I'm looking for my keys.*

look round (looks round, looking round, looked round) *v* If you **look round** a place, or if you **look around** it, you walk round it and look at the different parts of it. एखाद्या वस्तूच्या सभोवती फिरून पाहणे *We went to look round the show homes.*

look up (looks up, looking up, looked up) *v* If you **look up** a piece of information, you find it out by looking in a book or list. पुस्तक, वही इत्यादींमधून शोधणे *I looked your address up in your file.*

loose (looser, loosest) *adj* Something that is **loose** moves when it should not. ढिला ▷ *adj* **Loose** clothes are rather large and are not tight. ढगळ

lorry (lorries) n A **lorry** is a large vehicle used to transport goods by road. लॉरी

lorry driver (lorry drivers) n A **lorry driver** is someone who drives a lorry as their job. लॉरी चालक

lose (loses, losing, lost) v If you **lose** a game, you do not win it. हरणे ▷ vt If you **lose** something, you do not know where it is. हरवणे

loser (losers) n The **losers** of a contest or struggle are the people who are defeated. पराभूत खेळाडू किंवा संघ

loss (losses) n **Loss** is the fact of no longer having something or of having less of it than before. नुकसान, हानी

lost adj If you are **lost**, you do not know where you are or you are unable to find your way. रस्ता चुकलेली व्यक्ती

lot (lots) n A **lot** of something, or **lots** of something, is a large amount of it. खूप

lotion (lotions) n A **lotion** is a liquid that you use to clean, improve, or protect your skin or hair. द्रावण, लोशन

lottery (lotteries) n A **lottery** is a type of gambling in which people bet on a number or a series of numbers being chosen as the winner. Lotteries usually offer large cash prizes and are often organized so that a percentage of the profits is donated to good causes. लॉटरी (सोडत)

loud (louder, loudest) adj If a noise is **loud**, the level of sound is very high and it can be easily heard. Someone or something that is **loud** produces a lot of noise. मोठा (आवाज)

loudly adv If you do something **loudly**, you produce a lot of noise. मोठ्या आवाजात

loudspeaker (loudspeakers) n A **loudspeaker** is a piece of equipment, for example part of a radio, through which sound comes out. ध्वनिवर्धक

lounge (lounges) n A **lounge** is a room in a house, or in a hotel, where people sit and relax. लाऊंज

lousy (lousier, lousiest) adj If you describe something as **lousy**, you mean that it is of very bad quality. (informal) निकृष्ट

love (loves, loving, loved) n **Love** is the very strong warm feeling that you have when you care very much about someone, or you have strong romantic feelings for them. प्रेम ▷ vt If you **love** someone, you care very much about them. प्रेम करणे ▷ vt If you **love** something, you like it very much. आवडणे

lovely (lovelier, loveliest) adj If you describe someone or something as **lovely**, you mean that they are very beautiful or that you like them very much. आकर्षक, सुंदर

low (lower, lowest) adj Something that is **low** is close to the ground. खालच्या बाजूला ▷ adv If someone or something does something **low**, they do it close to the ground. खाली ▷ adj A **low** number is a small number. कमी

low-alcohol adj **Low-alcohol** beer or wine contains only a small amount of alcohol. मद्याचे कमी प्रमाण असलेली बिअर

lower (lowers, lowering, lowered) adj You can use **lower** to refer to the bottom one of a pair of things. खालचा ▷ vt If you **lower** something, you move it slowly downwards. खाली सरकवणे

low-fat adj **Low-fat** food and drinks contain only a very small amount of fat. कमी चरबीयुक्त

low season n The **low season** is the time of year when a place receives the fewest visitors, and fares and holiday accommodation are often cheaper. मंदीचा हंगाम

loyalty (loyalties) n **Loyalty** is behaviour in which you stay firm in your friendship or support for someone or something. निष्ठा

luck n **Luck** is success or good things that happen to you, which do not come from your own abilities or efforts. नशीब

luckily adv You add **luckily** to your statement to indicate that you are glad that something happened or is the case. सुदैवाने

lucky (luckier, luckiest) adj If someone is **lucky**, they are in a very desirable situation. नशीबवान

lucrative adj A **lucrative** business or activity earns you a lot of money. भरपूर कमाई असणारे काम

luggage *n* **Luggage** consists of the suitcases and bags that you take when you travel. सामान

luggage rack (**luggage racks**) *n* A **luggage rack** is a shelf for putting luggage on, on a vehicle such as a train or bus. सामान ठेवण्याची रॅक

lukewarm *adj* **Lukewarm** water is only slightly warm. कोमट

lullaby (**lullabies**) *n* A **lullaby** is a quietsong which is intended to be sung to babies and young children to help them go to sleep. अंगाई

lump (**lumps**) *n* A **lump** is a solid piece of something. गोळा

lunatic (**lunatics**) *n* If you describe someone as a **lunatic**, you think they behave in a dangerous, stupid, or annoying way. (*informal*) वेडसर

lunch (**lunches**) *n* **Lunch** is a meal that you have in the middle of the day. दुपारचे जेवण

lunch break (**lunch breaks**) *n* Your **lunch break** is the period in the middle of the day when you stop work in order to have a meal. दुपारच्या जेवणाची सुट्टी

lunchtime (**lunchtimes**) *n* **Lunchtime** is the period of the day when people have their lunch. दुपारच्या जेवणाची वेळ

lung (**lungs**) *n* Your **lungs** are the two organs inside your chest which you use for breathing. फुफ्फुस

lush (**lusher, lushest**) *adj* **Lush** fields or gardens have a lot of very healthy grass or plants. घनदाट

Luxembourg *n* **Luxembourg** is a small country in Western Europe. लक्झेम्बर्ग

luxurious *adj* Something that is **luxurious** is very comfortable and expensive. विलासी

luxury *n* **Luxury** is very great comfort, especially among beautiful and expensive surroundings. चैन

lyrics *npl* The **lyrics** of a song are its words. गाण्याचे बोल

m

mac (**macs**) *n* A **mac** is a raincoat, especially one made from a particular kind of waterproof cloth. (मेणकापडाचा) रेनकोट

macaroni *npl* **Macaroni** is a kind of pasta made in the shape of short hollow tubes. मॅकारोनी

machine (**machines**) *n* A **machine** is a piece of equipment which uses electricity or an engine in order to do a particular kind of work. यंत्र

machine gun (**machine guns**) *n* A **machine gun** is a gun which fires a lot of bullets very quickly one after the other. मशिनगन

machinery *n* **Machinery** is machines in general, or machines that are used in a factory. यंत्रसामग्री

machine washable *adj* **Machine washable** clothes are suitable for washing in a washing machine. यंत्राने धुलाई करण्याजोगे कपडे

mackerel (mackerel) n A **mackerel** is a sea fish with a dark, patterned back. बांगडा (एक मासा)

mad (madder, maddest) adj Someone who is **mad** has a mental illness which makes them behave in strange ways. वेडा ▷ adj You can say that someone is **mad** when they are very angry. (informal) रागावलेला

Madagascar n **Madagascar** is an island republic in the Indian Ocean, off the east coast of Africa. मादागास्कर

madam n **Madam** is a formal and polite way of addressing a woman. मॅडम/बाईसाहेब

madly adv If you do something **madly**, you do it in a fast, excited, or eager way. झपाटून, वेड्यासारखे

madman (madmen) n A **madman** is a man who is insane. वेडा

madness n If you describe a decision or an action as **madness**, you think it is very foolish. मूर्खपणा

magazine (magazines) n A **magazine** is a weekly or monthly publication which contains articles, stories, photographs, and advertisements. मासिक, नियतकालिक ▷ n In an automatic gun, the **magazine** is the part that contains the bullets. काडतूस

maggot (maggots) n **Maggots** are tiny creatures that look like very small worms and turn into flies. अळी

magic adj You use **magic** to describe something that does things, or appears to do things, by magic. जादुई ▷ n **Magic** is the power to use supernatural forces to make impossible things happen, such as making people disappear or controlling events in nature. जादू, गूढ विद्या

magical adj Something that is **magical** seems to use magic or to be able to produce magic. जादुई

magician (magicians) n A **magician** is a person who entertains people by doing magic tricks. जादुगार

magistrate (magistrates) n A **magistrate** is a person who is appointed to act as a judge

in law courts which deal with minor crimes or disputes. दंडाधिकारी

magnet (magnets) n A **magnet** is a piece of iron which attracts iron or steel towards it. लोहचुंबक

magnetic adj If something is **magnetic**, it has the power of a magnet or works like a magnet. चुंबकीय

magnificent adj Something or someone that is **magnificent** is extremely good, beautiful, or impressive. अत्युत्तम, दिमाखदार

magnifying glass (magnifying glasses) n A **magnifying glass** is a piece of glass which makes objects appear bigger than they actually are. भिंग

magpie (magpies) n A **magpie** is a black and white bird with a long tail. मेंगपाय पक्षी

mahogany n **Mahogany** is a dark reddish-brown wood that is used to make furniture. महोगनी लाकूड

maid (maids) n A **maid** is a woman who works as a servant in a hotel or private house. मोलकरीण

maiden name (maiden names) n A married woman's **maiden name** is her parents' surname, which she used before she got married and started using her husband's surname. लग्नापूर्वीचे नाव

mail (mails, mailing, mailed) n **Mail** is the letters and parcels that are delivered to you. टपाल ▷ vt If you **mail** something, you post it. टपालाने पाठविणे

mailing list (mailing lists) n A **mailing list** is a list of names and addresses that a company or organization keeps, so that they can send people information or advertisements. टपालपत्त्यांची यादी

m

main adj The **main** thing is the most important one. मुख्य

main course (main courses) n The **main course** is the most important dish of a meal. जेवणातला मुख्य पदार्थ

mainland n The **mainland** is the large main part of a country, in contrast to the islands around it. मुख्य भूप्रदेश

mainly adv You use **mainly** to say that a statement is true in most cases or to a large extent. मुख्यत:

main road (main roads) n A **main road** is an important road that leads from one town or city to another. मुख्य रस्ता

maintain (maintains, maintaining, maintained) vt If you **maintain** something, you continue to have it, and do not let it stop or grow weaker. राखणे

maintenance n The **maintenance** of a building, road, vehicle, or machine is the process of keeping it in good condition. देखभाल

maize n **Maize** is a tall plant which produces corn. मका

majesty (majesties) n You use majesty in expressions such as Your **Majesty** or Her **Majesty** when you are addressing or referring to a King or Queen. महाराज या अर्थाचे संबोधन

major adj You use **major** to describe something that is more important, serious, or significant than other things. महत्त्वाचा

majority n The **majority** of people or things in a group is more than half of them. बहुसंख्य

make (makes, making, made) n The **make** of a product is the name of the company that made it. वस्तू ज्या कंपनीची आहे, तिचे नाव किंवा ब्रॅंड ▷ vt You can use **make** to show that a person does or says something. करणे ▷ vt If you **make** something, you put it together or build it from other things. तयार करणे ▷ vt If you **make** a person do something, they must do it. करायला भाग पाडणे

makeover (makeovers) n If a person or room is given a **makeover**, their appearance is improved, usually by an expert. कायापालट

maker (makers) n The **maker** of something is the person or company that makes it. निर्माता

make up (makes up, making up, made up) v The people or things that **make up** something are the members or parts that form that thing. हिस्सा असणे Women officers make up 13 per cent of the police force. ▷ n **Make-up** consists of things such as lipstick or eye shadow which you can put on your face to make yourself look more attractive. आकर्षक दिसण्यासाठी सौंदर्यप्रसाधनांचा वापर करणे

malaria n **Malaria** is a serious disease caught from mosquitoes. हिवताप

Malawi n **Malawi** is a republic in east central Africa. मालावी

Malaysia n **Malaysia** is a country in South-East Asia. मलेशिया

Malaysian (Malaysians) adj **Malaysian** means belonging or relating to Malaysia, or to its people or culture. मलेशियन ▷ n A **Malaysian** is a person who comes from Malaysia. मलेशियन

male (males) adj Someone who is **male** is a man or a boy. पुरुष किंवा मुलगा ▷ n Men and boys are sometimes referred to as **males** when they are being considered as a type. पुरुष

malicious adj **Malicious** talk or behaviour is intended to harm people or their reputation, or to embarrass or upset them. द्वेषयुक्त

malignant adj A **malignant** tumour or disease is serious, spreads rapidly to other parts of the body, and may cause death. घातक (रोग)

malnutrition n If someone is suffering from **malnutrition**, they are physically weak and extremely thin because they have not eaten enough food or had a balanced diet. कुपोषण

Malta n **Malta** is a republic occupying the islands of Malta, Gozo, and Comino, in the Mediterranean. माल्टा

Maltese (Maltese) adj **Maltese** means belonging or relating to Malta, or to its people, language, or culture. माल्टिज़ ▷ n A **Maltese** is a person who comes from Malta.

माल्टिज ▷ n **Maltese** is a language spoken in Malta. माल्टिज

malt whisky (malt whiskies) n **Malt whisky** or **malt** is whisky that is made from malt. माल्ट व्हिस्की

mammal (mammals) n **Mammals** are animals such as dogs and humans that give birth to babies rather than laying eggs, and feed their young with milk. सस्तन

mammoth (mammoths) adj You can use **mammoth** to emphasize that a task is very great and needs a lot of effort to achieve. अगडबंब ▷ n A **mammoth** was a prehistoric animal like a large elephant with long curling tusks. पूर्वीच्या काळी अस्तित्वात असलेला प्रचंड हत्ती

man (men) n A **man** is an adult male human. पुरुष

manage (manages, managing, managed) vt If you **manage** an organization, business, or system, or the people who work in it, you are responsible for controlling them. व्यवस्थापन करणे

manageable adj Something that is **manageable** is of a size, quantity, or level of difficulty that people are able to deal with. आवाक्यातले

management (managements) n **Management** is the control and organizing of something. व्यवस्थापन

manager (managers) n A **manager** is the person responsible for running part of or the whole of a business organization. व्यवस्थापक

manageress (manageresses) n The **manageress** of a shop, restaurant, or other small business is the woman who is responsible for running it. व्यवस्थापिका

managing director (managing directors) n The **managing director** of a company is the senior working director, and is in charge of the way the company is managed. व्यवस्थापकीय संचालक

mandarin (mandarins) n Journalists sometimes use **mandarin** to refer to someone who has an important job working for a government department. महत्त्वाचा अधिकारी ▷ n A **mandarin** or a **mandarin orange** is a small orange whose skin comes off easily. छोटे संत्रे

mangetout (mangetout, mangetouts) n **Mangetout** are a type of pea whose pods are eaten as well as the peas inside them. मँगेआऊट (आतील बियांसकट खाता येऊ शकते अशी शेंग)

mango (mangoes, mangos) n A **mango** is a large, sweet yellowish fruit which grows in hot countries. आंबा

mania (manias) n If you say that a person or group has a **mania** for something, you mean that they enjoy it very much or devote a lot of time to it. ओढ, (एखाद्या गोष्टीचे) प्रचंड वेड

maniac (maniacs) n A **maniac** is a mad person who is violent and dangerous. माथेफिरू

manicure (manicures, manicuring, manicured) n A **manicure** is the cosmetic procedure of having the skin on your hands softened and your nails cut and polished. मेनिक्युअर ▷ vt If you **manicure** your hands or nails, you care for them by softening your skin and cutting your nails and polishing. मेनिक्युअर करणे

manipulate (manipulates, manipulating, manipulated) vt If you say that someone **manipulates** people or events, you disapprove of them because they control or influence them to produce a particular result. दबाव आणणे, चलाखी करून हवे तसे घडवून आणणे

mankind n You can refer to all human beings as **mankind** when you are considering them as a group. मानवजात

man-made adj **Man-made** things are created or caused by people, rather than occurring naturally. मनुष्यनिर्मित

manner n The **manner** in which you do something is the way that you do it. पद्धत

manners npl If someone has good **manners**, they are polite and observe social customs. If someone has bad **manners**, they are impolite and do not observe these customs. शिष्टाचार

manpower n Workers are sometimes referred to as **manpower** when they are being considered as a part of the process of producing goods or providing services. मनुष्यबळ

mansion (**mansions**) n A **mansion** is a very large, expensive house. मोठा वाडा

mantelpiece (**mantelpieces**) n A **mantelpiece** is a shelf over a fireplace. शेकोटीच्या वरती असणारी फळी

manual (**manuals**) n A **manual** is a book which tells you how to do something or how a piece of machinery works. माहितीपुस्तिका

manufacture (**manufactures, manufacturing, manufactured**) vt To **manufacture** something means to make it in a factory, usually in large quantities. कारखान्यात वस्तू तयार करणे

manufacturer (**manufacturers**) n A **manufacturer** is a business that makes goods in large quantities. निर्माता

manure n **Manure** is animal waste that is spread on the ground in order to improve the growth of plants. संद्रिय खत

manuscript (**manuscripts**) n A **manuscript** is a handwritten or typed document, especially a writer's first version of a book before it is published. हस्तलिखित प्रत

many det If there are **many** people or things, there are a lot of them. खूप *Does he have many friends?* ▷ pron **Many** is used to refer to a large number of people or things. अनेक *We thought about the possibilities. There weren't many.*

Maori (**Maoris**) adj **Maori** means belonging to or relating to the race of people who have lived in New Zealand and the Cook Islands since before Europeans arrived. मावरी जमात ▷ n The **Maori** or the **Maoris** are people who are Maori. मावरी ▷ n **Maori** is the language spoken by the Maori people. मावरी

map (**maps**) n A **map** is a drawing of a particular area, showing its main features as

they appear if you looked at them from above. नकाशा

maple (**maples**) n A **maple** is a tree with large leaves with five points. मेपल वृक्ष

marathon (**marathons**) n A **marathon** is a race in which people run a distance of 26 miles (about 42 km). मॅरेथॉन शर्यत

marble n **Marble** is a very hard rock used, for example, to make statues and fireplaces. संगमरवर

march (**marches, marching, marched**) n A **march** is the action, by a group of soldiers, of walking somewhere with very regular steps, as a group. कूच, कवाइत ▷ v When soldiers **march** somewhere, or when a commanding officer **marches** them somewhere, they walk there with very regular steps, as a group. कूच करणे

March (**Marches**) n **March** is the third month of the year in the Western calendar. मार्च महिना

mare (**mares**) n A **mare** is an adult female horse. घोडी

margarine n **Margarine** is a substance similar to butter, made from vegetable oil and sometimes animal fats. मार्गरिन (वनस्पती वा प्राण्यांच्या चरबीपासून तयार केलेला लोण्यासारखा एक पदार्थ)

margin (**margins**) n A **margin** is the difference between two amounts, especially the difference in the number of votes or points between the winner and the loser in a contest. फरक

marigold (marigolds) *n* A **marigold** is a type of yellow or orange flower. झेंडू

marina (marinas) *n* A **marina** is a small harbour for pleasure boats. मनोरंजनासाठी असलेल्या छोट्या नौका उभ्या करून ठेवण्याचे बंदर

marinade (marinades, marinading, marinaded) *n* A **marinade** is a sauce of oil, vinegar, and spices, which you soak meat or fish in before cooking it, in order to flavour it. मॅरिनेड (मांस वा मासे शिजवण्यापूर्वी त्यांना लावायचे एक मिश्रण) *v* If you **marinade** meat or fish, you keep it in a mixture of oil, vinegar, spices, and herbs, before cooking it, so that it can develop a special flavour. मॅरिनेड करणे

marital status *n* Your **marital status** is whether you are married, single, or divorced. *(formal)* वैवाहिक स्थिती

maritime *adj* **Maritime** means relating to the sea and to ships. जहाजे आणि समुद्राशी संबंधित

marjoram *n* **Marjoram** is a kind of herb. मर्जोरम (एक वनस्पती)

mark (marks, marking, marked) *n* A **mark** is a small dirty area on a surface. डाग ▷ *vt* If you **mark** something, you write a word or symbol on it. ठसा उमटवणे ▷ *vt* When a teacher **marks** a student's work, the teacher corrects it or gives it a grade. गुण देणे ▷ *n* A **mark** is a shape that you write or draw. खूण

market (markets) *n* A **market** is a place where goods are bought and sold, usually in the open air. बाजार

marketing *n* **Marketing** is the organization of the sale of a product, for example, deciding on its price, the areas it should be supplied to, and how it should be advertised. मालाच्या विक्री व वितरण संबंधीच्या बाबी हाताळणारा उद्योगाचा एक भाग

marketplace (marketplaces) *n* In business, the **marketplace** refers to the activity of buying and selling products. उत्पादनांची खरेदी-विक्री

market research *n* **Market research** is the activity of collecting and studying information about what people want, need, and buy. बाजार संशोधन

marmalade (marmalades) *n* **Marmalade** is a food like jam made from oranges or lemons. मर्मालेड (एक जॅम)

maroon *adj* Something that is **maroon** is dark reddish-purple in colour. तपकिरीसर तांबडा

marriage (marriages) *n* A **marriage** is the relationship between a husband and wife, or the state of being married. विवाह

marriage certificate (marriage certificates) *n* A **marriage certificate** is a legal document that proves two people are married. विवाह प्रमाणपत्र

married *adj* If you are **married**, you have a husband or wife. विवाहित

marrow (marrows) *n* A **marrow** is a long, thick, green vegetable with soft white flesh that is eaten cooked. मॅरो नावाची भाजी

marry (marries, marrying, married) *v* When two people **get married** or **marry**, they become each other's husband and wife during a special ceremony. विवाह करणे, लग्न करणे

marsh (marshes) *n* A **marsh** is a wet muddy area of land. दलदल

martyr (martyrs) *n* A **martyr** is someone who is killed or made to suffer greatly because of their religious or political beliefs. हुतात्मा

marvellous *adj* If you describe someone or something as **marvellous**, you are emphasizing that they are very good. अत्यंत छान

Marxism *n* **Marxism** is a political philosophy based on the writings of Karl Marx which stresses the importance of the struggle between different social classes. मार्क्सवाद

marzipan *n* **Marzipan** is a paste made of almonds, sugar, and egg which is sometimes put on top of cakes. मझिर्पिन (केकवर घालण्यात येणारी एक पेस्ट)

mascara (mascaras) *n* **Mascara** is a substance used to colour eyelashes. मस्कारा

masculine adj **Masculine** characteristics or things relate to or are considered typical of men, rather than women. पुरुषी

mashed potatoes npl **Mashed potatoes** are potatoes that have been boiled and crushed into a soft mass, often with butter and milk. उकडून कुस्करलेले बटाटे

mask (**masks**) n A **mask** is something which you wear over your face for protection or to disguise yourself. मुखवटा

masked adj Someone who is **masked** is wearing a mask. मुखवटा चढवलेली व्यक्ती

mass (**masses**) n A **mass** of something is a large amount of it. भरपूर

Mass (**masses**) n **Mass** is a Christian church ceremony during which people eat bread and drink wine in order to remember the last meal of Jesus Christ. ख्रिश्चनधर्मियांची सामुदायिक प्रार्थना

massacre (**massacres**) n A **massacre** is the killing of many people in a violent and cruel way. हत्याकांड

massive adj Something that is **massive** is very large in size. मोठ्या प्रमाणावरील

mast (**masts**) n The **masts** of a boat are the tall upright poles that support its sails. नौकेच्या शिडाचा खांब

master (**masters**, **mastering**, **mastered**) n A servant's **master** is the man that he or she works for. मालक ▷ vt If you **master** something, you manage to learn how to do it properly or understand it completely. प्रभुत्व मिळवणे

masterpiece (**masterpieces**) n A **masterpiece** is an extremely good painting, novel, film, or other work of art. कलेचा उत्कृष्ट नमुना

mat (**mats**) n A **mat** is a small piece of material which you put on a table to protect it from a hot plate or cup. चटई

match (**matches**, **matching**, **matched**) n A **match** is a game of football, cricket, or some other sport. कूच, कवाइत ▷ n If things or people are a good **match**, they look good together or go well together. जुळणे, तोड, जोडा

▷ v If one thing **matches** another, they look good together. जुळणे ▷ n A **match** is a small, thin stick that makes a flame when you rub it on a rough surface. आगकाडी

matching adj **Matching** is used to describe things which are of the same colour or design. (रंगसंगती, इ) जुळणारे

mate (**mates**) n You can refer to someone's friends as their **mates**. (informal) मित्र

material (**materials**) n A **material** is what something is made of, like rock, glass, or plastic. सहित्य, सामग्री ▷ n **Material** is cloth. कापड

maternal adj **Maternal** feelings or actions are typical of those of a mother towards her child. मातेश्वरी भावना

maternity hospital (**maternity hospitals**) n A **maternity hospital** is a hospital that provides help and medical care to women when they are pregnant and when they give birth. प्रसुती रुग्णालय

maternity leave n **Maternity leave** is a period of paid absence from work, to which a woman is legally entitled during the months immediately before and after childbirth. प्रसुती रजा

mathematical adj Something that is **mathematical** involves numbers and calculations. गणिती

mathematics npl **Mathematics** is the study of numbers, quantities, or shapes. गणित

maths npl Mathematics is usually referred to as **maths**. गणित

matter (**matters**, **mattering**, **mattered**) n A **matter** is a task, situation, or event which you have to deal with or think about. प्रकरण ▷ v If something **matters**, it is important because it has an effect on a situation. महत्त्वाचे असणे

mattress (**mattresses**) n A **mattress** is a large flat pad which is put on a bed to make it comfortable to sleep on. गादी

mature (**maturer**, **maturest**) adj A **mature** person or animal is fully grown. प्रौढ

mature student (mature students) *n* A **mature student** is a person who begins their studies at university or college a number of years after leaving school, so that they are older than most of the people they are studying with. प्रौढ विद्यार्थी

Mauritania *n* **Mauritania** is a republic in north-west Africa, on the Atlantic. मॉरिटानिया

Mauritius *n* **Mauritius** is an island and state in the Indian Ocean, east of Madagascar. मॉरिशस

mauve *adj* Something that is **mauve** is of a pale purple colour. फिकट जांभळा रंग

maximum *n* You use **maximum** to describe an amount which is the largest that is possible, allowed, or required. सर्वाधिक ▷ *n* A **maximum** is the greatest possible amount, degree, etc. सर्वाधिक

may *v* If you **may** do something, it is possible that you will do it. (एखादी गोष्ट) कदाचित होईल. *I may come back next year.* ▷ *v* If you **may** do something, you can do it because someone allows you to do it. करू शकणे *Please may I leave the room?*

May (Mays) *n* **May** is the fifth month of the year in the Western calendar. मे महिना

maybe *adv* You use **maybe** when you are not sure about something. इंग्रजी भाषेतील शक्यतादर्शक क्रियाविशेषण

mayonnaise *n* **Mayonnaise** is a sauce made from egg yolks, oil, and vinegar, eaten cold. मायोनेस (एक सॉस)

mayor (mayors) *n* The **mayor** of a town or city is the person who has been elected to represent it for a fixed period of time. महापौर

maze (mazes) *n* A **maze** is a complex system of passages or paths separated by walls or hedges. चक्रव्यूह, भूलभुलैय्या, कोडे

me *pron* You use **me** when you are talking about yourself. मला *Can you hear me?*

meadow (meadows) *n* A **meadow** is a field with grass and flowers growing in it. कुरण

meal (meals) *n* A **meal** is an occasion when people eat. जेवण

mealtime (mealtimes) *n* **Mealtimes** are occasions when you eat breakfast, lunch, or dinner. जेवणाची वेळ

mean (meaner, meanest, means, meaning, meant) *adj* Someone who is **mean** is not nice to other people. हलकट ▷ *vt* If you ask what something **means**, you want to understand it. अर्थ असणे ▷ *vt* If you **mean** what you are saying, it is not a joke. गंभीरपणे सांगणे ▷ *vt* If you **mean** to do something, it is not an accident. मनात हेतू असणे

meaning (meanings) *n* The **meaning** of something such as a word, symbol, or gesture is the thing that it refers to or the message that it conveys. अर्थ

means *npl* You can refer to the money that someone has as their **means**. साधने

meantime *adv* **In the meantime** means in the period of time between two events, or while an event is happening. दरम्यान

meanwhile *adv* **Meanwhile** means in the period of time between two events, or while an event is happening. दरम्यान

measles *npl* **Measles** is an infectious illness that gives you a high temperature and red spots. गोवर

measure (measures, measuring, measured) *vt* If you **measure** something, you find out its size. मोजणे

measurements *npl* Your **measurements** are the size of your chest, waist, hips, and other parts of your body. मोजमाप

meat (meats) *n* **Meat** is the flesh of a dead animal that people cook and eat. प्राण्यांचे मांस

meatball (meatballs) *n* **Meatballs** are small balls of chopped meat. They are usually eaten with a sauce. मीटबॉल (मांसाचे लहान गोळे)

Mecca *n* **Mecca** is a city in Saudi Arabia, which is the holiest city in Islam because the Prophet Mohammed was born there. All Muslims face towards Mecca when they pray. मक्का

mechanic (mechanics) *n* A **mechanic** is someone whose job is to repair and maintain

m

machines and engines, especially car engines. तंत्रज्ञ

mechanical adj A **mechanical** device has moving parts and uses power in order to do a particular task. तांत्रिक

mechanism (**mechanisms**) n A **mechanism** is a part of a machine that does a particular task. यंत्रांच्या भागाची रचना

medal (**medals**) n A **medal** is a small metal disc, given as an award for bravery or as a prize in a sporting event. पदक

medallion (**medallions**) n A **medallion** is a round metal disc which some people wear as an ornament, especially on a chain round their neck. मेंडालिअन (मुखवटा असलेले पदक)

media n You can refer to television, radio, and newspapers as the **media**. प्रसार माध्यमे

mediaeval adj **Mediaeval** things relate to or date from the period in European history between about 500 AD and about 1500 AD. मध्ययुगीन

medical (**medicals**) adj **Medical** means relating to illness and injuries and to their treatment or prevention. वैद्यकीय ▷ n A **medical** is a thorough examination of your body by a doctor. संपूर्ण वैद्यकीय चाचणी

medical certificate (**medical certificates**) n A **medical certificate** is a document stating the result of a satisfactory medical examination. वैद्यकीय प्रमाणपत्र

medicine n **Medicine** is the treatment of illness and injuries by doctors and nurses. वैद्यक शास्त्र

meditation n **Meditation** is the act of remaining in a silent and calm state for a period of time, as part of a religious training, or so that you are more able to deal with the problems of everyday life. ध्यानधारणा

Mediterranean n Something that is **Mediterranean** is characteristic of or belongs to the people or region around the Mediterranean Sea. भू-मध्य प्रदेशातील ▷ n The **Mediterranean** is the sea between southern Europe and North Africa. भू-मध्य समुद्र

medium adj You use **medium** to describe something which is average in size, degree, or amount, or approximately half way along a scale between two extremes. मध्यम

medium-sized adj **Medium-sized** means neither large nor small, but approximately halfway between the two. मध्यम आकाराचा

meet (**meets**, **meeting**, **met**) vt If you **meet** someone, you happen to be in the same place as them and start talking to them. You may know the other person, but be surprised to see them, or you may not know them at all. भेटणे ▷ vi If people **meet**, they happen to be in the same place and start talking to each other. They may know each other, but be surprised to see each other, or they may not know each other at all. भेटणे

meeting (**meetings**) n A **meeting** is an event at which a group of people come together to discuss things or make decisions. सभा

meet up (**meets up**, **meeting up**, **met up**) v If two or more people **meet up**, they go to the same place, which they have earlier arranged to do, so that they can talk or do something together. एकत्र जमणे We tend to meet up for lunch once a week.

mega adj Young people sometimes use **mega** in front of nouns in order to emphasize that the thing they are talking about is very good, very large, or very impressive. (informal) प्रचंड

melody (melodies) n A **melody** is a tune. *(formal)* धून

melon (melons) n A **melon** is a large, sweet, juicy fruit with a thick green or yellow skin. कलिंगड, खरबूज

melt (melts, melting, melted) vt When you **melt** a solid substance, it changes to a liquid because of being heated. वितळवणे ▷ vi When a solid substance **melts**, it changes to a liquid because of being heated. वितळणे

member (members) n A **member** of a group or organization is one of the people, animals, or things belonging to it. सभासद

membership n **Membership** is the fact or state of being a member of an organization. सभासदत्व

membership card (membership cards) n A **membership card** is a card that proves that you are a member of an organization. सभासदत्वाचे कार्ड

memento (mementos, mementoes) n A **memento** is an object which you keep because it reminds you of a person or a special occasion. स्मृतिचिन्ह

memo (memos) n A **memo** is an official note from one person to another within the same organization. औपचारिक चिठी (मेमो)

memorial (memorials) n A **memorial** is a structure built in order to remind people of a famous person or event. स्मारक

memorize (memorizes, memorizing, memorized) vt If you **memorize** something, you learn it so that you can remember it exactly. पाठ करणे

memory (memories) n Your **memory** is your ability to remember things. स्मृती ▷ n A **memory** is something you remember about the past. स्मृती

memory card (memory cards) n A **memory card** is a type of card containing computer memory that is used in digital cameras and other devices. मेमरी कार्ड

mend (mends, mending, mended) vt If you **mend** something that is damaged or broken,

you repair it so that it works properly or can be used. दुरुस्त करणे

meningitis n **Meningitis** is a serious infectious illness which affects your brain and spinal cord. मेंदूज्वर

menopause n The **menopause** is the time during which a woman's menstruation stops, usually when she is about fifty. स्त्रियांची ऋतुसमाप्ती

menstruation n **Menstruation** is the approximately monthly discharge of blood from the body by nonpregnant women. मासिक साव (पाळी)

mental adj **Mental** means relating to the mind and the process of thinking. मानसिक

mental hospital (mental hospitals) n A **mental hospital** is a hospital for people who are suffering from mental illness. मनोरुग्णालय

mentality (mentalities) n Your **mentality** is your attitudes or ways of thinking. मानसिकता

mention (mentions, mentioning, mentioned) vt If you **mention** something, you say something about it, usually briefly. उल्लेख करणे

menu (menus) n In a restaurant or café, the **menu** is a list of the available meals and drinks. हॉटेलातील खाद्यपदार्थांची यादी

merchant bank (merchant banks) n A **merchant bank** is a bank that deals mainly with firms, investment, and foreign trade, rather than with the public. व्यापारी बँक

mercury n **Mercury** is a silver-coloured liquid metal, used in thermometers. पारा

mercy n If someone in authority shows **mercy**, they choose not to harm or punish someone they have power over. दया

mere (merest) adj You use **mere** to say that something is small or not important. जेमतेम

merge (merges, merging, merged) v If one thing **merges** with another, or **is merged** with another, they combine or come together to make one whole thing. You can also say that two things **merge**, or **are merged**. एकत्र करणे

m

merger (**mergers**) *n* A **merger** is the joining together of two separate companies or organizations so that they become one. एकत्रिकरण

meringue (**meringues**) *n* **Meringue** is a mixture of beaten egg whites and sugar which is baked in the oven. मेरिंग(अंड्याचा पांढरा भाग व साखर यांचे मिश्रण)

mermaid (**mermaids**) *n* In fairy stories and legends, a **mermaid** is a woman with a fish's tail instead of legs, who lives in the sea. जलपरी

merry (**merrier, merriest**) *adj* **Merry** means happy and cheerful. (*old-fashioned*) उत्साही व आनंदी

merry-go-round (**merry-go-rounds**) *n* A **merry-go-round** is a large circular platform at a fairground on which there are model animals or vehicles for people to sit on or in as it turns round. मेरी-गो-राऊंड

mess (**messes**) *n* If something is a **mess** or in a **mess**, it is dirty or untidy. घाण, घसारा

mess about (**messes about, messing about, messed about**) *v* If you **mess about**, you spend time doing things without any particular purpose or without achieving anything. वेळ वाया घालवणे *The children scribbled with crayons at the table and messed about.*

message (**messages**) *n* A **message** is a piece of information or a request that you send to someone or leave for them when you cannot speak to them directly. निरोप

messenger (**messengers**) *n* A **messenger** takes a message to someone, or takes messages regularly as their job. संदेशवाहक

mess up (**messes up, messing up, messed up**) *v* If someone **messes** something **up**, or if they **mess up**, they cause something to fail or be spoiled. (*informal*) बिघडवणे *He had messed up his career.*

messy (**messier, messiest**) *adj* A **messy** person or activity makes things dirty or untidy. अव्यवस्थित

metabolism (**metabolisms**) *n* Your **metabolism** is the way that chemical processes in your body cause food to be used in an efficient way, for example to give you energy. चयापचय

metal (**metals**) *n* **Metal** is a hard substance such as iron, steel, copper, or lead. धातू

meteorite (**meteorites**) *n* A **meteorite** is a large piece of rock or metal from space that has landed on Earth. उल्का

meter (**meters**) *n* A **meter** is a device that measures and records something such as the amount of gas or electricity that you have used. मीटर (वीज, पाणी, इ.चा)

method (**methods**) *n* A **method** is a particular way of doing something. पद्धत

metre (**metres**) *n* A **metre** is a unit of length equal to 100 centimetres. मीटर (कापड, इ. मोजण्याचा)

metric *adj* The **metric** system of measurement uses metres, grammes, and litres. दशमान पद्धती

Mexican (**Mexicans**) *adj* **Mexican** means belonging to or relating to Mexico, or to its people or culture. मेक्सिकन ▷ *n* A **Mexican** is a Mexican citizen, or a person of Mexican origin. मेक्सिकन

Mexico *n* **Mexico** is a republic in North America, on the Gulf of Mexico and the Pacific. मेक्सिको

microchip (**microchips**) *n* A **microchip** is a small piece of silicon inside a computer, on which electronic circuits are printed. मायक्रोचिप

microphone (**microphones**) *n* A **microphone** is a device used to record sounds or make them louder. मायक्रोफोन

microscope (microscopes) n A **microscope** is an instrument which magnifies very small objects so that you can study them. सूक्ष्मदर्शी

microwave (microwaves) n A **microwave** or a **microwave oven** is an oven which cooks food very quickly by a kind of radiation rather than by heat. मायक्रोवेव्ह ओव्हन

mid adj Mid- is used to form nouns or adjectives that refer to the middle part of a particular period of time, or the middle point of a particular place. मध्य

midday n **Midday** is twelve o'clock in the middle of the day. मध्यान्ह

middle (middles) n The **middle** of something is the part that is farthest from its edges, ends, or outside surface. मध्यावर

middle-aged adj **Middle-aged** people are between the ages of about 40 and 60. मध्यमवयीन

Middle Ages npl In European history, the **Middle Ages** was the period between the end of the Roman Empire in 476 AD and about 1500 AD, especially the later part of this period. मध्ययुग

middle-class adj **Middle-class** people are the people in a society who are not working-class or upper-class, for example managers, doctors, and lawyers. मध्यमवर्गीय

Middle East n The **Middle East** is the area around the eastern Mediterranean that includes Iran and all the countries in Asia that are to the west and south-west of Iran. मध्य पूर्व

midge (midges) n **Midges** are very small insects which bite. मिजेस नावाचा कीटक

midnight n **Midnight** is twelve o'clock in the middle of the night. मध्यरात्र

midwife (midwives) n A **midwife** is a nurse who advises pregnant women and helps them to give birth. सुईण

might v You use **might** when something is possible. इंग्रजी भाषेतील शक्यतादर्शक सहाय्यकारी क्रियापद He might win the race.

migraine (migraines) n A **migraine** is a very severe headache. अर्धशिशी

migrant (migrants) n A **migrant** is a person who moves from one place to another, especially in order to find work. भटकी व्यक्ती

migration (migrations) n **Migration** is the act of people moving from one place to another, especially in order to find work. स्थलांतर

mild (milder, mildest) adj Something that is **mild** is not very strong or severe. सौम्य

mile (miles) n A **mile** is a unit of distance equal to approximately 1.6 kilometres. मैल

mileage (mileages) n **Mileage** refers to a distance that is travelled, measured in miles. प्रवास केलेले अंतर

mileometer (mileometers) n An **mileometer** is a device that records the number of miles that a bicycle or motor vehicle has travelled. मायलोमीटर

military adj **Military** means relating to a country's armed forces. सैनिकी

milk (milks, milking, milked) n **Milk** is the white liquid produced by cows and goats, which people drink and make into butter, cheese, and yoghurt. दूध ▷ vt When someone **milks** a cow or goat, they get milk from it from an organ called the udder, which hangs beneath its body. दूध काढणे

milk chocolate n **Milk chocolate** is chocolate that has been made with milk. It is lighter in colour and has a creamier taste than plain chocolate. मिल्क चॉकलेट

milkshake (milkshakes) n A **milkshake** is a cold drink made by mixing milk with a flavouring or fruit, and sometimes ice cream. मिल्कशेक

mill (mills) n A **mill** is a building where grain is crushed to make flour. गिरणी

millennium (millenniums, millennia) n A **millennium** is a thousand years. (formal) सहस्रक

millimetre (millimetres) n A **millimetre** is a metric unit of length equal to one tenth of a centimetre. मिलीमीटर

million (millions) num A **million** or one **million** is the number 1,000,000. दशलक्ष

millionaire (millionaires) n A **millionaire** is someone who has money or property worth at least a million pounds or dollars. लक्षाधीश

mimic (mimics, mimicking, mimicked) vt If you **mimic** someone's actions or voice, you imitate them in an amusing or entertaining way. नक्कल करणे

mince n **Mince** is meat cut into very small pieces. बारीक तुकडे करणे

mind (minds, minding, minded) n Your **mind** is the part of your brain that thinks, understands, and remembers. मन ▷ vt If you **mind** something, it annoys you. हरकत घेणे

mine (mines) n A **mine** is a deep hole or tunnel where people go to dig things like gold or diamonds out of rock. खाण ▷ pron **Mine** means belonging to me. माझा That isn't your bag, it's mine.

miner (miners) n A **miner** is a person who works underground in mines in order to obtain minerals such as coal, diamonds, or gold. खाणकामगार

mineral (minerals) adj **Mineral** means of, relating to, or containing minerals. खनिज ▷ n A **mineral** is a substance such as tin, salt, or coal that is formed naturally in rocks and in the earth. खनिज

mineral water (mineral waters) n **Mineral water** is water that comes out of the ground naturally and is considered healthy to drink. मिनरल वॉटर

miniature (miniatures) adj **Miniature** things are much smaller than other things of the same kind. लहान ▷ n A **miniature** is a very small detailed painting, often of a person. लहान प्रतिकृती

minibus (minibuses) n A **minibus** is a large van which has seats in the back and windows along its sides. मिनीबस

minicab (minicabs) n A **minicab** is a taxi which you have to arrange to pick you up by telephone. मिनीकॅब

minimal adj Something that is **minimal** is very small in quantity or degree. कमीत कमी

minimize (minimizes, minimizing, minimized) vt If you **minimize** a risk or problem, you reduce it to the lowest possible level. कमी करणे

minimum n You use **minimum** to describe an amount which is the smallest that is possible, allowed, or required. किमान ▷ n A **minimum** is the least possible amount, degree, or quantity. किमान

mining n **Mining** is the industry and activities connected with getting valuable or useful minerals from the ground, for example coal, diamonds, or gold. खाण उद्योग

minister (ministers) n A **minister** is a person who is in charge of a government department. मंत्री

ministry (ministries) n A **ministry** is a government department. मंत्रालय

mink (minks, mink) n A **mink** is a small furry animal with highly valued fur. मिंक (एक केसाळ प्राणी)

minor (minors) adj You use **minor** to describe something that is less important, serious, or significant than other things in a group or situation. क्षुल्लक ▷ n A **minor** is a person who is still legally a child. In Britain, people are minors until they reach the age of eighteen. प्रौढ नसलेली व्यक्ती

minority (minorities) n If you talk about a **minority** of people or things in a larger group, you are referring to a number of them that forms less than half of the larger group. अल्पसंख्याक

mint (mints) n The **mint** is the place where the official coins of a country are made. टांकसाळ ▷ n **Mint** is a fresh-tasting herb. पुदिना

minus prep You use **minus** when you take one number away from another number. वजा करणे Three minus two is one.

minute (minutest, minutes) adj Something that is **minute** is very small. कमी, बारीक ▷ n A

minute is used for measuring time. There are sixty seconds in one **minute**. मिनिट

miracle (**miracles**) *n* If you say that an event or invention is a **miracle**, you mean that it is very surprising and fortunate. चमत्कार

mirror (**mirrors**) *n* A **mirror** is an object made of glass in which you can see your reflection. आरसा

misbehave (**misbehaves, misbehaving, misbehaved**) *vi* If someone, especially a child, **misbehaves**, they behave in a way that is not acceptable to other people. गैरवर्तन करणे

miscarriage (**miscarriages**) *n* If a woman has a **miscarriage**, she gives birth to a foetus before it is properly formed and it dies. गर्भपात

miscellaneous *adj* A **miscellaneous** group consists of many different kinds of things or people that are difficult to put into a particular category. संकीर्ण

mischief *n* **Mischief** is playing harmless tricks on people or doing things you are not supposed to do. चेष्टा

mischievous *adj* A **mischievous** person is eager to have fun by embarrassing people or by playing harmless tricks. खोडकर

miser (**misers**) *n* If you say that someone is a **miser**, you disapprove of them because they seem to hate spending money, and try to spend as little as possible. कंजूष

miserable *adj* If you are **miserable**, you are very unhappy. दुःखी

misery (**miseries**) *n* **Misery** is great unhappiness. दुःख

misfortune (**misfortunes**) *n* A **misfortune** is something unpleasant or unlucky that happens to someone. दुर्दैव

mishap (**mishaps**) *n* A **mishap** is an unfortunate but not very serious event that happens to you. दुर्घटना

misjudge (**misjudges, misjudging, misjudged**) *vt* If you say that someone **has misjudged** a person or situation, you mean that they have formed an incorrect idea or opinion about them, and often that they have made a wrong decision as a result of this. चुकीचा अंदाज लावणे

mislay (**mislays, mislaying, mislaid**) *vt* If you **mislay** something, you put it somewhere and then forget where you have put it. एका ठिकाणी ठेवून विसरून जाणे

misleading *adj* If you describe something as **misleading**, you mean that it gives you a wrong idea or impression. दिशाभूल करणारे

misprint (**misprints**) *n* A **misprint** is a mistake in the way something is printed, for example a spelling mistake. चुकीचे छापलेले

miss (**misses, missing, missed**) *v* If you **miss** something that you are trying to hit or catch, you do not manage to hit it or catch it. चुकणे ▷ *vt* If you **miss** something, you do not notice it. लक्षात न येणे ▷ *vt* If you **miss** someone who is not with you, you feel sad that they are not there. आठवण येणे

Miss (**Misses**) *n* You use **Miss** in front of the name of a girl or unmarried woman when you are speaking to her or referring to her. कुमारी

missile (**missiles**) *n* A **missile** is a tube-shaped weapon that moves long distances through the air and explodes when it reaches its target. क्षेपणास्त्र

missing *adj* If someone or something is **missing** or has **gone missing**, they are not where you expect them to be, and you cannot find them. हरवलेले

mist (**mists**) *n* **Mist** consists of many tiny drops of water in the air, which make it difficult to see very far. धुके

m

mistake (mistakes, mistaking, mistook, mistaken) n A **mistake** is something you do which you did not intend to do, or which produces a result that you do not want. चूक ▷ vt If you **mistake** one person or thing **for** another, you wrongly think that they are the other person or thing. माणूस ओळखण्यात चूक करणे

mistaken adj If you are **mistaken**, or if you have a **mistaken** belief, you are wrong about something. चुकलेला

mistakenly adv If you do or think something **mistakenly**, you do something which you did not intend to do, or you are wrong about something. चुकून

mistletoe n **Mistletoe** is a plant with pale berries that grows on the branches of some trees. मिसलटो (एक झाड)

misty (mistier, mistiest) adj If it is **misty**, there is a lot of mist in the air. धुके असलेले

misunderstand (misunderstands, misunderstanding, misunderstood) v If you **misunderstand** someone or something, you do not understand them properly. गैरसमज होणे

misunderstanding (misunderstandings) n A **misunderstanding** is a failure to understand something such as a situation or a person's remarks. गैरसमज

mitten (mittens) n **Mittens** are gloves which have one section that covers your thumb and another section that covers your four fingers together. एक प्रकारचा हातमोजा

mix (mixes, mixing, mixed) n A **mix** is a powder containing all the substances that you need in order to make something, to which you add liquid. मिश्रण ▷ v If two substances **mix**, or if you **mix** one substance with another, they combine to form a single substance. मिसळणे

mixed adj If you have **mixed** feelings about something or someone, you feel uncertain about them because you can see both good and bad points about them. संमिश्र

mixed salad (mixed salads) n A **mixed salad** is a mixture of raw or cold foods such as lettuce, cucumber, and tomatoes. मिश्र सलाड

mixer (mixers) n A **mixer** is a machine used for mixing things together. मिक्सर

mixture (mixtures) n A **mixture** of things consists of several different things together. मिश्रण

mix up (mixes up, mixing up, mixed up, mix-ups) v If you **mix up** two things or people, you confuse them, so that you think that one of them is the other one. सरमिसळ I mixed her up with someone else. ▷ n A **mix-up** is a mistake or a failure in the way that something has been planned. (informal) नियोजन करूनही झालेला गोंधळ

MMS abbr **MMS** is a method of sending messages over wireless networks, especially on mobile phones. **MMS** is an abbreviation of 'Multimedia Messaging Service'. एमएमएस

moan (moans, moaning, moaned) vi If you **moan**, you make a low sound, usually because you are unhappy or in pain. विव्हळणे

moat (moats) n A **moat** is a deep, wide channel dug round a place such as a castle and filled with water, in order to protect the place from attack. खंदक

mobile adj Something or someone that is **mobile** is able to move or be moved easily. फिरता

mobile home (mobile homes) n A **mobile home** is a large caravan that people live in and that usually remains in the same place, but which can be pulled to another place using a car or van. फिरते घर

mobile number (mobile numbers) n Someone's **mobile number** is the series of numbers that you dial when you are making a telephone call to their mobile phone. मोबाईल क्रमांक

mobile phone (mobile phones) n A **mobile phone** is a small phone that you can take everywhere with you. भ्रमणध्वनी, मोबाईल फोन

mock (mocks, mocking, mocked) *adj* You use **mock** to describe something which is not genuine, but which is intended to be very similar to the real thing. लुटूपुटूचा ▷ *vt* If you **mock** someone, you laugh at them, tease them, or try to make them look foolish. वाकुल्या दाखविणे

mod cons *npl* **Mod cons** are the modern facilities in a house that make it easy and pleasant to live in. *(informal)* आधुनिक सुविधा

model (models, modelling, modelled) *adj* A **model** wife or a model teacher, for example, is an excellent wife or an excellent teacher. आदर्श ▷ *n* A **model** is a small copy of something. नमुना ▷ *vt* If one thing is **modelled** on another, the first thing is made so that it is like the second thing in some way. नमुन्याबरहुकूम बनविणे ▷ *n* A **model** is a person whose job is to wear and show new clothes. मॉडेल

modem (modems) *n* A **modem** is a device which uses a telephone line to connect computers or computer systems. मॉडेम

moderate *adj* **Moderate** political opinions or policies are not extreme. मध्यमवर्गीय, मवाळ

moderation *n* If someone's behaviour shows **moderation**, they act in a way that is reasonable and not extreme. मध्यममार्ग, मवाळ

modern *adj* **Modern** means relating to the present time. आधुनिक

modernize (modernizes, modernizing, modernized) *vt* To **modernize** a system means to replace old equipment or methods with new ones. आधुनिकीकरण करणे

modern languages *npl* **Modern languages** refers to the modern European languages, for example French, German, and Russian, which are studied at school or university. आधुनिक भाषा

modest *adj* A **modest** house or other building is not large or expensive. मध्यम

modification (modifications) *n* **Modification** is the act of changing something slightly in order to improve it. सुधारणा

modify (modifies, modifying, modified) *vt* If you **modify** something, you change it slightly in order to improve it. सुधारणा करणे

module (modules) *n* A **module** is one of the units that some university or college courses are divided into. मॉड्यूल

moist (moister, moistest) *adj* Something that is **moist** is slightly wet. दमट, ओलसर

moisture *n* **Moisture** is tiny drops of water in the air or on a surface. दमटपणा, आर्द्रता

moisturizer (moisturizers) *n* A **moisturizer** is a cream that you put on your skin to make it feel softer and smoother. मॉइश्चरायझर

Moldova *n* **Moldova** is a republic in south-east Europe. माल्डोव्हा

Moldovan (Moldovans) *adj* **Moldovan** means of or relating to Moldova or its inhabitants. माल्डोव्हन ▷ *n* A **Moldovan** is a native or inhabitant of Moldova. माल्डोव्हन

mole (moles) *n* A **mole** is a small animal with black fur that lives under the ground. चिचुंद्री ▷ *n* A **mole** is a person who works for an organization and gives secret information about it to other people or to its enemies. गुप्त महिती शत्रुदेशांना देणारा फितूर सरकारी अधिकारी ▷ *n* A **mole** is a natural dark spot on your skin. अंगावरील तीळ

molecule (molecules) *n* A **molecule** is the smallest amount of a chemical substance which can exist. रेणू

moment (moments) *n* A **moment** is a very short period of time. क्षण

momentarily *adv* **Momentarily** means for a short time. *(written)* क्षणिक

momentary *adj* Something that is **momentary** lasts for only a very short time. क्षणिक

m

momentous *adj* A **momentous** event is very important. महत्वाचा

Monaco *n* **Monaco** is a country in south-west Europe, on the Mediterranean. मोनॅको

monarch (monarchs) *n* A **monarch** is a king or queen. राजा, राणी

monarchy (monarchies) *n* A **monarchy** is a system in which a monarch rules over a country. राजेशाही

monastery (monasteries) *n* A **monastery** is a building in which monks live. धर्मशाळा

Monday (Mondays) *n* **Monday** is the day after Sunday and before Tuesday. सोमवार

monetary *adj* **Monetary** means relating to money. आर्थिक

money *n* **Money** consists of the coins or banknotes that you can spend, or a sum that can be represented by these. पैसे

Mongolia *n* **Mongolia** is a republic in east central Asia. मंगोलिया

Mongolian (Mongolians) *adj* **Mongolian** means belonging or relating to Mongolia, or to its people, language, or culture. मंगोलियन ▷ *n* A **Mongolian** is a person who comes from Mongolia. मंगोलियन ▷ *n* **Mongolian** is the language that is spoken in Mongolia. मंगोलियन

mongrel (mongrels) *n* A **mongrel** is a dog which is a mixture of different breeds. मॉंगेल जातीचा कुत्रा

monitor (monitors) *n* A **monitor** is a machine used to check or record things. मॉनिटर

monk (monks) *n* A **monk** is a member of a male religious community. भिक्षु, साधू

monkey (monkeys) *n* A **monkey** is an animal with a long tail which lives in hot countries and climbs trees. माकड

monopoly (monopolies) *n* If a company, person, or state has a **monopoly** on something such as an industry, they have complete control over it. मक्तेदारी

monotonous *adj* Something that is **monotonous** is very boring because it has a regular repeated pattern which never changes. कंटाळवाणे

monsoon (monsoons) *n* The **monsoon** is the season of very heavy rain in Southern Asia. वर्षा ऋतू

monster (monsters) *n* A **monster** is a large imaginary creature that is very frightening. राक्षस

month (months) *n* A **month** is one of the twelve periods of time that a year is divided into, for example January or February. महिना

monthly *adj* A **monthly** event or publication happens or appears every month. मासिक

monument (monuments) *n* A **monument** is a large structure, usually made of stone, which is built to remind people of an event in history or of a famous person. स्मारक

mood (moods) *n* Your **mood** is the way you are feeling at a particular time. मनाची अवस्था

moody (moodier, moodiest) *adj* A **moody** person often becomes depressed or angry without any warning. लहरी

moon *n* The **moon** is the object in the sky that goes round the Earth once every four weeks and that you can often see at night as a circle or part of a circle. चंद्र

moor (moors, mooring, moored) *n* A **moor** is an area of high open ground covered mainly with rough grass and heather. हिरवळ असलेली ओसाड जागा ▷ *v* If you **moor** or **moor** a boat, you attach it to the land with a rope or cable so that it cannot drift away. नौका दोरीने किनाऱ्यावरील जमिनीला बांधणे

mop (mops) *n* A **mop** consists of a sponge or many pieces of string attached to a long handle and is used for washing floors. पोतेरे

moped (mopeds) n A **moped** is a kind of motorcycle with a very small engine. छोटे इंजिन असलेली मोटर सायकल

mop up (mops up, mopping up, mopped up) v If you **mop up** a liquid, you clean it with a cloth so that the liquid is absorbed. पुसणे A waiter mopped up the mess.

moral adj **Moral** means relating to beliefs about what is right or wrong. नैतिक

morale n **Morale** is the amount of confidence and optimism that people have. मनोबल

morals npl **Morals** are principles and beliefs concerning right and wrong behaviour. नीतिमत्ता

more det You use **more** to talk about a greater amount of something. अधिक He has more chips than me. ▷ adv You can use **more** when something continues to happen for a further period of time. आणखी ▷ pron You use **more** to refer to an additional thing or amount. अधिक As the amount of work increased, workers ate more.

morgue (morgues) n A **morgue** is a building or room where dead bodies are kept before being cremated or buried. शवागार

morning (mornings) n The **morning** is the part of a day between the time that people wake up and noon. सकाळ

morning sickness n **Morning sickness** is a feeling of sickness that some women have, often in the morning, when they are pregnant. गरोदर स्त्रियांना येणाऱ्या उलट्या

Moroccan (Moroccans) adj **Moroccan** means belonging or relating to Morocco or to its people or culture. मोरक्कन ▷ n A **Moroccan** is a person who comes from Morocco. मोरक्कन

Morocco n **Morocco** is a kingdom in north-west Africa. मोरोक्को

morphine n **Morphine** is a drug used to relieve pain. मॉर्फिन, अफू

morse code n **Morse code** is a code used for sending messages. It represents each letter of the alphabet using short and long sounds or flashes of light, which can be written down as dots and dashes. मॉर्स कोड

mortar (mortars) n A **mortar** is a short cannon which fires shells high into the air for a short distance. लहान तोफ ▷ n **Mortar** is a mixture of sand, water, and cement, which is put between bricks to make them stay firmly together. रेती, सिमेंट व पाणी यांचे मिश्रण

mortgage (mortgages, mortgaging, mortgaged) n A **mortgage** is a loan of money which you get from a bank in order to buy a house. कर्ज ▷ vt If you **mortgage** your house or land, you use it as a guarantee to a company in order to borrow money from them. गहाण ठेवणे

mosaic (mosaics) n A **mosaic** is a design made of small pieces of coloured stone or glass set in concrete or plaster. लादीवरील ठिपक्यांची नक्षी

Moslem (Moslems) adj **Moslem** means relating to Islam or Moslems. मुस्लिम ▷ n A **Moslem** is someone who believes in Islam and lives according to its rules. मुस्लिम

mosque (mosques) n A **mosque** is a building where Muslims go to worship. मशीद

mosquito (mosquitoes, mosquitos) n **Mosquitoes** are small flying insects which bite people in order to suck their blood. डास

moss (mosses) n **Moss** is a very small, soft, green plant which grows on damp soil, or on wood or stone. शेवाळ

most adj You use **most** to talk about nearly all the people or things in a group. बहुतेक ▷ adv You use **most** to show that something is true or happens more than anything else. जास्त ▷ pron **Most** of a group of things or people means nearly all of them. बहुतेक Most of the houses here are very old.

mostly adv You use **mostly** to indicate that a statement is true about the majority of a group of things or people, true most of the time, or true in most respects. बहुधा

MOT (MOTs) abbr In Britain, an **MOT** is a test which, by law, must be made each year on all road vehicles that are more than three years

m

old, in order to check that they are safe to drive. वाहनांची एमओटी चाचणी

motel (motels) n A **motel** is a hotel intended for people who are travelling by car. मोटेल

moth (moths) n A **moth** is an insect like a butterfly, which usually flies about at night. पतंग

mother (mothers) n Your **mother** is your female parent. आई

mother-in-law (mothers-in-law) n Someone's **mother-in-law** is the mother of their husband or wife. सासू

mother tongue (mother tongues) n Your **mother tongue** is the language that you learn from your parents when you are a baby. मातृभाषा

motionless adj Someone or something that is **motionless** is not moving at all. स्थिर

motivated adj If you are **motivated**, you feel enthusiastic and determined to achieve success. प्रेरित

motivation (motivations) n Your **motivation** for doing something is what causes you to want to do it. प्रेरणा

motive (motives) n Your **motive** for doing something is your reason for doing it. उद्देश

motor (motors) n A **motor** in a machine, vehicle, or boat is the part that uses electricity or fuel to produce movement, so that the machine, vehicle, or boat can work. मोटर

motorbike (motorbikes) n A **motorbike** is a two-wheeled vehicle with an engine. मोटरसायकल

motorboat (motorboats) n A **motorboat** is a boat that is driven by an engine. यंत्रनौका

motorcycle (motorcycles) n A **motorcycle** is a two-wheeled vehicle with an engine. मोटरसायकल

motorcyclist (motorcyclists) n A **motorcyclist** is someone who rides a motorcycle. मोटरसायकलस्वार

motorist (motorists) n A **motorist** is someone who drives a car. कारचालक

motor mechanic (motor mechanics) n A **motor mechanic** is someone whose job is to repair and maintain car engines. मोटर दुरुस्त करणारा

motor racing n **Motor racing** is the sport of racing fast cars on a special track. मोटरगाड्यांची शर्यत

motorway (motorways) n A **motorway** is a wide road specially built for fast travel over long distances. मोटरवे

mould (moulds) n A **mould** is a container used to make something into a particular shape. साचा ▷ n **Mould** is a soft grey, green, or blue substance that sometimes forms in spots on old food or on damp walls or clothes. बुरशी

mouldy adj Something that is **mouldy** is covered with mould. बुरशी असलेले

mount (mounts, mounting, mounted) vt To **mount** a campaign or event means to organize it and make it take place. हाती घेणे

mountain (mountains) n A **mountain** is a very high area of land with steep sides. पर्वत

mountain bike (mountain bikes) n A **mountain bike** is a type of bicycle with a strong frame and thick tyres. मजबूत मोटरसायकल

mountaineer (mountaineers) n A **mountaineer** is someone who climbs mountains as a hobby or sport. पर्वतारोहण करणारी व्यक्ती

mountaineering n **Mountaineering** is the activity of climbing the steep sides of mountains as a hobby or sport. पर्वतारोहण

mountainous adj A **mountainous** place has a lot of mountains. डोंगराळ

mount up (mounts up, mounting up, mounted up) v If something **mounts up**, it increases in quantity. वाढणे _Her medical bills mounted up._

mourning n **Mourning** is behaviour in which you show sadness about a person's death. शोक

mouse (mice) n A **mouse** is a small animal with a long tail. उंदीर ▷ n You use a

mouse to move things on a computer screen. माऊस

mouse mat (mouse mats) *n* A **mouse mat** is a flat piece of plastic or some other material that you rest the mouse on while using a computer. माऊस मॅट

mousse (mousses) *n* Mousse is a sweet light food made from eggs and cream. अंडी आणि साय यापासून बनवलेला पदार्थ

moustache (moustaches) *n* A man's **moustache** is the hair that grows on his upper lip. मिशी

mouth (mouths) *n* Your **mouth** is your lips, or the space behind your lips where your teeth and tongue are. तोंड

mouth organ (mouth organs) *n* A **mouth organ** is a small musical instrument. You play it by moving it across your lips and blowing and sucking air through it. माऊथ ऑर्गन

mouthwash (mouthwashes) *n* Mouthwash is a liquid that you put in your mouth and then spit out in order to clean your mouth and make your breath smell pleasant. माऊथ वॉश

move (moves, moving, moved) *n* A **move** is an action that you take. चाल ▷ *vt* When you **move** something, you put it in a different place. हलवणे ▷ *vi* If you **move**, you go to live in a different place. दुसऱ्या ठिकाणी जाणे

move back (moves back, moving back, moved back) *v* If you **move back**, you change your position by going in a backward direction. मागे सरकणे *He moved back up the corridor.*

move forward (moves forward, moving forward, moved forward) *v* If you **move forward** an event, you arrange for it to take place at an earlier time than had been planned. अगोदर करणे/हलवणे *He had to move forward an 11 o'clock meeting.*

move in (moves in, moving in, moved in) *v* If you **move in** somewhere, or if you **move into** a new house or place, you begin to live in a different house or place. दुसऱ्या घरात राहायला

जाणे *A friend has moved in with me to rent my spare room.*

movement (movements) *n* Movement involves changing position or going from one place to another. हालचाल

movie (movies) *n* A **movie** is a film made for the cinema or TV. *(informal)* चित्रपट

moving *adj* If something is **moving**, it makes you feel a strong emotion such as pity. हेलावून टाकणारा

mow (mows, mowing, mowed, mown) *v* If you **mow** an area of grass, you cut it using a lawnmower or a mower. यंत्राने गवत कापणे

mower (mowers) *n* A **mower** is a machine for cutting grass, corn, or wheat. गवत कापणारे यंत्र

Mozambique *n* Mozambique is a republic in south-east Africa. मोझांबिक

MP3 player (MP3 players) *n* An **MP3 player** is a machine on which you can play music downloaded from the Internet. एमपी३ प्लेअर

MP4 player (MP4 players) *n* An **MP4 player** is a machine on which you can play music downloaded from the Internet. एमपी४ प्लेअर

mph *abbr* **mph** is written after a number to indicate the speed of something such as a vehicle. **mph** is an abbreviation for 'miles per hour'. मैल प्रतितास

Mr *n* **Mr** is used before a man's name when you are speaking or referring to him. श्रीयुत

Mrs *n* **Mrs** is used before the name of a married woman when you are speaking or referring to her. सौ

Ms *n* **Ms** is used before a woman's name when you are speaking to her or referring to her. If you use **Ms**, you are not specifying if the woman is married or not. श्रीमती

MS *abbr* **MS** is a serious disease of the nerves, which gradually makes a person weaker, and sometimes affects their sight or speech. **MS** is an abbreviation for 'multiple sclerosis'. एमएस

much *det* You use **much** to talk about a large amount of something. खूप *We don't have much food.* ▷ *adv* You use **much** with 'so', 'too', and 'very' to mean a very large amount of something. खूप ▷ *pron* You use **much** to mean a large amount of something. खूप *I didn't think much about it then.*

mud *n* Mud is a sticky mixture of earth and water. चिखल

muddle (muddles) *n* A **muddle** is a confused state or situation. गोंधळलेली स्थिती

muddy (muddier, muddiest) *adj* Something that is **muddy** contains, or is covered in, mud. चिखलाने माखलेले

mudguard (mudguards) *n* The **mudguards** of a bicycle or other vehicle are curved pieces of metal or plastic above the tyres, which stop mud getting on the rider or vehicle. मडगार्ड

muesli (mueslis) *n* **Muesli** is a breakfast cereal made from chopped nuts, dried fruit, and grains. म्यूसली (न्याहारी)

muffler (mufflers) *n* A **muffler** is a piece of cloth that you wear round your neck or head, usually to keep yourself warm. *(old-fashioned)* मफलर

mug (mugs, mugging, mugged) *n* A **mug** is a large deep cup with straight sides. मग ▷ *vt* If someone **mugs** you, they attack you in order to steal your money. पैसे हिसकावून घेण्यासाठी हल्ला करणे

mugger (muggers) *n* A **mugger** is a person who attacks someone violently in a street in order to steal money from them. पैसे हिसकावून घेण्यासाठी हल्ला करणारी व्यक्ती

mugging (muggings) *n* A **mugging** is an attack on somebody in order to steal their money. पैसे हिसकावून घेण्यासाठी केलेला हल्ला

mule (mules) *n* A **mule** is an animal whose parents are a horse and a donkey. खेचर

multinational (multinationals) *adj* A **multinational** company has branches or owns companies in many different countries. बहुराष्ट्रीय कंपनी ▷ *n* A **multinational** is a company that has branches or owns companies in many different countries. बहुराष्ट्रीय कंपनी

multiple sclerosis *n* **Multiple sclerosis** is a serious disease of the nerves. The abbreviation 'MS' is also used. मल्टिपल स्क्लेरोसिस, धमन्या आकसण्याचा रोग

multiplication *n* **Multiplication** is the process of increasing greatly in number or amount. गुणाकार

multiply (multiplies, multiplying, multiplied) *v* When something **multiplies**, or when you **multiply** it, it increases greatly in number or amount. मोठ्या प्रमाणात वाढविणे

mum (mums) *n* Your **mum** is your mother. You can call your mum 'Mum'. *(informal)* आई

mummy (mummies) *n* Some people, especially young children, call their mother **mummy**. *(informal)* आई ▷ *n* A **mummy** is a dead body which was preserved long ago by being rubbed with oils and wrapped in cloth. जतन करून ठेवलेला मृतदेह, ममी

mumps *n* **Mumps** is a disease usually caught by children. It causes a mild fever and painful swelling of the glands in the neck. गालगुंड

murder (murders, murdering, murdered) *n* **Murder** is the crime of deliberately killing a person. खून ▷ *vt* To **murder** someone means to commit the crime of killing them deliberately. खून करणे

murderer (murderers) *n* A **murderer** is a person who has murdered someone. खुनी

muscle (muscles) *n* Your **muscles** are the parts inside your body that connect your bones, and that help you to move. स्नायू

muscular *adj* **Muscular** means involving or affecting your muscles. स्नायूंचा

museum (museums) *n* A **museum** is a public building where interesting and valuable objects are kept and displayed. वस्तुसंग्रहालय

mushroom (mushrooms)
n **Mushrooms** are plants with short stems and round tops. You can eat some kinds of mushrooms अळंबी

music *n* **Music** is the pattern of sounds produced by people singing or playing instruments. संगीत

musical (musicals) *adj* **Musical** describes things that are concerned with playing or studying music. संगीताचा ▷ *n* A **musical** is a play or film that uses singing and dancing in the story. संगीत नाटक

musical instrument (musical instruments) *n* A **musical instrument** is an object such as a piano, guitar, or violin which you play in order to produce music. (संगीत) वाद्य

musician (musicians) *n* A **musician** is a person who plays a musical instrument as their job or hobby. संगीतकार

Muslim (Muslims) *adj* **Muslim** means relating to Islam or Muslims. मुस्लिम ▷ *n* A **Muslim** is someone who believes in Islam and lives according to its rules. मुसलमान

mussel (mussels) *n* A **mussel** is a kind of shellfish. कालव

must *v* You use **must** to show that you think something is very important. असलेच पहिजे (कर्तव्य वा आवश्यकता दाखवण्यास वापर) *You must tell the police all the facts.*

mustard *n* **Mustard** is a yellow or brown paste made from seeds which tastes spicy. मोहरीपासून बनवलेला एक पिवळसर पदार्थ

mutter (mutters, muttering, muttered) *v* If you **mutter**, you speak very quietly so that you cannot easily be heard, often because you are complaining about something. हळु आवाजात बोलणे

mutton *n* **Mutton** is meat from an adult sheep. मेंढ्याचे वा बकरीचे मांस

mutual *adj* You use **mutual** to describe a situation, feeling, or action that is experienced, felt, or done by both of two people mentioned. परस्पर, अन्योन्य

my *det* You use **my** to show that something belongs to you. माझा *I went to sleep in my room.*

Myanmar *n* **Myanmar** is a republic in south-east Asia. म्यानमार/ब्रह्मदेश

myself *pron* You use **myself** when you are talking about yourself. मी स्वतः *I hurt myself when I fell down.*

mysterious *adj* Someone or something that is **mysterious** is strange, not known about, or not understood. गूढ

mystery (mysteries) *n* A **mystery** is something that is not understood or known about. गूढ

myth (myths) *n* A **myth** is an ancient story about gods and magic. पुराणकथा

mythology *n* **Mythology** is a group of myths, especially those from a particular country, religion, or culture. पुराण

n

naff (naffer, naffest) *adj* If you say that something is **naff**, you mean it is very unfashionable or unsophisticated. *(informal)* गावंढळ

nag (nags, nagging, nagged) *v* If someone **nags** you, or if they **nag**, they keep asking you to do something you have not done yet or do not want to do. सतत उणेदुणे काढणे

nail (**nails**) n A **nail** is a thin piece of metal. It is flat at one end and it has a point at the other end. खिळा ▷n Your **nails** are the thin hard parts that grow at the ends of your fingers and toes. नख

nailbrush (**nailbrushes**) n A **nailbrush** is a small brush that you use to clean your nails when washing your hands. नखे साफ करण्याचा ब्रश

nailfile (**nailfiles**) n A **nailfile** is a small strip of rough metal or card that you rub across the ends of your nails to shorten them or shape them. नखांची कानस

nail polish (**nail polishes**) n **Nail polish** is a thick liquid that women paint on their nails. नेल पॉलिश

nail-polish remover (**nail-polish removers**) n **Nail-polish remover** is a solvent used to remove nail polish. नेल पॉलिश रिमूव्हर

nail scissors npl **Nail scissors** are small scissors that you use for cutting your nails. नखे कापण्याची कात्री

naive adj If you describe someone as **naive**, you think they lack experience, causing them to expect things to be uncomplicated or easy, or people to be honest or kind when they are not. भाबडा

naked adj Someone who is **naked** is not wearing any clothes. नग्न

name (**names**) n The **name** of a person, thing, or place is the word or words that you use to identify them. नाव

nanny (**nannies**) n A **nanny** is a person who is paid by parents to look after their children. दाई

nap (**naps**) n If you have a **nap**, you have a short sleep, usually during the day. डुलकी

napkin (**napkins**) n A **napkin** is a small piece of cloth or paper used to protect your clothes when you are eating. नॅपकीन

nappy (**nappies**) n A **nappy** is a piece of thick cloth or paper which is fastened round a baby's bottom in order to absorb its waste. नॅपी (लहान मुलांची लंगोट)

narrow (**narrower, narrowest**) adj Something that is **narrow** measures a very small distance from one side to the other, especially compared to its length or height. अरुंद

narrow-minded adj If you describe someone as **narrow-minded**, you are criticizing them because they are unwilling to consider new ideas or other people's opinions. कोत्या वृत्तीची व्यक्ती

nasty (**nastier, nastiest**) adj Something that is **nasty** is very unpleasant or unattractive. दुःखद, वाईट

nation (**nations**) n A **nation** is an individual country considered together with its social and political structures. राष्ट्र

national adj **National** means relating to the whole of a country, rather than to part of it or to other nations. राष्ट्रीय

national anthem (**national anthems**) n A **national anthem** is a nation's official song. राष्ट्रगीत

nationalism n **Nationalism** is the desire for political independence of people who feel they are historically or culturally a separate group within a country. राष्ट्रवाद

nationalist (**nationalists**) n A **nationalist** is someone who desires for the group of people to which they belong to gain political independence. राष्ट्रवादी

nationality (**nationalities**) n If you have the **nationality** of a particular country, you have the legal right to be a citizen of it. राष्ट्रीयत्व

nationalize (**nationalizes, nationalizing, nationalized**) vt If a government **nationalizes** a private industry, that industry becomes owned by the state and controlled by the government. राष्ट्रीयीकरण करणे

national park (**national parks**) n A **national park** is a large area of natural land protected by the government because of its natural beauty, plants, or animals. राष्ट्रीय उद्यान

native *adj* Your **native** country or area is the country or area where you were born and brought up. जन्मगाव, जन्मदेश

native speaker (**native speakers**) *n* A **native speaker** of a language is someone who speaks that language as their first language rather than having learned it as a foreign language. जन्मजात येणारी भाषा

NATO *n* **NATO** is an international organization which consists of the USA, Canada, Britain, and other European countries, all of whom have agreed to support one another if they are attacked. **NATO** is an abbreviation for 'North Atlantic Treaty Organization'. नाटो

natural *adj* If you say that it is **natural** for someone to act in a particular way, you mean that it is reasonable in the circumstances. नैसर्गिक

natural gas *n* **Natural gas** is gas which is found underground or under the sea. It is collected and stored, and piped into people's homes to be used for cooking and heating. नैसर्गिक वायू

naturalist (**naturalists**) *n* A **naturalist** is a person who studies plants, animals, and other living things. निसर्गाचा अभ्यासक

naturally *adv* You use **naturally** to indicate that you think something is very obvious and not at all surprising in the circumstances. साहजिक

natural resources *npl* The **natural resources** of a place are all its land, forests, energy sources, and minerals which exist naturally there and can be used by people. नैसर्गिक स्रोत

nature *n* **Nature** refers to all the animals, plants, and other things in the world that are not made by people, and all the events and processes that are not caused by people. निसर्ग

naughty (**naughtier, naughtiest**) *adj* You say that small children are **naughty** when they behave badly. द्वाट्य

nausea *n* **Nausea** is a feeling of sickness and dizziness. मळमळ

naval *adj* **Naval** people and things belong to a country's navy. नौदलविषयक

navel (**navels**) *n* Your **navel** is the small hollow in the centre of your stomach. नाभी

navy (**navies**) *n* A country's **navy** is the part of its armed forces that fights at sea. नौदल
▷ *adj* Something that is **navy** is very dark blue. गडद निळे

NB *abbr* You write **NB** to draw someone's attention to what you are going to write next. नीट लक्ष द्या

near (**nearer, nearest**) *adj* **Near** means at or in a place not far away. जवळचा ▷ *adv* **Near** means at or to a place not far away. जवळचा
▷ *prep* If something is **near** a place, thing, or person, it is not far away from them. जवळ *We are very near my house.*

nearby *adj* If something is **nearby**, it is only a short distance away. जवळपास ▷ *adv* If something is **nearby**, it is only a short distance away. जवळपास

nearly *adv* If something is **nearly** a quantity, it is very close to that quantity but slightly less than it. If something is **nearly** a certain state, it is very close to that state but has not quite reached it. सुमारे

near-sighted *adj* Someone who is **near-sighted** cannot see distant things clearly. लघुदृष्टी असलेली व्यक्ती

neat (**neater, neatest**) *adj* A **neat** place, thing, or person is tidy, smart, and orderly. नीटनेटके

neatly *adv* **Neatly** means in a tidy or smart manner. नीटनेटकेपणाने

necessarily *adv* If you say that something is **not necessarily** true, you mean that it may not be true or is not always true. अपरिहार्यपणे

necessary *adj* Something that is **necessary** is needed to get a particular result or effect. आवश्यक

necessity *n* **Necessity** is the need to do something. आवश्यकता

neck (**necks**) *n* Your **neck** is the part of your body which joins your head to the rest of your body. मान

necklace (necklaces) n A **necklace** is a piece of jewellery such as a chain or string of beads, which someone wears round their neck. हार, माळ

nectarine (nectarines) n A **nectarine** is a fruit similar to a peach with a smooth skin. नेक्टॅरीन नावाचे फळ

need (needs, needing, needed) n If you have a **need** for something, you cannot do what you want without it. गरज ▷ vt If you **need** something, you believe that you must have it or do it. गरज असणे

needle (needles) n A **needle** is a small very thin piece of metal with a hole at one end and a sharp point at the other, which is used for sewing. सुई

negative (negatives) adj A fact, situation, or experience that is **negative** is unpleasant, depressing, or harmful. दुःखदायक ▷ n A **negative** is a word, expression, or gesture that means 'no' or 'not'. नकारात्मक

neglect (neglects, neglecting, neglected) n **Neglect** is the failure to look after someone or something properly. दुर्लक्ष ▷ vt If you **neglect** someone or something, you fail to look after them properly. दुर्लक्ष करणे

neglected adj If someone is **neglected**, they have not been given enough love, attention or support. दुर्लक्षित

negotiate (negotiates, negotiating, negotiated) v If one person or group **negotiates** with another, they talk about a problem or a situation in order to solve the problem or complete the arrangement. बोलणी करणे

negotiations npl **Negotiations** are discussions that take place between people with different interests, in which they try to reach an agreement. बोलणी

negotiator (negotiators) n **Negotiators** are people who take part in political or financial negotiations. सौदेबाज

neighbour (neighbours) n Your **neighbours** are the people who live near you, especially the people who live in the house or flat which is next to yours. शेजारी

neighbourhood (neighbourhoods) n A **neighbourhood** is one of the parts of a town where people live. शेजारचा भाग

neither conj If you say that one person or thing does not do something and **neither** does another, what you say is true of both the people or things that you are mentioning. हेही नाही व तेही नाही I never learned to swim and neither did they. ▷ pron You use **neither** to refer to each of two things or people, when you are making a negative statement that includes both of them. हेही नाही व तेही नाही They both smiled; neither seemed likely to be aware of my absence for long. ▷ det **Neither** means not one or the other of two things or people. दोहोंपैकी एकही नाही

neither ... nor conj You use **neither ... nor** when you are talking about two or more things that are not true or that do not happen. हेही नाही व तेही नाही The play was neither as funny nor as exciting as she said it was.

neon n **Neon** is a gas which exists in very small amounts in the atmosphere. निऑन वायू

Nepal n **Nepal** is a republic in South Asia. नेपाळ

nephew (nephews) n Your **nephew** is the son of your sister or brother. भाचा/ पुतण्या

nerve (nerves) n **Nerves** are long thin fibres that transmit messages between your brain and other parts of your body. मज्जातंतू ▷ n **Nerve** is the courage you need to do something difficult or dangerous. धैर्य

nerve-racking *adj* A **nerve-racking** situation or experience makes you feel very tense and worried. पोटात गोळा आणणारे, काळजीत टाकणारे

nervous *adj* If you are **nervous**, you are worried and frightened, and show this in your behaviour. बेचैन, चिंतातूर

nest (**nests**) *n* A **nest** is a place that birds, insects, and other animals make to lay eggs in or give birth to their young in. घरटे

net (**nets**) *n* A **net** is made from pieces of string or rope tied together with holes between them. It is for catching things like fish, or the ball in some sports. जाळी

netball *n* **Netball** is a game played by two teams of seven players, usually women. Each team tries to score goals by throwing a ball through a net which is at the top of a pole at each end of the court. नेटबॉल

Netherlands *n* **The Netherlands** is a kingdom in north-west Europe, on the North Sea. नेदरलँड्स

nettle (**nettles**) *n* A **nettle** is a wild plant with leaves that sting when you touch them. खाजकुयली

network (**networks**) *n* A **network** of lines, roads, veins, or other long thin things is a large number of lines which cross each other and meet at many points. जाळे

neurotic *adj* If you say that someone is **neurotic**, you mean that they are always frightened or worried about things that you consider unimportant. फाजील गोष्टींची भीती बाळगणारी व्यक्ती

neutral *adj* A **neutral** person or country does not support anyone in a disagreement, war, or contest. तटस्थ ▷ *n* **Neutral** is the position between the gears of a vehicle, in which the gears are not connected to the engine. न्यूट्रल

never *adv* **Never** means at no time in the past or future. कधीही नाही

nevertheless *adv* You use **nevertheless** when saying something that contrasts with what has just been said. *(formal)* तथापि

new (**newer, newest**) *adj* Something that is **new** was not there before. नवीन ▷ *adj* If something is **new**, nobody has used it before. नवा ▷ *adj* A **new** thing or person is a different one from the one you had before. नवा

newborn *adj* A **newborn** baby or animal is one that has just been born. नवजात

newcomer (**newcomers**) *n* A **newcomer** is a person who has recently started a new activity, arrived in a place, or joined an organization. नवागत

news *npl* **News** is information about a recently changed situation or a recent event. बातमी

newsagent (**newsagents**) *n* A **newsagent** is the shopkeeper of a shop where newspapers, sweets, soft drinks, and stationery are sold. वर्तमानपत्राचे दुकान

newspaper (**newspapers**) *n* A **newspaper** is a publication consisting of large sheets of folded paper, on which news is printed. वर्तमानपत्र

newsreader (**newsreaders**) *n* A **newsreader** is a person who reads the news on the radio or on television. बातम्यांचे वाचन करणारी व्यक्ती

newt (**newts**) *n* A **newt** is a small creature that has four legs and a long tail and can live on land and in water. चार पाय व लांब शेपटी असणारा सरड्यासारखा उभयचर प्राणी

New Year *n* **New Year** or **the New Year** is the time when people celebrate the start of a year. नववर्ष

New Zealand *n* **New Zealand** is an island country, with two main islands (the North Island and the South Island), in the south-east Pacific. न्यूझीलंड

New Zealander (**New Zealanders**) *n* A **New Zealander** is a citizen of New Zealand, or a person of New Zealand origin. न्यूझीलंडर

next *adj* The **next** thing is the one that comes immediately after this one or after the last one. पुढील ▷ *adv* The thing that happens **next** happens immediately after something else. पुढील

next of kin n Your **next of kin** is your closest relative, especially in official or legal documents. *(formal)* जवळचा नातेवाईक

next to prep If one thing is **next to** another, it is at the side of it. बाजूला *She sat down next to him on the sofa.*

Nicaragua n **Nicaragua** is a republic in Central America. निकारागुआ

Nicaraguan (**Nicaraguans**) adj **Nicaraguan** means belonging or relating to Nicaragua, or to its people or culture. निकारागुअन ▷ n A **Nicaraguan** is a person who comes from Nicaragua. निकारागुअन

nice (**nicer, nicest**) adj If something is **nice**, you like it. छान

nickname (**nicknames**) n A **nickname** is an informal name for someone or something. टोपणनाव

nicotine n **Nicotine** is an addictive substance in tobacco. निकोटिन

niece (**nieces**) n Your **niece** is the daughter of your sister or brother. भाची / पुतणी

Niger n **Niger** is a republic in West Africa. नायजर

Nigeria n **Nigeria** is a republic in West Africa, on the Gulf of Guinea. नायजेरिया

Nigerian (**Nigerians**) adj **Nigerian** means belonging or relating to Nigeria, its people, or its culture. नायजेरियन ▷ n A **Nigerian** is a Nigerian citizen, or a person of Nigerian origin. नायजेरियन

night (**nights**) n The **night** is the part of each period of twenty-four hours when it is dark outside, especially the time when most people are sleeping. रात्र

nightclub (**nightclubs**) n A **nightclub** is a place where people go late in the evening to dance. नाईटक्लब

nightdress (**nightdresses**) n A **nightdress** is a sort of loose dress that a woman or girl wears in bed. स्त्रिया रात्री वापरतात ते कपडे

nightlife n The **nightlife** in a place is the entertainment and social activities that are available at night. नाईटलाईफ (रात्रीचे मनोरंजन)

nightmare (**nightmares**) n A **nightmare** is a very frightening dream. दु:स्वप्न

night school (**night schools**) n Someone who goes to **night school** does an educational course in the evenings. रात्रशाळा

night shift (**night shifts**) n If a group of factory workers, nurses, or other people work the **night shift**, they work during the night before being replaced by another group, so that there is always a group working. रात्रपाळी

nil n **Nil** means the same as zero. It is often used in scores of sports games. शून्य

nine num **Nine** is the number 9. नऊ

nineteen (**nineteens**) num **Nineteen** is the number 19. एकोणीस

nineteenth adj The **nineteenth** item in a series is the one that you count as number nineteen. एकोणीसावा

ninety num **Ninety** is the number 90. नव्वद

ninth (**ninths**) adj The **ninth** item in a series is the one that you count as number nine. नववा ▷ n A **ninth** is one of nine equal parts of something. एक नवमांश

nitrogen n **Nitrogen** is a colourless element that has no smell and is usually found as a gas. नत्रवायू

no det You use **no** to mean not any or not one person or thing. नाही *He had no idea where to go.* ▷ adv You use **no** to mean not in any way. नाही ▷ excl You use **no!** to give a negative response to a question. नाही!

nobody n **Nobody** means not one person. एकही नाही

nod (**nods, nodding, nodded**) v If you **nod**, you move your head downwards and upwards to show that you are answering 'yes' to a question, or to show agreement, understanding, or approval. होकारार्थी मान हलविणे

noise n **Noise** is a loud or unpleasant sound. गोंगाट

noisy (**noisier, noisiest**) adj Someone or something that is **noisy** makes a lot of loud or unpleasant noise. गोंगाटाचा

nominate (nominates, nominating, nominated) vt If someone **is nominated** for a job, position, or prize, their name is formally suggested as a candidate for it. नाव घोषित करणे, नामनिर्देशन करणे

nomination (nominations) n A **nomination** is an official suggestion of someone for a job, position, or prize. नामनिर्देश

none pron **None** means not one or not any. काहीही नाही, कोणीही नाही None of us knew her.

nonsense n If you say that something spoken or written is **nonsense**, you mean that you consider it to be untrue or silly. वायफळ बडबड

non-smoker (non-smokers) n A **non-smoker** is someone who does not smoke. धूम्रपान न करणारी व्यक्ती

non-smoking adj A **non-smoking** area in a public place is an area in which people are not allowed to smoke. धूम्रपान निषिद्ध असलेली जागा

non-stop adv If you do something **non-stop**, you continue to do it without any pauses or breaks. अखंड

noodles npl **Noodles** are long, thin pieces of pasta. नूडल्स

noon n **Noon** is twelve o'clock in the middle of the day. मध्यान्ह

no one pron **No one** means not a single person, or not a single member of a particular group or set. कोणीही नाही No one can predict what will happen in the months ahead.

nor conj You use **nor** after 'neither' to introduce the second of two things that are not true or that do not happen. आणि नाही ('neither' नंतर वापर) Neither her friends nor her family knew how old she was.

normal adj Something that is **normal** is usual and ordinary, and in accordance with what people expect. सामान्य

normally adv If you say that something **normally** happens or that you **normally** do a particular thing, you mean that it is what usually happens or what you usually do. सामान्यतः

north n The **north** edge, corner, or part of a place or country is the part which is towards the north. उत्तरेकडील ▷ n If you go **north**, you travel towards the north. उत्तरेकडील ▷ n The **north** is the direction on your left when you are looking towards the direction where the sun rises. उत्तर दिशा

North Africa n **North Africa** is the part of Africa between the Mediterranean and the Sahara. उत्तर आफ्रिका

North African (North Africans) adj **North African** means relating to North Africa or its inhabitants. उत्तर आफ्रिकन ▷ n A **North African** is a native or inhabitant of North Africa. उत्तर आफ्रिकन

North America n **North America** is a continent containing the United States, Canada, Greenland, Mexico, and Central America. उत्तर अमेरिका

North American (North Americans) adj **North American** means relating to North America or its inhabitants. उत्तर अमेरिकन ▷ n A **North American** is a native or inhabitant of North America. उत्तर अमेरिकन

northbound adj **Northbound** roads or vehicles lead or are travelling towards the north. उत्तर दिशेकडे जाणारे रस्ते किंवा वाहने

northeast n The **northeast** is the direction which is halfway between north and east. ईशान्य

northern adj **Northern** means in or from the north of a region or country. उत्तरेकडील

Northern Ireland n **Northern Ireland** is that part of the United Kingdom occupying the north-east part of Ireland. नॉर्दर्न आयर्लंड

North Korea n **North Korea** is a republic in north-east Asia. उत्तर कोरिया

North Pole n The **North Pole** is the place on the surface of the earth which is farthest towards the north. उत्तर ध्रुव

North Sea n **The North Sea** is the part of the Atlantic between Great Britain and the north European mainland. उत्तर समुद्र

northwest n The **northwest** is the direction which is halfway between north and west. वायव्य

Norway n **Norway** is a kingdom in north-west Europe. नॉर्वे

Norwegian (Norwegians) adj **Norwegian** means belonging or relating to Norway, or to its people, language, or culture. नॉर्वेजियन ▷ n A **Norwegian** is a person who comes from Norway. नॉर्वेजियन ▷ n **Norwegian** is the language spoken in Norway. नॉर्वेजियन

nose (noses) n Your **nose** is the part of your face which sticks out above your mouth. You use it for smelling and breathing. नाक

nosebleed (nosebleeds) n If someone has a **nosebleed**, blood comes out from inside their nose. नाकातील रक्तस्राव

nostril (nostrils) n Your **nostrils** are the two openings at the end of your nose. नाकपुड्या

nosy (nosier, nosiest) adj If you describe someone as **nosy**, you mean that they are interested in things which do not concern them. (informal) नाक खुपसणारी व्यक्ती

not adv You use **not** or **n't** to show that something is the opposite of true. नाही, नको (नकार दर्शविण्यासाठी वापरण्यात येणारा इंग्रजीतील शब्द)

note (notes) n A **note** is one musical sound. स्वरावली ▷ n A **note** is a piece of paper money. चलनी नोट ▷ n A **note** is a short letter or message. चिठ्ठी

notebook (notebooks) n A **notebook** is a small book for writing notes in. वही

note down (notes down, noting down, noted down) v When you **note** something **down**, you write it down so that you have a record of it. लिहून घेणे *She noted down the names.*

notepad (notepads) n A **notepad** is a pad of paper that you use for writing notes or letters on. नोटपॅड

notepaper n **Notepaper** is paper that you use for writing letters on. लिहिण्यासाठी असलेले कागद

nothing n **Nothing** means not anything. काहीही नाही

notice (notices, noticing, noticed) n A **notice** is a sign that gives information or instructions. सूचना ▷ n **Notice** is advance warning about something. सूचना ▷ vt If you **notice** something, you suddenly see or hear it. लक्षात येणे

noticeable adj Something that is **noticeable** is very obvious, so that it is easy to see or recognize. सहज दिसणारा

noticeboard (noticeboards) n A **noticeboard** is a board which is usually attached to a wall in order to display notices giving information about something. सूचना फलक

notify (notifies, notifying, notified) vt If you **notify** someone of something, you officially inform them of it. (formal) माहिती देणे

nought (noughts) n **Nought** is the number 0. शून्य

noun (nouns) n A **noun** is a word such as 'car', 'love', or 'man' which is used to refer to a person or thing. नाम

novel (novels) n A **novel** is a book containing a long story about imaginary people and events. कादंबरी

novelist (novelists) n A **novelist** is a person who writes novels. कादंबरीकार

November (Novembers) n **November** is the eleventh month of the year in the Western calendar. नोव्हेंबर महिना

now adv You use **now** to talk about the present time. आता

nowadays adv **Nowadays** means at the present time, in contrast with the past. अलीकडे

nowhere adv You use **nowhere** to mean not any place. कुठेही नाही

nuclear adj **Nuclear** means relating to the centres of atoms, or to the energy produced when these centres are split or combined. आण्विक

nude (**nudes**) *adj* A **nude** person is not wearing any clothes. नग्न ▷ *n* A **nude** is a picture or statue of a person who is not wearing any clothes. नग्न चित्र किंवा शिल्प

nuisance (**nuisances**) *n* If you say that someone or something is a **nuisance**, you mean that they annoy you or cause you problems. उपद्रव

numb *adj* If a part of your body is **numb**, you cannot feel anything there. बधीर

number (**numbers**) *n* A **number** is a word such as 'two', 'nine', or 'twelve', or a symbol such as 1, 3, or 47, which is used in counting something. संख्या

number plate (**number plates**) *n* A **number plate** is a sign on the front and back of a vehicle that shows its registration number. नंबर प्लेट

numerous *adj* If people or things are **numerous**, they exist or are present in large numbers. असंख्य

nun (**nuns**) *n* A **nun** is a member of a female religious community. नन

nurse (**nurses**) *n* A **nurse** is a person whose job is to care for people who are ill. परिचारिका, नर्स

nursery (**nurseries**) *n* A **nursery** is a place where children who are not old enough to go to school are looked after. बालवाडी

nursery rhyme (**nursery rhymes**) *n* A **nursery rhyme** is a traditional poem or song for young children. बडबडगीत

nursery school (**nursery schools**) *n* A **nursery school** is a school for very young children. बालवाडी

nursing home (**nursing homes**) *n* A **nursing home** is a private hospital for old people. खाजगी रुग्णालय, परिचर्या गृह

nut (**nuts**) *n* A **nut** is a small piece of metal with a hole through which you put a bolt. Nuts and bolts are used to hold things together such as pieces of machinery. बोल्टचा नट ▷ *n*

The firm shelled fruit of some trees and bushes are called **nuts**. कठीण कवचाचे फळ

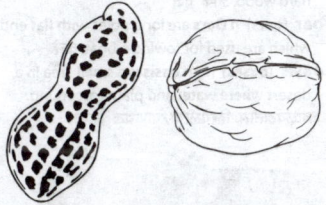

nut allergy (**nut allergies**) *n* If you have a **nut allergy**, you become ill if you eat nuts or come into contact with nuts. कठीण कवचाच्या फळांचे वावडे/ऍलर्जी

nutmeg *n* **Nutmeg** is a spice made from the seed of a tree that grows in hot countries. Nutmeg is usually used to flavour sweet food. जायफळ

nutrient (**nutrients**) *n* **Nutrients** are chemical substances that people and animals need from food and plants need from soil. पोषक घटक

nutrition *n* **Nutrition** is the process of taking and absorbing nutrients from food. पोषण

nutritious *adj* **Nutritious** food contains the proteins, vitamins, and minerals which help your body to be healthy. पोषक

nutter (**nutters**) *n* If you refer to someone as a **nutter**, you mean that they are mad or that their behaviour is very strange. *(informal)* वेडपट

nylon *n* **Nylon** is a strong, flexible, artificial material. नायलॉन

O

oak (oaks) *n* An **oak** is a large tree with strong, hard wood. ओक वृक्ष

oar (oars) *n* **Oars** are long poles with flat ends which are used for rowing a boat. वल्हे

oasis (oases) *n* An **oasis** is a small area in a desert where water and plants are found. वाळवंटातील हिरवळीची/पाणथळ जागा

oath (oaths) *n* An **oath** is a formal promise. शपथ

oatmeal *n* **Oatmeal** is a kind of flour made by crushing oats. ओटचे पीठ

oats *npl* **Oats** are a cereal crop or its grains, used for making porridge or feeding animals. ओटस्

obedient *adj* An **obedient** person or animal does what they are told to do. आज्ञाधारक

obese *adj* Someone who is **obese** is extremely fat. स्थूल

obey (obeys, obeying, obeyed) *v* If you **obey** a rule, instruction, or person, you do what you are told to do. सूचनांचे पालन करणे

obituary (obituaries) *n* Someone's **obituary** is an account of their character and achievements which is published shortly after they have died. मृत्युलेख/मृत्युवार्ता

object (objects) *n* An **object** is anything that has a fixed shape or form and that is not alive. वस्तू

objection (objections) *n* If you make an **objection** to something, you say that you do not like it or agree with it. हरकत

objective (objectives) *n* Your **objective** is what you are trying to achieve. उद्दिष्ट

oblong *adj* An **oblong** shape is one which has two long sides and two short sides and in which all the angles are right angles. आयताकृती

obnoxious *adj* If you describe someone as **obnoxious**, you think that they are very unpleasant. तिरस्करणीय, घृणास्पद

oboe (oboes) *n* An **oboe** is a musical instrument shaped like a tube which you play by blowing through the top end. ओबो नावाचे वाद्य

observant *adj* Someone who is **observant** pays a lot of attention to things and notices more about them than most people do. सूक्ष्म निरीक्षण करण्यात तरबेज

observatory (observatories) *n* An **observatory** is a building with a large telescope from which scientists study the stars and planets. वेधशाळा

observe (observes, observing, observed) *vt* If you **observe** someone or something, you watch them carefully. निरीक्षण करणे

observer (observers) *n* An **observer** is someone who sees or notices something. निरीक्षक

obsessed *adj* If someone is **obsessed** with a person or thing, they keep thinking about them and find it difficult to think about anything else. पछाडलेला

obsession (obsessions) *n* If you say that someone has an **obsession** with someone or something, you feel they are spending too much of their time thinking about that person or thing. मन व्यापून टाकणारी गोष्ट

obsolete adj Something that is **obsolete** is no longer needed because a better thing now exists. कालबाह्य, अप्रचलित

obstacle (obstacles) n An **obstacle** is something which makes it difficult for you to go forward or do something. अडथळा

obstinate adj If you describe someone as **obstinate**, you criticize them because they are very determined to do what they want, and refuse to be persuaded to do something else. हट्टी

obstruct (obstructs, obstructing, obstructed) vt To **obstruct** someone or something means to block their path, making it difficult for them to move forward. अडथळा करणे

obtain (obtains, obtaining, obtained) vt To **obtain** something means to get it or achieve it. (formal) प्राप्त करणे

obvious adj If something is **obvious**, it is easy to see or understand. स्पष्ट

obviously adv You use **obviously** when you are stating something that you expect your listener to know already. स्पष्टपणे, उघडपणे

occasion (occasions) n An **occasion** is a time when something happens. प्रसंग

occasional adj **Occasional** means happening sometimes, but not regularly or often. काही वेळा

occasionally adv **Occasionally** means from time to time. वेळोवेळी

occupation (occupations) n Your **occupation** is your job or profession. व्यवसाय ▷ n The **occupation** of a country is its invasion and control by a foreign army. आक्रमण

occupy (occupies, occupying, occupied) vt The people who **occupy** a building or place are the people who live or work there. ताबा घेणे

occur (occurs, occurring, occurred) vi When an event **occurs**, it happens. घडणे

occurrence (occurrences) n An **occurrence** is something that happens. (formal) घटना

ocean (oceans) n The **ocean** is the sea. महासागर

Oceania n **Oceania** is the islands of the central and South Pacific, including Melanesia, Micronesia, and Polynesia. ओशनिया

October (Octobers) n **October** is the tenth month of the year in the Western calendar. ऑक्टोबर महिना

octopus (octopuses) n An **octopus** is a sea creature with eight tentacles. ऑक्टोपस, अष्टपाद

odd (odder, oddest) adj If something is **odd**, it is strange or unusual. विचित्र ▷ adj You say that two things are **odd** when they do not belong to the same set or pair. भिन्न ▷ adj **Odd** numbers, such as three and seventeen, are numbers that cannot be divided by the number two. विषम

odour (odours) n An **odour** is a smell, especially one that is unpleasant. दुर्गंधी

of prep You use **of** to show that one thing belongs to another. चा …the holiday homes of the rich. ▷ prep You use **of** to talk about amounts. चा …a glass of milk. ▷ prep You use **of** to mean about. बद्दल He was thinking of her.

off adj When something that uses electricity is **off**, it is not using electricity. बंद ▷ prep If you take something **off** another thing, it is no longer on it. काढून घेणे He took his feet off the desk.

offence (offences) n An **offence** is a crime. गुन्हा

offend (offends, offending, offended) v If you **offend** someone, you upset or embarrass them. दुखावणे

offensive adj Something that is **offensive** upsets or embarrasses people because it is rude or insulting. विषादजनक

offer (**offers**, **offering**, **offered**) *n* An **offer** is something that someone says they will give you or do for you. देकार ▷ *vt* If you **offer** something to someone, you ask them if they would like to have it or to use it. देऊ करणे

office (**offices**) *n* An **office** is a room or a part of a building where people work sitting at desks. कार्यालय

office hours *npl* **Office hours** are the times when an office or similar place is open for business. कार्यालयाच्या कामकाजाची वेळ

officer (**officers**) *n* In the armed forces, an **officer** is a person in a position of authority. अधिकारी

official *adj* Something that is **official** is approved by the government or by someone else in authority. अधिकृत

off-peak *adv* If things are available **off-peak**, they are available at a time when there is less demand for them, so they are cheaper than usual. फारश गर्दी नसलेली वेळ

off-season *adj* If something is **off-season** it relates to the time of the year when not many people go on holiday and when things such as hotels and plane tickets are often cheaper. हंगाम नसलेला काळ ▷ *adv* If something happens **off-season** it happens at the time of the year when not many people go on holiday and when things such as hotels and plane tickets are often cheaper. हंगाम नसलेला काळ *Visiting hours are more flexible off-season.*

offside *adj* In games such as football or hockey, when an attacking player is **offside**, they have broken the rules by being nearer to the goal than a defending player when the ball is passed to them. ऑफसाईड (खेळात)

often *adv* If something happens **often**, it happens many times or much of the time. नेहमी

oil (**oils**, **oiling**, **oiled**) *n* **Oil** is a smooth thick liquid used as a fuel and for lubricating machines. Oil is found underground. तेल ▷ *vt* If you **oil** something, you put oil onto it or

into it in order to make it work smoothly or to protect it. तेल टाकणे

oil refinery (**oil refineries**) *n* An **oil refinery** is a factory where oil is prepared. तेलशुद्धिकरण कारखाना

oil rig (**oil rigs**) *n* An **oil rig** is a structure on land or in the sea that is used when getting oil from the ground. ऑईल रिग

oil slick (**oil slicks**) *n* An **oil slick** is a layer of oil that floats on the sea or on a lake. It is formed when oil accidentally spills out of a ship or container. पाण्यावरील तेलाचा तवंग

oil well (**oil wells**) *n* An **oil well** is a deep hole which is made in order to get oil out of the ground. तेलविहीर

ointment (**ointments**) *n* An **ointment** is a smooth thick substance that is put on sore skin or a wound to help it heal. मलम

OK! *excl* You can say '**OK!**' to show that you agree to something. ठीक !

okay *adj* If you say that something is **okay**, you find it satisfactory or acceptable. *(informal)* ठीक, योग्य ▷ *excl* You can say '**Okay!**' to show that you agree to something. ठीक!

old (**older**, **oldest**) *adj* An **old** person is someone who has lived for a long time. वृद्ध ▷ *adj* An **old** thing is something that somebody made a long time ago. जुना

old-age pensioner (**old-age pensioners**) *n* An **old-age pensioner** is a person who is old enough to receive a pension from their employer or the government. वृद्ध निवृतीवेतनधारक

old-fashioned *adj* Something that is **old-fashioned** is no longer used, done, or believed by most people, because it has been replaced by something that is more modern. जुन्या पद्धतीचे

olive (**olives**) *n* **Olives** are small green or black fruit with a bitter taste. ऑलिव्ह ▷ *n* An **olive** or an **olive tree** is a tree on which olives grow. ऑलिव्हचे झाड

olive oil (**olive oils**) *n* **Olive oil** is edible oil obtained by pressing olives. ऑलिव्ह तेल

Oman *n* **Oman** is a country in south-east Arabia, on the Gulf of Oman and the Arabian Sea. ओमान

omelette (**omelettes**) *n* An **omelette** is a food made by beating eggs and cooking them in a flat pan. ऑमलेट

on *adj* When something that uses electricity is **on**, it is using electricity. चालू ▷ *prep* If someone or something is **on** a surface, it is resting there. वर *There was a large box on the table.*

on behalf of *prep* If you do something **on behalf of** someone, you do it for that person. च्या वतीने

once *adv* If something happens **once**, it happens one time only. एकदा

one *num* **One** is the number 1. एक ▷ *pron* You can use **one** to refer to the first of two or more things. एक *One of the twins was thinner than the other.*

one-off (**one-offs**) *n* A **one-off** is something that is made or happens only once. एकदाच

one's *det* You use **one's** to show that something belongs to people in general. एखाद्याचा *It is natural to want to care for one's family and children.*

oneself *pron* Speakers or writers use **oneself** to say things about themselves and about other people. स्वतः *To work, one must have time to oneself.*

onion (**onions**) *n* An **onion** is a small round vegetable. It is white with a brown skin, and has a strong smell and taste. कांदा

online *adj* If you are **online**, your computer is connected to the Internet. ऑनलाईन ▷ *adv* If you do something **online**, you do it while connected to a computer or the Internet. ऑनलाईन

onlooker (**onlookers**) *n* An **onlooker** is someone who watches an event take place but does not take part in it. प्रेक्षक

only *adj* If you talk about the **only** thing or person, you mean that there are no others. एकमेव ▷ *adv* You use **only** when you are

saying how small or short something is. फक्त ▷ *adj* If you are an **only** child, you have no brothers or sisters. फक्त एक

on time *adj* If you are **on time**, you are not late. वेळेवर

onto *prep* If something moves **onto** a surface, it moves to a place on that surface. वर *The cat climbed onto her lap.* ▷ *prep* When you get **onto** a bus, train, or plane, you enter it. चढणे *He got onto the plane.*

open (**opens**, **opening**, **opened**) *adj* You use **open** to describe something which has been opened. उघडा ▷ *v* When you **open** something, or when it **opens**, you move it or it moves so that it is no longer closed. उघडणे ▷ *v* When a shop or office **opens**, people are able to go in. उघडणे

opening hours *npl* **Opening hours** are the times during which a shop, bank, library, or bar is open for business. उघडण्याची वेळ

opera (**operas**) *n* An **opera** is a musical entertainment. It is like a play, but most of the words are sung. ऑपेरा

operate (**operates**, **operating**, **operated**) *v* If you **operate** a business or organization, you work to keep it running properly. If a business or organization **operates**, it carries out its work. चालवणे ▷ *vi* When surgeons **operate** on a patient, they cut open the patient's body in order to remove, replace, or repair a diseased or damaged part. शस्त्रक्रिया करणे

operating theatre (**operating theatres**) *n* An **operating theatre** is a room in a hospital where surgeons carry out operations. शस्त्रक्रियागृह

operation (**operations**) *n* An **operation** is a highly organized activity that involves many people doing different things. कारवाई ▷ *n* If a patient has an **operation**, a surgeon cuts open their body in order to remove, replace, or repair a diseased or damaged part. शस्त्रक्रिया

operator (**operators**) *n* An **operator** is a person who works at a telephone exchange

o

or on the switchboard of an office or hotel. ऑपरेटर

opinion (opinions) *n* Your **opinion** about something is what you think or believe about it. मत

opinion poll (opinion polls) *n* An **opinion poll** involves asking people for their opinion on a particular subject, especially one concerning politics. लोकमत

opponent (opponents) *n* A politician's **opponents** are other politicians who belong to a different party or have different aims or policies. राजकीय विरोधक

opportunity (opportunities) *n* An **opportunity** is a situation in which it is possible for you to do something that you want to do. संधी

oppose (opposes, opposing, opposed) *vt* If you **oppose** someone or their plans or ideas, you disagree with what they want to do and try to prevent them from doing it. विरोध करणे

opposed *adj* If you are **opposed** to something, you disagree with it or disapprove of it. विरोधात

opposing *adj* **Opposing** ideas or tendencies are totally different from each other. विरोधी

opposite *adj* The **opposite** side or part of something is the side or part that is furthest away from you. विरुद्ध ▷ *adv* If one thing is **opposite** another, it is facing it. समोरासमोर ▷ *prep* If one thing is **opposite** another, it is across from it. समोर ▷ *adj* If things are **opposite**, they are as different as they can be. विरुद्ध

opposition *n* **Opposition** is strong, angry, or violent disagreement and disapproval. विरोध

optician (opticians) *n* An **optician** is someone whose job involves testing people's eyesight and making and selling glasses and contact lenses. चष्मे बनविणारा

optimism *n* **Optimism** is the feeling of being hopeful about the future or about the success of something. आशावाद

optimist (optimists) *n* An **optimist** is someone who is hopeful about the future. आशावादी

optimistic *adj* Someone who is **optimistic** is hopeful about the future or about the success of something. आशावादी

option (options) *n* An **option** is one of two or more things that you can choose between. पर्याय

optional *adj* If something is **optional**, you can choose whether or not you do it or have it. ऐच्छिक

opt out (opts out, opting out, opted out) *v* If you **opt out** of something, you choose not to be involved in it. अंग काढून घेणे *More and more people are opting out of the urban lifestyle.*

or *conj* You use **or** to show what you can choose or what is possible. किंवा *You can have tea or coffee.*

oral (orals) *adj* **Oral** is used to describe things that involve speaking rather than writing. तोंडी ▷ *n* An **oral** is an examination, especially in a foreign language, that is spoken rather than written. तोंडी

orange (oranges) *n* Something that is **orange** is of a colour between red and yellow. नारिंगी रंगाचे ▷ *n* An **orange** is a round fruit with a thick skin and lots of juice. संत्रे

orange juice (orange juices) *n* **Orange juice** is the liquid that can be obtained from an orange and drunk. संत्र्याचा रस

orchard (orchards) *n* An **orchard** is an area of land on which fruit trees are grown. फळांची बाग

orchestra (orchestras) *n* An **orchestra** is a large group of musicians who play a variety of different instruments together. वाद्यवृंद

orchid (orchids) *n* An **orchid** is a plant with brightly coloured, unusually shaped flowers. ऑर्किड

ordeal (ordeals) *n* An **ordeal** is an extremely unpleasant and difficult experience. भयावह अनुभव

order (orders, ordering, ordered) n If someone gives you an **order**, they tell you to do something. आदेश ▷ vt If you **order** someone to do something, you tell them to do it. आदेश देणे

order form (order forms) n An **order form** is a document filled in by customers when asking for goods. मागणी नोंदवण्याचा अर्ज

ordinary adj **Ordinary** people or things are not special or different in any way. सर्वसामान्य

oregano n **Oregano** is a herb that is used in cooking. स्वयंपाक करताना वापरण्यात येणारी ओरेगानो नावाची औषधी वनस्पती

organ (organs) n An **organ** is a large musical instrument with pipes of different lengths through which air is forced. It has keys and pedals rather like a piano, and is often found in a church. ऑर्गन नावाचे वाद्य ▷ n An **organ** is a part of your body that has a particular purpose, for example your heart or your lungs. शरीराचा अवयव

organic adj **Organic** food is grown without using chemicals. सेंद्रिय

organism (organisms) n An **organism** is a living thing. सूक्ष्म जीव

organization (organizations) n An **organization** is an official group of people, for example a business or a club. संघटना

organize (organizes, organizing, organized) vt If you **organize** an activity or event, you make all the arrangements for it. आयोजित करणे

Orient n The eastern part of Asia is sometimes referred to as the **Orient**. (literary, old-fashioned) पूर्व आशिया

oriental adj You use **oriental** to talk about things that come from places in eastern Asia. पूर्व आशियाकडील

origin (origins) n You can refer to the beginning, cause, or source of something as its **origin** or its **origins**. मूळ

original adj You use **original** to refer to something that existed at the beginning of a process or activity, or the characteristics that something had when it first existed. मूळचा

originally adv When you say what happened or was the case **originally**, you are saying what happened or was the case when something began or came into existence, often to contrast it with what happened later. सुरुवातीला

ornament (ornaments) n An **ornament** is an attractive object that you display in your home or garden. सजावटीची वस्तू

orphan (orphans) n An **orphan** is a child whose parents are dead. अनाथ

ostrich (ostriches) n An **ostrich** is a very large, long-necked African bird that cannot fly. शहामृग

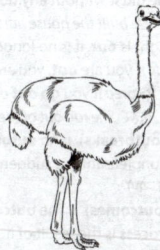

other adj **Other** people or things are different people or things. दुसरा

otherwise adv You use **otherwise** when stating the general condition or quality of something, when you are also mentioning an exception to this. अन्यथा ▷ conj You use **otherwise** after stating a situation or fact, to say what the result or consequence would be if this situation or fact was not the case. अन्यथा I'm lucky that I'm interested in school work; otherwise I'd go mad. ▷ adv You use **otherwise** to say what the result would be if things were different. नाहीतर

otter (otters) n An **otter** is a small animal with brown fur, short legs, and a long tail. Otters swim well and eat fish. पाणमांजर

ought v If someone **ought to** do something, it is the right thing to do. करायला हवे होते

ounce (**ounces**) n An **ounce** is a unit of weight. There are sixteen ounces in a pound and one ounce is equal to 28.35 grams. औंस

our det You use **our** to show that something belongs to you and one or more other people. आमचा *Our house is near the school.*

ours pron You use **ours** when you are talking about something that belongs to you and one or more other people. आमचा *That car is ours.*

ourselves pron You use **ourselves** when you are talking about yourself and one or more other people. आम्ही स्वतः *We sat by the fire to keep ourselves warm.* ▷ pron 'We did it **ourselves**' means that you and one or more other people did it without anymore help. आम्ही स्वतः *We built the house ourselves.*

out adj If a light is **out**, it is no longer shining. विझणे ▷ adv If you are **out**, you are not at home. बाहेर ▷ prep If you go **out** of a place, you leave it. बाहेर *She ran out of the house.*

outbreak (**outbreaks**) n An **outbreak** of something unpleasant is a sudden occurrence of it. उफाळून येणे

outcome (**outcomes**) n The **outcome** of an action or process is the result of it. निष्कर्ष

outdoor adj **Outdoor** activities or things take place or are used outside, rather than in a building. घराबाहेर, मैदानी

outdoors adv If something happens **outdoors**, it happens outside in the fresh air rather than in a building. मोकळ्या जागी

outfit (**outfits**) n An **outfit** is a set of clothes. कपड्यांचा संच

outgoing adj **Outgoing** things such as planes, mail, and passengers are leaving or being sent somewhere. बाहेर जाणारा

outing (**outings**) n An **outing** is a short enjoyable trip, usually with a group of people, away from your home, school, or place of work. सहल

outline (**outlines**) n An **outline** is a general explanation or description of something. वर्णन

outlook (**outlooks**) n Your **outlook** is your general attitude towards life. दृष्टिकोन

out of date adj Something that is **out of date** is old-fashioned and no longer useful. कालबाह्य

out-of-doors adv When you are **out-of-doors**, you are not inside a building, but in the open air. मोकळ्या जागी, बाहेर

outrageous adj If you describe something as **outrageous**, you are emphasizing that it is unacceptable or very shocking. धक्कादायक

outset n If something happens at the **outset** of an event, process, or period of time, it happens at the beginning of it. If something happens from the **outset**, it happens from the beginning and continues to happen. सुरुवातीपासून

outside (**outsides**) adj An **outside** thing surrounds another thing. बाहेर ▷ adv If you are **outside**, you are not in a building. बाहेर ▷ n The **outside** of something is the part that covers the rest of it. बाहेरची बाजू ▷ prep If you are **outside** something or somewhere, you are not inside it. बाहेर *The man was waiting outside a shop.*

outsize adj **Outsize** or **outsized** things are much larger than usual or much larger than you would expect. मोठ्या आकाराची वस्तू

outskirts npl The **outskirts** of a city or town are the parts that are farthest from its centre. शहरापासून दूरवरचा भाग

outspoken adj If you are **outspoken**, you give your opinions about things openly, even if they shock people. स्पष्टवक्ता

outstanding adj If you describe a person or their work as **outstanding**, you think that they are remarkable and impressive. उल्लेखनीय

oval adj **Oval** things have a shape that is like a circle but is wider in one direction than the other. लंबगोलाकार

ovary (**ovaries**) n A woman's **ovaries** are the two organs in her body that produce eggs. अंडाशय

oven (**ovens**) n An **oven** is a cooker or part of a cooker that is like a box with a door. You cook food inside an oven. ओव्हन

oven glove (oven gloves) *n* An **oven glove** is a glove made of thick material, used for holding hot dishes from an oven. ओव्हन ग्लोव्ह

ovenproof *adj* An **ovenproof** dish is one that has been specially made to be used in an oven without being damaged by the heat. ओव्हनप्रूफ

over *adj* If something is **over**, it has finished. संपलेला ▷ *prep* If one thing is **over** another thing, the first thing is above or higher than the second thing. वर *There was a lamp over the table.*

overall *adv* You use **overall** to indicate that you are talking about a situation in general or about the whole of something. एकंदरित

overalls *npl* **Overalls** consist of a single piece of clothing that combines trousers and a jacket. You wear overalls over your clothes in order to protect them while you are working. ओव्हरऑल्स (सदरा आणि विजार जोडून शिवलेले)

overcast *adj* If it is **overcast**, or if the sky or the day is **overcast**, the sky is completely covered with cloud and there is not much light. ढगांनी भरलेले आकाश

overcharge (overcharges, overcharging, overcharged) *vt* If someone **overcharges** you, they charge you too much for their goods or services. जास्त पैसे उकळणे

overcoat (overcoats) *n* An **overcoat** is a thick warm coat. ओव्हरकोट

overcome (overcomes, overcoming, overcame) *vt* If you **overcome** a problem or a feeling, you successfully deal with it and control it. मात करणे

overdone *adj* If food is **overdone**, it has been spoiled by being cooked for too long. जास्त शिजलेले

overdraft (overdrafts) *n* If you have an **overdraft**, you have spent more money than you have in your bank account. ओव्हरड्राफ्ट

overdrawn *adj* If you are **overdrawn** or if your bank account is **overdrawn**, you have spent more money than you have in your

account, and so you are in debt to the bank. बँक खात्यात शिल्लक असलेल्या रकमेपेक्षा काढलेली जास्त रक्कम

overdue *adj* If you say that a change or an event is **overdue**, you mean that it should have happened before now. वेळ टळून गेलेली गोष्ट

overestimate (overestimates, overestimating, overestimated) *vt* If you **overestimate** someone or something, you think that they are better, bigger, or more important than they really are. प्रत्यक्षापेक्षा एखाद्या गोष्टीला मोठे समजणे

overhead projector (overhead projectors) *n* An **overhead projector** is a machine that has a light inside it and makes the writing or pictures on a sheet of plastic appear on a screen or wall. The abbreviation 'OHP' is also used. ओव्हरहेड प्रोजेक्टर

overheads *npl* The **overheads** of a business are its regular and essential expenses. व्यवसायातील नेहमीचे खर्च

overlook (overlooks, overlooking, overlooked) *vt* If a building or window **overlooks** a place, you can see the place from the building or window. एखादी जागा वरून पाहणे वा दिसणे

overrule (overrules, overruling, overruled) *vt* If someone in authority **overrules** a person or their decision, they officially decide that the decision is incorrect or not valid. फेटाळून लावणे

overseas *adv* If something happens or exists **overseas**, it happens or exists abroad. परदेशात

oversight (oversights) *n* In business, **oversight** of a system or process is the responsibility for making sure that it works efficiently and correctly. लक्ष ठेवण्याची क्रिया ▷ *n* If there has been an **oversight**, someone has forgotten to do something which they should have done. नजरचूक

oversleep (oversleeps, oversleeping, overslept) *vi* If you **oversleep**, you sleep longer than you should have done. दीर्घ झोप

overtake (overtakes, overtaking, overtook, overtaken) v If you **overtake** or **overtake** a moving vehicle or person, you pass them because you are moving faster than they are. एखाद्या व्यक्तिस वा वाहनास मागे टाकून पुढे जाणे

overtime n **Overtime** is time that you spend doing your job in addition to your normal working hours. जास्तीचे काम

overweight adj Someone who is **overweight** weighs more than is considered healthy or attractive. नेहमीपेक्षा जास्त वजनाचे

owe (owes, owing, owed) vt If you **owe** money to someone, they have lent it to you and you have not yet paid it back. देणे असणे

owing to prep If something is **owing to** another thing, it is a result of that thing. च्या मुळे He was out of work owing to an injury.

owl (owls) n An **owl** is a bird with large eyes which hunts small animals at night. घुबड

own (owns, owning, owned) adj You use **own** to say that something belongs to you. स्वतःचा ▷ vt If you **own** something, it is your property. मालकीचे असणे

owner (owners) n The **owner** of something is the person to whom it belongs. मालक

own up (owns up, owning up, owned up) v If you **own up** to something wrong that you have done, you admit that you did it. मान्य करणे Own up to your failure, but don't dwell on it.

oxygen n **Oxygen** is a colourless gas in the air which is needed by all plants and animals. प्राणवायू, ऑक्सिजन

oyster (oysters) n An **oyster** is a large flat shellfish which produces pearls. शिंपला

ozone n **Ozone** is a form of oxygen. There is a layer of ozone high above the earth's surface. ओझोन

ozone layer n **The ozone layer** is the area high above the Earth's surface that protects living things from the harmful effects of the sun. ओझोनचा थर

p

PA (PAs) abbr A **PA** is a person who does office work and administrative work for someone. **PA** is an abbreviation for 'personal assistant'. पीए, वैयक्तिक सहायक

pace (paces) n The **pace** of something is the speed at which it happens or is done. गती

pacemaker (pacemakers) n A **pacemaker** is a device that is placed inside someone's body in order to help their heart beat in the right way. पेसमेकर

Pacific Ocean n **The Pacific Ocean** is a very large sea to the west of North and South America, and to the east of Asia and Australia. प्रशांत महासागर

pack (packs, packing, packed) n A **pack** of things is a collection of them that is sold or given together in a box or bag. एकत्र भरलेल्या वस्तू ▷ vt When you **pack** a bag, you put clothes and other things into it, because you are leaving a place or going on holiday. सामानाची बांधाबांध करणे

package (**packages**) *n* A **package** is a small parcel. पुडके

packaging *n* **Packaging** is the container or wrappings that something is sold in. सामान बांधून ठेवलेला डबा किंवा खोका

packed *adj* A place that is **packed** is very crowded. गच्च भरलेला

packed lunch (**packed lunches**) *n* A **packed lunch** is food, for example, sandwiches, which you take to work, to school, or on a trip and eat as your lunch. बांधलेले अन्नपदार्थ

packet (**packets**) *n* A **packet** is a small box, bag, or envelope in which a quantity of something is sold. विकीसाठी ठेवलेल्या वस्तूचे पाकीट

pad (**pads**) *n* A **pad** is a thick flat piece of a material such as cloth or foam rubber. पॅड

paddle (**paddles, paddling, paddled**) *n* A **paddle** is a short oar. You use it to move a small boat through water. पायाने हलवायचा वल्हा ▷ *vt* If someone **paddles** a boat, they move it using a paddle. पायाने वल्हे हलविणे ▷ *vi* If you **paddle**, you walk in shallow water. उथळ पाण्यातून चालणे

paddling pool (**paddling pools**) *n* A **paddling pool** is a shallow artificial pool for children to paddle in. नौका वल्हवण्यासाठी असलेला छोटा तलाव

padlock (**padlocks**) *n* A **padlock** is a lock which is used for fastening two things together. कुलूप

page (**pages, paging, paged**) *n* A **page** is a side of one of the pieces of paper in a book, magazine, or newspaper. पुस्तकाचे पान ▷ *v* If someone **is paged**, they receive a message over a speaker that someone is trying to contact them. पेजरवर निरोप पाठवणे

pager (**pagers**) *n* A **pager** is a small electronic device which gives you a message when someone is trying to contact you. पेजर

paid *adj* **Paid** means to do with the money a worker receives from his or her employer. You can say, for example, that someone is well **paid** when they receive a lot of money for the work that they do. भरपगारी

pail (**pails**) *n* A **pail** is a bucket, usually made of metal or wood. (*old-fashioned*) धातूची किंवा लाकडाची बादली

pain (**pains**) *n* If you feel **pain**, or if you are in **pain**, you feel great discomfort in a part of your body, because of illness or an injury. वेदना

painful *adj* If a part of your body is **painful**, it hurts. वेदनामय

painkiller (**painkillers**) *n* A **painkiller** is a drug which reduces or stops physical pain. वेदनाशामक

paint (**paints, painting, painted**) *n* **Paint** is a liquid used to decorate buildings, or to make a picture. रंग ▷ *v* If you **paint** a wall or a door, you cover it with **paint**. रंग लावणे ▷ *v* If you **paint** something on a piece of paper or cloth, you make a picture of it using paint. चित्र रंगवणे

paintbrush (**paintbrushes**) *n* A **paintbrush** is a brush which you use for painting. रंग लावण्याचा ब्रश

painter (**painters**) *n* A **painter** is an artist who paints pictures. चित्रकार

painting (**paintings**) *n* A **painting** is a picture which someone has painted. चित्रकला, पेंटिंग

pair (**pairs**) *n* A **pair** of things are two things of the same size and shape that are intended to be used together. जोडी

Pakistan n **Pakistan** is a republic in South Asia, on the Arabian Sea. पाकिस्तान

Pakistani (**Pakistanis**) adj **Pakistani** means belonging or relating to Pakistan, or to its people or culture. पाकिस्तानी ▷ n A **Pakistani** is a Pakistani citizen, or a person of Pakistani origin. पाकिस्तानी

pal (**pals**) n Your **pals** are your friends. (informal, old-fashioned) मित्र

palace (**palaces**) n A **palace** is a very large splendid house, especially the home of a king, queen, or president. राजवाडा

pale (**paler, palest**) adj Something that is **pale** is not strong or bright in colour. फिकट

Palestine n **Palestine** is an area between the Jordan River and the Mediterranean Sea. पॅलेस्टाईन

Palestinian (**Palestinians**) adj **Palestinian** means belonging or relating to the region between the River Jordan and the Mediterranean Sea. पॅलेस्टिनियन ▷ n A **Palestinian** is an Arab who comes from Palestine. पॅलेस्टिनियन

palm (**palms**) n The **palm** of your hand is the inside part of your hand, between your fingers and your wrist. तळहात ▷ n A **palm** or a **palm tree** is a tree that grows in hot countries. It has long leaves at the top, and no branches. पामवर्गातील झाड, ताडाच्या जातीचे झाड

pamphlet (**pamphlets**) n A **pamphlet** is a very thin book with a paper cover, which gives information about something. माहितीपुस्तिका

pan (**pans**) n A **pan** is a round metal container with a handle, which is used for cooking things, usually on top of a cooker. तवा

Panama n **Panama** is a republic in Central America. पनामा

pancake (**pancakes**) n A **pancake** is a thin, flat, circular piece of cooked batter that is eaten hot, often with a sweet or savoury filling. पॅनकेक

panda (**pandas**) n A **panda** is a large animal with black and white fur which lives in China. पांडा

panic (**panics, panicking, panicked**) n Panic is a strong feeling of anxiety or fear that makes you act without thinking carefully. तीव्र भीती ▷ v If you **panic**, or if someone or something **panics** you, you become anxious or afraid, and act without thinking carefully. एकदम घाबरून जाणे

panther (**panthers**) n A **panther** is a large wild animal that belongs to the cat family. Panthers are usually black. काळा बिबळ्या वाघ

pantomime (**pantomimes**) n A **pantomime** is a funny musical play for children, usually performed at Christmas. ख्रिसमसच्यावेळी मुलांसाठी सादर केलेले संगीत नाटक

pants npl **Pants** are a piece of underwear with two holes to put your legs through and elastic round the top. चड्डी

paper (**papers**) n Paper is a material that you write on or wrap things with. कागद ▷ n A **paper** is a newspaper. वृत्तपत्र

paperback (**paperbacks**) n A **paperback** is a book with a paper cover. कागदाचे वेष्टण असलेले पुस्तक

paperclip (**paperclips**) n A **paperclip** is a small piece of bent wire that is used to fasten papers together. पेपरक्लिप

paper round (**paper rounds**) n A **paper round** is a job of delivering newspapers to houses along a particular route. घरोघरी वर्तमानपत्रे टाकणे

paperweight (**paperweights**) n A **paperweight** is a small heavy object which you place on papers to prevent them from being disturbed or blown away. पेपरवेट

paperwork n **Paperwork** consists of the letters, reports, and records which have to be dealt with as the routine part of a job. दैनंदिन कामातील कागदपत्रे सांभाळणे व तयार करणे

paprika n **Paprika** is a red powder used for flavouring meat and other food. पॅप्रिका (लाल पावडर)

parachute (**parachutes**) n A **parachute** is a device which enables a person to jump from an aircraft and float safely to the ground. It consists of a large piece of thin cloth attached to your body by strings. पॅराशूट

parade (parades) n A **parade** is a line of people or vehicles moving together through a public place in order to celebrate an important day or event. संचलन

paradise n According to some religions, **paradise** is a wonderful place where people go after they die, if they have led good lives. नंदनवन

paraffin n **Paraffin** is a strong-smelling liquid which is used as a fuel in heaters, lamps, and engines. पॅरेफिन

paragraph (paragraphs) n A **paragraph** is a section of a piece of writing. A paragraph always begins on a new line and contains at least one sentence. परिच्छेद

Paraguay n Paraguay is an inland republic in South America. पॅराग्वे

Paraguayan (Paraguayans) adj **Paraguayan** means of or relating to Paraguay, its people, or its culture. पॅराग्वियन ▷ n A **Paraguayan** is a citizen of Paraguay, or a person of Paraguayan origin. पॅराग्वियन

parallel adj **Parallel** events or situations happen at the same time as one another, or are similar to one another. समांतर

paralysed adj If someone or part of their body is **paralysed**, they have no feeling in their body, or in part of their body, and are unable to move. अर्धांगवायू झालेला

paramedic (paramedics) n A **paramedic** is a person whose training is similar to that of a nurse and who helps to do medical work. परिचारिकेप्रमाणेच वैद्यकीय प्रशिक्षण घेतलेली व्यक्ती

parcel (parcels) n A **parcel** is something wrapped in paper, usually so that it can be sent to someone by post. पार्सल

pardon (pardons) excl You say '**Pardon?**' when you want someone to repeat what they have just said because you have not heard or understood it. पुन्हा एकदा सांगाल का? ▷ n If someone who has been found guilty of a

crime is given a **pardon**, they are officially allowed to go free and are not punished. दया

parent (parents) n A **parent** is a father or mother. आई किंवा वडील

park (parks, parking, parked) n A **park** is a place with grass and trees. People go to **parks** to take exercise or play games. उद्यान ▷ v When someone **parks** a car, they leave it somewhere. गाडी उभी/पार्क करणे

parking n **Parking** is the action of moving a vehicle into a place in a car park or by the side of the road where it can be left. वाहन उभे करून ठेवण्याची जागा

parking meter (parking meters) n A **parking meter** is a device which you have to put money into when you park in a parking space. पार्किंग मीटर

parking ticket (parking tickets) n A **parking ticket** is a piece of paper with instructions to pay a fine, and is put on your car when you have parked it somewhere illegally. पार्किंग तिकीट

parliament (parliaments) n The **parliament** of a country is the group of people who make or change its laws. संसद

parole n If a prisoner is given **parole**, he or she is released before the official end of their prison sentence and has to promise to behave well. पॅरोल (तुरुंगातून कैद्याला काही दिवसांसाठी दिलेली सुटटी)

parrot (parrots) n A **parrot** is a tropical bird with a curved beak and brightly coloured or grey feathers. Parrots can be kept as pets. पोपट

parsley n **Parsley** is a small plant with curly leaves used for flavouring or decorating savoury food. ओवा

parsnip (parsnips) n A **parsnip** is a root vegetable similar in shape to a carrot. पार्सनिप

part (parts) n **Part** of something is a piece or a section of it. भाग

partial adj You use **partial** to refer to something that is true or exists to some extent, but is not complete or total. अर्धवट

participate (participates, participating, participated) *vi* If you **participate** in an activity, you are involved in it with other people. सहभागी होणे

particular *adj* You use **particular** to emphasize that you are talking about one thing or one kind of thing rather than other similar ones. विशिष्ट

particularly *adv* You use **particularly** to indicate that what you are saying applies especially to one thing or situation. विशेषत:

parting (partings) *n* **Parting** is the act of leaving a particular person or place. सोडून देणे, अलग होणे

partly *adv* You use **partly** to indicate that something is true or exists to some extent, but not completely. अंशत:

partner (partners) *n* Your **partner** is the person you are married to or are having a long-term romantic relationship with. जोडीदार

partridge (partridges) *n* A **partridge** is a wild bird with brown feathers, a round body, and a short tail. कवडा/तितर पक्षी

part-time *adj* If someone is a **part-time** worker or has a **part-time** job, they work for only part of each day or week. अर्धवेळ ▷ *adv* If someone works **part-time**, they work for only part of each day or week. अर्धवेळ

part with (parts with, parting with, parted with) *v* If you **part with** something that you would prefer to keep, you give it or sell it to someone else. देऊन टाकणे, अलग होणे *Think carefully before parting with money.*

party (parties, partying, partied) *n* A **party** is a social event at which people enjoy themselves doing things such as eating or dancing. मेजवानी ▷ *n* A **party** of people is a group of them doing something together, for example travelling. समूह, गट ▷ *vi* If you **party**, you enjoy yourself doing things with other people such as eating and dancing. पार्टी करणे

pass (passes, passing, passed) *n* A **pass** is a document that allows you to do something.

परवानगी, परवाना ▷ *n* A **pass** is a narrow way between two mountains. खिंड ▷ *n* A **pass** in an examination, test, or course is a successful result in it. उत्तीर्ण होणे ▷ *vt* If you **pass** something to someone, you give it to them. देणे ▷ *vt* When you **pass** someone, you go by them. ओलांडणे ▷ *v* If you **pass** a test, you do well. उत्तीर्ण

passage (passages) *n* A **passage** is a long, narrow space between walls or fences connecting one room or place with another. रस्ता ▷ *n* A **passage** in a book, speech, or piece of music is a section of it. उतारा

passenger (passengers) *n* A **passenger** in a bus, boat, or plane is a person who is travelling in it, but who is not driving it or working on it. प्रवासी

passion fruit (passion fruit) *n* A **passion fruit** is a small, round, brown fruit that is produced by certain types of tropical flower. पेशन फ्रूट

passive *adj* If you describe someone as **passive**, you mean they do not take action but instead let things happen to them. निष्क्रिय, विरोध न करणारा

pass out (passes out, passing out, passed out) *v* If you **pass out**, you faint or collapse. बेशुद्ध होऊन कोसळणे *He felt sick and dizzy and then passed out.*

Passover *n* **Passover** is a Jewish festival beginning in March or April and lasting for seven or eight days. पासओव्हर (यहुदी सण)

passport (passports) *n* Your **passport** is an official document which you need to show when you enter or leave a country. पारपत्र

password (passwords) *n* A **password** is a secret word or phrase that enables you to enter a place or use a computer system. पासवर्ड

past *adj* **Past** events and things happened or existed before the present time. भूतकाळातील ▷ *n* The **past** is the period of time before now. भूतकाळ ▷ *prep* You use **past** when you are telling the time. ...वाजून ...मिनिटे *It was ten* past eleven. ▷ prep Something that is **past** a place is on the other side of it. दुसऱ्या बाजूला It's just past the school there.

pasta n **Pasta** is a type of food made from a mixture of flour, eggs, and water that is formed into different shapes. Spaghetti and macaroni are types of pasta. पास्ता

paste (pastes, pasting, pasted) n **Paste** is a soft, wet mixture, which you can spread easily. पेस्ट ▷ vt If you **paste** something on to a surface, you stick it with glue. चिकटविणे ▷ v If you **paste** words or pictures on a computer, you copy them from one place and put them somewhere new. पेस्ट

pasteurized adj **Pasteurized** milk, cream, or cheese has had bacteria removed from it by a special heating process to make it safer to eat or drink. पाश्चराईझ्ड

pastime (pastimes) n A **pastime** is something that you enjoy doing in your spare time. वेळ घालवण्याचे साधन

pastry n **Pastry** is a food made of flour, fat, and water that is used for making pies and flans. पेस्ट्री

patch (patches) n A **patch** on a surface is a part of it which is different in appearance from the area around it. ठिगळ

patched adj Something that is **patched** has been mended by having a piece of material fastened over a hole. ठिगळ लावलेले

paternity leave n If a man has **paternity leave**, his employer allows him some time off work because his child has just been born. पेटर्निटी लीव्ह (पितृत्व रजा)

path (paths) n A **path** is a strip of ground that people walk along. रस्ता

pathetic adj If you describe a person or animal as **pathetic**, you mean that they are sad and weak or helpless, and they make you feel very sorry for them. दयनीय

patience n If you have **patience**, you are able to stay calm and not get annoyed, for example when something takes a long time. शांत स्वभाव, धीर

patient (patients) adj If you are **patient**, you don't get angry quickly. सहनशील, शांत ▷ n A **patient** is someone that a nurse or a doctor is looking after. रुग्ण

patio (patios) n A **patio** is a paved area in a garden, where people can sit to eat or relax. पेशिओ (अंगणातील मोकळी फरसबंदीची जागा)

patriotic adj Someone who is **patriotic** loves their country and feels very loyal towards it. देशभक्त

patrol (patrols) n **Patrol** is the action of moving round an area or building in order to make sure that there is no trouble there. गस्त

patrol car (patrol cars) n A **patrol car** is a police car used for patrolling streets and roads. गस्त घालणारी कार

pattern (patterns) n A **pattern** is a particular way in which something is usually or repeatedly done. प्रकार, साचा

pause (pauses) n A **pause** is a short period when something stops before it continues again. विराम, खंड

pavement (pavements) n A **pavement** is a path with a hard surface by the side of a road. पदपथ

pavilion (pavilions) n A **pavilion** is a building on the edge of a sports field where players can change their clothes and wash. पॅव्हिलियन

paw (paws) n The **paws** of an animal such as a cat, dog, or bear are its feet. पंजा

pawnbroker (pawnbrokers) n A **pawnbroker** is a person who will lend you money if you give them something that you own. The pawnbroker can sell that thing if you do not pay back the money before a certain time. सावकार

pay (pays, paying, paid) n Your **pay** is the money that you get from your employer as wages or salary. पगार ▷ v When you **pay** an amount of money to someone, you give it to them because you are buying something from them or because you owe it to them. पैसे देणे

payable adj If an amount of money is **payable**, it has to be paid or it can be paid. देय

pay back (pays back, paying back, paid back) v If you **pay back** money that you have borrowed from someone, you give them an equal amount at a later time. पैसे परत देणे *He will have to pay back everything he has stolen.*

payment (payments) n Payment is the act of paying money to someone or of being paid. दिलेली किंवा देणे असलेली रक्कम

payphone (payphones) n A **payphone** is a telephone which you need to put coins or a card in before you can make a call. Payphones are usually in public places. पे फोन

PC (PCs) n A **PC** is a computer that is used by one person at a time in a business, a school, or at home. **PC** is an abbreviation for 'personal computer'. पीसी

PDF (PDFs) n **PDF** files are computer documents which look exactly like the original documents, regardless of which software or operating system was used to create them. **PDF** is an abbreviation for 'Portable Document Format'. पीडीएफ

peace n When there is **peace** in a country, it is not involved in a war. शांतता

peaceful adj Peaceful means not involving war or violence. शांततापूर्ण

peach (peaches) n A **peach** is a soft, round, juicy fruit with sweet yellow flesh and pinky-yellow skin. पीच नावाचे फळ

peacock (peacocks) n A **peacock** is a large bird. The male has a very large tail covered with blue and green spots, which it can spread out like a fan. मोर

peak (peaks) n The **peak** of a process or activity is the point at which it is at its strongest, most successful, or most fully developed. सर्वोच्च बिंदू

peak hours npl Peak hours are the busiest hours, for example in traffic. गर्दीची वेळ

peanut (peanuts) n Peanuts are small nuts often eaten as a snack. शेंगदाणे

peanut allergy (peanut allergies) n If you have a **peanut allergy**, you become ill if you eat peanuts or peanut butter, or come into contact with peanuts or peanut butter. शेंगदाण्याची ऍलर्जी

peanut butter n Peanut butter is a brown paste made out of crushed peanuts which you can spread on bread and eat. पीनट बटर (शेंगदाण्यापासून लोण्यासारखा बनवलेला पदार्थ)

pear (pears) n A **pear** is a juicy fruit which is narrow at the top and wider at the bottom. It has white flesh and green or yellow skin. नाशपती

pearl (pearls) n A **pearl** is a hard, shiny, white, ball-shaped object which grows inside the shell of an oyster. Pearls are used for making jewellery. मोती

peas npl Peas are small, round, green seeds eaten as a vegetable. वाटाणे

peat n Peat is dark decaying plant material which is found in some cool wet regions. It can be burned as a fuel or used for growing plants in. इंधन म्हणून वापरला जाणारा कुजलेला पालापाचोळा

pebble (pebbles) n A **pebble** is a small stone. गारगोटी, लहान दगड

peculiar adj If you describe someone or something as **peculiar**, you think that they are strange or unusual, often in an unpleasant way. विशिष्ट

pedal (pedals) n The **pedals** on a bicycle are the two parts that you push with your feet in order to make the bicycle move. पेडल

pedestrian (pedestrians) n A **pedestrian** is a person who is walking, especially in a town. पादचारी

pedestrian crossing (pedestrian crossings) n A **pedestrian crossing** is a place where pedestrians can cross a street and where motorists must stop to let them cross. पादचारी रस्ता ओलांडतात ती रस्त्यावरील जागा

pedestrianized adj A **pedestrianized** area is intended for pedestrians, not vehicles. पादचाऱ्यांसाठी राखून ठेवलेला भाग

pedestrian precinct (pedestrian precincts) n A **pedestrian precinct** is a street or part of a town where vehicles are not allowed. पादचाऱ्यांसाठी राखून ठेवलेला भाग

pedigree adj A **pedigree** animal is descended from animals which have all been of a particular breed, and is therefore considered to be of good quality. प्राण्यांची वंशावळ

peel (peels, peeling, peeled) n The **peel** of a fruit such as a lemon or apple is its skin. फळाची साल ▷ vt When you **peel** fruit or vegetables, you remove their skins. साल काढणे

peg (pegs) n A **peg** is a small hook or knob on a wall or door which is used for hanging things on. खुंटी

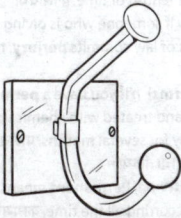

Pekinese (Pekineses) n A **Pekinese** is a type of small dog with long hair, short legs, and a short, flat nose. पेकिनिज जातीचा कुत्रा

pelican (pelicans) n A **pelican** is a type of large water bird. It catches fish and keeps them in the bottom part of its beak which is shaped like a large bag. पेलीकन पक्षी

pelican crossing (pelican crossings) n A **pelican crossing** is a place where pedestrians can cross a busy road. They press a button at the side of the road, which operates traffic lights to stop the traffic. पेलीकन क्रॉसिंग

pellet (pellets) n A **pellet** is a small ball of paper, mud, lead, or other material. (कागद, मेण, चिखल इ. वस्तूची) गोळी

pelvis (pelvises) n Your **pelvis** is the wide curved group of bones at the level of your hips. ओटीपोट

pen (pens) n A **pen** is a writing instrument, which you use to write in ink. पेन

penalize (penalizes, penalizing, penalized) vt If someone **is penalized** for something,

they are made to suffer some disadvantage because of it. शिक्षा करणे

penalty (penalties) n A **penalty** is a punishment for doing something which is against a law or rule. शिक्षा

pencil (pencils) n A **pencil** is a thin wooden rod with a black substance down the centre which is used for writing or drawing. पेन्सिल

pencil case (pencil cases) n A **pencil case** is a small bag, etc. for holding pencils and pens. पेन्सिल केस

pencil sharpener (pencil sharpeners) n A **pencil sharpener** is a small device with a blade inside, used for making pencils sharp. पेन्सिल शार्पनर

pendant (pendants) n A **pendant** is an ornament on a chain that you wear round your neck. पेंडंट (लॉकेटसारखा लोंबता दागिना)

penfriend (penfriends) n A **penfriend** is someone you write friendly letters to and receive letters from, although the two of you may never have met. पेनपाल (पत्रमित्र)

penguin (penguins) n A **penguin** is a black and white sea bird found mainly in the Antarctic. Penguins cannot fly. पेंग्विन पक्षी

penicillin n **Penicillin** is a drug that kills bacteria and is used to treat infections. पेनिसिलीन (प्रतिजैविक औषध)

peninsula (peninsulas) n A **peninsula** is a long narrow piece of land that is joined at one part to the mainland and is almost completely surrounded by water. द्वीपकल्प

penknife (penknives) n A **penknife** is a small knife with a blade that folds back into the handle. मिटून ठेवता येणारा छोटा चाकू

penny (pennies, pence) n In Britain, a **penny** is a coin or an amount which is worth one hundredth of a pound. पेनी

pension (pensions) n A **pension** is a sum of money which a retired, widowed, or disabled person regularly receives from the state or from a former employer. निवृत्तीवेतन

pensioner (pensioners) n A **pensioner** is a person who receives a pension. निवृत्तीवेतनधारक

pentathlon (pentathlons) *n* A **pentathlon** is an athletics competition in which each person must compete in five different events. पेंटॅथलन

penultimate *adj* The **penultimate** thing in a series is the one before the last. *(formal)* उपान्त्य

people *npl* **People** are men, women, and children. लोक

pepper (peppers) *n* **Pepper** is a spice with a hot taste which you put on food. मिरी ▷ *n* A **pepper** is a green, red, or yellow vegetable with seeds inside it. मिरीची भाजी

peppermill (peppermills) *n* A **peppermill** is a machine for grinding pepper into powder. पेपरमिल

peppermint *n* **Peppermint** is a strong fresh-tasting flavouring that is obtained from a plant or made artificially. पेपरमिंट

per *prep* You use **per** to talk about each one of something. For example, if a vehicle is travelling at 40 miles **per** hour, it travels 40 miles each hour. दर, प्रत्येक *Buses use much less fuel per person than cars.*

per cent *adv* You use **per cent** to talk about amounts. For example, if an amount is 10 per cent (10%) of a larger amount, it is equal to 10 hundredths of the larger amount. टक्के

percentage (percentages) *n* A **percentage** is a fraction of an amount expressed as a particular number of hundredths. टक्केवारी

percussion *n* **Percussion** instruments are musical instruments that you hit, such as drums. तालवाद्य

perfect *adj* Something that is **perfect** is as good as it can possibly be. परिपूर्ण, अचूक

perfection *n* **Perfection** is the quality of being perfect. परिपूर्णता

perfectly *adv* You can use **perfectly** to emphasize an adjective or adverb, especially when you think the person you are talking to might doubt what you are saying. अगदी बरोबर

perform (performs, performing, performed) *vt* When you **perform** a task or action, you complete it. एखादी कृती पूर्ण करणे

performance (performances) *n* A **performance** involves entertaining an audience by singing, dancing, or acting. सादरीकरण

perfume (perfumes) *n* **Perfume** is a pleasant-smelling liquid which women put on their necks and wrists to make themselves smell nice. अत्तर

perhaps *adv* You use **perhaps** when you are not sure about something. कदाचित

period (periods) *n* A particular **period** is a particular length of time. कालावधी

perjury *n* If someone who is giving evidence in a court of law commits **perjury**, they lie. खोटी साक्ष

perm (perms) *n* If you have a **perm**, your hair is curled and treated with chemicals so that it stays curly for several months. पर्मिंग (केसांना वळण देण्याची क्रिया)

permanent *adj* **Permanent** means lasting for ever or occurring all the time. कायमचा

permanently *adv* If something lasts or occurs **permanently**, it lasts for ever or occurs all the time. कायमस्वरूपी

permission *n* If you give someone **permission** to do something, you tell them that they can do it. परवानगी

permit (permits) *n* A **permit** is an official document allowing you to do something. परवाना

persecute (persecutes, persecuting, persecuted) *vt* If someone is **persecuted**, they are treated cruelly and unfairly, often because of their race or beliefs. छळणे

persevere (perseveres, persevering, persevered) *vi* If you **persevere** with something difficult, you continue doing it and do not give up. पिच्छा पुरविणे

Persian *adj* Something that is **Persian** belongs or relates to the ancient kingdom of Persia, or sometimes to the modern state of Iran. पर्शियन

persistent *adj* If something bad is **persistent**, it continues to exist or happen for a long time. सातत्यपूर्ण

person (**people, persons**) n A **person** is a man, woman, or child. व्यक्ती

personal adj A **personal** opinion, quality, or thing belongs or relates to a particular person. वैयक्तिक

personal assistant (**personal assistants**) n A **personal assistant** is a person who does office work and administrative work for someone. The abbreviation 'PA' is also used. वैयक्तिक सहायक

personality (**personalities**) n Your **personality** is your whole character and nature. व्यक्तिमत्त्व

personally adv You use **personally** to emphasize that you are giving your own opinion. व्यक्तिशः

personal organizer (**personal organizers**) n A **personal organizer** is a book containing personal or business information, which you can add pages to or remove pages from to keep the information up to date. Small computers used in a similar way are also called **personal organizers**. वैयक्तिक बाबींची नोंदवही

personal stereo (**personal stereos**) n A **personal stereo** is a small cassette or CD player with very light headphones, which people carry round so that they can listen to music while doing something else. पर्सनल स्टिरिओ

personnel npl The **personnel** of an organization are the people who work for it. कर्मचारी

perspective (**perspectives**) n A perspective is a particular way of thinking about something. एखाद्या गोष्टीविषयीचा दृष्टीकोन

perspiration n **Perspiration** is the liquid that appears on your skin when you are hot or frightened. (formal) घाम

persuade (**persuades, persuading, persuaded**) vt If you **persuade** someone to do a particular thing, you get them to do it, usually by convincing them that it is a good idea. मन वळवणे

persuasive adj Someone or something that is **persuasive** is likely to persuade you to do or believe a particular thing. मन वळवील असे

Peru n **Peru** is a republic in western South America, on the Pacific. पेरू

Peruvian (**Peruvians**) adj **Peruvian** means belonging or related to Peru, or to its people or culture. पेरुवियन ▷ n A **Peruvian** is a citizen of Peru, or a person of Peruvian origin. पेरवियन

pessimist (**pessimists**) n A **pessimist** is someone who thinks that bad things are going to happen. निराशावादी

pessimistic adj Someone who is **pessimistic** thinks that bad things are going to happen. निराशावादी

pest (**pests**) n A **pest** is an insect or small animal which damages crops or food supplies. कीटक

pester (**pesters, pestering, pestered**) vt If you say that someone **is pestering** you, you mean that they keep asking you to do something, or keep talking to you, and you find this annoying. भुणभुण लावणे

pesticide (**pesticides**) n **Pesticides** are chemicals which farmers put on their crops to kill harmful insects. कीटकनाशक

pet (**pets**) n A **pet** is an animal that you keep in your home to give you company and pleasure. पाळीव प्राणी

petition (**petitions**) n A **petition** is a document signed by a lot of people which asks for some official action to be taken. याचिका

petrified adj If you are **petrified**, you are extremely frightened. खूप घाबरलेला

petrol n **Petrol** is a liquid used as a fuel for motor vehicles. पेट्रोल

petrol station (**petrol stations**) n A **petrol station** is a garage by the side of the road where petrol is sold and put into vehicles. पेट्रोल पंप

petrol tank (**petrol tanks**) n The **petrol tank** in a motor vehicle is the container for petrol. पेट्रोलची टाकी

p

pewter n Pewter is a grey metal made by mixing tin and lead. कासे

pharmacist (pharmacists) n A **pharmacist** is a person who is qualified to prepare and sell medicines. औषधनिर्माता

pharmacy (pharmacies) n A **pharmacy** is a place where medicines are sold or given out. औषधांचे दुकान

PhD (PhDs) n A **PhD** is a degree awarded to people who have done advanced research. **PhD** is an abbreviation for 'Doctor of Philosophy'. पीएचडी

pheasant (pheasants, pheasant) n A **pheasant** is a bird with a long tail. तितरपक्षी

philosophy n Philosophy is the study or creation of theories about basic things such as the nature of existence or how people should live. तत्त्वज्ञान

phobia (phobias) n A **phobia** is an unreasonably strong fear of something. तीव्र भीती

phone (phones, phoning, phoned) n A **phone** is a piece of equipment that you use to talk to someone in another place. फोन ▷ v When you **phone** someone, you dial their phone number and speak to them by phone. दूरध्वनी करणे, फोन करणे

phone back (phones back, phoning back, phoned back) v If you **phone** someone **back**, you telephone them again or in return for a telephone call that they have made to you. प्रत्युत्तरादाखल फोन करणे I'll phone you back later.

phone bill (phone bills) n A **phone bill** is an account or bill for the charges for a telephone and line and for calls made from it. फोनचे बिल

phonebook (phonebooks) n A **phonebook** is a book that contains an alphabetical list of the names, addresses, and telephone numbers of the people in a town or area. फोन बुक

phonebox (phoneboxes) n A **phonebox** is a small shelter outdoors or in a building in which there is a public telephone. फोन बॉक्स

phone call (phone calls) n If you make a **phone call**, you dial someone's phone number and speak to them by phone. फोन कॉल

phonecard (phonecards) n A **phonecard** is a plastic card that you can use instead of money in some public telephones. फोन कार्ड

phone number (phone numbers) n Your **phone number** is the number that other people dial when they want to talk to you on the telephone. दूरध्वनी क्रमांक

photo (photos) n A **photo** is a picture that is made using a camera. छायाचित्र

photo album (photo albums) n A **photo album** is a book in which you keep photographs that you have collected. छायाचित्रसंग्रह

photocopier (photocopiers) n A **photocopier** is a machine which quickly copies documents by photographing them. फोटोकॉपिअर

photocopy (photocopies, photocopying, photocopied) n A **photocopy** is a document made by a photocopier. फोटोकॉपी ▷ vt If you **photocopy** a document, you make a copy of it with a photocopier. छायाप्रत

photograph (photographs, photographing, photographed) n A **photograph** is a picture that is made using a camera. छायाचित्र ▷ vt When you **photograph** someone or something, you use a camera to obtain a picture of them. छायाचित्र काढणे

photographer (photographers) n A **photographer** is someone who takes photographs, especially as their job. छायाचित्रकार

photography n Photography is the skill, job, or process of producing photographs. छायाचित्रण

phrase (phrases) n A **phrase** is a short group of words that are used as a unit and whose meaning is not always obvious from the words contained in it. वाक्प्रचार

phrasebook (phrasebooks) n A **phrasebook** is a book used by people travelling to a foreign country. It has lists of useful words and expressions, together with the translation of each word or expression in the language of that country. वाक्प्रचारांचे पुस्तक

physical (physicals) *adj* **Physical** means connected with a person's body, rather than with their mind. शारीरिक ▷ *n* A **physical** is a medical examination of the body to diagnose disease or check fitness. शारीरिक

physicist (physicists) *n* A **physicist** is a person who studies physics. भौतिकशास्त्रज्ञ

physics *n* **Physics** is the scientific study of forces such as heat, light, sound, pressure, gravity, and electricity. भौतिकशास्त्र

physiotherapist (physiotherapists) *n* A **physiotherapist** is a person whose job is using physiotherapy to treat people. फिजिओथेरपिस्ट

physiotherapy *n* **Physiotherapy** is medical treatment given to people who cannot move a part of their body and involves exercise, massage, or heat treatment. फिजिओथेरपी

pianist (pianists) *n* A **pianist** is a person who plays the piano. पियानोवादक

piano (pianos) *n* A **piano** is a large musical instrument with a row of black and white keys, which you strike with your fingers. पियानो

pick (picks, picking, picked) *n* The best things or people in a particular group are the **pick** of that group. निवडक चांगले लोक किंवा वस्तू ▷ *vt* If you **pick** someone, you choose them. निवडणे ▷ *vt* When you **pick** flowers, fruit, or leaves, you take them from a plant or tree. तोडणे

pick on (picks on, picking on, picked on) *v* If someone **picks on** you, they repeatedly criticize or attack you unfairly. *(informal)* दोष काढणे *They were always picking on her.*

pick out (picks out, picking out, picked out) *v* If you can **pick out** something or someone, you recognize them when it is difficult to see them. दूरवरून ओळखणे *With my binoculars, I pick out a figure a mile or so away.*

pickpocket (pickpockets) *n* A **pickpocket** is a person who steals things from people's pockets or bags in public places. खिसेकापू

pick up (picks up, picking up, picked up) *v* If you **pick** something **up**, you lift it upwards from a surface using your fingers. उचलणे *Ridley picked up the pencil.*

picnic (picnics) *n* When people have a **picnic**, they eat a meal out of doors. सहल

picture (pictures) *n* A **picture** consists of lines and shapes which are drawn, painted, or printed on a surface and show a person, thing, or scene. चित्र

picture frame (picture frames) *n* A **picture frame** is the wood, metal, or plastic that is fitted around a picture, especially when it is displayed or hung up on a wall. चित्राची चौकट

picturesque *adj* A **picturesque** place is attractive, interesting, and unspoiled. चित्रातल्यासारखी सुंदर जागा

pie (pies) *n* A **pie** consists of meat, vegetables, or fruit, baked in pastry. बेकरीमधील पाय

piece (pieces) *n* A **piece** of something is a portion, part, or section of it that has been removed, broken off, or cut off. तुकडा

pie chart (pie charts) *n* A **pie chart** is a circle divided into sections to show the relative proportions of a set of things. पाय चार्ट

pier (piers) *n* A **pier** is a large platform which sticks out into the sea and which people can walk along. समुद्रातील धक्का

pierce (pierces, piercing, pierced) *vt* If a sharp object **pierces** something, or if you **pierce** something with a sharp object, the object goes into it and makes a hole in it. टोचणे, खुपसणे

pierced *adj* If your ears or some other parts of your body are **pierced**, you have a small hole made through them so that you can wear a piece of jewellery in them. टोचलेले

piercing (piercings) *n* A **piercing** is a hole that has been made in part of someone's body that they can put jewellery in. टोचण्याची क्रिया

pig (pigs) *n* A **pig** is a farm animal with a pink, white, or black skin. Pigs are kept for their meat, which is called pork, ham, or bacon. डुक्कर

pigeon (pigeons) *n* A **pigeon** is a grey bird which is often seen in towns. कबुतर

piggybank (piggybanks) *n* A **piggybank** is a small container shaped like a pig, with a narrow hole in the top through which to put coins. Children often use piggybanks to save money. पिगी बँक

pigtail (pigtails) *n* If someone has a **pigtail** or **pigtails**, their hair is plaited or braided into one or two lengths. वेणी

pile (piles) *n* A **pile** of things is a quantity of them lying on top of one another. ढीग

piles *npl* **Piles** are painful swellings that can appear in the veins inside a person's anus. मूळव्याध

pile-up (pile-ups) *n* A **pile-up** is a road accident in which a lot of vehicles crash into each other. रस्त्यावरील अपघातात एकावर एक चढलेली वाहने

pilgrim (pilgrims) *n* A **pilgrim** is a person who makes a journey to a holy place. धार्मिक यात्रा करणारी व्यक्ती

pilgrimage (pilgrimages) *n* If someone makes a **pilgrimage** to a place, they make a journey there because the place is holy according to their religion, or very important to them personally. धार्मिक यात्रा

pill (pills) *n* **Pills** are small solid round masses of medicine or vitamins that you swallow. औषधाच्या गोळ्या

pillar (pillars) *n* A **pillar** is a tall solid structure which is usually used to support part of a building. खांब

pillow (pillows) *n* A **pillow** is a rectangular cushion which you rest your head on when you are in bed. उशी

pillowcase (pillowcases) *n* A **pillowcase** is a cover for a pillow, which can be removed and washed. उशीचा अभ्रा

pilot (pilots) *n* A **pilot** is a person who is trained to fly an aircraft. वैमानिक

pilot light (pilot lights) *n* A **pilot light** is a small gas flame in a cooker, stove, boiler, or fire. It burns all the time and lights the main

large flame when the gas is turned fully on. पायलट लाइट (सतत तेवत राहणारी वात)

pimple (pimples) *n* **Pimples** are small raised spots, especially on the face. मुरमे

pin (pins) *n* **Pins** are very small thin pieces of metal with points at one end, which are used to fasten things together. टाचणी

PIN *n* Someone's **PIN** or **PIN number** is a secret number which they can use, for example, with a bank card to withdraw money from a cash machine. **PIN** is an abbreviation for 'personal identification number'. पिन, वैयक्तिक ओळख क्रमांक

pinafore (pinafores) *n* A **pinafore** or a **pinafore dress** is a sleeveless dress. It is worn over a blouse or sweater. पिनाफोअर नावाचा स्त्रियांचा बिनबाह्यांचा वेश

pinch (pinches, pinching, pinched) *vt* If you **pinch** a part of someone's body, you take a piece of their skin between your thumb and first finger and give it a short squeeze. चिमटा घेणे

pine (pines) *n* A **pine** or a **pine tree** is a tall tree with long thin leaves which it keeps all year round. पाईन वृक्ष

pineapple (pineapples) n A **pineapple** is a large oval fruit with sweet, juicy, yellow flesh and thick, brown skin. अननस

pink (pinker, pinkest) adj Something that is **pink** is the colour between red and white. गुलाबी

pint (pints) n A **pint** is a unit of measurement for liquids. In Britain, it is equal to 568 cubic centimetres or one eighth of an imperial gallon. In America, it is equal to 473 cubic centimetres or one eighth of an American gallon. पिंट (द्रवपदार्थांचे एक परिमाण)

pip (pips) n **Pips** are the small hard seeds in a fruit such as an apple or orange. कठीण कवचाची लहान बी

pipe (pipes) n A **pipe** is a long, round, hollow object through which a liquid or gas can flow. नळी, नळ

pipeline (pipelines) n A **pipeline** is a large pipe used for carrying oil or gas over a long distance. पाईप लाईन, नलिकामार्ग

pirate (pirates) n **Pirates** are sailors who attack other ships and steal property from them. समुद्री चाचे

Pisces n **Pisces** is one of the twelve signs of the zodiac. Its symbol is two fish. People who are born between the 19th of February and the 20th of March come under this sign. मीन रास

pistol (pistols) n A **pistol** is a small gun. पिस्तूल

piston (pistons) n A **piston** is a cylinder or metal disc that is part of an engine. पिस्टन

pitch (pitches, pitching, pitched) n A **pitch** is an area of ground that is marked out and used for playing a game such as football, cricket, or hockey. खेळपट्टी ▷ n The **pitch** of a sound is how high or low it is. स्वरपट्टी ▷ vt If you **pitch** something somewhere, you throw it forcefully while aiming carefully. नेम धरून जोराने फेकणे

pity (pities, pitying, pitied) n If you feel **pity** for someone, you feel very sorry for them. दया ▷ vt If you **pity** someone, you feel very sorry for them. दया करणे

pixel (pixels) n A **pixel** is the smallest area on a computer screen which can be given a separate colour by the computer. पिक्सेल

pizza (pizzas) n A **pizza** is a flat piece of dough covered with tomatoes, cheese, and other savoury food, which is baked in an oven. पिझ्झा

place (places, placing, placed) n A **place** is a building, area, town, or country. ठिकाण ▷ vt If you **place** something somewhere, you put it in a particular position. एखाद्या जागी ठेवणे ▷ n A **place** is where something belongs. जागा

placement n The **placement** of something is the act of putting it in a particular place. एखाद्या जागी ठेवण्याची क्रिया

place of birth (places of birth) n Your **place of birth** is the place where you were born. जन्मठिकाण

plain (plainer, plainest, plains) adj A **plain** object, surface, or fabric is entirely in one colour and has no pattern, design, or writing on it. सपाट ▷ n A **plain** is a large, flat area of land with very few trees on it. सखल भूप्रदेश

plain chocolate n **Plain chocolate** is dark-brown chocolate that has a stronger and less sweet taste than milk chocolate. प्लेन चॉकलेट

plait (plaits) n A **plait** is a length of hair that has been twisted over and under two other lengths of hair to make one thick length of hair. वेणी

plan (plans, planning, planned) n A **plan** is a method of achieving something that you have worked out in detail beforehand. योजना ▷ v If you **plan** what you are going to do, you decide in detail what you are going to do, and you intend to do it. योजना आखणे

plane (planes) n A **plane** is a vehicle with wings and one or more engines which can fly. विमान ▷ n A **plane** is a flat level surface which may be sloping at a particular angle. सपाट/ समतल जागा ▷ n A **plane** is a tool that has a flat bottom with a sharp blade in it, used for shaping wood. रंधा

p

planet (planets) n A **planet** is a large, round object in space that moves around a star. The Earth is a planet. ग्रह

planning n **Planning** is the process of deciding in detail how to do something before you actually start to do it. नियोजन

plant (plants, planting, planted) n A **plant** is a factory or a place where power is produced. प्रकल्प ▷ n A **plant** is a living thing that grows in earth and has a stem, leaves, and roots. रोप ▷ vt When you **plant** a seed, plant, or young tree, you put it into earth so that it will grow. लागवड करणे

plant pot (plant pots) n A **plant pot** is a container that is used for growing plants. कुंडी

plaque (plaques) n A **plaque** is a flat piece of metal or wood, which is fixed to a wall or monument in memory of a person or event. स्मृतिशिला, कोनशिला

plasma screen (plasma screens) n A **plasma screen** is a type of thin television screen or computer screen that produces high-quality images. प्लाइमा स्क्रीन

plasma TV (plasma TVs) n A **plasma TV** is a type of television set with a thin screen that produces high-quality images. प्लाइमा टीव्ही

plaster (plasters) n **Plaster** is a paste which people put on walls and ceilings so that they are smooth. प्लॅस्टर ▷ n A **plaster** is a strip of material with a soft part in the middle. You can cover a cut on your body with a **plaster**. प्लास्टर

plastic (plastics) n **Plastic** is a light but strong material produced by a chemical process. प्लॅस्टिक

plastic bag (plastic bags) n A **plastic bag** is a bag made from a very thin flexible plastic. प्लॅस्टिकची पिशवी

plastic surgery n **Plastic surgery** is the practice of performing operations to repair or replace skin which has been damaged, or to improve people's appearance. प्लॅस्टिक सर्जरी

plate (plates) n A **plate** is a round or oval flat dish used to hold food. थाळी

platform (platforms) n A **platform** is a flat raised structure or area on which someone or something can stand. फलाट

platinum n **Platinum** is a very valuable silvery-grey metal. प्लॅटिनम

play (plays, playing, played) n A **play** is a piece of writing performed in a theatre, on the radio, or on television. नाटक ▷ vi When children **play**, they spend time using toys and taking part in games. खेळणे ▷ vt If you **play** an instrument, you make music with it. वाजवणे

player (players) n A **player** in a sport or game is a person who takes part. खेळाडू ▷ n You can use **player** to refer to a musician. वादक

playful adj A **playful** gesture is friendly and cheerful. मित्रत्वाचा, खेळकर

playground (playgrounds) n A **playground** is a piece of land where children can play. खेळाचे मैदान

playgroup (playgroups) n A **playgroup** is an informal kind of school for very young children where they learn by playing. प्लेग्रुप

playing card (playing cards) n Playing **cards** are thin pieces of card with numbers and pictures on them, which are used to play games. पत्ते

playing field (playing fields) n A **playing field** is a large area of grass where people play sports. हिरवळ असलेले खेळाचे मैदान

PlayStation® (PlayStations) n A PlayStation is a type of games console. प्लेस्टेशन

playtime n In a school for young children, **playtime** is the period of time between lessons when they can play outside. खेळण्याची वेळ

play truant (plays truant, playing truant, played truant) v If children **play truant**, they stay away from school without permission. शाळेला दांडी मारणे

playwright (playwrights) n A **playwright** is a person who writes plays. नाटककार

pleasant (pleasanter, pleasantest) adj Something that is **pleasant** is enjoyable or attractive. आल्हाददायक

please! excl You say **please!** when you are politely asking or inviting someone to do something.

pleased adj If you are **pleased**, you are happy about something or satisfied with it. समाधानी

pleasure n If something gives you **pleasure**, you get a feeling of happiness, satisfaction, or enjoyment from it. आनंद

plenty n If there is **plenty** of something, there is a lot of it. भरपूर

pliers npl Pliers are a tool with two handles at one end and two hard, flat, metal parts at the other. **Pliers** are used to hold or pull out things such as nails. पकड

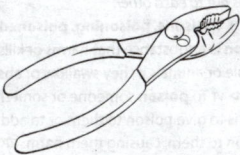

plot (plots, plotting, plotted) n A **plot** is a small piece of land, especially one that is intended for a purpose such as building houses or growing vegetables. भूखंड ▷ n A **plot** is a secret plan to do something that is illegal or wrong. गुप्त योजना

plough (ploughs, ploughing, ploughed) n A **plough** is a large farming tool with sharp blades, which is attached to a tractor or an animal and used to turn over the soil before planting. नांगर ▷ vt When a farmer **ploughs** an area of land, they turn over the soil using a plough. नांगरणे

plug (plugs) n A **plug** on a piece of electrical equipment is a small plastic object with two or three metal pins which fit into the holes of an electric socket. प्लग

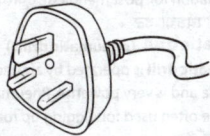

plughole (plugholes) n A **plughole** is a small hole in a bath or sink which allows the water to flow away and into which you can put a plug. प्लगहोल

plug in (plugs in, plugging in, plugged in) v If you **plug** a piece of electrical equipment **in**, you push its plug into an electric socket so that it can work. प्लग लावणे I filled the kettle and plugged it in.

plum (plums) n A **plum** is a small sweet fruit with a smooth red or yellow skin and a stone in the middle. आलुबुखार, मनुका

plumber (plumbers) n A **plumber** is a person whose job is to connect and repair things such as water and drainage pipes, baths, and toilets. नळजोडणी करणारा

plumbing n The **plumbing** in a building consists of the water and drainage pipes, baths, and toilets in it. नळजोडणीचे काम

plump (plumper, plumpest) adj A **plump** person is rather fat. जाडसर व्यक्ती

plunge (plunges, plunging, plunged) vi If something or someone **plunges** in a particular direction, especially into water, they fall, rush, or throw themselves in that direction. एखादी वस्तू वा व्यक्ती पाण्यात पडणे/कोसळणे/झोकून देणे

plural (plurals) n The **plural** of a noun is the form of it that is used to refer to more than one person or thing. अनेकवचन

plus *prep* You use **plus** to show that one number or quantity is being added to another. अधिक *Two plus two equals four.*

plywood *n* Plywood is wood that consists of thin layers of wood stuck together. प्लायवूड

p.m. *abbr* p.m. is used after a number to show that you are referring to a particular time between noon and midnight. **p.m.** is an abbreviation for 'post meridiem'. दुपारपासून मध्यरात्रीपर्यंतची वेळ

pneumatic drill (pneumatic drills) *n* A **pneumatic drill** is operated by air under pressure and is very powerful. Pneumatic drills are often used for digging up roads. न्यूमॅटिक ड्रील

pneumonia *n* Pneumonia is a serious disease which affects your lungs and makes breathing difficult. न्यूमोनिया

poached *adj* If fish, animals, or birds are **poached**, someone has caught them illegally on someone else's property. प्राण्यांचा बेकायदेशीर व्यापार ▷ *adj* Poached eggs, fish, or other foods are cooked gently in boiling water, milk, or other liquid. उकडलेले

pocket (pockets) *n* A **pocket** is a small bag or pouch that forms part of a piece of clothing. खिसा

pocket calculator (pocket calculators) *n* A **pocket calculator** is a very small electronic device that you use for making mathematical calculations. खिशात ठेवण्याजोगा कॅलक्युलेटर

pocket money *n* Pocket money is a small amount of money given regularly to children by their parents. मुलांना दरमहा खर्चासाठी मिळणारे पैसे

podcast (podcasts) *n* A **podcast** is an audio file that can be downloaded and listened to on a computer or iPod. पॉडकास्ट

poem (poems) *n* A **poem** is a piece of writing in which the words are chosen for their beauty and sound and are carefully arranged, often in short lines. कविता

poet (poets) *n* A **poet** is a person who writes poems. कवी

poetry *n* Poems, considered as a form of literature, are referred to as **poetry**. पद्य

point (points, pointing, pointed) *n* A **point** is an idea or a fact. मुद्दा ▷ *vi* If you **point** at something, you stick out your finger to show where it is. दर्शविणे. दाखविणे ▷ *n* The **point** of something is its thin, sharp end. Needles and knives have **points**. टोक ▷ *n* A **point** is a mark that you win in a game or a sport. गुण

pointless *adj* Something that is **pointless** has no purpose. निरुद्देश

point out (points out, pointing out, pointed out) *v* If you **point out** an object or place to someone, you direct their attention to it. बोट दाखवणे *Now and then they would stop to point things out to each other.*

poison (poisons, poisoning, poisoned) *n* **Poison** is a substance that harms or kills people or animals if they swallow or absorb it. विष ▷ *vt* To **poison** someone or something means to give poison to them or to add poison to them, causing them harm. विष देणे, विषप्रयोग करणे

poisonous *adj* Something that is **poisonous** will kill you or harm you if you swallow or absorb it. विषारी

poke (pokes, poking, poked) *vt* If you **poke** someone or something, you quickly push them with your finger or with a sharp object. टोचणे, ढोसणे

poker *n* Poker is a card game that people usually play in order to win money. पोकर खेळ

Poland n **Poland** is a republic in central Europe, on the Baltic. पोलंड

polar adj **Polar** refers to the area around the North and South Poles. ध्रुवीय

polar bear (polar bears) n A **polar bear** is a large white bear which is found near the North Pole. ध्रुवीय प्रदेशातील अस्वल

pole (poles) n A **pole** is a long, thin piece of wood or metal, used especially for supporting things. खांब

Pole (Poles) n A **Pole** is a citizen of Poland, or a person of Polish origin. पोलंडचा रहिवासी

pole vault n The **pole vault** is an athletics event in which athletes jump over a high bar, using a long flexible pole to help lift themselves up. पोल व्हॉल्ट नावाचा खेळ

police n The **police** are the official organization that is responsible for making sure that people obey the law. पोलीस

policeman (policemen) n A **policeman** is a man who is a member of the police force. पोलीस

police officer (police officers) n A **police officer** is a member of the police force. पोलीस अधिकारी

police station (police stations) n A **police station** is the local office of a police force in a particular area. पोलीस ठाणे

policewoman (policewomen) n A **policewoman** is a woman who is a member of the police force. महिला पोलीस

polio n **Polio** is a serious infectious disease which can make people paralysed. पोलिओ

polish (polishes, polishing, polished) n **Polish** is a substance that you put on the surface of an object in order to clean it, protect it, and make it shine. पॉलिश ▷ vt If you **polish** something, you put polish on it or rub it with a cloth to make it shine. चकचकीत/पॉलिश करणे

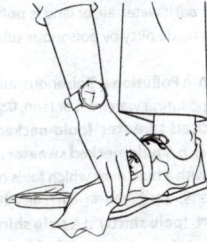

polish

Polish adj **Polish** means belonging or relating to Poland, or to its people, language, or culture. पोलंडचे रहिवासी ▷ n **Polish** is the language spoken by people in Poland. पोलिश भाषा

polite (politer, politest) adj A **polite** person has good manners and is not rude to other people. सभ्य

politely adv If you do something **politely**, you do it with good manners and without being rude to other people. सौम्यपणे, सभ्यपणे

politeness n **Politeness** is good manners in front of other people. सभ्यपणा

political adj **Political** means relating to the way power is achieved and used in a country or society. राजकीय

politician (politicians) n A **politician** is a person whose job is in politics, especially a member of parliament. राजकारणी

politics npl **Politics** is the actions or activities concerned with achieving and using power in a country or organization. राजकारण

poll (polls) n A **poll** is a survey in which people are asked their opinions about something. मतदान

pollen n **Pollen** is a powder produced by flowers in order to fertilize other flowers. पुष्पपराग

pollute (pollutes, polluting, polluted) vt To **pollute** water, air, or land means to make it dirty and dangerous to live in or to use, especially with poisonous chemicals. प्रदूषित करणे

polluted adj If water, air, or land is **polluted**, it has been made dirty by poisonous substances. प्रदूषित

pollution n **Pollution** is poisonous substances that are polluting water, air, or land. प्रदूषण

polo-necked sweater (polo-necked sweaters) n A **polo-necked sweater** is a sweater with a high neck which folds over. गळाबंद, जाड, उलटी केलेल्या कॉलरचा स्वेटर

polo shirt (polo shirts) n A **polo shirt** is a soft short-sleeved piece of clothing with a collar, which you put on over your head. पोलो शर्ट

Polynesia n **Polynesia** is the division of islands in the Pacific which includes Samoa, Tonga, the Cook Islands, and Tuvalu. पॉलिनेशिया

Polynesian (Polynesians) adj **Polynesian** means relating to Polynesia, its people, or any of their languages. पॉलिनेशियन ▷ n A **Polynesian** is a person who lives in Polynesia, or a person of Polynesian origin. पॉलिनेशियन ▷ n **Polynesian** is a branch of languages, which includes Maori, Hawaiian, and other languages of the South and central Pacific. पॉलिनेशियन

polythene bag (polythene bags) n A **polythene bag** is a bag made of thin plastic, especially one used to store or protect food or household articles. पॉलिथीनची पिशवी

pomegranate (pomegranates) n A **pomegranate** is a round fruit with a thick reddish skin. It contains lots of small seeds with juicy flesh around them. डाळिंब

pond (ponds) n A **pond** is a small, usually man-made, area of water. तळे

pony (ponies) n A **pony** is a type of small horse. छोटा घोडा

ponytail (ponytails) n If someone has their hair in a **ponytail**, it is tied up at the back so that it hangs down like a tail. पोनीटेल (मागे उंच बांधलेले केस)

pony trekking n **Pony trekking** is the act of riding ponies cross-country, especially as a pastime. छोट्या घोड्यावरून फिरणे

poodle (poodles) n A **poodle** is a type of dog with thick curly hair. पूडल जातीचा कुत्रा

pool (pools) n A **pool** of people, money, or things is a quantity or number of them that is available for use. संचय ▷ n A **pool** is a small area of still water. थारोळे, तळे

poor (poorer, poorest) adj Someone who is **poor** has very little money and few possessions. गरीब

poorly adj If someone is **poorly**, they are ill. आजारी

popcorn n **Popcorn** is a snack which consists of grains of maize that have been heated until they have burst and become large and light. लाह्या

pope (popes) n The **pope** is the head of part of the Christian Church. ख्रिश्चन धर्मगुरू

poplar (poplars) n A **poplar** or a **poplar tree** is a type of tall thin tree. पॉपलर वृक्ष

poppy (poppies) n A **poppy** is a plant with large, delicate, red flowers. अफूचे झुडूप

popular adj Someone or something that is **popular** is liked by a lot of people. लोकप्रिय

popularity n The **popularity** of someone or something is the degree to which they are liked by other people. लोकप्रियता

population (populations) n The **population** of a place is the people who live there, or the number of people living there. लोकसंख्या

pop-up (pop-ups) n On a computer screen, a **pop-up** is a small work area that appears on the screen when you perform particular operations. A **pop-up** may contain items such as a menu or advertisement. पॉप-अप

porch (porches) n A **porch** is a sheltered area at the entrance to a building. It has a roof and sometimes walls. पोर्च, इमारतीमध्ये प्रवेश करण्यापूर्वीचा भाग

porridge n **Porridge** is a thick sticky food made from oats cooked in water or milk and eaten hot, especially for breakfast. पॉरिज

port (ports) n **Port** is a type of strong, sweet red wine. पोर्ट वाईन ▷ n A **port** is a town or a harbour area with docks and warehouses, where ships load or unload goods or passengers. बंदर

portable *adj* A **portable** machine or device is designed to be easily carried or moved. उचलून दुसऱ्या ठिकाणी नेता येण्याजोगी वस्तू

porter (porters) *n* A **porter** is a person whose job is to be in charge of the entrance of a building such as a hotel. द्वारपाल

portfolio (portfolios) *n* A **portfolio** is a set of pictures or photographs of someone's work, which they show to potential employers. अवगत असलेल्या कलांचा संग्रह, पोर्टफोलिओ

portion (portions) *n* A **portion of** something is a part of it. भाग

portrait (portraits) *n* A **portrait** is a painting, drawing, or photograph of a person. व्यक्तिचित्र, शब्दचित्र

Portugal *n* **Portugal** is a republic in south-west Europe, on the Atlantic. पोर्तुगाल

Portuguese (Portuguese) *adj* **Portuguese** means belonging or relating to Portugal, or its people, language, or culture. पोर्तुगीज ▷ *n* The **Portuguese** are the people of Portugal. पोर्तुगीज ▷ *n* **Portuguese** is the language spoken in Portugal, Brazil, Angola, and Mozambique. पोर्तुगीज

position (positions) *n* The **position** of someone or something is the place where they are. ठिकाण

positive *adj* If you are **positive**, you are hopeful and confident, and think of the good aspects of a situation rather than the bad ones. आशावादी

possess (possesses, possessing, possessed) *vt* If you **possess** something, you have it or own it. मालकी असणे

possession *n* If you are in **possession** of something, you have it, because you have obtained it or because it belongs to you. (formal) ताबा

possibility (possibilities) *n* If you say there is a **possibility** that something is true or that something will happen, you mean that it might be true or it might happen. शक्यता

possible *adj* If it is **possible** to do something, it can be done. शक्य

possibly *adv* You use **possibly** to indicate that you are not sure whether something is true or will happen. शक्यतो

post (posts, posting, posted) *n* A **post** is a strong upright pole fixed into the ground. उभा खांब ▷ *n* A **post** is a job or official position in a company or organization. पद ▷ *n* The **post** is a system for collecting and delivering letters and parcels. टपाल ▷ *vt* If you **post** a letter, you put a stamp on it and send it to someone. पोस्टाने पाठविणे

postage *n* **Postage** is the money that you pay for sending letters and parcels by post. टपालखर्च

postal order (postal orders) *n* A **postal order** is a piece of paper representing a sum of money which you can buy at a post office and send to someone as a way of sending them money by post. पोस्टल ऑर्डर

postbox (postboxes) *n* A **postbox** is a metal box in a public place, where you put letters and packets to be collected. They are then sorted and delivered. टपाल पेटी

postcard (postcards) *n* A **postcard** is a piece of card, often with a picture on one side, which you can write on and post to someone without using an envelope. पोस्ट कार्ड

postcode (postcodes) *n* Your **postcode** is a short sequence of numbers and letters at the end of your address. टपाल सूची क्रमांक (पोस्टकोड)

poster (posters) *n* A **poster** is a large notice, advertisement, or picture that you stick on a wall. भित्तिपत्रक

postgraduate (postgraduates) *n* A **postgraduate** is a student with a first degree from a university who is studying or doing research at a more advanced level. स्नातकोत्तर, पदव्युत्तर

postman (postmen) *n* A **postman** is a man whose job is to collect and deliver letters and parcels that are sent by post. टपालवाहक पुरुष

p

postmark (**postmarks**) *n* A **postmark** is a mark which is printed on letters and packages at a post office. It shows the time and place at which something was posted. पोस्टमार्क

post office (**post offices**) *n* A **post office** is a building where you can buy stamps, post letters, and parcels, and use other services. टपाल कार्यालय

postpone (**postpones, postponing, postponed**) *vt* If you **postpone** an event, you arrange for it to take place at a later time than was originally planned. पुढे ढकलणे

postwoman (**postwomen**) *n* A **postwoman** is a woman whose job is to collect and deliver letters, etc. टपालवाहक स्त्री

pot (**pots**) *n* A **pot** is a deep round container for cooking food. भांडे

potato (**potatoes**) *n* **Potatoes** are vegetables with brown or red skins and white insides. बटाटा

potato peeler (**potato peelers**) *n* A **potato peeler** is a special tool used for removing the skin from potatoes. बटाटे सोलण्याचे साधन

potential *adj* You use **potential** to say that someone or something is capable of developing into the particular kind of person or thing. क्षमता ▷ *n* If something has **potential**, it is capable of being useful or successful in the future. क्षमता

pothole (**potholes**) *n* A **pothole** is a large hole in the surface of a road, caused by traffic and bad weather. रस्त्यावर वाहतुक आणि खराब हवामानामुळे पडलेला मोठा खड्डा

pot plant (**pot plants**) *n* A **pot plant** is a plant which is grown in a container, especially indoors. कुंडीतले रोप

pottery *n* **Pottery** is objects made from clay. मातीची वस्तू

potty (**potties**) *n* A **potty** is a deep bowl which a small child uses as a toilet. लहान मुलांना संडास करण्यासाठी देतात ते भांडे

pound (**pounds**) *n* The **pound** is the unit of money which is used in Britain. It is represented by the symbol £. Some other

countries, for example Egypt, also have a unit of money called a **pound**. पाऊंड

pound sterling (**pounds sterling**) *n* **Pound sterling** is the official name for the standard monetary unit of Britain. पाऊंड स्टर्लिंग

pour (**pours, pouring, poured**) *vt* If you **pour** a liquid, you make it flow steadily out of a container by holding the container at an angle. ओतणे

poverty *n* **Poverty** is the state of being very poor. गरिबी

powder (**powders**) *n* **Powder** consists of many tiny particles of a solid substance. भुकटी, पावडर

power *n* If someone has **power**, they have control over people. शक्ती ▷ *n* The **power** of something is its strength. शक्ती

power cut (**power cuts**) *n* A **power cut** is a period of time when the electricity supply to a particular building or area is stopped, sometimes deliberately. खंडित केलेली वीज

powerful *adj* A **powerful** person or organization is able to control or influence people and events. शक्तिशाली

practical *adj* **Practical** means involving real situations, rather than ideas and theories. व्यवहार्य

practically *adv* **Practically** means almost. जवळजवळ

practice (**practices**) *n* You can refer to something that people do regularly as a **practice**. नित्याचा व्यवहार, सराव

practise (practises, practising, practised) v
If you **practise** something, you keep doing it
regularly in order to do it better. नित्य सराव करणे

praise (praises, praising, praised) vt If you
praise someone or something, you express
approval for their achievements or qualities.
स्तुती करणे

pram (prams) n A **pram** is like a baby's cot
on wheels, which you can push along when
you want to take the baby somewhere. लहान
मुलांची चाके असलेली खाट

prank (pranks) n A **prank** is a childish trick.
(old-fashioned) पोरकट खोडी

prawn (prawns) n A **prawn** is a small edible
shellfish, similar to a shrimp. कोळंबी

pray (prays, praying, prayed) v When people
pray, they speak to God in order to give
thanks or to ask for help. प्रार्थना करणे

prayer (prayers) n **Prayer** is the activity of
speaking to God. प्रार्थना

precaution (precautions) n A **precaution**
is an action that is intended to prevent
something dangerous or unpleasant from
happening. सावधानता

preceding adj You refer to the period of time
or the thing immediately before the one that
you are talking about as the **preceding** one.
अगोदरचा

precinct (precincts) n A shopping **precinct**
is an area in the centre of a town in which cars
are not allowed. शहरातील बाजारपेठेचा मध्यवर्ती
भाग

precious adj If you say that something such
as a resource is **precious**, you mean that it is
valuable and should not be wasted or used
badly. मौल्यवान

precise adj You use **precise** to emphasize that
you are referring to an exact thing, rather than
something vague. तंतोतंत

precisely adv **Precisely** means accurately and
exactly. बरोबर

predecessor (predecessors) n Your
predecessor is the person who had your job
before you. पूर्वसुरी, पूर्वज

predict (predicts, predicting, predicted) vt
If you **predict** an event, you say that it will
happen. भविष्य वर्तवणे

predictable adj Something that is
predictable is obvious in advance and will
happen. भविष्य वर्तवण्याजोगे

prefect (prefects) n In some schools,
especially in Britain, a **prefect** is an older
pupil who does special duties and helps
the teachers to control the younger pupils.
ब्रिटनमधील शाळांमधील ज्येष्ठ विद्यार्थी जो कनिष्ठ
विद्यार्थ्यांवर लक्ष ठेवतो

prefer (prefers, preferring, preferred) vt If
you **prefer** someone or something, you like
that person or thing better than another. पसंत
करणे/असणे

preferably adv You use **preferably** to show
that something is more desirable or suitable.
शक्यतो

preference (preferences) n If you have a
preference for something, you would like to
have or do that thing rather than something
else. पसंती

pregnancy n **Pregnancy** is the condition
of being pregnant or the period of time
during which a female is pregnant.
गरोदरपण

pregnant adj If a woman or female animal
is **pregnant**, she has a baby or babies
developing in her body. गरोदर

prehistoric adj **Prehistoric** people and things
existed at a time before information was
written down. इतिहासपूर्वकालीन

prejudice (prejudices) n **Prejudice** is
an unreasonable dislike of someone or
something, or an unreasonable preference for
one group over another. पूर्वग्रह

prejudiced adj If someone is **prejudiced**
against a particular group, they have an
unreasonable dislike of them. पूर्वग्रह असलेली
व्यक्ती

premature adj Something that is **premature**
happens too early or earlier than expected.
मुदतपूर्व

premiere (**premieres**) n The **premiere** of a new play or film is the first public performance of it. शुभारंभाचा प्रयोग

premises npl The **premises** of a business or an institution are all the buildings and land that it occupies. वास्तू, जागा

premonition (**premonitions**) n If you have a **premonition**, you have a feeling that something is going to happen, often something unpleasant. मनाने दिलेली धोक्याची आगाऊ सूचना

preoccupied adj If you are **preoccupied**, you are thinking a lot about something or someone, and so you hardly notice other things. कामात व्यग्र असलेला

prepaid adj **Prepaid** items are paid for in advance, before the time when you would normally pay for them. आगोदरच पैसे दिलेला

preparation n **Preparation** is the process of getting something ready for use or for a particular purpose. तयारी

prepare (**prepares**, **preparing**, **prepared**) vt If you **prepare** something, you make it ready for something that is going to happen. तयार करणे

prepared adj If you are **prepared** to do something, you are willing to do it. तयार

prescribe (**prescribes**, **prescribing**, **prescribed**) vt If a doctor **prescribes** treatment, he or she states what medicine or treatment a patient should have. औषध लिहून देणे

prescription (**prescriptions**) n A **prescription** is a medicine which a doctor has told you to take, or the form on which the doctor has written the details of that medicine. औषधे लिहून दिलेली चिठ्ठी

presence n Someone's **presence** in a place is the fact that they are there. उपस्थिती

present (**presents**, **presenting**, **presented**) adj If someone is **present** somewhere, they are there. उपस्थित ▷ n A **present** is something that you give to someone for them to keep. भेटवस्तू ▷ n The **present** is the period of time that is taking place now.

वर्तमान ▷ vt If you **present** someone with a prize or with information, you give it to them. सादर करणे

presentation (**presentations**) n A **presentation** is the act of formally giving something such as a prize or document. प्रदान करण्याची क्रिया

presenter (**presenters**) n A radio or television **presenter** is a person who introduces the items in a particular programme. सादरकर्ता

presently adv If you say that something is **presently** happening, you mean that it is happening now. हल्ली

preservative (**preservatives**) n A **preservative** is a chemical that is added to substances to prevent them from decaying. पदार्थ टिकवून ठेवणारे रसायन

president (**presidents**) n The **president** of a country that has no king or queen is the person who is the head of state of that country. राष्ट्राध्यक्ष, अध्यक्ष

press (**presses**, **pressing**, **pressed**) n The **press** refers to newspapers and the journalists who write them. वर्तमानपत्र व त्यांचे बातमीदार ▷ vt If you **press** something somewhere, you push it firmly against something else. दाबणे

press conference (**press conferences**) n A **press conference** is a meeting held by a famous or important person in which they answer journalists' questions. पत्रकार परिषद

press-up (**press-ups**) n **Press-ups** are exercises that you do by lying with your face towards the floor and pushing with your hands to raise your body until your arms are straight. प्रेस अप्स् हा व्यायामाचा प्रकार

pressure (**pressures**, **pressuring**, **pressured**) n **Pressure** is the force produced when you press hard on something. दाब ▷ vt If you **pressure** someone to do something, you try forcefully to persuade them to do it. दबाव आणणे

prestige n If a person, a country, or an organization has **prestige**, they are admired and respected because they are important or successful. प्रतिष्ठा

prestigious *adj* A **prestigious** institution or activity is respected and admired by people. प्रतिष्ठित

presumably *adv* If you say that something is **presumably** true, you mean that you think it is true, although you are not certain. गृहीत धरून

presume (presumes, presuming, presumed) *vt* If you **presume** that something is true, you think that it is true, although you are not certain. गृहीत धरणे

pretend (pretends, pretending, pretended) *vt* If you **pretend** that something is true, you try to make people believe that it is true, although it is not. ढोंग करणे

pretext (pretexts) *n* A **pretext** is a reason which you pretend has caused you to do something. ढोंग

prettily *adv* If something is done or carried out **prettily** it is done or carried out in an attractive or pleasant manner. आकर्षकपणे

pretty (prettier, prettiest) *adj* If you describe someone, especially a girl, as **pretty**, you mean that they look nice and are attractive in a delicate way. आकर्षक ▷ *adv* You can use **pretty** before an adjective or adverb to mean 'quite' or 'rather'. अगदी

prevent (prevents, preventing, prevented) *vt* If you **prevent** something, you stop it happening or being done. आळा घालणे

prevention *n* **Prevention** is the act of stopping something happening or being done. आळा

previous *adj* A **previous** event or thing is one that occurred before the one you are talking about. अगोदरचा

previously *adv* **Previously** means at some time before the period that you are talking about. अगोदर

prey *n* A creature's **prey** are the creatures that it hunts and eats in order to live. भक्ष्य

price (prices) *n* The **price** of something is the amount of money that you must pay to buy it. किंमत

price list (price lists) *n* A **price list** is a list of the prices of goods or services. वस्तूंच्या किमतीची यादी

prick (pricks, pricking, pricked) *vt* If you **prick** something, you make small holes in it with a sharp object such as a pin. टाचणीने भोके पाडणे

pride *n* **Pride** is a feeling of satisfaction which you have because you or people close to you have done something good or possess something good. अभिमान

primarily *adv* You use **primarily** to say what is mainly true in a particular situation. मुख्यत:

primary *adj* You use **primary** to describe something that is extremely important or most important for someone or something. *(formal)* प्रमुख

primary school (primary schools) *n* A **primary school** is a school for children between the ages of 5 and 11. प्राथमिक शाळा

prime minister (prime ministers) *n* The leader of the government in some countries is called the **prime minister**. पंतप्रधान

primitive *adj* **Primitive** means belonging to a society in which people live in a very simple way, usually without industries or a writing system. प्राथमिक अवस्थेतील

primrose (primroses) *n* A **primrose** is a wild plant with pale yellow flowers. प्रिमरोझ नावाचे रानटी रोपटे

prince (princes) *n* A **prince** is a male member of a royal family, especially the son of the king or queen of a country. राजपुत्र

princess (princesses) *n* A **princess** is a female member of a royal family, usually the daughter of a king or queen or the wife of a prince. राजकन्या

principal (principals) *adj* **Principal** means first in order of importance. मुख्य ▷ *n* The **principal** of a school or college is the person in charge of it. प्राचार्य

principle (principles) *n* A **principle** is a belief that you have about the way you should behave. तत्त्व

print (prints, printing, printed) n Print is all the letters and numbers in a printed document. छपाई ▷ v If you **print** something, you use a machine to put words or pictures on paper. छापणे ▷ v If you **print** when you are writing, you do not join the letters together. अक्षरे एकमेकांना न जोडता दूरदूर लिहिणे

printer (printers) n A **printer** is a person or firm whose job is printing books, leaflets, or similar material. छापणारा ▷ n A **printer** is a machine that can be connected to a computer in order to make copies on paper of information held by the computer. प्रिंटर

printout (printouts) n A **printout** is a piece of paper on which information from a computer has been printed. प्रिंट आऊट

priority (priorities) n If something is a **priority**, it is the most important thing you have to achieve or deal with before everything else. प्राधान्यक्रमाची गोष्ट

prison (prisons) n A **prison** is a building where criminals are kept. तुरुंग

prisoner (prisoners) n A **prisoner** is a person who is kept in a prison as a punishment or because they have been captured by an enemy. कैदी

prison officer (prison officers) n A **prison officer** is someone who works as a guard at a prison. तुरुंग अधिकारी

privacy n **Privacy** is the fact of being alone so that you can do things without being seen or disturbed. एकांत

private adj **Private** industries and services are owned and controlled by an individual person or group, rather than by the state. खाजगी

private property n **Private property** is land or belongings owned by a person or group and kept for their exclusive use. खाजगी मालमत्ता

privatize (privatizes, privatizing, privatized) vt If an organization that is owned by the state **is privatized**, the government sells it to one or more private companies. खाजगीकरण करणे

privilege (privileges) n A **privilege** is a special right or advantage that only one person or group has. विशेष अधिकार

prize (prizes) n A **prize** is something valuable, such as money or a trophy, that is given to the winner of a game or competition. बक्षीस

prize-giving (prize-givings) n A **prize-giving** is a ceremony where prizes are awarded to people who have produced a very high standard of work. बक्षीस वितरण

prizewinner (prizewinners) n A **prizewinner** is a person, animal, or thing that wins a prize. बक्षीस विजेता

probability (probabilities) n The **probability** of something happening is how likely it is to happen, sometimes expressed as a fraction or a percentage. शक्यता

probable adj Something that is **probable** is likely to be true or likely to happen. शक्य

probably adv If you say that something is **probably** true, you think that it is likely to be true, although you are not sure. शक्यतो

problem (problems) n A **problem** is an unsatisfactory situation that causes difficulties for people. समस्या, अडचण

proceedings npl Legal **proceedings** are legal action taken against someone. (formal) कायदेशीर कारवाई

proceeds npl The **proceeds** of an event or activity are the money that has been obtained from it. कार्यक्रमाच्या आयोजनातून जमा झालेला पैसा

process (processes) n A **process** is a series of actions or events which have a particular result. प्रक्रिया

procession (processions) n A **procession** is a group of people who are walking, riding, or driving in a line as part of a public event. मिरवणूक

produce (produces, producing, produced) vt To **produce** something means to cause it to happen. कारणीभूत होणे

producer (producers) n A **producer** is a person whose job is to produce plays, films, programmes, or CDs. निर्माता

product (products) *n* A **product** is
something that is produced and sold in large
quantities. उत्पादन

production *n* **Production** is the process
of manufacturing or growing something
in large quantities, or the amount of goods
manufactured or grown. उत्पादन प्रक्रिया

productivity *n* **Productivity** is the rate at
which goods are produced. उत्पादनक्षमता

profession (professions) *n* A **profession** is a
type of job that requires advanced education
or training. पेशा, व्यवसाय

professional (professionals) *adj*
Professional means relating to a person's
work, especially work that requires special
training. व्यावसायिक *His professional career
started in a city law firm* ▷ *n* A **professional** is
a person who belongs to or engages in one of
the professions. व्यावसायिक

professionally *adv* If someone is
professionally trained or qualified it means
they have received special training that relates
to their job. व्यावसायिक दृष्ट्या

professor (professors) *n* A **professor** in a
British university is the most senior teacher in
a department. प्राध्यापक

profit (profits) *n* A **profit** is an amount of
money that you gain when you are paid more
for something than it cost you. नफा

profitable *adj* A **profitable** activity or
organization makes a profit. फायदेशीर

**program (programs, programming,
programmed)** *n* A **program** is a set of
instructions that a computer follows in order
to perform a particular task. कॉम्प्युटरचा प्रोग्रॅम
▷ *vt* When you **program** a computer, you
give it a set of instructions to make it able to
perform a particular task. कॉम्प्युटर प्रोग्रॅम करणे

programme (programmes) *n* A **programme**
of actions or events is a series of actions or
events that are planned to be done. कार्यक्रम

programmer (programmers) *n* A computer
programmer is a person whose job involves
writing programs for computers. प्रोग्रॅमर

programming *n* **Programming** is the
process of giving a set of instructions to
a computer to make it able to perform a
particular task. प्रोग्रॅमिंग

progress *n* **Progress** is the process of
gradually improving or getting nearer to
achieving or completing something. प्रगती

**prohibit (prohibits, prohibiting,
prohibited)** *vt* If someone **prohibits**
something, they forbid it or make it illegal.
(formal) मनाई करणे

prohibited *adj* If something is **prohibited**,
law or someone in authority forbids it or
makes it illegal. निषिद्ध

project (projects) *n* A **project** is a carefully
planned task that requires a lot of time and
effort. प्रकल्प

projector (projectors) *n* A **projector** is a
machine that uses light to make films or slides
appear on a screen or wall. प्रोजेक्टर

promenade (promenades) *n* In a seaside
town, the **promenade** is the road by the
sea where people go for a walk. समुद्रकिनारी
चालण्यासाठी बनवलेला मार्ग

promise (promises, promising, promised)
n A **promise** is a statement which you
make to a person in which you say that you
will definitely do something or give them
something. वचन ▷ *vt* If you **promise** that you
will do something, you say to someone that
you will definitely do it. वचन देणे

promising *adj* Someone or something that
is **promising** seems likely to be very good or
successful. प्रतिथयश

promote (promotes, promoting, promoted)
vt If people **promote** something, they help
to make it happen, increase, or become more
popular. चालना/बढती देणे

promotion (promotions) *n* A **promotion**
is a means of making something happen,
increase or become more popular. प्रसिद्धी
देणारा कार्यक्रम

prompt *adj* A **prompt** action is done without
any delay. विनाविलंब

promptly adv If you do something **promptly**, you do it immediately. तात्काळ

pronoun (pronouns) n A **pronoun** is a word which is used instead of a noun group to refer to someone or something. 'He', 'she', 'them', and 'something' are pronouns. सर्वनाम

pronounce (pronounces, pronouncing, pronounced) vt To **pronounce** a word means to say it. उच्चार करणे

pronunciation (pronunciations) n The **pronunciation** of words is the way they are pronounced. उच्चार

proof (proofs) n **Proof** is a fact or a piece of evidence which shows that something is true or exists. पुरावा ▷ n In publishing, the **proofs** of a book, magazine, or article are a first copy of it that is printed so that mistakes can be corrected before more copies are printed and published. कच्चे मुद्रण

propaganda n **Propaganda** is information, often inaccurate information, which an organization publishes or broadcasts in order to influence people. विरोधी प्रचार

proper adj You use **proper** to describe things that you consider to be real or satisfactory. योग्य

properly adv If something is done **properly**, it is done in a correct and satisfactory way. योग्यपणे

property n Someone's **property** consists of all the things that belong to them, or something that belongs to them. *(formal)* मालमता

proportion (proportions) n A **proportion** of an amount or group is a part of it. *(formal)* प्रमाण

proportional adj If one amount is **proportional** to another, the two amounts increase and decrease at the same rate so there is always the same relationship between them. *(formal)* प्रमाणात

proposal (proposals) n A **proposal** is a suggestion or plan, often a formal or written one. प्रस्ताव

propose (proposes, proposing, proposed) vt If you **propose** a plan or idea, you suggest it. प्रस्तावित

prosecute (prosecutes, prosecuting, prosecuted) v If the authorities **prosecute** someone, they charge them with a crime and put them on trial. आरोप ठेवणे

prospect (prospects) n A **prospect** is a possibility or a possible event. शक्यता

prospectus (prospectuses) n A **prospectus** is a document produced by a college, school, or company which gives details about it. शाळा, महाविद्यालयाचे माहितीपत्रक

prosperity n **Prosperity** is a condition in which a person or community is being financially successful. भरभराट

protect (protects, protecting, protected) vt To **protect** someone or something means to prevent them from being harmed or damaged. संरक्षण करणे

protection n If something gives **protection** against something unpleasant, it prevents people or things from being harmed or damaged by it. संरक्षण

protein (proteins) n **Protein** is a substance which the body needs and which is found in meat, eggs, and milk. प्रथिने

protest (protests, protesting, protested) n A **protest** is the act of saying or showing publicly that you do not approve of something. निषेध ▷ v To **protest** means to say or show publicly that you do not agree with something. निषेध करणे

proud (prouder, proudest) adj If you feel **proud**, you feel pleasure and satisfaction at something that you own, have done, or are connected with. अभिमान

prove (proves, proving, proved, proven) v If something **proves** to be true, it becomes clear after a period of time that it is true. सिद्ध होणे

proverb (proverbs) n A **proverb** is a short sentence that people often quote, which gives advice or tells you something about life. For example, 'A bird in the hand is worth two in the bush.' म्हण

provide (**provides, providing, provided**) *vt* If you **provide** something that someone needs or wants, you give it to them or make it available to them. पुरविणे

provided *conj* If something will happen **provided** that another thing happens, the first thing will happen only if the second thing also happens. जर असे घडले तर *He can go running, provided that he wears the right kind of shoes.*

provide for (**provides for, providing for, provided for**) *v* If you **provide for** someone, you support them financially and make sure that they have the things that they need. तरतूद करणे *She won't let him provide for her.*

provisional *adj* You use **provisional** to describe something that has been arranged or appointed for the present, but may be changed soon. तात्पुरता

proximity *n* **Proximity** to a place or person is the fact of being near to them. *(formal)* जवळीक

prune (**prunes**) *n* A **prune** is a dried plum. मनुका, सुके प्लम फळ

pry (**pries, prying, pried**) *vi* If you say that someone is **prying**, you disapprove of them because they are trying to find out about someone else's private affairs. खाजगी जीवनात चोरून लुडबूड करणे

pseudonym (**pseudonyms**) *n* A **pseudonym** is a name which someone, usually a writer, uses instead of his or her real name. टोपणनाव

psychiatric *adj* **Psychiatric** means relating to psychiatrists. मानसिक

psychiatrist (**psychiatrists**) *n* A **psychiatrist** is a doctor who treats people suffering from mental illness. मानसोपचारतज्ज्ञ

psychological *adj* **Psychological** means concerned with a person's mind and thoughts. मानसिक

psychologist (**psychologists**) *n* A **psychologist** is a person who studies the human mind and tries to explain why people behave in the way that they do. मानसशास्त्रज्ञ

psychology *n* **Psychology** is the scientific study of the human mind and the reasons for people's behaviour. मानसशास्त्र

psychotherapy *n* **Psychotherapy** is the use of psychological methods to treat people who are mentally ill. मानसोपचार

PTO *abbr* **PTO** is a written abbreviation for 'please turn over'. You write it at the bottom of a page to indicate that there is more writing on the other side. कृपया पान उलटा

public *n* **Public** means relating to all the people in a country or community. सार्वजनिक ▷ *n* You can refer to people in general as **the public**. जनता

publication (**publications**) *n* The **publication** of a book or magazine is the act of printing it and making it available. प्रकाशन

public holiday (**public holidays**) *n* A **public holiday** is a holiday for the whole country. सार्वजनिक सुट्टी

publicity *n* **Publicity** is advertising, information, or actions intended to attract the public's attention to someone or something. प्रसिद्धी

public opinion *n* **Public opinion** is the opinion or attitude of the public regarding a particular matter. जनतेचे मत

public relations *npl* **Public relations** are the state of the relationship between an organization and the public. जन संपर्क

public school (**public schools**) *n* In Britain, a **public school** is a private school that provides secondary education which parents have to pay for. ब्रिटनमधील खाजगी शाळा

public transport *n* **Public transport** is a system of buses, trains, etc, running on fixed routes, on which the public may travel. सार्वजनिक वाहतूक व्यवस्था

publish (**publishes, publishing, published**) *vt* When a company **publishes** a book or magazine, it prints copies of it, which are sent to shops and sold. प्रकाशित करणे

publisher (publishers) n A **publisher** is a person or company that publishes books, newspapers, or magazines. प्रकाशक

pudding (puddings) n A **pudding** is a cooked sweet food made with flour, fat, and eggs, and usually served hot. पुडिंग

puddle (puddles) n A **puddle** is a small shallow pool of rain or other liquid on the ground. डबके

Puerto Rico n **Puerto Rico** is an island in the Caribbean. पोर्टो रिको

puff pastry n **Puff pastry** is a type of pastry which is very light and consists of a lot of thin layers. पफ पेस्ट्री

pull (pulls, pulling, pulled) v When you **pull** something, you hold it and move it towards you. खेचणे

pull down (pulls down, pulling down, pulled down) v To **pull down** a building or statue means to deliberately destroy it. पाडून टाकणे *They pulled the offices down, leaving a large open space.*

pull out (pulls out, pulling out, pulled out) v When a vehicle or driver **pulls out**, the vehicle moves out into the road or nearer the centre of the road. रस्त्यावर मध्यभागी येणे *She pulled out into the street.*

pullover (pullovers) n A **pullover** is a woollen piece of clothing that covers the upper part of your body and your arms. पुलओव्हर (लोकरीचा तोकडा अंगरखा)

pull up (pulls up, pulling up, pulled up) v When a vehicle or driver **pulls up**, the vehicle slows down and stops. वेग कमी करून थांबणे *The car pulled up and the driver jumped out.*

pulse (pulses) n Your **pulse** is the regular beating of blood through your body, which you can feel, for example, at your wrist or neck. नाडी

pulses npl Some large dried seeds which can be cooked and eaten are called **pulses**, for example the seeds of peas, beans, and lentils. दिदल धान्ये

pump (pumps, pumping, pumped) n A **pump** is a machine that is used to force a liquid or gas to flow in strong regular movements in a particular direction. पंप ▷ vt To **pump** a liquid or gas in a certain direction means to force it to flow in that direction, using a pump. पंपाचा वापर करून पुढे ढकलणे

pumpkin (pumpkins) n A **pumpkin** is a large, round, orange-coloured vegetable with a thick skin. कोहळा, भोपळा

pump up (pumps up, pumping up, pumped up) v If you **pump up** something such as a tyre, you fill it with air, using a pump. हवा भरणे *Pump all the tyres up.*

punch (punches, punching, punched) n A **punch** is a blow with the fist. गुद्दा ▷ n **Punch** is a drink usually made from wine or spirits mixed with sugar, fruit, and spices. पंच नावाचे पेय ▷ vt If you **punch** someone or something, you hit them hard with your fist. गुद्दे मारणे

punctual adj Someone who is **punctual** arrives somewhere or does something at the right time and is not late. वक्तशीर

punctuation n **Punctuation** is the system of signs such as full stops, commas, and question marks that you use in writing to divide words into sentences and clauses. विरामचिह्नांचा वापर

puncture (punctures) n A **puncture** is a small hole in a car or bicycle tyre that has been made by a sharp object. टायरमध्ये झालेले छिद्र

punish (punishes, punishing, punished) vt
To **punish** someone means to make them
suffer in some way because they have done
something wrong. शिक्षा करणे

punishment n **Punishment** is the act of
punishing someone or being punished. शिक्षा

punk n **Punk** or **punk rock** is rock music that
is played in a fast, loud, and aggressive way.
Punk rock was particularly popular in the late
1970s. पंक रॉक संगीत

pupil (pupils) n The **pupils** of a school are the
children who go to it. विद्यार्थी ▷ n The **pupils**
of your eyes are the small, round, black holes
in the centre of them. डोळ्याची बाहुली

puppet (puppets) n A **puppet** is a doll that you
can move, either by pulling strings which are
attached to it, or by putting your hand inside its
body and moving your fingers. कळसुत्री बाहुली

puppy (puppies) n A **puppy** is a young dog.
कुत्र्याचे पिल्लू

**purchase (purchases, purchasing,
purchased)** vt When you **purchase**
something, you buy it. (formal) खरेदी करणे

pure (purer, purest) adj **Pure** means not
mixed with anything else. शुद्ध

purple adj Something that is **purple** is
reddish-blue in colour. जांभळा रंग

purpose (purposes) n The **purpose** of
something is the reason for which it is made
or done. हेतू

purr (purrs, purring, purred) vi When a cat
purrs, it makes a low vibrating sound with its
throat. मांजराच्या आनंदाने गुरगुरणे

purse (purses) n A **purse** is a very small bag
that people, especially women, keep their
money in. पर्स

pursue (pursues, pursuing, pursued) vt
If you **pursue** a particular aim or result, you
make efforts to achieve it or to progress in it.
(formal) पुढे चालू ठेवणे, सुरु ठेवणे

pursuit n Your **pursuit** of something that you
want consists of your attempts at achieving it.
प्राप्त करण्याचे प्रयत्न / पाठलाग

pus n **Pus** is a thick yellowish liquid that forms
in wounds when they are infected. पू

push (pushes, pushing, pushed) v When you
push something, you press it in order to move
it away from you. ढकलणे

pushchair (pushchairs) n A **pushchair** is a
small chair on wheels, in which a small child
can sit and be wheeled around. ढकलायची खुर्ची

push-up (push-ups) n **Push-ups** are exercises
to strengthen your arms and chest muscles.
They are done by lying with your face towards
the floor and pushing with your hands to raise
your body until your arms are straight. पुश-अप
व्यायाम प्रकार

put (puts, putting) vt When you **put**
something somewhere, you move it there.
ठेवणे

put aside (puts aside, putting aside) v If
you **put** something **aside**, you keep it to be
dealt with or used at a later time. भविष्यात
वापरण्यासाठी बाजूला काढून ठेवणे I put money
aside each month because I'm saving for a
holiday.

put away (puts away, putting away) v If you
put something **away**, you put it into the place
where it is normally kept when it is not being
used. बाजूला ठेवून देणे Put your maths books
away, it's time for your history lesson.

put back (puts back, putting back) v To
put something **back** means to delay it or
postpone it. पुढे ढकलणे The trip has been put
back to April.

put forward (puts forward, putting
forward) v If you **put forward** a plan,
proposal, or name, you suggest that it should
be considered for a particular purpose or job.
विचारार्थ पुढे मांडणे I asked my boss to put my
name forward for the job in head office.

put in (puts in, putting in) v If you **put in** an
amount of time or effort doing something,
you spend that time or effort doing it. (प्रयत्न
इ.) खर्ची घालणे We put in three hours' work
every evening.

put off (puts off, putting off) v If you
put something **off**, you delay doing it. पुढे
ढकलणे She put off telling him until the last
moment.

put up (puts up, putting up) v If people **put
up** a wall, building, tent, or other structure,
they construct it. उभारणे They put up their tents
and settled down for the night.

puzzle (puzzles) n A **puzzle** is a question,
game, or toy which you have to think about
carefully in order to answer it correctly or put
it together properly. कोडे

puzzled adj Someone who is **puzzled** is
confused because they do not understand
something. गोंधळलेला

puzzling adj If something is **puzzling**, it is
confusing or difficult to understand. गोंधळात
टाकणारे

pyjamas npl A pair of **pyjamas** consists of
loose trousers and a loose jacket that are worn
in bed. पायजमा

pylon (pylons) n Pylons are very tall metal
structures which hold electric cables high above
the ground so that electricity can be transmitted
over long distances. विजेच्या तारांचा उंच मोठा खांब

pyramid (pyramids) n A **pyramid** is a three-
dimensional shape with a flat base and flat
triangular sides which slope upwards to a
point. पिरॅमिड

q

Qatar n Qatar is a state in east Arabia, in the
Persian Gulf. कतार

quail (quails, quail) n A **quail** is a small bird
which is often shot and eaten. क्वेल नावाचा
लहान पक्षी

quaint (quainter, quaintest) adj Something
that is **quaint** is attractive because it is
unusual and rather old-fashioned. जुने
चमत्कारिक पण आकर्षक

qualification (qualifications) n Your
qualifications are the examinations that you
have passed. अर्हता, पात्रता

qualified adj If you give someone or something
qualified support or approval, you give support
or approval that is not total and suggests that
you have some doubts. सशर्त, मर्यादित

qualify (qualifies, qualifying, qualified)
v When someone **qualifies**, they pass the examinations that they need to pass in order to work in a particular profession. पात्र ठरणे

quality (qualities) *n* The **quality** of something is how good or bad it is. दर्जा

quantify (quantifies, quantifying, quantified)
v If you try to **quantify** something, you try to calculate how much of it there is. मोजणी करणे

quantity (quantities) *n* A **quantity** is an amount that you can measure or count. संख्या, प्रमाण

quarantine *n* If a person or animal is in **quarantine**, they are kept separate from other people or animals in case they have an infectious disease. साथीच्या काळात संसर्ग होऊ नये म्हणून वेगळे ठेवलेले

quarrel (quarrels, quarrelling, quarrelled) *n* A **quarrel** is an angry argument between two or more friends or family members. भांडण ▷ *vi* When two or more people **quarrel**, they have an angry argument. भांडणे

quarry (quarries) *n* A **quarry** is an area that is dug out from a piece of land or mountainside in order to extract stone, slate, or minerals. दगडाची खाण

quarter (quarters) *n* A **quarter** is one of four equal parts of something. चौथा हिस्सा

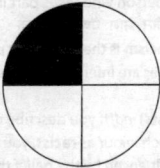

quarter final (quarter finals) *n* A **quarter final** is one of the four matches in a competition which decides which four players or teams will compete in the semifinal. उपांत्य फेरीपूर्वीच्या चार सामन्यांपैकीचा एक सामना

quartet (quartets) *n* A **quartet** is a group of four people who play musical instruments or sing together. चार वादक किंवा गायकांचा समूह

quay (quays) *n* A **quay** is a long platform beside the sea or a river where boats can be tied. समुद्रातील धक्का

queen (queens) *n* A **queen** is a woman who rules a country as its head of state. राणी

query (queries, querying, queried) *n* A **query** is a question about a particular point. शंका ▷ *vt* If you **query** something, you check it by asking about it because you are not sure if it is correct. शंका उपस्थित करणे

question (questions, questioning, questioned) *n* A **question** is something which you say or write in order to ask about a particular matter. प्रश्न ▷ *vt* If you **question** someone, you ask them questions about something. प्रश्न विचारणे

question mark (question marks) *n* A **question mark** is the punctuation mark (?) which is used in writing at the end of a question. प्रश्नचिन्ह

questionnaire (questionnaires) *n* A **questionnaire** is a written list of questions which are answered by a number of people in order to provide information for a report or survey. प्रश्नावली

queue (queues, queuing, queued) *n* A **queue** is a line of people or vehicles that are waiting for something. रांग ▷ *vi* When people **queue**, they stand in a line waiting for something. रांगेत उभे राहणे

quick (quicker, quickest) *adj* Someone or something that is **quick** moves or does things with great speed. जलद

quickly *adv* If someone or something moves or does something **quickly** they move or do something with great speed. त्वरित

quiet (quieter, quietest) *adj* Something or someone that is **quiet** makes only a small amount of noise. शांत

quietly *adv* If someone or something does something **quietly** they do it with only a small amount of noise. शांतपणे

quilt (quilts) *n* A **quilt** is a bed-cover filled with warm soft material, which is often decorated with lines of stitching. गोधडी

quit (quits, quitting, quit) v If you **quit** your job, you choose to leave it. *(informal)* सोडून देणे

quite adv Quite means a bit but not a lot. अगदी

quiz (quizzes) n A **quiz** is a game or competition in which someone tests your knowledge by asking you questions. प्रश्नमंजुषा

quota (quotas) n A **quota** is the limited number or quantity which is officially allowed. ठरलेले अधिकृत प्रमाण किंवा संख्या

quotation (quotations) n A **quotation** is a sentence or phrase taken from a book, poem, or play. उद्धरण

quotation marks npl Quotation marks are punctuation marks used in writing to show where speech or a quotation begins and ends. They are usually written or printed as (' ') and (" "). अवतरण चिन्ह

quote (quotes, quoting, quoted) n A **quote** from a book, poem, or play is a sentence or phrase from it. अवतरण ▷ v If you **quote** something, you repeat what someone has written or said. If you **quote** someone as saying something, you repeat what they have written or said. उदाहरण म्हणून उल्लेख करणे

r

rabbit (rabbits) n A **rabbit** is a small furry animal with long ears which is often kept as a pet. ससा

rabies n Rabies is a serious infectious disease which humans can get from the bite of an animal such as a dog which has the disease. कुत्रा चावल्याने होणारा रेबिज नावाचा आजार

race (races, racing, raced) n A **race** is a competition to see who is the fastest, for example in running or driving. शर्यत ▷ n A **race** is one of the major groups which human beings can be divided into according to their physical features, such as their skin colour. वंश ▷ v If you **race**, you take part in a race. शर्यतीत भाग घेणे

racecourse (racecourses) n A **racecourse** is a track on which horses race. घोड्यांच्या शर्यतीचे मैदान

racehorse (racehorses) n A **racehorse** is a horse that is trained to run in races. शर्यतीचा घोडा

racer (racers) n A **racer** is a person or animal that takes part in races. शर्यतीत भाग घेणारा

racetrack (racetracks) n A **racetrack** is a piece of ground that is used for races between runners, horses, dogs, cars, or motorcycles. शर्यतीची धावपट्टी/मैदान

racial adj Racial describes things relating to people's race. वांशिक/जातीय

racing car (racing cars) n A **racing car** is a car that has been specially designed for motor racing. शर्यतीची कार

racing driver (racing drivers) n A **racing driver** is a person who takes part in motor racing. शर्यतीत भाग घेणारा चालक

racism n Racism is the belief that people of some races are inferior to others. वंशद्वेष/जातीयवाद

racist (racists) adj If you describe people, things, or behaviour as **racist**, you mean that they are influenced by the belief that some people are inferior because they belong to a particular race. वंशवादी/जातीयवादी ▷ n A **racist**, or a person with **racist** views, believes that people of some races are inferior to others. वंशवादी/जातीयवादी

rack (racks) n A **rack** is a piece of equipment used for holding things or for hanging things on. खुंटी/खुंटाळे

racket (**rackets**) *n* A **racket** is a loud unpleasant noise. गोंगाट/गलका ▷ *n* A **racket** is an oval-shaped bat with strings across it. Rackets are used in tennis, squash, and badminton. रॅकेट

racoon (**racoons**) *n* A **racoon** is a small animal that has dark-coloured fur with white stripes on its face and on its long tail. Racoons live in forests in North and Central America and the West Indies. रॅकून नावाचा प्राणी

radar *n* **Radar** is a way of discovering the position or speed of objects such as aircraft or ships by using radio signals. रडार, दूरसंदेश यंत्रणा

radiation *n* **Radiation** is very small particles of a radioactive substance. Large amounts of radiation can cause illness and death. किरणोत्सर्ग

radiator (**radiators**) *n* A **radiator** is a hollow metal device which is connected to a central heating system and used to heat a room. रेडिएटर

radio *n* **Radio** is the broadcasting of programmes for the public to listen to. रेडिओ, आकाशवाणी

radioactive *adj* Something that is **radioactive** contains a substance that produces energy in the form of powerful rays which are harmful in large doses. किरणोत्सर्गी

radio-controlled *adj* A **radio-controlled** device works by receiving radio signals which operate it. ध्वनीलहरींनी नियंत्रित केलेले

radio station (**radio stations**) *n* A **radio station** is an installation consisting of one or more transmitters or receivers, etc, used for radiocommunications. आकाशवाणी केंद्र

radish (**radishes**) *n* **Radishes** are small red or white vegetables that are the roots of a plant. They are eaten raw in salads. मुळा

raffle (**raffles**) *n* A **raffle** is a competition in which you buy numbered tickets. Afterwards some numbers are chosen and if your ticket has one of these numbers on it, you win a prize. सोडत

raft (**rafts**) *n* A **raft** is a floating platform made from large pieces of wood tied together. तराफा

rag (**rags**) *n* A **rag** is a piece of old cloth which you can use to clean or wipe things. चिंधी

rage (**rages**) *n* **Rage** is strong, uncontrollable anger. क्रोध

raid (**raids, raiding, raided**) *n* A **raid** is a sudden surprise attack. धाड ▷ *vt* When soldiers **raid** a place, they make a sudden armed attack against it, with the aim of causing damage rather than occupying any of the enemy's land. धाड टाकणे

rail (**rails**) *n* A **rail** is a horizontal bar which is fixed to something and used as a fence or a support, or to hang things on. कठड

railcard (**railcards**) *n* A **railcard** is an identity card that allows people to buy train tickets cheaply. रेलकार्ड

railings *npl* A fence made from metal bars is called a **railing** or **railings**. धातूच्या सळ्यांचे कुंपण

railway (**railways**) *n* A **railway** is a route between two places along which trains travel on steel rails. लोहमार्ग, रेल्वेचे रूळ

railway station (**railway stations**) *n* A **railway station** is a building by a railway line where trains stop so that people can get on or off. रेल्वे स्थानक

rain (**rains, raining, rained**) *n* **Rain** is water that falls from the clouds in small drops. पाऊस ▷ *vi* When rain falls, you can say that it **is raining**. पाऊस पडणे

rainbow (**rainbows**) *n* A **rainbow** is the arch of different colours that you sometimes see in the sky when it is raining. इंद्रधनुष्य

raincoat (**raincoats**) *n* A **raincoat** is a waterproof coat. रेनकोट

rainforest (**rainforests**) *n* A **rainforest** is a thick forest of tall trees found in tropical areas where there is a lot of rain. पावसाळी प्रदेशातले घनदाट जंगल, पर्जन्यवन

rainy (**rainier, rainiest**) *adj* If it is **rainy**, it is raining a lot. पावसाळी

r

raise (raises, raising, raised) vt If you **raise** something, you move it to a higher position. उचलणे

raisin (raisins) n **Raisins** are dried grapes. बेदाणा

rake (rakes) n A **rake** is a garden tool consisting of a row of metal teeth attached to a long handle. दांताळे

rally (rallies) n A **rally** is a large public meeting held in support of something such as a political party. मेळावा, मोर्चा

ram (rams, ramming, rammed) n A **ram** is an adult male sheep. मेंढा ▷ vt If one vehicle **rams** another, it crashes into it with a lot of force. आदळणे

Ramadan n **Ramadan** is the ninth month of the Muslim year, when Muslims do not eat between the rising and setting of the sun. During Ramadan, Muslims celebrate the fact that it was in this month that God first revealed the words of the Quran to Mohammed. रमदान

rambler (ramblers) n A **rambler** is a person whose hobby is going on long walks in the countryside, often as part of an organized group. छंद म्हणून भटकणारा, भटक्या

ramp (ramps) n A **ramp** is a sloping surface between two places that are at different levels. दोन असमान पातळीवर असलेल्या जागांमधील उतार

random adj A **random** sample or method is one in which all the people or things involved have an equal chance of being chosen. सहगजत्या निवडलेला, यादृच्छिक

range (ranges, ranging, ranged) n The **range** of something is the maximum area within which it can reach things or detect things. मर्यादा, कक्षा ▷ n A **range** of mountains or hills is a line of them. पर्वतराजी ▷ vi If things **range between** two points or range from one point **to** another, they vary within these points on a scale of measurement or quality. विशिष्ट मर्यादेत बदलणे

rank (ranks, ranking, ranked) n Someone's **rank** is their position in an organization, or in society. दर्जा ▷ n A **rank** of people or things is a row of them. रांग ▷ v When someone or something **is ranked** a particular position, they are at that position on a scale. एका विशिष्ट क्रमांकावर किंवा स्थानावर असणे

ransom (ransoms) n A **ransom** is money that is demanded as payment for the return of someone who has been kidnapped. खंडणी

rape (rapes, raping, raped) n **Rape** is the crime of forcing someone to have sex. बलात्कार ▷ n **Rape** is a plant with yellow flowers which is grown as a crop. Its seeds are crushed to make cooking oil. एक प्रकारचे तेलबियांचे रोप ▷ vt If someone **is raped**, they are forced to have sex, usually by violence or threats of violence. बलात्कार करणे

rapids npl **Rapids** are a section of a river where the water moves very fast. पाण्याचा वेगवान प्रवाह

rapist (rapists) n A **rapist** is a man who has raped someone. बलात्कारी

rare (rarer, rarest) adj If something is **rare**, it is not common, and is therefore interesting, valuable, or unusual. दुर्मीळ ▷ adj Meat that is **rare** is cooked very lightly so that the inside is still red. कमी शिजवलेले

rarely adv **Rarely** means not very often. क्वचित

rash (rashes) n A **rash** is an area of red spots on your skin which appear when you are ill or have an allergy. अंगावरील पुरळ

raspberry (raspberries) n A **raspberry** is a small, soft, red fruit that grows on bushes. रास्पबेरी

rat (rats) n A **rat** is an animal which has a long tail and looks like a large mouse. घूस

rate (rates, rating, rated) n The **rate** at which something happens is the speed or frequency with which it happens. प्रमाण/दर ▷ vt If you **rate** someone or something as good or bad, you consider them to be good or bad. दर्जा देणे

rate of exchange (rates of exchange) n The **rate of exchange** of a country's unit of currency is the amount of another currency that you get in exchange for it. विनिमयाचा दर

rather adv You use **rather** to mean 'a little bit'. काहीसे, खरे म्हणजे

ratio (ratios) n The **ratio** of something is the relationship between two things expressed in numbers or amounts, to show how much greater one is than the other. गुणोत्तर प्रमाण

rational adj **Rational** decisions and thoughts are based on sensible judgment rather than on emotion. सुसंगत, तर्कनिष्ठ

rattle (rattles) n A **rattle** is a rapid succession of short sharp sounds. खडखड असा आवाज

rattlesnake (rattlesnakes) n A **rattlesnake** is a poisonous American snake which can make a rattling noise with its tail. शेपटीने खडखड आवाज करणारा अमेरिकेतील विषारी साप

rave (raves, raving, raved) n A **rave** is a big event at which young people dance to electronic music in a large building or in the open air. मोठ्या वा मोकळ्या जागी विद्युत संगीतावर बेधुंद नाचाचा मोठा कार्यक्रम ▷ v If someone **raves**, they talk in an excited and uncontrolled way. उत्तेजित होऊन वा पिसाटासारखे बोलणे

raven (ravens) n A **raven** is a large bird with shiny black feathers and a deep harsh call. डोंब कावळा

ravenous adj If you are **ravenous**, you are extremely hungry. भुकेलेली व्यक्ती

ravine (ravines) n A **ravine** is a very deep, narrow valley with steep sides. अरुंद खोल दरी

raw (rawer, rawest) adj A **raw** substance is in its natural state before being processed. कच्चा माल, नैसर्गिक अवस्थेतील

razor (razors) n A **razor** is a tool that people use for shaving. वस्त्रा, रेझर

razor blade (razor blades) n A **razor blade** is a small flat piece of metal with a very sharp edge which is put into a razor and used for shaving. रेझरचे पाते

reach (reaches, reaching, reached) vt When you **reach** a place, you arrive there. पोहोचणे ▷ vi If you **reach** somewhere, you move your arm and hand to take or touch something. एखादी गोष्ट घेण्यासाठी हात पुढे करणे

react (reacts, reacting, reacted) vi When you **react** to something that has happened to you, you behave in a particular way because of it. प्रतिक्रिया देणे/होणे

reaction (reactions) n Your **reaction** to something that has happened or something that you have experienced is what you feel, say, or do because of it. प्रतिक्रिया

reactor (reactors) n A **reactor** is a device which produces nuclear energy. अणुभट्टी

read (reads, reading) v When you **read** something such as a book or article, you look at and understand the words that are written there. वाचणे

reader (readers) n The **readers** of a book, newspaper, or magazine are the people who read it. वाचक

readily adv If you do something **readily**, you do it willingly. स्वेच्छेने

reading n **Reading** is the activity of reading books. वाचन

read out (reads out, reading out) v If you **read** something **out**, you say the words aloud, especially in a loud, clear voice. मोठ्याने वाचन करणे *We read plays out in class.*

ready (readier, readiest) adj If someone or something is **ready**, they have reached the required stage for something or they are properly prepared for action or use. तयार, सज्ज

ready-cooked adj If food that you buy is **ready-cooked**, you only have to heat it before eating it because it has already been cooked. अगोदरच शिजवलेले

real adj Something that is **real** is true and is not imagined. खरा ▷ adj If something is **real**, it is not a copy. खरा

realistic adj If you are **realistic** about a situation, you recognize and accept its true nature and try to deal with it. वास्तववादी

reality n You use **reality** to refer to real things or the real nature of things rather than imagined or invented ideas. वास्तवात

reality TV n **Reality TV** is a type of television which aims to show how ordinary people behave in everyday life, or in situations, often created by the programme makers, which are intended to be like everyday life. दूरदर्शनवर दाखवलेले वास्तव जीवनदर्शन

realize (realizes, realizing, realized) v If you **realize** that something is true, you become aware of that fact or understand it. समजणे, उमजणे

really adv You say **really** to show how much you mean something. *(spoken)* खरोखर ▷ adv You say **really** to show that what you are saying is true. खरोखर

rear n **Rear** means situated in the back part of something or refers to the back part of something. पाठीमागील ▷ n The **rear** of something is the back part of it. पिछाड, मागची बाजू

rear-view mirror (rear-view mirrors) n Inside a car, the **rear-view mirror** is the mirror that enables you to see the traffic behind when you are driving. मागून येणारी वाहने दिसावीत म्हणून वाहनाला लावलेला आरसा

reason (reasons) n The **reason** for something is a fact or situation which explains why it happens. कारण

reasonable adj If you think that someone is fair and sensible you can say they are **reasonable**. रास्त, योग्य

reasonably adv If someone behaves or acts **reasonably** they behave or act fairly and sensibly. रास्तपणे, योग्यपणे

reassure (reassures, reassuring, reassured) vt If you **reassure** someone, you say or do things to make them stop worrying about something. आश्वासित करणे, दिलासा देणे

reassuring adj If you find someone's words or actions **reassuring**, they make you feel less worried. आश्वासित करणारे, दिलासा देणारे

rebate (rebates) n A **rebate** is an amount of money which is paid to you when you have paid more tax, rent, or rates than you needed to. सूट

rebellious adj A **rebellious** person behaves in an unacceptable way and does not do what they are told. बंडखोर

rebuild (rebuilds, rebuilding, rebuilt) vt When people **rebuild** something such as a building, they build it again after it has been damaged or destroyed. पुनर्बांधणी करणे

receipt (receipts) n A **receipt** is a piece of paper that you get from someone as confirmation that they have received money or goods from you. पावती

receive (receives, receiving, received) vt When you **receive** something, you get it after someone gives it to you or sends it to you. मिळणे

receiver (receivers) n A telephone **receiver** is the part that you hold near to your ear and speak into. रिसिव्हर ▷ n A **receiver** is someone who is officially appointed to manage the affairs of a business, usually when it is facing financial failure. दिवाळे निघालेल्या

कंपनीचे कामकाज पाहण्यासाठी नियुक्त केलेला आधिकारी

recent adj A **recent** event or period of time happened only a short while ago. अलीकडचा

recently adv If you have done something **recently** or if something happened **recently**, it happened only a short time ago. अलीकडे

reception (receptions) n In a hotel, office, or hospital, the **reception** is the place where people are received and their reservations, appointments, and inquiries are dealt with. स्वागत कक्ष

receptionist (receptionists) n In a hotel, office, or hospital, the **receptionist** is the person whose job is to answer the telephone, arrange reservations, or appointments, and deal with people when they first arrive. स्वागतकार

recession (recessions) n A **recession** is a period when the economy of a country is not very successful. मंदी

recharge (recharges, recharging, recharged) vt If you **recharge** a battery, you put an electrical charge back into the battery by connecting it to a machine that draws power from another source of electricity. पुनर्भारित करणे

recipe (recipes) n A **recipe** is a list of ingredients and a set of instructions that tell you how to cook something. पाककृतिया

recipient (recipients) n The **recipient** of something is the person who receives it. (formal) प्राप्त करणारी व्यक्ती

reckon (reckons, reckoning, reckoned) vt If you **reckon** that something is true, you think that it is true. (informal) वाटणे

reclining adj A **reclining** seat has a back that you can lower so that it is more comfortable to sit in. मागे रेलणारा

recognizable adj Something that is **recognizable** is easy to recognize or identify. ओळखता येणारा

recognize (recognizes, recognizing, recognized) vt If you **recognize** someone or

something, you know who or what they are, because you have seen or heard them before or because they have been described to you. ओळखणे

recommend (recommends, recommending, recommended) vt If someone **recommends** something or someone to you, they suggest that you would find them good or useful. शिफारस करणे

recommendation (recommendations) n The **recommendations** of a person or a committee are their suggestions or advice on what is the best thing to do. शिफारस

reconsider (reconsiders, reconsidering, reconsidered) v If you **reconsider** a decision or method, you think about it and try to decide whether it should be changed. पुनर्विचार करणे

record (records, recording, recorded) n If you keep a **record** of something, you keep a written account or photographs of it so that it can be looked at later. नोंद ▷ vt If you **record** a piece of information or an event, you write it down or photograph it so that in the future people can look at it. नोंद करणे ▷ n A **record** is the best result ever. विक्रम ▷ vt If you **record** something like a TV programme, you make a copy of it so that you can watch it later. रेकॉर्ड करणे

recorded delivery n If you send a letter or parcel **recorded delivery**, you send it using a Post Office service which gives you an official record of the fact that it has been posted and delivered. टपाल कार्यालयात नोंद केलेला बटवडा

recorder (recorders) n A **recorder** is a hollow musical instrument that you play by blowing down one end and covering a series of holes with your fingers. रेकॉर्डर ▷ n A **recorder** is a machine or instrument that keeps a record of something, for example, in an experiment or on a vehicle. नोंद करणारे यंत्र

recording (recordings) n A **recording** of something such as moving pictures and sounds is a computer file or a disk on which they are stored. ध्वनिमुद्रण, चित्रमुद्रण

recover (**recovers, recovering, recovered**) *vi* When you **recover** from an illness or an injury, you become well again. आजारातून बरे होणे

recovery (**recoveries**) *n* If a sick person makes a **recovery**, he or she becomes well again. तब्बेतीतील सुधारणा

recruitment *n* The **recruitment** of workers, soldiers, or members is the act or process of selecting them for an organization or army and persuading them to join. भरती

rectangle (**rectangles**) *n* A **rectangle** is a shape with four sides whose angles are all right angles. Each side of a rectangle is the same length as the one opposite to it. आयत

rectangular *adj* Something that is **rectangular** is shaped like a rectangle. आयताकृती

rectify (**rectifies, rectifying, rectified**) *vt* If you **rectify** something that is wrong, you change it so that it becomes correct or satisfactory. चूक दुरुस्त करणे

recurring *adj* Something that is **recurring** happens more than once. पुनरावृती होणारा

recycle (**recycles, recycling, recycled**) *vt* If you **recycle** things that have already been used, such as bottles or sheets of paper, you do things to them so that they can be used again. पुन्हा उपयोगात आणण्यासाठी प्रक्रिया करणे

recycling *n* **Recycling** is the means by which things that have already been used, such as bottles or sheets of paper, are made ready to be used again. पुन्हा उपयोगात आणण्यासाठी करण्याची प्रक्रिया

red (**redder, reddest**) *adj* Something that is **red** is the colour of blood or tomatoes. लाल

Red Cross *n* The **Red Cross** is an international organization that helps people who are suffering, for example, as a result of war, floods, or disease. रेड क्रॉस

redcurrant (**redcurrants**) *n* **Redcurrants** are very small, bright red berries that grow in bunches on a bush and can be eaten as a fruit or cooked to make a sauce for meat. रेड करंट नावाची फळे

redecorate (**redecorates, redecorating, redecorated**) *v* If you **redecorate** a room or a building, you put new paint or wallpaper on it. पुन्हा सजवणे

red-haired *adj* A **red-haired** person is a person whose hair is between red and brown in colour. तपकिरी केसांची व्यक्ती

redhead (**redheads**) *n* A **redhead** is person, especially a woman, whose hair is a colour that is between red and brown. तपकिरी केसांची स्री

red meat (**red meats**) *n* **Red meat** is meat such as beef or lamb, which is dark brown in colour after it has been cooked. शिजवून तपकिरी रंगाचे केलेले (गायीचे वा कोकराचे) मांस

redo (**redoes, redoing, redid, redone**) *vt* If you **redo** a piece of work, you do it again in order to improve it or change it. पुन्हा करणे

Red Sea *n* The **Red Sea** is a long narrow sea between Arabia and north-east Africa. तांबडा समुद्र

reduce (**reduces, reducing, reduced**) *vt* If you **reduce** something, you make it smaller. कमी करणे

reduction (**reductions**) *n* When there is a **reduction** in something, it is made smaller. घट

redundancy (**redundancies**) *n* If there are **redundancies** within an organization, some of its employees are dismissed because their jobs are no longer necessary or because the organization can no longer afford to pay them. कपात

redundant *adj* If you are made **redundant**, you lose your job because it is no longer necessary or because your employer cannot afford to keep paying you. कामावरून कमी केलेला

red wine (**red wines**) *n* **Red wine** is wine that gets its red colour from the skins of the grapes. रेड वाईन

reed (**reeds**) *n* **Reeds** are tall plants that grow in shallow water or wet ground. बोरूचे गवत, लव्हाळे

reel (reels) n A **reel** is a cylinder-shaped object around which you wrap something such as thread or cinema film. रीळ

refer (refers, referring, referred) vi If you **refer** to a particular subject or person, you mention them. उल्लेख करणे

referee (referees) n The **referee** is the official who controls a sports match. खेळामधील पंच

reference (references) n **Reference** to someone or something is the act of talking about them or mentioning them. A **reference** is a particular example of this. संदर्भ

reference number (reference numbers) n A **reference number** is a number that tells you where you can obtain the information you want. संदर्भ क्रमांक

refill (refills, refilling, refilled) vt If you **refill** something, you fill it again after it has been emptied. पुन्हा भरणे

refinery (refineries) n A **refinery** is a factory which prepares a substance such as oil or sugar. शुद्धिकरण कारखाना

reflect (reflects, reflecting, reflected) vt If something **reflects** an attitude or situation, it shows that the attitude or situation exists. प्रतिबिंबित होणे

reflection (reflections) n A **reflection** is an image that you can see in a mirror or in water. प्रतिबिंब

reflex (reflexes) n A **reflex** or a **reflex action** is a normal uncontrollable reaction of your body to something that you feel, see, or experience. तीव्र प्रतिक्षिप्त क्रिया

refresher course (refresher courses) n A **refresher course** is a training course in which people improve their knowledge or skills and learn about new developments that are related to the job that they do. नोकरीत असताना नवीन गोष्टींचे ज्ञान होण्यासाठी प्रशिक्षण कार्यक्रम

refreshing adj A **refreshing** bath or drink makes you feel energetic or cool again after you have been tired or hot. ताजेतवाने करणारे

refreshments npl **Refreshments** are drinks and small amounts of food that are provided,

for example, during a meeting or journey. अल्पोपाहार

refrigerator (refrigerators) n A **refrigerator** is a large container which is kept cool inside, usually by electricity, so that the food and drink in it stays fresh. रेफ्रिजरेटर

refuel (refuels, refuelling, refuelled) v When an aircraft or other vehicle **refuels**, it is filled with more fuel so that it can continue its journey. वाहनात इंधन भरणे

refuge n If you take **refuge** somewhere, you try to protect yourself from physical harm by going there. आश्रय

refugee (refugees) n **Refugees** are people who have been forced to leave their country because there is a war there or because of their political or religious beliefs. निर्वासित

refund (refunds, refunding, refunded) n A **refund** is a sum of money which is returned to you, for example because you have returned goods to a shop. परत मिळालेले पैसे ▷ vt If someone **refunds** your money, they return it to you. पैसे परत करणे

refusal (refusals) n A **refusal** is the fact of firmly saying or showing that you will not do, allow, or accept something. नकार

refuse (refuses, refusing, refused) n **Refuse** consists of the rubbish and unwanted things in a house, shop, or factory that are regularly thrown away. कचरा ▷ v If you **refuse** to do something, you deliberately do not do it, or say firmly that you will not do it. नकार देणे

regain (regains, regaining, regained) vt If you **regain** something that you have lost, you get it back again. पुन्हा मिळवणे

regard (regards, regarding, regarded) n If you have a high **regard** for someone, you have a lot of respect for them. आदर ▷ vt If you **regard** someone or something in a particular way, you think of them in that way, or have that opinion of them. समजणे

regarding prep You can use **regarding** to say what people are talking or writing about.

विषयी *They refused to give any information regarding the accident.*

regiment (regiments) *n* A **regiment** is a large group of soldiers commanded by a colonel. सैन्याची तुकडी

region (regions) *n* A **region** is an area of a country or of the world. प्रदेश

regional *adj* **Regional** is used to describe things which relate to a particular area of a country or of the world. प्रादेशिक

register (registers, registering, registered) *n* A **register** is an official list or record. नोंद असलेली यादी ▷ *vi* If you **register** for something, you put your name on an official list. नोंदणी करणे

registered *adj* A **registered** letter or parcel is sent by a special postal service, for which you pay extra money for insurance in case it gets lost. नोंदणीकृत

registration *n* The **registration** of something is the recording of it in an official list. नोंदणी

registry office (registry offices) *n* A **registry office** is a place where births, marriages, and deaths are officially recorded, and where people can get married without a religious ceremony. नोंदणी कार्यालय

regret (regrets, regretting, regretted) *n* **Regret** is a feeling of sadness or disappointment. दु:ख ▷ *vt* If you **regret** something that you have done, you wish that you had not done it. दु:ख/पश्चाताप वाटणे

regular *adj* **Regular** things happen at equal intervals, or involve things happening at equal intervals. नियमित

regularly *adv* If you do something **regularly** or something happens **regularly**, you do it or it happens at equal intervals. नियमितपणे

regulation *n* **Regulation** is the controlling of an activity or process, usually by means of rules. नियम

rehearsal (rehearsals) *n* A **rehearsal** of a play, dance, or piece of music is the time when those taking part practise it. तालीम

rehearse (rehearses, rehearsing, rehearsed) *v* When people **rehearse** a play, dance, or piece of music, they practise it. तालीम करणे

reimburse (reimburses, reimbursing, reimbursed) *vt* If you **reimburse** someone for something, you pay them back the money that they have spent or lost because of it. *(formal)* केलेला खर्च परत देणे

reindeer (reindeer) *n* A **reindeer** is a type of deer that lives in northern areas of Europe, Asia, and America. मोठे काळवीट

reins *npl* **Reins** are the long leather straps attached to a horse's head which are used to make it go faster or stop. लगाम

reject (rejects, rejecting, rejected) *vt* If you **reject** something such as a proposal or request, you do not accept it or agree to it. नाकारणे

relapse (relapses) *n* If someone has a **relapse** or if there is a **relapse** then that person starts to behave in a particular way again or a situation returns to how it was before. ढासळणे, मूळ पदावर येणे

related *adj* If two or more things are **related**, there is a connection between them. एकमेकांशी संबंधित

relation (relations) *n* **Relations** between people, groups, or countries are contacts between them and the way they behave towards each other. नाते, संबंध

relationship (relationships) *n* The **relationship** between two people or groups is the way they feel and behave towards each other. नातेसंबंध

relative (relatives) n Your **relatives** are the members of your family. नातेवाईक

relatively adv **Relatively** means to a certain degree, especially when compared with other things of the same kind. तुलनात्मकरीत्या

relax (relaxes, relaxing, relaxed) v If you **relax**, or if something **relaxes** you, you feel calmer and less worried or tense. शांत होणे

relaxation n **Relaxation** is a way of spending time in which you rest and feel comfortable. शांततेत/आरामात घालवलेला मोकळा वेळ

relaxed adj If you are **relaxed**, you are calm and not worried or tense. तणावरहित

relaxing adj Something that is **relaxing** is pleasant and helps you to relax. आरामदायी

relay (relays) n A **relay** or a **relay race** is a race between two or more teams in which each member of the team runs or swims one section of the race. रिले शर्यत

release (releases, releasing, released) n When someone is released, you refer to their **release**. सुटका ▷ vt If a person or animal **is released** from somewhere where they have been locked up or looked after, they are set free or allowed to go. सुटका करणे

relegate (relegates, relegating, relegated) vt If a team that competes in a league **is relegated**, it is moved to a lower division because it finished at or near the bottom of its division at the end of a season. खालच्या स्थानावर ढकलणे

relevant adj If something is **relevant** to a situation or person, it is important or significant in that situation or to that person. महत्त्वाचे, सुसंबद्ध

reliable adj **Reliable** people or things can be trusted to work well or to behave in the way that you want them to. विश्वासू

relief n If you feel a sense of **relief**, you feel glad because something unpleasant has not happened or is no longer happening. सुटका

relieve (relieves, relieving, relieved) vt If something **relieves** an unpleasant feeling or situation, it makes it less unpleasant or causes it to disappear completely. वेदनामुक्त करणे

relieved adj If you are **relieved**, you feel glad because something unpleasant has not happened or is no longer happening. मनावरचा ताण गेल्यामुळे आनंद होण्याची भावना

religion n **Religion** is belief in a god or gods. धर्म

religious adj **Religious** means connected with religion or with one particular religion. धार्मिक

reluctant adj If you are **reluctant** to do something, you do not really want to do it. नाखूष

reluctantly adv If you do something **reluctantly**, you do not really want to do it. नाखुषीने

rely on (relies on, relying on, relied on) v If you **rely on** someone or something, you need them and depend on them in order to live or work properly. अवलंबून असणे The country relies heavily on tourism.

remain (remains, remaining, remained) v To **remain** in a particular state means to stay in that state and not change. आहे त्या स्थितीत राहणे

remaining adj The **remaining** things or people out of a group are the things or people that still exist, are still present, or have not yet been dealt with. उर्वरित

remains npl The **remains** of something are the parts of it that are left after most of it has been taken away or destroyed. अवशेष

remake (remakes) n A **remake** is a film that has the same story, and often the same title, as a film that was made earlier. जुन्या चित्रपटावर आधारित नव्याने तयार केलेला नवा चित्रपट

remark (remarks) n If you make a **remark** about something, you say something about it. अभिप्राय

remarkable adj Someone or something that is **remarkable** is very impressive or unusual. उल्लेखनीय

remarkably adv **Remarkably** means impressively or unusually. उल्लेखनीयरीत्या

remarry (remarries, remarrying, remarried)
vi If someone **remarries**, they marry again after they have obtained a divorce from their previous husband or wife, or after their previous husband or wife has died. पुनर्विवाह करणे

remedy (remedies) *n* A **remedy** is a successful way of dealing with a problem. उपाय

remember (remembers, remembering, remembered) *vt* If you **remember** people or events from the past, you still have an idea of them in your mind and you are able to think about them. आठवणे

remind (reminds, reminding, reminded) *vt* If someone **reminds** you of a fact or event that you already know about, they say something which makes you think about it. आठवण करून देणे

reminder (reminders) *n* If one thing is a **reminder** of another, the first thing makes you think about the second. *(written)* आठवण

remorse *n* **Remorse** is a strong feeling of guilt and regret about something wrong that you have done. पश्चातापाची भावना

remote (remoter, remotest) *adj* **Remote** areas are far away from places where most people live. दूरवरचा

remote control *n* **Remote control** is a system of controlling a machine or vehicle from a distance by using radio or electronic signals. दूरनियंत्रक

remotely *adv* You use **remotely** to emphasize a negative statement. अल्पांशाने

removable *adj* A **removable** part of something is a part that can easily be moved from its place or position. काढून घेण्याजोगा

removal *n* The **removal** of something is the act of removing it. काढून टाकण्याची क्रिया

removal van (removal vans) *n* A **removal van** is a large vehicle that is used to transport furniture or equipment from one building to another. सामान वाहून नेण्याची गाडी

remove (removes, removing, removed) *vt* If you **remove** something from a place, you take it away. *(written)* काढणे

rendezvous (rendezvous) *n* A **rendezvous** is a meeting, often a secret one, that you have arranged with someone for a particular time and place. भेटण्याचे संकेतस्थळ

renew (renews, renewing, renewed) *vt* If you **renew** an activity or a relationship, you begin it again. पुन्हा सुरू करणे

renewable *adj* **Renewable** resources are ones such as wind, water, and sunlight, which are constantly replacing themselves and therefore do not become used up. पुनर्वापर करता येण्याजोगे

renovate (renovates, renovating, renovated) *vt* If someone **renovates** an old building or machine, they repair it and get it back into good condition. नूतनीकरण करणे

renowned *adj* A person or place that is **renowned** for something, usually something good, is well known because of it. सुप्रसिद्ध

rent (rents, renting, rented) *n* **Rent** is the amount of money that you pay regularly to use a house, flat, or piece of land. भाडे ▷ *vt* If you **rent** something, you regularly pay its owner in order to have it and use it yourself. भाड्याने घेणे

rental (rentals) *n* The **rental** of something such as a car or television is the fact of paying an amount of money in order to have and use it. भाडे

reorganize (reorganizes, reorganizing, reorganized) *vt* To **reorganize** something means to change the way in which it is organized or done. पुन्हा जुळणी/पुनर्संघटन करणे

rep (reps) *n* A **rep** is a person who travels round selling their company's products or services to other companies. कंपनीची उत्पादने विकणारा प्रतिनिधी

repair (repairs, repairing, repaired) *n* A **repair** is something that you do to mend something that has been damaged. दुरुस्ती ▷ *vt* If you **repair** something that has been damaged or is not working properly, you mend it. दुरुस्त करणे

repair kit (repair kits) *n* A **repair kit** is a group of items that you keep together, usually in the same container, in case you need to repair something. दुरुस्ती संच

repay (repays, repaying, repaid) *vt* If you **repay** a debt, you pay back the money you owe to somebody. परतफेड करणे

repayment (repayments) *n* A **repayment** is an amount of money paid at regular intervals in order to repay a debt. परतफेड

repeat (repeats, repeating, repeated) *n* If there is a **repeat** of an event, usually an undesirable event, it happens again. पुनरावृती ▷ *vt* If you **repeat** something, you say or write it again. पुन्हा करणे

repeatedly *adv* If you do something **repeatedly**, you do it many times. पुन:पुन्हा

repellent *adj* If you think that something is horrible and disgusting, you can say it is **repellent**. *(formal)* भयानक

repercussions *npl* If an action or event has **repercussions**, it causes unpleasant things to happen some time after the original action or event. *(formal)* (दूरगामी) वाईट परिणाम

repetitive *adj* **Repetitive** actions are repeated many times and are therefore boring. तोचतोपणा असलेले

replace (replaces, replacing, replaced) *vt* To **replace** a person or thing means to put another person or thing in their place. बदलणे

replacement *n* If you refer to the **replacement** of one thing by another, you mean that the second thing takes the place of the first. बदललेली वस्तू

replay (replays, replaying, replayed) *n* A **replay** is a showing again of a sequence of action, esp part of a sporting contest immediately after it happens. कॅमेऱ्यात पकडलेला खेळाचा प्रसंग पुन्हा दाखविणे ▷ *vt* If a match between two sports teams **is replayed**, the two teams play it again, because neither team won the first time, or because the match was stopped because of bad weather. पुन्हा खेळवणे

replica (replicas) *n* A **replica** of something such as a statue, machine, or weapon is an accurate copy of it. प्रतिकृती

reply (replies, replying, replied) *n* A **reply** is something that you say or write when you answer someone or answer a letter or advertisement. उत्तर ▷ *vi* When you **reply** to something that someone has said or written to you, you say or write an answer to them. उत्तर देणे

report (reports, reporting, reported) *n* A **report** is a news article or broadcast which gives information about something that has just happened. वर्तमानपत्रातली किंवा दूरदर्शनवरील बातमी ▷ *vt* If you **report** something that has happened, you tell people about it. माहिती देणे ▷ *n* A **report** is an official written account of how well or how badly a pupil has done during the term or year that has just finished. गुणपत्रक

reporter (reporters) *n* A **reporter** is someone who writes news articles or broadcasts news reports. बातमीदार

represent (represents, representing, represented) *vt* If someone **represents** you, they act for you. प्रतिनिधित्व करणे

representative *adj* A **representative** group acts for a larger group. प्रतिनिधी

reproduction (reproductions) *n* A **reproduction** is a copy of something such as an antique or a painting. तयार केलेली दुसरी प्रत

reptile (reptiles) *n* **Reptiles** are a group of animals which have scales on their skin and lay eggs. Snakes and crocodiles are reptiles. सरपटणारा प्राणी

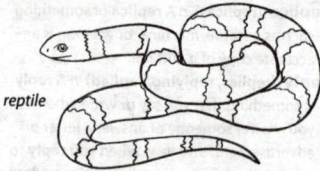

reptile

republic (**republics**) n A **republic** is a country that has a president or whose system of government is based on the idea that every citizen has equal status. प्रजासत्ताक

repulsive adj **Repulsive** means horrible and disgusting. भयानक

reputable adj A **reputable** company or person is reliable and trustworthy. विश्वासू

reputation (**reputations**) n To have a **reputation** for something means to be known or remembered for it. ख्याती, नावलौकिक

request (**requests, requesting, requested**) n If you make a **request**, you politely ask for something or ask someone to do something. (formal) विनंती ▷ vt If you **request** something, you ask for it politely or formally. (formal) विनंती करणे

require (**requires, requiring, required**) vt To **require** something means to need it. (formal) आवश्यक असणे

requirement (**requirements**) n A **requirement** is something that you must have in order to be allowed to do something or to be suitable for something. आवश्यकता

rescue (**rescues, rescuing, rescued**) n A **rescue** is an attempt to save someone from a dangerous or unpleasant situation. संकटातून सोडविण्याची क्रिया ▷ vt If you **rescue** someone, you get them out of a dangerous or unpleasant situation. संकटातून सोडविणे

research n **Research** is work that involves studying something and trying to discover facts about it. संशोधन

resemblance (**resemblances**) n If there is a **resemblance** between two people or things, they are similar to each other. सारखेपणा

resemble (**resembles, resembling, resembled**) vt If one thing or person **resembles** another, they are similar to that thing or person. एक दुस-याशारखे दिसणे

resent (**resents, resenting, resented**) vt If you **resent** someone or something, you feel bitter and angry about them. संताप येणे

resentful adj If you are **resentful**, you feel resentment. संताप आलेला

reservation (**reservations**) n If you have **reservations** about something, you are not sure that it is entirely good or right. शंका

reserve (**reserves, reserving, reserved**) n A **reserve** is a supply of something that is available for use when needed. गरजेच्यावेळी वापरण्यासाठी ठेवलेला साठा ▷ n A nature **reserve** is an area of land where animals, birds, and plants are officially protected. अभयारण्य ▷ vt If something **is reserved** for a particular person or purpose, it is kept specially for that person or purpose. राखून ठेवणे

reserved adj Someone who is **reserved** keeps their feelings hidden. मितभाषी, संकोची

reservoir (**reservoirs**) n A **reservoir** is a lake used for storing water before it is supplied to people. पाण्याची टाकी/जलाशय

resident (**residents**) n The **residents** of a house or area are the people who live there. रहिवासी

residential adj A **residential** area contains houses rather than offices or factories. निवासी

resign (**resigns, resigning, resigned**) vi If you **resign** from a job or position, you formally announce that you are leaving it. राजीनामा देणे

resin (**resins**) n **Resin** is a sticky substance produced by some trees. राळ

resist (**resists, resisting, resisted**) vt If you **resist** a change, you refuse to accept it and try to prevent it. प्रतिकार करणे

resistance n **Resistance** to a change or a new idea is a refusal to accept it. प्रतिकार

resit (**resits, resitting, resat**) v If someone **resits** a test or examination, they take it again, usually because they failed the first time. पुन्हा बसणे

resolution (**resolutions**) *n* A **resolution** is a formal decision taken at a meeting by means of a vote. ठराव

resort (**resorts**) *n* A holiday **resort** is a place where people can spend their holidays. रिसॉर्ट

resort to (**resorts to, resorting to, resorted to**) *v* If you **resort to** a course of action that you do not really approve of, you adopt it because you cannot see any other way of achieving what you want. अवलंब करणे *Some schools have resorted to recruiting teachers from overseas.*

resource (**resources**) *n* The **resources** of a country, organization, or person are the materials, money, and other things they have and can use. स्रोत

respect (**respects, respecting, respected**) *n* If you have **respect** for someone, you have a good opinion of them. आदर ▷ *vt* If you **respect** someone, you have a good opinion of their character or ideas. आदर करणे

respectable *adj* Someone or something that is **respectable** is approved of by society and considered to be morally correct. आदरणीय

respectively *adv* **Respectively** means in the same order as the items you have just mentioned. क्रमशः

respond (**responds, responding, responded**) *vi* When you **respond** to something that is done or said, you react by doing or saying something. प्रतिसाद देणे

response (**responses**) *n* Your **response** to an event or to something that is said is your reply or reaction to it. प्रतिसाद

responsibility (**responsibilities**) *n* If you have **responsibility** for something or someone, it is your job or duty to deal with them. जबाबदारी

responsible *adj* If you are **responsible** for something bad that has happened, it is your fault. जबाबदार

rest (**rests, resting, rested**) *det* The **rest** is the parts of something that are left. उर्वरित ▷ *v* If you **rest** or if you **rest** your body, you sit or lie down and do not do anything active for a while. विश्रांती घेणे

restaurant (**restaurants**) *n* A **restaurant** is a place where you can buy and eat a meal. रेस्टॉरंट, उपहारगृह

restful *adj* Something that is **restful** helps you to feel calm and relaxed. आरामदायी

restless *adj* If you are **restless**, you are bored or dissatisfied, and want to do something else. बेचैन

restore (**restores, restoring, restored**) *vt* To **restore** something means to cause it to exist again. अगोदर होते तसे पुन्हा करणे

restrict (**restricts, restricting, restricted**) *vt* If you **restrict** something, you put a limit on it to stop it becoming too large. आळा घालणे

restructure (**restructures, restructuring, restructured**) *vt* To **restructure** an organization or system means to change the way it is organized, usually in order to make it work more effectively. पुनर्रचना करणे

result (**results, resulting, resulted**) *n* A **result** is something that happens or exists because of something else that has happened. परिणाम ▷ *vi* If something **results in** a particular situation or event, it causes that situation or event to happen. परिणाम/निष्पत्ती होणे

resume (**resumes, resuming, resumed**) *v* If you **resume** an activity, it begins again. (*formal*) पुन्हा सुरू करणे

retail (**retails, retailing, retailed**) *n* **Retail** is the activity of selling goods direct to the public. किरकोळ विक्री ▷ *vi* If an item in a shop **retails** at or for a particular price, it is for sale at that price. किरकोळ विक्रीस ठेवणे

retailer (**retailers**) *n* A **retailer** is a person or business that sells goods to the public. किरकोळ विक्रेता

retail price (**retail prices**) *n* The **retail price** of something is the price it is on sale for in a shop. किरकोळ विक्रीची किंमत

retire (retires, retiring, retired) vi When older people **retire**, they leave their job and stop working. निवृत्त होणे

retired adj A **retired** person is an older person who has left his or her job and has usually stopped working completely. निवृत्त

retirement n **Retirement** is the time when a worker retires. निवृत्ती

retrace (retraces, retracing, retraced) vt If you **retrace** your steps , you return to where you started from, using the same route. आलेल्या मार्गावरून परत जाणे

return (returns, returning, returned) n Your **return** is when you arrive back at a place where you were before. परत येणे ▷ n The **return** on an investment is the amount of money you gain from it. परतावा ▷ vt If you **return** something to someone, you give it back to them. परत करणे ▷ vi When you **return** to a place, you go back to it after you have been away. परत येणे ▷ n A **return** or a **return ticket** is a ticket that allows you to travel to a place and then back again. परतीचे तिकीट

reunion (reunions) n A **reunion** is a party or occasion when people who have not seen each other for a long time meet again. पुनर्भेट

reuse (reuses, reusing, reused) vt When you **reuse** something, you use it again instead of throwing it away. पुनर्वापर करणे

reveal (reveals, revealing, revealed) vt To **reveal** something means to make people aware of it. उघड करणे

revenge n **Revenge** involves hurting someone who has hurt you. बदला

revenue n **Revenue** is money that a company, organization, or government receives from people. महसूल

reverse (reverses, reversing, reversed) n If your car is in **reverse**, you have changed gear so that you can drive it backwards. उलटा ▷ vt To **reverse** a process, decision, or policy means to change it to its opposite. उलट फिरवणे

review (reviews) n A **review** of a situation or system is its formal examination by people in authority. This is usually done in order to see whether it can be improved or corrected. पुनरावलोकन

revise (revises, revising, revised) vt If you **revise** something, you alter it in order to make it better or more accurate. सुधारणा करणे

revision (revisions) n To make a **revision** of something that is written or something that has been decided means to make changes to it in order to improve it, make it more modern, or make it more suitable for a particular purpose. सुधारणा

revive (revives, reviving, revived) v When something such as a feeling or a practice **revives** or **is revived**, it becomes active or successful again. पुनरुज्जीवित करणे

revolting adj **Revolting** means horrible and disgusting. भयंकर

revolution (revolutions) n A **revolution** is a successful attempt by a large group of people to change their country's political system, using force. क्रांती

revolutionary adj **Revolutionary** activities, organizations, or people have the aim of causing a political revolution. क्रांतीकारी

revolver (revolvers) n A **revolver** is a kind of small gun. रिव्हॉल्व्हर

reward (rewards) n A **reward** is something that you are given because you have behaved well, worked hard, or provided a service to the community. बक्षीस

rewarding adj Something that is **rewarding** gives you satisfaction or brings you benefits. समाधानकारक

rewind (rewinds, rewinding, rewound) v When a recording on a tape, computer file, or disk **rewinds**, or when you **rewind** it, the recording goes backwards so that you can play it again. पुन्हा गुंडाळणे

rheumatism n **Rheumatism** is an illness that makes your joints or muscles stiff and painful. Older people, especially, suffer from rheumatism. संधिवात

rhubarb n **Rhubarb** is a plant with large leaves and long red stems. रूबार्ब

rhythm (**rhythms**) n A **rhythm** is a regular series of sounds, movements, or actions. लय

rib (**ribs**) n Your **ribs** are the curved bones that go from your backbone around your chest. बरगडी

ribbon (**ribbons**) n A **ribbon** is a long, narrow piece of cloth used as a fastening or decoration, for example on a birthday present. फीत

rice n **Rice** consists of white or brown grains taken from a cereal plant. भात

rich (**richer, richest**) adj A **rich** person has a lot of money or valuable possessions. श्रीमंत

ride (**rides, riding, rode, ridden**) n A **ride** is a journey on a horse or bicycle, or in a vehicle. दुचाकी किंवा घोड्यावरील स्वारी ▷ v If you **ride** a horse, you sit on it and control its movements. दुचाकी किंवा घोडा चालवणे

rider (**riders**) n A **rider** is someone who rides a horse, bicycle, or motorcycle. दुचाकी किंवा घोडा चालवता येणारा

ridiculous adj If you say that something or someone is **ridiculous**, you mean that they are very foolish. मूर्खपणाची

riding n **Riding** is the activity or sport of riding horses. घोडेस्वारी

rifle (**rifles**) n A **rifle** is a gun with a long barrel. बंदूक

rig (**rigs**) n A **rig** is a large structure that is used for extracting oil or gas from the ground or under the sea. तेल किंवा वायू काढण्यासाठी केलेले बांधकाम

right adj If something is **right**, it is correct and there have been no mistakes. बरोबर ▷ adj The **right** side is the side that is towards the east when you look north. उजवा ▷ adv If someone is **right** about something, they are correct. बरोबर ▷ n **Right** is used to talk about actions that are good and acceptable. बरोबर

right angle (**right angles**) n A **right angle** is an angle of ninety degrees. काटकोन

right-hand adj If something is on the **right-hand** side of something, it is positioned on the right of it. उजवीकडील

right-hand drive n In a motor vehicle, **right-hand drive** is a driving system in which the steering wheel is on the right side. Cars with **right-hand drive** are designed to be driven in countries where people drive on the left side of the road. चालकाची जागा उजवीकडे असते ते वाहन

right-handed adj Someone who is **right-handed** uses their right hand rather than their left hand for activities such as writing and sports, and for picking things up. उजव्या हाताचा वापर करणारा

rightly adv If you do something **rightly** you do it in accordance with the facts or correctly. योग्यपणे

right of way (**rights of way**) n A **right of way** is a public path across private land. खाजगी जागेतून गेलेला सार्वजनिक रस्ता

right-wing adj A **right-wing** person or group has conservative or capitalist views. उजवी विचारसरणी असलेले

rim (**rims**) n The **rim** of a container or a circular object is the edge which goes all the way round the top or round the outside. कडा, धाव

ring (**rings, ringing, rang, rung**) n A **ring** is a round piece of metal that you wear on a finger. अंगठी ▷ vt When you **ring** someone, you telephone them. फोन करणे ▷ v When a bell **rings**, or when you **ring** it, it makes a clear, loud sound. वाजणे

ring back (rings back, ringing back, rang back, rung back) v If you **ring** someone **back**, you phone them, either because they phoned you earlier and you were out or because you did not finish an earlier conversation. उत्तरादाखल फोन करणे *Tell her I'll ring back in a few minutes.*

ring binder (ring binders) n A **ring binder** is a file with hard covers, which you can insert pages into. The pages are held in by metal rings on a bar attached to the inside of the file. रिंग बायंडर फाईल.

ring road (ring roads) n A **ring road** is a road that goes round the edge of a town so that traffic does not have to go through the town centre. शहरासभोवतालून बनवलेला मार्ग

ringtone (ringtones) n A **ringtone** is a musical tune played by a mobile phone when a call is received. रिंगटोन

ring up (rings up, ringing up, rang up, rung up) v When you **ring** someone **up** you telephone them. फोन करणे *He rang up and invited us over for dinner.*

rink (rinks) n A **rink** is a large area where people go to skate. स्केटिंग करण्याची विस्तीर्ण जागा

rinse (rinses, rinsing, rinsed) n When you give something a **rinse**, you wash it in clean water in order to remove dirt or soap from it. खळखळून धुण्याची क्रिया ▷ vt When you **rinse** something, you wash it in clean water in order to remove dirt or soap from it. खळखळून धुणे

riot (riots, rioting, rioted) n When there is a **riot**, a crowd of people behave violently in a public place, for example they fight, throw stones, or damage buildings and vehicles. दंगल ▷ vi If people **riot**, they behave violently in a public place. दंगल करणे

rip (rips, ripping, ripped) v If you **rip** something, you tear it forcefully with your hands or with a tool such as a knife. If something **rips**, it is torn forcefully. जोराने फाडणे

ripe (riper, ripest) adj **Ripe** fruit or grain is fully grown and ready to be harvested or eaten. पिकलेले

rip off (rips off, ripping off, ripped off, rip-offs) v If someone **rips** you **off**, they cheat you by charging too much for goods or services. (informal) जास्त किंमत घेऊन फसवणे *People are buying these products and getting ripped off.* ▷ n If you say that something that you bought was a **rip-off**, you mean that you were charged too much money or that it was of very poor quality. (informal) भरमसाट किंमत देऊन विकत घेतलेले

rip up (rips up, ripping up, ripped up) v If you **rip** something **up**, you tear it into small pieces. तुकडे तुकडे करणे *He ripped up the letter.*

rise (rises, rising, rose, risen) n If there is a **rise** in an amount, the amount increases. वाढ, वाढणे ▷ vi If something **rises** or **rises up**, it moves upwards. उठणे

risk (risks, risking, risked) n If there is a **risk** of something unpleasant, there is a possibility that it will happen. जोखीम ▷ v If you **risk** something unpleasant, you do something knowing that the unpleasant thing might happen as a result. धोका पत्करणे

risky (riskier, riskiest) adj If an activity or action is **risky**, it is dangerous or could fail. धोकादायक

ritual (rituals) n **Ritual** activities happen as part of a ritual or tradition. पारंपरिक, कर्मकांडाशी ▷ n A **ritual** is a religious service or other ceremony which involves a series of actions performed in a fixed order. धर्मिक विधी/कर्मकांड

rival (rivals) adj **Rival** groups are groups of people that compete against each other. विरोधी गट ▷ n Your **rival** is a person, business, or organization who you are competing or fighting against in the same area or for the same things. प्रतिस्पर्धी

rivalry (rivalries) n **Rivalry** is competition or conflict between people or groups. शत्रुत्व

river (rivers) n A **river** is a large amount of fresh water flowing continuously in a long line across land, such as the Amazon or the Nile. नदी

road (roads) n A **road** is a long piece of hard ground built between two places so that people can drive or ride easily from one to the other. रस्ता

roadblock (roadblocks) n When the police or the army put a **roadblock** across a road, they stop all the traffic going through, for example because they are looking for a criminal. रस्त्यावरचा अडथळा

road map (road maps) n A **road map** is a map which shows the roads in a particular area in detail. रस्त्यांचा नकाशा

road rage n **Road rage** is an angry or violent reaction by a driver towards another road user. एका वाहन चालकाचा दुसऱ्या चालकावरचा राग

road sign (road signs) n A road sign is a sign near a road giving information or instructions to drivers. वाहतुकीच्या खुणा

road tax n **Road tax** is a tax paid every year by the owners of every motor vehicle which is being used on the roads. पथकर

roadworks npl **Roadworks** are repairs or other work being done on a road. रस्तादुरूस्तीचे काम

roast adj **Roast** meat has been cooked by dry heat. भाजलेले

rob (robs, robbing, robbed) vt If a person or place **is robbed**, money or property is stolen from them, often using force. लुटणे

robber (robbers) n A **robber** is someone who steals money or property from a bank, a shop, or a vehicle, often by using force or threats. लुटारू, दरोडेखोर

robbery (robberies) n **Robbery** is the crime of stealing money or property, often using force. दरोडा, चोरी

robin (robins) n A **robin** is a small brown bird with a red breast. रॉबिन पक्षी

robot (robots) n A **robot** is a machine which moves and performs certain tasks automatically. यंत्रमानव

rock (rocks, rocking, rocked) n Rock is the hard material that is in the ground and in mountains. खडक ▷ n A **rock** is a piece of this material. दगड ▷ v If something **rocks**, it moves from side to side. हेलकावे खाणे

rock climbing n **Rock climbing** is the activity of climbing cliffs or large rocks, as a hobby or sport. प्रस्तरारोहण

rocket (rockets) n A **rocket** is a space vehicle shaped like a long tube. अग्निबाण

rocking chair (rocking chairs) n A **rocking chair** is a chair that is built on two curved pieces of wood so that you can rock yourself backwards and forwards when you are sitting in it. झुलती खुर्ची, डोलखुर्ची

rocking horse (rocking horses) n A **rocking horse** is a toy horse which a child can sit on and which can be made to rock backwards and forwards. खेळण्यातील झुलता/डोलता लाकडी घोडा

rod (rods) n A **rod** is a long thin bar made of metal or wood. दांडा

rodent (rodents) n **Rodents** are small mammals, for example rats and squirrels, with sharp front teeth. कुरतडणारा प्राणी

role (roles) n The **role** of someone or something in a situation is their job or position in it. भूमिका

roll (rolls, rolling, rolled) n A **roll** of paper, plastic, cloth, or wire is a long piece of it that has been wrapped many times around itself or around a tube. गुंडाळी ▷ v If something **rolls** or if you **roll** it, it moves along a surface, turning over many times. गुंडाळी करणे

roll call (roll calls) n If you take a **roll call**, you check which of the members of a group are present by reading their names out. हजेरी

roller (rollers) n A **roller** is a cylinder that turns round in a machine or device. रोलर

rollercoaster (rollercoasters) n A **rollercoaster** is a small railway at a fair that goes up and down steep slopes fast and that people ride on for pleasure or excitement. रोलरकोस्टर

r

rollerskates *npl* **Rollerskates** are shoes with four small wheels on the bottom. रोलरस्केटस्

rollerskating *n* **Rollerskating** is the activity of moving over a flat surface wearing rollerskates. रोलरस्केटिंग करणे

rolling pin (rolling pins) *n* A **rolling pin** is a cylinder that you roll backwards and forwards over uncooked pastry in order to make the pastry flat. लाटणे

Roman *adj* **Roman** means related to or connected with ancient Rome and its empire. रोमन

romance (romances) *n* A **romance** is a relationship between two people who are in love with each other but who are not married to each other. प्रणय

Romanesque *adj* **Romanesque** architecture is in the style that was common in western Europe around the eleventh century. It is characterized by rounded arches and thick pillars. रोमनेस्क शिल्पकला

Romania *n* **Romania** is a republic in south-east Europe. रोमानिया

Romanian (Romanians) *adj* **Romanian** means belonging or relating to Romania, or to its people, language, or culture. रोमानियन ▷ *n* A **Romanian** is a person who comes from Romania. रोमानियन ▷ *n* **Romanian** is the language spoken in Romania. रोमानियन

romantic *adj* Someone who is **romantic** or does **romantic** things says and does things that make their partner feel special and loved. प्रणयरम्य

roof (roofs) *n* The **roof** of a building or car is the covering on top of it. छत

room (rooms) *n* A **room** is a part of a building that has its own walls. खोली ▷ *n* If there is **room** somewhere, there is a enough empty space. मोकळी जागा

roommate (roommates) *n* Your **roommate** is the person you share an apartment or house with. एकाच खोलीत सोबत राहणारा सोबती

room service *n* **Room service** is a service in a hotel by which meals or drinks are provided for guests in their rooms. हॉटेलमधल्या भाड्याने घेतलेल्या खोलीपर्यंत दिल्या जाणाऱ्या सेवा

root (roots) *n* The **roots** of a plant are the parts that grow underground. मूळ

rope (ropes) *n* A **rope** is a very thick cord, made by twisting together several thinner cords. दोर

rope in (ropes in, roping in, roped in) *v* If you say that you **were roped in** to do a particular task, you mean that someone persuaded you to help them do that task. *(informal)* कामात ओढणे/सामील करून घेणे *Visitors were roped in to help pick tomatoes.*

rose (roses) *n* A **rose** is a flower which has a pleasant smell and grows on a bush with thorns. गुलाब

rosé (rosés) *n* **Rosé** is wine which is pink in colour. रोझ वाईन

rosemary *n* **Rosemary** is a herb used in cooking. It comes from an evergreen plant with small narrow leaves. रोझमेरी नावाचे झुडुप

rot (rots, rotting, rotted) *v* When food, wood, or other substances **rot**, or when something **rots** them, they decay and fall apart. सडणे

rotten *adj* If food, wood, or another substance is **rotten**, it has decayed and can no longer be used. सडलेले

rough (rougher, roughest) *adj* If something is **rough**, it is not smooth or even. ओबडधोबड ▷ *adj* If you are **rough**, you are not being careful or gentle. उद्धट

roughly *adv* If you do something **roughly** you do it with too much force. धसमुसळेपणा

roulette *n* **Roulette** is a gambling game in which a ball is dropped onto a revolving wheel with numbered holes in it. The players bet on which hole the ball will end up in. रौलेट नावाचा खेळ

round (rounder, roundest, rounds) *adj* Something **round** is in the shape of a ball or a circle. गोल ▷ *n* A **round** of events is a series of similar events, especially one which comes after or before a similar series. फेरी ▷ *n* A **round** is a circular shape. गोल ▷ *prep* **Round** a place or object means on all sides of it. संभोवती *They were sitting round the kitchen table.*

roundabout (roundabouts) *n* A **roundabout** is a circle at a place where several roads meet. ज्या ठिकाणी अनेक रस्ते एकत्र येतात अशी रस्त्यावरील वर्तुळाकार जागा

round trip (round trips) *n* If you make a **round trip**, you travel to a place and then back again. एका ठिकाणाहून जाऊन पुन्हा त्याच ठिकाणी येणे

round up (rounds up, rounding up, rounded up) *v* If people or animals **are rounded up**, someone gathers them together. एकत्र करणे *He had sought work as a cowboy, rounding up cattle.*

route (routes) *n* A **route** is a way from one place to another. मार्ग

routine (routines) *n* A **routine** is the usual series of things that you do at a particular time in a particular order. दैनंदिन काम

row (rows, rowing, rowed) *n* A **row** is a line of things or people. रांग ▷ *n* A **row** is a serious disagreement or noisy argument. वादविवाद ▷ *v* When you **row**, or when you **row** a boat, you make it move through the water by using oars. नौका वल्हविणे ▷ *vi* If two people **row**, they have a noisy argument. वादविवाद करणे

rowing *n* **Rowing** is a sport in which people or teams race against each other in boats with oars. नौका वल्हविण्याची स्पर्धा

rowing boat (rowing boats) *n* A **rowing boat** is a small boat that you move through the water by using oars. वल्हे असलेली नौका

royal *adj* **Royal** means related to or belonging to a king, queen, or emperor, or to a member of their family. राजेशाही, राजघराण्याचा

rub (rubs, rubbing, rubbed) *vt* If you **rub** something, you move your hand or a cloth

backwards and forwards over it while pressing firmly. घासणे

rubber (rubbers) *n* **Rubber** is a strong material that stretches. **Rubber** is used to make things like tyres and boots for wet weather. रबर ▷ *n* A **rubber** is a small piece of rubber used to remove pencil mistakes. खोडरबर

rubber band (rubber bands) *n* A **rubber band** is a thin circle of very elastic rubber. You put it around things such as papers in order to keep them together. रबर बँड

rubber gloves *npl* **Rubber gloves** are gloves made of rubber that you wear to protect your hands, for example when you are washing up or gardening. रबरी हातमोजे

rubbish *adj* If you think that someone is not very good at something, you can say that they are **rubbish** at it. *(informal)* बिनकामाचा ▷ *n* **Rubbish** consists of unwanted things or waste material such as old food. टाकाऊ पदार्थ

rubbish dump (rubbish dumps) *n* A **rubbish dump** is a place where rubbish is left, for example on open ground outside a town. टाकाऊ पदार्थ टाकण्याचे ठिकाण

rucksack (rucksacks) *n* A **rucksack** is a bag, often on a frame, used for carrying things on your back. रकसॅक

rude (ruder, rudest) *adj* If someone is **rude**, they behave in a way that is not polite. उद्धट, मग्रूर

rug (rugs) *n* A **rug** is a piece of thick material that you put on the floor and use like a carpet. गालिचा

rugby *n* **Rugby** is a game played by two teams, who try to get an oval ball past a line at their opponents' end of the pitch. रग्बी नावाचा खेळ

ruin (ruins, ruining, ruined) *n* **Ruin** is the state of no longer having any money. कंगाल ▷ *vt* To **ruin** something means to severely harm, damage, or spoil it. उध्वस्त करणे

rule (rules, ruling, ruled) *n* **Rules** are instructions that tell you what you must do or must not do. नियम ▷ v Someone who **rules** a country controls it. राज्य करणे

rule out (**rules out, ruling out, ruled out**) v If you **rule out** an idea or course of action, you reject it because it is impossible or unsuitable. नाकारणे *The Prime Minister is believed to have ruled out cuts in child benefit or pensions.*

ruler (**rulers**) n A **ruler** is a person who rules a country. राज्यकर्ता ▷ n A **ruler** is a long, flat piece of wood or plastic with straight edges. You use a **ruler** for measuring things or drawing straight lines. फूटपट्टी

rum (**rums**) n **Rum** is an alcoholic drink made from sugar cane juice. रम

rumour (**rumours**) n A **rumour** is a piece of information that may or may not be true, but that people are talking about. अफवा

run (**runs, running, ran, run**) n A **run** is a journey you make by running. धाव ▷ vi You say that something long, such as a road, **runs** in a particular direction when you are describing its course or position. एका विशिष्ट दिशेने जाणे वा पसरणे ▷ vi When you **run**, you move very quickly on your legs. धावणे

run away (**runs away, running away, ran away, run away**) v If you **run away** from a place, you secretly leave it. पळून जाणे *I ran away from home when I was sixteen.*

runner (**runners**) n A **runner** is a person who runs, especially for sport or pleasure. धावपटू

runner bean (**runner beans**) n **Runner beans** are long green beans that are eaten as a vegetable. एक प्रकारची भाजी

runner-up (**runners-up**) n A **runner-up** is someone who finishes in second place in a race or competition. उप विजेता

running n **Running** is the activity of moving fast on foot, especially as a sport. धावण्याची शर्यत

run out (**runs out, running out, ran out, run out**) v If you **run out** of something, you have no more of it left. संपणे *By now the plane was running out of fuel.*

run over (**runs over, running over, ran over, run over**) v If a vehicle **runs over** someone or something, it knocks them down. वाहनाने ठोकर मारणे *He ran over an elderly man.*

runway (**runways**) n At an airport, the **runway** is the long strip of ground with a hard surface which an aeroplane takes off from or lands on. विमानतळावरील धावपट्टी

rural adj **Rural** means relating to country areas as opposed to large towns. ग्रामीण

rush (**rushes, rushing, rushed**) n A **rush** is a situation in which you need to go somewhere or do something very quickly. घाई ▷ vi If you **rush** somewhere, you go there quickly. घाईने धावत जाणे

rush hour (**rush hours**) n The **rush hour** is one of the periods of the day when most people are travelling to or from work. गर्दीची वेळ

rusk (**rusks**) n **Rusks** are hard, dry biscuits that are given to babies and young children. कुरकुरीत बिस्कीट

Russia n **Russia** is the largest country in the world, covering north Eurasia. **Russia** borders on the Pacific and Arctic Oceans, and the Baltic, Black, and Caspian Seas. रशिया

Russian (**Russians**) adj **Russian** means belonging or relating to Russia, or to its people, language, or culture. रशियन ▷ n A **Russian** is a person who comes from Russia. रशियन ▷ n **Russian** is the language spoken in Russia, and other countries such as Belarus, Kazakhstan, and Kyrgyzstan. रशियन

rust n **Rust** is a brown substance that forms on iron or steel when it comes into contact with water. गंज

rusty (**rustier, rustiest**) adj A **rusty** metal object has a lot of rust on it. गंजलेला

ruthless adj Someone who is **ruthless** is very harsh or determined, and will do anything that is necessary to achieve their aim. निर्दय

rye n **Rye** is a cereal grown in cold countries. Its grains can be used to make flour, bread, or other foods. राय नावाचे धान्य

S

sabotage (sabotages, sabotaging, sabotaged) n Sabotage is the deliberate damage or destruction of equipment or property which belongs to your enemy or opponent. विध्वंस ▷ vt If a machine, railway line, or bridge **is sabotaged**, it is deliberately damaged or destroyed, for example in a war or as a protest. विध्वंस करणे

sachet (sachets) n A **sachet** is a small closed plastic or paper bag, containing a small quantity of something. छोटे कागदी पाकीट

sack (sacks, sacking, sacked) n A **sack** is a large bag made of rough woven material. गोण ▷ n If your employers give you the **sack**, they tell you to leave your job. कामावरून काढून टाकलेला ▷ vt If your employers **sack** you, they tell you to leave your job. कामावरून काढून टाकणे

sacred adj Something that is **sacred** is believed to be holy. पवित्र

sacrifice (sacrifices) n To offer an animal as a **sacrifice**, means to kill it in a special religious ceremony. बळी

sad (sadder, saddest) adj If you are **sad**, you feel unhappy. दुःखी

saddle (saddles) n A **saddle** is a leather seat that you put on the back of an animal so that you can ride the animal. खोगीर

saddlebag (saddlebags) n A **saddlebag** is a bag fastened to the saddle of a bicycle or

motorcycle, or the saddle of a horse. दुचाकी किंवा घोड्याला बांधून ठेवायची पिशवी

sadly adv If you feel or do something sadly, you feel or do it unhappily. खिन्नपणे, दुःखाने

safari (safaris) n A **safari** is an expedition for hunting or observing wild animals, especially in East Africa. शिकारीची मोहीम

safe (safer, safest, safes) adj Something that is **safe** does not cause physical harm or danger. सुरक्षित ▷ n A **safe** is a strong metal cupboard with special locks, in which you keep money, jewellery, or other valuable things. तिजोरी

safety n Safety is the state of being safe from harm or danger. सुरक्षितता

safety belt (safety belts) n A **safety belt** is a strap that you fasten across your body for safety when travelling in a car or plane. सुरक्षितता पट्टा

safety pin (safety pins) n A **safety pin** is a bent metal pin used for fastening things together. The point of the pin has a cover so that when the pin is closed it cannot hurt anyone. सेफ्टी पिन

saffron n Saffron is a yellowish-orange powder obtained from a flower and used to give flavour and colouring to some foods. केशर

Sagittarius n Sagittarius is one of the twelve signs of the zodiac. Its symbol is a creature that is half horse, half man, shooting an arrow. People who are born between the 22nd of November and the 21st of December come under this sign. धनु रास

Sahara n The Sahara is a desert in North Africa. सहारा वाळवंट

sail (sails, sailing, sailed) n Sails are large pieces of material attached to the mast of a boat. शीड ▷ v If you **sail** a boat, or if a boat **sails**, it moves across water. शिडाची नौका पाण्यात घेऊन जाणे

sailing (sailings) n A **sailing** is a voyage made by a ship carrying passengers. समुद्रपर्यटन

sailing boat (sailing boats) n A **sailing boat** is a boat with sails. शिडाची नौका

sailor (sailors) n A **sailor** is a person who works on a ship as a member of its crew. खलाशी

saint (saints) n A **saint** is someone who has died and been officially recognized and honoured by the Christian church because his or her life was a perfect example of the way Christians should live. संत

salad (salads) n A **salad** is a mixture of uncooked vegetables, eaten as part of a meal. कोशिंबीर

salad dressing (salad dressings) n Salad **dressing** is a mixture of oil, vinegar, herbs, and other flavourings, which you pour over a salad. सेलाड ड्रेसिंग

salami (salamis) n Salami is a type of strong-flavoured sausage. It is usually thinly sliced and eaten cold. सलामी

salary (salaries) n Your **salary** is the money that you are paid each month by your employer. पगार

sale n The **sale** of goods is the selling of them for money. विक्री

sales assistant (sales assistants) n A **sales assistant** is a person who works in a shop selling things to customers. विक्री सहायक

salesman (salesmen) n A **salesman** is a man whose job is selling things to people. विक्रेता

salesperson (salespeople, salespersons) n A **salesperson** is a person whose job is selling things to people. विक्रेता

sales rep (sales reps) n A **sales rep** is an employee of a company who travels around a particular area selling the company's goods to shops, etc. विक्री प्रतिनिधी

saleswoman (saleswomen) n A **saleswoman** is a woman whose job is selling things to people. विक्रेती

saliva n **Saliva** is the watery liquid that forms in your mouth. लाळ

salmon (salmon) n A **salmon** is a large edible silver-coloured fish with pink flesh. साल्मन नावाचा खाण्याचा मासा

saloon (saloons) n A **saloon** or a **saloon car** is a car with seats for four or more people, a

fixed roof, and a boot that is separated from the rear seats. सलून कार

saloon car (saloons) n A **saloon** or a **saloon car** is a car with seats for four or more people, a fixed roof, and a boot that is separated from the rear seats. सलून कार

salt n Salt is a substance in the form of white powder or crystals, used to improve the flavour of food or to preserve it. Salt occurs naturally in sea water. मीठ

saltwater adj Saltwater fish live in water which is salty. **Saltwater** lakes contain salty water. खाऱ्या पाण्यातील

salty (saltier, saltiest) adj Salty things contain salt or taste of salt. खारट, क्षारयुक्त

salute (salutes, saluting, saluted) v If you **salute** someone, you greet them or show your respect with a formal sign. Soldiers usually salute officers by raising their right hand so that their fingers touch their forehead. सलाम करणे

same adj If two things are the **same**, they are like one another. सारखेच

sample (samples) n A **sample** of a substance or product is a small quantity of it, showing you what it is like. नमुना

sand n **Sand** is a powder that consists of extremely small pieces of stone. वाळू

sandal (sandals) n Sandals are light shoes that have straps instead of a solid part over the top of your foot. सँडल

sandcastle (sandcastles) n A **sandcastle** is a pile of sand made to look like a castle, usually by a child on a beach. लहान मुलांनी बनविलेला वाळूचा किल्ला

sand dune (sand dunes) n A **sand dune** is a hill of sand near the sea or in a sand desert. वाळूची टेकडी

sandpaper n **Sandpaper** is strong paper that has a coating of sand on it. It is used for rubbing wood or metal surfaces to make them smoother. सँडपेपर, खरखरीत कागद

sandpit (sandpits) n A **sandpit** is a shallow hole or box in the ground with sand in it where small children can play. लहान मुलांना खेळण्यासाठी बनविलेला वाळूचा खड्डा

sandstone n **Sandstone** is a type of rock which contains a lot of sand. वाळूचा खडक

sandwich (sandwiches) n A **sandwich** consists of two slices of bread with a layer of food between them. सँडविच नावाचा खाण्याचा पदार्थ

sanitary towel (sanitary towels) n A **sanitary towel** is a pad of thick soft material which women wear to absorb the blood during menstruation. सॅनिटरी टॉवेल

San Marino n **San Marino** is a republic in south central Europe in the Apennines. सॅन मरिनो

sapphire (sapphires) n A **sapphire** is a precious stone which is blue in colour. नीलमणी

sarcastic adj Someone who is **sarcastic** says the opposite of what they really mean in order to mock or insult someone. उपरोधिक

sardine (sardines) n **Sardines** are a kind of small sea fish, often eaten as food. सार्डीन मासा

satchel (satchels) n A **satchel** is a bag with a long strap that schoolchildren use for carrying books. दप्तर

satellite (satellites) n A **satellite** is an object which has been sent into space in order to collect information or to be part of a communications system. कृत्रिम उपग्रह

satellite dish (satellite dishes) n A **satellite dish** is a piece of equipment which receives satellite television signals. उपग्रह तबकडी

satisfaction n **Satisfaction** is the pleasure you feel when you do something you wanted or needed to do. समाधान

satisfactory adj If something is **satisfactory**, it is acceptable to you or fulfils a particular need or purpose. समाधानकारक

satisfied adj If you are **satisfied** with something, you are pleased because you have got what you wanted. समाधानी

satnav n **Satnav** is a system that uses information from satellites to find the best way of getting to a place. It is often found in cars. **Satnav** is an abbreviation for 'satellite navigation'. उपग्रहामार्फत माहिती मिळविण्याची प्रणाली, सॅट-नॅव्ह

Saturday (Saturdays) n **Saturday** is the day after Friday and before Sunday. शनिवार

sauce (sauces) n A **sauce** is a thick liquid which is served with other food. सॉस

saucepan (saucepans) n A **saucepan** is a deep metal cooking pot, usually with a long handle and a lid. सॉसपॅन

saucer (saucers) n A **saucer** is a small curved plate on which you stand a cup. बशी

Saudi (Saudis) adj **Saudi** or **Saudi Arabian** means belonging or relating to Saudi Arabia or to its people, language, or culture. सौदी ▷ n The **Saudis** or **Saudi Arabians** are the people who come from Saudi Arabia. सौदी

Saudi Arabia n **Saudi Arabia** is a kingdom in south-west Asia, between the Persian Gulf and the Red Sea. सौदी अरेबिया

Saudi Arabian (Saudi Arabians) adj **Saudi** or **Saudi Arabian** means belonging or relating to Saudi Arabia or to its people, language, or culture. सौदी अरेबियन ▷ n The **Saudi Arabians** or **Saudis** are the people who come from Saudi Arabia. सौदी अरेबियन

sauna (saunas) n A **sauna** is a hot steam bath. सोना

sausage (sausages) n A **sausage** consists of minced meat, mixed with other ingredients, inside a long thin skin. सॉसेज

save (saves, saving, saved) vt If you **save** someone or something, you help them to escape from danger. वाचवणे ▷ vt If you **save** something, you keep it because you will need it later. बचत करणे

save up (saves up, saving up, saved up) v If you **save up**, you gradually collect money by spending less than you get, usually in order to buy something that you want. बचत करणे She is saving up to buy a car.

savings npl Your **savings** are the money that you have saved, especially in a bank. बचत

savoury adj **Savoury** food has a salty or spicy flavour rather than a sweet one. तिखटमिठाचा

saw (saws) n A **saw** is a tool for cutting wood, which has a blade with sharp teeth along one edge. करवत

sawdust n **Sawdust** is the very fine fragments of wood which are produced when you saw wood. लाकडाचा भुसा

saxophone (saxophones) n A **saxophone** is a musical wind instrument in the shape of a curved metal tube with keys and a curved mouthpiece. सॅक्सोफोन

say (says, saying, said) vt When you **say** something, you talk. बोलणे

saying (sayings) n A **saying** is a traditional sentence that people often say and that gives advice or information about life. जुनी म्हण

scaffolding n **Scaffolding** is a temporary framework of poles and boards that is used by workmen to stand on while they are working on the outside structure of a building. परांची

scale (scales) n A **scale** is a set of levels or numbers which are used in a particular system of measuring things or comparing things. मोजपट्टी ▷ n The **scales** of a fish or reptile are the small, flat pieces of hard skin that cover its body. खवले

scales npl **Scales** are a piece of equipment for weighing things or people. वजने

scallop (scallops) n **Scallops** are large shellfish with two flat fan-shaped shells. Scallops can be eaten. स्कॅलोप नावाचा मासा

scam (scams) n A **scam** is an illegal trick, usually with the purpose of getting money from people or avoiding paying tax. (informal) आर्थिक फसवणूक

scampi npl **Scampi** are large prawns, often served fried in breadcrumbs. मोठ्या कोळंब्या

scan (scans, scanning, scanned) n A **scan** is a medical test in which a machine sends a beam of X-rays over a part of your body in order to check whether your organs are healthy. स्कॅन

▷ **vt** When you **scan** an area, a group of things, or a piece of writing, you look at it carefully, usually because you are looking for something in particular. बारकाईने पाहणे

scandal (scandals) n A **scandal** is a situation, event, or someone's behaviour that shocks a lot of people because they think it is immoral. लोकापवाद, घोटाळा

Scandinavia n **Scandinavia** is a group of northern European countries that includes Denmark, Norway, and Sweden. स्कँडिनेव्हिया

Scandinavian adj **Scandinavian** means belonging or relating to a group of northern European countries that includes Denmark, Norway, and Sweden, or to the people, languages, or culture of those countries. स्कँडिनेव्हियन

scanner (scanners) n A **scanner** is a machine which is used to examine, identify, or record things, for example by moving a beam of light, sound, or X-rays over them. स्कॅनर

scar (scars) n A **scar** is a mark on the skin which is left after a wound has healed. व्रण

scarce (scarcer, scarcest) adj If something is **scarce**, there is not enough of it. तुटपुंजा, दुष्प्राप्य

scarcely adv You use **scarcely** to emphasize that something is only just true. कसाबसा

scare (scares, scaring, scared) n If someone or something gives you a **scare**, they frighten you. भीती ▷ **vt** If something **scares** you, it frightens or worries you. घाबरवणे

scarecrow (scarecrows) n A **scarecrow** is an object in the shape of a person, which is put in a field where crops are growing in order to frighten birds away. बुजगावणे

scared adj If you are **scared** of someone or something, you are frightened of them. घाबरलेला

scarf (scarfs, scarves) n A **scarf** is a piece of cloth that you wear round your neck or head, usually to keep yourself warm. रुमाल

scarlet adj Something that is **scarlet** is bright red. शेंदरी, लालजर्द

scary (scarier, scariest) adj Something that is **scary** is rather frightening. घाबरवणारे, भीतीदायक

scene (scenes) n A **scene** in a play, film, or book is part of it in which a series of events happen in the same place. दृश्य

scenery n The **scenery** in a country area is the land, water, or plants that you can see around you. देखावा

scent (scents) n The **scent** of something is the pleasant smell that it has. सुगंध

sceptical adj If you are **sceptical** about something, you have doubts about it. संशयवादी

schedule (schedules) n A **schedule** is a plan that gives a list of events or tasks and the times at which each one should happen or be done. कामाचे वेळापत्रक

scheme (schemes) n A **scheme** is a plan or arrangement, especially one produced by a government or other organization. योजना

schizophrenic adj Someone who is **schizophrenic** is suffering from a serious mental illness called schizophrenia. स्किझोफ्रेनिया झालेली व्यक्ती

scholarship (scholarships) n If you get a **scholarship** to a school or university, your studies are paid for by the school or university, or by some other organization. शिष्यवृती

school (schools) n A **school** is a place where people go to learn. शाळा

schoolbag (schoolbags) n A **schoolbag** is a bag that children use to carry books and other things to and from school. विद्यार्थी शाळेत नेतात ते दसर

schoolbook (schoolbooks) n **Schoolbooks** are books giving information about a particular subject, which children use at school. पाठ्यपुस्तक

schoolboy (schoolboys) n A **schoolboy** is a boy who goes to school. शाळकरी मुलगा

schoolchildren npl **Schoolchildren** are children who go to school. शाळकरी मुले

schoolgirl (schoolgirls) n A **schoolgirl** is a girl who goes to school. शाळकरी मुलगी

schoolteacher (schoolteachers) n A **schoolteacher** is a person who gives lessons in a school. शाळेतील शिक्षक

school uniform (school uniforms) n A **school uniform** is a special set of clothes which some children wear at school. शाळेचा गणवेश

science n **Science** is the study of the nature and behaviour of natural things and the knowledge that we obtain about them. विज्ञान

science fiction n **Science fiction** consists of stories and films about events that take place in the future or in other parts of the universe. वैज्ञानिक कल्पित कथा वा चित्रपट

scientific adj **Scientific** is used to describe things that relate to science or to a particular science. शास्त्रीय

scientist (scientists) n A **scientist** is someone who has studied science and whose job is to teach or do research in science. शास्त्रज्ञ

sci-fi n **Sci-fi** consists of stories in books, magazines, and films about events that take place in the future or in other parts of the universe. **Sci-fi** is short for 'science fiction'. (informal) वैज्ञानिक कल्पित कथा

scissors npl **Scissors** are a small tool with two sharp blades which are screwed together. You use scissors for cutting things such as paper and cloth. कात्री

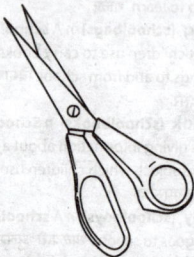

scoff (scoffs, scoffing, scoffed) vi If you **scoff**, you speak in a ridiculing way about something. उपहास करणे

scold (scolds, scolding, scolded) vt If you **scold** someone, you speak angrily to them because they have done something wrong. (formal) खरडपट्टी काढणे

scooter (scooters) n A **scooter** is a small lightweight motorcycle. स्कूटर

score (scores, scoring, scored) n The **score** in a game is the number of points that each team or player has. गुण ▷ n The **score** of a piece of music is the written version of it. संगीताची लिखित स्वरावली ▷ v If you **score** in a game, you get a goal, run, or point. गुणसंख्या

Scorpio n **Scorpio** is one of the twelve signs of the zodiac. Its symbol is a scorpion. People who are born between the 23rd of October and the 21st of November come under this sign. वृश्चिक रास

scorpion (scorpions) n A **scorpion** is a small creature which looks like a large insect. Scorpions have a long curved tail, and some of them are poisonous. विंचू

Scot (Scots) n A **Scot** is a Scottish person. स्कॉटलंडमधील

Scotland n **Scotland** is a country that is part of the United Kingdom, occupying the north of Great Britain. स्कॉटलंड

Scots adj **Scots** means belonging or relating to Scotland, its people, language, or culture. स्कॉटलंडचा

Scotsman (Scotsmen) n A **Scotsman** is a Scottish man. स्कॉटलंडमधील पुरुष

Scotswoman (Scotswomen) n A **Scotswoman** is a Scottish woman. स्कॉटलंडमधील स्त्री

Scottish adj **Scottish** means belonging or relating to Scotland, its people, language, or culture. स्कॉटलंडमधील

scout (scouts) n A **scout** is someone who is sent to an area of countryside to find out the position of an enemy army. स्काऊट

scrambled eggs npl **Scrambled eggs** are eggs that have been broken, mixed together, and then heated and stirred in a pan. फोडून एकत्र करून शिजवलेली अंडी

scrap (scraps, scrapping, scrapped) *n* A **scrap** of something is a very small piece or amount of it. लहान तुकडा ▷ *n* You can refer to a fight or an argument as a **scrap**. भांडण ▷ *vt* If you **scrap** something, you get rid of it or cancel it. रद्द करणे

scrapbook (scrapbooks) *n* A **scrapbook** is a book with empty pages on which you can stick things such as pictures or newspaper articles in order to keep them. स्क्रैपबुक

scrap paper *n* **Scrap paper** is loose pieces of paper used for writing notes on. लिखाणासाठी वापरण्यात येणारा कागद

scratch (scratches, scratching, scratched) *n* **Scratches** on someone or something are small cuts. ओरखडे ▷ *v* If you **scratch** part of your body, you rub your nails against your skin. खाजवणे ▷ *vt* If a sharp thing **scratches** someone or something, it makes small cuts on their skin or on its surface. ओरखडा

scream (screams, screaming, screamed) *n* A **scream** is a sharp piercing cry or sound, especially one caused by fear or pain. किंकाळी ▷ *vi* When someone **screams**, they make a very loud, high-pitched cry, for example because they are in pain or are very frightened. किंकाळी मारणे

screen (screens, screening, screened) *n* A **screen** is the flat vertical surface on which pictures or words are shown on a television, on a computer, or in a cinema. चित्रपट दाखविण्याचा पडदा ▷ *vt* When a film or a television programme **is screened**, it is shown in the cinema or broadcast on television. चित्रपट दाखविणे

screensaver (screensavers) *n* A **screensaver** is a moving picture which appears on a computer screen when the computer is not being used. स्क्रीन सेव्हर

screw (screws) *n* A **screw** is a small metal device for fixing things together. It has a wide top, a pointed end, and a groove along its length. स्क्रू

screwdriver (screwdrivers) *n* A **screwdriver** is a tool for fixing screws into place. स्क्रू ड्रायव्हर

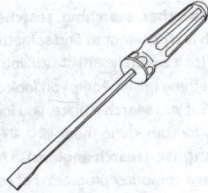

scribble (scribbles, scribbling, scribbled) *v* If you **scribble** or **scribble** something, you write it quickly and untidily. घाईघाईने लिहिणे

scrub (scrubs, scrubbing, scrubbed) *vt* If you **scrub** something, you rub it hard in order to clean it, using a stiff brush and water. घासणे

scuba diving *n* **Scuba diving** is the activity of swimming underwater using special breathing equipment. स्कूबा डायव्हिंग

sculptor (sculptors) *n* A **sculptor** is someone who creates sculptures. शिल्पकार

sculpture (sculptures) *n* A **sculpture** is a work of art that is produced by carving or shaping materials such as stone or clay. शिल्प

sea *n* The **sea** is the salty water that covers much of the earth's surface. समुद्र

seafood *n* **Seafood** refers to shellfish and other sea creatures that you can eat. खाण्यासाठी समुद्रातील पकडतात ते मासे इत्यादी

seagull (seagulls) *n* A **seagull** is a type of bird that lives near the sea. सीगल नावाचा पक्षी

seal (seals, sealing, sealed) *n* A **seal** is an animal which eats fish and lives partly on land and partly in the sea. सील नावाचा प्राणी ▷ *n* A **seal** is an official stamp on a document. मोहर ▷ *vt* When you **seal** an envelope, you close it by folding part of it and sticking it down. बंद करणे

sea level *n* If you are at **sea level**, you are at the same level as the surface of the sea. समुद्रसपाटी

seam (**seams**) *n* A **seam** is a line of stitches joining two pieces of cloth together. शिवण

seaman (**seamen**) *n* A **seaman** is a sailor. खलाशी

search (**searches, searching, searched**) *n* A **search** is an attempt to find something by looking for it carefully. शोध ▷ *v* If you **search for** something or someone, you look carefully for them. If you **search** a place, you look carefully for something there. शोध घेणे

search engine (**search engines**) *n* A **search engine** is a computer program that searches for documents on the Internet. सर्च इंजिन

search party (**search parties**) *n* A **search party** is an organized group of people who are searching for someone who is missing. हरवलेल्या व्यक्तीचा शोध घेणारा गट

seashore (**seashores**) *n* The **seashore** is the part of a coast where the land slopes down into the sea. समुद्रकिनारा

seasick *adj* If someone is **seasick** when they are travelling in a boat, they vomit or feel sick because of the way the boat is moving. समुद्रप्रवासामुळे उलट्या होणे

seaside *n* You can refer to an area that is close to the sea, especially where people go for their holidays, as the **seaside**. समुद्राच्या काठचा प्रदेश

season (**seasons**) *n* The **seasons** are the periods into which a year is divided and which each have their own typical weather conditions. ऋतू

seasonal *adj* **Seasonal** means happening during one particular time of the year. हंगामी

seasoning *n* **Seasoning** is salt, pepper, or spices that are added to food to improve its flavour. अन्नाची चव वाढविण्यासाठी त्यात टाकलेला मीठ, मसाला इत्यादी.

season ticket (**season tickets**) *n* A **season ticket** is a ticket for a series of events, such as football matches, or a number of journeys, that you usually buy at a reduced rate. सिजन तिकीट

seat (**seats**) *n* A **seat** is an object that you can sit on, for example a chair. आसन ▷ *n* When

someone is elected to parliament, you can say that they or their party have won a **seat**. मतदारसंघातील जागा

seatbelt (**seatbelts**) *n* A **seatbelt** is a strap that you fasten across your body for safety when travelling in a car or plane. सीटबेल्ट

sea water *n* **Sea water** is salt water from the sea. खारे पाणी

seaweed (**seaweeds**) *n* **Seaweed** is a plant that grows in the sea. समुद्रात वाढणारे गवत

second (**seconds**) *adj* The **second** thing in a number of things is the one that you count as number two. दुसरा ▷ *n* A **second** is an amount of time. There are sixty seconds in one minute. सेकंद

secondary school (**secondary schools**) *n* A **secondary school** is a school for pupils between the ages of 11 or 12 and 17 or 18. माध्यमिक शाळा

second class *n* **Second class** is accommodation on a train or ship which is cheaper and less comfortable than the first-class accommodation. दुसरा वर्ग ▷ *adj* **Second-class** things are regarded as less valuable or less important than others of the same kind. दुय्यम दर्जाचे

secondhand *adj* **Secondhand** things are not new and have been owned by someone else. पूर्वी दुसऱ्याच्या मालकीचे असलेले

secondly *adv* You say **secondly** when you want to make a second point or give a second reason for something. दुसरे म्हणजे

second-rate *adj* If you describe something as **second-rate**, you mean that it is of poor quality. हलक्या प्रतीचा

secret (**secrets**) *adj* If something is **secret**, it is known about by only a small number of people, and is not told or shown to anyone else. गुप्त ▷ *n* A **secret** is a fact that is known by only a small number of people, and is not told to anyone else. गुपित

secretary (**secretaries**) *n* A **secretary** is a person who is employed to do office work, such as typing letters or answering phone calls. सचिव

secretly *adv* If you do something **secretly**, it is known about by only a small number of people. गुप्तपणे

secret service (secret services) *n* A country's **secret service** is a government department whose job is to find out enemy secrets and to prevent its own government's secrets from being discovered. हेरसंस्था

sect (sects) *n* A **sect** is a group of people that has separated from a larger group and has a particular set of religious or political beliefs. पंथ

section (sections) *n* A **section** of something is one of the parts that it is divided into. हिस्सा

sector (sectors) *n* A **sector** of something, especially a country's economy, is a particular part of it. क्षेत्र

secure *adj* If something such as a job or institution is **secure**, it is safe and reliable, and unlikely to be lost or fail. सुरक्षित

security *n* **Security** refers to all the precautions that are taken to protect a place. सुरक्षाव्यवस्था

security guard (security guards) *n* A **security guard** is someone whose job is to protect a building or to collect and deliver large amounts of money. सुरक्षारक्षक

sedative (sedatives) *n* A **sedative** is a drug that calms you or makes you sleep. गुंगी आणणारे औषध

see (sees, seeing, saw, seen) *v* If you **see** something, you are looking at it or you notice it. पाहणे ▷ *vt* If you **see** someone, you meet them. भेटणे

seed (seeds) *n* A **seed** is one of the small hard parts of a plant from which a new plant grows. बी

seek (seeks, seeking, sought) *vt* If you **seek** something, you try to find it or obtain it. *(formal)* शोधणे

seem (seems, seeming, seemed) *v* You use **seem** to say that someone or something

gives the impression of having a particular quality, or that something gives the impression of happening in the way you describe. वाटणे

seesaw (seesaws) *n* A **seesaw** is a long board which is balanced on a fixed part in the middle. To play on it, a child sits on each end, and when one end goes up, the other goes down. सीसॉ

see-through *adj* **See-through** clothes are made of thin cloth, so that you can see a person's body or underwear through them. (ज्यातून पाहिले जाऊ शकते असे) पातळ/पारदर्शी कपडे

seize (seizes, seizing, seized) *vt* If you **seize** something, you take hold of it quickly and firmly. जबरदस्तीने (घट्ट) पकडणे

seizure (seizures) *n* If someone has a **seizure**, they have a heart attack or a fit. झटका

seldom *adv* If something **seldom** happens, it does not happen very often. क्वचित

select (selects, selecting, selected) *vt* If you **select** something, you choose it from a number of things of the same kind. निवडणे

selection *n* **Selection** is the act of selecting one or more people or things from a group. निवड

self-assured *adj* Someone who is **self-assured** shows confidence in what they say and do because they are sure of their own abilities. स्वतःच्या क्षमतेवर विश्वास असलेला

self-catering *n* If you go on a **self-catering** holiday or you stay in **self-catering** accommodation, you stay in a place where you have to make your own meals. स्वतः अन्न शिजवून खावे लागते असे सहलीचे ठिकाण

self-centred *adj* Someone who is **self-centred** is only concerned with their own wants and needs and never thinks about other people. स्वयंकेंद्री

self-conscious *adj* Someone who is **self-conscious** is easily embarrassed and nervous about the way they look or appear. स्वतःविषयी जागरूक असलेला

self-contained *adj* You can describe someone as **self-contained** when they do not need help or resources from other people. समाधानी

self-control *n* Your **self-control** is your ability to control your feelings and appear calm. स्वतःवरील ताबा

self-defence *n* **Self-defence** is the use of force to protect yourself against someone who is attacking you. स्वसंरक्षण

self-discipline *n* **Self-discipline** is the ability to control yourself and to make yourself work hard or behave in a particular way without needing anyone else to tell you what to do. स्वयंशिस्त

self-employed *adj* If you are **self-employed**, you work for yourself, rather than for someone else. स्वयंरोजगार असणारा

selfish *adj* If you say that someone is **selfish**, you disapprove of them because they care only about themselves, and not about other people. स्वार्थी

self-service *adj* A **self-service** shop, restaurant, or garage is one where you get things for yourself rather than being served by another person. सेल्फ-सर्व्हिस

sell (sells, selling, sold) *vt* If you **sell** something that you own, you let someone have it in return for money. विकणे

sell-by date (sell-by dates) *n* The **sell-by date** on a food container is the date by which the food should be sold or eaten before it starts to decay. तयार पदार्थ ज्या तारखेपूर्वी खाल्ला पाहिजे ती तारीख

selling price (selling prices) *n* The **selling price** of something is the price for which it is sold. विक्रीची किंमत

sell off (sells off, selling off, sold off) *v* If you **sell** something **off**, you sell it because you need the money. विकून टाकणे *The company is selling off some sites and concentrating on cutting debts.*

Sellotape® *n* **Sellotape** is a clear sticky tape that you use to stick paper or card together or onto a wall. सेलोटेप

sell out (sells out, selling out, sold out) *v* If a shop **sells out** of something, it sells all its stocks of it. सर्व वस्तू विकून टाकणे *The supermarket sold out of flour in a single day.*

semester (semesters) *n* In colleges and universities, a **semester** is one of two periods into which the year is divided. सत्र

semicircle (semicircles) *n* A **semicircle** is one half of a circle, or something having the shape of half a circle. अर्धवर्तुळ

semi-colon (semi-colons) *n* A **semi-colon** is the punctuation mark (;) which you use in writing to separate different parts of a sentence. अर्धविराम

semi-detached house (semi-detached houses) *n* A **semi-detached house** is a house that is joined to another house on one side by a shared wall. सामाईक भिंत असलेले दुसरे जोडलेले घर

semifinal (semifinals) *n* A **semifinal** is one of the two matches or races in a competition that are held to decide who will compete in the final. उपांत्य फेरी

semi-skimmed milk *n* **Semi-skimmed milk** or **semi-skimmed** is milk from which some of the cream has been removed. अर्धवट साय काढून घेतलेले दूध

send (sends, sending, sent) *vt* When you **send** someone something, you arrange for them to receive it, for example by post. पाठविणे

send back (sends back, sending back, sent back) *v* When you **send** something **back**, you arrange for it to be taken and delivered to the person who sent it to you, for example by post. परत पाठविणे *The camera was damaged, so I sent it back to the manufacturer.*

sender (senders) *n* The **sender** of a letter, package, or radio message is the person who sent it. प्रेषक

send off (sends off, sending off, sent off) *v* If you **send off** a letter or parcel, you send it somewhere by post. टपालाने पाठवून देणे *He sent off copies to various people.*

send out (**sends out, sending out, sent out**) v If you **send out** things such as leaflets or bills, you send them to a large number of people at the same time. वाटणे *She sent out four hundred invitations to the party.*

Senegal n **Senegal** is a republic in West Africa, on the Atlantic. सेनेगल

Senegalese (**Senegalese**) adj **Senegalese** means belonging or relating to Senegal, or to its people or culture. सेनेगलिज ▷ n A **Senegalese** is a Senegalese citizen, or a person of Senegalese origin. सेनेगलिज

senior adj The **senior** people in an organization have the highest and most important jobs in it. वरिष्ठ

senior citizen (**senior citizens**) n A **senior citizen** is a person who is old enough to receive an old-age pension. ज्येष्ठ नागरिक

sensational adj A **sensational** event or situation is so remarkable that it causes great excitement and interest. सनसनाटी

sense (**senses**) n Your **senses** are the physical abilities of sight, smell, hearing, touch, and taste. जाणीव

senseless adj A **senseless** action seems to have no meaning or purpose. निरर्थक

sense of humour n Someone's **sense of humour** is the fact that they find certain things amusing. विनोदबुद्धी

sensible adj A **sensible** person is able to make good decisions and judgements based on reason. समजूतदार

sensitive adj If you are **sensitive** to other people's problems and feelings, you understand and are aware of them. समज असलेले, संवेदनशील

sensuous adj **Sensuous** things give pleasure to the mind or body through the senses. इंद्रियांना सुखद वाटणारा

sentence (**sentences, sentencing, sentenced**) n A **sentence** is a group of words which, when they are written down, begin with a capital letter and end with a full stop, question mark, or exclamation mark. Most sentences contain a subject and a verb. वाक्य ▷ n In a law court, a **sentence** is the punishment that a person receives after they have been found guilty of a crime. शिक्षा ▷ vt When a judge **sentences** someone, he or she states in court what their punishment will be. शिक्षा सुनावणे

sentimental adj A **sentimental** person or thing feels or makes you feel emotions such as tenderness, affection, or sadness, sometimes in a way that is exaggerated or foolish. भावनाप्रधान

separate (**separates, separating, separated**) adj If one thing is **separate** from another, the two things are apart and are not connected. वेगळे ▷ v If you **separate** people or things that are together, or if they **separate**, they move apart. वेगळे करणे

separately adv If people or things are dealt with **separately** or do something **separately**, they are dealt with or do something at different times or places, rather than together. स्वतंत्रपणे

separation (**separations**) n The **separation** of two or more things or groups is the fact that they are separate or become separate, and are not linked. वेगळे होणे

September (**Septembers**) n **September** is the ninth month of the year in the Western calendar. सप्टेंबर

septic tank (**septic tanks**) n A **septic tank** is an underground tank where faeces, urine, and other waste matter is made harmless using bacteria. मलमूत्र साठविण्याची टाकी

sequel (**sequels**) n The **sequel** to a book or film is another book or film which continues the story. पुस्तक किंवा चित्रपटाच्या मालिकेतील पुढील भाग

sequence (**sequences**) n A **sequence** of things is a number of them that come one after another in a particular order. क्रम

Serbia n **Serbia** is a republic in south-east Europe. सर्बिया

S

Serbian (**Serbians**) *adj* **Serbian** means of, relating to, or characteristic of Serbia, its people, or their language. सर्बियन ▷ *n* A **Serbian** is a native or inhabitant of Serbia. सर्बियन ▷ *n* **Serbian** is the language spoken in Serbia. सर्बियन

sergeant (**sergeants**) *n* A **sergeant** is an officer in the army or the police. सैन्यातील साजेंट

serial (**serials**) *n* A **serial** is a story which is broadcast or published in a number of parts over a period of time. मालिका

series (**series**) *n* A **series** of things or events is a number of them that come one after the other. घटनांची मालिका

serious *adj* **Serious** problems or situations are very bad and cause people to be worried or afraid. गंभीर

seriously *adv* **Seriously** means that something is done in a serious manner or to a serious degree. गंभीरपणे

servant (**servants**) *n* A **servant** is someone who is employed to work in another person's house, for example to cook or clean. नोकर

serve (**serves, serving, served**) *n* A **serve** is when you hit a ball or a shuttlecock in a game of tennis or badminton in order to start the game. खेळातील सर्व्ह ▷ *vt* If you **serve** your country, an organization, or a person, you do useful work for them. सेवा करणे

server (**servers**) *n* A **server** is part of a computer network which does a particular task, for example storing or working on information, for all or part of the network. सर्व्हर ▷ *n* In tennis and badminton, the **server** is the player whose turn it is to hit the ball or shuttlecock to start play. खेळातील सर्व्ह करणारा

service (**services, servicing, serviced**) *n* A **service** is an organization or system that provides something for the public. सेवा ▷ *vt* If you have a vehicle or machine **serviced**, you arrange for someone to examine, adjust, and clean it so that it will keep working efficiently and safely. वाहनाची सर्व्हिसिंग

service area (**service areas**) *n* A **service area** is a place beside a motorway where you can buy petrol and other things, or have a meal. रस्त्याच्या कडेला पेट्रोल, जेवण आदि मिळते ते ठिकाण

service charge (**service charges**) *n* A **service charge** is an amount that is added to your bill in a restaurant to pay for the work of the person who comes and serves you. सेवा आकार

serviceman (**servicemen**) *n* A **serviceman** is a man who is in the army, navy, or air force. सैन्यातील माणूस

service station (**service stations**) *n* A **service station** is a place that sells things such as petrol, oil, and spare parts. Service stations often sell food, drink, and other goods. सेवा केंद्र

servicewoman (**servicewomen**) *n* A **servicewoman** is a woman who is in the army, navy, or air force. सैन्यातील स्त्री

serviette (**serviettes**) *n* A **serviette** is a square of cloth or paper that you use to protect your clothes or to wipe your mouth when you are eating. सर्व्हिएट (जेवताना अंगावर घ्यायचा वा तोंड पुसायचा कपडा)

session (**sessions**) *n* A **session** is a meeting or series of meetings of a court, parliament, or other official group. सत्र

set (**sets, setting**) *n* A **set** of things is a number of things that belong together. संच ▷ *vt* If you **set** something somewhere, you put it there. बसविणे

setback (**setbacks**) *n* A **setback** is an event that delays your progress or reverses some of the progress that you have made. पीछेहाट

set off (**sets off, setting off**) *v* When you **set off**, you start a journey. प्रवास सुरू करणे *He set off for the station.*

set out (**sets out, setting out**) *v* When you **set out**, you start a journey. प्रवास सुरू करणे *I set out for home.*

settee (**settees**) *n* A **settee** is a long comfortable seat with a back and arms, for two or three people. तीन माणसांसाठी रेलून बसण्याचे आसन

settle (settles, settling, settled) *vt* If two people **settle** an argument or problem, or if someone or something **settles** it, they solve it by making a decision about who is right or about what to do. मिटवणे

settle down (settles down, settling down, settled down) *v* When someone **settles down**, they start living a quiet life in one place, especially when they get married or buy a house. स्थिरस्थावर होणे *One day I'll settle down and have a family.*

seven *num* **Seven** is the number 7. सात

seventeen *num* **Seventeen** is the number 17. सतरा

seventeenth *adj* The **seventeenth** item in a series is the one that you count as number seventeen. सतरावा

seventh (sevenths) *adj* The **seventh** item in a series is the one that you count as number seven. सातवा ▷ *n* A **seventh** is one of seven equal parts of something. सातवा भाग

seventy *num* **Seventy** is the number 70. सत्तर

several *det* **Several** is used to talk about a number of people or things that is not large but is greater than two. अनेक *I lived there for several years.* ▷ *pron* **Several** means a small number of people or things that is greater than two. अनेक *You may have to try several before you find the right treatment.*

sew (sews, sewing, sewed, sewn) *v* When you **sew** something such as clothes, you make them or repair them by joining pieces of cloth together by passing thread through them with a needle. शिवणे

sewer (sewers) *n* A **sewer** is a large underground channel that carries waste matter and rainwater away. गटाराचा पाईप

sewing *n* **Sewing** is the activity of making or mending clothes or other things using a needle and thread. शिवणकाम

sewing machine (sewing machines) *n* A **sewing machine** is a machine that you use for sewing. शिलाई यंत्र

sew up (sews up, sewing up, sewed up, sewn up) *v* If you **sew up** pieces of cloth or tears in cloth or skin, you join them together using a needle and thread. शिवून एकत्र जोडणे *Next day, Miss Stone decided to sew up the rip.*

sex (sexes) *n* The **sexes** are the two groups, male and female, into which people and animals are divided. लिंग

sexism *n* **Sexism** is the belief that men and women need not be treated fairly and equally. स्त्रियांना गौण समजणे

sexist *adj* If you describe people or their behaviour as **sexist**, you disapprove of the fact that they believe that men and women need not be treated fairly and equally. स्त्रियांना गौण समजणारा

shabby (shabbier, shabbiest) *adj* **Shabby** things or places look old and in bad condition. गबाळा

shade *n* **Shade** is a cool area of darkness where the sun does not reach. छाया

shadow (shadows) *n* A **shadow** is a dark shape on a surface that is made when something stands between a light and the surface. सावली

shake (shakes, shaking, shook, shaken) *vt* If you **shake** something, you hold it and move it quickly up and down. हलविणे ▷ *vi* If someone or something **shakes**, they move quickly backwards and forwards or up and down. हलणे

shaken *adj* If you are **shaken**, you are upset and unable to think calmly. हादरलेला

shaky (shakier, shakiest) *adj* If your body or your voice is **shaky**, you cannot control it properly and it trembles, for example because you are ill or nervous. थरथरणारा

shall *v* You use **shall**, usually with 'I' and 'we', when you are talking about something that will happen in the future. एखादी कृती करीन, करू *I shall know more tomorrow.*

shallow (shallower, shallowest) *adj* A **shallow** hole, container, or layer of water measures only a short distance from the top to the bottom. उथळ

shambles *n* If a place, event, or situation is a **shambles**, everything is in disorder. गोंधळ

shame *n* **Shame** is the very uncomfortable feeling that you have when you have done something wrong or stupid. लाज

shampoo (shampoos) *n* **Shampoo** is a liquid that you use for washing your hair. शेंप्

shape (shapes) *n* The **shape** of an object, a person, or an area is the form or pattern of its outline. आकार

circle

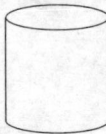

cylinder

oval

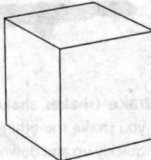

cube

square

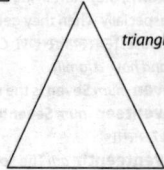

triangle

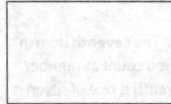

rectangle

share (shares, sharing, shared) *n* If you have or do your **share** of something, you have or do the amount that is reasonable or fair. वाटा ▷ *vt* If you **share** something with another person, you both have it, use it, do it, or experience it. विभागून घेणे

shareholder (shareholders) *n* A **shareholder** is a person who owns shares in a company. भागधारक

share out (shares out, sharing out, shared out) *v* If you **share** something **out**, you give each person in a group an equal or fair part of it. हिस्सा देणे *The funding will be shared out between universities, hospitals, and research bodies.*

shark (sharks) *n* **Sharks** are very large fish with sharp teeth. शार्क मासा

sharp (sharper, sharpest) *adj* A **sharp** point or edge is very thin and can cut through things quickly. धारदार ▷ *adj* A **sharp** feeling is sudden and is very big or strong. तीव्र

shave (shaves, shaving, shaved) *v* When a man **shaves**, he removes the hair from his face using a razor or shaver so that his face is smooth. दाढी करणे

shaver (**shavers**) *n* A shaver is an electric device used for shaving hair from the face and body. दाढी करण्याचे विजेवर चालणारे साधन

shaving cream (**shaving creams**) *n* Shaving cream is a soft soapy substance which men put on their face before they shave. शेव्हिंग क्रीम

shaving foam (**shaving foams**) *n* Shaving foam is a soft soapy substance which men put on their face before they shave. शेव्हिंग फोम

shawl (**shawls**) *n* A shawl is a large piece of woollen cloth worn over a woman's shoulders or head, or wrapped around a baby to keep it warm. शाल

she *pron* You use she to talk about a woman, a girl, or a female animal. ती *She's seventeen years old.*

shed (**sheds**) *n* A shed is a small building used for storing things such as garden tools. पडवी, टपरी

sheep (**sheep**) *n* A sheep is a farm animal with a thick woolly coat. मेंढी

sheepdog (**sheepdogs**) *n* A sheepdog is a breed of dog. Some sheepdogs are used for controlling sheep. शिपडॉग जातीचा कुत्रा

sheepskin (**sheepskins**) *n* Sheepskin is the skin of a sheep with the wool still attached to it, used especially for making coats and rugs. मेंढीची लोकरीसहित असलेली कातडी

sheer (**sheerer, sheerest**) *adj* You can use sheer to emphasize that a state or situation is complete and does not involve anything else. निव्वळ, केवळ

sheet (**sheets**) *n* A sheet is a large piece of cloth that you sleep on or cover yourself with in bed. चादर ▷ *n* A sheet is a piece of paper, glass, plastic, or metal. कागद

shelf (**shelves**) *n* A shelf is a flat piece of wood, metal, or glass which is attached to a wall or to the sides of a cupboard. फळी, कोनाडा

shell (**shells**) *n* The shell of an egg or nut is its hard part. कवच ▷ *n* The shell of an animal such as a snail is the hard part that covers its back and protects it. खवले

shellfish (**shellfish**) *n* A shellfish is a small creature with a shell that lives in the sea. कवचातील मासे

shell suit (**shell suits**) *n* A shell suit is a casual suit which is made of thin nylon. शेल सूट

shelter (**shelters**) *n* A shelter is a small building or covered place which is made to protect people from bad weather or danger. निवाऱ्याची जागा

shepherd (**shepherds**) *n* A shepherd is a person whose job is to look after sheep. धनगर

sherry (**sherries**) *n* Sherry is a type of strong wine that is made in south-western Spain. शेरी नावाचे मद्य

shield (**shields**) *n* A shield is a large piece of metal or leather which soldiers carried in the past to protect their bodies. ढाल

shift (**shifts, shifting, shifted**) *n* If someone's opinion, a situation, or a policy changes slightly, the change is called a shift. बदल ▷ *v* If you shift something, or if it shifts, it moves slightly. सरकणे

shifty (**shiftier, shiftiest**) *adj* Someone who looks shifty gives the impression of being dishonest. (*informal*) अप्रामाणिक

shin (**shins**) *n* Your shin is the front part of your leg between your knee and ankle. पायाची नळी, नडगी

shine (**shines, shining, shined, shone**) *vi* When the sun or a light shines, it gives out bright light. चमकणे

shiny (**shinier, shiniest**) *adj* Shiny things are bright and reflect light. चमकदार

ship (**ships**) *n* A ship is a large boat which carries passengers or cargo. जहाज

shipbuilding *n* Shipbuilding is the industry of building ships. जहाजबांधणी उद्योग

shipment (**shipments**) *n* A shipment is an amount of a particular kind of cargo that is sent to another country on a ship, train,

S

aeroplane, or other vehicle. जहाज, विमान इत्यादीमधून न्यायचे सामान

shipwreck (shipwrecks) n When there is a **shipwreck**, a ship is destroyed in an accident at sea. जहाज फुटण्याची क्रिया

shipwrecked adj If someone is **shipwrecked**, their ship is destroyed in an accident at sea but they survive and manage to reach land. फुटलेल्या जहाजातून वाचलेले (व्यक्ती, सामान, इ.)

shipyard (shipyards) n A **shipyard** is a place where ships are built and repaired. जहाज बांधण्याची व दुरुस्त करण्याची जागा

shirt (shirts) n A **shirt** is a piece of clothing worn on the upper part of your body with a collar, sleeves, and buttons down the front. सदरा, शर्ट

shiver (shivers, shivering, shivered) vi When you **shiver**, your body shakes slightly because you are cold or frightened. थरथर कापणे

shock (shocks, shocking, shocked) n If you have a **shock**, you suddenly have an unpleasant or surprising experience. धक्कादायक अनुभव ▷ vt If something **shocks** you, it makes you feel very upset. अस्वस्थ करणे

shocking adj You can say that something is **shocking** if you think that it is very bad. (informal) धक्कादायक

shoe (shoes) n **Shoes** are objects worn on your feet. शू, पादत्राण

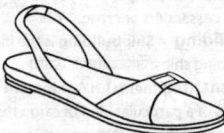

shoelace (shoelaces) n **Shoelaces** are long, narrow pieces of material like pieces of string that you use to fasten your shoes. शू लेस, बुटाची नाडी

shoe polish (shoe polishes) n **Shoe polish** is a substance that you put on your shoes in order to clean them, protect them, and make them shine. शू पॉलिश

shoe shop (shoe shops) n A **shoe shop** is a shop that sells shoes. पादत्राणांचे दुकान

shoot (shoots, shooting, shot) vt To **shoot** a person or animal means to kill or injure them by firing a gun at them. गोळी घालणे

shooting (shootings) n A **shooting** is an occasion when someone is killed or injured by being shot with a gun. गोळीबार

shop (shops) n A **shop** is a building or part of a building where things are sold. दुकान

shop assistant (shop assistants) n A **shop assistant** is a person who works in a shop selling things to customers. दुकानात काम करणारा

shopkeeper (shopkeepers) n A **shopkeeper** is a person who owns a small shop. दुकानदार

shoplifting n **Shoplifting** is stealing from a shop by hiding things in a bag or in your clothes. दुकानातून वस्तू चोरणे

shopping n When you do the **shopping**, you go to shops and buy things. खरेदी

shopping bag (shopping bags) n A **shopping bag** is a strong container with one or two handles, used to carry things in when you go shopping. खरेदीची पिशवी

shopping centre (shopping centres) n A **shopping centre** is an area in a town where a lot of shops have been built close together. शॉपिंग सेंटर

shopping trolley (shopping trolleys) n A **shopping trolley** is a large metal basket on wheels which is provided by shops such as supermarkets for customers to use while they are in the shop. शॉपिंग ट्रॉली

shop window (shop windows) n A **shop window** is a large piece of glass along the front of a shop, behind which some of the goods that the shop sells are displayed. दुकानातील सामानाचे प्रदर्शन व्हावे म्हणून लावलेली काच

shore (shores) n The **shores** or the **shore** of a sea, lake, or wide river is the land along the edge of it. किनारा

short (shorter, shortest) adj If something is **short**, it does not last very long. अल्पकालीन ▷ adj A **short** thing is small in length, distance, or height. आखूड

shortage (shortages) n If there is a **shortage** of something, there is not enough of it. तुटवडा

shortcoming (shortcomings) n The **shortcomings** of a person or thing are their faults or weaknesses. कमतरता, दोष

shortcrust pastry n **Shortcrust pastry** is a type of pastry that is used to make pies and tarts. शॉर्टक्रस्ट पेस्ट्री

shortcut (shortcuts) n A **shortcut** is a quicker way of getting somewhere than the usual route. जवळचा रस्ता

shortfall (shortfalls) n If there is a **shortfall** in something, there is not enough of it. तुटवडा

shorthand n **Shorthand** is a quick way of writing which uses signs to represent words or syllables. लघुलेखन

shortlist (shortlists) n A **shortlist** is a list of people or things which have been chosen

from a larger group, for example for a job or a prize. The successful person or thing is then chosen from the small group. निवडक गोष्टींची यादी

shortly adv If something happens **shortly** after or before something else, it happens a short amount of time after or before it. थोड्या वेळापूर्वी, थोडक्यात

shorts npl **Shorts** are trousers with short legs. आखूड चड्डी

short-sighted adj If you are **short-sighted**, you cannot see things properly when they are far away, because there is something wrong with your eyes. दूरचे न दिसणारा

short-sleeved adj A **short-sleeved** shirt, dress, or other item of clothing has sleeves that cover the top part of your arms. आखूड बाह्यांचा

short story (short stories) n A **short story** is a written story about imaginary events that is only a few pages long. लघुकथा

shot (shots) n If you fire a **shot**, you fire a gun once. बंदुकीचा बार

shotgun (shotguns) n A **shotgun** is a gun which fires a lot of small metal balls at one time. शॉटगन

should v You use **should** when you are saying what is the right thing to do. .... करावे He should tell us what happened.

shoulder (shoulders) n Your **shoulders** are the parts of your body between your neck and the tops of your arms. खांदा

shoulder blade (shoulder blades) n Your **shoulder blades** are the two large, flat, triangular bones that you have in the upper part of your back, below your shoulders. पाठीच्या वरच्या भागातील खांदाखालची दोन हाडे

shout (shouts, shouting, shouted) n A **shout** is the noise made when someone speaks very loudly. मोठा आवाज, आरोळी ▷ v If you **shout**, you say something very loudly, usually because you want people a long distance away to hear you or because you are angry. मोठ्या आवाजात ओरडणे

S

shovel (shovels) n A **shovel** is a tool like a spade, used for lifting and moving earth, coal, or snow. फावडे

show (shows, showing, showed, shown) n A **show** of a feeling is an attempt by someone to make it clear that they have that feeling. दाखवून देणे ▷ vt If information or a fact **shows** that a situation exists, it proves it. दाखवणे ▷ v If you **show** someone something, you let them see it. दाखवणे ▷ vt If you **show** someone how to do something, you teach them how to do it. दाखवणे

show business n **Show business** is the entertainment industry. मनोरंजन उद्योग

shower (showers) n A **shower** is a thing that you stand under, that covers you with water so you can wash yourself. शॉवर ▷ n A **shower** is a short period of rain. पावसाची सर

shower cap (shower caps) n A **shower cap** is a waterproof cap that you wear in the shower to keep your hair dry. शॉवर कॅप

shower gel (shower gels) n **Shower gel** is liquid soap you use in the shower. शॉवर जेल

showerproof adj If a coat or jacket is **showerproof**, it keeps you dry in light rain, but not in heavy rain. पाणी आत न येणारे, जलरोधक

showing (showings) n A **showing** is a presentation, exhibition, or display. प्रदर्शन

show jumping n **Show jumping** is a sport in which horses are ridden in competitions to demonstrate their skill in jumping over fences and walls. शो जंपिंग

show off (shows off, showing off, showed off, shown off, show-offs) v If you say that someone **is showing off**, you are criticizing them for trying to impress people by showing in a very obvious way what they can do or what they own. दिखाऊपणा करणे All right, there's no need to show off. ▷ n If you say that someone is a **show-off**, you are criticizing them for trying to impress people by showing in a very obvious way what they can do or what they own. (informal) दिखाऊपणा

show up (shows up, showing up, showed up, shown up) v If a person you are expecting to meet does not **show up**, they do not arrive at the place where you expect to meet them. येणे, तोंड दाखवणे We waited until five o'clock, but he did not show up.

shriek (shrieks, shrieking, shrieked) vi When someone **shrieks**, they make a short, very loud cry, for example, because they are suddenly surprised, are in pain, or are laughing. किंकाळी मारणे

shrimp (shrimps, shrimp) n **Shrimps** are small shellfish with long tails and many legs. कोळंबी मासा

shrine (shrines) n A **shrine** is a holy place associated with a sacred person or object. प्रार्थनास्थळ, पवित्र स्थळ

shrink (shrinks, shrinking, shrank, shrunk) v If something **shrinks** or you **shrink** it, becomes smaller. आखडणे

shrub (shrubs) n **Shrubs** are low plants like small trees with several stems instead of a trunk. झुडूप

shrug (shrugs, shrugging, shrugged) vi If you **shrug**, you raise your shoulders to show that you are not interested in something or that you do not know or care about something. खांदे उडवणे

shrunken adj Someone or something that is **shrunken** has become smaller than they used to be. आखडलेला

shudder (shudders, shuddering, shuddered) vi If you **shudder**, you shake with fear, horror, or disgust, or because you are cold. थरकाप उडणे, कापरे भरणे

shuffle (shuffles, shuffling, shuffled) *vi* If you **shuffle** somewhere, you walk there without lifting your feet properly off the ground. पाय घाशीत चालणे

shut (shuts, shutting) *v* If you **shut** something such as a door or if it **shuts**, it moves so that it fills a hole or a space. बंद करणे

shut down (shuts down, shutting down) *v* If a factory or business **is shut down**, it is closed permanently. बंद करणे *Smaller contractors were forced to shut down.*

shutters *npl* **Shutters** are wooden or metal covers fitted on the outside of a window. They can be opened to let in the light, or closed to keep out the sun or the cold. शटर्स

shuttle (shuttles) *n* A **shuttle** is a spacecraft that is designed to travel into space and back to earth several times. अवकाश यान

shuttlecock (shuttlecocks) *n* A **shuttlecock** is the small object that you hit over the net in a game of badminton. शटलकॉक

shut up (shuts up, shutting up) *v* If you **shut up**, you stop talking. If you say '**shut up**' to someone, you are rudely telling them to stop talking. बोलणे बंद करणे *He wished she would shut up.*

shy (shyer, shyest) *adj* A **shy** person is nervous and uncomfortable in the company of other people. लाजाळू

Siberia *n* **Siberia** is a vast region of Russia and north Kazakhstan. सायबेरिया

siblings *npl* Your **siblings** are your brothers and sisters. *(formal)* भावंडे

sick (sicker, sickest) *adj* If you are **sick**, you are ill. आजारी

sickening *adj* You describe something as **sickening** when it gives you feelings of horror or disgust, or makes you feel sick in your stomach. शिसारी आणणारा

sick leave *n* **Sick leave** is the time that a person spends away from work because of illness or injury. आजारपणात घेतलेली रजा,

sickness *n* **Sickness** is the state of being ill or unhealthy. आजारपण

sick note (sick notes) *n* A **sick note** is an official note signed by a doctor which states that someone is ill and needs to stay off work for a particular period of time. आजारपणाचे प्रमाणपत्र, सीक नोट

sick pay *n* When you are ill and unable to work, **sick pay** is the money that you get from your employer instead of your normal wages. आजारपणात घेतलेला पगार

side (sides) *n* The **side** of something is a place to the left or right of it. बाजू ▷ *n* The **side** of something is its edge. बाजू ▷ *n* The different **sides** in a game are the groups of people who are playing against each other. बाजू

sideboard (sideboards) *n* A **sideboard** is a long cupboard which is about the same height as a table. Sideboards are usually kept in dining rooms to put plates and glasses in. साईडबोर्ड

side effect (side effects) *n* The **side effects** of a drug are the effects, usually bad ones, that the drug has on you in addition to its job of curing illness or pain. दुष्परिणाम

sidelight (sidelights) *n* The **sidelights** on a vehicle are the small lights at the front that help other drivers to notice the vehicle and to judge its width. वाहनाच्या साईडलाईट्स

side street (side streets) *n* A **side street** is a quiet, often narrow street which leads off a busier street. मुख्य रस्त्याला सोडून जाणारा बाजूचा रस्ता उपरस्ता

sideways *adv* **Sideways** means from or towards the side of something or someone. बाजूला

sieve (sieves) *n* A **sieve** is a tool consisting of a metal or plastic ring with a fine wire net attached. It is used for separating liquids from solids or larger pieces of something from smaller pieces. चाळण

sigh (sighs, sighing, sighed) *n* When you let out a **sigh**, you let out a deep breath.

निःश्वास ▷ *vi* When you **sigh**, you let out a deep breath, as a way of expressing feelings such as disappointment, tiredness, or pleasure. निःश्वास टाकणे

sight (**sights**) *n* Your **sight** is your ability to see. दृष्टी

sightseeing *n* **Sightseeing** is the activity of visiting the interesting places that tourists usually visit. प्रेक्षणीय स्थळे पाहणे

sign (**signs, signing, signed**) *n* A **sign** is a mark or a shape that has a special meaning. चिन्ह ▷ *v* When you **sign** a document, you write your name on it. सही ▷ *n* You can make a **sign** to somebody by moving something. खाणाखुणा

signal (**signals, signalling, signalled**) *n* A **signal** is a sound or action which is intended to send a particular message. संकेत ▷ *v* If you **signal** something, or if you **signal** to someone, you make a gesture or sound in order to give someone a particular message. खूण दाखवणे

signature (**signatures**) *n* Your **signature** is your name, written in your own characteristic way. सही

significance *n* The **significance** of something is its importance. महत्त्व

significant *adj* A **significant** amount of something is large enough to be important or noticeable. महत्त्वाचे

sign language (**sign languages**) *n* **Sign language** is movements of your hands and arms used to communicate. There are several official systems of sign language, used, for example, by deaf people. खुणांची भाषा

sign on (**signs on, signing on, signed on**) *v* In the UK, when an unemployed person **signs on**, they officially inform the authorities that they are unemployed, so that they can receive money from the government in order to live. बेरोजगारी घोषित करणे *He has signed on at the job centre.*

signpost (**signposts**) *n* A **signpost** is a sign where roads meet that tells you which direction to go in to reach a particular place or different places. कोणता रस्ता कुठे जातो ते सांगणारा फलक

Sikh (**Sikhs**) *adj* **Sikh** means of or relating to Sikhs or their religious beliefs and customs. शीख ▷ *n* A **Sikh** is a member of an Indian religion which separated from Hinduism in the sixteenth century and which teaches that there is only one God. शीख

silence (**silences**) *n* If there is **silence**, it is completely quiet. शांतता

silencer (**silencers**) *n* A **silencer** is a device that is fitted onto a gun to make it very quiet when it is fired. सायलेन्सर

silent *adj* If something is **silent**, it is quiet, with no sound at all. शांत ▷ *adj* If you are **silent**, you are not talking. गप्प

silicon chip (**silicon chips**) *n* A **silicon chip** is a very small piece of material inside a computer. It has electronic circuits on it and can hold large quantities of information or perform mathematical or logical operations. सिलिकॉन चिप

silk (**silks**) *n* **Silk** is a very smooth, fine cloth made from a substance produced by a kind of moth. रेशीम

silly (**sillier, silliest**) *adj* Someone who is being **silly** is behaving in a foolish or childish way. मूर्ख

silver *n* **Silver** is a valuable greyish-white metal used for making jewellery and ornaments. चांदी

similar *adj* If one thing is **similar to** another, or if a number of things are **similar**, they have features that are the same. सारखा

similarity (**similarities**) *n* If there is a **similarity** between two or more things, they share some features that are the same. सारखेपणा

simmer (**simmers, simmering, simmered**) *v* When you **simmer** food, you cook it gently at just below boiling point. मंद उकळणे

simple (**simpler, simplest**) *adj* If something is **simple**, it is not complicated, and is therefore easy to understand or do. सोपा

simplify (simplifies, simplifying, simplified) *vt* If you **simplify** something, you make it easier to understand. सोपे करणे

simply *adv* **Simply** means in a simple and uncomplicated manner. सोपेपणाने, सोप्या रीतीने

simultaneous *adj* Things which are **simultaneous** happen or exist at the same time. एकाच वेळी

simultaneously *adv* If things happen or exist **simultaneously** they happen or exist at the same time. एकाच वेळी

since *adv* You use **since** when you are talking about something that started in the past, and that has not stopped from then until now. तेव्हा पासून ▷ *conj* You use **since** when you are talking about something that started in the past, and that has not stopped from then until now. तेव्हा पासून *I've lived here since I was six years old.* ▷ *prep* You use **since** when you are talking about something that started in the past, and that has not stopped from then until now. पासून *I've not seen her since my birthday.*

sincere *adj* If you say that someone is **sincere**, you approve of them because they really mean the things they say. प्रामाणिक

sincerely *adv* If you say or feel something **sincerely**, you really mean it or feel it. प्रामाणिकपणे

sing (sings, singing, sang, sung) *v* If you **sing**, you make musical sounds with your voice, usually producing words that fit a tune. गाणे

singer (singers) *n* A **singer** is a person who sings, especially as a job. गायक

singing *n* **Singing** is the activity of making musical sounds with your voice. गायन

single *adj* You use **single** to emphasize that you are referring to one thing, and no more than one thing. एकच, एकही

single parent (single parents) *n* A **single parent** is someone who is bringing up a child or children on their own, because the other parent is not living with them. एकटा पालक

singles *npl* **Singles** is a game of tennis or badminton in which one player plays another. एकेरी स्पर्धा

single ticket (single tickets) *n* A **single ticket** is a ticket for a journey from one place to another but not back again. एकेरी तिकीट

singular *n* **The singular** of a noun is the form of it that is used to refer to one person or thing. एकवचन

sinister *adj* Someone or something that is **sinister** seems evil or harmful. अभद्र, अशुभ

sink (sinks, sinking, sank, sunk) *n* A **sink** is a basin with taps that supply water. सिंक ▷ *v* If a boat **sinks**, or if something **sinks** it, it disappears below the surface of a mass of water. बुडणे

sinus (sinuses) *n* Your **sinuses** are the spaces in the bone behind your nose. नाकामागील पोकळी

sir (sirs) *n* People sometimes say **sir** as a polite way of addressing a man. सर, महाशय

siren (sirens) *n* A **siren** is a warning device which makes a long, loud, wailing noise. Most fire engines, ambulances, and police cars have sirens. भोंगा

sister (sisters) *n* Your **sister** is a girl or woman who has the same parents as you. बहीण

sister-in-law (sisters-in-law) *n* Your **sister-in-law** is the sister of your husband or wife, or the woman who is married to your brother. मेहुणी, नणंद, वहिनी

sit (sits, sitting, sat) *vi* If you **are sitting** somewhere, for example in a chair, your weight is supported by your buttocks rather than your feet. बसणे

sitcom (sitcoms) *n* A **sitcom** is an amusing television drama series about a set of characters. **Sitcom** is an abbreviation for 'situation comedy'. सय स्थितीवर भाष्य करणारा विनोदी कार्यक्रम

sit down (sits down, sitting down, sat down) *v* When you **sit down** somewhere, you lower your body until you are sitting on something. खाली बसणे *He sat down beside me.*

s

site (sites) *n* A **site** is a piece of ground that is used for a particular purpose or where a particular thing happens or is situated. एखादी विशिष्ट जागा

sitting room (sitting rooms) *n* A **sitting room** is a room in a house where people sit and relax. दिवाणखाना

situated *adj* If something is **situated** somewhere, it is in a particular place or position. स्थित

situation (situations) *n* You use **situation** to refer generally to what is happening at a particular place and time, or to refer to what is happening to you. परिस्थिती

six *num* Six is the number 6. सहा

sixteen *num* Sixteen is the number 16. सोळा

sixteenth *adj* The **sixteenth** item in a series is the one that you count as number sixteen. सोळावा

sixth *adj* The **sixth** item in a series is the one that you count as number six. सहावा

sixty *num* Sixty is the number 60. साठ

size (sizes) *n* The **size** of something is how big or small it is. आकार

skate (skates, skating, skated) *vi* If you **skate**, you move about wearing ice-skates or roller-skates. स्केट

skateboard (skateboards) *n* A **skateboard** is a narrow board with wheels at each end, which people stand on and ride for pleasure. स्केट बोर्ड

skateboarding *n* **Skateboarding** is the activity of riding on a skateboard. स्केटबोर्डिंग

skates *npl* **Skates** are boots with a thin metal blade underneath that people wear to move quickly on ice. बर्फावर घसरत चालण्यासाठी असलेले बूट, स्केट्स

skating *n* **Skating** is the act or process of moving about wearing ice-skates or roller-skates. स्केटिंग करणे

skating rink (skating rinks) *n* A **skating rink** is a large area covered with ice where people go to ice-skate, or a large area of concrete where people go to roller-skate. स्केटिंगचे मैदान

skeleton (skeletons) *n* Your **skeleton** is the framework of bones in your body. हाडांचा सांगाडा

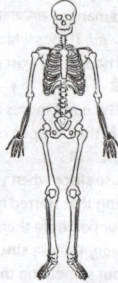

sketch (sketches, sketching, sketched) *n* A **sketch** is a drawing that is done quickly without a lot of details. रेखाचित्र ▷ *v* If you **sketch** something, you make a quick rough drawing of it. रेखाचित्र तयार करणे

skewer (skewers) *n* A **skewer** is a long metal pin which is used to hold pieces of food together during cooking. चिमटा

ski (skis, skiing, skied) *n* Skis are long, flat, narrow pieces of wood, metal, or plastic that are fastened to boots so that you can move easily over snow. स्कीईंग करण्यासाठी वापरायच्या टोकदार काठ्या ▷ *vi* When people **ski**, they move over snow on skis. स्कि करणे

skid (skids, skidding, skidded) *vi* If a vehicle **skids**, it slides sideways or forwards while moving, for example when you are trying to stop it suddenly on a wet road. घसरणे

skier (skiers) *n* A **skier** is a person who moves over snow on skis. स्कीईंग करणारी व्यक्ती

skiing *n* **Skiing** is the act or process of moving over snow on skis. बर्फावरून घसरण्याचा खेळ, स्कीईंग

skilful *adj* Someone who is **skilful** at something does it very well. कुशल

ski lift (ski lifts) *n* A **ski lift** is a machine for taking people to the top of a slope so that they can ski down it. It consists of a series of seats hanging down from a moving wire. स्की लिफ्ट

skill (skills) n A **skill** is a type of activity or work which requires special training or knowledge. कौशल्य

skilled adj Someone who is **skilled** has the knowledge and ability to do something well. कुशल

skimmed milk n **Skimmed milk** is milk from which the cream has been removed. साय काढून घेतलेले दूध

skimpy (skimpier, skimpiest) adj **Skimpy** means too small in size or quantity. तोकडा

skin (skins) n Your **skin** covers your whole body. त्वचा ▷ n The **skin** of a fruit or vegetable covers the outside of it. साल

skinhead (skinheads) n A **skinhead** is a young person whose hair is shaved or cut very short. Skinheads are usually regarded as violent and aggressive. डोक्यावरील केस काढलेला तरण माणूस

skinny (skinnier, skinniest) adj If you say that someone is **skinny**, you mean that they are very thin in a way you find unattractive. (informal) हडकुळा

skin-tight adj **Skin-tight** clothes fit very tightly so that they show the shape of your body. अंगाला चिकटणारे घट्ट कपडे

skip (skips, skipping, skipped) vi If you **skip** along, you move along jumping from one foot to the other. उड्या मारणे ▷ vt If you **skip** something, you decide not to do it. टाळणे

skirt (skirts) n A **skirt** is a piece of clothing worn by women and girls. It fastens at the waist and hangs down around the legs. स्कर्ट

skirting board (skirting boards) n **Skirting board** or **skirting** is a narrow length of wood which goes along the bottom of a wall in a room and makes a border between the walls and the floor. स्कर्टिंग (जमिनीपासून वर भिंतीला ठोकलेली पट्टी)

skive (skives, skiving, skived) v If you **skive**, you avoid working, especially by staying away

from the place where you should be working. (informal) काम करण्याचे टाळणे, कामचुकारपणा करणे

skull (skulls) n Your **skull** is the bony part of your head which holds your brain. कवटी

sky (skies) n The **sky** is the space around the earth which you can see when you stand outside and look upwards. आकाश

skyscraper (skyscrapers) n A **skyscraper** is a very tall building in a city. गगनचुंबी इमारत

slack (slacker, slackest) adj Something that is **slack** is loose and not tightly stretched. ढिला

slag off (slags off, slagging off, slagged off) v To **slag** someone **off** means to criticize them in an unpleasant way. (informal) शिव्याशाप देणे All bands slag off their record companies. It's just the way it is.

slam (slams, slamming, slammed) v If you **slam** a door or window, or if it **slams**, it shuts noisily and with great force. धाडकन बंद करणे

slang n **Slang** is words, expressions, and meanings that are informal and are used by people who know each other very well or who have the same interests. अनौपचारिक भाषा

slap (slaps, slapping, slapped) vt If you **slap** someone, you hit them with the palm of your hand. चापट मारणे

slate n **Slate** is a dark grey rock that can be easily split into thin layers. पातळ थरांमध्ये कापता येणारा निळसर करडा खडक

slave (slaves, slaving, slaved) n A **slave** is a person who is owned by another person and has to work for that person without pay. गुलाम ▷ vi If you **slave**, you work very hard. मेहनत करणे

sledge (sledges) n A **sledge** is an object that you sit on in order to travel over snow. स्लेज, बर्फावरून सामान खेचण्यासाठी बनवलेली छोट्या चौकटीची गाडी

sledging n **Sledging** is the activity of riding over snow on a sledge. बर्फावरून छाट्या गाडीवरून सामान खेचण्याची क्रिया

sleep (sleeps, sleeping, slept) n **Sleep** is the natural state of rest in which your eyes are

closed, your body is inactive, and your mind
does not think. झोप ▷ *vi* When you **sleep**, you
rest with your eyes closed and your mind and
body inactive. झोपणें

sleep in (**sleeps in, sleeping in, slept in**) *v* If
you **sleep in**, you sleep longer than usual. खूप
उशिरापर्यंत झोपणें *Yesterday, few players turned
up because most slept in.*

sleeping bag (**sleeping bags**) *n* A **sleeping
bag** is a large warm bag for sleeping in,
especially when you are camping. स्लिपिंग बॅग

sleeping car (**sleeping cars**) *n* A **sleeping
car** is a railway carriage containing beds for
passengers to sleep in at night. रेल्वेगाडीतील
झोपण्याची व्यवस्था असलेला डबा

sleeping pill (**sleeping pills**) *n* A **sleeping
pill** is a pill that you can take to help you sleep.
झोपेची गोळी

sleepwalk (**sleepwalks, sleepwalking,
sleepwalked**) *vi* If someone **sleepwalks**,
they walk around while they are asleep. झोपेत
चालण्याची क्रिया

sleepy (**sleepier, sleepiest**) *adj* If you feel
sleepy, you feel tired and ready to go to sleep.
झोपाळू

sleet (**sleets, sleeting, sleeted**) *n* Sleet is
rain that is partly frozen. बर्फ आणि गारांनी युक्त
पाऊस ▷ *v* When partly melted snow or hail,
or partly frozen rain, falls from the clouds, you
can say that it is **sleeting**. बर्फ आणि गारांनी युक्त
पाऊस पडणें

sleeve (**sleeves**) *n* The **sleeves** of a coat, shirt,
or other item of clothing are the parts that
cover your arms. कपड्याची बाही

sleeveless *adj* A **sleeveless** dress, top,
or other item of clothing has no sleeves.
बिनबाह्यांचा

slender *adj* A **slender** person is thin and
graceful in an attractive way. *(written)* सडपातळ

slice (**slices, slicing, sliced**) *n* A **slice** of bread,
meat, fruit, or other food is a thin piece that
has been cut from a larger piece. फळ किंवा ब्रेड
यांची चकती ▷ *vt* If you **slice** food, you cut it
into thin pieces. चकत्या करणें

slide (**slides, sliding, slid**) *n* A **slide** in a
playground is a structure that has a steep
slope for children to slide down. घसरगुंडी
▷ *v* When something **slides** somewhere, or
when you **slide** it somewhere, it moves there
smoothly over or against something else.
घसरणें, सरकणें

slight (**slighter, slightest**) *adj* Something that
is **slight** is very small in degree or quantity.
किरकोळ

slightly *adv* **Slightly** means to some degree
but not much. थोडेसे

slim (**slimmer, slimmest**) *adj* A **slim** person
has a nicely shaped body. सडपातळ

sling (**slings**) *n* A **sling** is an object made of
ropes, straps, or cloth that is used for carrying
things. झोळी

slip (**slips, slipping, slipped**) *n* A **slip** is a small
or unimportant mistake. छोटीशी चूक ▷ *n* A
slip of paper is a small piece of paper. कागदाचा
तुकडा ▷ *n* A **slip** is a thin piece of clothing
that a woman wears under her dress or skirt.
महिलांचे अंतर्वस्त्र, स्लीप ▷ *vi* If you **slip**, you
accidentally slide and lose your balance. घसरणें

slipped disc (slipped discs) *n* If you have a **slipped disc**, you have a bad back because one of the discs in your spine has moved out of its proper position. मणका सरकण्याचा आजार

slipper (slippers) *n* **Slippers** are loose soft shoes that you wear in the house. घरात घालण्याचे पादत्राण

slippery *adj* Something that is **slippery** is smooth, wet, or greasy, making it difficult to walk on or to hold. निसरडे

slip road (slip roads) *n* A **slip road** is a road which cars use to drive on and off a motorway. मुख्य रस्त्याला जोडणारा बाजूचा रस्ता

slip up (slips up, slipping up, slipped up, slip-ups) *v* If you **slip up**, you make a small or unimportant mistake. छोटीशी चूक करणे *We slipped up a few times.* ▷ *n* A **slip-up** is a small or unimportant mistake. *(informal)* छोटीशी चूक

slope (slopes) *n* A **slope** is a surface that is at an angle, so that one end is higher than the other. उतार

sloppy (sloppier, sloppiest) *adj* Work that is **sloppy** is messy and careless. निष्काळजीपणे केलेले, गचाळ

slot (slots) *n* A **slot** is a narrow opening in a machine or container, for example a hole that you put coins in to make a machine work. खोबण

slot machine (slot machines) *n* A **slot machine** is a machine from which you can get food or cigarettes or on which you can gamble. You make it work by putting coins into a slot. स्लॉट मशीन

Slovak (Slovaks) *adj* **Slovak** means of, relating to, or characteristic of Slovakia, its people, or their language. स्लोव्हाक ▷ *n* **Slovak** is the official language of Slovakia. स्लोव्हाक ▷ *n* A **Slovak** is a native or inhabitant of Slovakia. स्लोव्हाक

Slovakia *n* **Slovakia** is a country in central Europe. स्लोव्हाकियन

Slovenia *n* **Slovenia** is a republic in south central Europe. स्लोव्हाकियन

Slovenian (Slovenians) *adj* **Slovenian** means belonging or relating to Slovenia, or to its people, language, or culture. स्लोव्हाकियन ▷ *n* A **Slovenian** is a person of Slovenian origin. स्लोव्हाकियन ▷ *n* **Slovenian** is the language spoken in Slovenia. स्लोव्हाकियन

slow (slower, slowest) *adj* Something that is **slow** moves, happens, or is done without much speed. मंद

slow down (slows down, slowed down, slowing down) *v* If something **slows down**, or if you slow it **down**, it starts to move or happen more slowly. वेग कमी करणे *The car slowed down.*

slowly *adv* If something happens or is done **slowly**, it happens or is done without much speed. हळूहळू

slug (slugs) *n* A **slug** is a small slow-moving creature, with a long slippery body, like a snail without a shell. कवच नसलेली एक प्रकारची गोगलगाय

slum (slums) *n* A **slum** is an area of a city where living conditions are very bad. झोपडपट्टी

slush *n* **Slush** is snow that has begun to melt and is therefore very wet and dirty. वितळू लागलेला बर्फ

sly *adj* A **sly** look, expression, or remark shows that you know something that other people do not know. गुपचुप केलेला

smack (smacks, smacking, smacked) *vt* If you **smack** someone, you hit them with your hand. हाताचा फटका मारणे

small (smaller, smallest) *adj* If something is **small**, it is not large in size or amount. लहान

small ads *npl* The **small ads** in a newspaper are short advertisements in which you can advertise something such as an object for sale or a room to let. छोट्या जाहिराती

smart (smarter, smartest) *adj* Smart people and things are pleasantly neat and clean in appearance. चुणचुणीत

smart phone (smart phones) *n* A smart phone is a type of mobile phone that can do some of the things that a computer does, such as using the Internet. स्मार्ट फोन

smash (smashes, smashing, smashed) *v* If something smashes, or if you smash it, it breaks into many pieces, for example when it is hit or dropped. तुकडे करणे/होणे

smashing *adj* If you describe something or someone as smashing, you mean that you like them very much. (*informal*) आवडते

smear (smears) *n* A smear or a smear test is a medical test in which a few cells are taken from a woman's body and examined to see if any cancer cells are present. गर्भाशयमुखाच्या पेशींच्या पातळ थराची वैद्यकीय तपासणी

smell (smells, smelling, smelled, smelt) *n* You become aware of the smell of something through your nose. वास ▷ *vt* If you smell something, you become aware of it through your nose. वास घेणे ▷ *vi* If something smells of a particular thing, you become aware of this through your nose. वास येणे

smelly (smellier, smelliest) *adj* Something that is smelly has an unpleasant smell. दुर्गंधीयुक्त

smile (smiles, smiling, smiled) *n* A smile is the expression that you have on your face when you smile. हास्य, हसू ▷ *vi* When you smile, the corners of your mouth curve up and you sometimes show your teeth. People smile when they are pleased or amused, or when they are being friendly. हसणे

smiley (smileys) *n* A smiley is a symbol used in email to show how someone is feeling. :-) is a smiley showing happiness. (*informal*) स्मायली, ई-मेलमधून भावना व्यक्त करण्याचे चिन्ह

smoke (smokes, smoking, smoked) *n* Smoke consists of gas and small bits of solid material that are sent into the air when

something burns. धूर ▷ *vi* If something is smoking, smoke is coming from it. धूर येणे

smoke alarm (smoke alarms) *n* A smoke alarm or a smoke detector is a device fixed to the ceiling of a room which makes a loud noise if there is smoke in the air, to warn people. धूर निघत असल्यास मिळणारा सावधानतेचा इशारा

smoked *adj* Smoked glass has been made darker by being treated with smoke. धुराने प्रक्रिया केलेली गडद काच

smoker (smoker) *n* A smoker is a person who habitually smokes tobacco. धूम्रपान करणारी व्यक्ती

smoking *n* Smoking is the act or habit of smoking cigarettes, cigars, or a pipe. धूम्रपान

smooth (smoother, smoothest) *adj* A smooth surface has no roughness or holes. गुळगुळीत

SMS *n* SMS is a way of sending short written messages from one mobile phone to another. SMS is an abbreviation for 'short message system'. एसएमएस

smudge (smudges) *n* A smudge is a dirty, blurred mark. डाग

smug *adj* If you say that someone is smug, you are criticizing the fact they seem very pleased with how good, clever, or fortunate they are. अल्पसंतुष्ट

smuggle (smuggles, smuggling, smuggled) *vt* If someone smuggles things or people into a place or out of it, they take them there illegally or secretly. तस्करी करणे

smuggler (smugglers) *n* Smugglers are people who take goods into or out of a country illegally. तस्कर

smuggling *n* Smuggling is the act of taking things or people into a place or out of it, illegally or secretly. तस्करी

snack (snacks) *n* A snack is a small, quick meal, or something eaten between meals. नाश्ता

snack bar (snack bars) *n* A snack bar is a place where you can buy drinks and simple meals such as sandwiches. उपाहार गृह

snail (snails) *n* A **snail** is a small animal that has a spiral shell. It moves slowly, leaving behind a trail of slime. गोगलगाय

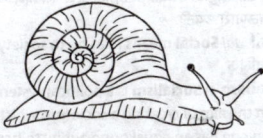

snake (snakes) *n* A **snake** is a long, thin reptile with no legs. साप

snap (snaps, snapping, snapped) *v* If something **snaps** or if you **snap** it, it breaks suddenly, usually with a sharp cracking noise. धाडकन उघडणे, बंद करणे किंवा मोडणे

snapshot (snapshots) *n* A **snapshot** is a photograph that is taken quickly and casually. छायाचित्र खेचणे

snarl (snarls, snarling, snarled) *vi* When an animal **snarls**, it makes a fierce, rough sound in its throat while showing its teeth. दात विचकून गुरगुरणे

snatch (snatches, snatching, snatched) *v* If you **snatch** something, or if you **snatch at** it, you take it or pull it away quickly. हिसकावून घेणे

sneeze (sneezes, sneezing, sneezed) *vi* When you **sneeze**, you suddenly take in your breath and then blow it down your nose noisily without being able to stop yourself, for example because you have a cold. शिंकणे

sniff (sniffs, sniffing, sniffed) *v* When you **sniff**, you suddenly and quickly breathe in air through your nose. हुंगणे, सूंस् करणे

snigger (sniggers, sniggering, sniggered) *vi* If someone **sniggers**, they laugh quietly in a disrespectful way, for example at something rude or unkind. मिस्किलपणे हळूच हसणे

snob (snobs) *n* A **snob** is someone who feels that they are better than other people because of their behaviour or social class. शिष्ट, अहंकारी

snooker *n* **Snooker** is a game involving balls on a large table. The players use long sticks called cues to hit a white ball, and score points by knocking coloured balls into the pockets at the sides of the table. स्नूकर खेळ

snooze (snoozes, snoozing, snoozed) *n* A **snooze** is a short, light sleep, especially during the day. *(informal)* डुलकी ▷ *vi* If you **snooze**, you sleep lightly for a short period of time. *(informal)* डुलकी घेणे

snore (snores, snoring, snored) *vi* When someone who is asleep **snores**, they make a loud noise each time they breathe. घोरणे

snorkel (snorkels) *n* A **snorkel** is a tube through which a person swimming just under the surface of the sea can breathe. पाण्याखाली पोहणाऱ्याला शुद्ध हवा मिळावी म्हणून पृष्ठभागाच्यावर काढलेली नळी

snow (snows, snowing, snowed) *n* **Snow** is the soft white bits of frozen water that fall from the sky in cold weather. हिम ▷ *vi* When it **snows**, snow falls from the sky. हिमवर्षाव होणे

snowball (snowballs) *n* A **snowball** is a ball of snow. बर्फाचा गोळा

snowflake (snowflakes) *n* A **snowflake** is one of the soft, white bits of frozen water that fall as snow. हिमकण

snowman (snowmen) *n* A **snowman** is a large shape which is made out of snow, especially by children, and is supposed to look like a person. बर्फापासून बनवलेला माणसाचा आकार, स्नोमॅन

snowplough (snowploughs) n A **snowplough** is a vehicle which is used to push snow off roads or railway lines. साठलेले बर्फ काढून टाकण्यासाठी असलेले अवजार

snowstorm (snowstorms) n A **snowstorm** is a very heavy fall of snow, usually when there is also a strong wind blowing at the same time. हिमवादळ

so adv You use **so** to talk about something without repeating the same words. म्हणून ▷ conj You use **so** and **so that** to talk about the reason for doing something. म्हणजे They went outside so that nobody would see them. ▷ adv You can use **so** in front of adjectives and adverbs to make them stronger. एवढे की

soak (soaks, soaking, soaked) v When you **soak** something, or when you leave it to **soak**, you put it into a liquid and leave it there. भिजत ठेवणे

soaked adj If someone or something gets **soaked** or **soaked through**, water or some other liquid makes them extremely wet. भिजलेला

soap (soaps) n **Soap** is a substance that you use with water for washing yourself or sometimes for washing clothes. साबण

soap dish (soap dishes) n A **soap dish** is a shallow container with a wide uncovered top, used in a bathroom for holding soap. साबण ठेवण्यासाठी असलेले भांडे

soap opera (soap operas) n A **soap opera** is a television drama serial about the daily lives of a group of people. लोकांच्या दैनंदिन जीवनावर आधारित दूरदर्शनवरील मालिका

soap powder (soap powders) n **Soap powder** is a powder made from soap and other substances that you use for washing your clothes, especially in a machine. साबण चुरा

sob (sobs, sobbing, sobbed) vi When someone **sobs**, they cry in a noisy way, breathing in short breaths. हुंदके देत रडणे

sober adj When you are **sober**, you are not drunk. सभ्य, मद्य न प्यालेला

sociable adj **Sociable** people enjoy meeting and talking to other people. इतर लोकांमध्ये मिसळणारी व्यक्ती

social adj **Social** means relating to society. सामाजिक

socialism n **Socialism** is a political system with the aim of creating a society in which everyone has an equal opportunity to benefit from a country's wealth. Under socialism, the country's main industries are usually owned by the state. समाजवाद

socialist (socialists) adj **Socialist** means based on socialism or relating to socialism. समाजवादी ▷ n A **socialist** is a person who believes in socialism or who is a member of a socialist party. समाजवादी

social security n **Social security** is money that is paid by the government to people who are unemployed, poor, or ill. सामाजिक सुरक्षितता

social services npl **Social services** are services provided by the local authority to help people who have serious family problems or financial problems. समाजसेवा

social worker (social workers) n A **social worker** is a person whose job is to help people who have serious family problems or financial problems. सामाजिक कार्यकर्ता

society (societies) n **Society** consists of all the people in a country or region, considered as a group. समाज

sociology n **Sociology** is the study of society or of the way society is organized. समाजशास्त्र

sock (socks) n **Socks** are pieces of clothing which cover your foot and ankle and are worn inside shoes. पायमोजा

socket (sockets) n A **socket** is a device on a piece of electrical equipment into which you can put a plug or bulb. सॉकेट

sofa (sofas) n A **sofa** is a long, comfortable seat with a back and arms, which two or three people can sit on. सोफा

sofa bed (sofa beds) n A **sofa bed** is a type of sofa whose seat folds out so that it can also be used as a bed. सोफा बेड

soft (softer, softest) adj Something that is **soft** is nice to touch, and not rough or hard. मऊ ▷ adj A **soft** sound or light is very gentle. नरम

soft drink (soft drinks) n A **soft drink** is a sweet drink that contains no alcohol. मद्यविरहित पेय

software n Computer programs are referred to as **software**. सॉफ्टवेअर

soggy (soggier, soggiest) adj Something that is **soggy** is unpleasantly wet. ओलसर

soil n **Soil** is the substance on the surface of the earth in which plants grow. माती

solar adj **Solar** is used to describe things relating to the sun. सौर

solar power n **Solar power** is heat radiation from the sun converted into electrical power. सौर ऊर्जा

solar system (solar systems) n The **solar system** is the sun and all the planets that go round it. सूर्यमाला

soldier (soldiers) n A **soldier** is a person who works in an army. सैनिक

sold out adj If a performance, sports event, or other entertainment is **sold out**, all the tickets for it have been sold. संपूर्ण विकली गेलेली

solicitor (solicitors) n A **solicitor** is a lawyer who gives legal advice. वकील, अधिवक्ता

solid adj Something that is **solid** stays the same shape whether it is in a container or not. घनपदार्थ ▷ adj Something that is **solid** is not hollow. भरीव

solid   hollow

solo (solos) n A **solo** is a piece of music or a dance performed by one person. एका व्यक्तीने म्हटलेले गीत

soloist (soloists) n A **soloist** is a person who performs a solo, usually a piece of music. गाणे म्हणणारी एकटी व्यक्ती

soluble adj A substance that is **soluble** will dissolve in a liquid. विद्राव्य, विरघळणारा

solution (solutions) n A **solution** to a problem is a way of dealing with it so that the difficulty is removed. उकल, उत्तर

solve (solves, solving, solved) vt If you **solve** a problem or a question, you find a solution or an answer to it. समस्या सोडविणे

solvent (solvents) n A **solvent** is a liquid that can dissolve other substances. द्रावक

Somali (Somalis) adj **Somali** means of, relating to, or characteristic of Somalia, the Somalis, or their language. सोमाली ▷ n A **Somali** is a member of a people living in Somalia or other countries in north-east Africa. सोमाली ▷ n **Somali** is the language spoken by the Somali people. सोमाली

Somalia n **Somalia** is a republic in north-east Africa. सोमालिया

some det You use **some** to talk about an amount of something. काही Can I have some orange juice, please? ▷ pron **Some** means a quantity of something or a number of people or things. काही The apples are ripe and we are going to pick some.

somebody pron You use **somebody** to talk about a person without saying who you mean. कोणीतरी

somehow adv You use **somehow** when you cannot say how somebody did something, or how somebody will do something. कसेतरी

someone pron You use **someone** to talk about a person without saying who you mean. कोणीतरी I need someone to help me.

someplace adv You use **someplace** to talk about a place without saying where you mean. कोठेतरी

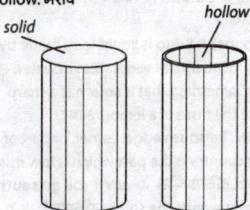

something *pron* You use **something** to talk about a thing without saying what it is. काहीतरी *He knew that there was something wrong.*

sometime *adv* You use **sometime** to talk about a time in the future or the past that is not known. कधीतरी

sometimes *adv* You use **sometimes** to talk about things that do not take place all the time. कधीकधी

somewhere *adv* You use **somewhere** to talk about a place without saying where you mean. कोठेतरी

son (**sons**) *n* A person's **son** is their male child. स्वतःचा मुलगा, पुत्र

song (**songs**) *n* A **song** is a piece of music with words and music sung together. गाणे

son-in-law (**sons-in-law**) *n* A person's **son-in-law** is the husband of their daughter. जावई

soon (**sooner, soonest**) *adv* If something is going to happen **soon**, it will happen after a short time. लवकर

soot *n* **Soot** is black powder which rises in the smoke from a fire and collects on the inside of chimneys. काजळी

sophisticated *adj* A **sophisticated** person is comfortable in social situations and knows about culture, fashion, and other matters that are considered socially important. सुसंस्कृत व उच्च अभिरुची असलेली व्यक्ती

soppy (**soppier, soppiest**) *adj* If you describe someone or something as **soppy**, you mean that they are foolishly sentimental. भावनाप्रधान, भडक भावनांचा

soprano (**sopranos**) *n* A **soprano** is a woman, girl, or boy with a high singing voice. तारस्वरात गाणारी स्त्री किंवा मुलगा किंवा मुलगी

sorbet (**sorbets**) *n* **Sorbet** is a frozen dessert made with fruit juice, sugar, and water. सॉर्बेट नावाचा खाद्यपदार्थ

sorcerer (**sorcerers**) *n* In fairy stories, a **sorcerer** is a person who performs magic by using the power of evil spirits. भुताटकी करणारी व्यक्ती, जादूगार

sore (**sorer, sorest, sores**) *adj* If part of your body is **sore**, it causes you pain and discomfort. दुखरा ▷ *n* A **sore** is a painful spot on your body where the skin is infected. जखम

sorry *excl* You say '**Sorry!**' as a way of apologizing to someone for something that you have done which has upset them or caused them difficulties, or when you bump into them accidentally. माफ करा! ▷ *adj* If you are **sorry** about something, you feel sad about it. दुःखी ▷ *adj* If you feel **sorry** for someone, you feel sad for them. खेद

sort (**sorts**) *n* A particular **sort** of something is one of its different kinds or types. प्रकार

sort out (**sorts out, sorting out, sorted out**) *v* If you **sort out** a group of things, you organize or tidy them. सोडवणे, निवडणे *We try to sort out the truth from the lies.*

SOS *n* An **SOS** is a signal which indicates to other people that you are in danger and need help quickly. संकटात असल्यासंबंधीचा संकेत

so-so *adv* **So-so** means in an average or indifferent manner. *(informal)* यथातथा

soul (**souls**) *n* A person's **soul** is the spiritual part of them which some people believe continues existing after their body is dead. आत्मा

sound (**sounder, soundest, sounds**) *adj* If something is **sound**, it is in good condition or healthy. चांगला, मजबूत ▷ *n* A **sound** is something that you hear. आवाज

soundtrack (**soundtracks**) *n* The **soundtrack** of a film is its sound, speech, and especially the music. चित्रपटाचे संवाद, गीत, संगीत इत्यादी

soup (**soups**) *n* **Soup** is liquid food made by cooking meat, fish, or vegetables in water. सूप

sour *adj* Something that is **sour** has a sharp taste like the taste of a lemon. आंबट

south *adj* The **south** edge, corner, or part of a place or country is the part which is towards the south. दक्षिणेकडील ▷ *adv* If you go **south**, you travel towards the south. दक्षिणेकडे ▷ *n*

The south is the direction on your right when you are looking towards the place where the sun rises. दक्षिण दिशा

South Africa *n* **South Africa** is a republic in the southernmost part of the African continent. दक्षिण आफ्रिका

South African (**South Africans**) *adj* **South African** means of or relating to the Republic of South Africa, its inhabitants, or any of their languages. दक्षिण आफ्रिकेचा ▷ *n* A **South African** is a native or inhabitant of the Republic of South Africa. दक्षिण आफ्रिकेतील

South America *n* **South America** is the fourth largest continent in the world, bordering on the Caribbean in the north, the Pacific in the west, and the Atlantic in the east. दक्षिण अमेरिका

South American (**South Americans**) *adj* **South American** means of or relating to the continent of South America or its inhabitants. दक्षिण अमेरिकेतील ▷ *n* A **South American** is a native or inhabitant of South America. दक्षिण अमेरिकेचा

southbound *adj* **Southbound** roads or vehicles lead or are travelling towards the south. दक्षिणकडे जाणारा

southeast *n* The **southeast** is the direction which is halfway between south and east. आग्नेय दिशा

southern *adj* **Southern** means in or from the south of a region or country. दक्षिणेकडील

South Korea *n* **South Korea** is a republic in north-east Asia. दक्षिण कोरिया

South Pole *n* The **South Pole** is the place on the surface of the earth which is farthest towards the south. दक्षिण ध्रुव

southwest *n* The **southwest** is the direction which is halfway between south and west. नैऋत्य दिशा

souvenir (**souvenirs**) *n* A **souvenir** is something which you buy or keep to remind you of a holiday, place, or event. स्मरणिका

soya *n* **Soya** flour, butter, or other food is made from soya beans. सोयाबिन

soy sauce *n* **Soy sauce** is a dark brown liquid made from soya beans and used as a flavouring, especially in Chinese cooking. सोय सॉस

spa (**spas**) *n* A **spa** is a place where water with minerals in it bubbles out of the ground. खनिज पाण्याचा झरा

space (**spaces**) *n* You use **space** to talk about an area that is empty. जागा ▷ *n* **Space** is the area past the Earth, where the stars and planets are. अवकाश

spacecraft (**spacecraft**) *n* A **spacecraft** is a rocket or other vehicle that can travel in space. अवकाश यान

spade (**spades**) *n* A **spade** is a tool used for digging, with a flat metal blade and a long handle. फावडा

spaghetti *n* **Spaghetti** is a type of pasta which looks like long pieces of string. स्पघेटी

Spain *n* **Spain** is a kingdom in south-west Europe. स्पेन

spam (**spams**) *n* **Spam** is unwanted email that is sent to a large number of people, usually as advertising. नको असलेले ई-मेल

Spaniard (**Spaniards**) *n* A **Spaniard** is a Spanish citizen, or a person of Spanish origin. स्पेनमधील व्यक्ती

spaniel (**spaniels**) *n* A **spaniel** is a type of dog with long ears that hang down. स्पॅनियल जातीचा कुत्रा

Spanish *adj* **Spanish** means belonging or relating to Spain, or to its people, language, or culture. स्पॅनिश ▷ *n* **Spanish** is the main language spoken in Spain, and in many countries in South and Central America. स्पॅनिश

spank (**spanks, spanking, spanked**) *vt* If someone **spanks** a child, they punish them by hitting them on the bottom several times. कुल्ल्यांवर फटके मारणे

spanner (**spanners**) *n* A **spanner** is a metal tool used for tightening a nut. पाना

spare (**spares, sparing, spared**) *adj* You use **spare** to describe something that is the same as things that you are already using, but that

S

you do not need yet and are keeping ready in case another one is needed. जादा ▷ vt If you **spare** time or money, you make it available. जादा असणे

spare part (spare parts) n Spare parts are parts that you can buy separately to replace old or broken parts in a piece of equipment. सुटे भाग

spare room (spare rooms) n A **spare room** is a bedroom which is kept especially for visitors to sleep in. पाहुण्यांची झोपायची खोली

spare time n Your **spare time** is the time during which you do not have to work and you can do whatever you like. फावला वेळ

spare tyre (spare tyres) n A **spare tyre** is a wheel with a tyre on it that you keep in your car in case you get a flat tyre and need to replace one of your wheels. अतिरिक्त टायर

spare wheel (spare wheels) n A **spare wheel** is a wheel with a tyre on it that you keep in your car in case you get a flat tyre and need to replace one of your wheels. अतिरिक टायर

spark (sparks) n A **spark** is a tiny bright piece of burning material that flies up from something that is burning. ठिणगी

sparkling water (sparkling waters) n **Sparkling water** is slightly fizzy water. फसफसणारे पाणी

spark plug (spark plugs) n A **spark plug** is a device in the engine of a motor vehicle, which produces electric sparks to make the petrol burn. स्पार्क प्लग

sparrow (sparrows) n A **sparrow** is a small brown bird that is common in Britain. चिमणी

spasm (spasms) n A **spasm** is a sudden tightening of your muscles, which you cannot control. स्नायूंचे अचानक झालेले आकुंचन

spatula (spatulas) n A **spatula** is an object like a knife with a wide, flat blade. Spatulas are used in cooking. बोथट सुरी

speak (speaks, speaking, spoke, spoken) v When you **speak**, you use your voice in order to say something. बोलणे

speaker (speakers) n A **speaker** at a meeting, conference, or other gathering is a person who is making a speech or giving a talk. वका

speak up (speaks up, speaking up, spoke up, spoken up) v If you ask someone to **speak up**, you are asking them to speak more loudly. मोठ्याने बोलणे I'm quite deaf – you'll have to speak up.

special adj Someone or something that is **special** is different from normal, often in a way that makes them better or more important than other people or things. खास

specialist (specialists) n A **specialist** is a person who has a particular skill or knows a lot about a particular subject. विशेषज्ञ

speciality (specialities) n Someone's **speciality** is the kind of work they do best or the subject they know most about. वैशिष्ट्य

specialize (specializes, specializing, specialized) vi If you **specialize in** an area of study or a type of work, you know a lot about it and spend a lot of your time and attention on it. विशेष ज्ञान प्राप्त करणे

specially adv If something has been done **specially** for a particular person or purpose, it has been done only for that person or purpose. खास करून, विशेषत:

special offer (special offers) n A **special offer** is a product, service, or programme that is offered at reduced prices or rates. खास देकार

species (species) n A **species** is a class of plants or animals whose members have the same characteristics and are able to breed with each other. प्रजाती

specific adj You use **specific** to emphasize that you are talking about a particular thing or subject. विशिष्ट

specifically adv You use **specifically** to emphasize that a subject is being considered separately from other subjects. खास

specify (specifies, specifying, specified) vt If you **specify** something, you state it precisely. स्पष्ट करणे

spectacles npl **Spectacles** are two lenses in a frame that some people wear in front of their eyes in order to help them see better. *(formal)* चष्मा

spectacular adj Something that is **spectacular** is very impressive or dramatic. नेत्रसुखद

spectator (spectators) n A **spectator** is someone who watches something, especially a sporting event. प्रेक्षक

speculate (speculates, speculating, speculated) v If you **speculate** about something, you guess about its nature or identity, or about what might happen. अंदाज बांधणे

speech n **Speech** is the ability to speak or the act of speaking. बोलणे

speechless adj If you are **speechless**, you are temporarily unable to speak, usually because something has shocked you. नि:शब्द, अवाक्

speed (speeds) n The **speed** of something is the rate at which it moves, happens, or is done. वेग

speedboat (speedboats) n A **speedboat** is a boat that can go very fast because it has a powerful engine. स्पीडबोट

speeding n **Speeding** means the act or process of moving or travelling quickly. वेगाने जाण्याची क्रिया

speed limit (speed limits) n The **speed limit** on a road is the maximum speed at which you are legally allowed to drive. वेगमर्यादा

speedometer (speedometers) n A **speedometer** is the instrument in a vehicle which shows how fast the vehicle is moving. वाहनाचा वेग दर्शविणारा मीटर

speed up (speeds up, speeding up, speeded up) v When something **speeds up**, it moves, happens, or is done more quickly. वेग वाढणे *Try to speed up your breathing and stretch your legs.*

spell (spells, spelling, spelled, spelt) n A **spell** of a particular type of weather or a particular activity is a short period of time during which this type of weather or activity occurs. कालावधी ▷ n A **spell** is a situation in which events are controlled by a magical power. मंत्र ▷ vt When you **spell** a word, you write or speak each letter in the word in the correct order. शब्दाचे घटक वर्ण योग्य क्रमाने लिहिणे

spellchecker (spellcheckers) n A **spellchecker** is a special program on a computer which you can use to check for spelling mistakes. शब्दाचे घटक वर्ण योग्य क्रमाने लिहिले आहेत किंवा नाहीत हे दर्शविणारा कॉन्प्युटर प्रोग्रॅम

spelling (spellings) n The **spelling** of a word is the correct sequence of letters in it. स्पेलिंग, शब्दातील वर्णानुक्रम

spend (spends, spending, spent) vt When you **spend** money, you buy things with it. खर्च करणे ▷ vt To **spend** time or energy is to use it doing something. घालवणे

sperm (sperms, sperm) n A **sperm** is a cell produced in the sex organs of a male animal which can enter a female animal's egg and fertilize it. शुक्रजंतू

spice (spices) n A **spice** is a part of a plant, or a powder made from that part, which you put in food to give it flavour. मसाला

spicy (spicier, spiciest) adj **Spicy** food is strongly flavoured with spices. मसालेदार

spider (spiders) n A **spider** is a small creature with eight legs. कोळी

spill (spills, spilling, spilled, spilt) v If a liquid **spills** or if you **spill** it, it accidentally flows over the edge of a container. सांडणे, ऊतू जाणे

spinach n **Spinach** is a vegetable with large green leaves. पालक भाजी

spinal cord (spinal cords) n Your **spinal cord** is a thick bundle of nerves inside your spine which connects your brain to nerves in all parts of your body. पृष्ठमज्जारज्जू

spin drier (spin driers) n A **spin drier** is a machine that partly dries clothes that you have washed by turning them round and round very fast to remove the water. स्पिन ड्रायर

S

spine (spines) n Your **spine** is the row of bones down your back. मणका

spinster (spinsters) n A **spinster** is a woman who has never been married; used especially when talking about an old or middle-aged woman. (old-fashioned) अविवाहित स्त्री

spire (spires) n The **spire** of a church is a tall cone-shaped structure on top of a tower. चर्चची सुळक्यासारखे शिखर वा मनोरा

spirit (spirits) n Your **spirit** is the part of you that is not physical and that is connected with your deepest thoughts and feelings. मन

spirits npl You can refer to your **spirits** when saying how happy or unhappy you are. For example, if your spirits are high, you are happy. मनस्थिती

spiritual adj **Spiritual** means relating to people's deepest thoughts and beliefs, rather than to their bodies and physical surroundings. आध्यात्मिक

spit (spits, spitting, spat) n **Spit** is the watery liquid produced in your mouth. थुंकी ▷ v If someone **spits**, they force an amount of spit out of their mouth. If you **spit** liquid or food somewhere, you force a small amount of it out of your mouth. थुंकणे

spite n If you do something cruel out of **spite**, you do it because you want to hurt or upset someone. द्वेष ▷ vt If you do something cruel to **spite** someone, you do it in order to hurt or upset them. द्वेष करणे

spiteful adj Someone who is **spiteful** does cruel things to hurt people they dislike. मत्सरी, दुष्ट

splash (splashes, splashing, splashed) vi If you **splash** about or **splash** around in water, you hit or disturb the water in a noisy way, causing some of it to fly up into the air. पाण्याचा फवारा मारणे, शिंतोडे उडवणे

splendid adj If you say that something is **splendid**, you mean that it is very good. उत्तम, उत्कृष्ट

splint (splints) n A **splint** is a long piece of wood or metal that is fastened to a broken arm, leg, or back to keep it still. मोडलेल्या हाडाला आधार देण्यासाठी बांधलेली लाकडाची किंवा धातूची पट्टी

splinter (splinters) n A **splinter** is a very thin sharp piece of wood or glass which has broken off from a larger piece. लाकडाचा किंवा काचेचा तुकडा/कपची

split (splits, splitting) v If something **splits**, or if you **split** it, it is divided into two or more parts. फुटणे, भंगणे

split up (splits up, splitting up) v If two people **split up**, they end their relationship or marriage. विभक्त होणे I split up with my boyfriend.

spoil (spoils, spoiling, spoiled, spoilt) vt If you **spoil** something, you damage it or stop it from working as it should. खराब करणे ▷ vt If you **spoil** children, you give them everything they want or ask for. बिघडवणे

spoilsport (spoilsports) n If you say that someone is a **spoilsport**, you mean that they are behaving in a way that ruins other people's pleasure or enjoyment. (informal) इतरांच्या आनंदाचा रसभंग करणारा माणूस

spoilt adj A **spoilt** child is a child who has been given everything he wants, which has a bad effect on his character. लाडामुळे बिघडलेले मूल

spoke (spokes) n The **spokes** of a wheel are the bars that join the outer ring to the centre. आरा

spokesman (spokesmen) n A **spokesman** is a male spokesperson. प्रवक्ता

spokesperson (spokespersons, spokespeople) n A **spokesperson** is a person who speaks as the representative of a group or organization. प्रवक्ता

spokeswoman (spokeswomen) n A **spokeswoman** is a female spokesperson. प्रवक्ती

sponge (sponges) n A **sponge** is a piece of sponge that you use for washing yourself or for cleaning things. स्पंज ▷ n A **sponge** is a light cake or pudding made from flour, eggs, sugar, and sometimes fat. स्पंज केक

sponge bag (sponge bags) n A **sponge bag** is a small bag in which you keep things such as soap and a toothbrush when you are travelling. स्पंज बॅग

sponsor (sponsors, sponsoring, sponsored) n A **sponsor** is a person or organization that sponsors something or someone. प्रायोजक ▷ vt If an organization **sponsors** something such as an event, it pays some or all of the expenses connected with it, often in order to get publicity for itself. प्रायोजित करणे

sponsorship n **Sponsorship** is financial support given by a sponsor. प्रायोजकत्व

spontaneous adj **Spontaneous** acts are not planned or arranged, but are done because someone suddenly wants to do them. उत्स्फूर्त

spooky (spookier, spookiest) adj If something is **spooky**, it has a frightening and unnatural atmosphere. (informal) घाबरवणारा, भयाण

spoon (spoons) n A **spoon** is a tool used for eating, stirring, and serving food. It is shaped like a small shallow bowl with a long handle. चमचा

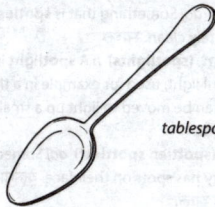

tablespoon

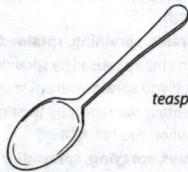

teaspoon

spoonful (spoonfuls) n You can refer to an amount of food resting on a spoon as a **spoonful** of food. चमचाभर

sport (sports) n **Sports** are games and other competitive activities which need physical effort and skill. खेळ

sportsman (sportsmen) n A **sportsman** is a man who takes part in sports. खेळाडू

sportswear n **Sportswear** is the special clothing worn for playing sports or for informal leisure activities. खेळताना किंवा काहीबाही काम करताना घालावयाचे कपडे

sportswoman (sportswomen) n A **sportswoman** is a woman who takes part in sports. महिला खेळाडू

sporty (sportier, sportiest) adj A **sporty** person enjoys playing sports. खेळाची आवड असलेली व्यक्ती

spot (spots, spotting, spotted) n **Spots** are small, round, coloured areas on a surface. डाग, ठिपके ▷ n You can refer to a particular place as a **spot**. विशिष्ट जागा ▷ vt If you **spot** something or someone, you notice them. दृष्टीस पडणे

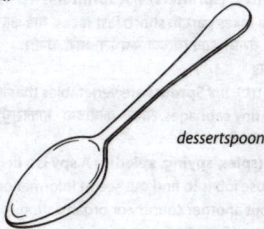

dessertspoon

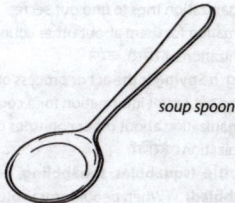

soup spoon

S

spotless *adj* Something that is **spotless** is completely clean. स्वच्छ

spotlight (spotlights) *n* A **spotlight** is a powerful light, used for example in a theatre, which can be moved to light up a small area. स्पॉट लाईट

spotty (spottier, spottiest) *adj* Someone who is **spotty** has spots on their face. चेहऱ्यावर डाग असलेली व्यक्ती

spouse (spouses) *n* Someone's **spouse** is the person they are married to. वैवाहिक जोडीदार, पती किंवा पत्नी

sprain (sprains, spraining, sprained) *n* A **sprain** is the injury caused by spraining a joint. लचक ▷ *vt* If you **sprain** your ankle or wrist, you accidentally damage it by twisting it, for example, when you fall. मुरगळणे

spray (sprays, spraying, sprayed) *n* Spray consists of a lot of small drops of water which are being splashed or forced into the air. फवारा ▷ *v* If you **spray** drops of a liquid or small pieces of something somewhere, or if they **spray** somewhere, they cover a place or shower someone. फवारा मारणे

spread (spreads, spreading) *n* A **spread** is a soft food which you put on bread. ब्रेडवर पसरण्याचा मऊ पदार्थ ▷ *vt* If you **spread** something somewhere, you open it out. पसरणे ▷ *vt* If you **spread** something on a surface, you put it all over the surface. पसरणे ▷ *vi* If something **spreads**, it reaches a larger area. पसरणे

spread out (spreads out, spreading out) *v* If people, animals, or vehicles **spread out**, they move apart from each other. पांगणे *They spread out to search the area.*

spreadsheet (spreadsheets) *n* A **spreadsheet** is a computer program that is used for displaying and dealing with numbers. Spreadsheets are used mainly for financial planning. स्प्रेडशीट

spring (springs) *n* Spring is the season between winter and summer when the weather becomes warmer and plants start to grow again. वसंत ऋतू ▷ *n* A **spring** is a long piece of metal that goes round and round. It goes back to the same shape after you pull it. स्प्रिंग

spring-cleaning *n* **Spring-cleaning** is the process of thoroughly cleaning a place, especially your home. पूर्णपणे साफ करण्याची क्रिया

spring onion (spring onions) *n* **Spring onions** are small onions with long green leaves. They are often eaten raw in salads. पातीसहित असलेले कांदे

springtime *n* **Springtime** is the period of time during which spring lasts. वसंत ऋतूचा कालावधी

sprinkler (sprinklers) *n* A **sprinkler** is a device used to spray water. Sprinklers are used to water plants or grass, or to put out fires in buildings. पाण्याची झारी

sprint (sprints, sprinting, sprinted) *n* A **sprint** is a short fast race. थोडे अंतर खूप वेगाने धावण्याची स्पर्धा ▷ *vi* If you **sprint**, you run or ride as fast as you can over a short distance. थोडे अंतर खूप वेगाने धावणे

sprinter (sprinters) *n* A **sprinter** is a person who takes part in short, fast races. थोडे अंतर खूप वेगाने धावण्याच्या स्पर्धेत भाग घेणारा खेळाडू

sprouts *npl* **Sprouts** are vegetables that look like tiny cabbages. लहान कोबीच्या आकाराची एक भाजी

spy (spies, spying, spied) *n* A **spy** is a person whose job is to find out secret information about another country or organization. हेर ▷ *vi* Someone who **spies** for a country or organization tries to find out secret information for them about other countries or organizations. हेरगिरी करणे

spying *n* **Spying** is the act or process of finding out secret information for a country or organization about other countries or organizations. हेरगिरी

squabble (squabbles, squabbling, squabbled) *vi* When people **squabble**, they quarrel about something that is not really important. बिनमहत्त्वाच्या कारणावरून भांडणे

squander (**squanders, squandering, squandered**) *vt* If you **squander** money, resources, or opportunities, you waste them. पैसे वाया घालवणे, उडवणे

square (**squares**) *adj* If something is **square**, it has a shape similar to a square. चौकोनी ▷ *n* A **square** is a shape with four sides of the same length and four corners that are all right angles. चौकोन

squash (**squashes, squashing, squashed**) *n* **Squash** is a game in which two players hit a small rubber ball against the walls of a court using rackets. स्क्वेश नावाचा खेळ ▷ *vt* If someone or something **is squashed**, they are pressed or crushed with such force that they become injured or lose their shape. चेंगरणे, चिरडणे

squeak (**squeaks, squeaking, squeaked**) *vi* If something or someone **squeaks**, they make a short, high-pitched sound. कर्कश आवाज करणे

squeeze (**squeezes, squeezing, squeezed**) *vt* If you **squeeze** something, you press it firmly, usually with your hands. पिळून काढणे, घट्ट दाबणे

squeeze in (**squeezes in, squeezing in, squeezed in**) *v* If you **squeeze** a person or thing **in** somewhere or if they **squeeze in** there, they manage to get through or into a small space. कसेबसे घुसणे, चेंबटणे *They squeezed down in the lift, squeezing in with half a dozen guests.*

squid (**squids, squid**) *n* A **squid** is a sea creature with a long soft body and many tentacles. स्क्वीड नावाचा सागरी प्राणी

squint (**squints, squinting, squinted**) *vi* If you **squint** at something, you look at it with your eyes partly closed. डोळे तिरळे करून पाहणे

squirrel (**squirrels**) *n* A **squirrel** is a small furry wild animal with a long bushy tail. खार

Sri Lanka *n* **Sri Lanka** is a republic in South Asia, on the island of Ceylon. श्रीलंका

stab (**stabs, stabbing, stabbed**) *vt* If someone **stabs** another person, they push a knife into their body. भोसकणे

stability *n* **Stability** is the quality of being stable. स्थैर्य

stable (**stabler, stablest, stables**) *adj* If something is **stable**, it is not likely to change or come to an end suddenly. स्थिर ▷ *n* A **stable** or **stables** is a building in which horses are kept. तबेला

stack (**stacks**) *n* A **stack** of things is a neat pile of them. ढीग

stadium (**stadiums, stadia**) *n* A **stadium** is a large sports ground with rows of seats all round it. क्रीडाप्रेक्षागृह

staff (**staffs**) *npl* The **staff** of an organization are the people who work for it. कर्मचारीवृंद/ कर्मचारीवर्ग ▷ *n* A **staff** is a stout rod or stick. दणकट काठी वा दांडा

staffroom (**staffrooms**) *n* The **staffroom** is a room that an organization provides for the use of the people who work for it. कर्मचाऱ्यांसाठी असलेली खोली

stage (**stages**) *n* A **stage** of an activity, process, or period is one part of it. व्यासपीठ, मंच

stagger (**staggers, staggering, staggered**) *vi* If you **stagger**, you walk very unsteadily, for example because you are ill or drunk. झोकांड्या देत चालणे

stag night (**stag nights**) *n* A **stag night** is a party for a man who is getting married very soon, to which only men are invited. ज्याचे लग्न ठरले आहे अशा पुरुषाला दिली जाणारी मेजवानी, ज्यात फक्त पुरुषांनाच निमंत्रण असते

stain (**stains, staining, stained**) *n* A **stain** is a mark on something that is difficult to remove. डाग ▷ *vt* If a liquid **stains** something, the thing becomes coloured or marked by the liquid. डाग पडणे

stained glass *n* **Stained glass** consists of pieces of glass of different colours used to make decorative windows or other objects. रंगीबेरंगी काच

s

stainless steel n Stainless steel is a metal which does not rust. स्टेनलेस स्टील

stain remover (stain removers) n Stain remover is a substance that you use for removing an unwanted stain from a surface. डाग घालवणारे रसायन

staircase (staircases) n A staircase is a set of stairs inside a house. जिना

stairs npl Stairs are a set of steps inside a building which go from one floor to another. जिना

stale (staler, stalest) adj Stale food or air is no longer fresh. शिळा

stalemate (stalemates) n Stalemate is a situation in which neither side in an argument or contest can make progress. कुंठित अवस्था

stall (stalls) n A stall is a large table on which you put goods that you want to sell, or information that you want to give people. ठेला, स्टॉल

stamina n Stamina is the physical or mental energy needed to do a tiring activity for a long time. शारीरिक क्षमता

stammer (stammers, stammering, stammered) v If you stammer, you speak with difficulty, hesitating and repeating words or sounds. तोतरे बोलणे

stamp (stamps, stamping, stamped) n A stamp or a postage stamp is a small piece of paper which you stick on an envelope or parcel, to show that you have paid the cost of posting it. पोस्टाचे तिकीट ▷ vt If you stamp a mark or word on an object, you press the mark or word onto the object, using a stamp. शिक्का मारणे

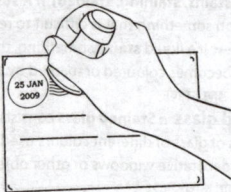
stamp

stand (stands, standing, stood) vi When you are standing, you are on your feet. उभे राहणे ▷ n A stand at a sports ground is where people sit or stand to watch. प्रेक्षक बसतात तो सज्जा

standard (standards) adj Standard means usual and normal. नेहमीचा ▷ n A standard is a level of quality or achievement, especially a level that is thought to be acceptable. दर्जा

standard of living (standards of living) n Your standard of living is the level of comfort and wealth which you have. राहणीमान

stand for (stands for, standing for, stood for) v If letters stand for particular words, they are an abbreviation for those words. ...चे संक्षिप्त रूप असणे UN stands for United Nations.

standing order (standing orders) n A standing order is an instruction to your bank to pay a fixed amount of money to someone at regular times. एखाद्या व्यक्तिला वेळेवर पैसे देण्याची बँकेला दिली गेलेली कायमस्वरूपी सूचना

stand out (stands out, standing out, stood out) v If something stands out, it can be clearly noticed or is clearly better or more important than other similar things. उठून दिसणे The dark shape of the castle stands out clearly on the skyline.

standpoint (standpoints) n If you look at an event, situation, or idea from a particular standpoint, you look at it in a particular way. दृष्टिकोन

stand up (stands up, standing up, stood up) v When you are standing up, your body is upright, your legs are straight, and your weight is supported by your feet. उभे राहणे Shop assistants have to stand up all day.

staple (staples, stapling, stapled) n **Staples** are small pieces of bent wire that are used mainly for holding sheets of paper together firmly. स्टेपल ▷ n A **staple** is a food, product, or activity that is basic and important in people's everyday lives. मुख्य आहार ▷ vt If you **staple** something, you fasten it to something else or fix it in place using staples. स्टेपलने एकत्र जोडणे

stapler (staplers) n A **stapler** is a device used for putting staples into sheets of paper. स्टेपलर नावाचे साधन

star (stars, starring, starred) n A **star** is a large ball of burning gas in space. Stars look like small points of light in the sky. तारा ▷ n A **star** is somebody who is famous for doing something, for example acting or singing. प्रसिद्ध कलाकार ▷ v If an actor or actress **stars** in a play or film, he or she has one of the most important parts in it. मुख्य भूमिका करणे ▷ n A **star** is a shape that has four, five, or more points sticking out of it in a pattern. तारा

starch (starches) n **Starch** is a carbohydrate found in foods such as bread, potatoes, and rice. पिष्टमय पदार्थ

stare (stares, staring, stared) vi If you **stare** at someone or something, you look at them for a long time. एकटक पाहणे

stark (starker, starkest) adj **Stark** choices or statements are harsh and unpleasant. कडक, स्वच्छ/उघड ताशेरे

start (starts, starting, started) n If you make a **start** on doing something, you begin to do it. सुरुवात ▷ vt If you **start** to do something, you begin to do it. सर्वात करणे ▷ v When something **starts**, it begins. सुरुवात होणे

starter (starters) n A **starter** is a small quantity of food served as the first course of a meal. मुख्य जेवणापूर्वी खाण्याचा पदार्थ

startle (startles, startling, startled) vt If something sudden and unexpected **startles** you, it surprises you and frightens you slightly. आश्चर्ययुक्त भीती वाटणे

start off (starts off, starting off, started off) v If you **start off** by doing something, you do

it as the first part of an activity. सुरुवात करणे / started off by setting out the facts.

starve (starves, starving, starved) vi If people **starve**, they suffer greatly and may die from lack of food. उपासमार होणे

state (states, stating, stated) n You can refer to countries as **states**, particularly when you are discussing politics. देश ▷ vt If you **state** something, you say or write it in a formal or definite way. सांगणे

stately home (stately homes) n A **stately home** is a very large old house, especially one that people can pay to visit. प्रशस्त घर

statement (statements) n A **statement** is something that you say or write which gives information in a formal or definite way. म्हणणे, जबाब

station (stations) n A **station** is a building by a railway line where a train stops. स्थानक

stationer (stationers) n A **stationer** or a **stationer's** is a shop that sells paper, envelopes, and other materials or equipment used for writing. लेखनसामग्रीचे दुकान

stationery n **Stationery** is paper, envelopes, and writing equipment. लेखनसामग्री

statistics npl **Statistics** are facts obtained from analyzing information that is expressed in numbers. आकडेवारी

statue (statues) n A **statue** is a large sculpture of a person or an animal, made of stone, bronze, or some other hard material. पुतळा

S

status quo n The **status quo** is the situation that exists at a particular time. जशी आहे तशी स्थिती

stay (stays, staying, stayed) n The time you spend in a place is your **stay** there. मुक्कामाचा कालावधी ▷ vi If you **stay** in a place, you do not move away from it. राहणे ▷ vi If you **stay** somewhere, you live there for a short time. थांबणे

stay in (stays in, staying in, stayed in) v If you **stay in**, you remain at home during the evening and do not go out. घरी थांबणे We decided to stay in and have dinner at home.

stay up (stays up, staying up, stayed up) v If you **stay up**, you remain out of bed at a later time than normal. जागे राहणे I used to stay up late with my mum and watch TV.

steady (steadier, steadiest) adj Something that is **steady** continues or develops gradually without any interruptions and is unlikely to change suddenly. स्थिर

steak (steaks) n **Steak** is beef without much fat on it. कमी चरबी असलेला गायीच्या मांसाचा तुकडा

steal (steals, stealing, stole, stolen) v If you **steal** something from someone, you take it away from them without their permission and without intending to return it. चोरणे

steam n **Steam** is the hot mist that forms when water boils. **Steam** vehicles and machines are powered by steam. वाफ

steel n **Steel** is a very strong metal made mainly from iron. पोलाद

steep (steeper, steepest) adj A **steep** slope rises at a very sharp angle and is difficult to go up. मोठा चढाव

steeple (steeples) n A **steeple** is a tall pointed structure on top of the tower of a church. चर्चच्या छतावरील टोकदार मनोरा

steering n The **steering** in a car or other vehicle is the mechanical parts of it which make it possible to guide it. स्टिअरिंग, सुकाणू

steering wheel (steering wheels) n The **steering wheel** in a vehicle is the wheel which

the driver holds to guide the vehicle. स्टिअरिंग व्हिल, सुकाणू

step (steps) n If you take a **step**, you lift your foot and put it down in a different place. पाऊल ▷ n A **step** is a flat surface that you put your feet on to walk up or down to somewhere. पायरी

stepbrother (stepbrothers) n Someone's **stepbrother** is the son of their stepfather or stepmother. सावत्र भाऊ

stepdaughter (stepdaughters) n Someone's **stepdaughter** is a daughter that was born to their husband or wife during a previous relationship. सावत्र मुलगी

stepfather (stepfathers) n Your **stepfather** is the man who has married your mother after the death of your father or divorce of your parents. सावत्र बाप

stepladder (stepladders) n A **stepladder** is a portable ladder that is made of two sloping parts that are hinged together at the top so that it will stand up on its own. घडीची शिडी

stepmother (stepmothers) n Your **stepmother** is the woman who has married your father after the death of your mother or divorce of your parents. सावत्र आई

stepsister (stepsisters) n Someone's **stepsister** is the daughter of their stepfather or stepmother. सावत्र बहीण

stepson (stepsons) n Someone's **stepson** is a son born to their husband or wife during a previous relationship. सावत्र मुलगा

stereo (stereos) n A **stereo** is a CD or MP3 player with two speakers. स्टिरिओ

stereotype (stereotypes) n A **stereotype** is a fixed general image or set of characteristics representing a particular type of person or thing, but which may not be true in reality. एखाद्या व्यक्तिविषयी/गोष्टीविषयी केलेली एकाच प्रकारची कायमची कल्पना

sterile adj Something that is **sterile** is completely clean and free of germs. निर्जंतुक

sterilize (sterilizes, sterilizing, sterilized) vt If you **sterilize** a thing or place, you make it completely clean and free from germs. निर्जंतुक करणे

sterling *n* **Sterling** is the money system of Great Britain. स्टर्लिंग, ब्रिटिश चलन

steroid (**steroids**) *n* A **steroid** is a type of chemical substance which occurs naturally in the body, and can also be made artificially. स्टिरॉईड

stew (**stews**) *n* A **stew** is a meal made by cooking meat and vegetables in liquid at a low temperature. भाजी आणि मांस एकत्र शिजवलेला अन्नपदार्थ

steward (**stewards**) *n* A **steward** is a man whose job is to look after passengers on a ship, plane, or train. स्टिवर्ड (जहाज, विमान किंवा ट्रेनमध्ये प्रवाशांना मदत करण्यासाठी ठेवलेली व्यक्ती)

stick (**sticks, sticking, stuck**) *n* A **stick** is a long, thin piece of wood. काठी ▷ *vt* If you **stick** one thing to another, you join them together using glue. चिकटवणे

sticker (**stickers**) *n* A **sticker** is a small piece of paper or plastic with writing or a picture on it, that you can stick onto a surface. स्टिकर

stick insect (**stick insects**) *n* A **stick insect** is an insect with a long thin body and legs. एक प्रकारचा कीटक

stick out (**sticks out, sticking out, stuck out**) *v* If something **sticks out**, or if you stick it **out**, it extends beyond something else. एखादी वस्तू बाहेर डोकावणे *A newspaper was sticking out of his back pocket.*

sticky (**stickier, stickiest**) *adj* A **sticky** substance can stick to other things. **Sticky** things are covered with a sticky substance. चिकट

stiff (**stiffer, stiffest**) *adj* Something that is **stiff** is firm and does not bend easily. कडक

stifling *adj* **Stifling** heat is so hot that it makes you feel uncomfortable. उकाडा

still (**stiller, stillest**) *adj* If you are **still**, you are not moving. स्थिर ▷ *adv* If a situation **still** exists, it has continued and exists now. अजूनही

sting (**stings, stinging, stung**) *n* The **sting** of an insect is the part that stings you. कीटकाची नांगी ▷ *v* If an insect or plant **stings** you, it pricks your skin, usually with poison, so that you feel a sharp pain. विषारी काटा किंवा नांगी टोचणे

stingy (**stingier, stingiest**) *adj* If you describe someone as **stingy**, you are criticizing them for being unwilling to spend money. *(informal)* चिक्कू, कंजूष

stink (**stinks, stinking, stank, stunk**) *n* A **stink** is a strong foul smell or stench. दुर्गंधी ▷ *vi* To **stink** means to smell extremely unpleasant. दुर्गंधी येणे

stir (**stirs, stirring, stirred**) *vt* When you **stir** a liquid, you mix it inside a container using something such as a spoon. हलवणे

stitch (**stitches, stitching, stitched**) *n* **Stitches** are the pieces of thread that have been sewn in a piece of cloth. टाका ▷ *vt* If you **stitch** cloth, you use a needle and thread to join two pieces together or to make a decoration. शिवणे, टाके घालणे

stock (**stocks, stocking, stocked**) *n* **Stocks** are shares in the ownership of a company. A company's **stock** consists of all the shares that people have bought in it. कंपनीचे शेअर्स ▷ *vt* A shop that **stocks** particular goods keeps a supply of them to sell. साठा करणे

stockbroker (**stockbrokers**) *n* A **stockbroker** is someone whose profession is buying and selling stocks and shares for clients. शेअर दलाल

stock cube (**stock cubes**) *n* A **stock cube** is a solid cube made from dried meat or vegetable juices and other flavourings. Stock cubes are used to add flavour to dishes such as stews and soups. स्टॉक क्यूब

stock exchange (**stock exchanges**) *n* A **stock exchange** is a place where people buy and sell stocks and shares. शेअर बाजार

stock market (**stock markets**) *n* The **stock market** consists of the activity of buying stocks and shares, and the people and institutions that organize it. शेअर बाजार

stock up (**stocks up, stocking up, stocked up**) *v* If you **stock up** with something or **stock**

S

up on it, you buy a lot of it, in case you cannot get it later. साठा करून ठेवणे *People are stocking up on fuel.*

stomach (stomachs) *n* Your **stomach** is the organ inside your body where food is digested. पोट

stomachache (stomachaches) *n* If you have a **stomachache**, you have a pain in your stomach. पोटदुखी

stone (stones) *n* Stone is a hard solid material that is found in the ground. It is often used for building. दगड ▷ *n* A **stone** is a small piece of rock that is found on the ground. दगड

stool (stools) *n* A **stool** is a seat with legs but no support for your back or arms. स्टूल

stop (stops, stopping, stopped) *n* If something that is moving comes to a **stop**, it slows down and no longer moves. थांबण्याची क्रिया ▷ *vi* If you **stop** doing something, you do not do it any more. थांबवणे ▷ *vi* If something **stops**, it does not do what it did any more. थांबणे

stopover (stopovers) *n* A **stopover** is a short stay in a place in between parts of a journey. प्रवासात मध्येच विश्रांतीसाठी घेतलेला थांबा

stopwatch (stopwatches) *n* A **stopwatch** is a watch with buttons which you press at the beginning and end of an event, so that you can measure exactly how long it takes. स्टॉपवॉच

storage *n* Storage is the process of keeping something in a particular place until it is needed. साठा

store (stores, storing, stored) *n* A **store** is a shop. Store is used mainly to refer to a large shop selling a variety of goods, but in American English, a **store** can be any shop. दुकान ▷ *vt* When you **store** things, you put them in a container or other place and leave them there until they are needed. साठवून ठेवणे

storm (storms) *n* A **storm** is very bad weather, with heavy rain, strong winds, and often thunder and lightning. वादळ

stormy (stormier, stormiest) *adj* If there is **stormy** weather, there is a strong wind and heavy rain. वादळी

story (stories) *n* A **story** is a description of imaginary people and events, which is written or told in order to entertain. गोष्ट, कथा

stove (stoves) *n* A **stove** is a piece of equipment for heating a room or cooking. स्टोव्ह

straight (straighter, straightest) *adj* A **straight** line or edge continues in the same direction and does not bend or curve. सरळ

straighteners *npl* **Straighteners** are a heated device that you use to make your hair straight. केस सरळ करणारे साधन

straightforward *adj* If something is **straightforward**, it is not complicated to do or understand. साधेसरळ

straight on *adv* You use **straight on** to indicate that the way from one place to another is forward. सरळ

strain (strains, straining, strained) *n* If **strain** is put on a person or organization, they have to do more than they are really able to do. तणाव ▷ *vt* To **strain** something means to make it do more than it is really able to do. ताण आणणे

strained *adj* If someone's appearance, voice, or behaviour is **strained**, they seem worried and nervous. ताणतणाव असलेले

stranded *adj* If you are **stranded**, you are prevented from leaving a place, for example because of bad weather. अडकून पडलेला

strange (stranger, strangest) *adj* Strange means unusual or unexpected. विचित्र

stranger (strangers) *n* A **stranger** is someone you have not met before or do not know at all. If two people are **strangers**, they have never met or do not know each other at all. अनोळखी

strangle (strangles, strangling, strangled) *vt* To **strangle** someone means to kill them by tightly squeezing their throat. गळा आवळून ठार मारणे

strap (straps) n A **strap** is a narrow piece of leather, cloth, or other material. Straps are used to carry things or hold them in place. पट्टा

strategic adj **Strategic** means relating to the most important, general aspects of something such as a military operation or political policy. धोरणात्मक

strategy (strategies) n A **strategy** is a general plan or set of plans intended to achieve something, especially over a long period. धोरण

straw (straws) n **Straw** is the dry, yellow stems of crops. पेंढा ▷ n A **straw** is a thin tube that you use to suck a drink into your mouth. स्ट्रॉ

strawberry (strawberries) n A **strawberry** is a small red fruit with tiny seeds in its skin. स्ट्रॉबेरी

stray (strays) n A **stray** is a domestic animal, fowl, etc, that has wandered away and is lost. भटका प्राणी

stream (streams) n A **stream** is a small narrow river. ओढा

street (streets) n A **street** is a road in a town or village, usually with houses along it. (दोन्ही बाजूला घरे असलेला) रस्ता

streetlamp (streetlamps) n A **streetlamp** is a tall post with a light at the top, which stands by the side of the road to light it up, usually in a town. पथदीप

street map (street maps) n A **street map** is a map of a town or city, showing the positions and names of all the streets. रस्त्याचा नकाशा

streetwise adj Someone who is **streetwise** knows how to deal with difficult or dangerous situations in big cities. (informal) स्ट्रीटव्हाइज़ (मोठ्या शहरातील खडतर किंवा धोकादायक प्रसंग नीट हाताळू शकणारा)

strength n Your **strength** is the physical energy that you have, which gives you the ability to do things such as lift heavy objects. शक्ती

strengthen (strengthens, strengthening, strengthened) vt To **strengthen** something means to make it stronger. मजबूत करणे

stress (stresses, stressing, stressed) n If you lay **stress** on a point, you emphasize it because you think it is important. जोर ▷ vt If you **stress** a point in a discussion, you emphasize it because you think it is important. एखाद्या मुद्यावर जोर देणे

stressed adj If you feel **stressed**, you feel tension and anxiety because of difficulties in your life. ताणतणाव असलेले

stressful adj A **stressful** situation or experience causes someone to feel stress. ताणतणावयुक्त

stretch (stretches, stretching, stretched) vi Something that **stretches** over an area covers all of it. विस्तारणे, पसरणे ▷ vi When you **stretch**, you hold out part of your body as far as you can. ताणणे

stretcher (stretchers) n A **stretcher** is a long piece of canvas with a pole along each side, which is used to carry an injured person. स्ट्रेचर

stretchy (stretchier, stretchiest) adj **Stretchy** material is slightly elastic and stretches easily. ताणणारे

strict (stricter, strictest) adj A **strict** rule or order is very precise or severe and must be obeyed absolutely. काटेकोर

strictly adv If something is done **strictly** it is done severely and must be obeyed absolutely. काटेकोरपणे

strike (strikes, striking, struck, stricken) n When there is a **strike**, workers stop doing their work for a period of time, usually in order to try to get better pay or conditions for themselves. संप ▷ vt If you **strike** someone or something, you deliberately hit them. फटका मारणे ▷ vi When workers **strike**, they stop working for a period of time, usually to try to get better pay or conditions. संप पुकारणे ▷ v To **strike** someone or something means to attack them or to affect them, quickly and violently. हल्ला करणे

striker (strikers) n A **striker** is a person who is on strike. संपावरील व्यक्ती

striking adj Something that is **striking** is very noticeable or unusual. वेगळेपणाने उठून दिसणारे

string (strings) n **String** is thin rope that is made of twisted threads. दोरी ▷ n The **strings** on an instrument are the thin pieces of wire that are stretched across it and that make sounds when the instrument is played. तार

strip (strips, stripping, stripped) n A **strip** of something is a long narrow piece of it. पट्टा ▷ v If you **strip**, or if someone **strips** you, your clothes are removed from your body. विवस्त्र करणे

stripe (stripes) n A **stripe** is a long line which is a different colour from the areas next to it. वेगळ्या रंगाचा पट्टा

striped adj Something that is **striped** has stripes on it. पट्टे असलेले

stripy adj Something that is **stripy** has stripes on it. (informal) पट्टे असलेला

stroke (strokes, stroking, stroked) n If someone has a **stroke**, a blood vessel in their brain bursts or gets blocked, which may kill them or cause one side of their body to be paralysed. झटका ▷ vt If you **stroke** someone or something, you move your hand slowly and gently over them. हळुवारपणे हात फिरवणे

stroll (strolls) n A **stroll** is a leisurely walk. आरामशीरपणे चालणे

strong (stronger, strongest) adj Someone who is **strong** is healthy with good muscles. बलवान ▷ adj **Strong** things are not easy to break. मजबूत

strongly adv If something is built **strongly**, it means it is not easily broken. मजबूतपणे

structure (structures) n The **structure** of something is the way in which it is made, built, or organized. रचना

struggle (struggles, struggling, struggled) n A **struggle** is an attempt to obtain something or to defeat someone who is denying you something. संघर्ष ▷ v If you **struggle** or **struggle** to do something difficult, you try hard to do it. संघर्ष करणे

stub (stubs) n The **stub** of a cigarette or a pencil is the short piece which remains when the rest has been used. थोटूक

stubborn adj A **stubborn** person is determined to do what they want and refuses to change their mind. हट्टी

stub out (stubs out, stubbing out, stubbed out) v When someone **stubs out** a cigarette, they put it out by pressing it against something hard. थोटूक चुरगळणे A sign told visitors to stub out their cigarettes.

stuck adj If something is **stuck** in a place, it cannot move. अडकलेला ▷ adj If you get **stuck**, you can't go on doing something because it is too difficult. अडकलेला

stuck-up adj If you say that someone is **stuck-up**, you mean that are very proud and unfriendly because they think they are very important. (informal) गर्विष्ठ, स्वत:विषयी अवास्तव कल्पना असलेला

stud (studs) n **Studs** are small pieces of metal which are attached to a surface for decoration. छोटे खिळे/बटन

student (students) n A **student** is a person who is studying at a university, college, or school. विद्यार्थी

student discount (student discounts) n A **student discount** is a reduction in the usual price of something that only students are allowed. विद्यार्थ्यांना दिलेली सूट

studio (studios) n A **studio** is a room where a designer, painter, or photographer works. स्टुडिओ

studio flat (studio flats) n A **studio flat** is a small flat with one room for living and sleeping in, a kitchen, and a bathroom. स्वयंपाकघर व बैठकीची खोली असलेला फ्लॅट

study (studies, studying, studied) v If you **study**, you spend time learning about a particular subject or subjects. अभ्यास करणे

stuff n You can use **stuff** to refer to things in a general way, without mentioning the things themselves by name. *(informal)* वस्तू, गोष्ट

stuffy (stuffier, stuffiest) adj If you describe a person or institution as **stuffy**, you are criticizing them for being formal and old-fashioned. जुनाट वळणाची व्यक्ती

stumble (stumbles, stumbling, stumbled) vi If you **stumble**, you nearly fall while walking or running. धडपडणे

stunned adj **Stunned** means shocked or astonished. विस्मयचकित

stunning adj A **stunning** person or thing is extremely beautiful or impressive. अत्यंत सुंदर

stunt (stunts) n A **stunt** is something interesting that someone does to get attention or publicity. लोकांचे लक्ष वेधून घेण्यासाठी केलेले धाडसाचे काम

stuntman (stuntmen) n A **stuntman** is a man whose job is to do dangerous things, either for publicity, or in a film instead of an actor so that the actor does not risk being injured. लोकांचे लक्ष वेधून घेण्यासाठी धाडसाचे काम करणारा

stupid (stupider, stupidest) adj If you say that someone or something is **stupid**, you mean that they show a lack of good judgement or intelligence and they are not at all sensible. मूर्ख

stutter (stutters, stuttering, stuttered) vi If someone **stutters**, they have difficulty speaking because they find it hard to say the first sound of a word. तोतरे बोलणे

style (styles) n The **style** of something is the general way it is done or presented. शैली

stylist (stylists) n A **stylist** is a person whose job is to cut and arrange people's hair. केशरचनाकार

subject (subjects) n The **subject** of a conversation, letter, or book is the person or thing that is being discussed or written about. विषय

submarine (submarines) n A **submarine** is a ship that can travel below the surface of the sea. पाणबुडी

subscription (subscriptions) n A **subscription** is an amount of money that you pay regularly to receive a service or magazine, or to belong to or support an organization. वर्गणी

subsidiary (subsidiaries) n A **subsidiary** is a company which is part of a larger and more important company. दुय्यम कंपनी

subsidize (subsidizes, subsidizing, subsidized) vt If an authority **subsidizes** something, they pay part of the cost of it. (मदत म्हणून) अर्थसहाय्य करणे/किमतीचा काही भाग भरणे

subsidy (subsidies) n A **subsidy** is money paid by an authority in order to help an industry or business, or to pay for a public service. अनुदान

substance (substances) n A **substance** is a solid, powder, liquid, or gas. पदार्थ

substitute (substitutes, substituting, substituted) n A **substitute** is something or someone that you use instead of something or someone else. बदली वस्तू ▷ v If you **substitute** one thing for another, you use it instead of the other thing. एखाद्या गोष्टीच्या बदली वापरणे

subtitled adj If a foreign film is **subtitled**, a printed translation of the words is shown at the bottom of the picture. उपशीर्षक असलेला

subtitles npl **Subtitles** are a printed translation of the words of a foreign film that are shown at the bottom of the picture. उपशीर्षके

subtle (subtler, subtlest) adj Something **subtle** is not immediately obvious or noticeable. सूक्ष्म

subtract (subtracts, subtracting, subtracted) vt If you **subtract** one number from another,

you take the first number away from the
second. वजा करणे

suburb (suburbs) n The **suburbs** of a city
are the areas on the edge of it where people
live. उपनगर

suburban adj **Suburban** means relating to a
suburb. उपनगरी

subway (subways) n A **subway** is a passage
for pedestrians underneath a busy road. भुयारी
रस्ता

succeed (succeeds, succeeding, succeeded)
vi To **succeed** means to achieve the result that
you wanted or to perform in a satisfactory
way. यशस्वी होणे

success n **Success** is the achievement of
something you have wanted to achieve. यश

successful adj Someone or something that
is **successful** achieves a desired result or
performs in a satisfactory way. यशस्वी

successfully adv If something happens or is
carried out successfully, it achieves a desired
result or performs in a satisfactory way.
यशस्वीपणे

successive adj **Successive** means happening
or existing one after another without a break.
लागोपाठचा

successor (successors) n Someone's
successor is the person who takes their job
after they have left. उत्तराधिकारी

such det You use **such** to refer back to the
thing or person that you have just mentioned,
or a thing or person like the one that you have
just mentioned. अशा प्रकारचा We regard such
methods as entirely unacceptable. ▷ det You
use **such** in front of an adjective followed by
a noun to make the adjective stronger. असा
They're such good friends. ▷ det **Such** means
like this or like that. असे, तसे How could you do
such a thing? ▷ det You use **such a** or **such an**
in front of an adjective followed by a noun to
make the adjective stronger. इतका.... की It's
such an ugly building.

suck (sucks, sucking, sucked) v If you **suck**
something, you hold it in your mouth and

pull at it with the muscles in your cheeks and
tongue, for example in order to get liquid out
of it. चोखणे

Sudan n **Sudan** is a republic in north-east
Africa, on the Red Sea. सुदान

Sudanese (Sudanese) adj **Sudanese**
means belonging or relating to Sudan, or
to its people or culture. सुदानिज ▷ npl The
Sudanese are the people of Sudan. सुदानिज

sudden adj Something that is **sudden**
happens quickly and unexpectedly. अचानकपणे

suddenly adv If something happens
suddenly, it happens quickly and
unexpectedly. अचानकपणे

sue (sues, suing, sued) v If you **sue**
someone, you start a legal case against them
to claim money from them because they
have harmed you in some way. न्यायालयात
खटला भरणे

suede n **Suede** is thin soft leather with a
slightly rough surface. पृष्ठभाग थोडा खरखरीत
असलेले पातळ मऊ चामडे

suffer (suffers, suffering, suffered) v If you
suffer pain or an illness, or if you **suffer** from
a pain or illness, you are badly affected by it.
वेदना होणे

**suffocate (suffocates, suffocating,
suffocated)** vi If someone **suffocates**, they
die because there is no air for them to breathe.
गुदमरणे

sugar n **Sugar** is a sweet substance, often in
the form of white or brown crystals, used to
sweeten food and drink. साखर

sugar-free adj **Sugar-free** drinks do not
contain any sugar. साखररहित

suggest (suggests, suggesting, suggested)
vt If you **suggest** something, you put forward
a plan or idea for someone to consider. सूचना
करणे

suggestion (suggestions) n If you make a
suggestion, you put forward an idea or plan
for someone to think about. सूचना

suicide (suicides) n People who commit
suicide deliberately kill themselves. आत्महत्या

suicide bomber (suicide bombers) n A **suicide bomber** is a terrorist who carries out a bomb attack, knowing that he or she will be killed in the explosion. आत्मघातकी मानवी बॉम्ब

suit (suits, suiting, suited) n A **suit** is a matching jacket and trousers, or a matching jacket and skirt. सूट ▷ vt If a piece of clothing or a particular style or colour **suits** you, it makes you look attractive. शोभून दिसणे

suitable adj Someone or something that is **suitable** for a particular purpose or occasion is right or acceptable for it. योग्य

suitcase (suitcases) n A **suitcase** is a case for carrying clothes when you are travelling. कपडे ठेवण्याची पेटी, सूटकेस

suite (suites) n A **suite** is a set of rooms in a hotel or other building. स्वीट (हॉटेलमधील वा इतरकडील दोन-तीन खोल्या असणारी खास प्रशस्त खोली)

sulk (sulks, sulking, sulked) vi If you **sulk**, you are silent and bad-tempered for a while because you are annoyed about something. चिडणे, फुगून बसणे

sulky adj Someone who is **sulky** is sulking or is unwilling to enjoy themselves. चिडलेला, फुरंगटलेला

sultana (sultanas) n **Sultanas** are dried white grapes. सुकवलेली पांढरी द्राक्षे, बेदाणा

sum (sums) n A **sum** of money is an amount of money. रक्कम ▷ n In maths, a **sum** is a problem you work out using numbers. बेरीज

summarize (summarizes, summarizing, summarized) v If you **summarize** something, you give a brief description of its main points. सारांशरूपाने सांगणे

summary (summaries) n A **summary** is a short account of something giving the main points but not the details. सारांश

summer (summers) n **Summer** is the season between spring and autumn. In summer the weather is usually warm or hot. उन्हाळा

summer holidays npl Your **summer holidays** are a period of time in the summer during which you relax and enjoy yourself away from home. उन्हाळी सुट्ट्या

summertime n **Summertime** is the period of time during which summer lasts. उन्हाळ्याचा कालावधी

summit (summits) n A **summit** is a meeting between the leaders of two or more countries to discuss important matters. शिखर परिषद

sum up (sums up, summing up, summed up) v If you **sum up** or **sum** something **up**, you briefly describe the main features of something. सारांशरूपाने सांगणे Well, to sum up, what is the message that you are trying to communicate?

sun n The **sun** is the ball of fire in the sky that the Earth goes round, and that gives us heat and light. सूर्य

sunbathe (sunbathes, sunbathing, sunbathed) vi When people **sunbathe**, they sit or lie in a place where the sun shines on them, in order to get a suntan. सूर्यस्नान करणे

sunbed (sunbeds) n A **sunbed** is a piece of equipment with special lights. You lie on it to make your skin browner. सनबेड

sunblock (sunblocks) n **Sunblock** is a cream which you put on your skin to protect it completely from the sun. उन्हापासून संरक्षण देणारे क्रीम

sunburn (sunburns) n If someone has **sunburn**, their skin is sore because they have spent too much time in the sun. उन्हामुळे त्वचा जळणे

sunburnt adj Someone who is **sunburnt** has sore skin because they have spent too much time in hot sunshine. उन्हामुळे करपलेली त्वचा

suncream (suncreams) n **Suncream** is a cream that protects your skin from the sun's rays, especially in hot weather. उन्हापासून संरक्षण देणारे क्रीम

Sunday (Sundays) n **Sunday** is the day after Saturday and before Monday. रविवार

sunflower (sunflowers) n A **sunflower** is a tall plant with large yellow flowers. सूर्यफूल

S

sunglasses *npl* **Sunglasses** are spectacles with dark lenses to protect your eyes from bright sunlight. सनग्लासेस, उन्हापासून संरक्षण करणारा चष्मा

sunlight *n* **Sunlight** is the light that comes from the sun. सूर्यप्रकाश

sunny (**sunnier, sunniest**) *adj* When it is **sunny**, the sun is shining brightly. कडक ऊन पडलेला दिवस

sunrise *n* **Sunrise** is the time in the morning when the sun first appears. सूर्योदय

sunroof (**sunroofs**) *n* A **sunroof** is a part of the roof of a car that opens to let sunshine and air enter the car. सूर्यप्रकाश व हवा आत येण्यासाठी असलेले कारचे छत

sunscreen (**sunscreens**) *n* A **sunscreen** is a cream that protects your skin from the sun's rays in hot weather. उन्हापासून संरक्षण देणारे क्रीम

sunset *n* **Sunset** is the time in the evening when the sun disappears. सूर्यास्त

sunshine *n* **Sunshine** is the light and heat that comes from the sun. ऊन

sunstroke *n* **Sunstroke** is an illness caused by spending too much time in hot sunshine. उष्माघात

suntan (**suntans**) *n* If you have a **suntan**, the sun has turned your skin a brown colour. उन्हामुळे त्वचेवर चढलेला राप

suntan lotion (**suntan lotions**) *n* **Suntan lotion** protects your skin from the sun. उन्हापासून संरक्षण देणारे द्रावण/ लोशन

suntan oil (**suntan oils**) *n* **Suntan oil** protects your skin from the sun. उन्हापासून संरक्षण देणारे तेल

super *adj* **Super** means very nice or good. *(informal, old-fashioned)* उत्तम

superb *adj* If something is **superb**, it is very good indeed. सर्वोत्कृष्ट

superficial *adj* If you describe someone as **superficial**, you disapprove of them because they do not think deeply, and have little understanding of anything serious or important. उथळपणे वागणारे

superior (**superiors**) *adj* You use **superior** to describe someone or something that is better than other similar people or things. वरचढ ▷ *n* Your **superior** in an organization that you work for is a person who has a higher rank than you. वरिष्ठ

supermarket (**supermarkets**) *n* A **supermarket** is a large shop which sells all kinds of food and some household goods. सुपरमार्केट

supernatural *adj* **Supernatural** creatures, forces, and events are believed by some people to exist or happen, although they are impossible according to scientific laws. गूढ, देवी, अलौकिक

superstitious *adj* People who are **superstitious** believe in things that are not real or possible, for example magic. अंधश्रद्धाळू

supervise (**supervises, supervising, supervised**) *vt* If you **supervise** an activity or a person, you make sure that the activity is done correctly or that the person is behaving correctly. देखरेख करणे

supervisor (**supervisors**) *n* A **supervisor** is a person who supervises activities or people, especially workers or students. पर्यवेक्षक

supper (**suppers**) *n* Some people refer to the main meal eaten in the early part of the evening as **supper**. रात्रीचे जेवण

supplement (**supplements**) *n* A **supplement** is something which is added to another thing in order to improve it. जोड, पुरवणी

supplier (**suppliers**) *n* A **supplier** is a person or company that provides you with goods or equipment. पुरवठादार

supplies *npl* You can use **supplies** to refer to food, equipment, and other essential things that people need, especially when these are provided in large quantities. जीवनावश्यक वस्तू

supply (**supplies, supplying, supplied**) *n* A **supply** of something is an amount of it which is available for use. If something is **in short**

supply, there is very little of it available. पुरवठा
▷ *vt* If you **supply** someone with something, you provide them with it. पुरवणे

supply teacher (**supply teachers**) *n* A **supply teacher** is a teacher whose job is to take the place of other teachers at different schools when they are unable to be there. बदली शिक्षक

support (**supports, supporting, supported**) *n* If you give someone your **support**, you agree with them, and perhaps try to help them because you want them to succeed. पाठिंबा ▷ *vt* If you **support** someone or their ideas or aims, you agree with them, and perhaps help them because you want them to succeed. पाठिंबा देणे

supporter (**supporters**) *n* **Supporters** are people who support someone or something, for example a political leader or a sports team. समर्थक

suppose (**supposes, supposing, supposed**) *vt* You use **suppose** or **supposing** when you are considering a possible situation or action and trying to think what effects it would have. समजून चालणे

supposedly *adv* **Supposedly** means that the following word or description is misleading and is not definitely known to be true. कल्पना केल्याप्रमाणे

supposing *conj* You say **supposing** to ask someone to pretend that something is true or to imagine that something will happen. जर असे मानले तर *Supposing he sees us?*

surcharge (**surcharges**) *n* A **surcharge** is an extra payment of money in addition to the usual payment for something. It is added for a specific reason, for example by a company because costs have risen or by a government as a tax. अधिभार

sure (**surer, surest**) *adj* If you are **sure** that something is true, you are certain that it is true. If you are not **sure** about something, you do not know for certain what the true situation is. खात्री असलेला

surely *adv* You use **surely** to emphasize that you think something should be true, and you would be surprised if it was not true. खात्रीपूर्वक

surf (**surfs, surfing, surfed**) *n* **Surf** is the mass of white foam formed by waves as they fall on the shore. लाटांमुळे तयार झालेला फेस ▷ *vi* If you **surf**, you ride on big waves on a special board. खास बोर्डच्या सहाय्याने समुद्राच्या लाटांवर स्वार होणे

surface (**surfaces**) *n* The **surface** of something is the top part of it or the outside of it. पृष्ठभाग

surfboard (**surfboards**) *n* A **surfboard** is a long narrow board that is used for surfing. सर्फबोर्ड

surfer (**surfers**) *n* A **surfer** rides on big waves on a special board. सर्फबोर्डच्या सहाय्याने लाटांवर स्वार होणारा

surfing *n* **Surfing** is the sport of riding on the top of a wave while standing or lying on a special board. सर्फिंग नावाचा खेळ

surge (**surges**) *n* A **surge** is a sudden large increase in something that has previously been steady, or has only increased or developed slowly. अचानक झालेली वाढ

surgeon (**surgeons**) *n* A **surgeon** is a doctor who performs surgery. शस्त्रक्रिया करणारे डॉक्टर

surgery (**surgeries**) *n* **Surgery** is medical treatment which involves cutting open a person's body in order to repair or remove a diseased or damaged part. शस्त्रक्रिया ▷ *n* A **surgery** is the room or house where a doctor or dentist works. डॉक्टर काम करतात ती जागा

surname (**surnames**) *n* Your **surname** is the name that you share with other members of your family. आडनाव

surplus (**surpluses**) *n* **Surplus** is used to describe something that is extra or that is more than is needed. जादा ▷ *n* If there is a **surplus** of something, there is more than is needed. जादा

surprise (**surprises**) *n* A **surprise** is an unexpected event, fact, or piece of news. आश्चर्य

S

surprised adj If you are **surprised** at something, you feel that it is unexpected or unusual. आश्चर्यचकित झालेली व्यक्ती

surprising adj Something that is **surprising** is unexpected or unusual. आश्चर्यचकित करणारे

surprisingly adv **Surprisingly** means unexpectedly or unusually. आश्चर्यकारकरीत्या

surrender (**surrenders, surrendering, surrendered**) vi If you **surrender**, you stop fighting or resisting someone and agree that you have been beaten. शरणागती पत्करणे

surrogate mother (**surrogate mothers**) n A **surrogate mother** is a woman who has agreed to give birth to a baby on behalf of another woman. मूल होण्यासाठी जिचे गर्भाशय भाड्याने घेतले आहे अशी स्त्री

surround (**surrounds, surrounding, surrounded**) vt If something or someone **is surrounded** by something, that thing is situated all around them. वेढणे

surroundings npl The place where someone or something is can be referred to as their **surroundings**. परिसर

survey (**surveys**) n If you carry out a **survey**, you try to find out detailed information about a lot of different people or things, usually by asking people a series of questions. सर्वेक्षण

surveyor (**surveyors**) n A **surveyor** is a person whose job is to inspect land or buildings. सर्वेक्षक

survival n **Survival** is the fact of continuing to live or exist in spite of great danger or difficulty. जगण्याची धडपड

survive (**survives, surviving, survived**) v If someone **survives** in a dangerous situation, they do not die. वाचणे

survivor (**survivors**) n A **survivor** of a disaster, accident, or illness is someone who continues to live afterwards in spite of coming close to death. संकटातून वाचलेली व्यक्ती

suspect (**suspects, suspecting, suspected**) n A **suspect** is a person who the police think may be guilty of a crime. संशयित ▷ vt If you

say that you **suspect** that something is true, you mean that you believe it is probably true, but you want to make it sound less strong or direct. संशय घेणे

suspend (**suspends, suspending, suspended**) vt If you **suspend** something, you delay or stop it for a while. काही काळासाठी थांबवणे

suspense n **Suspense** is a state of excitement or anxiety about something that is going to happen very soon. उत्कंठा

suspension n The **suspension** of something is the act of delaying or stopping it for a while. काही काळासाठीची स्थगिती

suspension bridge (**suspension bridges**) n A **suspension bridge** is a type of bridge that is supported from above by cables. लोखंडी दोरखंडांच्या आधारी बांधलेला तरंगता पूल

suspicious adj If you are **suspicious** of someone or something, you do not trust them. संशयास्पद

swallow (**swallows, swallowing, swallowed**) n When you take a **swallow**, you cause something to go from your mouth down into your stomach. गिळण्याची क्रिया ▷ vt If you **swallow** something, you cause it to go from your mouth down into your stomach. गिळणे ▷ vi When you **swallow**, you cause something to go from your mouth down into your stomach. गिळणे

swamp (**swamps**) n A **swamp** is an area of wet land with wild plants growing in it. दलदलीचा प्रदेश

swan (**swans**) n A **swan** is a large white bird with a long neck that lives on rivers and lakes. राजहंस

swap (**swaps, swapping, swapped**) v If you **swap** something with someone, you give it to them and receive a different thing in exchange. वस्तूंची देवाणघेवाण करणे

swat (**swats, swatting, swatted**) vt If you **swat** an insect, you hit it with a quick, swinging movement. जलद फटका मारून चिरडून टाकणे

sway (sways, swaying, swayed) *vi* When people or things **sway**, they lean or swing slowly from one side to the other. हेलकावे खाणे

Swaziland *n* Swaziland is a kingdom in southern Africa. स्वाझीलँड

swear (swears, swearing, swore, sworn) *vi* If someone **swears**, they use language that is considered to be rude or offensive. वाईट भाषेचा वापर करणे

swearword (swearwords) *n* A **swearword** is a word which is considered to be rude or offensive. Swearwords are usually used when people are angry. वाईट शब्द

sweat (sweats, sweating, sweated) *n* Sweat is the salty colourless liquid which comes through your skin when you are hot, ill, or afraid. घाम ▷ *vi* When you **sweat**, sweat comes through your skin. घाम येणे

sweater (sweaters) *n* A **sweater** is a warm piece of clothing which covers the upper part of your body and your arms. स्वेटर

sweatshirt (sweatshirts) *n* A **sweatshirt** is a loose warm piece of casual clothing, usually made of thick cotton, which covers the upper part of your body and your arms. स्वेटशर्ट

sweaty (sweatier, sweatiest) *adj* If your clothing or body is **sweaty**, it is soaked or covered with sweat. घामेजलेले

swede (swedes) *n* A **swede** is a round yellow root vegetable with a brown or purple skin. स्वीड नावाची भाजी

Swede (Swedes) *n* A **Swede** is a person who comes from Sweden. स्वीडनचा रहिवासी

Sweden *n* Sweden is a kingdom in north-west Europe, occupying the eastern part of the Scandinavian Peninsula, on the Gulf of Bothnia and the Baltic. स्वीडन

Swedish *adj* Swedish means belonging or relating to Sweden, or to its people, language, or culture. स्वीडिश ▷ *n* Swedish is the language spoken in Sweden. स्वीडिश भाषा

sweep (sweeps, sweeping, swept) *vt* If you **sweep** an area of ground, you push dirt or rubbish off it with a broom. झाडणे

sweet (sweeter, sweetest, sweets) *adj* Sweet food or drink contains a lot of sugar. गोड ▷ *adj* If you describe something as **sweet**, you mean that it gives you great pleasure and satisfaction. प्रसन्न ▷ *n* A **sweet** is something sweet, such as fruit or a pudding, that you eat at the end of a meal. गोड पदार्थ

sweetcorn *n* Sweetcorn consists of the yellow seeds of the maize plant, which are eaten as a vegetable. गोड मका

sweetener (sweeteners) *n* A **sweetener** is an artificial substance that can be used instead of sugar. गोडवा आणणारा पदार्थ

sweets *npl* Sweets are small sweet things such as toffees, chocolates, and mints. मिठाई

sweltering *adj* If the weather is **sweltering**, it is very hot. अंगाची लाही लाही करणारा, घामाघूम करणारा

swerve (swerves, swerving, swerved) *v* If a vehicle or other moving thing **swerves**, it suddenly changes direction, often in order to avoid hitting something. चकवणे, एकदम वळणे

swim (swims, swimming, swam, swum) *vi* When you **swim**, you move through water by making movements with your arms and legs. पोहणे

swimmer (swimmers) *n* A **swimmer** is a person who swims, especially for sport or pleasure, or a person who is swimming. पोहणारी व्यक्ती

swimming *n* Swimming is the activity of swimming, especially as a sport or for pleasure. पोहण्याची क्रिया

swimming costume (swimming costumes) *n* A **swimming costume** is a piece of clothing that is worn for swimming, especially by women and girls. पोहण्याचा स्त्रियांचा पोषाख

swimming pool (swimming pools) *n* A **swimming pool** is a place that has been built for people to swim in. It consists of a large

S

hole that has been tiled and filled with water. पोहण्यासाठी बांधलेला तलाव

swimming trunks npl **Swimming trunks** are the shorts that a man wears when he goes swimming. पोहताना पुरुष वापरतात ती चड्डी

swimsuit (swimsuits) n A **swimsuit** is a piece of clothing that is worn for swimming, especially by women and girls. पोहण्याचा (स्त्रियांसाठी) पोषाख

swing (swings, swinging, swung) n A **swing** is the action of moving backward and forward or from side to side. हेलकावा ▷ v If something **swings** or if you **swing** it, it moves repeatedly backwards and forwards or from side to side from a fixed point. झोके घेणे

Swiss adj **Swiss** means belonging or relating to Switzerland, or to its people or culture. स्विस ▷ npl The **Swiss** are the people of Switzerland. स्विस

switch (switches, switching, switched) n A **switch** is a small control for an electrical device which you use to turn the device on or off. स्वीच ▷ vi If you **switch** to something different, for example to a different system, task, or subject of conversation, you change to it from what you were doing or saying before. कामात झटकन केलेला बदल

switchboard (switchboards) n A **switchboard** is a place in a large office or business where all the telephone calls are connected. स्विचबोर्ड

switch off (switches off, switching off, switched off) v If you **switch off** an electrical device, you stop it working by operating a switch. दिवा किंवा पंखा इत्यादी बंद करणे The driver switched off the headlights.

switch on (switches on, switching on, switched on) v If you **switch on** an electrical device, you make it start working by operating a switch. चालू करणे We switched on the radio.

Switzerland n **Switzerland** is a republic in west central Europe. स्वीत्झर्लंड

swollen adj If a part of your body is **swollen**, it is larger and rounder than normal, usually as a result of injury or illness. सुजलेला

sword (swords) n A **sword** is a weapon with a handle and a long blade. तलवार

swordfish (swordfish) n A **swordfish** is a large sea fish with a very long upper jaw. स्वर्डफिश नावाचा मासा

swot (swots, swotting, swotted) vi If you **swot**, you study very hard, especially when you are preparing for an examination. (informal) खूप अभ्यास करणे

syllable (syllables) n A **syllable** is a part of a word that contains a single vowel sound and that is pronounced as a unit. एकच स्वरयुक्त उच्चार असलेला शब्द

syllabus (syllabuses) n You can refer to the subjects that are studied in a particular course as the **syllabus**. अभ्यासक्रम

symbol (symbols) n A **symbol** of something such as an idea is a shape or design that is used to represent it. चिन्ह

symmetrical adj If something is **symmetrical**, it has two halves which are exactly the same, except that one half is the mirror image of the other. दोन्ही बाजूंची एकसमानता

sympathetic adj If you are **sympathetic** to someone who has had a misfortune, you are kind to them and show that you understand how they are feeling. सहानुभूतिपूर्वक वागणारा

sympathize (sympathizes, sympathizing, sympathized) vi If you **sympathize** with someone who has had a misfortune, you show that you are sorry for them. सहानुभूती दाखविणे

sympathy (sympathies) *n* If you have **sympathy** for someone who has had a misfortune, you are sorry for them, and show this in the way you behave towards them. सहानुभूती

symphony (symphonies) *n* A **symphony** is a piece of music written to be played by an orchestra, usually in four parts. वाद्यवृंदाचे संगीत

symptom (symptoms) *n* A **symptom** of an illness is something wrong with your body that is a sign of the illness. लक्षण

synagogue (synagogues) *n* A **synagogue** is a building where Jewish people worship. यहुदी धर्मीयांचे प्रार्थनास्थळ

Syria *n* Syria is a republic in West Asia, on the Mediterranean. सिरिया

Syrian (Syrians) *adj* Syrian means belonging or relating to Syria, or to its people or culture. सिरियन ▷ *n* A **Syrian** is a Syrian citizen, or a person of Syrian origin. सिरियन

syringe (syringes) *n* A **syringe** is a small tube with a fine hollow needle, used for injecting drugs or for taking blood from someone's body. सिरिंज

syrup (syrups) *n* Syrup is a sweet liquid made by cooking sugar with water or fruit juice. गोड द्रवरूप औषध

system (systems) *n* A **system** is a way of working, organizing, or doing something which follows a fixed plan or set of rules. प्रणाली, पद्धत

systematic *adj* Something that is done in a **systematic** way is done according to a fixed plan, in a thorough and efficient way. पद्धतशीर

systems analyst (systems analysts) *n* A **systems analyst** is someone whose job is to decide what computer equipment and software a company needs, and to provide it. सिस्टीम ॲनॅलिस्ट

t

table (tables) *n* A **table** is a piece of furniture with a flat top that you put things on or sit at. मेज ▷ *n* A **table** is a set of facts or figures arranged in columns and rows. तक्ता

tablecloth (tablecloths) *n* A **tablecloth** is a large piece of material used to cover a table, especially during a meal. टेबलवर घालायचे कापड

tablespoon (tablespoons) *n* A **tablespoon** is a fairly large spoon used for serving food and in cookery. मोठा चमचा

tablet (tablets) *n* A **tablet** is a small, solid, round mass of medicine which you swallow. औषधाची गोळी

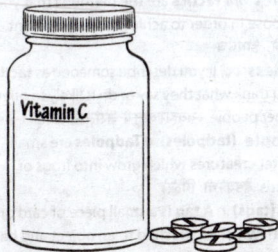

Vitamin C

table tennis *n* Table tennis is a game played inside by two or four people. The players stand at each end of a table which has a low net across the middle and hit a small light ball over the net, using small bats. टेबल टेनिस

table wine (table wines) *n* Table wine is fairly cheap wine that is drunk with meals. टेबल वाइन

taboo (taboos) *adj* If a subject or activity is **taboo**, it is a social custom to avoid doing that activity or talking about that subject, because people find it embarrassing or offensive. निषेधार्ह, निषिद्ध ▷ *n* If there is a **taboo** on a subject or activity, it is a social custom to avoid doing that activity or talking about that subject, because people find it embarrassing or offensive. निषेधार्ह,

tackle (tackles, tackling, tackled) *n* A **tackle** is when you try to take the ball away from someone in a game such as football. (फुटबॉल वगैरे) खेळात चेंडू पळवणे ▷ *vt* If you **tackle** a difficult task, you start dealing with it in a determined way. समस्या सोडवणे

tact *n* **Tact** is the ability to avoid upsetting or offending people by being careful not to say or do things that would hurt their feelings. व्यवहारचातुर्य

tactful *adj* If you describe someone as **tactful**, you approve of them because they are careful not to say or do anything that would offend or upset other people. व्यवहारचातुर्यपूर्ण, (वागण्या-बोलण्यात)पटाईत

tactics *npl* **Tactics** are the methods that you choose in order to achieve what you want. युक्ती, डावपेच

tactless *adj* If you describe someone as **tactless**, you think what they say or do is likely to offend other people. व्यवहारचातुर्य नसलेली व्यक्ती

tadpole (tadpoles) *n* **Tadpoles** are small water creatures which grow into frogs or toads. बेडकाची पिल्ले

tag (tags) *n* A **tag** is a small piece of card or cloth which is attached to an object and has information about that object on it. वस्तूला बांधलेले किंमत दर्शवणारे लेबल

Tahiti *n* **Tahiti** is an island in the South Pacific, in the Windward group of the Society Islands. ताहिती

tail (tails) *n* The **tail** of an animal is the part extending beyond the end of its body. शेपूट

tailor (tailors) *n* A **tailor** is a person who makes clothes, especially for men. शिंपी

Taiwan *n* **Taiwan** is an island in south-east Asia between the East China Sea and the South China Sea, off the south-east coast of the People's Republic of China. तैवान

Taiwanese (Taiwanese) *adj* **Taiwanese** means of or relating to Taiwan or its inhabitants. तैवानीज ▷ *n* A **Taiwanese** is a native or inhabitant of Taiwan. तैवानीज

Tajikistan *n* **Tajikistan** is a republic in central Asia. ताजिकिस्तान

take (takes, taking, took, taken) *vt* If you **take** a vehicle, you ride in it from one place to another. प्रवास करण्यासाठी वाहनात बसणे ▷ *vt* If you **take** something, you move it or carry it. घेऊन जाणे ▷ *vt* If you **take** something that does not belong to you, you steal it. घेणे

take after (takes after, taking after, took after, taken after) *v* If you **take after** a member of your family, you look or behave like them. कुटुंबातल्या एखाद्या व्यक्तिप्रमाणे (स्वभावाने) असणे वा दिसणे *He takes after his dad.*

take apart (takes apart, taking apart, took apart, taken apart) *v* If you **take** something **apart**, you separate it into its different parts. सुटे करणे *When the clock stopped, he took it apart.*

take away (takes away, taking away, took away, taken away, takeaways) *v* If you **take** something **away** from someone, you remove it from them. काढून घेणे *If you don't like it, we'll take it away for free.* ▷ *n* A **takeaway** is a shop or restaurant which sells hot food to be eaten elsewhere. A meal that you buy there is also called a **takeaway**. गरम पदार्थ (पार्सल) मिळण्याचे उपहारगृह

take back (takes back, taking back, took back, taken back) *v* If you **take** something **back**, you return it. परत घेणे *I once took back a pair of shoes that fell apart after a week.*

take off (takes off, taking off, took off, taken off, takeoffs) *v* When an aircraft **takes off**, it leaves the ground and starts flying.

विमान हवेत उडणे *We took off at 11 o'clock.* ▷ *n* **Takeoff** is the beginning of a flight, when an aircraft leaves the ground. उड्डाण

take over (**takes over, taking over, took over, taken over, takeovers**) *v* To **take over** something such as a company or country means to gain control of it. एक कंपनी दुसऱ्या कंपनीने ताब्यात घेणे *The company has been taken over by a multinational corporation.* ▷ *n* A **takeover** is the act of gaining control of a company by buying a majority of its shares. दुसऱ्या कंपनीचा घेतलेला ताबा वा ताबा घेण्याची कृती

takings *npl* The **takings** of a business such as a shop or cinema consist of the amount of money it gets from selling its goods or tickets during a certain period. वस्तूंच्या विक्रीतून मिळालेला पैसा, आवक

talcum powder *n* **Talcum powder** is fine powder with a pleasant smell which people put on their bodies after they have had a bath or a shower. टॅल्कम पावडर

tale (**tales**) *n* A **tale** is a story, especially one involving adventure or magic. गोष्ट

talent (**talents**) *n* **Talent** is the natural ability to do something well. बुद्धी, प्रतिभा

talented *adj* Someone who is **talented** has a natural ability to do something well. बुद्धिमान, प्रतिभावान

talk (**talks, talking, talked**) *n* **Talk** is the things you say to someone when you talk. बोलणे, संभाषण, चर्चा ▷ *vi* When you **talk**, you use spoken language to express your thoughts, ideas, or feelings. बोलणे

talkative *adj* Someone who is **talkative** talks a lot. बोलघेवडी व्यक्ती

talk to (**talks to, talking to, talked to**) *v* If you **talk to** someone, you have a conversation with them. संवाद साधणे, बोलणे *I talked to him yesterday.*

tall (**taller, tallest**) *adj* Someone or something that is **tall** is above average height. उंच

tame (**tamer, tamest**) *adj* A **tame** animal or bird is not afraid of humans. पाळीव

tampon (**tampons**) *n* A **tampon** is a firm piece of cotton wool that a woman puts inside her body during menstruation, in order to absorb the blood. टॅम्पोन

tan (**tans**) *n* If you have a **tan**, your skin has become darker than usual because you have been in the sun. त्वचेवरील राप

tandem (**tandems**) *n* A **tandem** is a bicycle designed for two riders. दोन माणसे बसतील अशी सायकल

tangerine (**tangerines**) *n* A **tangerine** is a small sweet orange. छोटे संत्रे

tank (**tanks**) *n* A **tank** is a large container for holding liquid or gas. टाकी, हौद ▷ *n* A **tank** is a military vehicle equipped with guns or rockets. रणगाडा

tanker (**tankers**) *n* A **tanker** is a ship or lorry used for transporting large quantities of gas or liquid, especially oil. तेल किंवा वायू वाहून नेणारा मोठा ट्रक किंवा जहाज

tanned *adj* If someone is **tanned**, his or her skin is darker because of the time he or she has spent in the sun. उन्हात रापलेली त्वचा असलेली व्यक्ती

tantrum (**tantrums**) *n* If a child has a **tantrum**, it suddenly becomes angry in a noisy way. क्रोधाचा झटका

Tanzania *n* **Tanzania** is a republic in East Africa, on the Indian Ocean. टांझानिया

Tanzanian (**Tanzanians**) *adj* **Tanzanian** means of or relating to Tanzania or its inhabitants. टांझानियन ▷ *n* A **Tanzanian** is a native or inhabitant of Tanzania. टांझानियन

tap (**taps**) *n* A **tap** is a device that controls the flow of a liquid or gas from a pipe or container. नळ

tap-dancing *n* **Tap-dancing** is a style of dancing in which the dancers wear special shoes with pieces of metal on the heels and toes. The shoes make loud sharp sounds as the dancers move their feet. टॅप डान्सिंग

tape (**tapes, taping, taped**) *n* **Tape** is a narrow plastic strip covered with a magnetic substance. It is used to record sounds, pictures, and computer information. ध्वनिफीत ▷ vt If you **tape** music, sounds, or television pictures, you record them using a tape recorder or a video recorder. ध्वनिमुद्रित किंवा चित्रमुद्रित करणे

tape measure (tape measures) n A **tape measure** is a strip of metal, plastic, or cloth with marks on it, used for measuring, especially for clothes and DIY. मोजपट्टी

tape recorder (tape recorders) n A **tape recorder** is a machine used for recording and playing music, speech, or other sounds. ध्वनिमुद्रण यंत्र

target (targets) n A **target** is something that someone is trying to hit with a weapon or other object. लक्ष्य

tariff (tariffs) n A **tariff** is a tax on goods coming into a country. कर, जकात

tarmac n **Tarmac** is a material used for making road surfaces, consisting of crushed stones mixed with tar. **Tarmac** is a trademark. टारमॅक

tarpaulin n **Tarpaulin** is a fabric made of canvas or similar material coated with tar, wax, paint, or some other waterproof substance. ताडपत्री, जलरोधक कापड/आवरण

tarragon n **Tarragon** is a European herb with narrow leaves which are used to add flavour to food. टॅरॅगॉन नावाची वनस्पती

tart (tarts) n A **tart** is a shallow pastry case with a filling of sweet food or fruit. टार्ट

tartan adj **Tartan** cloth, which traditionally comes from Scotland, has different coloured stripes crossing each other. टारटॅन नावाचे कापड

task (tasks) n A **task** is an activity or piece of work which you have to do. काम, कार्यभाग

Tasmania n **Tasmania** is an island in the South Pacific, south of mainland Australia. टास्मानिया

taste (tastes, tasting, tasted) n Your sense of **taste** is your ability to recognize the flavour of things with your tongue. चव ▷ vi If food or drink **tastes** of something, it has that particular flavour. चव असणे

tasteful adj If you describe something as **tasteful**, you mean that it is attractive and elegant. आकर्षक

tasteless adj If you describe something as **tasteless**, you mean that it is vulgar and unattractive. अनाकर्षक

tasty (tastier, tastiest) adj If you say that food, especially savoury food, is **tasty**, you mean that it has a pleasant and fairly strong flavour which makes it good to eat. चवदार

tattoo (tattoos) n A **tattoo** is a design on someone's skin, made by pricking little holes and filling them with coloured dye. गोंदण

Taurus n **Taurus** is one of the twelve signs of the zodiac. Its symbol is a bull. People who are born between the 20th of April and the 20th of May come under this sign. वृषभ रास

tax (taxes) n **Tax** is an amount of money that you have to pay to the government so that it can pay for public services. कर

taxi (taxis) n A **taxi** is a car driven by a person whose job is to take people where they want to go in return for money. टॅक्सी, भाड्याचा गाडी

taxi driver (taxi drivers) n A **taxi driver** is a person whose job is to take people in a car to the place they want to go to in return for money. टॅक्सी चालक

taxpayer (taxpayers) n **Taxpayers** are people who pay a percentage of their income to the government as tax. करदाता

tax return (tax returns) n A **tax return** is an official form that you fill in with details about your income and personal situation, so that the tax you owe can be calculated. कर विवरण

TB n **TB** is a very serious infectious disease that affects someone's lungs and other parts of their body. **TB** is an abbreviation for 'tuberculosis'. क्षयरोग

tea (teas) n **Tea** is a drink. You make it by pouring hot water on to the dry leaves of a plant called the tea bush. चहा ▷ n **Tea** is a meal that you eat in the afternoon or the early evening. टी

tea bag (tea bags) n **Tea bags** are small paper bags with tea leaves in them. You put them into hot water to make tea. टी बॅग

teach (teaches, teaching, taught) vt If you **teach** someone something, you give them instructions so that they know about it or know how to do it. शिकवणे

teacher (teachers) n A **teacher** is a person who teaches, usually as a job at a school or similar institution. शिक्षक

teaching n **Teaching** is the work that a teacher does in helping students to learn. अध्यापन

teacup (teacups) n A **teacup** is a cup that you use for drinking tea. चहाचा कप

team (teams) n A **team** is a group of people who play together against another group in a sport or game. संघ

teapot (teapots) n A **teapot** is a container with a lid, a handle, and a spout, used for making and serving tea. चहाची किटली

tear (tears, tearing, tore, torn) n **Tears** are the liquid that comes out of your eyes when you cry. अश्रू ▷ n A **tear** in something is a hole that has been made in it. छिद्र ▷ vt If you **tear** something, you pull it into pieces or make a hole in it. फाडणे

tear gas n **Tear gas** is a gas that causes your eyes to sting and fill with tears so that you cannot see. It is sometimes used by the police or army to control crowds. अश्रूधूर

tear up (tears up, tearing up, tore up, torn up) v If you **tear up** a piece of paper, you tear it into a lot of small pieces. तुकडे तुकडे करणे
Don't you dare tear up her ticket.

tease (teases, teasing, teased) vt To **tease** someone means to laugh at them or make jokes about them in order to embarrass, annoy, or upset them. खिजवणे

teaspoon (teaspoons) n A **teaspoon** is a small spoon that you use to put sugar into tea or coffee. छोटा चमचा

teatime (teatimes) n **Teatime** is the period of the day when people have their tea. It can be in the late afternoon or in the early part of the evening. चहाची वेळ

tea towel (tea towels) n A **tea towel** is a cloth used to dry dishes after they have been washed. ताटे पुसायाचा कपडा

technical adj **Technical** means involving the sorts of machines, processes, and materials used in industry, transport, and communications. तांत्रिक

technician (technicians) n A **technician** is someone whose job involves skilled practical work with scientific equipment, for example in a laboratory. तंत्रज्ञ

technique (techniques) n A **technique** is a particular method of doing an activity, usually a method that involves practical skills. तंत्र

techno n **Techno** is a form of modern electronic music with a very fast beat. टेक्नो संगीत

technological adj **Technological** means relating to or associated with technology. तंत्रज्ञानविषयक

technology (technologies) n **Technology** refers to things which are the result of scientific knowledge being used for practical purposes. तंत्रज्ञान

teddy bear (teddy bears) n A **teddy bear** or a **teddy** is a soft toy that looks like a bear. टेडी बेअर नावाचे खेळणे

tee (tees) n In golf, a **tee** is a small piece of wood or plastic which is used to support the ball before it is hit at the start of each hole. टी (गोल्फमधील लाकडाचा किंवा प्लॅस्टिकचा तुकडा)

teenager (teenagers) n A **teenager** is someone between 13 and 19 years of age. तेरा ते एकोणीस वर्षांपर्यंत वय असलेले

teens npl If you are in your **teens**, you are between 13 and 19 years old. तेरा ते एकोणीस वर्षांपर्यंत वय असलेले

tee-shirt (tee-shirts) n A **tee-shirt** is a cotton shirt with short sleeves and no collar or buttons. टी-शर्ट

teethe (teethes, teething, teethed) *vi* When babies **are teething**, their teeth are starting to appear through their gums. दुधाचे दात येणे

teetotal *adj* Someone who is **teetotal** does not drink alcohol. मद्य न पिणारा

telecommunications *npl* **Telecommunications** is the technology of sending signals and messages over long distances using electronic equipment, for example by radio and telephone. दूरसंचरण

telegram (telegrams) *n* A **telegram** is a message that is sent by electricity or radio and then printed and delivered to someone's home or office. तार

telephone (telephones) *n* The **telephone** is an electrical system used to talk to someone in another place by dialling a number on a piece of equipment and speaking into it. दूरध्वनी

telephone directory (telephone directories) *n* The **telephone directory** is a book that contains an alphabetical list of the names, addresses, and telephone numbers of the people in a particular area. दूरध्वनी ग्राहकांची सूची

telesales *n* **Telesales** is a method of selling in which someone employed by a company telephones people to try to persuade them to buy the company's products or services. दूरध्वनीवरून संपर्क साधून उत्पादने विकणारा

telescope (telescopes) *n* A **telescope** is an instrument shaped like a tube. It has lenses inside it that make distant things seem larger and nearer when you look through it. दुर्बीण

television (televisions) *n* A **television** or a **television set** is a piece of electrical equipment consisting of a box with a screen on which you can watch programmes with pictures and sounds. दूरदर्शन संच

tell (tells, telling, told) *vt* If you **tell** someone something, you let them know about it. सांगणे ▷ *vt* If you **tell** someone to do something, you say that they must do it. सांगणे ▷ *vt* If you can **tell** something, you know it. सांगणे

teller (tellers) *n* A **teller** is someone who works in a bank and who customers pay money to or get money from. बँकेत पैशांची देवाण-घेवाण करणारी व्यक्ती

tell off (tells off, telling off, told off) *v* If you **tell** someone **off**, you speak to them angrily or seriously because they have done something wrong. रागाने सांगणे *I'm always getting told off for being late.*

telly (tellies) *n* A **telly** is a piece of equipment consisting of a box with a glass screen on it on which you can watch programmes with pictures and sounds. *(informal)* दूरदर्शन संच

temp (temps) *n* A **temp** is a person who is employed by an agency that sends them to work in different offices for short periods of time, for example to replace someone who is ill or on holiday. तात्पुरते कामावर ठेवलेली व्यक्ती

temper (tempers) *n* If you say that someone has a **temper**, you mean that they become angry very easily. राग

temperature (temperatures) *n* The **temperature** of something is how hot or cold it is. तापमान

temple (temples) *n* A **temple** is a building used for the worship of a god or gods, especially in the Buddhist and Hindu religions. मंदिर, देऊळ

temporary *adj* Something that is **temporary** lasts for only a limited time. तात्पुरते

tempt (tempts, tempting, tempted) *v* Something that **tempts** you attracts you and makes you want it, even though it may be wrong or harmful. मोहात पाडणे

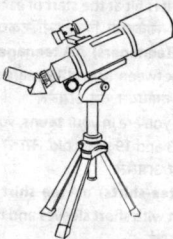

temptation (temptations) n **Temptation** is the state you are in when you want to do or have something, although you know it might be wrong or harmful. मोह

tempting adj If something is **tempting**, it makes you want to do it or have it. मोहात पाडणारे

ten num **Ten** is the number 10. दहा

tenant (tenants) n A **tenant** is someone who pays rent for the place they live in, or for land or buildings that they use. भाडेकरू

tend (tends, tending, tended) vi If something **tends** to happen, it usually happens or it happens often. कल असणे

tendency (tendencies) n A **tendency** is a worrying or unpleasant habit or action that keeps occurring. कल

tender (tenderer, tenderest) adj Someone or something that is **tender** is kind and gentle. नाजूक

tendon (tendons) n A **tendon** is a strong cord of tissue in your body joining a muscle to a bone. स्नायुबंध

tennis n **Tennis** is a game played by two or four players on a rectangular court with a net across the middle. The players use rackets to hit a ball over the net. टेनिस

tennis court (tennis courts) n A **tennis court** is an area in which you play the game of tennis. टेनिस कोर्ट

tennis player (tennis players) n A **tennis player** is a person who plays tennis, either as a job or for fun. टेनिस खेळाडू

tennis racket (tennis rackets) n A **tennis racket** is the racket that you use when you play tennis. टेनिस रॅकेट

tenor (tenors) n A **tenor** is a male singer with a fairly high voice. मोठा वा खडा आवाज असलेला गायक

tenpin bowling n **Tenpin bowling** is a game in which you try to knock down ten objects shaped like bottles by rolling a heavy ball towards them. It is usually played in a place called a bowling alley. टेनपिन बोलिंग

(बाटलीसारखा आकार असलेल्या दहा वस्तू जड बॉल त्यांच्या दिशेने घरंगळून खाली पाडण्याचा खेळ)

tense (tenser, tensest, tenses) adj If you are **tense**, you are worried and nervous, and cannot relax. तणावग्रस्त ▷ n The **tense** of a verb group is its form, which usually shows whether you are referring to past, present, or future time. काळ

tension (tensions) n **Tension** is a feeling of fear or nervousness produced before a difficult, dangerous, or important event. ताणतणाव

tent (tents) n A **tent** is a shelter made of canvas or nylon and held up by poles and ropes, used mainly by people who are camping. तंबू

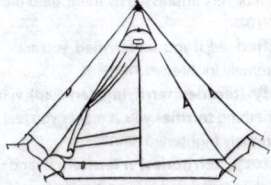

tenth (tenths) adj The **tenth** item in a series is the one that you count as number ten. दहावा ▷ n A **tenth** is one of ten equal parts of something. दहावा भाग

term (terms) n A **term** is a word or expression with a specific meaning. पारिभाषिक शब्द, संज्ञा ▷ n A **term** is one of the periods of time that a school, college, or university year is divided into. सत्र

terminal (terminals) adj A **terminal** illness or disease cannot be cured and eventually causes death. प्राणघातक, असाध्य ▷ n A **terminal** is a place where vehicles, passengers, or goods begin or end a journey. जेथून वाहने सुटतात किंवा पोहोचतात ते ठिकाण (बसस्थानक, विमानतळ, इ.)

terminally adv If someone is **terminally** ill, it means that they will die of an illness or disease that cannot be cured. प्राणघातक, असाध्य रोगाने

terrace (terraces) *n* A **terrace** is a row of similar houses joined together by their side walls. सामाईक भिंत असलेल्या घरांची रांग

terraced *adj* A **terraced** slope or side of a hill has flat areas like steps cut into it, where crops or other plants can be grown. टेकडीवरील पायऱ्यांसारखे उतार

terrible *adj* **Terrible** means extremely bad. भयानक, असह्य

terribly *adv* **Terribly** means in an extremely bad manner. भयानकपणे, अतिशय

terrier (terriers) *n* A **terrier** is a small breed of dog. There are many different types of terrier. टेरिअर जातीचा कुत्रा

terrific *adj* If you describe something or someone as **terrific**, you are very pleased with them or very impressed by them. *(informal)* खूप (छान)

terrified *adj* If you are **terrified**, you are extremely frightened. घाबरलेला

terrify (terrifies, terrifying, terrified) *vt* If something **terrifies** you, it makes you feel extremely frightened. घाबरणे

territory (territories) *n* **Territory** is land which is controlled by a particular country or ruler. एखाद्या देशाची वा राजाची हद्द

terrorism *n* **Terrorism** is the use of violence in order to achieve political aims or to force a government to do something. दहशतवाद

terrorist (terrorists) *n* A **terrorist** is a person who uses violence in order to achieve political aims. दहशतवादी

terrorist attack (terrorist attacks) *n* A **terrorist attack** is a violent incident, usually involving murder and bombing, carried out by people who are trying to achieve political aims. दहशतवादी हल्ले

test (tests, testing, tested) *n* A **test** is an action or experiment to find out how well something works. चाचणी ▷ *vt* If you **test** something, you try it to see what it is like, or how it works. चाचणी घेणे ▷ *n* A **test** is something you do to show how much you know or what you can do. चाचणी

testicle (testicles) *n* A man's **testicles** are the two sex glands that produce sperm. अंडकोष, वृषण

test tube (test tubes) *n* A **test tube** is a small tube-shaped container made from glass. Test tubes are used in laboratories. परीक्षा नळी

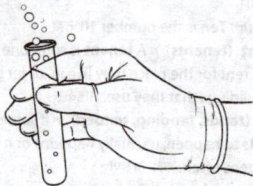

tetanus *n* **Tetanus** is a serious painful disease caused by bacteria getting into wounds. It makes your muscles, especially your jaw muscles, go stiff. धनुर्वात

text (texts, texting, texted) *n* **Text** is any written material. लिखाण, मजकूर ▷ *vt* If you **text** someone, you send them a text message on a mobile phone. एसएमएस पाठवणे

textbook (textbooks) *n* A **textbook** is a book about a particular subject that is intended for students. पाठ्यपुस्तक

textile (textiles) *n* **Textiles** are types of woven cloth. विणलेले कपडे

text message (text messages) *n* A **text message** is a written message that you send using a mobile phone. एसएमएस

Thai (Thais) *adj* **Thai** means belonging or relating to Thailand, or to its people, language, or culture. थाय ▷ *n* A **Thai** is a person who comes from Thailand. थाय ▷ *n* **Thai** is the language spoken in Thailand. थाय

Thailand *n* **Thailand** is a kingdom in south-east Asia, on the Andaman Sea and the Gulf of Thailand. थायलंड

than *prep* You use **than** when you are talking about the difference between two people or things. पेक्षा *Children learn faster than adults.*

thank (thanks, thanking, thanked) *vt* When you **thank** someone for something, you show

that you are grateful to them for it. आभार
मानणे

thanks! *excl* You can say '**thanks!**' to show that
you are grateful to someone for something
they have done. धन्यवाद!

that *det* You use **that** to talk about something
that you have mentioned before. ते (निर्देशक)
*For that reason the claims procedure is as simple
and helpful as possible.* ▷ *conj* You use **that**
to join two different things you are saying.
की, असे *I felt sad that he was leaving.* ▷ *pron*
You use **that** to talk about something that
you have mentioned before. ते (सर्वनाम) *They
said you wanted to talk to me. Why was that?*
▷ *det* You use **that** to talk about somebody
or something a distance away from you. तो,
ती, ते *Look at that car over there.* ❑ *Who's that
beautiful girl?* ▷ *pron* You use **that** to talk
about somebody or something a distance
away from you. तो, ती, ते *Who's that?* ▷ *pron*
You use **that** to show which person or thing
you are talking about. जो, जी, जे *There's the
girl that I told you about.*

thatched *adj* A **thatched** house has a roof
made of straw or reeds. बांबूचे किंवा वाशांचे छत
असलेले घर

the *det* You use **the** before a noun when it is
clear which person or thing you are talking
about. इंग्रजी भाषेतील निश्चिततादर्शी उपपद *It's
always hard to think about the future.* ▷ *det*
You use **the** before a noun to talk about
things of that type in general. (इंग्रजीत) एका
ठराविक गोष्टीकडे निर्देश करताना वापर. *The
computer has developed very quickly in recent
years.*

theatre (**theatres**) *n* A **theatre** is a building
with a stage on which plays and other
entertainments are performed. नाट्यगृह,
चित्रपटगृह

theft (**thefts**) *n* **Theft** is the criminal act of
stealing. चोरी

their *det* You use **their** to say that something
belongs to a group of people, animals, or
things. त्यांचा *They took off their coats.*

theirs *pron* You use **theirs** to say that
something belongs to a group of people,
animals, or things. त्यांच्या, त्यांचा *The house
next to theirs was empty.*

them *pron* You use **them** to talk about more
than one person, animal, or thing. त्यांना *I've
lost my keys. Have you seen them?*

theme (**themes**) *n* A **theme** in a piece of
writing, a discussion, or a work of art is an
important idea or subject in it. मध्यवर्ती
संकल्पना

theme park (**theme parks**) *n* A **theme park**
is a large outdoor area where people pay
to go to enjoy themselves. All the different
activities in a theme park are usually based
on a particular idea or theme. मनोरंजनासाठी
असलेले उद्यान

themselves *pron* You use **themselves** to talk
about people, animals, or things that you have
just talked about. ते स्वतःच *They all seemed
to be enjoying themselves.*

then *adv* **Then** means at that time. त्या वेळी
▷ *conj* You use **then** to say that one thing
happens after another. *(informal)* त्या
नंतर, मग *She said good night, then went to
bed.*

theology *n* **Theology** is the study of religion.
धर्म व देव यांच्या विषयीचा अभ्यास, धर्मशास्त्र

theory (**theories**) *n* A **theory** is a formal idea
or set of ideas intended to explain something.
सिद्धांत

therapy *n* **Therapy** is the treatment of mental
or physical illness without the use of drugs or
operations. उपचारपद्धती

there *adv* **There** means to a place, or at a
place. तेथे ▷ *pron* You use **there** to say that
something is in a place or is happening,
or to make someone notice it. Cannot be
translated *There are flowers on the table.* तेथे

therefore *adv* You use **therefore** when you
are talking about the result of something.
म्हणून

thermometer (**thermometers**) *n* A
thermometer is an instrument for measuring

the temperature of a room or of a person's body. तापमापक

Thermos® (Thermoses) n A **Thermos** or **Thermos flask** is a container which is used to keep hot drinks hot or cold drinks cold. It has two thin shiny glass walls with no air between them. थरमॉस

thermostat (thermostats) n A **thermostat** is a device that switches a system or motor on or off according to the temperature. Thermostats are used, for example, in central heating systems and fridges. तापनियंत्रक

these det You use **these** to talk about someone or something that you have already mentioned. हे *These people need more support.* ▷ pron You use **these** to talk about people or things that are near you. हे *I like these, on this table.* ▷ det You use **these** to talk about people or things that are near you. हे, ह्या, हा *These bags are very heavy.* ▷ det You use **these** to introduce people or things that you are going to talk about. हे, ह्या, हा *If you're looking for a builder, these phone numbers will be useful.*

they pron You use **they** when you are talking about more than one person, animal, or thing. ते *They are all in the same class.*

thick (thicker, thickest) adj If something is **thick**, it is deep or wide between one side and the other. जाड ▷ adj If a liquid is **thick**, it flows slowly. घट्ट

thickness (thicknesses) n The **thickness** of something is the distance between its two opposite surfaces. जाडी

thief (thieves) n A **thief** is a person who steals something from another person. चोर

thigh (thighs) n Your **thighs** are the top parts of your legs, between your knees and your hips. मांडी

thin (thinner, thinnest) adj If something is **thin**, it is narrow between one side and the other. पातळ ▷ adj If a person or animal is **thin**, they are not fat and they do not weigh much. लुकडा

thing (things) n You use **thing** as a substitute for another word when you are unable to be more precise, or you do not need or want to be more precise. ही/ती वस्तू

think (thinks, thinking, thought) v If you **think** something, you believe that it is true. वाटणे ▷ vi When you **think**, you use your mind. विचार करणे

third (thirds) adj The **third** item in a series is the one that you count as number three. तिसरा ▷ n A **third** is one of three equal parts of something. तिसरा हिस्सा

thirdly adv You use **thirdly** when you are about to mention the third thing in a series of items. तिसरे म्हणजे ...

third-party insurance n **Third-party insurance** is insurance that covers you if you injure someone or damage someone's property. दुसऱ्या कुणाच्या नुकसान झाल्यास त्यासाठी असलेला विमा

thirst (thirsts) n **Thirst** is the feeling that you need to drink something. तहान

thirsty (thirstier, thirstiest) adj If you are **thirsty**, you feel a need to drink something. तहानलेली व्यक्ती

thirteen num **Thirteen** is the number 13. तेरा

thirteenth adj The **thirteenth** item in a series is the one that you count as number thirteen. तेरावा

thirty num **Thirty** is the number 30. तीस

this det You use **this** to talk about someone or something that you have already mentioned. हा *How can we resolve this problem?* ▷ pron You use **this** to talk about someone or something near you. हा *'Would you like a different one?'—'No, this is great.'* ▷ det You use **this** followed by a noun, or followed by an adjective and a noun, to talk about somebody or something that is near you. हा, ही, हे *I* like this room much better than the other one. ▷ *pron* You use **this** to introduce someone or something that you are going to talk about. हा, ही, हे *This is what I will do. I will call her and explain.*

thistle (thistles) *n* A **thistle** is a wild plant which has leaves with sharp points and purple flowers. कोटधोतरा

thorn (thorns) *n* **Thorns** are the sharp points on some plants and trees such as roses and holly. काटा

thorough *adj* A **thorough** action is done very carefully and methodically. संपूर्ण

thoroughly *adv* If somebody does something **thoroughly**, they do it with great care. संपूर्णपणे

those *det* You use **those** to talk about people or things that have already been mentioned. ते *I don't know any of those people you mentioned.* ▷ *pron* You use **those** to talk about people or things a distance away from you. ते *Those are nice shoes.* ▷ *det* You use **those** to talk about people or things a distance away from you. ते, त्या, ती *What are those buildings?*

though *adv* You use **though** when talking about an idea that is not what you would expect. जरी, आणि तरीही ▷ *conj* You use **though** to add information that changes what you have already said. जरी, तथापि *They went to the same school, though they never met there.* ▷ *conj* You use **though** to start talking about an idea that is not what you would expect. जरी *He plays in adult tennis games even though he is only 15.*

thought (thoughts) *n* A **thought** is an idea or opinion. विचार

thoughtful *adj* If you are **thoughtful**, you are quiet and serious because you are thinking about something. विचारमग्न

thoughtless *adj* If you describe someone as **thoughtless**, you are critical of them because they forget or ignore other people's wants, needs, or feelings. अविचारी

thousand *num* A **thousand** or one **thousand** is the number 1,000. हजार

thousandth (thousandths) *adj* The **thousandth** item in a series is the one you count as number one thousand. हजारावा ▷ *n* A **thousandth** is one of a thousand equal parts of something. एक सहस्रांश

thread (threads) *n* **Thread** or a **thread** is a long very thin piece of a material such as cotton, nylon, or silk, especially one that is used in sewing. धागा

threat (threats) *n* A **threat** to someone or something is a danger that something unpleasant might happen to them. धोका

threaten (threatens, threatening, threatened) *vt* If someone **threatens** to do something unpleasant to you, or if they **threaten** you, they say that they will do something unpleasant to you, especially if you do not do what they want. धमकी देणे

threatening *adj* You can describe someone's behaviour as **threatening** when you think that they are trying to harm you. धमकी देणारा

three *num* **Three** is the number 3. तीन

three-dimensional *adj* A **three-dimensional** object is solid rather than flat, because it can be measured in three dimensions, usually the height, length, and width. त्रिमितीय

thrifty (thriftier, thriftiest) *adj* If you say that someone is **thrifty**, you are praising them for saving money, not buying unnecessary things, and not wasting things. काटकसरी

thrill (thrills) *n* If something gives you a **thrill**, it gives you a sudden feeling of great excitement, pleasure, or fear. थरार, उत्सुकता वा भीतीची भावना

thrilled *adj* If you are **thrilled** about something, you are pleased and excited about it. उत्तेजित झालेला

t

thriller (thrillers) n A **thriller** is a book, film, or play that tells an exciting story about something such as criminal activities or spying. थरारक अनुभव देणारा

thrilling adj Something that is **thrilling** is very exciting and enjoyable. थरारक, खळबळजनक

throat (throats) n Your **throat** is the back part of your mouth that you use to swallow and to breathe. घसा ▷ n Your **throat** is the front part of your neck. गळा

throb (throbs, throbbing, throbbed) vi If part of your body **throbs**, you feel a series of strong and usually painful beats there. धडधडणे, ठणकणे

throne (thrones) n A **throne** is a special chair used by a king, queen, or emperor on important occasions. सिंहासन

through prep **Through** means going all the way from one side of something to the other side. च्या मधून We walked through the forest.

throughout prep If something happens **throughout** a period of time, it happens for all of that period. सर्वत्र, सर्ववेळ, …. भर It rained heavily throughout the game.

throw (throws, throwing, threw, thrown) vt If you **throw** an object that you are holding, you move your hand quickly and let go of the object, so that it moves through the air. फेकणे

throw away (throws away, throwing away, threw away, thrown away) v If you **throw away** or **throw out** something you do not want, you get rid of it. फेकून देणे I never throw anything away.

throw out (throws out, throwing out, threw out, thrown out) v When you **throw out** something that you do not want, you get rid of it. फेकून देणे

throw up (throws up, throwing up, threw up, thrown up) v To **throw up** means to vomit. (informal) उलटी करणे, ओकारी करणे She threw up after reading reports of the trial.

thrush (thrushes) n A **thrush** is a small brown bird with small marks on its chest. थ्रश नावाचा पक्षी

thug (thugs) n If you refer to someone as a **thug**, you think they are violent or a criminal. ठक

thumb (thumbs) n Your **thumb** is the short, thick part on the side of your hand next to your first finger. अंगठा

thumbtack (thumbtacks) n A **thumbtack** is a short pin with a broad flat top which is used for fastening papers or pictures to a board, wall, or other surface. सपाट माथ्याची टाचणी

thump (thumps, thumping, thumped) v If you **thump** something, you hit it hard, usually with your fist. गुद्दा/धपका मारणे

thunder n **Thunder** is the loud noise that you hear from the sky after a flash of lightning, especially during a storm. गडगडाट

thunderstorm (thunderstorms) n A **thunderstorm** is a storm in which there is thunder, lightning, and heavy rain. गडगडाट व जोरदार पाऊस यांसहित आलेले वादळ

thundery adj When the weather is **thundery**, there is a lot of thunder, or there are heavy clouds which make you think that there will be thunder soon. गडगडाटी, वादळी

Thursday (Thursdays) n **Thursday** is the day after Wednesday and before Friday. गुरुवार

thyme n **Thyme** is a type of herb. एक प्रकारची अन्नात वापरली जाणारी वनस्पती

Tibet n **Tibet** is a region of south-west China. तिबेट

Tibetan (Tibetans) adj **Tibetan** means of, relating to, or characteristic of Tibet, its people, or their language. तिबेटी ▷ n A **Tibetan** is a native or inhabitant of Tibet. तिबेटी ▷ n **Tibetan** is a language spoken by people who live in Tibet. तिबेटी

tick (ticks, ticking, ticked) n A **tick** is a written mark like a V with the right side extended. You use it to show that something is correct or has been dealt with. बरोबरची खूण ▷ vt If you **tick** something that is written on a piece of paper, you put a tick next to it. बरोबरची खूण करणे

ticket (tickets) n A **ticket** is an official piece of paper or card which shows that you have paid for a journey or have paid to enter a place of entertainment. तिकीट

ticket machine (ticket machines) n A **ticket machine** is a machine, for example in a railway station, from which you can get tickets by putting in money and pressing a button. तिकीट देणारे यंत्र

ticket office (ticket offices) n A **ticket office** is a place, for example at a theatre, cinema, or railway station, where tickets are sold. तिकीट कार्यालय

tickle (tickles, tickling, tickled) vt When you **tickle** someone, you move your fingers lightly over their body, often in order to make them laugh. गुदगुल्या करणे

ticklish adj A **ticklish** problem, situation, or task is difficult and needs to be dealt with carefully. गुंतागुंतीचा प्रश्न

tick off (ticks off, ticking off, ticked off) v If you **tick off** an item on a list, you put a tick by it to show that it has been dealt with. ठरवलेले काम पूर्ण झाल्यानंतर त्यावर खूण करणे He ticked off my name on a piece of paper.

tide (tides) n The **tide** is the regular change in the level of the sea on the shore. समुद्राची भरती-ओहोटी

tidy (tidier, tidiest, tidies, tidying, tidied) adj Something that is **tidy** is neat and arranged in an orderly way. नीटनेटके ▷ vt When you **tidy** a place, you make it neat by putting things in their proper places. नीटनेटके करणे

tidy up (tidies up, tidying up, tidied up) v When you **tidy up** or tidy a place **up**, you put things back in their proper places so that everything is neat. नीटनेटके करणे She spent an hour tidying up the shop.

tie (ties, tying, tied) n A **tie** is a long, narrow piece of cloth that you tie a knot in and wear around your neck with a shirt. टाय ▷ vt If you **tie** something, you fasten it with string or a rope. बांधणे

tie up (ties up, tying up, tied up) v When you **tie** something **up**, you fasten string or rope round it so that it is firm or secure. बांधणे He tied up the bag and took it outside.

tiger (tigers) n A **tiger** is a large fierce animal belonging to the cat family. Tigers are orange with black stripes. वाघ

tight (tighter, tightest) adj If clothes are **tight**, they are so small that they fit very close to your body. घट्ट ▷ adj Something that is **tight** is fastened so that it is not easy to move it. घट्ट

tighten (tightens, tightening, tightened) v If you **tighten** your grip on something, or if your grip on something **tightens**, you hold it more firmly or securely. घट्ट करणे

tights npl **Tights** are a piece of clothing made of thin material such as nylon that covers your hips and each of your legs and feet separately. टाइट्स

tile (tiles) n **Tiles** are flat square pieces of baked clay, carpet, cork, or other substance, which are fixed as a covering onto a floor, wall, or roof. लादी, फरशी, कौल

tiled adj A **tiled** surface is covered with tiles. लाद्या/कौल बसवलेली

till (tills) conj If something happens **till** something else happens, the first thing happens before the other thing and stops when the other thing happens. (informal) जोपर्यंत, तोपर्यंत They slept till the alarm woke them. ▷ n In a shop, a **till** is a cash register where money is kept, and where customers pay for what they have bought. पैशाची देवाण-घेवाण करण्यासाठी असलेली पेटी वा गल्ला ▷ prep If something happens **till** a time, it happens before that time and stops at that time. (informal) पर्यंत She lived there till last year. ▷ prep If something does not happen **till** a time, it does not happen before that time and only starts happening at that time. (informal) पर्यंत The shop doesn't open till half past nine.

timber n **Timber** is wood used for building houses and making furniture. इमारती लाकूड

time n Time is how long something takes to happen. We measure **time** in minutes, hours, days, weeks, months, and years. काळ ▷ n The **time** is a moment in the day that you describe in hours and minutes. वेळ

time bomb (time bombs) n A **time bomb** is a bomb with a mechanism that causes it to explode at a particular time. ठराविक वेळी फुटणारा बॉंब

time off n If you have **time off**, you do not go to work or school, for example, because you are ill or it is a day when you do not usually work. सवड

timer (timers) n A **timer** is a device that measures time, especially one that is part of a machine and causes it to start or stop working at specific times. ठराविक वेळेवर ठराविक गोष्ट करणारे यंत्र

timetable (timetables) n A **timetable** is a plan of the times when particular events are to take place. वेळापत्रक

time zone (time zones) n A **time zone** is one of the areas into which the world is divided where the time is calculated as being a particular number of hours behind or ahead of GMT. ग्रिनिच वेळेनुसार जगभरात विभागलेली वेळ

tin (tins) n Tin is a kind of soft, pale grey metal. पत्रा ▷ n A tin is a metal container for food. डबा

tinfoil n Tinfoil consists of shiny metal in the form of a thin sheet which is used for wrapping food. टिनफॉइल

tinned adj Tinned food has been preserved by being sealed in a tin. डबाबंद

tin opener (tin openers) n A **tin opener** is a tool that is used for opening tins of food. टिन ओपनर

tinsel n Tinsel consists of small strips of shiny paper attached to long pieces of thread. People use tinsel as a decoration. नाताळसणाच्या सजावटीसाठी वापरली जाणारी चकाकत्या कागदाची पट्टी

tinted adj If something is **tinted**, it has a small amount of a particular colour or dye in it. रंगछटा असलेला

tiny (tinier, tiniest) adj Someone or something that is **tiny** is extremely small. अतिशय लहान, छोटा

tip (tips, tipping, tipped) n The **tip** of something long and narrow is the end of it. टोक ▷ n If you give someone such as a waiter a **tip**, you give them some money for their services. वेटरला दिलेली बक्षिसी ▷ n A **tip** is a useful piece of advice. सल्ला ▷ v If an object or part of your body **tips**, or if you **tip** it, it moves into a sloping position with one end or side higher than the other. झुकवणे, कलणे ▷ v If you **tip** someone such as a waiter, you give them some money for their services. वेटरला बक्षिसी देणे

tipsy adj If someone is **tipsy**, they are slightly drunk. किंचित झिंगलेला

tired adj If you are **tired**, you feel that you want to rest or sleep. थकलेला

tiring adj If you describe something as **tiring**, you mean that it makes you tired so that you want to rest or sleep. थकविणारे

tissue (tissues) n In animals and plants, tissue consists of cells that are similar in appearance and function. स्नायू

title (titles) n The **title** of a book, play, film, or piece of music is its name. शीर्षक

to prep You use **to** when you are talking about the position or direction of something. ...ला, कडे, साठी She went to the window and looked out. ▷ prep You use **to** before the infinitive (= the simple form of a verb). (इंग्रजीत) क्रियापदाच्या मूळ रूपापुढे लावतात It was time to leave.

toad (toads) n A **toad** is an animal like a frog, but with a drier skin. जमिनीवर राहणारा बेडकासारखा प्राणी

toadstool (toadstools) n A **toadstool** is a plant that you cannot eat because it is poisonous. विषारी अळंबी

toast (toasts) n Toast is slices of bread heated until they are brown and crisp. टोस्ट ▷ n When you drink a **toast** to someone, you wish them success or good health, and then drink some alcoholic drink. सुयश चिंतणे

oaster (toasters) n A **toaster** is a piece of electric equipment used to toast bread. ब्रेड भाजण्याचे विद्युत उपकरण

obacco (tobaccos) n **Tobacco** is the dried leaves of a plant which people smoke in pipes, cigars, and cigarettes. तंबाखू

obacconist (tobacconists) n A **tobacconist** or a **tobacconist's** is a shop that sells cigarettes, tobacco, etc. तंबाखूचे दुकान

oboggan (toboggans) n A **toboggan** is a light wooden board with a curved front, used for travelling down hills on snow or ice. टोबोगन

obogganing n **Tobogganing** is the activity of travelling down a slope on snow or ice using a toboggan. टोबोगनींग

oday adv You use **today** to refer to the day on which you are speaking or writing. आज

oddler (toddlers) n A **toddler** is a young child who has only just learnt to walk. नुकतेच चालू लागलेले मूल

oe (toes) n Your **toes** are the five movable parts at the end of each foot. पायाचे बोट

offee (toffees) n A **toffee** is a sweet made by boiling sugar and butter together with water. साखरयुक्त मिठाई

ogether adv If people do something **together**, they do it with each other. एकत्र

ogo n **Togo** is a republic in West Africa, on the Gulf of Guinea. टोगो

oilet (toilets) n A **toilet** is a large bowl connected to the drains which you use when you want to get rid of urine or waste from your body. प्रसाधनगृह

oilet bag (toilet bags) n A **toilet bag** is a small bag in which you keep things such as soap, a flannel, and a toothbrush when you are travelling. प्रसाधनासाठी आवश्यक असलेले सामान असलेली पिशवी

oilet paper n **Toilet paper** is paper that you use to clean yourself after getting rid of urine or faeces from your body. प्रसाधनगृहात वापरायचा कागद

oiletries npl **Toiletries** are products such as soap and toothpaste that you use

when cleaning or taking care of your body. प्रसाधनासाठी आवश्यक असलेली उत्पादने

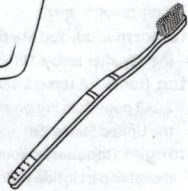

toilet roll (toilet rolls) n A **toilet roll** is a long narrow strip of toilet paper that is wound around a small cardboard tube. प्रसाधनगृहात वापरायच्या कागदाची गुंडाळी

token (tokens) n A **token** is a piece of paper, plastic, or metal which can be used instead of money. टोकन

tolerant adj If you are **tolerant**, you let other people say and do what they like, even if you do not agree with it or approve of it. सहनशील

toll (**tolls**) n A **toll** is a sum of money that you have to pay in order to use a particular bridge or road. पथकर

tomato (**tomatoes**) n A **tomato** is a small, soft, red fruit that is used in cooking as a vegetable or eaten raw in salads. टोमॅटो

tomato sauce n Tomato sauce is a thick sauce made with tomatoes and often served with pasta. टोमॅटो सॉस

tomb (**tombs**) n A **tomb** is a stone structure containing the body of a dead person. थडगे

tomboy (**tomboys**) n If you say that a girl is a **tomboy**, you mean that she likes playing rough or noisy games, or doing things that were considered to be things that boys enjoy. पुरुषी वागणारी मुलगी

tomorrow adv You use **tomorrow** to refer to the day after today. उद्या

ton (**tons**) n A **ton** is a unit of weight equal to 2,240 pounds in Britain and 2,000 pounds in the United States. टन

tongue (**tongues**) n Your **tongue** is the soft movable part inside your mouth that you use for tasting, licking, and speaking. जीभ

tonic (**tonics**) n Tonic or **tonic water** is a colourless, fizzy drink that has a slightly bitter flavour. शक्तिवर्धक औषध

tonight adv **Tonight** is used to refer to the evening of today or the night that follows today. आज रात्री

tonsillitis n Tonsillitis is a painful swelling of your tonsils caused by an infection. घशातील गाठींची सूज

tonsils npl Your **tonsils** are the two small soft lumps in your throat at the back of your mouth. घशातील गाठी, टॉन्सिलस्

too adv Too means also. सुद्धा ▷ adv You use **too** to mean more than you want or need. खूप

tool (**tools**) n A **tool** is any instrument or simple piece of equipment, for example, a hammer or a knife, that you hold in your hands and use to do a particular kind of work. उपकरण

tooth (**teeth**) n Your **teeth** are the hard, white things in your mouth that you use to bite and chew food. दात ▷ n The **teeth** of a comb, a saw, or a zip are the parts that are in a row along its edge. दात

toothache n Toothache is pain in one of your teeth. दातदुखी

toothbrush (**toothbrushes**) n A **toothbrush** is a small brush used for cleaning your teeth. दात घासण्याचा ब्रश

toothpaste (**toothpastes**) n Toothpaste is a thick substance which you use to clean your teeth. दातांना लावायची पेस्ट

toothpick (**toothpicks**) n A **toothpick** is a small stick which you use to remove food from between your teeth. दातकोरणे

top (**tops**) adj The **top** thing is the highest one. सर्वांत वरचा ▷ n The **top** of something is the highest part of it. माथा ▷ n The **top** of something is the part that fits over the end of it. झाकण

topic (**topics**) n A **topic** is a particular subject that you write about or discuss. प्रकरण

topical adj Topical means relating to events that are happening at the time when you are speaking or writing. प्रकरणांशी संबंधित

top-secret adj Top-secret information or activity is intended to be kept completely secret. अत्यंत गुप्त बाब

top-up card (**top-up cards**) n A **top-up card** is a card bought by a mobile-phone user entitling him or her to an amount of credit for future calls. टॉप-अप कार्ड

torch (**torches**) n A **torch** is a small, battery-powered electric light which you carry in your hand. विजेरी

tornado (**tornadoes, tornados**) n A **tornado** is a violent storm with strong circular winds. तुफानी वावटळ

tortoise (**tortoises**) n A **tortoise** is a slow-moving animal with a shell into which it can pull its head and legs for protection. कासव

torture (tortures, torturing, tortured) *n*
If someone is made to experience **torture**,
another person deliberately causes them great
pain, in order to punish them or make them
reveal information. छळ ▷ *vt* If someone **is
tortured**, another person deliberately causes
them great pain over a period of time, in
order to punish them or to make them reveal
information. छळ करणे

toss (tosses, tossing, tossed) *vt* If you **toss**
something somewhere, you throw it there
lightly and carelessly. भिरकावणे

total (totals) *adj* The **total** number or cost of
something is the number or cost that you get
when you add together or count all the parts
in it. एकूण ▷ *n* A **total** is the number that you
get when you add several numbers together
or when you count how many things there are
in a group. एकूण

totally *adv* **Totally** means completely.
संपूर्णपणे

touch (touches, touching, touched) *vt* If
you **touch** something, you put your fingers or
your hand on it. स्पर्श करणे ▷ *v* If one thing
touches another, or two things **touch**, they
are so close that there is no space between
them. स्पर्श करणे

touchdown (touchdowns) *n* **Touchdown** is
the landing of an aircraft or spacecraft. विमान
जमिनीवर उतरवणे

touched *adj* If you are **touched**, you are
affected or moved to sympathy or emotion.
हेलावून गेलेला

touching *adj* If something is **touching**, it
causes feelings of sadness or sympathy. हेलावून
टाकणारा

touchline *n* In sports such as rugby and
football, the **touchline** is one of the two
lines which mark the side of the playing area.
टचलाईन

touch pad (touch pads) *n* A **touch pad** is
a flat pad on some computers that you slide
your finger over in order to move the cursor.
टच पॅड

touchy (touchier, touchiest) *adj* **Touchy**
people are easily upset or irritated. सहजगत्या
अस्वस्थ होणारे

tough (tougher, toughest) *adj* A **tough**
person has a strong character and can tolerate
difficulty or hardship. कणखर

toupee (toupees) *n* A **toupee** is a piece of
artificial hair worn by a man to cover a patch
on his head where he has lost his hair. पुरुषांनी
वापरायचा केसांचा टोप

tour (tours, touring, toured) *n* A **tour**
is an organized trip that people such as
musicians, politicians, or theatre companies
go on to several different places, stopping
to meet people or perform. दौरा ▷ *v* When
people such as musicians, politicians, or
theatre companies **tour**, they go on a tour,
for example in order to perform or to meet
people. दौरा करणे

tour guide (tour guides) *n* A **tour guide**
is someone who helps tourists who are on
holiday or shows them round a place. प्रवाशांचा
मार्गदर्शक

tourism *n* **Tourism** is the business of providing
services for people on holiday. पर्यटन व्यवसाय

tourist (tourists) *n* A **tourist** is a person who
is visiting a place for pleasure, especially when
they are on holiday. पर्यटक

tourist office (tourist offices) *n* A **tourist
office** is a place where tourists can go to
get information, to make bookings, etc. यात्रा
कंपनीचे कार्यालय

tournament (tournaments) *n* A
tournament is a sports competition in which
players who win a match continue to play
further matches until just one person or team
is left. स्पर्धा

towards *prep* **Towards** means in the direction
of something. ...कडे *He moved towards the
door.*

**tow away (tows away, towing away, towed
away)** *v* If one vehicle **tows away** another, it
removes it by pulling it along behind it. वाहन
खेचून नेणे *They threatened to tow away my car.*

towel (towels) n A **towel** is a piece of thick, soft cloth that you use to dry yourself with. टॉवेल, पंचा

tower (towers) n A **tower** is a tall narrow structure that is often part of a castle. मनोरा

town (towns) n A **town** is a place with many streets and buildings where people live and work. शहर

town centre (town centres) n The **town centre** is the main part of a town, where the shops are. शहरातील मध्यवर्ती विभाग

town hall (town halls) n The **town hall** in a town is a large building owned and used by the town council, often as its headquarters. नगरपरिषदेचे मुख्यालय

town planning n **Town planning** is the planning and design of all the new buildings, roads, and parks in a place in order to make them attractive and convenient for the people who live there. नगररचना आयोजन

toxic adj A **toxic** substance is poisonous. विषारी

toy (toys) n A **toy** is an object that children play with, for example, a doll or a model car. खेळणे

trace (traces) n A **trace** of something is a very small amount of it. अंश

tracing paper n **Tracing paper** is transparent paper which you put over a picture so that you can draw over its lines in order to produce a copy of it. ट्रेसिंग पेपर

track (tracks) n A **track** is a narrow road or path. अरुंद रस्ता

track down (tracks down, tracking down, tracked down) v If you **track down** someone or something, you find them after a long and difficult search. शोधून काढणे It took two years to track him down.

tracksuit (tracksuits) n A **tracksuit** is a loose, warm suit consisting of trousers and a top, worn mainly when exercising. ट्रॅक सूट

tractor (tractors) n A **tractor** is a farm vehicle that is used for pulling farm machinery. यांत्रिक नांगर, ट्रॅक्टर

trade (trades) n **Trade** is the activity of buying, selling, or exchanging goods or services between people, firms, or countries. व्यापार

trademark (trademarks) n A **trademark** is a name or symbol that a company uses on its products and that cannot legally be used by another company. ट्रेडमार्क

trade union (trade unions) n A **trade union** is an organization formed by workers in order to represent their rights and interests to their employers. कामगार संघटना

trade unionist (trade unionists) n A **trade unionist** is an active member of a trade union. कामगार संघटनेचा सक्रिय सभासद

tradition (traditions) n A **tradition** is a custom or belief that has existed for a long time. परंपरा

traditional adj **Traditional** customs, beliefs, or methods are ones that have existed for a long time without changing. परंपरागत

traffic n **Traffic** refers to all the vehicles that are moving along the roads in an area. रहदारी

traffic jam (traffic jams) n A **traffic jam** is a long line of vehicles that cannot move because there is too much traffic, or because the road is blocked. वाहतूक कोंडी

traffic lights npl **Traffic lights** are the coloured lights at road junctions which control the flow of traffic. वाहतूक नियंत्रित करणारे दिवे, सिग्नल

traffic warden (traffic wardens) n A **traffic warden** is a person whose job is to make sure that cars are not parked illegally. (बेकायदेशीर पार्किंग होऊ नये म्हणून काम करणारा) ट्रॅफिक वार्डेन

tragedy (tragedies) n A **tragedy** is an extremely sad event or situation. दुःखद घटना, शोकान्तिका

tragic adj Something that is **tragic** is extremely sad, usually because it involves suffering. दुःखद, शोकात्म

trailer (trailers) n A **trailer** is a vehicle without an engine which is pulled by a car or lorry. ट्रेलर

train (**trains, training, trained**) *n* A **train** is a long vehicle that is pulled by an engine along a railway line. ट्रेन ▷ *vt* If you **train** to do something, you learn the skills that you need in order to do it. प्रशिक्षण घेणे

trained *adj* A person who is **trained** in a particular kind of work has learned the skills that you need in order to do it. प्रशिक्षित

trainee (**trainees**) *n* A **trainee** is a junior employee who is being taught how to do a job. प्रशिक्षणार्थी

trainer (**trainers**) *n* A **trainer** is someone who teaches you the skills you need to be able to do something. प्रशिक्षक

trainers *npl* **Trainers** are shoes that people wear, especially for running and other sports. धावताना व खेळताना वापरायचे बूट

training *n* **Training** is the process of learning the skills that you need for a particular job or activity. प्रशिक्षण

training course (**training courses**) *n* A **training course** is a series of lessons or lectures teaching the skills that you need for a particular job or activity. प्रशिक्षण पाठ्यक्रम

tram (**trams**) *n* A **tram** is a public transport vehicle, usually powered by electricity, which travels along rails laid in the surface of a street. ट्राम

tramp (**tramps**) *n* A **tramp** is a person with no home or job who travels around and gets money by doing occasional work or by begging. कामधंदा व घरदार नसलेला भटक्या ▷ *n* A **tramp** is a difficult and long walk. दूरवरचा कष्टाचा प्रवास

trampoline (**trampolines**) *n* A **trampoline** is a piece of equipment on which you jump up and down as a sport. It consists of a large piece of strong cloth held by springs in a frame. ट्रँपोलीन

tranquillizer (**tranquillizers**) *n* A **tranquillizer** is a drug that is used to make people or animals become sleepy or unconscious. मन शांत करणारे औषध

transaction (**transactions**) *n* A **transaction** is a business deal. *(formal)* व्यवहार

transcript (**transcripts**) *n* A **transcript** of something that is spoken is a written copy of it. जे बोलले गेले त्याची लेखी प्रत

transfer (**transfers**) *n* The **transfer** of something or someone is the act of transferring them. हस्तांतरण

transform (**transforms, transforming, transformed**) *vt* To **transform** someone or something means to change them completely. परिवर्तन करणे

transfusion (**transfusions**) *n* A blood **transfusion** is a process in which blood is injected into the body of a person who is badly injured or ill. रक्तधानप्रयोग, रक्तदान

transistor (**transistors**) *n* A **transistor** is a small electronic component in something such as a television or radio, which is used to control electronic signals. ट्रांझिस्टर

transit *n* **Transit** is the carrying of goods or people by vehicle from one place to another. वस्तू किंवा माणसे एका जागेवरून दुसऱ्या जागेवर हलवणे

transition (**transitions**) *n* **Transition** is the process in which something changes from one state to another. संक्रमण

translate (**translates, translating, translated**) *vt* If something that someone has said or written **is translated**, it is said or written again in a different language. भाषांतर करणे

translation (**translations**) *n* A **translation** is a piece of writing or speech that has been translated from a different language. भाषांतर

translator (**translators**) *n* A **translator** is a person whose job is translating writing or speech from one language to another. भाषांतरकार

transparent *adj* If an object or substance is **transparent**, you can see through it. पारदर्शक

transplant (**transplants**) *n* A **transplant** is a surgical operation in which a part of a person's body is replaced because it is diseased. प्रत्यारोपण

transport (**transports, transporting, transported**) *n* **Transport** refers to any type of vehicle that you can travel in. वाहतूक, वाहन ▷ *vt* When goods or people **are transported** from one place to another, they are moved there. वाहतूक करणे

transvestite (**transvestites**) *n* A **transvestite** is a person, usually a man, who enjoys wearing clothes normally worn by people of the other sex. भिन्न लिंगीयांचे कपडे घालणारी व्यक्ती

trap (**traps**) *n* A **trap** is a device which is placed somewhere or a hole which is dug somewhere in order to catch animals or birds. सापळा

traumatic *adj* A **traumatic** experience is very shocking or upsetting, and may cause psychological damage. अत्यंत क्लेशकारक, आघाताचा

travel (**travels, travelling, travelled**) *n* Travel is the act of travelling. प्रवास ▷ *vi* If you **travel**, you go from one place to another, often to a place that is far away. प्रवास करणे

travel agency (**travel agencies**) *n* A **travel agency** is a business which makes arrangements for people's holidays and journeys. प्रवासाची व्यवस्था करून देणारी एजन्सी वा कंपनी

travel agent *n* A **travel agent** is a person who arranges people's holidays and journeys. प्रवासाची व्यवस्था करून देणारा एजन्ट वा माणूस

travel insurance *n* Travel insurance is an arrangement in which you pay money to a company, and they pay money to you if your property is stolen or damaged, or if you get a serious illness. प्रवासात अपघात झाल्यास संरक्षण देणारा विमा

traveller (**travellers**) *n* A **traveller** is a person who is making a journey or who travels a lot. प्रवासी

traveller's cheque (**traveller's cheques**) *n* **Traveller's cheques** are special cheques that you can exchange for local currency when you are abroad. प्रवासी धनादेश

travelling *n* **Travelling** is the process of going from one place to another, often one that is far away. प्रवास

tray (**trays**) *n* A **tray** is a flat piece of wood, plastic, or metal that has raised edges and that is used for carrying food or drinks. तबक, ट्रे

treacle *n* **Treacle** is a thick, sweet, sticky liquid that is obtained from sugar. It is used in making cakes and puddings. काकवी

tread (**treads, treading, trod, trodden**) *vi* If you **tread on** something, you put your foot on it when you are walking or standing. पायावर पाय पडणे/टाकणे, चिरडणे

treasure *n* In children's stories, **treasure** is a collection of valuable old objects, such as gold coins and jewels. (*literary*) खजिना

treasurer (**treasurers**) *n* The **treasurer** of a society or organization is the person in charge of its finances. खजिनदार

treat (**treats, treating, treated**) *n* If you give someone a **treat**, you buy or arrange something special for them which they will enjoy. मेजवानी ▷ *vt* If you **treat** someone or something in a particular way, you behave towards them in that way. वागणूक देणे

treatment (**treatments**) *n* **Treatment** is medical attention given to a sick or injured person or animal. वैद्यकीय इलाज

treaty (**treaties**) *n* A **treaty** is a written agreement between countries. देशांमधील करार

treble (**trebles, trebling, trebled**) *v* If something **trebles**, or if you **treble** it, it becomes three times greater in number or amount. तिप्पट करणे

tree (**trees**) *n* A **tree** is a tall plant with a hard trunk, branches, and leaves. झाड

trek (**treks, trekking, trekked**) *n* A **trek** is a long and often difficult journey. पायी केलेला दूरवरचा खडतर प्रवास ▷ *vi* If you **trek** somewhere, you go on a journey across difficult country, usually on foot. पायी (खडतर) प्रवास करणे

tremble (**trembles, trembling, trembled**) *vi* If you **tremble**, you shake slightly, usually because you are frightened or cold. थरथर कापणे

tremendous adj You use **tremendous** to emphasize how strong a feeling or quality is, or how large an amount is. प्रचंड

trench (**trenches**) n A **trench** is a long narrow channel dug in the ground. खंदक

trend (**trends**) n A **trend** is a change towards something different. कल

trendy (**trendier, trendiest**) adj If you say that something or someone is **trendy**, you mean that they are very fashionable and modern. (informal) आधुनिकतेचे अनुकरण करणारे

trial (**trials**) n A **trial** is a formal meeting in a law court, at which a judge and jury listen to evidence and decide whether a person is guilty of a crime. तपासणी

trial period (**trial periods**) n If you are on a **trial period** for a job, you do the job for a short period of time to see if you are suitable for it. नोकरीचा चाचणीचा कालावधी

triangle (**triangles**) n A **triangle** is a shape with three straight sides. त्रिकोण ▷ n A **triangle** is an instrument made of metal in the shape of a **triangle** that you hit with a stick to make music. त्रिकोणी आकाराचे वाद्य

tribe (**tribes**) n **Tribe** is sometimes used to refer to a group of people of the same race, language, and customs, especially in a developing country. जमात

tribunal (**tribunals**) n A **tribunal** is a special court or committee that is appointed to deal with particular problems. लवाद

trick (**tricks, tricking, tricked**) n A **trick** is an action that is intended to deceive someone. चलाखी ▷ vt If someone **tricks** you, they deceive you, often in order to make you do something. चलाखी करणे

tricky (**trickier, trickiest**) adj A **tricky** task or problem is difficult to deal with. कठीण काम

tricycle (**tricycles**) n A **tricycle** is a cycle with three wheels, two at the back and one at the front. Tricycles are usually ridden by children. तीनचाकी सायकल

trifle (**trifles**) n **Trifles** are things that are not considered important. क्षुल्लक गोष्ट

trim (**trims, trimming, trimmed**) vt If you **trim** something, for example, someone's hair, you cut off small amounts of it in order to make it look neater and tidier. छाटणे, नीट कापणे

Trinidad and Tobago n **Trinidad and Tobago** is an independent republic in the Caribbean. त्रिनिदाद आणि टोबेगो

trip (**trips, tripping, tripped**) n A **trip** is a journey that you make to a place and back again. सहल ▷ vi If you **trip** when you are walking, you knock your foot against something and fall or nearly fall. चालताना अडखळणे

triple adj **Triple** means consisting of three things or parts. तिहेरी

triplets npl **Triplets** are three children born at the same time to the same mother. तिळी मुले

triumph (**triumphs, triumphing, triumphed**) n A **triumph** is a great success or achievement. विजय ▷ vi If you **triumph**, you win a victory or succeed in overcoming something. विजय होणे

trivial adj If you describe something as **trivial**, you think that it is unimportant and not serious. क्षुल्लक

trolley (**trolleys**) n A **trolley** is a small cart on wheels that you use to carry things such as shopping or luggage. ट्रॉली

trombone (**trombones**) n A **trombone** is a long brass musical instrument which you play by blowing into it and sliding part of it backwards and forwards. ट्रॉंबोन नावाचे वाद्य

troops npl **Troops** are soldiers. सैनिक, सैन्यदल

trophy (**trophies**) n A **trophy** is a prize such as a cup, given to the winner of a competition. चषक

tropical adj **Tropical** means belonging to or typical of the tropics. विषुववृत्तीय

trot (**trots, trotting, trotted**) vi If you **trot** somewhere, you move fairly fast at a speed between walking and running, taking small quick steps. दुडक्या चालीने चालणे

trouble (**troubles**) n You can refer to problems or difficulties as **trouble**. त्रास

troublemaker (troublemakers) n A **troublemaker** is someone who causes trouble. त्रास देणारा

trough (troughs) n A **trough** is a long container from which farm animals drink or eat. गव्हाण,पन्हाळ

trousers npl **Trousers** are a piece of clothing that you wear over your body from the waist downwards, and that cover each leg separately. You can also say **a pair of trousers**. पायजमा, पँट

trout (trout, trouts) n A **trout** is a kind of fish that lives in rivers and streams. ट्राऊट नावाचा मासा

trowel (trowels) n A **trowel** is a small garden tool which you use for digging small holes or removing weeds. खुरपे

truce (truces) n A **truce** is an agreement between two people or groups to stop fighting or quarrelling for a short time. तह

truck (trucks) n A **truck** is a large vehicle that is used to transport goods by road. ट्रक

truck driver (truck drivers) n A **truck driver** is someone who drives a truck as their job. ट्रक चालक

true (truer, truest) adj If a story is **true**, it really happened. खरा ▷ adj If something is **true**, it is right or correct. बरोबर

truly adv **Truly** means completely and genuinely. खरोखर

trumpet (trumpets) n A **trumpet** is a brass wind instrument. तुतारी

trunk (trunks) n A **trunk** is the thick stem of a tree. The branches and roots grow from the **trunk**. खोड ▷ n An elephant's **trunk** is its long nose. Elephants use their **trunks** to suck up water and to lift things. सोंड ▷ n A **trunk** is a large, strong box that you use to keep things in. मोठी पेटी

trunks npl **Trunks** are shorts that a man wears when he goes swimming. चड्डी

trust (trusts, trusting, trusted) n Your **trust** in someone is your belief that they are honest and sincere and will not deliberately do anything to harm you. विश्वास ▷ vt If you **trust** someone, you believe that they are honest and sincere and will not deliberately do anything to harm you. विश्वास ठेवणे

trusting adj A **trusting** person believes that people are honest and sincere and do not intend to harm him or her. विश्वास ठेवणारा

truth n The **truth** about something is all the facts about it, rather than things that are imagined or invented. सत्य

truthful adj If a person or their comments are **truthful**, they are honest and do not tell any lies. सत्य

try (tries, trying, tried) n If you have a **try** at doing something, you make an effort to do it. प्रयत्न ▷ vi If you **try** to do something, you do it as well as you can. प्रयत्न करणे ▷ vt If you **try** something, you test it to see what it is like or how it works. आजमावून पाहणे

try on (tries on, trying on, tried on) v If you **try on** a piece of clothing, you put it on to see if it fits you or if it looks nice. कपडे अंगावर चढवून बरोबर होतात का ते पाहणे *Try on clothing and shoes to make sure they fit.*

try out (tries out, trying out, tried out) v If you **try** something **out**, you test it in order to find out how useful or effective it is. चाचपणी करणे *The company hopes to try out the system in September.*

T-shirt (T-shirts) n A **T-shirt** is a cotton shirt with short sleeves and no collar or buttons. टी- शर्ट

tsunami (tsunamis) n A **tsunami** is a very large wave, often caused by an earthquake, that flows onto the land and destroys things. सुनामी

tube (tubes) n A **tube** is a long, round, hollow piece of metal, rubber, or plastic. नळी ▷ n A **tube** is a soft metal or plastic container that you press to make what is in it come out. ट्यूब

tuberculosis n **Tuberculosis**, or **TB**, is a serious infectious disease that affects the lungs. क्षयरोग

Tuesday (Tuesdays) n **Tuesday** is the day after Monday and before Wednesday. मंगळवार

tug-of-war (tugs-of-war) n A **tug-of-war** is a sports event in which two teams test their strength by pulling against each other on opposite ends of a rope. रस्सीखेच

tuition n If you are given **tuition** in a particular subject, you are taught about that subject, especially on your own or in a small group. शिकवणी

tuition fees npl **Tuition fees** are the money that you pay to be taught, especially in a college or university. शिकवणीसाठी दिलेले पैसे

tulip (tulips) n **Tulips** are garden flowers that grow in the spring. ट्युलिप

tumble dryer (tumble dryers) n A **tumble dryer** is an electric machine which dries washing by turning it over and over and blowing warm air onto it. टंबल ड्रायर

tummy (tummies) n Your **tummy** is your stomach. पोट

tumour (tumours) n A **tumour** is a mass of diseased or abnormal cells that has grown in someone's body. गाठ

tuna (tuna, tunas) n A **tuna** or a **tuna fish** is a large fish that lives in warm seas. (खाऱ्या पाण्यातील एक मोठा मासा) ट्यूना

tune (tunes) n A **tune** is a series of musical notes that is pleasant to listen to. संगीताची धून

Tunisia n Tunisia is a republic in North Africa, on the Mediterranean. ट्युनिशिया

Tunisian (Tunisians) adj **Tunisian** means belonging to or relating to Tunisia, or to its people or culture. ट्युनिशियन ▷ n A **Tunisian** is a person who comes from Tunisia. ट्युनिशियन

tunnel (tunnels) n A **tunnel** is a long passage which has been made under the ground, usually through a hill or under the sea. बोगदा

turbulence n **Turbulence** is a state of confusion and disorganized change. प्रक्षुब्धता

Turk (Turks) n A **Turk** is a person who comes from Turkey. तुर्क

turkey (turkeys) n A **turkey** is a large bird that is kept on a farm for its meat. टर्की नावाचा पक्षी

Turkey n Turkey is a republic in western Asia and south-eastern Europe. तुर्कस्थान

Turkish adj **Turkish** means belonging or relating to Turkey, or to its people, language, or culture. तुर्की ▷ n **Turkish** is the main language spoken in Turkey. तुर्की भाषा

turn (turns, turning, turned) n A **turn** is a change of direction. वळण ▷ v When you **turn**, you move in a different direction. वळणे ▷ v When something **turns**, it moves around in a circle. वळणे ▷ vi If one thing **turns into** another thing, it becomes that thing. रूप बदलणे

turn around (turns around, turning around, turned around) v To **turn around** means to move in a different direction or to move into a different position. जागा बदलणे, वळणे She turned around to see a woman standing there. ❑ I felt a tapping on wmy shoulder and I turned around.

turn back (turns back, turning back, turned back) v If you **turn back**, or if someone turns you **back** when you are going somewhere, you change direction and go towards where you started from. मागे वळणे Police attempted to turn back protesters.

turn down (turns down, turning down, turned down) v If you **turn down** a person or their request or offer, you refuse their request or offer. नाकारणे, धुडकावून लावणे After careful consideration I turned the invitation down.

turning (turnings) n If you take a particular **turning**, you go along a road which leads away from the side of another road. वळण

turnip (turnips) n A **turnip** is a round vegetable with a green and white skin. सलगम नावाची कंदभाजी

turn off (turns off, turning off, turned off) v If you **turn off** the road or path you are going along, you start going along a different road or path which leads away from it. एक रस्ता सोडून दुसऱ्या रस्त्यावर जाणे Turn off at the bridge.

turn on (turns on, turning on, turned on) v When you **turn on** a piece of equipment or a supply of something, you cause heat, sound, or water to be produced by adjusting the controls. चालू करणे *She asked them why they hadn't turned the lights on.*

turn out (turns out, turning out, turned out) v If something **turns out** a particular way, it happens in that way or has the result or degree of success indicated. निष्पन्न होणे *I was positive things were going to turn out fine.*

turnover n The **turnover** of a company is the value of goods or services sold during a particular period of time. उलाढाल

turn up (turns up, turning up, turned up) v If you say that someone or something **turns up**, you mean that they arrive, often unexpectedly, or after you have been waiting a long time. येणे *We waited for the bus, but it never turned up.*

turquoise adj **Turquoise** is used to describe things that are of a light greenish-blue colour. फिकट हिरवट-निळसर रंगाचा

turtle (turtles) n A **turtle** is a large reptile with a thick shell which lives in the sea. कासव

tutor (tutors) n A **tutor** is a teacher at a British university or college. ब्रिटिश विद्यापीठातील शिक्षक

tutorial (tutorials) n In a British university or college, a **tutorial** is a regular meeting between a tutor and one or several students for discussion of a subject that is being studied. शिक्षक व विद्यार्थी यांची एखाद्या विषयावर चर्चा करण्यासाठी भेट

tuxedo (tuxedos) n A **tuxedo** is a black or white jacket worn by men for formal social events. टक्सेडो नावाचे काळे जाकीट

TV (TVs) n A **TV** is a piece of electrical equipment with a glass screen on which you can watch programmes with pictures and sounds. **TV** is an abbreviation for 'television'. दूरदर्शन संच

tweezers npl **Tweezers** are a small tool that you use for tasks such as picking up small objects or pulling out hairs. Tweezers consist of two strips of metal or plastic joined together at one end. एक प्रकारची चिमटा

twelfth adj The **twelfth** item in a series is the one that you count as number twelve. बारावा

twelve num **Twelve** is the number 12. बारा

twentieth adj The **twentieth** item in a series is the one that you count as number twenty. विसावा

twenty num **Twenty** is the number 20. वीस

twice adv If something happens **twice**, it happens two times. दोनदा

twin (twins) n If two people are **twins**, they have the same mother and were born on the same day. जुळे

twin beds npl **Twin beds** are two single beds in one bedroom. एकाच शयनकक्षातील दोन (वेगळे) बिछाने

twinned adj When a place or organization in one country is **twinned** with a place or organization in another country, a special relationship is formally established between them. दुसऱ्या देशाशी किंवा त्यातील संस्थेशी असलेले जवळकीचे संबंध

twist (twists, twisting, twisted) vt If you **twist** something, you turn it to make a spiral shape, for example by turning the two ends of it in opposite directions. पिळणे

twit (twits) n If you call someone a **twit**, you are insulting them and saying that they are silly or stupid. *(informal)* अपमानास्पद बोलणे

two num **Two** is the number 2. दोन

type (types, typing, typed) n A **type** of something is the kind of thing that it is. प्रकार ▷ v If you **type** something, you write it with a machine, for example a computer. टाईप करणे, छापणे

typewriter (typewriters) n A **typewriter** is a machine with keys which are pressed in order to print letters, numbers, or other characters onto paper. टंकण यंत्र

typhoid *n* **Typhoid** or **typhoid fever** is a serious infectious disease that produces fever and diarrhoea and can cause death. It is spread by dirty water or food. विषमज्वर

typical *adj* You use **typical** to describe someone or something that shows the most usual characteristics of a particular type of person or thing, and is therefore a good example of that type. नमुनेदार

typist (**typists**) *n* A **typist** is someone who works in an office typing letters and other documents. टंकलेखक

tyre (**tyres**) *n* A **tyre** is a thick ring of rubber filled with air and fitted round the wheel of a vehicle. टायर

u

UFO (**UFOs**) *abbr* A **UFO** is an object seen in the sky or landing on Earth which cannot be identified and which is often believed to be from another planet. **UFO** is an abbreviation for 'unidentified flying object'. (युएफओ) उडती तबकडी

Uganda *n* **Uganda** is a republic in East Africa. युगांडा

Ugandan (**Ugandans**) *adj* **Ugandan** means belonging or relating to Uganda or to its people or culture. युगांडन ▷ *n* A **Ugandan** is a Ugandan citizen, or a person of Ugandan origin. युगांडन

ugh! *excl* **Ugh!** is used in writing to represent the sound that people make if they think something is unpleasant, horrible, or disgusting. ई !

ugly (**uglier, ugliest**) *adj* If you say that someone or something is **ugly**, you mean that they are unattractive and unpleasant to look at. कुरूप

UHT milk *n* **UHT milk** is milk which has been treated at a very high temperature so that it can be kept for a long time if the container is not opened. **UHT** is an abbreviation for 'ultra-heat-treated'. यू. एच. टी. दूध

UK *n* The **UK** is Great Britain and Northern Ireland. **UK** is an abbreviation for 'United Kingdom'. यू.के., युनायटेड किंगडम

Ukraine *n* **Ukraine** is a republic in south-east Europe, on the Black Sea and the Sea of Azov. युक्रेन

Ukrainian (**Ukrainians**) *adj* **Ukrainian** means of or relating to Ukraine, its people, or their language. युक्रेनियन ▷ *n* A **Ukrainian** is a Ukrainian citizen, or a person of Ukrainian origin. युक्रेनियन ▷ *n* **Ukrainian** is the official language of Ukraine. युक्रेनियन

ulcer (**ulcers**) *n* An **ulcer** is a sore area on or inside a part of your body which is very painful and may bleed. शरीराच्या अंतर्भागात झालेली जखम किंवा व्रण

Ulster *n* **Ulster** is a region and former kingdom of Northern Ireland. अल्स्टर

ultimate *adj* You use **ultimate** to describe the final result or the original cause of a long series of events. अंतिम

ultimately *adv* **Ultimately** means finally, after a long series of events. शेवटी

ultimatum (**ultimatums, ultimata**) *n* An **ultimatum** is a warning that unless someone acts in a particular way within a particular time limit, action will be taken against them. शेवटची कालमर्यादा, निर्वाणीचा इशारा

ultrasound *n* **Ultrasound** refers to sound waves which travel at such a high frequency that they cannot be heard by humans. अतिसूक्ष्म ध्वनिलहरी

umbrella (**umbrellas**) *n* An **umbrella** is an object which you use to protect yourself from the rain. It consists of a long stick with a folding frame covered in cloth. छत्री

umpire (**umpires**) *n* An **umpire** is a person whose job is to make sure that a sports match or contest is played fairly and that the rules are not broken. खेळातील पंच

UN *abbr* The **UN** is an organization which most countries belong to. Its role is to encourage international peace, cooperation, and friendship. **UN** is an abbreviation for 'United Nations'. संयुक्त राष्ट्रसंघ

unable *adj* If you are **unable** to do something, it is impossible for you to do it. असमर्थ

unacceptable *adj* If you describe something as **unacceptable**, you strongly disapprove of it or object to it and feel that it should not be allowed to happen or continue. अस्वीकाराई

unanimous *adj* When a group of people or their opinion is **unanimous**, they all agree about something. एकमुखाने

unattended *adj* When people or things are left **unattended**, they are not being watched or looked after. दुर्लक्षित

unavoidable *adj* If something bad is **unavoidable**, it cannot be avoided or prevented. अपरिहार्य

unbearable *adj* If you describe something as **unbearable**, you mean that it is so unpleasant, painful, or upsetting that you feel unable to accept it or deal with it. असह्य

unbeatable *adj* If you describe something as **unbeatable**, you mean that it is the best thing of its kind. सर्वोत्कृष्ट

unbelievable *adj* If you say that something is **unbelievable**, you are emphasizing that it is very extreme, impressive, or shocking. अविश्वसनीय

unbreakable *adj* **Unbreakable** objects cannot be broken, usually because they are made of a very strong material. न तुटणारे, न मोडणारे

uncanny *adj* If something is **uncanny**, it is strange and difficult to explain. अस्वाभाविक

uncertain *adj* If you are **uncertain** about something, you do not know what to do. अनिश्चित

uncertainty (**uncertainties**) *n* **Uncertainty** is a state of doubt about the future or about what is the right thing to do. अनिश्चितता

unchanged *adj* Something that is **unchanged** has stayed the same during a period of time. बदल न झालेले

uncivilized *adj* If you describe someone's behaviour as **uncivilized**, you find it unacceptable, for example because it is very cruel or very rude. असंस्कृत

uncle (**uncles**) *n* Your **uncle** is the brother of your mother or father, or the husband of your aunt. काका, मामा

unclear *adj* If something is **unclear**, it is not known or not certain. अस्पष्ट

uncomfortable *adj* If you are **uncomfortable**, you are not physically relaxed, and feel slight pain or discomfort. अस्वस्थ

unconditional *adj* Something that is **unconditional** is done or given to someone freely, without anything being required in return. बिनशर्त

unconscious *adj* Someone who is **unconscious** is in a state similar to sleep, as a result of a shock, accident, or injury. बेशुद्ध

uncontrollable *adj* If something such as an emotion is **uncontrollable**, you can do nothing to prevent it or control it. अनावर

unconventional adj If someone is **unconventional**, they do not behave in the same way as most other people in their society. अपारंपरिक

undecided adj If you are **undecided** about something, you have not yet made a decision about it. अनिर्णित

undeniable adj If something is **undeniable**, it is definitely true or definitely exists. नाकारता न येणाऱ्या

under prep If one thing is **under** another thing, it is lower down than it, or the second thing covers the first thing. ...च्याखाली *There was a dog under the table.* ❑ *He was standing under a large painting.*

underage adj Someone who is **underage** is not legally old enough to do something. कायद्याच्या दृष्टीने अज्ञान

underestimate (**underestimates, underestimating, underestimated**) vt If you **underestimate** something, you do not realize how large it is or will be. अंदाज न लागणे, कमी लेखणे

undergo (**undergoes, undergoing, underwent, undergone**) vt If you **undergo** something necessary or unpleasant, it happens to you. भोगणे (दुःख, वेदना इत्यादी), (अनुभव)

undergraduate (**undergraduates**) n An **undergraduate** is a student at a university or college who is studying for his or her first degree. प्रथम पदवीसाठी शिकणारा महाविद्यालीन विद्यार्थी

underground n Something that is **underground** is below the surface of the ground. जमिनीखाली, भूमिगत ▷ n The **underground** in a city is the railway system in which electric trains travel below the ground in tunnels. भुयारी रेल्वे

underground station (**underground stations**) n An **underground station** is a station of an underground railway system. भुयारी रेल्वे स्थानक

underline (**underlines, underlining, underlined**) vt If a person or event **underlines**

something, they draw attention to it and emphasize its importance. अधोरेखित करणे

underneath adv If one thing is **underneath** another thing, the second thing covers the first thing. ...च्याखाली ▷ prep If one thing is **underneath** another thing, the second thing covers the first thing. खाली *The ring was underneath the sofa.*

underpaid adj People who are **underpaid** are not paid enough money for the job that they do. कमी मोबदला मिळणारे

underpants npl **Underpants** are a piece of underwear with two holes for your legs and elastic around the waist. **Underpants** refers only to men's underwear. पुरुषांसाठीची आत घालायची चड्डी

underpass (**underpasses**) n An **underpass** is a road or path that goes underneath a railway or another road. एका रस्त्याच्या किंवा रेल्वे रूळाच्या खालून गेलेला रस्ता

underskirt (**underskirts**) n An **underskirt** is any skirtlike garment worn under a skirt. स्कर्टच्या खालचे अंतर्वस्त्र

understand (**understands, understanding, understood**) vt If you **understand** someone, or if you **understand** what they are saying, you know what they mean. आकलन होणे, समजणे

understandable adj If you describe someone's behaviour or feelings as **understandable**, you mean that they have reacted to a situation in a natural way or in the way you would expect. समजण्याजोगे, साहजिक

understanding adj If you are **understanding** towards someone, you are kind and forgiving. समजूतदार

undertaker (**undertakers**) n An **undertaker** is a person whose job is to deal with the bodies of people who have died and to arrange funerals. शव ताब्यात घेऊन त्याची व्यवस्था लावणारा

underwater adv Something that exists or happens **underwater** exists or happens

u

below the surface of the sea, a river, or a lake. पाण्याच्या पृष्ठभागाखाली

underwear *n* **Underwear** is clothing which you wear next to your skin under your other clothes. अंतर्वस्त्र

undisputed *adj* If you describe something as **undisputed**, you mean that everyone accepts that it exists or is true. निर्विवाद

undo (**undoes, undoing, undid, undone**) *vt* If you **undo** something, you loosen or untie it. सैल सोडणे, सोडणे

undoubtedly *adv* **Undoubtedly** means certainly, definitely, or unquestionably. नि:संशयपणे

undress (**undresses, undressing, undressed**) *v* When you **undress**, you take off your clothes. If you **undress** someone, you take off their clothes. कपडे उतरवणे

unemployed *adj* Someone who is **unemployed** does not have a job. बेकार

unemployment *n* **Unemployment** is the fact that people who want jobs cannot get them. बेकारी

unexpected *adj* Something that is **unexpected** surprises you because you did not think it was likely to happen. अनपेक्षित

unexpectedly *adv* **Unexpectedly** means surprisingly. अनपेक्षितरीत्या

unfair *adj* Something that is **unfair** is not right or not just. अयोग्य, अन्याय्य

unfaithful *adj* If someone is **unfaithful** to their partner or to the person they are married to, they have a romantic relationship with someone else. बेइमान

unfamiliar *adj* If something is **unfamiliar** to you, or if you are **unfamiliar** with it, you know very little about it and have not seen or experienced it before. अपरिचित

unfashionable *adj* If something is **unfashionable**, it is not approved of or done by most people. काळानुरूप नसलेले

unfavourable *adj* **Unfavourable** conditions or circumstances cause problems and reduce the chance of success. प्रतिकूल

unfit *adj* If you are **unfit**, your body is not in good condition because you have not been taking regular exercise. तंदुरुस्त नसलेला

unforgettable *adj* If something is **unforgettable**, it is so impressive that you are likely to remember it for a long time. अविस्मरणीय

unfortunately *adv* You can use **unfortunately** to express regret about what you are saying. दुर्दैवाने

unfriendly *adj* If you describe someone as **unfriendly**, you mean that they behave in a cruel or hostile way. दु:स्वास करणारा, शत्रुभावाचा

ungrateful *adj* If you describe someone as **ungrateful**, you are criticizing them for not showing thanks or for being cruel to someone who has helped them. कृतघ्न

unhappy (**unhappier, unhappiest**) *adj* If you are **unhappy**, you are sad and depressed. दु:खी

unhealthy (**unhealthier, unhealthiest**) *adj* Something that is **unhealthy** is likely to cause illness or poor health. अनारोग्यकारक

unhelpful *adj* If you say that someone or something is **unhelpful**, you mean that they do not help you or improve a situation, and may even make things worse. निरुपयोगी, बिनकामाचा

uni (**unis**) *n* A **uni** is an institution where students study for degrees and where academic research is done. **Uni** is short for 'university'. *(informal)* विद्यापीठ

unidentified *adj* If you describe someone or something as **unidentified**, you mean that no-one knows who or what they are. अज्ञात, ओळख न पटलेला

uniform (**uniforms**) *n* A **uniform** is a special set of clothes which some people wear to work in, and which some children wear at school. गणवेश

unimportant *adj* If you describe something or someone as **unimportant**, you mean that they do not have much effect or value, and are therefore not worth considering. बिनमहत्त्वाचा

uninhabited adj An **uninhabited** place is one where no-one lives. कोणीही राहत नसलेला

unintentional adj Something that is **unintentional** is not done deliberately, but happens by accident. निरुद्देशी

union (unions) n A **union** is an organization that has been formed by workers in order to represent their rights and interests to their employers, for example in order to improve working conditions or wages. संघटना

unique adj Something that is **unique** is the only one of its kind. अद्वितीय, खास

unit (units) n If you consider something as a **unit**, you consider it as a single complete thing. एकक

unite (unites, uniting, united) v If a group of people or things **unite**, they join together and act as a group. एक होणे

United Arab Emirates n The **United Arab Emirates** are a group of seven countries in south-west Asia, on the Persian Gulf, consisting of Abu Dhabi, Dubai, Sharjah, Ajman, Umm al Qaiwain, Ras el Khaimah, and Fujairah. संयुक्त अरब अमिरात

United Kingdom n The **United Kingdom** is the official name for the country consisting of Great Britain and Northern Ireland. युनायटेड किंगडम

United Nations n The **United Nations** is a worldwide organization which most countries belong to. Its role is to encourage international peace, cooperation, and friendship. संयुक्त राष्ट्रसंघ

United States of America n The **United States of America** is the official name for the country in North America that consists of 50 states and the District of Columbia. It is bordered by Canada in the north and Mexico in the south. The form **United States** is also used. युनायटेड स्टेट्स

universe n The **universe** is the whole of space, and all the stars, planets, and other forms of energy in it. विश्व, ब्रम्हांड

university (universities) n A **university** is an institution where students study for degrees and where academic research is done. विश्वविद्यापीठ

unknown adj If something is **unknown** to you, you have no knowledge of it. अज्ञात

unleaded adj **Unleaded** fuels contain a reduced amount of lead in order to reduce the pollution caused when they are burned. You can refer to such fuels as **unleaded**. शिसेरहित

unleaded petrol n **Unleaded petrol** contains a smaller amount of lead than most fuels so that it produces fewer harmful substances when it is burned. शिसेरहित पेट्रोल

unless conj **Unless** means if the thing you are talking about does not happen. जर नाही... तर He says he won't go to the party, unless I go too.

unlike prep If one thing is **unlike** another thing, the two things are different. ...च्या सारखे नसलेले, वेगळा You're so unlike your father!

unlikely (unlikelier, unlikeliest) adj If you say that something is **unlikely** to happen or **unlikely** to be true, you believe that it will not happen or that it is not true, although you are not completely sure. असंभवनीय

unlisted adj If a person or their telephone number is **unlisted**, the number is not listed in the telephone book, and the telephone company will refuse to give it to people who ask for it. यादीत समावेश नसलेला

unload (unloads, unloading, unloaded) vt If you **unload** goods from a vehicle, you remove the goods from the vehicle. सामान उतरवून घेणे

unlock (unlocks, unlocking, unlocked) vt If you **unlock** something such as a door, a room, or a container, you open it using a key. उघडणे (कुलूप, कडी इत्यादी)

unlucky (unluckier, unluckiest) adj If you are **unlucky**, you have bad luck. दुर्दैवी

unmarried adj Someone who is **unmarried** is not married. अविवाहित

unnecessary adj If you describe something as **unnecessary**, you mean that it is not needed or does not have to be done. अनावश्यक

unofficial *adj* An **unofficial** action is not authorized, approved, or organized by a person in authority. अनधिकृत

unpack (unpacks, unpacking, unpacked) *v* When you **unpack** a suitcase, box, or bag, you take the things out of it. वेष्टनातून बाहेर काढणे

unpaid *adj* If you do **unpaid** work, you do a job without receiving any money for it. पैसे न मिळालेला

unpleasant *adj* If something is **unpleasant**, it gives you bad feelings, for example by making you feel upset or uncomfortable. त्रासदायक

unplug (unplugs, unplugging, unplugged) *vt* If you **unplug** a piece of electrical equipment, you take its plug out of the socket. प्लग काढून घेणे

unpopular *adj* If something or someone is **unpopular**, most people do not like them. लोकप्रिय नसलेला

unprecedented *adj* If something is **unprecedented**, it has never happened before. अभूतपूर्व

unpredictable *adj* If someone or something is **unpredictable**, you cannot tell what they are going to do or how they are going to behave. वर्तवता न येणारे

unreal *adj* If you say that a situation is **unreal**, you mean that it is so strange that you find it difficult to believe it is happening. विश्वास न बसण्याजोगे

unrealistic *adj* If you say that someone is being **unrealistic**, you mean that they do not recognize the truth about a situation, especially about the difficulties involved. वस्तुस्थितीची जाणीव नसलेला

unreasonable *adj* If you say that someone is being **unreasonable**, you mean that they are behaving in a way that is not fair or sensible. अवास्तव, अवाजवी

unreliable *adj* If you describe a person, machine, or method as **unreliable**, you mean that you cannot trust them to do or provide what you want. विश्वास न ठेवण्याजोगा

unroll (unrolls, unrolling, unrolled) *v* If you **unroll** something such as a sheet of paper or cloth, it opens up and becomes flat when it was previously rolled in a cylindrical shape. गुंडाळी उलगडणे

unsatisfactory *adj* If you describe something as **unsatisfactory**, you mean that it is not as good as it should be, and cannot be considered acceptable. असमाधानकारक

unscrew (unscrews, unscrewing, unscrewed) *v* If you **unscrew** something such as a lid, or if it **unscrews**, you keep turning it until you can remove it. फिरवून उघडणे

unshaven *adj* If a man is **unshaven**, he has not shaved recently and there are short hairs on his face or chin. दाढी न केलेला

unskilled *adj* People who are **unskilled** do not have any special training for a job. अकुशल

unstable *adj* You can describe something as **unstable** if it is likely to change suddenly, especially if this creates difficulty. अस्थिर

unsteady *adj* If you are **unsteady**, you have difficulty doing something because you cannot completely control your body. अस्थिर

unsuccessful *adj* Something that is **unsuccessful** does not achieve what it was intended to achieve. अयशस्वी

unsuitable *adj* Someone or something that is **unsuitable** for a particular purpose or situation does not have the right qualities for it. अयोग्य

unsure *adj* If you are **unsure** of yourself, you don't have much confidence. आत्मविश्वास नसलेला

untidy *adj* Something that is **untidy** is messy, and not neatly arranged. अस्ताव्यस्त

untie (unties, untying, untied) *vt* If you **untie** something that is tied to another thing, or if you **untie** two things that are tied together, you remove the string or rope that holds them. सोडणे

until *conj* **Until** a particular time means during the period before that time. जो पर्यंत, तो पर्यंत *I waited until it got dark.* ▷ *prep* If something happens **until** a time, it happens before that time and then stops at that time. पर्यंत *I worked until midnight.*

unusual *adj* If something is **unusual**, it does not happen very often or you do not see it or hear it very often. नेहमीचे नसणारे, असाधारण

unwell *adj* If you are **unwell**, you are ill. आजारी

unwind (**unwinds, unwinding, unwound**) *vi* When you **unwind** after working hard, you relax. आराम करणे

unwise *adj* Something that is **unwise** is foolish. वेडेपणाचे

unwrap (**unwraps, unwrapping, unwrapped**) *vt* When you **unwrap** something, you take off the paper or covering that is around it. वेष्टन काढून टाकणे

unzip (**unzips, unzipping, unzipped**) *vt* To **unzip** an item of clothing or a bag means to unfasten its zip. झिप उघडणे

up *adv* When something moves **up**, it moves from a lower place to a higher place. वर

upbringing *n* Your **upbringing** is the way your parents treat you and the things that they teach you when you are growing up. मूल वाढवणे, संगोपन करणे

update (**updates, updating, updated**) *vt* If you **update** something, you make it more modern, usually by adding newer parts to it. अद्ययावत करणे

uphill *adv* If something or someone is **uphill** or is moving **uphill**, they are near the top of a hill or are going up a slope. टेकडीच्या शिखराकडे

upon *prep* **Upon** means the same as **on**. च्या वर *He stood upon the bridge.*

upper *adj* You use **upper** to describe something that is above something else. वरचा

upright *adv* If you are sitting or standing **upright**, you have your back straight and are not bending or lying down. सरळ

upset (**upsets, upsetting, upset**) *adj* If you are **upset**, you are unhappy or disappointed because something unpleasant has happened. अस्वस्थ ▷ *vt* If something **upsets** you, it makes you feel worried or unhappy. अस्वस्थ करणे

upside down *adv* If you hang **upside down**, your head is below your feet. आपलेच डोके खाली ठेऊन उलटे उभे राहणे ▷ *adj* If something is **upside down**, the part that is usually at the bottom is at the top. उलटा

upstairs *adv* If you go **upstairs** in a building, you go up a staircase towards a higher floor. वरच्या मजल्यावर

uptight *adj* If someone is **uptight**, they are very tense, because they are worried or annoyed about something. (*informal*) तणावग्रस्त

up-to-date *adj* If something is **up-to-date**, it is the newest thing of its kind. अद्ययावत

upwards *adv* If someone moves or looks **upwards**, they move or look up towards a higher place. वरच्या दिशेने

uranium *n* **Uranium** is a radioactive metal that is used to produce nuclear energy and weapons. युरेनियम

urgency *n* **Urgency** is the quality of being urgent or pressing. तातडी, निकड

urgent *adj* If something is **urgent**, it needs to be dealt with as soon as possible. तातडीचे

urine *n* **Urine** is the liquid that you get rid of from your body when you go to the toilet. लघवी

URL (**URLs**) *n* A **URL** is an address that shows where a particular page can be found on the World Wide Web. **URL** is an abbreviation for 'Uniform Resource Locator'. यूआरएल

Uruguay *n* **Uruguay** is a republic in South America, on the Atlantic. उरुग्वे

Uruguayan (**Uruguayans**) *adj* **Uruguayan** means of or relating to Uruguay or its inhabitants. उरुग्वियन ▷ *n* A **Uruguayan** is a native or inhabitant of Uruguay. उरुग्वियन

us *pron* You use **us** to talk about yourself and the person or people with you. आम्ही *He has invited us to a party.*

u

US *n* The **US** is an abbreviation for the 'United States'. यूएस

USA *n* The **USA** is an abbreviation for the 'United States of America'. यूएसए

use (uses, using, used) *n* Your **use** of something is the action or fact of your using it. वापर ▷ *vt* If you **use** something, you do something with it. वापरणे

used *adj* A **used** handkerchief, glass, or other object is dirty or spoiled because it has been used. वापरलेले ▷ *v* You use **used to** to talk about something that was true in the past but is not true now. करीत असे/असू

useful *adj* If something is **useful**, you can use it to do something or to help you. उपयुक्त

useless *adj* If something is **useless**, you cannot use it. निरुपयोगी

user (users) *n* The **users** of a product, machine, service, or place are the people who use it. उपयोगकर्ता

user-friendly *adj* If you describe something such as a machine or system as **user-friendly**, you mean that it is well designed and easy to use. वापरण्यास सुलभ

use up (uses up, using up, used up) *v* If you **use up** a supply of something, you finish it so that none of it is left. वापरून संपवणे *Did you use up the milk?*

usual *adj* **Usual** is used to describe what happens or what is done most often in a particular situation. नेहमीचे

usually *adv* If something **usually** happens, it is the thing that most often happens in a particular situation. सामान्यत:

utility room (utility rooms) *n* A **utility room** is a room in a house which is usually connected to the kitchen and which contains things such as a washing machine, sink, and cleaning equipment. नेहमीच्या वापराचे सामान ठेवण्याची खोली

U-turn (U-turns) *n* If you make a **U-turn** when you are driving or cycling, you turn in a half-circle in one movement, so that you are then going in the opposite direction. यू टर्न

Uzbekistan *n* **Uzbekistan** is a republic in central Asia. उझबकिस्तान

V

vacancy (vacancies) *n* A **vacancy** is a job or position which has not been filled. नोकरीसाठी असलेले रिक्त पद

vacant *adj* If something is **vacant**, it is not being used by anyone. रिकामा

vacate (vacates, vacating, vacated) *vt* If you **vacate** a place or a job, you leave it and make it available for other people. *(formal)* रिकामे करणे

vaccinate (vaccinates, vaccinating, vaccinated) *vt* If a person or animal **is vaccinated**, they are given, usually by injection, a substance containing a harmless form of a disease, to prevent them from getting that disease. लसीकरण करणे

vaccination (vaccinations) *n* **Vaccination** is the process of giving a person or animal, usually by injection, a substance containing a harmless form of a disease, to prevent them from getting that disease लसीकरण

vacuum (vacuums, vacuuming, vacuumed) *v* If you **vacuum** something, you clean it using a vacuum cleaner. व्हॅक्यूम क्लिनरने साफ करणे

vacuum cleaner (vacuum cleaners) n A **vacuum cleaner** or a **vacuum** is an electric machine which sucks up dust and dirt from carpets. व्हॅक्यूम क्लिनर

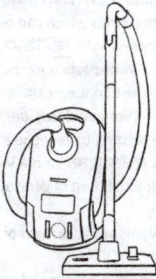

vague (vaguer, vaguest) adj If something is **vague**, it is not clear, distinct, or definite. संदिग्ध

vain (vainer, vainest) adj A **vain** attempt or action is one that fails to achieve what was intended. निष्फळ

Valentine's Day n On **Valentine's Day**, the 14th of February, people send a greetings card to someone that they are in love with or are attracted to, usually without signing their name. व्हॅलेंटाईन्स डे

valid adj A **valid** reason or argument is logical and reasonable, and therefore worth taking seriously. वैध

valley (valleys) n A **valley** is a low area of land between hills, often with a river flowing through it. दरी

valuable adj Something that is **valuable** is very useful. मौल्यवान

valuables npl **Valuables** are things that you own that are worth a lot of money, especially small objects such as jewellery. मौल्यवान वस्तू

value n The **value** of something such as a method is its importance or usefulness. मूल्य

vampire (vampires) n In fiction, **vampires** are creatures who come out of their graves at night and suck the blood of living people. रक्तपिपासू भूत

van (vans) n A **van** is a medium-sized road vehicle that is used for carrying goods. व्हॅन

vandal (vandals) n A **vandal** is someone who deliberately damages things, especially public property. गुंड

vandalism n **Vandalism** is the deliberate damaging of things, especially public property. सार्वजनिक मालमत्तेची नासधूस

vandalize (vandalizes, vandalizing, vandalized) v If something **is vandalized** by someone, they deliberately damage it. सार्वजनिक मालमत्तेची नासधूस करणे

vanilla n **Vanilla** is a flavouring used in ice cream and other sweet food. व्हॅनिला

vanish (vanishes, vanishing, vanished) vi If someone or something **vanishes**, they disappear suddenly or cease to exist altogether. नाहीसे होणे

variable adj Something that is **variable** is likely to change at any time. बदलणारे

varied adj Something that is **varied** consists of things of different types, sizes, or qualities. वैविध्यपूर्ण

variety (varieties) n If something has **variety**, it consists of things which are different from each other. विविधता

various adj If you say that there are **various** things, you mean there are several different things of the type mentioned. विविध

varnish (varnishes, varnishing, varnished) n **Varnish** is an oily liquid which is painted onto wood to give it a hard, clear, shiny surface. वॉर्निश ▷ vt If you **varnish** something, you paint it with varnish. वॉर्निश लावणे

vary (varies, varying, varied) vi If things **vary**, they are different in size, amount, or degree. फरक असणे

vase (vases) n A **vase** is a jar used for holding cut flowers or as an ornament. फुलदाणी

V

VAT *abbr* VAT is a tax that is added to the price of goods or services. **VAT** is an abbreviation for 'value added tax'. मूल्य वर्धित कर

Vatican n **The Vatican** is the city state in Rome ruled by the pope which is the centre of the Roman Catholic Church. व्हॅटिकन

veal n **Veal** is meat from a calf. वासराचे मांस

vegan (**vegans**) n A **vegan** is someone who never eats meat or any animal products such as milk, butter, or cheese. कोणतीही प्राणीजन्य वस्तू न वापरणारा

vegetable (**vegetables**) n **Vegetables** are edible plants such as cabbages, potatoes, and onions. भाजी

vegetarian (**vegetarians**) adj Someone who is **vegetarian** never eats meat or fish. शाकाहारी ▷ n A **vegetarian** is someone who does not eat meat or fish. शाकाहारी

vegetation n **Vegetation** is plants, trees, and flowers. *(formal)* वनस्पती

vehicle (**vehicles**) n A **vehicle** is a machine with an engine, for example a car, that carries people or things from place to place. वाहन

veil (**veils**) n A **veil** is a piece of thin soft cloth that women sometimes wear over their heads and which can also cover their face. स्त्रिया डोक्यावर घेतात तो पडदा

vein (**veins**) n Your **veins** are the tubes in your body through which your blood flows towards your heart. रक्तवाहिनी

Velcro® n **Velcro** is a material consisting of two strips of nylon fabric which you press together to close things such as pockets and bags. वेलक्रो

velvet n **Velvet** is a soft fabric with a thick layer of short cut threads on one side. मखमल

vending machine (**vending machines**) n A **vending machine** is a machine from which you can get things such as cigarettes, chocolate, or coffee by putting in money and pressing a button. पैशाच्या बदल्यात ठरावीक वस्तू देणारे यंत्र

vendor (**vendors**) n A **vendor** is someone who sells things such as newspapers or hamburgers from a small stall or cart. विक्रेता

Venetian blind (**Venetian blinds**) n A **Venetian blind** is a window blind made of thin horizontal strips which can be adjusted to let in more or less light. विनिशिअन ब्लाइंड

Venezuela n **Venezuela** is a republic in South America, on the Caribbean. व्हेनीझुएला

Venezuelan (**Venezuelans**) adj **Venezuelan** means of or relating to Venezuela or its inhabitants. व्हेनीझुएलन ▷ n A **Venezuelan** is a native or inhabitant of Venezuela. व्हेनीझुएलन

venison n **Venison** is the meat of a deer. हरणाचे मांस

venom n **Venom** is a feeling of great bitterness or anger towards someone. विखारी भावना

ventilation n **Ventilation** is the act or process of allowing fresh air to get into a room or building. वायुवीजन

venue (**venues**) n The **venue** for an event or activity is the place where it will happen. ठिकाण

verb (**verbs**) n A **verb** is a word such as 'sing' or 'feel' which is used to say what someone or something does or what happens to them, or to give information about them. क्रियापद

verdict (**verdicts**) n In a law court, a **verdict** is the decision that is given by the jury or judge at the end of a trial. न्यायमूर्तींनी दिलेला निर्णय

versatile adj If you say that a person is **versatile**, you approve of them because they have many different skills. अष्टपैलू

version (**versions**) n A **version** of something is a form of it in which some details are different from earlier or later forms. आवृती

versus prep **Versus** is used for showing that two teams or people are on different sides in a game. विरुद्ध ... *the Italy versus Paraguay game*.

vertical adj Something that is **vertical** stands or points straight upwards. उभा, वरच्या दिशेने

vertigo n If you get **vertigo** when you look down from a high place, you feel unsteady and sick. उंचावरून खाली पाहिल्याने येणारी भोवळ

very adv **Very** is used before a word to make it stronger. खूप

vest (vests) n A **vest** is a piece of underwear which is worn to keep the top part of your body warm. वरचे शरीर गरम रहावे म्हणून घातले जाणारे अंतर्वस्त्र

vet (vets) n A **vet** is someone who is qualified to treat sick or injured animals. पशुवैद्य

veteran (veterans) adj A **veteran** campaigner, actor, or other person is someone who has been involved in their particular activity for a long time. जुनाजाणता, मातबर ▷ n A **veteran** is someone who has served in the armed forces of their country, especially during a war. जुना सैनिक

veto (vetoes) n If someone in authority puts a **veto** on something, they forbid it, or stop it being put into action. नकाराधिकार

via prep If you go somewhere **via** a place, you go through that place on the way. मार्गे He will return home via Hungary.

vice (vices) n A **vice** is a habit which is regarded as a weakness in someone's character, but not usually as a serious fault. दोष

vice versa adv **Vice versa** is used to indicate that the reverse of what you have said is also true. For example, 'Women may bring their husbands with them, and vice versa' means that men may also bring their wives with them. उलटपक्षी

vicinity n If something is in the **vicinity** of a place, it is in the nearby area. (formal) जवळपासचा भाग

vicious adj A **vicious** person is violent and cruel. दुष्ट

victim (victims) n A **victim** is someone who has been hurt or killed by someone or something. बळी

victory (victories) n A **victory** is a success in a war or a competition. विजय

video (videos) n A **video** is a film or television programme recorded on magnetic tape. चित्रफीत

video camera (video cameras) n A **video camera** is a camera that you use to record something that is happening so that you can watch it later. व्हिडिओ कॅमेरा

videophone (videophones) n A **videophone** is a telephone which has a camera and screen so that people who are using the phone can see and hear each other. व्हिडिओ फोन

Vietnam n **Vietnam** is a republic in south-east Asia. व्हिएतनाम

Vietnamese (Vietnamese) adj **Vietnamese** means of, relating to, or characteristic of Vietnam, its people, or their language. व्हिएतनामी ▷ n A **Vietnamese** is a native or inhabitant of Vietnam. व्हिएतनामी ▷ n **Vietnamese** is the language spoken in Vietnam. व्हिएतनामी

view (views) n Your **views** on something are the opinions or beliefs that you have about it. मत

viewer (viewers) n **Viewers** are people who watch television. प्रेक्षक

viewpoint (viewpoints) n Someone's **viewpoint** is the way they think about things in general or about a particular thing. दृष्टिकोन

vile (viler, vilest) adj If you say that someone or something is **vile**, you mean that they are extremely unpleasant. अत्यंत वाईट

villa (villas) n A **villa** is a fairly large house, especially one that is used for holidays in Mediterranean countries. सुट्टी घालवण्यासाठी असलेले प्रशस्त घर

village (villages) n A **village** consists of a group of houses, together with other buildings such as a school, in a country area. खेडे

villain (villains) n A **villain** is someone who deliberately harms other people or breaks the law in order to get what he or she wants. खलनायक

vinaigrette (**vinaigrettes**) n **Vinaigrette** is a salad dressing made by mixing oil, vinegar, salt, pepper, and herbs, which is put on salad. व्हिनेगरेट

vine (**vines**) n A **vine** is a climbing plant, especially one which produces grapes. द्राक्षाची वेल

vinegar n **Vinegar** is a sharp-tasting liquid, usually made from sour wine or malt, which is used to make things such as salad dressing. व्हिनिगर

vineyard (**vineyards**) n A **vineyard** is an area of land where vines are grown in order to produce wine. मद्यासाठी तयार केलेला द्राक्षाचा मळा

viola (**violas**) n A **viola** is a musical instrument which looks like a violin but is slightly larger. व्हायोला नावाचे वाद्य

violence n **Violence** is behaviour which is intended to hurt or kill people. हिंसा

violent adj If someone is **violent**, or if they do something which is **violent**, they use physical force or weapons to hurt other people. हिंसक

violin (**violins**) n A **violin** is a musical instrument with four strings stretched over a shaped hollow box. You hold a violin under your chin and play it with a bow. व्हायोलिन

violinist (**violinists**) n A **violinist** is someone who plays the violin. व्हायोलिन वादक

virgin (**virgins**) n A **virgin** is someone who has never had sex. कुमारी

Virgo n **Virgo** is one of the twelve signs of the zodiac. Its symbol is a young woman. People who are born between approximately the 23rd of August and the 22nd of September come under this sign. कन्या रास

virtual adj You can use **virtual** to indicate that something is so nearly true that for most purposes it can be regarded as being true. तत्वतः, वास्तविक

virtual reality n **Virtual reality** is an environment which is produced by a computer and seems very like reality to the person experiencing it. वास्तव वाटावे असे, जवळजवळ

virus (**viruses**) n A **virus** is a kind of germ that can cause disease. विषाणू

visa (**visas**) n A **visa** is an official document or a stamp put in your passport which allows you to enter or leave a particular country. व्हिसा

visibility n **Visibility** is how far or how clearly you can see in particular weather conditions. दृग्गोचरता

visible adj If an object is **visible**, it can be seen. दृग्गोचर, दृश्यमान

visit (**visits, visiting, visited**) n If you pay someone a **visit**, you go to see them and spend time with them. भेट ▷ vt If you **visit** someone, you go to see them and spend time with them. भेट देणे

visiting hours npl In an institution such as a hospital or prison, **visiting hours** are the times during which people from outside the institution are officially allowed to visit people who are staying at the institution. बाहेरच्या लोकांनी भेट देण्याची वेळ

visitor (**visitors**) n A **visitor** is someone who is visiting a person or place. अभ्यागत, भेटायला येणारा

visitor centre (**visitor centres**) n A **visitor centre** at a place of interest is a building or group of buildings that provides information, often with video displays and exhibitions. माहिती देणारे केंद्र

visual adj **Visual** means relating to sight, or to things that you can see. दृक

visualize (**visualizes, visualizing, visualized**) vt If you **visualize** something, you imagine what it is like by forming a mental picture of it. मनःचक्षूसमोर आणणे

vital adj If something is **vital**, it is necessary or very important. महत्त्वपूर्ण

vitamin (**vitamins**) n **Vitamins** are substances in food which you need in order to remain healthy. जीवनसत्त्व

vivid adj **Vivid** memories and descriptions are very clear and detailed. सुस्पष्ट

vocabulary (vocabularies) *n* Your **vocabulary** is the total number of words you know in a particular language. शब्दसंग्रह

vocational *adj* **Vocational** training and skills are the training and skills needed for a particular job or profession. व्यावसायिक वा धंद्याचे प्रशिक्षण

vodka (vodkas) *n* **Vodka** is a strong, clear, alcoholic drink. व्होडका नावाचे मद्य

voice (voices) *n* When someone speaks or sings, you hear their **voice**. आवाज

voicemail *n* **Voicemail** is an electronic system which can store telephone messages, so that someone can listen to them later. व्हाईसमेल

void (voids) *adj* Something that is **void** is officially considered to have no value or authority. अवैध ▷ *n* If you describe a situation or a feeling as a **void**, you mean that it seems empty because there is nothing interesting or worthwhile about it. पोकळी

volcano (volcanoes) *n* A **volcano** is a mountain from which hot melted rock, gas, steam, and ash sometimes burst. ज्वालामुखी

volleyball *n* **Volleyball** is a sport in which two teams use their hands to hit a large ball over a high net. व्हॉलीबॉल

volt (volts) *n* A **volt** is a unit used to measure the force of an electric current. व्होल्ट

voltage (voltages) *n* The **voltage** of an electrical current is its force measured in volts. व्होल्टेज

volume (volumes) *n* The **volume** of something is the amount of it that there is. आकारमान, धनफळ

voluntarily *adv* If something is done **voluntarily**, it is done because you choose to do it and not because you have to do it. स्वेच्छेने

voluntary *adj* **Voluntary** is used to describe actions and activities that you do because you choose them, rather than because you have to do them. ऐच्छिक

volunteer (volunteers, volunteering, volunteered) *n* A **volunteer** is someone who does work without being paid for it, especially for an organization such as a charity. स्वयंसेवक ▷ *v* If you **volunteer** to do something, you offer to do it without being forced to do it. एखादे काम स्वेच्छेने करणे

vomit (vomits, vomiting, vomited) *vi* If you **vomit**, food and drink comes back up from your stomach and out through your mouth. उलटी करणे

vote (votes, voting, voted) *n* A **vote** is a choice made by a particular person or group in a meeting or an election. मत ▷ *v* When you **vote**, you indicate your choice officially at a meeting or in an election, for example, by raising your hand or writing on a piece of paper. मत देणे

voucher (vouchers) *n* A **voucher** is a piece of paper that can be used instead of money to pay for something. व्हाऊचर

vowel (vowels) *n* A **vowel** is a sound such as the ones represented in writing by the letters 'a', 'e', 'i', 'o', and 'u', which you pronounce with your mouth open, allowing the air to flow through it. स्वर

vulgar *adj* If you describe something as **vulgar**, you think it is in bad taste or of poor artistic quality. अश्लील

vulnerable *adj* If someone or something is **vulnerable** to something, they have some weakness or disadvantage which makes them more likely to be harmed or affected by that thing. बळी पडण्याजोगे

vulture (**vultures**) *n* A **vulture** is a large bird which lives in hot countries and eats dead animals. गिधाड

W

wafer (**wafers**) *n* A **wafer** is a thin crisp biscuit, often eaten with ice cream. वेफर

waffle (**waffles, waffling, waffled**) *n* If someone talks or writes a lot without saying anything clear or important, you can call what they say or write **waffle**. (*informal*) वायफळ बडबड किंवा लेखन ▷ *vi* If you say that someone **waffles**, you are critical of them because they talk or write a lot without actually making any clear or important points. (*informal*) वायफळ बडबड किंवा लेखन करणे

wage (**wages**) *n* Someone's **wages** are the amount of money that is regularly paid to them for the work that they do. मजुरी/वेतन

waist (**waists**) *n* Your **waist** is the middle part of your body, above your hips. कंबर

waistcoat (**waistcoats**) *n* A **waistcoat** is a sleeveless piece of clothing with buttons, usually worn over a shirt. वेस्टकोट

wait (**waits, waiting, waited**) *vi* If you say that something can **wait**, you mean that it is not important, so you will do it later. वाट पाहणे

waiter (**waiters**) *n* A **waiter** is a man who serves food and drink in a restaurant. वेटर

waiting list (**waiting lists**) *n* A **waiting list** is a list of people who have asked for something which they cannot receive immediately, for example medical treatment or housing, and so who must wait until it is available. प्रतीक्षा यादी

waiting room (**waiting rooms**) *n* A **waiting room** is a room in a place such as a railway station or a clinic, where people can sit down while they wait. प्रतीक्षा कक्ष

waitress (**waitresses**) *n* A **waitress** is a woman who serves food and drink in a restaurant. वेट्रेस

wait up (**waits up, waiting up, waited up**) *v* If you **wait up**, you deliberately do not go to bed, especially because you are expecting someone to return home late at night. रात्री उशिरापर्यंत वाट पाहणे *I hope he doesn't expect you to wait up for him.*

waive (**waives, waiving, waived**) *vt* If you **waive** your right to something, for example legal representation, or if someone else **waives** it, you no longer have the right to receive it. (हक्क) सोडून देणे

wake up (**wakes up, waking up, woke up**) *v* When you **wake up**, you become conscious again after being asleep. जागे होणे *It's lovely to wake up every morning and see a blue sky.*

Wales *n* **Wales** is a part of the United Kingdom, in the west of Great Britain. वेल्स

walk (**walks, walking, walked**) *n* A **walk** is a journey that you make by walking. फेरफटका ▷ *vi* When you **walk**, you move along by putting one foot in front of the other. चालणे

walkie-talkie (**walkie-talkies**) *n* A **walkie-talkie** is a small portable radio which you can talk into and hear messages through so that you can communicate with someone far away. वॉकी-टॉकी

walking *n* **Walking** is the activity of going for walks in the country. फिरायला जाणे

walking stick (**walking sticks**) *n* A **walking stick** is a long wooden stick which a person can lean on while walking. फिरायला जाताना वापरायची काठी

walkway (walkways) n A **walkway** is a path or passage for pedestrians, especially one which is raised above the ground. पदपथ

wall (walls) n A **wall** is one of the vertical sides of a building or room. भिंत

wallet (wallets) n A **wallet** is a small flat folded case where you can keep banknotes and credit cards. पैशाचे पाकीट

wallpaper (wallpapers) n **Wallpaper** is thick coloured or patterned paper that is used to decorate the walls of rooms. वॉलपेपर

walnut (walnuts) n **Walnuts** are light brown edible nuts which have a wrinkled shape and a very hard round shell. अक्रोड

walrus (walruses) n A **walrus** is a large, fat animal which lives in the sea. It has two long teeth called tusks that point downwards. वॉलरस नावाचा प्राणी

waltz (waltzes, waltzing, waltzed) n A **waltz** is a piece of music which people can dance to. वॉल्ट्झ् नृत्य ▷ vi If you **waltz** with someone, you dance a waltz with them. वॉल्ट्झ् नृत्य करणे

wander (wanders, wandering, wandered) vi If you **wander** in a place, you walk around there in a casual way, often without intending to go in any particular direction. भटकणे

want (wants, wanting, wanted) vt If you **want** something, you would like to have it. हवे असणे

war (wars) n A **war** is a period of fighting between countries. युद्ध

ward (wards) n A **ward** is a room in a hospital which has beds for many people, often people who need similar treatment. रूग्णालयातील कक्ष ▷ n A **ward** is a district which forms part of a political constituency or local council. प्रभाग

warden (wardens) n A **warden** is an official who is responsible for a particular place or thing, and for making sure that certain laws are obeyed. अधिक्षक

wardrobe (wardrobes) n A **wardrobe** is a tall cupboard in which you hang your clothes. कपड्यांचे कपाट

warehouse (warehouses) n A **warehouse** is a large building where raw materials or manufactured goods are stored before they are taken to a shop. वखार

warm (warmer, warmest) adj Something that is **warm** has some heat but not enough to be hot. उबदार

warm up (warms up, warming up, warmed up) v If you **warm** something up, or if it **warms up**, it gets hotter. तापवणे *Have you warmed the milk up, Mum?*

warn (warns, warning, warned) v If you **warn** someone about a possible danger or problem, you tell them about it so that they are aware of it. सावधानतेची किंवा धोक्याची सूचना देणे

warning (warnings) n A **warning** is something which is said or written to tell people of a possible danger, problem, or other unpleasant thing that might happen. सावधानतेची किंवा धोक्याची सूचना

warranty (warranties) n A **warranty** is a written guarantee which enables you to get a product repaired or replaced free of charge within a certain period of time. लेखी हमी

wart (warts) n A **wart** is a small lump which grows on your skin and which is usually caused by a virus. चामखीळ

wash (washes, washing, washed) vt If you **wash** something, you clean it using water and usually a substance such as soap or detergent. धुणे

washbasin (washbasins) n A **washbasin** is a large bowl for washing your hands and face. It is usually fixed to a wall, with taps for hot and cold water. वॉश बेसिन

washing n **Washing** is clothes, sheets, and other things that need to be washed, are being washed, or have just been washed. धुणे

washing line (washing lines) n A **washing line** is a strong cord which you can hang clothes on while they dry. वळणी

W

washing machine (**washing machines**) *n* A **washing machine** is a machine that you use to wash clothes in. धुलाई यंत्र

washing powder (**washing powders**) *n* **Washing powder** is a powder that you use with water to wash clothes. कपडे धुण्याची पावडर

washing-up *n* To do the **washing-up** means to wash the pans, plates, cups, and cutlery which have been used in cooking and eating a meal. खरकटी भांडी घासण्याची क्रिया

washing-up liquid (**washing-up liquids**) *n* **Washing-up liquid** is a thick soapy liquid which you add to hot water to clean dirty dishes. खरकटी भांडी धुण्याचा द्रवपदार्थ

wash up (**washes up, washing up, washed up**) *v* If you **wash up**, you wash the pans, plates, cups, and cutlery which have been used in cooking and eating a meal. खरकटी भांडी धुणे *I made breakfast and then washed up the plates.*

wasp (**wasps**) *n* A **wasp** is a small insect with a painful sting. It has yellow and black stripes across its body. गांधीलमाशी

waste (**wastes, wasting, wasted**) *n* If you waste something such as time, money, or energy, you use too much of it doing something that is not important or necessary, or is unlikely to succeed. You can say that doing this is a **waste** of time, money, or energy. अपव्यय ▷ *vt* If you **waste** something such as time, money, or energy, you use too much of it doing something that is not important or necessary, or is unlikely to succeed. अपव्यय करणे

wastepaper basket (**wastepaper baskets**) *n* A **wastepaper basket** is a container for rubbish, especially paper, which is usually placed on the floor in the corner of a room or next to a desk. केराची टोपली

watch (**watches, watching, watched**) *n* A **watch** is a small clock that you wear on your wrist. घड्याळ ▷ *vt* If you **watch** something, you look at it for a period of time. पाहणे

watch out (**watches out, watching out, watched out**) *v* If you tell someone to **watch out**, you are warning them to be careful, because something unpleasant might happen to them or they might get into difficulties. लक्ष ठेवणे/काळजी घेणे *You have to watch out – there are dangers everywhere.*

watch strap (**watch straps**) *n* A **watch strap** is a strap of leather, cloth, etc, attached to a watch for fastening it round the wrist. घड्याळाचा पट्टा

water (**waters, watering, watered**) *n* Water is a clear thin liquid that has no colour or taste when it is pure. It falls from clouds as rain. पाणी ▷ *vt* If you **water** plants, you pour water over them in order to help them to grow. पाणी घालणे

watercolour (**watercolours**) *n* **Watercolours** are coloured paints, used for painting pictures, which you apply with a wet brush or dissolve in water first. जलरंग

watercress *n* **Watercress** is a small plant with white flowers which grows in streams and pools. Its leaves taste hot and are eaten raw in salads. वॉटरक्रेस नावाची वनस्पती

waterfall (**waterfalls**) *n* A **waterfall** is a place where water flows over the edge of a steep cliff or rocks and falls into a pool below. धबधबा

watering can (**watering cans**) *n* A **watering can** is a container with a long spout which is used to water plants. झारी

watermelon (**watermelons**) *n* A **watermelon** is a large, round fruit with green skin, pink flesh, and black seeds. कलिंगड

waterproof *adj* Something that is **waterproof** does not let water pass through it. जलरोधक

water-skiing *n* **Water-skiing** is the act of standing on skis in the water while being pulled along by a boat. वॉटर स्कीईंग

wave (**waves, waving, waved**) *n* If you give a **wave**, you move your hand from side to side in the air, usually to say hello or goodbye to someone. हात हलवून निरोप देण्याची क्रिया ▷ *v* If you **wave** your hand, you move it from side to side, usually to say hello or goodbye. निरोपासाठी हात हलवणे ▷ *n* **Waves** on the surface of the sea are the parts that move up and down. लाट

wavelength (wavelengths) *n* A **wavelength** is the distance between the same point on two waves of energy such as light or sound that are next to each other. तरंगलांबी

wavy (wavier, waviest) *adj* **Wavy** hair is not straight or curly, but curves slightly. लाटांप्रमाणे केसांची ठेवण

wax *n* **Wax** is a solid, slightly shiny substance made of fat or oil which is used to make candles and polish. मेण

way (ways) *n* A **way** of doing something is how you do it. पद्धत ▷ *n* The **way** to a place is how you get there. रस्ता

way in (ways in) *n* The **way in** is the point where you enter a place, for example, a door or gate. आत जाण्याचा मार्ग

way out (ways out) *n* The **way out** is the point where you leave a place, for example, a door or gate. बाहेर पडण्याचा मार्ग

we *pron* You use **we** to talk about yourself and one or more other people as a group. आम्ही *We said we would always be friends.*

weak (weaker, weakest) *adj* If someone is **weak**, they do not have very much strength or energy. अशक्त

weakness (weaknesses) *n* **Weakness** is the state of having little strength or energy. अशक्तपणा

wealth *n* **Wealth** is a large amount of money or property owned by someone, or the possession of it. संपत्ती

wealthy (wealthier, wealthiest) *adj* Someone who is **wealthy** has a large amount of money, property, or valuable things. श्रीमंत, धनवान

weapon (weapons) *n* A **weapon** is an object such as a gun, knife, or missile. शस्त्र

wear (wears, wearing, wore, worn) *vt* When you **wear** clothes, shoes, or jewellery, you have them on your body. अंगावर चढवणे/घालणे

weasel (weasels) *n* A **weasel** is a small wild animal with a long thin body, a tail, short legs, and reddish-brown fur. विझूळ नावाचा प्राणी

weather *n* The **weather** is the condition of the atmosphere in an area at a particular time, for example, if it is raining, hot, or windy. हवामान

weather forecast (weather forecasts) *n* A **weather forecast** is a statement saying what the weather will be like the next day or for the next few days. हवामानाचा अंदाज

web (webs) *n* A **web** is the thin net made by a spider from a string that comes out of its body. जाळे

W

Web *n* The **Web** is made up of a very large number of websites all joined together. You can use it anywhere in the world to search for information. **Web** is short for World Wide Web. वेब, संगणकीय जाळे

Web 2.0 *n* **Web 2.0** is the Internet viewed as a medium in which interactive experience, in the form of blogs, wikis, forums, etc, plays a more important role than simply accessing information. वेब २.०

web address (**web addresses**) *n* A **web address** is a website's location on the Internet. वेब ॲड्रेस

web browser (**web browsers**) *n* A **web browser** is a piece of computer software that you use to search for information on the Internet, especially on the World Wide Web. वेब ब्राऊझर

webcam (**webcams**) *n* A **webcam** is a video camera that takes pictures which can be viewed on a website. The pictures are often of something that is happening while you watch. वेबकॅम

webmaster (**webmasters**) *n* A **webmaster** is someone who is in charge of a website, especially someone who does that as their job. वेब मास्टर

website (**websites**) *n* A **website** is a set of data and information about a particular subject which is available on the Internet. वेबसाईट

webzine (**webzines**) *n* A **webzine** is a website which contains the kind of articles, pictures, and advertisements that you would find in a magazine. वेबझाईन

wedding (**weddings**) *n* A **wedding** is a marriage ceremony and the celebration that often takes place afterwards. लग्न/विवाहसमारंभ

wedding anniversary (**wedding anniversaries**) *n* Your **wedding anniversary** is a date that you remember or celebrate because you got married on that date in a previous year. लग्नाचा वाढदिवस

wedding dress (**wedding dresses**) *n* A **wedding dress** is a special dress that a woman wears at her wedding. खास लग्नासाठी शिवलेले कपडे

wedding ring (**wedding rings**) *n* A **wedding ring** is a ring that you wear to show that you are married. लग्नाची अंगठी

Wednesday (**Wednesdays**) *n* **Wednesday** is the day after Tuesday and before Thursday. बुधवार

weed (**weeds**) *n* A **weed** is a wild plant growing where it is not wanted, for example in a garden. रानगवत

weedkiller (**weedkillers**) *n* **Weedkiller** is a substance you put on your garden to kill weeds. रानगवत नाशक

week (**weeks**) *n* A **week** is a period of seven days, which is often considered to start on Monday and end on Sunday. आठवडा

weekday (**weekdays**) *n* A **weekday** is any day of the week except Saturday and Sunday. शनिवार व रविवार सोडून आठवड्यातील इतर कोणताही दिवस

weekend (**weekends**) *n* A **weekend** is Saturday and Sunday. शनिवार-रविवार

weep (**weeps**, **weeping**, **wept**) *v* If someone **weeps**, they cry. *(literary)* रडणे

weigh (**weighs**, **weighing**, **weighed**) *vt* If someone or something **weighs** a particular amount, that is how heavy they are. वजन करणे

weight (**weights**) *n* The **weight** of a person or thing is how heavy they are, measured in units such as kilos or pounds. वजन

weightlifter (**weightlifters**) *n* A **weightlifter** is a person who does weightlifting. भारोत्तोलक

weightlifting *n* **Weightlifting** is a sport in which the competitor who can lift the heaviest weight wins. भारोत्तोलन

weird (**weirder**, **weirdest**) *adj* **Weird** means strange and peculiar. *(informal)* विचित्र

welcome! (**welcomes**, **welcoming**, **welcomed**) *excl* You say '**Welcome!**' when you are greeting someone who has just arrived somewhere. स्वागत असो! ▷ *n* If you give someone a **welcome**, you greet them in a friendly way when they arrive somewhere. स्वागत ▷ *vt* If you **welcome** someone, you greet them in a friendly way when you arrive somewhere. स्वागत करणे

well (better, best, wells) *adj* If you are **well**, you are healthy and not ill. बरा/कुशल ▷ *adv* If you do something **well**, you do it in a good way. चांगल्या रीतीने ▷ *n* A **well** is a deep hole in the ground from which people take water, oil, or gas. विहीर

well-behaved *adj* If you describe someone, especially a child, as **well-behaved**, you mean that they behave in a way that adults generally like and think is correct. सद्वर्तनी

well done! *excl* You say 'Well done!' to indicate that you are pleased that someone has done something good. छान केले!/शाब्बास!

wellingtons *npl* **Wellingtons** are long rubber boots which you wear to keep your feet dry. वेलिंग्टन्स नावाचे बूट

well-known *adj* Something or someone that is **well-known** is famous or familiar. सुप्रसिद्ध

well-off *adj* Someone who is **well-off** is rich enough to be able to do and buy most of the things that they want. *(informal)* सुखवस्तू

well-paid *adj* If you say that a person or their job is **well-paid**, you mean that they receive a lot of money for the work that they do. भरपूर पगार असलेला

Welsh *adj* **Welsh** means belonging or relating to Wales, or to its people, language, or culture. वेल्श ▷ *n* **Welsh** is a language of Wales. वेल्श

west *n* The **west** part of a place, country, or region is the part which is towards the west. पश्चिमेकडचा ▷ *n* If you go **west**, you travel towards the west. पश्चिमेकडे ▷ *n* The **west** is the direction in which you look to see the sun set. पश्चिम

westbound *adj* **Westbound** roads or vehicles lead to or are travelling towards the west. पश्चिमेला जाणारा

western (westerns) *adj* **Western** means in or from the west of a region or country. पाश्चिमात्य ▷ *n* A **western** is a film or book about the life of cowboys. पश्चिम अमेरिकेतील गुराख्याबाबतचा पुस्तक किंवा चित्रपट

West Indian (West Indians) *adj* **West Indian** means belonging or relating to the West Indies, or to its people or culture. वेस्ट इंडियन ▷ *n* A **West Indian** is a person who comes from the West Indies. वेस्ट इंडियन

West Indies *n* The **West Indies** is a group of islands off Central America, extending in an arc from Florida to Venezuela, separating the Caribbean Sea from the Atlantic Ocean. वेस्ट इंडिज

wet (wetter, wettest) *adj* If something is **wet**, it is covered in water or another liquid. ओला

wetsuit (wetsuits) *n* A **wetsuit** is a close-fitting rubber suit which an underwater swimmer wears in order to keep their body warm. वेट सूट

whale (whales) *n* A **whale** is a very large sea mammal. देवमासा

what *det* You use **what** with a noun, when you ask for information. काय *What time is it?* ▷ *pron* You use **what** in questions when you ask for information. काय *What do you want?*

whatever *conj* You use **whatever** to talk about anything or everything of a type. जे काही असेल ते *We can do whatever you want.*

wheat *n* **Wheat** is a cereal crop grown for its grain, which is ground into flour to make bread. गहू

wheat intolerance *n* If you have a **wheat intolerance**, you become ill if you eat food containing wheat. गव्हाची ॲलर्जी

wheel (wheels) *n* A **wheel** is a circular object which turns round on a rod attached to its centre. Wheels are fixed underneath vehicles so that they can move along. चाक

wheelbarrow (wheelbarrows) *n* A **wheelbarrow** is a small open cart with one wheel and handles that is used for carrying

W

things, for example in the garden. एका चाकाची
दोन दांडे असलेली ढकलगाडी

wheelchair (**wheelchairs**) n A **wheelchair**
is a chair with wheels that sick or disabled
people use in order to move about. चाके
असलेली खुर्ची

when adv You use **when** to ask what time
something happened or will happen. कधी
▷ conj You use **when** to talk about the time at
which something happens. केव्हा/जेव्हा I asked
him when he'd be back.

whenever conj You use **whenever** to talk
about any time or every time that something
happens. ज्या-ज्या वेळी Whenever I talked to
him, he seemed quite nice.

where adv You use **where** to ask questions
about the place something is in. कुठे ▷ conj
You use **where** to talk about the place in
which something is situated or happens. जेथे
People were wondering where the noise was
coming from.

whether conj You use **whether** when you are
talking about a choice between two or more
things. की They now have two weeks to decide
whether or not to buy the house.

which det You use **which** when you want
help to choose between things. कोणता Which
shoes should I put on? ▷ pron You use **which**
to ask questions when there are two or more
possible answers. कोणता Which is your room?

whichever det **Whichever** means any person
or thing. कोणताही Whichever way we do this, it
isn't going to work.

while n If one thing happens **while** another
thing is happening, the two things are
happening at the same time. त्याच वेळी She
goes to work while her children are at school.
▷ n A **while** is a period of time. काळ/वेळ

whip (**whips**) n A **whip** is a long thin piece of
leather or rope fastened to a handle. It is used
for hitting animals or people. चाबूक

whipped cream n **Whipped cream** is cream
that has been stirred very fast until it is thick or
stiff. खूप घोटलेली साय

whisk (**whisks**) n A **whisk** is a kitchen tool
used for stirring eggs or cream. व्हिस्क

whiskers npl The **whiskers** of an animal such
as a cat or a mouse are the long stiff hairs that
grow near its mouth. प्राण्यांच्या मिशा

whisky (**whiskies**) n **Whisky** is a strong
alcoholic drink made, especially in Scotland,
from grain such as barley or rye. व्हिस्की

whisper (**whispers, whispering, whispered**)
v When you **whisper**, you say something very
quietly, using your breath rather than your
throat, so that only one person can hear you.
कुजबुजणे

whistle (**whistles, whistling, whistled**) n A
whistle is a small metal tube which you blow
in order to produce a loud sound and attract
someone's attention. शिट्टी ▷ v When you
whistle, you make sounds by forcing your
breath out between your lips or teeth. शिट्टी
वाजवणे

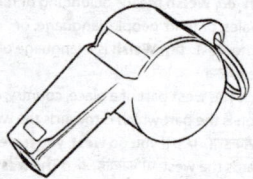

white (**whiter, whitest**) adj Something that is
white is the colour of snow or milk. पांढरा/शुभ्र

whiteboard (**whiteboards**) n A **whiteboard**
is a shiny white board on which people draw

or write using special pens. Whiteboards are often used for teaching or giving talks. पांढरा फळा

whitewash *n* **Whitewash** is a mixture of lime or chalk and water used for painting walls white. भिंतींना लावायचा चुना

whiting (**whitings, whiting**) *n* A **whiting** is a black and silver fish that lives in the sea. व्हायटिंग नावाचा मासा

who *pron* You use **who** in questions when you ask about someone's name. कोण *Who won the quiz?*

whoever *conj* You use **whoever** to talk about somebody when you do not know who they are. कोणीही *Whoever wins the prize is going to be famous for life.*

whole *adj* You use **whole** before a noun to refer to all of that thing. संपूर्ण ▷ *n* A **whole** is a single thing which contains several different parts. अखंड

wholefoods *npl* **Wholefoods** are foods which have not been through many processes and which have not had artificial ingredients added. प्रक्रिया न केलेले अन्न

wholemeal *adj* **Wholemeal** flour is made from the complete grain of the wheat plant, including the outer part. **Wholemeal** bread or pasta is made from wholemeal flour. सालपटे न काढता दळलेले धान्य

wholesale *adj* **Wholesale** goods are bought cheaply in large quantities and then sold again to shops. घाऊक ▷ *n* **Wholesale** is the activity of buying and selling goods in large quantities and therefore at cheaper prices, usually to shopkeepers who then sell them to the public. घाऊक विक्री

whom *pron* **Whom** is used in formal or written English instead of 'who' when somebody does something to somebody. *(formal)* कोणाला *The book is about her husband, whom she married ten years ago.*

whose *det* You use **whose** to ask who something belongs to. कोणाचा *Whose bag is this?* ▷ *pron* You use **whose** to explain who

something belongs to. ज्याचा *He shouted at the driver whose car was blocking the street.*

why *adv* You use **why** when you are asking about the reason for something. का

wicked *adj* You use **wicked** to describe someone or something that is very bad in a way that is deliberately harmful to people. दुष्ट

wide (**wider, widest**) *adj* Something that is **wide** is a large distance from one side to the other. रुंद ▷ *adv* If you open something **wide**, you open it fully. पूर्ण उघडलेले

widespread *adj* Something that is **widespread** exists or happens over a large area or to a very great extent. सर्वत्र पसरलेले

widow (**widows**) *n* A **widow** is a woman whose husband has died. विधवा

widower (**widowers**) *n* A **widower** is a man whose wife has died. विधूर

width (**widths**) *n* The **width** of something is the distance that it measures from one side to the other. रुंदी

wife (**wives**) *n* A man's **wife** is the woman he is married to. पत्नी

Wi-Fi *n* **Wi-Fi** is a system for using the Internet from laptop computers with wireless connections. **Wi-Fi** is an abbreviation of 'wireless fidelity'. वाय-फाय

wig (**wigs**) *n* A **wig** is a mass of false hair which is worn on your head. केसांचा टोप

wild (**wilder, wildest**) *adj* **Wild** animals and plants live or grow in natural surroundings and are not looked after by people. जंगली

wildlife *n* You can use **wildlife** to refer to animals and other living things that live in natural surroundings. जंगलातील प्राणीसंपदा

will (**wills**) *n* **Will** is the determination to do something. इच्छा ▷ *n* A **will** is a legal document stating what you want to happen to your money when you die. मृत्युपत्र ▷ *v* You use **will** to talk about things that are going to happen in the future. भविष्यकाळात वापरण्याचे इंग्रजी भाषेतील सहाय्यकारी क्रियापद *Mum will be angry.*

w

willing adj If someone is **willing** to do something, they do not mind doing it or have no objection to doing it. इच्छुक

willingly adv If someone does something **willingly**, they have no objection to doing it. स्वेच्छेने

willow (willows) n A **willow** is a tree with long narrow leaves and branches that hang down. विलो नावाचा वृक्ष

willpower n **Willpower** is a very strong determination to do something. इच्छाशक्ती

wilt (wilts, wilting, wilted) vi If a plant **wilts**, it gradually bends downwards and becomes weak, because it needs more water or is dying. कोमेजणे

win (wins, winning, won) v If you **win** something such as a competition, battle, or argument, you defeat those people you are competing or fighting against, or you do better than everyone else involved. जिंकणे

wind (winds, winding, winded, wound) n **Wind** is air that moves. वारा ▷ vt If you are **winded** by something, you have difficulty breathing for a short time. श्वास अडकणे ▷ vi If a road or river **winds**, it twists and turns. वळण घेणे ▷ vt When you **wind** something long around something, you wrap it around several times. गुंडाळणे

windmill (windmills) n A **windmill** is a tall building with sails which turn as the wind blows. Windmills are used to grind grain or pump water. पवनचक्की

window (windows) n A **window** is a space in the wall of a building or in the side of a vehicle, which has glass in it so that light can pass through and people can see in or out. खिडकी

window pane (window panes) n A **window pane** is a piece of glass in the window of a building. तावदान

window seat (window seats) n A **window seat** is a seat which is fixed to the wall underneath a window in a room. खिडकीजवळ घट्ट बसवलेले आसन

windowsill (windowsills) n A **windowsill** is a shelf along the bottom of a window, either inside or outside a building. खिडकीखालचा कोनाडा वा कट्टा

windscreen (windscreens) n The **windscreen** of a car or other vehicle is the glass window at the front through which the driver looks. वाहनाची पुढची काच

windscreen wiper (windscreen wipers) n A **windscreen wiper** is a device that wipes rain from a vehicle's windscreen. विंडस्क्रीन वायपर

windsurfing n **Windsurfing** is a sport in which you move along the surface of the sea or a lake on a long narrow board with a sail on it. विंडसर्फिंग नावाचा खेळ

windy (windier, windiest) adj If it is **windy**, the wind is blowing a lot. सोसाट्याचा वारा सुटलेला

wine (wines) n **Wine** is an alcoholic drink, usually made from grapes. वाइन

wineglass (wineglasses) n A **wineglass** is a glass drinking vessel, typically having a small bowl on a stem. वाईनग्लास

wine list (wine lists) n A restaurant's **wine list** is a list of all the wines that it has available. वाइन लिस्ट

wing (wings) n The **wings** of a bird or insect are the parts of its body that it uses for flying. पंख

wing mirror (wing mirrors) n The **wing mirrors** on a car are the mirrors on each side of the car on the outside. वाहनाच्या दोन्ही बाजूचे आरसे

wink (winks, winking, winked) vi When you **wink** at someone, you look towards them and close one eye very briefly, usually as a signal that something is a joke or a secret. डोळे मिचकावणे

winner (winners) n The **winner** of a prize, race, or competition is the person, animal, or thing that wins it. विजेता

winning adj You can use **winning** to describe a person or thing that wins something such as a competition, game, or election. जिंकणारा

winter (**winters**) *n* **Winter** is the season between autumn and spring. In winter the weather is usually cold. हिवाळा

winter sports *npl* **Winter sports** are sports that take place on ice or snow, for example skating and skiing. हिवाळ्यातील खेळ

wipe (**wipes, wiping, wiped**) *vt* If you **wipe** something, you rub its surface to remove dirt or liquid from it. पुसणे

wipe up (**wipes up, wiping up, wiped up**) *v* If you **wipe up** dirt or liquid from something, you remove it using a cloth. कापडाने पुसणे *Wipe up spills immediately.*

wire (**wires**) *n* A **wire** is a long thin piece of metal that is used to fasten things or to carry electric current. तार

wisdom *n* **Wisdom** is the ability to use your experience and knowledge to make sensible decisions and judgments. अक्कल, शहाणपण

wisdom tooth (**wisdom teeth**) *n* Your **wisdom teeth** are the four large teeth at the back of your mouth which usually grow much later than your other teeth. अक्कल दाढ

wise (**wiser, wisest**) *adj* A **wise** person is able to use their experience and knowledge to make sensible decisions and judgments. शहाणा

wish (**wishes, wishing, wished**) *n* A **wish** is a desire for something. इच्छा ▷ *vt* If you **wish** to do something, you want to do it. इच्छा असणे

wit *n* **Wit** is the ability to use words or ideas in an amusing and clever way. (चतुर) विनोदबुद्धि

witch (**witches**) *n* A **witch** is a woman who is believed to have magic powers, especially evil ones. चेटकीण

with *prep* If one person is **with** another, they are together in one place. सहित, सोबत *He's watching a film with his friends.* ▷ *prep* You use **with** to say that someone has something. असलेला *My daughter is the girl with brown hair.*

withdraw (**withdraws, withdrawing, withdrew, withdrawn**) *vt* If you **withdraw** something from a place, you remove it or take it away. (*formal*) काढून घेणे

withdrawal (**withdrawals**) *n* The **withdrawal** of something is the act or process of removing it or ending it. (*formal*) काढून घेण्याची क्रिया

within *prep* If something is **within** a place, area, or object, it is inside it or surrounded by it. (*formal*) ...च्या आत *The sports fields must be within the city.*

without *prep* If you do something **without** someone, they are not in the same place as you are, or they are not doing the same thing as you. शिवाय *He went without me.*

witness (**witnesses**) *n* A **witness** to an event such as an accident or crime is a person who saw it. साक्षीदार

witty (**wittier, wittiest**) *adj* Someone or something that is **witty** is amusing in a clever way. चतुर व विनोदी

wolf (**wolves**) *n* A **wolf** is a wild animal that looks like a large dog. लांडगा

woman (**women**) *n* A **woman** is an adult female human being. स्त्री

wonder (**wonders, wondering, wondered**) *vt* If you **wonder** about something, you think about it and try to guess or understand more about it. स्वत:शीच विचार करणे

wonderful *adj* If you describe something or someone as **wonderful**, you think they are extremely good. विस्मयकारक, फार छान

wood (**woods**) *n* **Wood** is the hard material that trees are made of. लाकूड ▷ *n* A **wood** is a large area of trees growing near each other. वन, जंगल

wooden *adj* A **wooden** object is made of wood. लाकडापासून बनवलेली वस्तू

woodwind *adj* **Woodwind** instruments are musical instruments such as flutes, clarinets, and recorders that you play by blowing into them. फुंकून वाजवायचे वाद्य

woodwork *n* You can refer to the doors and other wooden parts of a house as the **woodwork**. लाकूडकाम

wool *n* **Wool** is the hair that grows on sheep and on some other animals. लोकर

W

woollen *adj* **Woollen** clothes are made from wool. लोकरीपासून बनवलेली वस्तू

woollens *npl* **Woollens** are clothes, especially sweaters, that are made of wool. लोकरीचे कपडे

word (**words**) *n* **Words** are things that you say or write. शब्द

work (**works, working, worked**) *n* People who have **work** have a job. काम ▷ *vi* When you **work**, you do something that uses a lot of your time or effort. काम करणे ▷ *vi* If a machine **works**, it does its job. चालू असणे

worker (**workers**) *n* **Workers** are people who are employed in industry or business and who are not managers. कामगार, कर्मचारी

work experience *n* **Work experience** is a period of time that a young person, especially a student, spends working in a company as a form of training. कामाचा अनुभव

workforce (**workforces**) *n* The **workforce** is the total number of people in a country or region who are physically able to do a job and are available for work. काम करण्यास योग्य माणसे

working-class *adj* If you are **working-class**, you are a member of the group of people in a society who do not own much property, who have low social status, and who do jobs which involve using physical skills rather than intellectual skills. कामगार वर्ग

workman (**workmen**) *n* A **workman** is a man who works with his hands, for example a builder or plumber. कामगार

work of art (**works of art**) *n* A **work of art** is a painting or piece of sculpture of high quality. कलाकारी

work out (**works out, working out, worked out**) *v* If you **work out** a solution to a problem or mystery, you find the solution by thinking or talking about it. शोधून काढणे, प्रश्न सोडवणे *They are planning to meet later today to work out a solution.*

work permit (**work permits**) *n* A **work permit** is an official document that someone needs in order to work in a particular foreign country. दुसऱ्या देशात काम करण्याचा परवाना

workplace (**workplaces**) *n* Your **workplace** is the place where you work. कामाचे ठिकाण

workshop (**workshops**) *n* A **workshop** is a room or building containing tools or machinery for making or repairing things. कार्यशाळा

workspace *n* A person's **workspace** is the area, especially in an office, that is for them to work in. कामासाठी ठेवलेली जागा

workstation (**workstations**) *n* A **workstation** is a computer. संगणक

world *n* The **world** is the planet that we live on. विश्व, पृथ्वी

World Cup *n* The **World Cup** is an international competition held between national teams in various sports, most notably association football. विश्व चषक

worm (**worms**) *n* A **worm** is a small thin animal without bones or legs which lives in the soil. किडा, कृमी

worn *adj* **Worn** things are damaged or thin because they are old and have been used a lot. विटलेले

worried *adj* When you are **worried**, you are unhappy because you keep thinking about problems that you have or about unpleasant things that might happen in the future. चिंताग्रस्त

worry (**worries, worrying, worried**) *vi* If you **worry**, you keep thinking about a problem or about something unpleasant that might happen in the future. चिंता करणे

worrying *adj* If something is **worrying**, it causes people to worry. चिंताजनक

worse *adj* **Worse** is the comparative of bad. It means more bad. अधिक/फार वाईट ▷ *adv* **Worse** is the comparative of **badly**. It means more badly. अधिक वाईट

worsen (**worsens, worsening, worsened**) *v* If a situation **worsens**, it becomes more difficult, unpleasant, or unacceptable. अधिक वाईट होणे

worship (worships, worshipping, worshipped) v If you **worship** a god, you show your respect to the god, for example by saying prayers. (देवाला) भजणे

worst adj **Worst** is the superlative of bad. It means most bad. सर्वाधिक वाईट

worth n Someone's **worth** is their value, usefulness, or importance. किंमत

worthless adj Something that is **worthless** is of no real use or value. बिनकामी, कुचकामी

would v You use **would** to say that someone agreed to do something. करीन, करील *They said they would come to my party.*

wound (wounds, wounding, wounded) n A **wound** is a part of your body that you have hurt with something like a knife or a gun. जखम ▷ vt If somebody or something **wounds** you, they hurt you. जखमी करणे

wrap (wraps, wrapping, wrapped) vt When you **wrap** something, you fold paper or cloth tightly round it to cover it completely, for example in order to protect it or so that you can give it to someone as a present. आच्छादणे

wrapping paper (wrapping papers) n **Wrapping paper** is special paper which is used for wrapping presents. भेटवस्तू गुंडाळण्याचा कागद

wrap up (wraps up, wrapping up, wrapped up) v If you **wrap** something **up**, you fold paper or cloth tightly round it to cover it. गुंडाळणे *I'll take the opportunity to wrap up some presents.*

wreck (wrecks, wrecking, wrecked) n A **wreck** is something such as ship, car, plane, or building which has been destroyed, usually in an accident. अपघातामुळे मोडतोड झालेली गाडी, इमारत इ. ▷ vt To **wreck** something means to completely destroy or ruin it. नाश करणे

wreckage n When a plane, car, or building has been destroyed, you can refer to what remains as the **wreckage**. भग्नावशेष

wren (wrens) n A **wren** is a very small brown bird. रेन नावाचा पक्षी

wrench (wrenches, wrenching, wrenched) n If you say that leaving someone or something

is a **wrench**, you feel very sad about it. दुःखकारक ▷ vt If you **wrench** something, usually something that is in a fixed position, you pull or twist it violently. हिसकावूनू घेणे

wrestler (wrestlers) n A **wrestler** is someone who does wrestling as a sport. कुस्तीगीर

wrestling n **Wrestling** is a sport in which two people try to force each other into painful positions and throw each other to the ground. कुस्ती

wrinkle (wrinkles) n **Wrinkles** are lines which form on someone's face as they grow old. सुरकुती

wrinkled adj Someone who has **wrinkled** skin has a lot of wrinkles. सुरकुतलेला

wrist (wrists) n Your **wrist** is the part of your body between your hand and arm which bends when you move your hand. मनगट

write (writes, writing, wrote, written) v When you **write** something on a surface, you use something such as a pen or pencil to produce words, letters, or numbers on it. लिहिणे

write down (writes down, writing down, wrote down, written down) v When you **write** something **down**, you record it on a piece of paper using a pen or pencil. लिहून घेणे *I wrote down exactly what I thought.*

writer (writers) n A **writer** is a person whose job is writing books, stories, or articles. लेखक

writing n **Writing** is something that has been written or printed. लिखाण

writing paper (writing papers) n **Writing paper** is paper for writing letters on. It is usually of good, smooth quality. लिखाणासाठी वापरायचा कागद

wrong adj If there is something **wrong**, there is something that is not as it should be. चूक ▷ adj If you say that an answer is **wrong**, you mean that it is not right. चूक ▷ adj If you say that something someone does is **wrong**, you mean that it is bad. चुकीचे

wrong number (wrong numbers) n A **wrong number** is a telephone number dialled in error. फोनवरून लावलेला चुकीचा क्रमांक

X

Xmas (Xmases) *n* **Xmas** is used in written English to represent the word Christmas. *(informal)* नाताळ

X-ray (X-rays, X-raying, X-rayed) *n* An **X-ray** is a type of radiation that can pass through most solid materials. X-rays are used by doctors to examine the bones or organs inside your body, and at airports to see inside people's luggage. क्ष-किरण ▷ *vt* If someone or something **is X-rayed**, an X-ray picture is taken of them. एक्स रे काढणे

xylophone (xylophones) *n* A **xylophone** is a musical instrument which consists of a row of wooden bars of different lengths. You play the xylophone by hitting the bars with special hammers. झायलोफोन नावाचे वाद्य

y

yacht (yachts) *n* A **yacht** is a large boat with sails or a motor, used for racing or for pleasure trips. क्रिडानौका

yard (yards) *n* A **yard** is a unit of length equal to 36 inches or approximately 91.4 centimetres. याई ▷ *n* A **yard** is a flat area of concrete or stone that is next to a building and often has a wall around it. बंदिस्त अंगण

yawn (yawns, yawning, yawned) *vi* If you **yawn**, you open your mouth very wide and breathe in more air than usual, often when you are tired or when you are not interested in something. जांभई देणे

year (years) *n* A **year** is a period of twelve months, beginning on the first of January and ending on the thirty-first of December. वर्ष

yearly *adj* A **yearly** event happens once a year or every year. वार्षिक ▷ *adv* If something happens **yearly**, it happens once a year or every year. वार्षिक

yeast (yeasts) *n* **Yeast** is a kind of plant which is used to make bread rise, and in making alcoholic drinks such as beer. किण्व

yell (yells, yelling, yelled) *v* If you **yell**, you shout loudly, usually because you are excited, angry, or in pain. मोठ्याने ओरडणे

yellow *adj* Something that is **yellow** is the colour of lemons, butter, or the middle part of an egg. पिवळा

Yellow Pages® *n* **Yellow Pages** is a book that contains advertisements and telephone numbers for businesses and organizations in a particular area, grouped according to the type of business they do. यलो पेजेस

Yemen *n* **Yemen** is a republic in south-west Arabia, on the Red Sea and the Gulf of Aden. येमेन

yes! *excl* You say **'yes!'** to give a positive response to a question. हो!

yesterday *adv* You use **yesterday** to refer to the day before today. काल

yet *adv* You use **yet** when you expect something to happen, but it hasn't happened. अद्याप

yew (yews) *n* A **yew** or a **yew tree** is an evergreen tree. It has sharp leaves which are broad and flat, and red berries. यू नावाचा सदाहरित वृक्ष

yield (yields, yielding, yielded) *vi* If you **yield** to someone or something, you stop resisting them. *(formal)* शरण जाणे

yoga *n* **Yoga** is a type of exercise in which you move your body into various positions in order to become more fit or flexible, to improve your breathing, and to relax your mind. योग

yoghurt (yoghurts) *n* **Yoghurt** is a slightly sour thick liquid made by adding bacteria to milk. दही

yolk (yolks) *n* The **yolk** of an egg is the yellow part in the middle. अंड्यातील पिवळा बलक

you *pron* **You** means the person or people that someone is talking or writing to. तू, तुम्ही, आपण *Can I help you?*

young (younger, youngest) *adj* A **young** person, animal, or plant has not lived for very long. तरुण

younger *adj* A **younger** person or animal has lived for a shorter time than another. लहान

youngest *adj* The **youngest** person or animal of a group has lived for the shortest time of all of them. सर्वात लहान

your *det* You use **your** to show that something belongs to the people that you are talking to. तुझा, तुमचा, आपला *I do like your name.*

yours *pron* **Yours** refers to something belonging to the people that you are talking to. तुझा, तुमचा, आपला *His hair is longer than yours.*

yourself *pron* **Yourself** means you alone. तू स्वतः *You'll hurt yourself.*

yourselves *pron* A speaker or writer uses **yourselves** to refer to the people that they are talking or writing to. **Yourselves** is used when the object of a verb or preposition refers to the same people as the subject of the verb. तुम्ही स्वतः *Treat yourselves to an ice cream.*

youth *n* Someone's **youth** is the period of their life when they are a child, before they are a fully mature adult. तरुण्याचा काळ

youth club (youth clubs) *n* A **youth club** is a club where young people can go to meet each other and take part in various leisure activities. Youth clubs are often run by a church or local authority. तरुणांसाठी मनोरंजनाची जागा

youth hostel (youth hostels) *n* A **youth hostel** is a place where people can stay cheaply when they are travelling. तरुणांसाठी असलेले निवासगृह

Z

Zambia *n* **Zambia** is a republic in southern Africa. झांबिया

Zambian (Zambians) *adj* **Zambian** means of or relating to Zambia or its inhabitants. झांबियन ▷ *n* A **Zambian** is a native or inhabitant of Zambia. झांबियन

zebra (zebras, zebra) *n* A **zebra** is an African wild horse which has black and white stripes. झेब्रा

zebra crossing (zebra crossings) *n* In Britain, a **zebra crossing** is a place on the road that is marked with black and white stripes, where vehicles are supposed to stop so that people can walk across. झेब्रा क्रॉसिंग

zero *n* **Zero** is freezing point on the Centigrade scale. It is often written as 0°C. शून्य अंश

zest *n* **Zest** is a feeling of pleasure and enthusiasm. उत्साह ▷ *n* The **zest** of a lemon, orange, or lime is the outer skin when it is used to give flavour to something such as a cake or drink. लिंबाची साल

Zimbabwe n **Zimbabwe** is a country in south-east Africa. झिंबाब्वे

Zimbabwean (**Zimbabweans**) adj **Zimbabwean** means of or relating to Zimbabwe or its inhabitants. झिंबाब्विअन ▷ n A **Zimbabwean** is a native or inhabitant of Zimbabwe. झिंबाब्विअन

Zimmer® frame (**Zimmer frames**) n A **Zimmer frame** or a **Zimmer** is a frame that old or ill people sometimes use to help them walk. झिमर फ्रेम

zinc n **Zinc** is a bluish-white metal which is used to make other metals such as brass, or to cover other metals such as iron to stop them rusting. जस्त

zip (**zips, zipping, zipped**) n A **zip** is a device used to open and close parts of clothes and bags. It consists of two rows of metal or plastic teeth which separate or fasten together as you pull a small tag along them. चेन ▷ vt When you **zip** something, you fasten it using a zip. चेन बंद करणे

zit (**zits**) n **Zits** are spots on someone's skin, especially a young person's. (informal) त्वचेवरील डाग

zodiac n The **zodiac** is a diagram used by astrologers to represent the positions of the planets and stars. It is divided into twelve sections, each with a special name and symbol. राशिचक्र

zone (**zones**) n A **zone** is an area that has particular features or characteristics. विभाग/ क्षेत्र

zoo (**zoos**) n A **zoo** is a park where live animals are kept so that people can look at them. प्राणिसंग्रहालय

zoology n **Zoology** is the scientific study of animals. प्राणिशास्त्र

zoom lens (**zoom lenses**) n A **zoom lens** is a lens that you can attach to a camera, which allows you to make the details larger or smaller while always keeping the picture clear. झूम लेन्स

Index

तेथे there
अंग काढून घेणे back out, opt out
अंगठा thumb
अंगठी ring
अंगण courtyard
अंगरक्षक bodyguard
अंगाई lullaby
अंगाची लाही लाही करणारा sweltering
अंगावर चढवणे/घालणे wear
अंगावरील तीळ mole
अंगावरील पुरळ rash
अंजीर fig
अंडकोष testicle
अंडाशय ovary
अंडे egg
अंड्यातील पांढरा भाग egg white
अंड्यातील पिवळा बलक egg yolk
अंतर distance
अंतराळयात्री astronaut
अंतर्गत internal
अंतर्गत सजावटकार interior designer
अंतर्भूत गोष्ट content
अंतर्मनातील भावना intuition
अंतर्वस्त्र underwear
अंतिम final, ultimate
अंतिम तारीख deadline
अंतिम सामना final
अंत्यसंस्कार funeral
अंथरायची शोभिवंत चादर bedspread
अंथरुणे bedclothes
अंथरूण व पांघरूण bedding
अंदाज forecast, guess
अंदाज करणे estimate
अंदाज न लागणे underestimate
अंदाज बांधणे speculate
अंदाज वर्तवणे guess
अंदाजित approximate
अंदाजित मूल्य estimate

अंदाजे approximately
अंधश्रद्धाळू superstitious
अंधार dark, darkness
अंधारकोठडी dungeon
अंधारी gloomy
अंधूक dim
अंश trace
अंशतः partly
अंश सेल्सिअस degree Celsius
अकरा eleven
अकरावा eleventh
अकारण चिंता fuss
अकार्यक्षम incompetent, inefficient
अकुशल clumsy, unskilled
अक्कल wisdom
अक्कल दाढ wisdom tooth
अक्षय eternal
अक्षर letter
अक्षरशः literally
अक्षांश latitude
अखंड non-stop, whole
अखेरीस eventually
अगडबंब mammoth
अगदी absolutely, dead, even, exactly, pretty, quite
अगदी अलिकडचा last
अगदी बरोबर perfectly
अगोदर before, earlier, formerly, previously
अगोदर आणणे/ठेवणे bring forward
अगोदर करणे/हलवणे move forward
अगोदरच already, beforehand
अगोदरच शिजवलेले ready-cooked
अगोदरचा preceding, previous
अग्निबाण rocket
अग्निशमन दलातील जवान fireman

अग्निशामक extinguisher, fire extinguisher
अग्निशामक दल fire brigade
अचानक abrupt
अचानक झालेली वाढ surge
अचानकपणे sudden, suddenly
अचानक बिघडणे crash
अचानक भेटणे bump into
अचूक accurate, exact, perfect
अचूकपणा accuracy
अचूकपणे accurately, exactly
अजूनही still
अज्ञात unidentified, unknown
अज्ञान ignorance
अज्ञानी ignorant
अटक arrest
अटक करणे arrest
अठरा eighteen
अठरावा eighteenth
अडकलेला stuck
अडकून पडलेला stranded
अडगळीत टाकणे dump
अडचण problem
अडथळा barrier, block, blockage, hurdle, interruption, obstacle
अडथळा आणणे disrupt, interrupt
अडथळा करणे obstruct
अडवून धरणे hold up
अडसर bolt
अढी grudge
अणुभट्टी reactor
अणू atom
अणूबॉंब atom bomb
अणूसंबंधी atomic
अति थंड chilly, icy
अतिथीगृह guesthouse
अति दक्षता विभाग intensive care unit
अतिरिक्त additional

अतिरिक्त टायर spare tyre, spare wheel
अतिशय excessive, extreme, extremely, terribly
अतिशय लहान tiny
अतिशयोक्ति exaggeration
अतिशयोक्ति करणे exaggerate
अति शहाणा know-all
अतिशहाणा bigheaded
अतिसार diarrhoea
अतिसूक्ष्म ध्वनिलहरी ultrasound
अतुल्य incredible
अत्तर perfume
अत्यंत awfully
अत्यंत एकाकी lonesome
अत्यंत क्लेशकारक traumatic
अत्यंत गुप्त बाब top-secret
अत्यंत छान marvellous
अत्यंत वाईट vile
अत्यंत सुंदर glorious, stunning
अत्यावश्यक essential
अत्युत्तम magnificent
अदलाबदल करणे exchange
अदृश्य invisible
अदृश्य होणे disappearance
अद्भूत fabulous
अययावत up-to-date
अययावत करणे update
अद्याप yet
अद्वितीय unique
अधिक more, plus
अधिक चांगला better
अधिक/फार वाईट worse
अधिक बरे better
अधिक वाईट worse
अधिक वाईट होणे worsen
अधिकारी executive, officer
अधिकृत official
अधिकृत परवानगी देणे authorize
अधिक्षक warden
अधिभार surcharge

अधिवक्ता solicitor
अधोरेखित करणे underline
अध्यक्ष chairman
अध्यापन teaching
अनंत काल eternity
अनधिकृत unofficial
अननस pineapple
अननुभवी green, inexperienced
अनपेक्षित unexpected
अनपेक्षितरीत्या unexpectedly
अनपेक्षित संकट/अरिष्ट catastrophe
अनवधानी absent-minded
अनवाणी barefoot
अनवाणी चालणे barefoot
अनाकर्षक drab, tasteless
अनागोंदी chaos
अनाथ orphan
अनादर contempt
अनामिक anonymous
अनारोग्यकारक unhealthy
अनावर uncontrollable
अनावश्यक unnecessary
अनियमित irregular
अनिर्णित undecided
अनिवार्य compulsory
अनिश्चित uncertain
अनिश्चितता uncertainty
अनुकरणीय व्यक्ती icon
अनुक्रमणिका index
अनुदान grant, subsidy
अनुपस्थिती absent
अनुपस्थिती absence
(अनुभव) undergo
अनुभव experience
अनुभवी experienced
अनुरूप compatible
अनुसार according to
अनेक many, several
अनेकवचन plural
अनैतिक immoral
अनोळखी stranger
अनौपचारिक casual, informal

अनौपचारिक भाषा slang
अनौपचारिकरीत्या casually
अन्न food
अन्न पचणे digest
अन्नाचे पचन digestion
अन्नातून झालेली विषबाधा food poisoning
अन्यत्र elsewhere
अन्यथा otherwise
अन्याय injustice
अन्याय्य unfair
अन्योन्य mutual
अपंग disabled
अपंगत्व disability
अपघात accident
अपघात विमा accident insurance
अपघाती accidental
अपचन indigestion
अपमान insult
अपमान करणे insult
अपमानास्पद बोलणे twit
अपयश failure
अपयशी flop
अपराधी guilty
अपराधीपणाची भावना guilt
अपरिचित unfamiliar
अपरिहार्य inevitable, unavoidable
अपरिहार्यपणे necessarily
अपवाद exception
अपवादात्मक exceptional
अपव्यय waste
अपव्यय करणे waste
अपसव्य anticlockwise
अपहरण करणे kidnap
अपहरणकर्ता hijacker
अपात्र ठरविणे disqualify
अपारंपरिक unconventional
अपुरा inadequate, insufficient
अपूर्ण incomplete
अपेक्षा करणे expect
अप्रचलित obsolete
अप्रत्यक्ष indirect

अप्रत्यक्षपणे सुचवणे hint	अर्थशास्त्र economics	अवलंब करणे resort to
अप्रामाणिक bent, dishonest, shifty	अर्थशास्त्रज्ञ economist	अवलंबून असणे count on, depend, lean on, rely on
अफवा rumour	अर्थशास्त्रासंबंधी economic	अवशेष remains
अफूचे झुडूप poppy	अर्थसहाय्य finance	अवहेलना contempt
अफू morphine	अर्थसहाय्य करणे finance	अवाक् speechless
अबू धाबी Abu Dhabi	अर्धपुतळा bust	अवाजवी unreasonable
अब्ज billion	अर्धवट partial	अवाढव्य gigantic
अभद्र sinister	अर्धवर्तुळ semicircle	अवास्तव unreasonable
अभयारण्य reserve	अर्धविराम semi-colon	अविकसित immature
अभाव lack	अर्धवेळ part-time	अविचारी thoughtless
अभिनंदन congratulations	अर्धशिशी migraine	अविवाहित bachelor, unmarried
अभिनंदन करणे congratulate	अर्धा half	
अभिनय acting	अर्धागवायू झालेला paralysed	अविवाहित स्त्री spinster
अभिनय करणे act	अर्धा तास half-hour	अविश्वसनीय unbelievable
अभिनेता actor	अर्ध्या किमतीत half-price	अविस्मरणीय unforgettable
अभिनेत्री actress	अर्हता qualification	अवैध void
अभिप्राय remark	अलग होणे parting, part with	अव्यवस्थित messy
अभिमान pride, proud		अव्यवहार्य impractical
अभियंता engineer	अलिस राहणे keep out	अशक्त frail, weak
अभियांत्रिकी engineering	अलीकडचा recent	अशक्तपणा weakness
अभूतपूर्व unprecedented	अलीकडे lately, nowadays, recently	अशक्य impossible
अभ्यागत visitor		अशा प्रकारचा such
अभ्यास exercise	अलौकिक supernatural	अशुभ sinister
अभ्यास करणे study	अलौकिक बुद्धिमत्ता genius	अश्रुधूर tear gas
अभ्यासक्रम curriculum, syllabus	अल्प brief	अश्रू tear
	अल्पकालीन short	अश्लील vulgar
अमूर्त abstract	अल्पसंख्याक minority	अष्टपाद octopus
अयशस्वी unsuccessful	अल्पसंतुष्ट smug	अष्टपैलू versatile
अयशस्वी होणे fail	अल्पांशाने remotely	असंख्य numerous
अयोग्य unfair, unsuitable	अल्पोपाहार refreshments	असंबद्ध irrelevant
अरब Arab	अल्ला Allah	असंभवनीय unlikely
अरबी Arabic	अळंबी mushroom	असंवेदनशील insensitive
अरुंद narrow	अळी maggot	असंस्कृत uncivilized
अरुंद रस्ता track	अवकाश space	असणे be
अरुंद खोल दरी ravine	अवकाश यान shuttle, spacecraft	असभ्य gross
अर्ज application		असभ्यपणे grossly
अर्ज करणे apply	अवघड hard	असमर्थ unable
अर्जदार applicant	अवजड वाहन HGV	असमाधानकारक unsatisfactory
अर्जाचा नमुना application form	अवज्ञा करणारा disobedient	
	अवज्ञा करणे disobey	असमाधानी dissatisfied
अर्थ meaning	अवतरण quote	असलेला with
अर्थ असणे mean	अवतरण चिन्ह inverted commas, quotation marks	असहमती disagreement
अर्थ लावणे interpret		असहमती दर्शवणे contradict
अर्थव्यवस्था economy	अवमूल्यन devaluation	असहिष्णू intolerant

असह्य terrible, unbearable
असाधारण abnormal, unusual
असाध्य terminal
असामान्य extraordinary, fancy
असुरक्षित insecure
असे असूनसुद्धा despite
अस्खलित fluent
अस्तर lining
अस्ताव्यस्त untidy
अस्तित्वात असणे exist
अस्तित्वात नसणे anymore
अस्तित्वात नसलेला extinct
अस्थिर unstable, unsteady
अस्थिरता instability
अस्पष्ट unclear
अस्वल bear
अस्वस्थ uncomfortable, upset
अस्वस्थ करणे shock, upset
अस्वाभाविक abnormal, uncanny
अस्वीकारार्ह unacceptable
अस्सल authentic, genuine
अहंकारी snob
अहवाल account
आंघोळ करणे bathe
आंघोळीची टॉवेल bath towel
आंतरराष्ट्रीय international
आंत्रपुच्छाचा रोग appendicitis
आंधळा blind
आंबट sour
आंबा mango
आई mother, mum, mummy
आई किंवा वडील parent
आईसलंड Iceland
आकडेमोड calculation
आकडेमोड करणे calculate
आकडेवारी figure, statistics
आकर्षक attractive, charming, cute, gorgeous, lovely, pretty, tasteful

आकर्षकपणा charm
आकर्षकपणे prettily
आकर्षण attraction
आकर्षित करणे attract
आकलन comprehension
आकलन होणे understand
आकार shape, size
आकारमान volume
आकारलेली किंमत charge
आकाश sky
आकाशवाणी radio
आकाशवाणी केंद्र radio station
आकृती diagram
आक्रमक aggressive, hostile
आक्रमण occupation
आक्रमण करणे invade
आखडणे shrink
आखडलेला shrunken
आखाती देश Gulf States
आखूड short
आखूड बाह्यांचा short-sleeved
आख्यायिका legend
आग fire
आगकाडी match
आगमन advent, arrival
आगमन होणे arrive
आगाऊ रक्कम advance
आगाऊ समजणे foresee
आगीचा इशारा fire alarm
आगेकूच करणे advance
आगोदरच पैसे दिलेला prepaid
आग्नेय दिशा southeast
आग्रह धरणे insist
आघाडी frontier, lead
आघाताचा traumatic
आच्छादणे wrap
आज today
आजमावून पाहणे try
आज रात्री tonight
आजारपण illness, sickness
आजारपणाचे प्रमाणपत्र sick note

आजारपणात घेतलेली रजा sick leave
आजार होणे catch
आजारातून बरे होणे recover
आजारी ill, poorly, sick, unwell
आजी grandma, grandmother, granny
आजी-आजोबा grandparents
आजोबा granddad, grandfather, grandpa
आज्ञा command
आज्ञाधारक obedient
आटोपशीर compact
आठ eight
आठवडा week
आठवण reminder
आठवण करून देणे remind
आठवण येणे miss
आठवण remember
आठवा eighth
आडनाव surname
आडवे होणे lie
आणखी more
आणखी else
आणणे bring, get
आणि and
आणीबाणी emergency
आण्विक nuclear
आत in, indoors, inside, into
आत जाण्याचा मार्ग way in
आतडे gut
आतमध्ये inside
आत येऊ देणे let in
आतला भाग interior
आतली बाजू inside
आता now
आतील indoor, inner
आताचा last
आत्मघातकी मानवी बॉम्ब suicide bomber
आत्मचरित्र autobiography
आत्मविश्वास confidence
आत्मविश्वास नसलेला unsure
आत्महत्या suicide

आत्मा soul
आत्या aunt, auntie
आदर regard, respect
आदर करणे respect
आदरणीय respectable
आदरातिथ्य hospitality
आदर्श ideal, model
आदर्श रीतीने ideally
आदळणे ram
आदेश order
आदेश देणे order
आयाखरांनी सही करणे initial
आयाक्षरे initials
आधार basis, ground
आधारित based
आधी before, early
आधुनिक modern
आधुनिकतेचे अनुकरण करणारे trendy
आधुनिक भाषा modern languages
आधुनिक सुविधा mod cons
आधुनिकीकरण करणे modernize
आध्यात्मिक spiritual
आनंद delight, happiness, joy, pleasure
आनंददायक enjoyable
आनंद लुटणे enjoy
आनंदाने happily
आनंदित delighted
आनंदित होणे flattered
आनंदी cheerful, delightful, glad, happy, jolly
आनुवंशिक genetic, hereditary
आनुवंशिकतेचा अभ्यास genetics
आपत्कालीन अपघात विभाग accident and emergency
आपत्ती disaster
आपत्तीजनक disastrous
आपला your, yours
आपोआप automatically
आभार मानणे thank

आभास illusion
आमंत्रण invitation
आमंत्रित करणे invite
आमचा our, ours
आमटी curry
आमूलाग्र drastic
आम्ल acid
आम्ही us, we
आम्ही स्वतः ourselves
आम्ही स्वतःच ourselves
आयकर income tax
आयत rectangle
आयताकृती oblong, rectangular
आयात import
आयात करणे import
आयोजित करणे arrange, conduct, organize
आरक्षण booking
आरक्षित करणे book
आरसा mirror
आरा spoke
आराखडा design, layout
आराखडा तयार करणे design
आराम करणे unwind
आरामखुर्ची armchair, easy chair
आरामदायी relaxing, restful
आरामशीर comfortable
आरामशीरपणे चालणे stroll
आरोग्य health, hygiene
आरोग्यदायी healthy
आरोप accusation, allegation, charge
आरोप ठेवणे accuse, charge, prosecute
आरोपी accused
आरोळी shout
आरोहण climbing
आर्थिक financial, fiscal, monetary
आर्थिक फसवणूक scam
आर्थिक वर्ष financial year, fiscal year
आर्द्रता humidity, moisture

आलटून पालटून alternate
आलुबुखार plum
आले ginger
आलेख graph
आल्हाददायक pleasant
आळशी lazy
आळा prevention
आळा घालणे prevent, restrict
आळीव cress
आवडणे like, love
आवडता favourite
आवडते smashing
आवड निर्माण होणे interest
आवडीचा interesting
आवश्यक necessary
आवश्यक असणे require
आवश्यकता necessity, requirement
आवाक्यातले manageable
आवाज sound, voice
आवाहन appeal
आवाहन करणे appeal
आवृत्ती edition, version
आव्हान challenge
आव्हान देणे challenge
आव्हानात्मक challenging, demanding
आशा hope
आशावाद optimism
आशावादी hopeful, optimist, optimistic, positive
आशा व्यक्त करणे hope
आशिया Asia
आशीर्वाद देणे bless
आश्चर्य surprise
आश्चर्यकारक amazing
आश्चर्यकारकरीत्या surprisingly
आश्चर्यचकित amazed
आश्चर्यचकित करणारे surprising
आश्चर्ययुक्त भीती वाटणे startle
आश्रय refuge
आश्वासित करणारे reassuring

आश्वासित करणे reassure
आस axle
आसन seat
आहार diet
आहारनियंत्रण करणे diet
इंग्रज English, Englishman
इंग्रज स्त्री Englishwoman
इंग्रजी English
इंग्लंड England
इंच inch
इंजिन engine
इंजिनाशिवाय तरंगणारे
   आकाशयान glider
इंजेक्शन देणे inject
इंटरनेटचा वापरकर्ता Internet
   user
इंटरनेटसंबंधी गुन्हे
   cybercrime
इंद्रधनुष्य rainbow
इंद्रियांना सुखद वाटणारा
   sensuous
इंधन fuel
इक्वाडोर Ecuador
इच्छा desire, will, wish
इच्छा असणे desire, wish
इच्छाशक्ती willpower
इच्छुक willing
जुळणारे matching
इतिहास history
इतिहासतज्ज्ञ historian
इतिहासपूर्वकालीन prehistoric
इत्यादी etc
इथिओपिआ Ethiopia
इन्व्हॉईस पाठविणे invoice
इमारत building
इमारतीची देखभाल करणारा
   janitor
इमारती लाकूड timber
इसवी सन AD
इस्त्री iron
इस्त्री करणे iron
इस्लाम Islam
ईशान्य northeast
उंच high, tall
उंच उडी high jump

उंच खुर्ची highchair
उंच टाचांचे high-heeled,
   high heels
उंची height
उंट camel
उंदीर mouse
उकडणे boil
उकडलेले boiled, poached
उकडलेले अंडे boiled egg
उकडून कुस्करलेले बटाटे
   mashed potatoes
उकल solution
उकळणे boil
उकळते boiling
उकाडा stifling
उघड apparent, blatant
उघडउघड grossly
उघड करणे disclose, reveal
उघडणे open
उघडण्याची वेळ opening
   hours
उघडपणे obviously
उघडा bare
उघडा open
उघडे करणे bare
उचकी hiccups
उचलणे lift, pick up, raise
उच्चशिक्षण higher
   education
उच्चार pronunciation
उच्चार करणे pronounce
उच्छिष्ट leftovers
उजवा right
उजवीकडील right-hand
उजवी विचारसरणी असलेले
   right-wing
उठणे rise
उठून दिसणे stand out
उडणे bounce, fly
उडवणे squander
उडी मारणे jump, leap
उडून जाणे fly away
उड्डाण take off
उड्या मारणे skip
उतार slope

उतारा passage
उतावीळ impatient
उतावीळपणा impatience
उतावीळपणे impatiently
उतू जाणे boil over, spill
उत्कंठा suspense
उत्कर्ष होणे blossom
उत्कृष्ट excellent, splendid
उत्क्रांती evolution
उत्तम splendid, super
उत्तम प्रकारची लोकर
   cashmere
उत्तर answer, reply, solution
उत्तर दिशा north
उत्तर देणारे यंत्र answering
   machine
उत्तर देणे answer, reply
उत्तर ध्रुव North Pole
उत्तर समुद्र North Sea
उत्तरादाखल फोन करणे ring
   back
उत्तराधिकारी successor
उत्तरेकडील north, northern
उत्तीर्ण pass
उत्तीर्ण होणे pass
उत्तेजन encouragement
उत्तेजन देणारा encouraging
उत्तेजन देणे encourage
उत्तेजित करणारे exciting
उत्तेजित झालेला thrilled
उत्पादन product
उत्पादनक्षमता productivity
उत्पादन प्रक्रिया production
उत्पादनांची खरेदी-विक्री
   marketplace
उत्सव celebration, festival
उत्साह enthusiasm, zest
उत्साहपूर्ण energetic
उत्साही enthusiastic, jolly,
   lively
उत्साही व आनंदी merry
उत्सुक excited, keen
उत्सुकता वा भीतीची भावना
   thrill
उत्स्फूर्त spontaneous

उथळ shallow
उथळपणे वागणारे superficial
उथळ पाण्यातून चालणे paddle
उदरनिर्वाह living
उदा. (उदाहरणार्थ) e.g.
उदारमतवादी broad-minded
उदास depressing
उदाहरण example, illustration, instance
उद्गारचिन्ह exclamation mark
उद्दिष्ट aim, objective
उद्दिष्ट ठेवणे aim
उद्देश motive
उद्धट arrogant, blunt, cheeky, rough, rude
उद्धरण quotation
उद्या tomorrow
उद्योग industry
उद्वाहन (लिफ्ट) lift
उद्विग्न झालेला frustrated
उद्वेगजनक dismal
उधळ्या extravagant
उधार credit
उध्वस्त करणे ruin
उध्वस्त होणे devastated
उन्हामुळे करपलेली त्वचा sunburnt
उन्हामुळे त्वचा जळणे sunburn
उन्हाळा summer
उन्हाळी सुट्ट्या summer holidays
उन्हाळ्याचा कालावधी summertime
उपकरण apparatus, appliance, device, equipment, instrument, tool
उपक्रम activity
उपग्रह तबकडी satellite dish
उपचार cure
उपचारपद्धती therapy
उपद्रव nuisance
उपनगर suburb

उपनगरी suburban
उप मुख्याध्यापक deputy head
उपयुक्त handy, useful
उपयोगकर्ता user
उपरोध irony
उपरोधिक ironic, sarcastic
उपलब्ध accessible, available
उपलब्धता availability
उपलब्ध होणे come out
उप विजेता runner-up
उपशीर्षक असलेला subtitled
उपशीर्षके subtitles
उपसागर bay
उपस्थित present
उपस्थित राहणे attend
उपस्थिती appearance, attendance, presence
उपहारगृह café, restaurant
उपहास करणे scoff
उपांत्य फेरी semifinal
उपान्त्य penultimate
उपाय remedy
उपाय शोधून काढणे figure out
उपासमार होणे starve
उपाहार गृह snack bar
उपाहारगृह canteen
उफाळून येणे outbreak
उबदार cosy, warm
उभा vertical
उभा खांब post
उभारणे put up
उभे राहणे get up, stand, stand up
उमजणे realize
उमेदवार candidate
उर्फ alias
उर्वरित remaining, rest
उलट backwards
उलटणे backfire
उलटपक्षी contrary, vice versa
उलट फिरवणे reverse
उलटा reverse, upside down
उलटी करणे throw up, vomit

उलाढाल turnover
उल्का meteorite
उल्लेख करणे mention, refer
उल्लेखनीय outstanding, remarkable
उल्लेखनीयरीत्या remarkably
उवा lice
उशिरा late
उशी cushion, pillow
उशीचा अभ्रा pillowcase
उशीर delay
उशीर करणे delay
उष्णता heat
उष्णता देणे heat
उष्मांक calorie
उष्माघात sunstroke
उसने घेणे borrow
उसने देणे lend
उसळणे bounce
ऊन sunshine
ऊर्जा energy
ऋतू season
ऍलर्जिक allergic
ऍलर्जी allergy
ऍसिड acid
एक one
एकदरित altogether, overall
एक अष्टमांश eighth
एकक unit
एक काटेरी झुडूप hawthorn
एकच single
एकटक पाहणे stare
एकटा alone
एकटा पालक single parent
एकत्र together
एकत्र करणे combine, merge, round up
एकत्र गोळा होणे gather
एकत्र जमणे get together, meet up
एकत्र येणे join
एकत्रिकरण merger
एकत्रीकरण combination
एकदम घाबरून जाणे panic
एकदम वळणे swerve

एकदा once
एकदाच one-off
एक दुसऱ्यासारखे दिसणे resemble
एक-दोन couple
एक नवमांश ninth
एकनिष्ठ faithful
एकनिष्ठेने faithfully
एक प्रकारचा कीटक beetle, stick insect
एक प्रकारचा चिमटा tweezers
एक प्रकारचा मुळा horseradish
एक प्रकारचा हातमोजा mitten
एक प्रकारचे लिंबू lime
एकमत consensus
एकमुखाने unanimous
एकमेकांशी संबंधित related
एकमेव only
एकर acre
एकवचन singular
एक सहस्रांश thousandth
एकसारखा identical
फक्त एक single
कोणीही नाही nobody
एक होणे unite
एकांत privacy
एकाएकी abruptly
एकाएकी आणि अनपेक्षित abrupt
एकाकी isolated, lonely
एकाकीपणा loneliness
एकाग्रता concentration
एकाग्र होणे concentrate
एकाच वेळी simultaneous, simultaneously
एकूण gross, total
एकेरी तिकीट single ticket
एकेरी स्पर्धा singles
एकोणीस nineteen
एकोणीसावा nineteenth
एक्का ace
एखादी विशिष्ट जागा site
(एखाद्या गोष्टीचे) प्रचंड वेड mania

एखाद्याचा one's
एखाद्या जागी ठेवणे place
एखाद्या व्यक्तीसंबंधी individual
एजन्ट agent
एजन्सी agency
एरिट्रिया Eritrea
एवढे as ... as
ऐंशी eighty
ऐकणे hear, listen
ऐच्छिक optional, voluntary
ऐटबाज cool
ऐतिहासिक historical
ऑक्टोपस octopus
प्राणवायू oxygen
ऑंगळ foul
ऑडका log
ओक वृक्ष oak
ओकारी करणे throw up
ओझे burden
ओझोनचा थर ozone layer
ओटचे पीठ oatmeal
ओटीपोट pelvis
ओठ lip
ओठांच्या हालचालीवरून बोलणे समजून घेणे lip-read
ओढ mania
ओढणे draw
ओढा stream
ओतणे pour
ओबडधोबड crude, rough
ओरखडा scratch
ओरबडे scratch
ओरडणे cry
ओलसर damp, moist, soggy
ओला wet
ओलांडणे cross, pass
ओलीस ठेवलेली व्यक्ती hostage
ओळख identification, identity
ओळखणे identify, recognize
ओळखता येणारा recognizable
ओळख न पटलेला unidentified

ओळखपत्र ID card, identity card
ओवा parsley
ऑंस ounce
औदार्य generosity
औद्योगिक industrial
औद्योगिक वसाहत industrial estate
औपचारिक formal
औपचारिक चिठी (मेमो) memo
औपचारिकता formality
औपचारिक पेहराव evening dress
औषध drug
औषधनिर्मिता pharmacist
औषध लिहून देणे prescribe
औषधविक्रेता chemist
औषधांचे दुकान chemist, pharmacy
औषधाची गोळी tablet
औषधांची मात्रा dose
औषधाचे बाह्य वेष्टन capsule
औषधाच्या गोळ्या pill
कंगवा comb
कंगाल hard up, ruin
कंजूष miser, stingy
कंटाळलेला bored
कंटाळवाणा boring
कंटाळवाणे monotonous
कंटाळा boredom
कंटाळा आणणे bore
कंद bulb
कंबर waist
कंबोडिया Cambodia
कंस brackets
कक्षा range
(कचऱ्याची) होळी bonfire
कचरा litter, refuse
कचरा कुंडी litter bin
कचरा टाकण्याची जागा dump
कचरापेटी dustbin
कच्चा माल raw
कच्चे मुद्रण proof
कट conspiracy

कठडा rail
कठीण difficult, hard
कठीण कवचाचे फळ nut
कठीण काम tricky
कठोर harsh
कड edge
कडक stiff
कडक कारवाई करणे crack down on
कडबा hay
कडवट bitter
कडा rim
कडून from
कडे चालत येणे come up
कढी curry
कढी मसाला curry powder
कणखर tough
कणीक dough
कतार Qatar
कथा story
कदाचित perhaps
कधी when
कधीकधी sometimes
कधीतरी sometime
कधीही ever
कधीही नाही never
कनिष्ठ inferior, junior
कनिष्ठ सहयोगी associate
कन्या रास Virgo
कपची chip
कपडा cloth
कपडे clothes, clothing
कपडे अंगावर चढणे dress
कपडे उतरवणे undress
कपडे घातलेली व्यक्ती dressed
कपडे धुण्याची पावडर washing powder
कपडे बदलणे change
कपड्यांचा संच outfit
कपड्यांचे कपाट wardrobe
कपड्याची बाही sleeve
कपाट cabinet, cupboard
कपात redundancy
कपाळ forehead

कपाळावर आठ्या घालणे frown
कप्पा compartment, drawer
कबाब kebab
कबुतर pigeon
कबुली acknowledgement, confession
कबुली देणे confess
कमतरता shortcoming
कमाई earnings
कमान arch
कमावणे earn
कमी fewer, less, low, minute
कमी करणे cutback, cut down, minimize, reduce
कमी कालावधीची सुट्टी half-term
कमी खर्चाचे inexpensive
कमी चरबीयुक्त low-fat
कमीजास्त करता येण्याजोगे adjustable
कमीत कमी at least, minimal
कमी मोबदला मिळणारे underpaid
कमी लेखणे underestimate
कमी शिजवलेले rare
कमी होणे come down, diminish, go down
कम्युनिस्ट पक्ष communist
कर tariff, tax
करडा रंग grey
करणे do, make
करदाता taxpayer
करमणुकीची जागा amusement arcade
करमणूक करणारा entertainer
करमणूक करणे amuse, entertain
करमुक्त duty-free
करवत saw
करवली bridesmaid

कर विवरण tax return
करायला भाग पाडणे make
करार agreement, contract
... करावे should
करिता for
करीत राहणे keep
करू देणे let
करू शकणे may
कर्क रास Cancer
कर्करोग cancer
कर्कश आवाज करणे squeak
कर्ज debt, loan, mortgage
कर्जाऊ देणे loan
कर्णभूषण earring
कर्णशूळ earache
कर्णा horn
कर्बोदक carbohydrate
कर्मकांडाचा ritual
कर्मचारी employee, personnel, worker
कर्मचारीवृंद/कर्मचारीवर्ग staff
कल tendency, trend
कल असणे tend
कलणे tip
कलम clause
कला art
कलाकार artist
कलाकारी work of art
कलात्मक artistic
कला दालन art gallery
कलादालन gallery
कला महाविद्यालय art school
कलाशाखेचा पदवीधर BA
कलिंगड melon, watermelon
कलेचा उत्कृष्ट नमुना masterpiece
कल्पक creative
कल्पकतापूर्ण ingenious
कल्पना idea, imagination
कल्पना करणे imagine
कल्पना केल्याप्रमाणे supposedly
कळप flock
कळसुत्री बाहुली puppet

कवच shell
कवचातील मासे shellfish
कवटी skull
कवडा/तितर पक्षी partridge
कवळी dentures
कवाइत march, March
कविता poem
कवी poet
कशिदाकाम embroidery
कशिदाकाम करणे embroider
कसरत करणारा athletic
कसरतपटू acrobat, athlete,
  gymnast
कसरतीचे खेळ athletics
कसरतीचे व्यायामप्रकार
  gymnastics
कसा how
कसाबसा scarcely
कसेतरी somehow
कसेसे घुसणे squeeze in
कसेही anyhow
कस्टम्स customs
कस्टम्स अधिकारी customs
  officer
का why
कांजिण्या chickenpox
कांति complexion
कांदा onion
कांस्य bronze
काकडी cucumber
काकवी treacle
काकू auntie
काख armpit
कागद paper, sheet
कागदपत्र document
कागदपत्रे documents
कागदपत्रे बनविणे
  documentation
कागदाचा तुकडा slip
काच glass
काचफोड blister
काचोळी bra
काजळी soot
काजू cashew
काटकसर करणे economize

काटकसरी thrifty
काटकसरीचा economical
काटकुळा व अनाकर्षक lanky
काटकोन right angle
काटा fork, thorn
काटेकोर strict
काटेकोरपणे strictly
काटेरी तार barbed wire
काठ edge
काठी stick
काठोकाठ भरणे fill up
काडतूस cartridge,
  magazine
काढणे remove
काढून घेणे off, take away,
  withdraw
काढून घेण्याची क्रिया
  withdrawal
काढून घेण्याजोगा removable
काढून टाकणे cut off, dismiss,
  eliminate
कातरण cutting
कातरी scissors
कादंबरी novel
कादंबरीकार novelist
कान ear
कानस file
कानसीने घासणे file
कानाचा पडदा eardrum
कापड cloth, fabric, material
कापडाने पुसणे wipe up
कापणी करणे harvest
कापणे cut
कापरे भरणे shudder
कापल्याने झालेली जखम cut
काम task, work
काम करणे work
काम करण्याचे टाळणे skive
कामगार worker, workman
कामगार वर्ग working-class
कामगार संघटना trade union
कामचुकारपणा करणे skive
कामधंदा job
कामाचा अनुभव work
  experience

कामाचे ठिकाण workplace
कामाचे वेळापत्रक schedule
कामात ओढणे rope in
कामात व्यग्र असलेला
  preoccupied
कामावरून कमी केलेला
  redundant
कामावरून काढून टाकणे
  sack
कामावरून काढून टाकलेला
  sack
कामासाठी ठेवलेली जागा
  workspace
काय what
कायदा law
कायदेशीर legal
कायदेशीर कारवाई
  proceedings
कायद्याच्या दृष्टीने अज्ञानी
  underage
कायमचा permanent
कायमस्वरूपी permanently
कायापालट makeover
कार car
कारंजे fountain
कारखाना factory
कारचालक motorist
कारचे भाडे car rental
कारच्या चाव्या car keys
कारण cause, reason
कारण की because
कारणीभूत होणे cause,
  produce
कार धुण्याची जागा car
  wash
कारवाई action, operation
कारविमा car insurance
कारस्थान conspiracy
कारागीर craftsman
कार्ड card
कार्यक्रम activity,
  programme
कार्यक्षम efficient
कार्यक्षमतापूर्वक efficiently
कार्यभाग task

कार्यशाळा workshop
कार्यालय office
काल yesterday
कालबाह्य obsolete, out of date
कालव mussel
कालवा canal
कालावधी duration, period, spell
काल्पनिक imaginary
काल्पनिक कथा fiction
काळ tense, time
काळजी care, concern
काळजी करणे fret
काळजी घेणे care, look after, watch out
काळजीत टाकणारे nerve-racking
काळजीत पडलेला concerned
काळवीट antelope
काळ/वेळ while
काळा black
काळानुरूप नसलेले unfashionable
काळा बिबळ्या वाघ panther
काळी तुती blackberry
काळ्या मनुका currant
कावळा crow
कावीळ hepatitis, jaundice
कासव tortoise, turtle
कासे pewter
काही any, couple, few, some
काही काळासाठीची स्थगिती suspension
काही काळासाठी थांबवणे suspend
काही घडण्याची शक्यता likely
काहीतरी something
काही वेळा occasional
काहीही anything
काहीही नाही none, nothing
किंकाळी scream
किंकाळी मारणे scream, shriek
किंचित झिंगलेला tipsy

किंमत cost, price, worth
किंमत आकारणे charge
किंमत मोजणे cost
किंमतीत होणारी वाढ inflation
किंवा or
किटली kettle
किडा worm
किण्व yeast
किती how
किनारा bank, shore
किमान least, minimum
किरकोळ slight
किरकोळ विक्री retail
किरकोळ विकेता retailer
किरण beam
किरणोत्सर्ग radiation
किरणोत्सर्गी radioactive
किराणा दुकानदार grocer
किराणा सामान groceries
किराणा सामानाचे दुकान grocer
किल्ला castle, fort
किल्ली key
किळस loathe
किळस आलेला disgusted
किळसवाणा disgusting
किसणे grate
की whether
कीटक insect, pest
कीटकनाशक pesticide
कीटकाची नांगी sting
कुंचला brush
कुंठित अवस्था stalemate
कुंडली horoscope
कुंडी plant pot
कुंडीतले रोप pot plant
कुंपण fence
कुंभ रास Aquarius
कुचकामी worthless
कुचकामी वस्तूंचा पसारा clutter
कुजणे decay
कुजबुजणे whisper
कुटाळक्या gossip

कुटुंब family, household
कुठे where
कुठेही नाही nowhere
कुणाच्यातरी मागे जाणे follow
कुत्रा dog
कुत्री bitch
कुत्र्याचे पिल्लू puppy
कुपोषण malnutrition
कुबडी crutch
कुमारी Miss, virgin
कुरकुरीत बिस्कीट rusk
कुरण meadow
कुरतडणारा प्राणी rodent
कुरळे curly
कुऱ्हाड axe
कुराण Koran
कुरूप ugly
कुलूप lock, padlock
कुलूप लावणे lock
कुलूपवाला locksmith
कुल्ले buttocks
कुल्ल्यांवर फटके मारणे spank
कुशल skilful, skilled
कुस्ती wrestling
कुस्तीगीर wrestler
कूच march, March
कूच करणे march
कृतघ्न ungrateful
कृतज्ञ grateful
कृती act
कृती करणे act
कृत्रिम artificial
कृत्रिम उपग्रह satellite
कृपया please!
कृपया पान उलटा PTO
कृमी worm
कॅटलॉग catalogue
कॅन can
कॅनडा Canada
कॅनरी पक्षी canary
कॅनरी लोक Canaries
कॅमेरून Cameroon
कॅरिबिअन समुद्र Caribbean

केंद्र centre
केकाटणे howl
केबल दूरदर्शन cable television
केर भरण्याची सुपळी dustpan
केराची टोपली bin, wastepaper basket
केलेला खर्च परत देणे reimburse
केलेला फोन call
केळे banana
केवळ exclusively, sheer
केव्हा/जेव्हा when
केशर saffron
केशरचना hairdo, hairstyle
केशरचनाकार hairdresser, stylist
केशरचनेचे दुकान hairdresser
केस hair
केसांचा टोप wig
केसांची झुलपे fringe
केसांची बट lock
केसातील कोंडा dandruff
केसाळ hairy
कैदी inmate, prisoner
काँगो Congo
कॉफीचे भांडे coffeepot
कोंडा bran
कोंबडा cock
कोंबडी chicken, hen
कोंबडीचे मांस chicken
कोंबणे cram
कोकरू lamb
कोकीळ cuckoo
कोटपोतरा thistle
कोठार barn
कोठेतरी someplace, somewhere
कोठेही anywhere
कोडे maze, puzzle
कोण who
कोणता which
कोणताही whichever
कोणताही any
कोणत्याही वेळी anytime

कोणाचा whose
कोणाला whom
कोणालाही anyone
कोणी anybody
कोणीतरी somebody, someone
कोणीही whoever
कोणीही नाही none, no one
कोणीही राहत नसलेला uninhabited
कोत्या वृत्तीची व्यक्ती narrow-minded
कोथिंबीर coriander
कोन angle
कोनशिला plaque
कोनाडा shelf
कोपर elbow
कोपरा corner
कोबी cabbage
कोमट lukewarm
कोमा coma
कोमेजणे wilt
कोरडा dry
कोरडा ठणठणीत bone dry
कोरडे करणे dry
कोरणे engrave
कोरा blank
कोरी कॉफी black coffee
कोलंबिया Colombia
कोल्हा fox
कोळंबी prawn
कोळंबी मासा shrimp
कोळशाची खाण colliery
कोळसा charcoal
कोळी spider
कोळ्याचे जाळे cobweb
कोशिंबीर salad
कोसळणे collapse
कोस्टा रिका Costa Rica
कोहळा pumpkin
कौतुक admiration
कौल tile
कौशल्य skill
क्युबा Cuba
क्रम sequence

क्रमशः respectively
क्रांती revolution
क्रांतिकारी revolutionary
क्रिडानौका yacht
क्रियापद verb
क्रियाविशेषण adverb
क्रीडाप्रेक्षागृह stadium
क्रूर brutal, cruel
क्रूरता cruelty
क्रूरपणे वागणे ill-treat
क्रोध anger, rage
क्रोधाचा झटका tantrum
क्रोधित angry
क्वचित hardly, rarely, seldom
क्ष-किरण X-ray
क्षण moment
क्षणचित्रे highlight
क्षणिक momentarily, momentary
क्षमता ability, capacity, potential
क्षमा apology
क्षमा करणे forgive
क्षमा मागणे apologize
क्षयरोग TB, tuberculosis
क्षारयुक्त salty
क्षितिज horizon
क्षितिजासमांतर आडवी horizontal
क्षुल्लक minor, trivial
क्षुल्लक गोष्ट trifle
क्षेत्र area, sector
क्षेपणास्त्र missile
खंड continent, pause
खंडणी ransom
खंडित broken
खंडित केलेली वीज power cut
खंड्या पक्षी kingfisher
खंदक moat, trench
खगोलशास्त्र astronomy
खच्चून भरलेला crammed
खजिनदार treasurer
खजिना treasure
खडक rock

खडबडीत coarse
खडबडीत वाळू gravel
खडू chalk
खड्डा खणणे dig
खणणारे यंत्र digger
खत fertilizer
खनिज mineral
खनिज पाण्याचा झरा spa
खबऱ्या grass
खरकटी भांडी धुणे wash up
खरडपट्टी काढणे scold
खरबूज melon
खरा real, true
खराब bad
खराब करणे spoil
खरेदी shopping
खरेदी करणे purchase
खरेदीची पिशवी shopping
  bag
खरेदीदार buyer
खरोखर actually, indeed,
  really, truly
खर्च expenditure, expenses
खर्च करणे spend
खर्चाचे अंदाजपत्रक budget
खर्चिक expensive
खर्जातील आवाज bass
खलनायक villain
खलाशी sailor, seaman
खळखळून धुणे rinse
खळबळजनक thrilling
खवले scale, shell
खांदा shoulder
खांदे उडवणे shrug
खांब column, pillar, pole
खाचखळगे असलेला bumpy
खाजकुयली nettle
खाजगी private
खाजगीकरण करणे privatize
खाजगी मालमत्ता private
  property
खाजगी रुग्णालय nursing
  home
खाजण lagoon

खाजवणे itch, scratch
खाटकाचे दुकान butcher
खाटीक butcher
खाण mine
खाण उद्योग mining
खाणकामगार miner
खाणाखुणा sign
खाणावळ inn
खाणे eat
खाण्यायोग्य edible
खाण्यायोग्य पूरक पदार्थ
  additive
खातरजमा करणे check
खाते account
खाते क्रमांक account
  number
खात्री असलेला sure
खात्री असलेला confident
खात्री करणे ensure
खात्री देणे assure
खात्रीपूर्वक surely
खानपानसेवा catering
खार squirrel
खारट salty
खाऱ्या पाण्यातील saltwater
खारे पाणी sea water
खालचा lower
खालच्या बाजूला low
खालच्या मजला downstairs
खाली below, down,
  underneath
खाली उतरणे descend
खाली झुकणे bend down,
  bend over
खाली पडणे fall, fall down
खाली बसणे sit down
खाली वाकणे crouch down
खाली सरकवणे lower
खास special, specifically,
  unique
खास करून specially
खास देकार special offer
खास वैशिष्ट्य feature
खिंड pass
खिजवणे tease

खिडकी window
खिन्न depressed
खिन्नपणे sadly
खिळवून ठेवणारे gripping
खिळा nail
खिसा pocket
खिसेकापू pickpocket
खुंटी peg
खुंटी/बुटाळे rack
खुणांची भाषा sign language
खुनी murderer
खुपसणे pierce
खुरपे trowel
खुर्ची chair
खुलासा करणे account for
खुळचट absurd
खुशामत करणे flatter
खुसखुशीत crisp, crispy
खूण mark
खूण दाखवणे signal
खून murder
खून करणे murder
खूनी killer
खूप high, lot, many, much,
  too, very
खूप अभ्यास करणे swot
खूप उंच इमारत high-rise
खूप घाबरलेला petrified
खूप घोटलेली साय whipped
  cream
खूप (छान) terrific
खूप दूर far
खूप मोठा गोंगाट din
खूप वेळ long
खेकडा crab, lobster
खेचणे drag, pull
खेचर mule
खेडे village
खेडेगाव country
खेद sorry
खेरीज besides
खेळ game, sport
खेळकर playful
खेळणे play, toy
खेळण्याची वेळ playtime

खेळपट्टी pitch
खेळाचे मैदान playground
खेळाडू player, sportsman
खेळातील पंच umpire
खेळातील पते card
खेळातील विश्रांतीची वेळ half-time
खेळामधील पंच referee
खोकणे cough
खोकला cough
खोकल्याचे औषध cough mixture
खोका carton
खोगीर saddle
खोटा fake
खोटारडा liar
खोटी भीती false alarm
खोटी साक्ष perjury
खोटे lie
खोड trunk
खोडकर mischievous
खोडणे cross out
खोडरबर rubber
खोडून टाकणे erase
खोबण slot
खोल deep
खोलवर deeply
खोली depth, room
ख्याती reputation
ख्रिस्त Christ
ख्रिस्तपूर्व BC
ख्रिस्ती Christian
ख्रिस्ती धर्म Christianity
गंज rust
गंजलेला rusty
गंभीर serious
गंभीरपणे seriously
गंभीरपणे सांगणे mean
गंमत fun
गगनचुंबी इमारत skyscraper
गचाळ sloppy
गच्च भरलेला packed
गज bar
गजकर्ण eczema
गजबजलेला busy, crowded

गजराचे घड्याळ alarm clock
गट group, party
गटार drain
गटाराचा पाईप sewer
गडगडाट thunder
गडगडाटी thundery
गडद dark
गडद निळे navy
गणनयंत्र calculator
गणवेश uniform
गणित mathematics, maths
गणिती mathematical
गतिवर्धन acceleration
गती pace
गप्प silent
गप्पागोष्टी chat
गप्पागोष्टी करणे chat
गबाळा shabby
गर core
गरज need
गरज असणे need
गरम hot
गरम करणे heat up
गरम करण्याची क्रिया heating
गरम पाण्याची बाटली hot-water bottle
गरिबी poverty
गरीब poor
गरूड eagle
गरोदर pregnant
गरोदरपण pregnancy
गर्दीचा हंगाम high season
गर्दीची वेळ peak hours, rush hour
गर्भ foetus
गर्भनिरोधनाचे साधन contraceptive
गर्भपात miscarriage
गर्भरोध contraception
गलिचा rug
गल्ली alley, lane
गळणे drip, leak
गळती leak
गळपट्टा collar

गळा throat
गळा काढणे howl
गळू abscess
गवंडी bricklayer
गवत grass
गवत कापणारे यंत्र mower
गवताची गंजी haystack
गव्हाण trough
गस्त patrol
गस्त घालणारी कार patrol car
गहाण ठेवणे mortgage
गहू wheat
गांधीलमाशी wasp
गांबिया Gambia
गाजर carrot
गाठ cyst, knot, tumour
गाठणे catch up
गाडणे bury
गाडी car
गाडी उभी/पार्क करणे park
गाडीतील झोपण्याची जागा berth
गाढव donkey
गाणे sing, song
गाण्याचे बोल lyrics
गादी mattress
गाभा core
गाय cow
गायक singer
गायकसमूह choir
गायन singing
गारगोटी pebble
गारा hail
गाल cheek
गालगुंड mumps
गालफड cheekbone
गाळणी colander, filter
गाळणे filter
गाळलेली जागा blank
गावंढळ naff
गाशा गुंडाळणे pack
गिधाड vulture
गिनी Guinea
गिरणी mill

गिळणे swallow
गिळण्याची क्रिया swallow
गुंगी आणणारे औषध sedative
गुंजन करणे hum
गुंड vandal
गुंडांच्या टोळीतील माणूस gangster
गुंडाळणे wind, wrap up
गुंडाळी roll
गुंडाळी उलगडणे unroll
गुंडाळी करणे roll
गुंतलेला engaged
गुंतलेले busy
गुंतवणूक investment
गुंतवणूक करणे invest
गुंतवणूकदार investor
गुंतागुंत complication
गुंतागुंतीचा प्रश्न ticklish
गुंतागुंतीचे complex, complicated
गुजरणे करणे live on
गुडघा knee
गुडघे टेकणे kneel, kneel down
गुडघ्याची वाटी kneecap
गुण credentials, point, score
गुण देणे mark
गुणधर्म characteristic
गुणपत्रक report
गुणसंख्या score
गुणाकार multiplication
गुणोत्तर प्रमाण ratio
गुदगुल्या करणे tickle
गुदमरणे choke, suffocate
गुद्दा punch
गुद्दा/धपका मारणे thump
गुद्दे मारणे punch
गुन्हा crime, offence
गुन्हेगार criminal, culprit
गुन्हेगारी criminal
गुपचूप केलेला sly
गुपित secret
गुस confidence, secret
गुसपणे secretly

गुस योजना plot
गुमहेर detective
गुयाना Guyana
गुरगुरणे growl
गुरुवार Thursday
गुरे cattle
गुलनार carnation
गुलाब rose
गुलाबी pink
गुलाम slave
गुळगुळीत smooth
गुहा cave
गूढ mysterious, mystery, supernatural
गूढ विद्या magic
गृहपाठ homework
गृहिणी housewife
गृहीत धरणे assume, presume
गृहीत धरून presumably
गॅबन Gabon
गॅरेज garage
गेलेला gone
गैरवर्तन करणे misbehave
गैरसमज misunderstanding
गैरसमज होणे misunderstand
गैरसोय inconvenience
गैरसोयीचा awkward
गैरसोयीचा inconvenient
गोंगाट noise
गोंगाट/गलका racket
गोंगाटाचा noisy
गोंद glue
गोंदण tattoo
गोंधळ chaos, confusion, shambles
गोंधळलेला baffled, bewildered, puzzled
गोंधळलेला confused
गोंधळलेली स्थिती muddle
गोंधळाचा chaotic
गोंधळात टाकणारा confusing
गोंधळात टाकणारे puzzling

गोंधळात टाकणे confuse
गोगलगाय snail
गोठणे freeze
गोठण्याची स्थिती condensation
गोठनरोधी antifreeze
गोठलेले frosty, frozen
गोठलेले दव frost
गोठवणे freeze
गोठविणारा freezing
गोड sweet
गोड दाट चटणी dip
गोड द्रवरूप औषध syrup
गोड पदार्थ sweet
गोड मका sweetcorn
गोडवा आणणारा पदार्थ sweetener
गोडे fresh
गोण sack
गोदी dock
गोधडी quilt
गोपनीय confidential
गोल round
गोल्फची काठी golf club
गोल्फचे मैदान golf course
गोळा lump
गोळी घालणे shoot
गोळीबार shooting
गोवर German measles
गोष्ट story, stuff, tale
गोरीफळ blackberry
ग्रंथपाल librarian
ग्रंथालय library
ग्रंथी gland
ग्रह planet
ग्रामीण rural
ग्रामीण भाग countryside
ग्राहक client, consumer, customer
ग्रेट ब्रिटन Great Britain
ग्लास glass
ग्वाटेमाला Guatemala
घंटा bell
घट decrease, drop, reduction

घटक component, element, ingredient
घटना occurrence
घटनांची मालिका series
घटनापूर्ण eventful
घटनेचा एक भाग episode
घटस्फोट divorce
घटस्फोटित divorced
घट होणे decrease, drop
घट्ट fit, thick, tight
घट्ट करणे tighten
घट्ट दाबणे squeeze
घट्ट बसवणे fix
घट्ट लावणे do up
घडणे go, happen, occur
घडणे अपेक्षित due
घडी fold
घडी घालणे fold
घडीची शिडी stepladder
घड्याळ clock, watch
घड्याळाचा पट्टा watch strap
घन cube
घनता density
घनदाट dense, lush
घनपदार्थ solid
घन (परिमाण) cubic
घर home, house
घरकाम housework
घरचा पत्ता home address
घरटे nest
घरफोडी burglary
घरफोडी करणारा चोर burglar
घरफोडी करणे burgle
घरमालक landlord
घराबाहेर outdoor
घरी home
घरी थांबणे stay in
घरी बनवलेला home-made
घरोघरी वर्तमानपत्रे टाकणे paper round
घर्मरोधी antiperspirant
घशाची सूज laryngitis
घशातील गाठी tonsils
घशातील गाठींची सूज tonsillitis

घसरगुंडी slide
घसरणे skid, slide, slip
घसा throat
घसारा mess
घाई hurry, rush
घाई करणे hurry up
घाईघाईने hastily
घाईघाईने जाणे hurry
घाईघाईने लिहिणे scribble
घाईने धावत जाणे rush
घाऊक wholesale
घाऊक विक्री wholesale
घाण mess
घाणेरडा filthy
घातक (रोग) malignant
घाना Ghana
घाबरणे terrify
घाबरलेला scared, terrified
घाबरलेला frightened
घाबरवणारा frightening, spooky
घाबरवणारे scary
घाबरवणे scare
घाबरविणे frighten
घाम perspiration, sweat
घाम येणे sweat
घामाघूम करणारा sweltering
घामेजलेले sweaty
घालणे lay
घालवणे spend
घाव घालणे hack
घास bite
घासणे rub, scrub
घासाघीस करणे haggle
घुबड owl
घुसखोर intruder
घुसखोरी break in
घुसणे break in
घुसमटणे choke
घूस rat
घृणास्पद obnoxious
घेऊन जाणे lead, take
घेणे take
घोंगडी blanket
घोंगावणे hum

घोटा ankle
घोटाळा scandal
घोडचूक blunder
घोडा horse
घोडागाडी cart
घोडी mare
घोडेस्वार jockey
घोडेस्वारी riding
घोड्यांची शर्यत horse racing
घोड्यांच्या शर्यतीचे मैदान racecourse
घोड्याचा नाल horseshoe
घोड्याची चौखूर धाव gallop
घोड्यावर केलेली रपेट horse riding
घोरणे snore
घोषणा announcement
चंद्र moon
चकत्या करणे slice
चकवणे swerve
चकाट्या पिटणे gossip
चकित करणारे astonishing
चकित करणे astonish
चकित झालेला astonished
चक्कर येणे faint
चक्र cycle
चक्रव्यूह maze
चक्रीवादळ cyclone
चटई mat
चड्डी briefs, pants, trunks
चढणारा climber
चढणे climb, onto
चतुर व विनोदी witty
(चतुर) विनोदबुद्धि wit
चप्पल flip-flops
चमक flash
चमकणे shine
चमकदार fluorescent, shiny
चमचा spoon
चमचाभर spoonful
चमत्कार miracle
चमत्कारिक funny
चयापचय metabolism
चरित्र biography, character
चर्चा debate, discussion, talk

Marathi	English
चर्चा करणे	debate, discuss
चलन	currency
चलनी नोट	note
चलाखी	trick
चलाखी करणे	trick
चव	flavour, taste
चव असणे	taste
चवदार	tasty
चषक	trophy
चष्मा	glasses, spectacles
चष्मे बनविणारा	optician
चहा	tea
चहाचा कप	teacup
चहाची किटली	teapot
चहाची वेळ	teatime
चांगला	fine, good, sound
चांगले कपडे घालणे	dress up
चांगले वागणे	behave
चांगल्या रीतीने	well
चांदी	silver
चाक	wheel
चाके असलेली खुर्ची	wheelchair
चाचणी	test
चाचणी घेणे	test
चाचपडणे	grope
चाचपणी करणे	try out
चाटणे	lick
चाड	Chad
चादर	sheet
चादर व उशांचे अभे	bed linen
चाप	clasp, clip
चापट मारणे	slap
चाबूक	whip
चामखीळ	wart
चामडे	leather
चार	four
चाल	move
चालक	driver
चालक परवाना	driving licence
चालणे	walk
चालताना अडखळणे	trip
चालना/गती देणे	accelerate
चालना देणे	boost
चालना/बढती देणे	promote
चालवणे	operate
चालू	on
चालू असणे	work
चालू करणे	switch on, turn on
चालू खाते	current account
चालू घडामोडी	current affairs
चालू ठेवणे	continue, go on
चालू राहणे	continue
चाळण	sieve
चाळीस	forty
चावणे	chew
चावा घेणे	bite
चा विचार करता	considering
चावून चोथा करणे	chew
चाहता	fan
चिंता	anxiety
चिंता करणे	worry
चिंताग्रस्त	worried
चिंताजनक	worrying
चिंतातूर	nervous
चिंधी	rag
चिकट	sticky
चिकटवणे	attach, glue, stick
चिकटवणे	paste
चिकणमाती	clay
चिक्कू	stingy
चिखल	mud
चिखलाने माखलेले	muddy
चिचुंद्री	mole
चिठ्ठी	note
चिडखोर	grumpy, irritable
चिडचिडा	bad-tempered
चिडणे	sulk
चिडलेला	sulky
चिता	leopard
चित्र	drawing, picture
चित्रकला	painting
चित्र काढणे	draw
चित्रकार	painter
चित्रपट	film, movie
चित्रपट अभिनेता/अभिनेत्री	film star
चित्रपटगृह	cinema, theatre
चित्रपट दाखविणे	screen
चित्रपट दाखविण्याचा पडदा	screen
चित्रफित	video
चित्रमुद्रण	recording
चित्र रंगवणे	paint
चित्रलेख	graphics
चित्राची चौकट	picture frame
चित्रातल्यासारखी सुंदर जागा	picturesque
चिनी	Chinese
चिनीमाती	china
चिन्ह	sign, symbol
चिमटा	clothes peg, skewer
चिमटा घेणे	pinch
चिमणी	sparrow
चिरडणे	crush, squash
चिलखत	armour
चिली	Chile
चीन	China
चुंबकीय	magnetic
चुंबन	kiss
चुंबन घेणे	kiss
चुकणे	miss
चुकलेला	mistaken
चुकीचा	false, inaccurate, incorrect
चुकीचा अंदाज लावणे	misjudge
चुकीचे	wrong
चुकीचे छापलेले	misprint
चुकून	inadvertently, mistakenly
चुणचुणीत	smart
चुनखडक	chalk
चुनखडी	limestone
चुना	lime
चुरा	crumb
चुलत भाऊ/बहीण	cousin
चुलती	aunt
चूक	error, fault, mistake, wrong
चूक दुरुस्त करणे	rectify

चेंगरणे squash
चेंडू ball
चेंडूफेक bowling
चेंबटणे squeeze in
चेटकीण witch
चेन zip
चेन बंद करणे zip
चे बनलेले असणे consist of
-चे रहिवासी असणे come from
चेष्टा mischief
चेहऱ्याशी संबंधित facial
चेहरा face
चैतन्यशील dynamic
चैन luxury
चोखणे suck
चोच beak
चोप देणे bash
चोर thief
चोरणे steal
चोरी robbery, theft
चौक crossroads, junction
चौकट diamond, frame
चौकटीची जाळी grid
चौकडीचे checked
चौकशी enquiry, inquiry
चौकशी करणे enquire, inquire
चौकशी करण्याची जागा inquiry desk
चौकशी कार्यालय inquiries office
चौकोन diamond, square
चौकोनी square
चौखूर धावणे gallop
चौथा fourth
चौथा हिस्सा quarter
चौदा fourteen
चौदावा fourteenth
...च्या आत within
च्या कारणाने due to
च्या खाली below, beneath
च्या मधून through
च्या मागे behind
च्या मुळे owing to

च्या वतीने on behalf of
च्या सारखा like
छंद hobby
छंद म्हणून भटकणारा rambler
छत ceiling, roof
छत्री umbrella
छपाई print
छळ harassment, torture
छळ करणे torture
छळणे persecute
छाटणे trim
छाती chest
छान nice
छाप impression
छापणारा printer
छापणे print, type
छाप पाडणारे impressive
छाप पाडणे impress
छाया shade
छायाचित्र photo, photograph
छायाचित्र काढणे photograph
छायाचित्रकार cameraman, photographer
छायाचित्र खेचणे snapshot
छायाचित्रण photography
छायाचित्रसंग्रह photo album
छायाप्रत photocopy
छावणी camp
छावणीची जागा campsite
छावणी टाकणे camp
छावणीतील वास्तव्य camping
छावा cub
छिद्र tear
छिन्नी chisel
छोटा tiny
छोटा गोल पाव bun
छोटा घोडा pony
छोटा चमचा teaspoon
छोटा मचवा dinghy
छोटी तिजोरी locker
छोटी नोंदवही jotter
छोटीशी चूक slip up
छोटी समस्या hitch

छोटीशी चूक slip
छोटे कागदी पाकीट sachet
छोटे खिळे/बटण stud
छोटे छिद्र aperture
छोटे संत्रे tangerine
छोट्या घोड्यावरून फिरणे pony trekking
छोट्या जाहिराती small ads
जंक्शन junction
जंगल forest, jungle, wood
जंगलातील प्राणीसंपदा wildlife
जंगली wild
जंतुनाशक antiseptic, disinfectant
जकात tariff
जखम injury, sore, wound
जखम बरी होणे heal
जखमी hurt, injured
जखमी करणे hurt, injure, wound
जगणे live
जगण्याची धडपड survival
जड heavy
जडजवाहीर jewellery
जत्रा fair
जत्रेचे मैदान fairground
जनगणना census
जनता public
जनतेचे मत public opinion
जन संपर्क public relations
जनुक gene
जनुकीयदृष्ट्या सुधारित genetically-modified, GM
जन्म birth
जन्मगाव native
जन्मजात born
जन्मजात येणारी भाषा native speaker
जन्मठिकाण birthplace, place of birth
जन्मदेश native
जन्म प्रमाणपत्र birth certificate
जस करणे confiscate
जबडा jaw

जबरदस्ती करणे force
जबरदस्तीने (घट्ट) पकडणे seize
जबाब statement
जबाबदार accountable, responsible
जबाबदारी responsibility
जमा करणे collect
जमात tribe
जमाव assembly, crowd
जमिनीखाली underground
जमिनीवर उतरणे land
जमीन floor, ground, land
जमीनदार landowner
जर if
जरी although
जर्दाळू apricot
जर्मन German
जर्मनी Germany
जलद fast, quick
जलपरी mermaid
जलपर्यटन cruise
जलरंग watercolour
जलरोधक showerproof, waterproof
जलसा concert
जलाशय reservoir
जळणे burn
जवळ close, near
जवळचा near
जवळचा नातेवाईक next of kin
जवळचा रस्ता shortcut
जवळजवळ approximate, practically, virtual reality
जवळ जाणे approach
जवळपास around, close by, nearby
जवळपासचा भाग vicinity
जवळीक proximity
जवळून closely
जवळून जाणे go past
जवाहिऱ्या jeweller
जशी आहे तशी स्थिती status quo

जसे as
जसेच्या तसे intact
जस्त zinc
जहाज ship
जहाज फुटण्याची क्रिया shipwreck
जहाजबांधणी उद्योग shipbuilding
जहाजांचा ताफा fleet
जहाजाचा नांगर anchor
जहालमतवाद extremism
जहालमतवादी extremist
जांभई देणे yawn
जांभळा रंग purple
जाऊन आणणे fetch
जागतिक global
जागतिक तापमानवाढ global warming
जागतिकीकरण globalization
जागा place, premises, space
जागा बदलणे turn around
जागे awake
जागे राहणे awake, stay up
जागेवर away
जागे होणे wake up
जाजम carpet
जाड thick
जाडसर व्यक्ती plump
जाडी thickness
जाणवणे feel
जाणीव consciousness, sense
जाणीव असलेला conscious
जाणीव असलेले aware
जाणून बुजून intentional
जाणूनबुजून केलेले deliberate
जाणे go
जादा extra, spare, surplus
जादा असणे spare
जादा आधार back up
जादुई magic, magical
जादूगार magician
जादू magic

जादूगार conjurer, sorcerer
जामीन bail
जायफळ nutmeg
जाळणे burn
जाळपोळ arson
जाळी net
जाळून टाकणे burn down
जाळे network, web
जावई son-in-law
जास्त most
जास्त पैसे उकळणे overcharge
जास्त शिजलेले overdone
जास्तीचे काम overtime
जाहिरात ad, advert, advertisement, commercial
जाहिरात देणे advertise
जाहिरातबाजी advertising
जाहीर करणे announce, declare, issue
जिंकणारा winning
जिंकणे conquer, win
जिज्ञासू curious, inquisitive
जिना staircase, stairs
जिप्सी gypsy
जिराफ giraffe
जिरे cumin
जिल्हा district
जिवंत alive, lively
जिवलग intimate
जिवावर उदार होऊन desperately
जीभ tongue
जीवजंतू creature
जीवन life
जीवनशैली lifestyle
जीवनसत्त्व vitamin
जीवनावश्यक वस्तू supplies
जीवरक्षक lifeguard, life-saving
जीवरक्षक नौका lifeboat
जीवरसायन शास्त्र biochemistry

जीवशास्त्र biology	ज्ञान knowledge	झोपेची गोळी sleeping pill
जीवाणू bacteria	ज्ञानकोश encyclopaedia	झोपेत चालण्याची क्रिया
जुगार gambling	ज्ञानी knowledgeable	sleepwalk
जुगार खेळणे gamble	ज्याचा whose	झोळी sling
जुगारी gambler	ज्या-ज्या वेळी whenever	टंकण यंत्र typewriter
जुना old	ज्यावेळी as	टंकलेखक typist
जुनाजाणता veteran	ज्येष्ठ eldest	टकटक आवाज knock
जुनाट chronic	ज्येष्ठ नागरिक senior	टक लावून पाहणे gaze
जुनाट वळणाची व्यक्ती stuffy	citizen	टक्कर collision, crash
जुना सैनिक veteran	ज्योतिषशास्त्र astrology	टक्कर होणे collide
जुनी म्हण saying	ज्वाला flame	टक्कल पडलेला bald
जुन्या पढतीचे old-fashioned	ज्वालाग्राही flammable	टक्के per cent
जुळणे fit in, match	ज्वालामुखी volcano	टक्केवारी percentage
जुळवून घेणे adapt, adjust	ज्वाळा blaze	टपरी kiosk, shed
जुळे twin	झटका seizure, stroke	टपाल mail, post
जे काही असेल ते whatever	झपाटून madly	टपाल कार्यालय post office
जेट विमान jet	झांजा cymbals	टपालखर्च postage
जेथे where	झाकण cover, cover charge,	टपालपत्त्यांची यादी mailing
जेमतेम barely, mere	lid, top	list
जेवण meal	झाकणे cover	टपाल पेटी postbox
जेवणाची वेळ mealtime	झाकले जाणे go in	टपालवाहक पुरुष postman
जेवणातला मुख्य पदार्थ main	झाड tree	टपालवाहक स्त्री postwoman
course	झाडणे sweep	टपाल सूची क्रमांक
जेव्हा as	झाडाचे पान leaf	postcode
जैवमितिक biometric	झाडू broom	टपालाने पाठविणे mail
जैवरासायनिक अभ्यास	झारी watering can	टपालाने पाठवून देणे send off
biochemistry	झिप उघडणे unzip	टवका chip
जैविक biological	झुकणे bend, bow, lean	टांकसाळ mint
जोखीम risk	झुकवणे tip	टांगलेला कापडी बिछाना
जोड supplement	झुडपांचे कुंपण hedge	hammock
जोडणे attach, fix, link	झुडूप bush, shrub	टाईप करणे type
जोडपे couple	झुरळ cockroach	टाका stitch
जोडरेघ hyphen	झुलती खुर्ची rocking chair	टाकाऊ पदार्थ rubbish
जोडा match	झेंडा flag	टाकी tank
जोडी couple, pair	झेंडू marigold	टाके घालणे stitch
जोडीदार partner	झेलणे catch	टाच heel
एकत्र काम करणे	झोकांड्या देत चालणे stagger	टाचणी pin
collaborate	झोके घेणे swing	टाचणीने भोके पाडणे prick
जोडून ठेवलेली चादर fitted	झोप sleep	टायरच्या आतील ट्यूब inner
sheet	झोपडपट्टी slum	tube
जोपर्यंत till	झोपडी hut	टायरमध्ये झालेले छिद्र
जोर stress	झोपणे sleep	puncture
जोराने heavily	झोपण्याची वेळ bedtime	टाळणे avoid, skip
जोराने फाडणे rip	झोपलेला asleep	टाळ्यांचा गजर applause
जोराने फेकणे fling	झोपाळू sleepy	टाळ्या वाजवणे applaud, clap

टिकणे last	ठिपके spot	डोळे तिरळे करून पाहणे
टीका criticism	ठिबकणे drip	squint
टीका करणे criticize	ठीक आहे all right, okay	डोळे मिचकावणे wink
टॅक्सी cab, taxi	ठीक! OK!	डोळ्यांवर पट्टी बांधणे
टॅक्सी चालक taxi driver	ठीक! okay	blindfold
टेकडी hill	ठेकेदार contractor	डोळ्यांवर बांधलेली पट्टी
टेकडीच्या शिखराकडे uphill	ठेला stall	blindfold
टेकड्यांवरून भटकणे hill-	ठेव deposit	डोळ्याची बाहुली pupil
walking	ठेवणे keep, lay, put	डोळ्यातील बुबूळ iris
टेनिस खेळाडू tennis player	ठोकळा block	डौलदार graceful
टेबलवर घालायचे कापड	ठोका beat	ड्रम वाजविणारा drummer
tablecloth	ठोठावणे knock	ढकलणे push
टॉन्सिल्स tonsils	डबके puddle	ढकलायची खुर्ची pushchair
टॉवेल towel	डबा carton, tin	ढग cloud
टोक point, tip	डबाबंद tinned	ढगळ loose
टोचणे pierce, poke	डबी case	ढगांनी भरलेले आकाश
टोचण्याची क्रिया piercing	डाग dirt, mark, smudge,	overcast
टोचलेले pierced	spot, stain	ढगाळ cloudy
टोपणनाव nickname,	डाग घालवणारे रसायन stain	ढाल shield
pseudonym	remover	ढासळणे relapse
टोपली basket	डाग पडणे stain	ढिला loose, slack
टोपी cap	डाळिंब pomegranate	ढीग heap, pile, stack
टोळासारखा एक कीटक	डावखुरी व्यक्ती left-handed	ढेकर burp
cricket	डावपेच tactics	ढेकर देणे burp
टोळी gang	डावीकडे left	ढोंग pretext
ट्यूब tube	डावी बाजू left	ढोंग करणे pretend
ट्रक truck	डावे पक्ष left-wing	ढोसणे poke
ट्रक चालक truck driver	डाव्या बाजूचे left-hand	तंतू fibre
ट्रॅक्टर tractor	डास mosquito	तंतूमय काच fibreglass
तबक tray	डिजिटल घड्याळ digital	तंतोतंत precise
ट्रेन train	watch	तंत्र technique
ठक thug	डुक्कर pig	तंत्रज्ञ mechanic, technician
ठकवणे bluff	डुलकी nap, snooze	तंत्रज्ञान technology
ठणकणे throb	डुलकी घेणे doze, snooze	तंत्रज्ञानविषयक technological
ठरविणे decide	डुलकी लागणे doze off	तंदुरुस्त नसलेला unfit
ठराव resolution	डेन्मार्क Denmark	तंबाखू tobacco
ठराविक कामगिरी	डोंगराळ mountainous	तंबाखूचे दुकान tobacconist
assignment	डोंब कावळा raven	तंबू tent
ठसा उमटवणे mark	डोकावणे browse	तकलादू fragile
ठार मारणे kill	डोके head	तक्ता chart, table
ठिकाण location, place,	डोकेदुखी headache	तक्रार complaint, grouse
position, venue	डोक्याला बांधण्याचा रुमाल	तक्रार करणे complain
ठिगळ patch	headscarf	तज्ज्ञ expert
ठिगळ लावलेले patched	डोलखुर्ची rocking chair	तटरक्षक coastguard
ठिणगी spark	डोळा eye	तटस्थ neutral

तडजोड compromise	तळणे fry	ताबडतोब immediately
तडा crack, fracture	तळण्याचा तवा frying pan	ताबा custody, possession
तडा गेलेला cracked	तळमजला ground floor	ताबा घेणे occupy
तडा जाणे crack	तळमजल्यावरचा downstairs	तार string, telegram, wire
तणाव strain	तळलेला fried	तारा star
तणावग्रस्त tense, uptight	तळहात palm	तारीख date
तणावरहित relaxed	तळे pond, pool	तारुण्याचा काळ youth
तत्त्व principle	तवा pan	तार्किक logical
तत्त्वज्ञान philosophy	तसराळे basin	तालवाद्य percussion
तत्त्वतः virtual	तस्कर smuggler	तालिका catalogue
तथापि however,	तस्करी smuggling	तालीम rehearsal
nevertheless, though	तस्करी करणे smuggle	तालीम करणे rehearse
तपकिरी brown	तह truce	ताळेबंद balance sheet
तपकिरी केस auburn	तहान thirst	तावदान window pane
तपकिरीसर तांबडा maroon	तहानलेली व्यक्ती thirsty	तास hour
तपशील detail	तांत्रिक mechanical,	तासागणिक hourly
तपशीलवार detailed	technical	तासिका lesson
तपास investigation	तांत्रिक ज्ञान know-how	तिकीट ticket
तपासणी check-up, trial	तांबडा समुद्र Red Sea	तिकीट कार्यालय ticket office
तपासणे examine, inspect	तांबे copper	तिकीट देणारे यंत्र ticket
तफावत contrast	ताजा fresh, last	machine
तबक tray	ताजेतवाने करणारे refreshing	तिखटमिठाचा savoury
तबकडी disc	ताजेतवाने करणे freshen up	तिचा hers
तबेला stable	ताटे पुसायचा कपडा tea towel	तिजोरी chest, safe
तब्येतीतील सुधारणा recovery	ताठर inflexible	तिटकारा loathe
तमालपत्र bay leaf	ताण आणणे strain	तितरपक्षी pheasant
तयार prepared, ready	ताणणारे stretchy	तिने स्वतः herself
तयार करणे make, prepare	ताणणे stretch	तिप्पट करणे treble
तयार केलेली दुसरी प्रत	ताणतणाव tension	तिरपा diagonal
reproduction	ताणतणाव असलेले strained,	तिरस्कार करणे despise
तयारी preparation	stressed	तिला her
तरंगणे float	ताणतणावयुक्त stressful	तिळी मुले triplets
तरंगलांबी wavelength	तातडी urgency	तिसरा third
तरतूद करणे provide for	तातडीचे urgent	तिसरा हिस्सा third
तराफा float, raft	तात्काळ immediate, instant,	तिरस्करणीय obnoxious
तरुण young	instantly, promptly	तिहेरी triple
तरुण मनुष्य lad	तात्पुरता provisional	ती her, she
तरुणी lass	तात्पुरते temporary	तीन three
तर्कनिष्ठ rational	ताप fever	तीनचाकी सायकल tricycle
तर्कशुद्ध logical	तापदायक annoying	तीव्र intense, sharp
तर्जनी index finger	तापनियंत्रक thermostat	तीव्रता degree
तलवार sword	तापमान temperature	तीव्र दुःख grief
तलाव lake	तापमापक thermometer	तीव्र प्रतिक्षिप्त क्रिया reflex
तळ base, bottom	तापवणे warm up	तीव्र भीती panic, phobia
तळघर basement, cellar	ताफा convoy	तीस thirty

तुकडा piece
तुकडे करणे cut up
तुकडे करणे/होणे smash
तुकडे तुकडे करणे rip up, tear up
तुकड्यांमध्ये विभागणे apart
तुझा your, yours
तुटणे break
तुटपुंजा scarce
तुटवडा shortage, shortfall
तुतारी trumpet
तुफानी वावटळ tornado
तुमचा your, yours
तुम्ही स्वतः yourselves
तुरुंग prison
तुरुंग अधिकारी prison officer
तुरुंगात अडकवून ठेवणे detention
तुरुंगात टाकणे jail
तुरुंग jail
तुलना comparison
तुलना करणे compare
तुलना करण्याजोगा comparable
तुलनात्मकरीत्या comparatively, relatively
तूट deficit
तूळ रास Libra
तू स्वतः yourself
तृणधान्याचे रोप cereal
ते they, those
तेजस्वी bright
तेथे there
तेरा thirteen
तेरावा thirteenth
तेल oil
तेल टाकणे oil
तेलविहीर oil well
तेलशुद्धिकरण कारखाना oil refinery
तेव्हा पासून since
ते स्वतःच themselves
तैलस्फटिक amber
तो he
तोंड mouth

तोंड दाखवणे show up
तोंडी oral
तोकडा skimpy
तोचतोपणा असलेले repetitive
तोटा disadvantage
तोड match
तोडणे break up, pick
तोतरे बोलणे stammer, stutter
तोपर्यंत till
तोल balance
तो स्वतः himself
त्यांचा theirs
त्यांचा their
त्यांना them
त्या ऐवजी instead, instead of
त्याग करणे abandon, ditch
त्याच वेळी while
त्याचा his
त्याचा its
त्याचे स्वतःचे itself
त्या नंतर then
त्यानंतर afterwards
त्यानुसार accordingly
त्याला him
त्या वेळी then
त्रास trouble
त्रासदायक unpleasant
त्रास देणारा troublemaker
त्रास देणे annoy, disturb
त्रिकोण triangle
त्रिकोणी आकाराचे वाद्य triangle
त्रिमितीय three-dimensional
त्रुटी flaw
त्वचा skin
काचफोड blister
त्वचेवरील डाग zit
त्वचेवरील राप tan
त्वरित quickly
थंड cold, cool
थंड करणे chill
थकबाकी arrears
थकलेला tired

थकविणारे tiring
थडगे grave, tomb
थडग्यावरील चिरा gravestone
थर layer
थरकाप उडणे shudder
थरथर कापणे shiver, tremble
थरथरणारा shaky
थरार thrill
थरारक thrilling
थरारक अनुभव देणारा thriller
थर्मास flask
थवा flock
थांबणे stay, stop
थांबण्याची क्रिया stop
थांबवणे stop
थांबा halt
थापा मारणे bluff
थारोळे pool
थाळी dish, plate
थुंकणे spit
थुंकी spit
थुलथुलीत flabby
थेट direct, directly
थोटूक stub
थोटूक चुरगळणे stub out
थोडक्यात shortly
थोडा अंश bit
थोडा वेळ वाट पहाणे hang on
थोडेसे briefly, slightly
थोड्या वेळापूर्वी shortly
दंगल riot
दंगल करणे riot
दंड fine
दंडगोल cylinder
दंडाधिकारी magistrate
दंतकथा legend
दंतविषयक dental
दंतवैद्य dentist
दक्ष careful
दक्षिणकडे जाणारा southbound
दक्षिण दिशा south
दक्षिण ध्रुव South Pole
दक्षिणेकडील south, southern

दक्षिणेकडे south
दगड rock, stone
दगडाची खाण quarry
दगडी कोळसा coal
दडपण inhibition
दडपणाखाली असलेली व्यक्ती edgy
दडपशाही करणे bully
दणकट काठी वा दांडा staff
दत्तक adopted
दत्तक घेणे adopt
दत्तक घेण्याची क्रिया adoption
दसर satchel
दफनभूमी cemetery, graveyard
दबाव influence
दबाव आणणे manipulate, pressure
दबाव टाकणे influence
दमट humid, moist
दमटपणा moisture
दमलेला exhausted
दमा asthma
दयनीय pathetic
दयनीयता austerity
दया mercy, pardon, pity
दया करणे pity
दयाळू kind
दयाळूपणा kindness
दर per
दरम्यान between, during, meantime, meanwhile
दररोज daily
दररोज प्रवास करणे commute
दरवर्षी annually
दरवाजा door
दरवाजाची घंटा doorbell
दरवाजाची मूठ door handle
दरी valley
दरोडा robbery
दरोडेखोर robber
दर्जा grade, quality, rank, standard

दर्जा देणे rate
दर्जेदार classic
दर्शनी भाग hallway
दर्शविणे indicate, point
दलदल marsh
दलदलीचा प्रदेश bog, swamp
दलाल broker
दलाली commission
दळणवळण communication
दळणे grind
दवाखाना clinic
दशक decade
दशमान decimal
दशमान पद्धती metric
दशलक्ष million
दहशतवाद terrorism
दहशतवादी terrorist
दहशतवादी हल्ले terrorist attack
दहा ten
दहावा tenth
दहावा भाग tenth
दही yoghurt
दांडा rod
दांताळे rake
दाई nanny
दाखवणे show
दाखविणे point
दाखवून देणे show
दागदागिने jewellery
दागदागिन्यांचे दुकान jeweller
दागिने jewel
दाट/खोळंबा झालेला jammed
दाटीवाटी congestion
दाढी beard
दाढी असलेला bearded
दाढी करणे shave
दाढी न केलेला unshaven
दाणे grain
दात tooth
दातकोरणे toothpick
दात घासण्याचा ब्रश toothbrush

दातदुखी toothache
दात विचकून गुरगुरणे snarl
दाता donor
दातांना लावायची पेस्ट toothpaste
दान करणे donate
दानशूर generous
दाब pressure
दाबणे press
दाबून ठेवलेल्या भावना inhibition
दालचिनी cinnamon
दावा claim
दावा करणे claim
दावा प्रपत्र claim form
दाह inflammation
दाहकारक inflamed
दिखाऊपणा show off
दिखाऊपणा करणे show off
दिग्दर्शक director
दिनदर्शिका calendar
दिमाखदार magnificent
दिलासा देणारे reassuring
दिलासा देणे reassure
दिवस day
दिवसाची वेळ daytime
दिवा lamp
दिवाणखाना hall, living room, sitting room
दिवाळखोर bankrupt
दिशा direction
दिशाभूल करणारे misleading
दिसणे appear, look
दीपस्तंभ lighthouse
दीर brother-in-law
दीर्घ long
दीर्घकाळपर्यंत longer
दीर्घ झोप oversleep
दीर्घ मिठी cuddle
दुःखाने sadly
दुकान shop, store
दुकानदार shopkeeper
दुकानात काम करणारा shop assistant

दुकानातून वस्तू चोरणे shoplifting

दुःख misery, regret

दुःखकारक wrench

दुःखद grim, nasty, tragic

दुःखद घटना tragedy

दुःखदायक negative

पश्चाताप वाटणे regret

दुखरा sore

दुखावणे offend

दुःखी heartbroken, miserable, sad, sorry, unhappy

दुग्धालय dairy

दुग्धोत्पादने dairy produce, dairy products

दुचाकी bike

दुडक्या चालीने चालणे trot

दुधाचे दात येणे teethe

दुपदरी रस्ता dual carriageway

दुपार afternoon

दुपारचे जेवण lunch

दुपारच्या जेवणाची वेळ lunchtime

दुपारच्या जेवणाची सुट्टी lunch break

दुपारपासून मध्यरात्रीपर्यंतची वेळ p.m.

दुप्पट होणे double

दुभाषी interpreter

दुय्यम कंपनी subsidiary

दुय्यम दर्जाचे second class

दुराग्रही fanatic

दुराभिमानी chauvinist

दुरुस्त करणे mend, repair

दुरुस्ती correction, repair

दुरुस्ती संच repair kit

दुर्गंधी odour, stink

दुर्गंधीयुक्त smelly

दुर्गंधी येणे stink

दुर्घटना mishap

दुर्दैव misfortune

दुर्दैवाने unfortunately

दुर्दैवी unlucky

दुर्बिण binoculars, telescope

दुर्मीळ rare

दुर्लक्ष neglect

दुर्लक्ष करणे ignore, neglect

दुर्लक्षित neglected, unattended

दुष्काळ drought, famine

दुष्कृत्य करण्यातील साथीदार accomplice

दुष्ट evil, spiteful, vicious, wicked

दुष्परिणाम side effect

दुष्प्राप्य scarce

दुसऱ्या ठिकाणी जाणे move

दुसऱ्या बाजूला beyond, past

दुसरा another, second

दुसरा other

दुसरा वर्ग second class

दुसरे म्हणजे secondly

दुःस्वप्न nightmare

दुःस्वास करणारा unfriendly

दुहेरी double

दूध milk

दूध काढणे milk

दूधपावडर baby milk

दूर apart, far

दूर अंतरावरील distant

(दूरगामी) वाईट परिणाम repercussions

दूरचे न दिसणारा short-sighted

दूर जाणे go away

दूरदर्शन संच television, telly, TV

दूरध्वनी telephone

दूरध्वनी करणे phone

दूरध्वनी क्रमांक phone number

दूरध्वनी ग्राहकांची सूची telephone directory

दूरनियंत्रक remote control

बाजूला ठेवणे exclude

दूरवर away

दूरवरचा remote

दूरवरचा कष्टाचा प्रवास tramp

दूरवरून ओळखणे pick out

दूरसंचरण telecommunications

दृक् visual

दृग्गोचर visible

दृग्गोचरता visibility

दृढनिश्चयी determined

दृश्य scene

दृश्यमान visible

दृष्टिकोन attitude, outlook, standpoint, viewpoint

दृष्टिक्षेप glance

दृष्टिक्षेप टाकणे glance

दृष्टी eyesight

दृष्टीस पडणे spot

देऊ करणे offer

देऊन टाकणे part with

देऊळ temple

देकार offer

देखणा handsome

देखभाल maintenance

देखरेख करणे supervise

देखावा scenery

देणे give, hand, pass

देणे असणे owe

देण्यासाठी पैसे काढणे debit

देय payable

देयक bill

देव God

देवदूत angel

देवमासा whale

(देवाला) भजणे worship

देश country, state

देशभक्त patriotic

देशांमधील करार treaty

देशबाहेर घालवून देणे deport

देहदंड execution

देहांत शासन करणे execute

दैनंदिन काम routine

दररोज daily

दैनंदिन प्रवासी commuter

दैनंदिनी diary

दैव fate

दैवी supernatural

दोघेही **both**
दोन **two**
दोनदा **twice**
दोन्ही **both**
दोन्ही बाजूंची एकसमानता **symmetrical**
दोर **rope**
दोरी **string**
दोष **defect, drawback, shortcoming, vice**
दोष काढणे **pick on**
दोषारोप **blame**
दोषारोप ठेवणे **blame**
दोहोंपैकी कोणताही एक **either**
दौऱ्याचा कार्यक्रम **itinerary**
दौरा **tour**
दौरा करणे **tour**
द्रवपदार्थ **liquid**
द्रवीभवन **condensation**
द्राक्षाची वेल **vine**
द्राक्षे **grape**
द्रावक **solvent**
द्रावण **lotion**
द्वारपाल **porter**
द्विदल धान्ये **pulses**
द्विधा मन:स्थिती **dilemma**
द्विबिंदुचिन्ह **colon**
द्विभाषी **bilingual**
द्वीपकल्प **peninsula**
द्वेष **hatred, spite**
द्वेष करणे **hate, spite**
द्वेषयुक्त **malicious**
धक्कादायक **outrageous, shocking**
धक्कादायक अनुभव **shock**
धक्का वा ठोकर **bump**
धडक **dash**
धडकणे **crash**
धडधडणे **throb**
धडधडीत **gross**
धडपडणे **stumble**
धडा **lesson**
धणे **coriander**
धनगर **shepherd**

घनफळ **volume**
धनवान **wealthy**
धनादेश **cheque**
धनादेश पुस्तिका **chequebook**
धनु रास **Sagittarius**
धनुर्वात **tetanus**
धनुष्य **bow**
धन्यवाद! **thanks!**
धबधबा **cataract, waterfall**
धमकी देणारा **threatening**
धमकी देणे **threaten**
धमनी **artery**
धरण **dam**
धर्म **religion**
धर्मशाळा **monastery**
धर्मशास्त्र **theology**
धर्मादाय संस्था **charity**
धार्मिक विधी/कर्मकांड **ritual**
धसमुसळेपणा **roughly**
धागा **thread**
धागादोरा **clue**
धाड **raid**
धाडकन उघडणे **snap**
धाड टाकणे **raid**
धाडकन बंद करणे **slam**
धातू **metal**
धातूचा डबा **canister**
धातूची किंवा लाकडाची बादली **pail**
धातूच्या सळयांचे कुंपण **railings**
धान्य **grain**
धामधूम **activity**
धारदार **sharp**
धार्मिक **religious**
धार्मिक यात्रा **pilgrimage**
धाव **run**
धावणे **run**
धावण्याची शर्यत **running**
धावपटू **runner**
धावा! मदत करा! **help**
धिक्कार करणे **condemn**
धीट **courageous**
धीर **patience**

धुके **fog, mist**
धुके असलेले **misty**
धुके भरलेले **foggy**
धुडकावून लावणे **turn down**
धुणे **wash, washing**
धुराचा लोट **fumes**
धुराडे **chimney, exhaust**
धुलाई यंत्र **washing machine**
धून **melody**
धूमकेतू **comet**
धूम्रपान **smoking**
धूम्रपान करणारी व्यक्ती **smoker**
धूर **smoke**
धूर येणे **smoke**
धूर्त **cunning**
धूळ **dust**
धूळ झटकणे **dust**
धूळ साचलेला **dusty**
धैर्य **courage, nerve**
धोका **danger, threat**
धोकादायक **dangerous, risky**
धोका पत्करणे **risk**
धोरण **strategy**
धोरणात्मक **strategic**
ध्यानधारणा **meditation**
ध्येय **cause**
ध्रुवीय **polar**
ध्वनिफीत **cassette, tape**
ध्वनिमुद्रण **recording**
ध्वनिमुद्रण यंत्र **tape recorder**
ध्वनिवर्धक **loudspeaker**
नंतर **after, later**
नंदनवन **paradise**
नऊ **nine**
नकली **fake**
नकार **refusal**
नकार देणे **refuse**
नकारात्मक **negative**
नकाराधिकार **veto**
नकाशा **layout, map**
नकाशापुस्तिका **atlas**

नको असलेली पत्रे junk mail
नक्कल imitation
नक्कल करणे copy, imitate, mimic
नख fingernail
नखांची कानस nailfile
नगरपरिषदेचे मुख्यालय town hall
नगररचना आयोजन town planning
नगरसेवक councillor
नग्न naked, nude
नजर look
नजरचुकीने accidentally
नजरचूक oversight
नडगी shin
न तुटणारे unbreakable
नत्रवायू nitrogen
नदी river
नफा profit
नमस्कार hello!
बरे आहे, नमस्कार! farewell!
नमुना example, format, model, sample
नमुनेदार classic, typical
नमुन्याबरहुकूम बनविणे model
न मोडणारे unbreakable
नम्र humble
नरक hell
नरम soft
नरसाळे funnel
नर्तक dancer
नर्स nurse
नलिकामार्ग pipeline
नळ pipe, tap
नळजोडणी करणारा plumber
नळजोडणीचे काम plumbing
नळी pipe, tube
नखवा green
नवजात newborn
नवरदेव groom
नवरा bridegroom
नवरी bride
नववर्ष New Year

नववा ninth
नवशिक्या beginner
नवा new
नवा कोरा brand-new
नवागत newcomer
नवी कल्पना innovation
नवीन new
नवीन बाबीची सुरुवात introduction
नवी पद्धत innovation
नव्वद ninety
नशीब luck
नशीबवान lucky
नष्ट करणे destroy
न संपणारे endless
नांगर plough
नांगरणे plough
नाऊमेद करणे discourage
नाक nose
नाक खुपसणारी व्यकी nosy
नाकतोडा grasshopper
नाकपुड्या nostril
नाकातील रक्तस्राव nosebleed
नाकामागील पोकळी sinus
नाकारणे deny, reject, rule out, turn down
नाकारता न येणारा undeniable
नाखुषीने reluctantly
नाखूष reluctant
नागरिक citizen, civilian
नागरिकत्व citizenship
नागरी संस्कृती civilization
नागरी हक्क civil rights
नाचणे dance
नाजूक delicate, fragile, tender
नाटक drama, play
नाटककार playwright
नाट्यगृह theatre
नाट्यमय dramatic
नाडी lace, pulse
नाणे coin
नात granddaughter
नातवंड grandchild

नाताळ Christmas, Xmas
नातू grandson
नाते relation
नातेवाईक relative
नातेसंबंध relationship
नादुरुस्त होणे break
नाभी navel
नाम noun
नामनिर्देश nomination
नामनिर्देशन करणे nominate
नायक hero
नायिका heroine
नारळ coconut
नारिंगी रंगाचे orange
नाव name
नाव घोषित करणे nominate
नावड असणे dislike
नावतौकिक reputation
नावीन्यपूर्ण innovative
नाश करणे wreck
नाशपती pear
नाश्ता snack
नासधूस करणारा devastating
नास्तिक atheist
नाही no
नाहीतर otherwise
नाहीतरी anyway
नाहीसे होणे disappear, vanish
निःश्वास sigh
निःश्वास टाकणे sigh
निःसंशय certain
निकड urgency
निकष criterion
निकृष्ट lousy
निघून जाणे get out
नितंब hip
नित्य सराव करणे practise
नित्याचा व्यवहार practice
निदर्शक demonstrator, indicator
निदर्शने demo
निदान diagnosis
निदानाश insomnia

निधी funds
नि:पक्षपाती impartial
निपज करणे breed
निबंध essay
नियंत्रण check, clutch, control
नियंत्रित करणे control
नियतकालिक magazine
नियती destiny
नियम regulation, rule
नियमित regular
नियमितपणे regularly
नियोजन planning
निरंतर continually, continuous, eternal
निरक्षर illiterate
निरर्थक absurd, senseless
निराश disappointed, hopeless
निराश करणारे disappointing
निराश करणे disappoint, let down
निराशावादी pessimist, pessimistic
निरीक्षक inspector, observer
निरीक्षण करणे observe
निरुद्देश pointless
निरुद्देशी unintentional
निरुपद्रवी harmless
निरुपयोगी unhelpful, useless
निरोगी healthy
निरोध condom
निरोप message
निरोपासाठी हात हलवणे wave
निर्जंतुक sterile
निर्जंतुक करणे sterilize
निर्जलीकरण केलेले dehydrated
निर्णय decision
निर्णायक decisive
निर्दय ruthless
निर्देश करणे direct
निर्देशांक index
निर्दोष innocent

निर्धन broke
निर्माण करणे create
निर्माता producer
निर्माता maker, manufacturer
निर्मिती creation
निर्मूलन abolition
निर्मूलन करणे abolish
निर्यात export
निर्यात करणे export
निर्लज्ज blatant
निर्वाणीचा इशारा ultimatum
निर्वासित refugee
निर्वासित बेट desert island
निर्विवाद undisputed
निळा रंग blue
निवड selection
निवडक गोष्टींची यादी shortlist
निवड करणे choose
निवडणूक election
निवडणूकीतील प्रचंड विजय landslide
निवडणे pick, select, sort out
निवडलेला chosen
निवडुंग cactus
निवडून देणे elect
निवाऱ्याची जागा shelter
निवासी residential
निवृत्त retired
निवृत्त होणे retire
निवृत्ती retirement
निवृत्तीवेतन pension
निवृत्तीवेतनधारक pensioner
निव्वळ sheer
नि:शब्द speechless
निश्चित easy-going
निश्चित certain, definite
निश्चितता certainty
निश्चितपणे certainly, definitely
निषिद्ध prohibited, taboo
निषेध protest
निषेध करणे protest
निषेधार्ह taboo

निष्कर्ष conclusion, outcome
निष्कर्ष काढणे conclude
निष्काळजी careless
निष्काळजीपणे केलेले sloppy
निष्क्रिय passive
निष्ठा loyalty
निष्पन्न होणे turn out
निष्पाप innocent
निष्फळ break down, vain
नि:संशयपणे undoubtedly
निसटणे escape, get away
निसरडे slippery
निसर्ग nature
निसर्गदृश्य landscape
निसर्गाचा अभ्यासक naturalist
निस्तेज fade, faint
नीट कापणे trim
नीटनेटका decent
नीटनेटके neat, tidy
नीटनेटके tidy, tidy up
नीटनेटकेपणाने neatly
नीतिमत्ता morals
नीरस dull
नीलमणी sapphire
नुकतेच just
नुकसान loss
नुकसानभरपाई compensation
नुकसानभरपाई देणे compensate
नूतनीकरण करणे renovate
नृत्य dance, dancing
नेऊन देणे deliver
नेचे fern
नेता leader
नेतृत्व करणे head
नेत्रसुखद spectacular
नेमणूक appointment
नेमणूक करणे appoint
नेम धरून जोराने फेकणे pitch
नेहमी always, often
नेहमीचा standard
नेहमीचे usual

नेहमीचे नसणारे unusual
नेहमीपेक्षा जास्त वजनाचे overweight
नैतिक ethical, moral
नैराश्य depression, despair, disappointment
नैराश्य दूर करणारे औषध antidepressant
नैऋत्य दिशा southwest
नैसर्गिक natural
नैसर्गिक अवस्थेतील raw
नैसर्गिक देणगी लाभलेले gifted
नैसर्गिक प्रवृती instinct
नैसर्गिक वायू natural gas
नैसर्गिक स्रोत natural resources
नोंद record
नोंद असलेली यादी register
नोंद करणारे यंत्र recorder
नोंद करणे record
नोंदणी registration
नोंदणी करणे register
नोंदणी कार्यालय register office
नोंदणीकृत registered
नोकर servant
नोकरशाही bureaucracy
नोकरी duty, employment
नोकरीचा चाचणीचा कालावधी trial period
नोकरीवर ठेवणे employ
नौका boat, ferry
नौका वल्हविणे row
नौकेच्या शिडाचा खांब mast
नौदल navy
नौदलविषयक naval
न्याय justice
न्याय देणे judge
न्यायमंडळ jury
न्यायमूर्तींनी दिलेला निर्णय verdict
न्यायाधीश judge
न्यायालय court
न्यायालयात खटला भरणे sue

न्याहारी breakfast
न्हाणीघर bathroom
न्हावी barber
पंख wing
पंचा towel
पंजा paw
पंतप्रधान prime minister
पंथ sect
पंधरवडा fortnight
पंधरा fifteen
पंधरावा fifteenth
पकड pliers
पकडणे capture, catch, grab, grasp, hold
पकडून ठेवणे grip, hold on
पक्षपाती biased
पक्षी bird
पक्षीनिरीक्षण birdwatching
पक्ष्याचे पिल्लू chick
पगार pay, salary
पछाडलेला obsessed
पटणारा convincing
पटवून देणे convince
पटाशी chisel
पट्टा belt, strap, strip
पट्टी band
पट्टे असलेला stripy
पट्टे असलेले striped
पाठिंबा backing
पडण्याची क्रिया fall
पडदा curtain
पडवी shed
पडसे catarrh
पडून जाणे fall out
पणजी great-grandmother
पणजोबा great-grandfather
पतंग kite, moth
पतंग (कीटक) dragonfly
पती husband
पती किंवा पत्नी spouse
पता address
पत्ते playing card
पत्नी wife
पत्र letter
पत्रकार journalist

पत्रकार परिषद press conference
पत्रकारिता journalism
पत्रपेटी letterbox
पत्रव्यवहार correspondence
पत्रा tin
पथकर road tax, toll
पथदीप streetlamp
पद post
पदक medal
पदपथ footpath, pavement, walkway
पदपथाचा कठडा kerb
पदविका diploma
पदवीधर graduate
पदव्युत्तर postgraduate
पदार्थ substance
पढत manner, method, system, way
पढतशीर systematic
पद्य poetry
पन्नास fifty
पन्हाळ trough
परंतु but
परंपरा heritage, tradition
परंपरागत traditional
परंपरावादी conventional
परकीय alien
परकीय चलनदर exchange rate
परत करणे return
परत घेणे take back
परत देणे give back
परत पाठविणे send back
परतफेड repayment
परतफेड करणे repay
परत मिळणे get back
परत मिळालेले पैसे refund
परत येणे come back, return
परतावा return
परतीचे तिकीट day return
परदेश abroad
परदेशात overseas
परदेशी foreign, foreigner

परमानंद bliss, ecstasy
पररराष्ट्रनीतीसंबंधी diplomatic
परवडणे afford
परवडण्याजोगे affordable
परवानगी pass, permission
परवानगी देणे allow
परवाना licence, pass, permit
परस्पर mutual
परस्पर संबंध link
परांची scaffolding
पराभव defeat
पराभव करणे defeat
पराभव मान्य करणे give in
पराभूत करणे beat
परिकथा fairytale
परिगणक calculator
परिचयाचा known
परिचर्या गृह nursing home
परिचारिका nurse
परिचित familiar
परिच्छेद paragraph
परिणाम consequence, effect, result
परिणाम करणे/होणे affect
परिणामकारक effective
परिणामकारक रीतीने effectively
परिणामत: consequently
परिणाम/निष्पत्ती होणे result
परिपूर्णता perfection
परिपूर्ण complete, perfect
परिमाण gauge
परिवर्तन करणे convert, transform
परिवर्तनशील changeable, convertible
परिषद conference, council
परिसर surroundings
परिस्थिती circumstances, situation
परी fairy
परीक्षक examiner
परीक्षा exam, examination
परीक्षा नळी test tube

पर्यंत till, until
पर्यटक tourist
पर्यटन व्यवसाय tourism
पर्यवेक्षक invigilator, supervisor
पर्याय alternative, choice, option
पर्यायाने alternatively
पर्यायी alternative
पर्यायी मार्ग diversion
पर्यावरण environment
पर्यावरणविषयक environmental
पर्यावरणशास्त्र ecology
पर्यावरणस्नेही ecofriendly, environmentally friendly
पर्यावरणीय ecological
पर्वत mountain
पर्वतराजी range
पर्वतारोहण mountaineering
पर्वा करणे care
पलंग bed, cot
पलिकडे beyond
पलीकडे across
पळवून नेणे abduct
पळून जाणे flee, run away
पवनचक्की windmill
पवित्र holy, sacred
पवित्र स्थळ shrine
पशुवैद्य vet
पश्चातापाची भावना remorse
पश्चिम west
पश्चिमेला जाणारा westbound
पसंत करणे/असणे prefer
पसंती favour, preference
पसरणे spread, stretch
पसरवणे spread
पहाट dawn
पांगणे spread out
पांडा panda
पांढरा फळा whiteboard
पांढरा/शुभ white
पाईप लाईन pipeline
पाऊल foot, step
पाऊस rain

पाऊस पडणे rain
पाककृया recipe
पाककृयेवरील पुस्तक cookbook, cookery book
पाकोळी bat
पाच five
पाचवा fifth
पाठ back
पाठ करणे memorize
पाठदुखी backache
पाठपुरावा करणे go after
पाठमोरी back
पाठलाग chase
पाठलाग करणे chase
पाठविणे send
पाठिंबा support
पाठिंबा देणे support
पाठीचा कणा backbone
पाठीतील वेदना back pain
पाठीमागची बाजू backside
पाठीमागील rear
पाठीमागे after, behind
पाठीराखा defender
पाठीवर पोहणे backstroke
पाठ्यपुस्तक schoolbook, textbook
पाडून टाकणे knock down, pull down
पाणघोडा hippo, hippopotamus
पाणबुडी submarine
पाणमांजर otter
पाणी water
पाणी आत न येणारे showerproof
पाणी काढून टाकणे drain
पाणी घालणे water
पाण्याचा फवारा मारणे splash
पाण्याचा वेगवान प्रवाह rapids
पाण्याची झारी sprinkler
पाण्याची टाकी reservoir
पाण्याच्या पृष्ठभागाखाली underwater
पाण्यात सूर मारणे dive

पाण्यावरील तेलाचा तवंग oil slick
पातळ thin
पातळ कचऱ्या chips
पातळी level
पातीसहित असलेले कांदे spring onion
पाते blade
पात्र character
पात्र ठरणे qualify
पात्रता qualification
पात्रता credentials
पात्र/लायक/योग्य असणे deserve
पादचारी pedestrian
पादत्राण boot
पादत्राणांचे दुकान shoe shop
पाना spanner
पापणी eyelid
पापणीचा केस eyelash
पाय leg
पाय घाशीत चालणे shuffle
पायजमा pyjamas
पायदळ infantry
पायमोजा sock
पायरी doorstep
पाया foundations
पायाची नळी shin
पायाचे बोट toe
पायाने वल्हे हलविणे paddle
पायाभूत सुविधा infrastructure
पारंपरिक ritual
पारदर्शक transparent
पारपत्र passport
पारवा dove
पारा mercury
पारितोषिक award
पारिभाषिक शब्द term
पार्क park
पार्टी करणे party
पार्श्वभाग behind, bottom, bum
पार्श्वभूमी background
पाल lizard

पालक भाजी spinach
पाळणा cradle
पाळणाघर babysitting, crèche
पाळणाघर चालवणारी व्यक्ती babysitter
पाळणाघर चालवणे babysit
पाळीव tame
पाळीव प्राणी pet
पाव bread
पाव ठेवण्याची टोपली bread bin
पावडर powder
पावती receipt
पावलांचा आवाज footstep
पावलाचा ठसा footprint
पावले feet
पावसाची सर shower
पावसाळी rainy
पावांचा रोल bread roll
पावाची लादी loaf
पावाचे तुकडे breadcrumbs
पाश्चिमात्य western
पासून since
पाहणे look, see, watch
पाहुणा guest
पाहुण्यांची झोपायची खोली spare room
पिंगट केस fair
पिंजरा cage
पिंप barrel
पिकलेले ripe
पिच्छा पुरविणे persevere
पिच्छाड rear
पिढी generation
पिणे drink
पिण्याचे पाणी drinking water
पितळ brass
पिताशय gall bladder
पिताशयातील खडा gallstone
पियानोवादक pianist
पिळणे twist
पिळून काढणे squeeze
पिवळा yellow

पिशवी bag
पिष्टमय पदार्थ starch
पिसू flea
पिस्तूल pistol
पीए PA
पीक crop
पीछेहाट setback
पीठ flour
पीस feather
पुंड bully
पुडके package
पुढचा ahead
पुढची बाजू front
पुढाकार initiative
पुढील further, next
पुढे forward, further
पुढे चालू ठेवणे pursue
पुढे जाणे go ahead
पुढे झुकणे lean forward
पुढे ढकलणे postpone, put back, put off
पुढे पाठवणे forward
पुतळा statue
पुत्र son
पुदिना mint
पुनःपुन्हा repeatedly
पुनरावलोकन review
पुनरावृत्ती repeat
पुनरावृत्ती होणारा recurring
पुनरुज्जीवित करणे revive
पुनर्बांधणी करणे rebuild
पुनर्भारित करणे recharge
पुनर्भेट reunion
पुनर्रचना करणे restructure
पुनर्वापर करणे reuse
पुनर्वापर करता येण्याजोगे renewable
पुनर्विचार करणे reconsider
पुनर्विवाह करणे remarry
पुन्हा again
पुन्हा करणे redo, repeat
पुन्हा खेळवणे replay
पुन्हा गुंडाळणे rewind
पुन्हा बसणे resit
पुन्हा भरणे refill

पुन्हा मिळवणे regain
पुन्हा सजवणे redecorate
पुन्हा सुरू करणे renew, resume
पुरवठा supply
पुरवठादार supplier
पुरवणी supplement
पुरवणे supply
पुरविणे provide
पुराण mythology
पुराणकथा myth
पुराणमतवादी conservative
पुरातत्व शास्त्र archaeology
पुरातत्व शास्त्रज्ञ archaeologist
पुराभिलेख archive
पुरावा evidence, proof
पुरुष guy, male, man
पुरुषवादी chauvinist
पुरुषी masculine
पुरुषी वागणारी मुलगी tomboy
पुरेसा enough
पुष्टी confirmation
पुष्टी करणे confirm
पुष्पगुच्छ bouquet
पुष्पपराग pollen
पुसणे mop up, wipe
पुस्तक book
पुस्तकांचे कपाट bookcase, bookshelf
पुस्तकांचे दुकान bookshop
पुस्तकाचे पान page
पुस्तकातील खूण bookmark
पुस्तिका booklet
पू pus
पूज्य मानणे adore
पूर flood, flooding
पूर आणणे flood
पूरक complementary
पूर येणे flood
पूर्ण entire
पूर्ण उघडलेले wide
पूर्ण करणे fulfil
पूर्ण केलेले done

पूर्णतः fully
पूर्णपणे dead, entirely
पूर्ण विराम full stop
पूर्ण वेळ full-time
पूर्व आशिया Orient
पूर्व आशियाकडील oriental
पूर्वग्रह prejudice
पूर्वग्रह असलेली व्यक्ती prejudiced
पूर्वज ancestor, predecessor
पूर्व दिशा east
पूर्वसंध्या eve
पूर्वसुरी predecessor
पूर्वी ago, before
पूर्वीचा former
पूर्वीच्या कामगिऱ्या credentials
पूर्वीपासून चालू असणे go back
पूर्वेकडील east, eastern
पूर्वेकडे east
पूर्वेकडे जाणारा eastbound
पूल bridge
पृथ्वी earth, globe, world
पृष्ठभाग surface
पृष्ठमज्जारज्जू spinal cord
पेंगणारा drowsy
चित्रकला painting
पेंढा straw
पेचप्रसंग crisis
पेटवणे light
पेटी box, case
पेट्यांतून भरलेले सामान baggage
पेट्रोलची टाकी petrol tank
पेय drink
पेरू Peru
पेला cup
पेशा career, profession
पेशी cell
पेस्ट paste
पैज bet
पैज लावणे bet
पैलू aspect, dimension
पैशाचे पाकीट wallet

पैसे money
पैसे जमवणे club together
पैसे देणे pay
पैसे न मिळालेला unpaid
पैसे परत करणे refund
पैसे परत देणे pay back
पैसे वाया घालवणे squander
पॉलिनेशिया Polynesia
पोकळ hollow
पोकळी void
पोचपावती acknowledgement
पोचा dent
पोचा पाडणे dent
पोट abdomen, belly, stomach, tummy
पोटदुखी stomachache
पोटमाळा attic, loft
पोटरी calf
पोटात गोळा आणणारे nerve-racking
पोटातला coeliac
पोतेरे mop
पोपट parrot
पोरकट childish
पोरकट खोडी prank
पोलंड Poland
पोलका blouse
पोलाद steel
पोलीस cop, policeman
पोलीस अधिकारी police officer
पोलीस ठाणे police station
पोवळे coral
पोशाख dress
पोषक nutritious
पोषक घटक nutrient
पोषण nutrition
पोस्टाचे तिकीट stamp
पोस्टाने पाठविणे post
पोहणारी व्यक्ती swimmer
पोहणे swim
पोहण्याची क्रिया swimming
पोहताना घालावयाचे कपडे bathing suit

पोहोचणे get, get in, reach
पोहोचण्याचे ठिकाण destination
पौगंडावस्था adolescence
पौगंडावस्थेतील मूल adolescent
पौर्णिमा full moon
पौर्वात्य eastern, Far East
प्रकरण affair, case, chapter, episode, matter, topic
प्रकरणांशी संबंधित topical
प्रकल्प plant, project
प्रकार form, kind, pattern, sort, type
प्रकाश light
प्रकाशक publisher
प्रकाशन publication
प्रकाशमान light
प्रकाशित light
प्रकाशित करणे publish
प्रक्रिया process
प्रक्षुब्धता turbulence
प्रक्षेपण broadcast
प्रक्षेपित करणे broadcast
प्रगत advanced
प्रगत होणे develop
प्रगती progress
प्रचंड enormous, huge, mega, tremendous
प्रचार करणे canvass
प्रजाती species
प्रजासत्ताक republic
प्रणय romance
प्रणयरम्य romantic
प्रणाली system
प्रत copy
प्रतवारी assortment
प्रतिकार resistance
प्रतिकार करणे resist
प्रतिकूल harsh, hostile, unfavourable
प्रतिकृती replica
प्रतिक्रिया reaction
प्रतिक्रिया देणे/होणे react
प्रतिगामी closed

प्रतिजैविक antibiotic
प्रतिथयश promising
प्रतिध्वनि echo
प्रतिनिधित्व करणे represent
प्रतिनिधी agent, representative
प्रतिपिंड antibody
प्रतिबंधात्मक इंजेक्शन jab
प्रतिबिंब reflection
प्रतिबिंबित होणे reflect
प्रतिभा talent
प्रतिभावान talented
प्रतिमा image
प्रतिवादी defendant
प्रतिष्ठा dignity, prestige
प्रतिष्ठित prestigious
प्रतिसाद feedback, response
प्रतिसाद देणे respond
प्रतिस्पर्धी rival
प्रतीक्षा कक्ष waiting room
प्रतीक्षा यादी waiting list
प्रत्यारोपण transplant
प्रत्येक each, per
प्रत्येक गोष्ट everything
प्रत्येकजण everybody, everyone
प्रथम first
प्रथमतः firstly
प्रथम नाम first name
प्रथम श्रेणी first-class
प्रथमोपचार first aid
प्रथमोपचार पेटी first-aid kit
प्रथिने protein
प्रदर्शन display, exhibition, showing
प्रदर्शन करणे display
प्रदान करण्याची क्रिया presentation
प्रदूषण pollution
प्रदूषित polluted
प्रदूषित करणे pollute
प्रदेश region
प्रभरण charge
प्रभरण करणे charge

प्रभाग ward
प्रभाव impact, influence
प्रभावित करणे influence
प्रभावित झालेला impressed
प्रभुत्व मिळवणे master
प्रमाण degree, extent, proportion, quantity
प्रमाण/दर rate
प्रमाणपत्र certificate
प्रमाणात proportional
प्रमाणापेक्षा मोठा extortionate
प्रमाणे as
प्रमुख chief, head, primary
प्रयत्न attempt, effort, try
प्रयत्न करणे attempt, try
प्रयोग experiment
प्रयोगशाळा lab, laboratory
प्रवक्ता spokesman, spokesperson
प्रवक्ती spokeswoman
प्रवाशांचा मार्गदर्शक tour guide
प्रवास journey, travel, travelling
प्रवास करणे travel
प्रवास केलेले अंतर mileage
प्रवास सुरू करणे set off, set out
प्रवासाचे भाडे fare
प्रवासास निघणे depart
प्रवासी passenger, traveller
प्रवासी धनादेश traveller's cheque
प्रवाह current
प्रवीण good
प्रवेश admission
प्रवेश करणे enter
प्रवेश देणे admit
प्रवेशद्वार entrance
प्रवेशद्वारावरील फोन entry phone
प्रवेश शुल्क entrance fee
प्रवेशाचा हक्क admittance
प्रवेशास बंदी करणे lock out

प्रवेशिका entry
प्रशंसा compliment
प्रशंसा करणे appreciate, compliment
प्रशस्त extensive
प्रशस्त घर stately home
प्रशांत महासागर Pacific Ocean
प्रशासकीय administrative
प्रशासन administration
प्रशिक्षक coach, instructor, trainer
प्रशिक्षण training
प्रशिक्षण घेणे train
प्रशिक्षण पाठ्यक्रम training course
प्रशिक्षणार्थी trainee
प्रशिक्षित trained
प्रश्न question
प्रश्नचिन्ह question mark
प्रश्नमंजुषा quiz
प्रश्न विचारणे question
प्रश्न सोडवणे work out
प्रश्नावली questionnaire
प्रसंग event, incident, occasion
प्रसन्न sweet
प्रसाधनगृह toilet
प्रसाधनगृहात वापरायचा कागद toilet paper
प्रसार माध्यमे media
प्रसिद्ध कलाकार star
प्रसिद्धी fame, publicity
प्रसिद्धी देणारा कार्यक्रम promotion
प्रसूति रजा maternity leave
प्रसूति रुग्णालय maternity hospital
प्रसूतिपूर्व antenatal
प्रस्तरारोहण rock climbing
प्रस्ताव proposal
प्रस्तावित propose
प्रस्थान departure
प्रस्थान कक्ष departure lounge

प्राचार्य principal
प्राचीन ancient
प्राणघातक fatal, terminal
प्राणघातक/असाध्य रोगाने terminally
प्राणरक्षक life-saving
प्राणवायू oxygen
प्राणिशास्त्र zoology
प्राणिसंग्रहालय zoo
प्राणी animal
प्राण्यांचा बेकायदेशीर व्यापार poached
प्राण्यांची मिशी whiskers
प्राण्यांची वंशावळ pedigree
प्राण्यांचे मांस meat
प्रात्यक्षिक demonstration
प्राथमिक अवस्थेतील primitive
प्राथमिक शाळा primary school
प्रादेशिक regional
प्राधान्यक्रमाची गोष्ट priority
प्राध्यापक professor
प्राप्त करणारी व्यक्ती recipient
प्राप्त करणे achieve, obtain
प्राप्त होणे come in
प्रामाणिक conscientious, honest, sincere
प्रामाणिकपणा honesty
प्रामाणिकपणे honestly, sincerely
प्रायोजक sponsor
प्रायोजकत्व sponsorship
प्रायोजित करणे sponsor
प्रार्थना prayer
प्रार्थना करणे pray
प्रार्थनास्थळ shrine
प्रिय darling, dear
प्रियकर boyfriend
प्रेक्षक onlooker, spectator, viewer
प्रेक्षणीय स्थळे पाहणे sightseeing
प्रेत corpse
प्रेम love

प्रेम करणे love
प्रेमळ caring
प्रेमाचे ढोंग करणे flirt
प्रेमात पडणे fall for
प्रेमाने मिठी मारणे hug
प्रेयसी girlfriend
प्रेरणा motivation
प्रेरित motivated
प्रेषक sender
प्रोत्साहन cheer, incentive
प्रोत्साहित करणे cheer
प्रौढ adult, grown-up, mature
प्रौढ नसलेली व्यक्ती minor
प्रौढ विद्यार्थी mature student
प्रौढ शिक्षण adult education
प्लग काढून घेणे unplug
प्लग लावणे plug in
फक्त only
फट gap
फटका blow, hit
फटका मारणे hit, strike
फटाके fireworks
फडफडवणे flap
फरक difference, distinction, margin
फरक असणे vary
फरक करणे distinguish
फर fur
फरचा कोट fur coat
फरशी tile
फरो बेटे Faroe Islands
फलाट platform
फळ fruit
फळा blackboard
फळांची बाग orchard
फळाचा रस fruit juice
फळाची साल peel
फळी shelf
फवारा spray
फवारा मारणे spray
फसवणूक करणारी व्यक्ती cheat
फसवणे cheat
फसवणे deceive

फांदी branch
फाईलमध्ये ठेवणे file
फाटक gate
फाडणे tear
फायदा advantage, benefit
फायदा होणे benefit
फायदेशीर profitable
फार छान wonderful
फावडा spade
फावडे shovel
फावला वेळ spare time
फाशीची शिक्षा capital punishment
फासा clasp, dice
फिकट dull, light, pale
फिकट जांभळा रंग mauve
फिकट तपकिरी रंगाचे beige
फिकट होणे fade
फिजी Fiji
फिदीफिदी हसणे giggle
फिनलंड Finland
फिरता mobile
फिरता जिना escalator
फिरता पट्टा conveyor belt
फिरते घर mobile home
फिरून उघडणे unscrew
फिरायला जाणे walking
फीत lace, ribbon
फुंकर मारणे blow
फुंकायचे शिंग horn
फुगवता येण्याजोगी वस्तू inflatable
फुगा balloon, bubble
फुगून बसणे sulk
फुटणे blow up, break, burst, go off, split
फुप्फुस lung
फुरगटलेला sulky
फुरसतीचा/मोकळा वेळ leisure
फुलणे flower
फुलदाणी vase
फुलपाखरू butterfly
फुले विकणारा florist
फूटपट्टी ruler

फूटबॉलचा सामना football match
फूटबॉलपटू footballer, football player
फूल flower
फेकणे throw
फेकून देणे throw away, throw out
फेटाळणे dismiss
फेटाळून लावणे overrule
फेरफटका walk
फेरफार करणे alter
फेरी round
फेरीबोट car ferry
फोन phone
फोन करणे call, phone, ring, ring up
फोनचा नंबर फिरविणे dial
फोन ठेवून देणे hang up
फ्रान्स France
फ्रेंच French
बँकखाते bank account
बँक प्रभार bank charges
बँक विवरण bank statement
बँकेतील वरिष्ठ अधिकारी banker
बँकेतील शिल्लक bank balance
बंगला bungalow
बंडखोर rebellious
बंद off
बंद करणे close, seal, shut, shut down
बंद करणे किंवा मोडणे snap
बंद करण्याची वेळ closing time
बंदर dock, harbour, port
बंदिस्त अंगण yard
बंदी ban
बंदी घातलेला forbidden
बंदी घातलेले banned
बंदी घालणे ban, forbid
बंदुकीचा बार shot
बंदुकीच्या गोळ्या bullet
बंदूक gun, rifle

बंध bond
बंधन clutch, curb
बंब boiler
बकरा goat
बकल buckle
बक्षीस prize, reward
बक्षीस विजेता prizewinner
बक्षीस वितरण prize-giving
बगळा heron
बचत savings
बचत करणे save, save up
बछडा cub
बटन button
बटवडा delivery
बटाटा potato
बडबडगीत nursery rhyme
बडीशेपपासून बनवलेला पदार्थ aniseed
वढाई मारणे boast
बदक duck
बदल change, shift
बदलणारा variable
बदलणे change, replace
बदल न झालेले unchanged
बदललेली वस्तू replacement
बदला revenge
बदली शिक्षक supply teacher
बदली वस्तू substitute
बदाम almond
बद्धकोष्ठता असलेली व्यक्ती constipated
बधीर numb
बनवाबनवी fraud
बरंय... येतो आता goodbye!
बरगडी rib
बरणी jar
बरा/कुशल well
बरे आहे farewell!
बरोबर correct, precisely, right, true
बरोबरची खूण tick
बरोबरची खूण करणे tick
बरोबरी (उंचीने) level
बरोबरी करणे equal

बरोबरीच्या पातळीवर आणणे equalize

बर्फ ice

बर्फाचा गोळा snowball

बर्फाची पेटी icebox

बर्फाचे जोरदार वादळ blizzard

बलवान strong

बलात्कार rape

बलात्कार करणे rape

बलात्कारी rapist

बल्गेरिया Bulgaria

बळ force

बळी sacrifice, victim

बळी पडण्याजोगे vulnerable

बशी saucer

बस bus

बसचे तिकीट bus ticket

बसणे sit

बसथांबा bus stop

बसविणे set

बसस्थानक bus station

बहर blossom

बहिरा deaf

बहीण sister

बहुतेक almost

बहुधा mostly

बहुभाषाभिज्ञ linguist

बहुराष्ट्रीय कंपनी multinational

बहुसंख्य majority

बांगडा (एक मासा) mackerel

बांगलादेश Bangladesh

बांगलादेशी Bangladeshi

बांध embankment

बांधकाम construction

बांधकाम पाडून टाकणे demolish

बांधकाम व्यावसायिक builder

बांधणे build, construct, tie, tie up

बांधलेले अन्नपदार्थ packed lunch

बांबू bamboo

बाक bench

बाकडे bench

बाग garden

बागकाम gardening

बाजार market

बाजार संशोधन market research

बाजू side

बाजूने along

बाजूला aside, beside, next to, sideways

बाजूला ठेवून देणे put away

बाटली bottle

बाण arrow

बाणाचे चिन्ह arrow

बातमी news

बातमीदार reporter

बादली bucket

बाबा daddy

बायपास शस्त्रक्रिया bypass

बायबल Bible

बारकाईने पाहणे scan

बारा twelve

बारावा twelfth

बारीक fine, minute

बारीक तुकडे करणे mince

बालक baby

बालपण childhood

बालवाडी nursery, nursery school

बालसंगोपन childcare

बाल्कन Balkan

बासरी flute

बाहुली doll

बाहू arm

बाहेर out, out-of-doors, outside

बाहेर घालवणे expel

बाहेरची बाजू outside

बाहेरच्या बाजूस झुकणे lean out

बाहेर जाणारा outgoing

बाहेर पडणे get away

बाहेर पडण्याचा मार्ग exit, way out

बाह्य exterior, external

बिंदू dot

बिघडणे break down

बिघडलेला broken down

बिघडवणे mess up, spoil

बिजागरे hinge

बिजिंग Beijing

बिनकामाचा idle, rubbish, unhelpful

बिनकामी worthless

बिनबाह्यांचा sleeveless

बिनमहत्त्वाचा unimportant

बिनशर्त unconditional

बिल्ला badge

बिस्किट biscuit

बी seed

बीअरचा कारखाना brewery

बी. ए. BA

बीझी सिग्नल busy signal

बीट beetroot

बुजगावणे scarecrow

बुटका dwarf

बुडणे drown, sink

बुडबुडेयुक्त fizzy

बुडविणे dip

बुद्ध Buddha

बुद्धिबळ chess

बुद्धिमत्ता intelligence

बुद्धिमान brainy, brilliant, intelligent

बुद्धिमान व्यक्ती intellectual

प्रतिभा talent

प्रतिभावान talented

बुद्ध्यांक IQ

बुधवार Wednesday

बुरशी mould

बुरशी असलेले mouldy

बूट boot

बूड bottom

जादा आधार back up

बेंबी belly button

बेइमान unfaithful

बेकरीवाला baker

बेकायदेशीर illegal

बेकार unemployed

बेकारी unemployment
बेकारीभत्ता dole
बेघर homeless
बेचैन nervous, restless
बेजबाबदार irresponsible
बेट island
बेडकाची पिल्ले tadpole
बेडूक frog
बेड्या handcuffs
बेताल desperate
बेदाणा raisin, sultana
बेरीज sum
बेरीज करणे add, add up
बेरोजगार jobless
बेरोजगारी घोषित करणे
   sign on
बेलारूस Belarus
बेशुद्ध unconscious
बेशुद्ध पाडणे knock out
बेशुद्ध होऊन कोसळणे pass
   out
बेशुद्धी coma
बेसिन basin
बैल bull
बैलगाडी cart
बॉम्ब टाकणे bomb
बॉम्बफेक bombing
बोगदा tunnel
बोट finger
बोट दाखवणे point out
बोटाचा ठसा fingerprint
बोथट सुरी spatula
बोरूचे गवत reed
बोलघेवडी व्यक्ती talkative
बोलणी negotiations
बोलणी करणे negotiate
बोलणे say, speak, speech,
   talk, talk to
बोलणे बंद करणे shut up
बोली bid
बोली भाषा dialect
बोली लावणे bid
बोल्टचा नट nut
बौद्ध Buddhist
बौद्धिक intellectual

बौद्ध धर्म Buddhism
ब्रम्हांड universe
ब्रशने घासणे brush
ब्रह्मदेशी Burmese
ब्राझील Brazil
ब्रिटन Britain
ब्रिटिश British
ब्रिटिश विद्यापीठातील शिक्षक
   tutor
ब्रेक brake
ब्रेक लावणे brake
ब्लँकेट blanket
भंगणे split
भंगार junk
भक्कम firm
भक्ष्य prey
भग्नावशेष wreckage
भटकणे wander
भटका प्राणी stray
भटकी व्यक्ती migrant
भटक्या rambler
भडक bright
भडक भावनांचा soppy
भपकेदार fancy
भपकेदार पोषाख fancy
   dress
भयंकर fierce, gruesome,
   horrible, horrifying,
   revolting
भयपट horror film
भयभीत afraid,
   apprehensive
भयसूचक alarming
भयसूचक भावना alarm
भयाण spooky
भयानक awful, horrendous,
   repellent, repulsive,
   terrible
भयानकपणे terribly
भयावह अनुभव ordeal
- भर throughout
भरणे fill, fill in
भरती recruitment
भरपगारी paid
भरपूर plenty

भरपूर पगार असलेला
   well-paid
भरपूर विक्री होणारे पुस्तक
   bestseller
भरभराट prosperity
भरलेला full
भरवणे feed
भरीव solid
भलतेच होणे backfire
भविष्य वर्तवणे predict
भविष्य वर्तवण्याजोगे
   predictable
भविष्यातील future
भव्य grand
भस्म्यारोग bulimia
भांडण quarrel, scrap
भांडणे quarrel
भांडवल capital
भांडवलशाही capitalism
भांडे pot
भाऊ brother
भाग part, portion
भागधारक shareholder
भाग लावणे divide
भागीदार associate
भाचा/ पुतण्या nephew
भाची/ पुतणी niece
भाजणे bake, baking, grill
भाजलेला baked, grilled
भाजलेला मोठा बटाटा jacket
   potato
भाजलेले roast
भाजी vegetable
भाजी विक्रेता greengrocer
भाडे hire, rent, rental
भाडेकरू lodger, tenant
भाडेपट्टी lease
भाडेपट्टीने देणे lease
भाड्याची गाडी taxi
भाड्याने घेणे rent
भाड्याने देणे hire
भात rice
भाबडा naive
भार load
भारत India

भारतीय Indian
भारतीय महासागर Indian Ocean
भारोतोलक weightlifter
भारोतोलन weightlifting
भाला javelin
भावंडे siblings
भावना emotion, feeling
भावनाप्रधान sentimental, soppy
भावनिक emotional
भाषण address
भाषा language
भाषांतर translation
भाषांतर करणे translate
भाषांतरकार translator
भाषिक linguistic
भाष्य करणे comment
भिंग magnifying glass
भिंत wall
भिंतींना लावायचा चुना whitewash
भिकारी beggar
भिक्षु monk
भिजत ठेवणे soak
भिजलेला soaked
भिजून चिंब होणे drench
भित्तीपत्रक poster
भिन्न odd
भिरकावणे toss
भीती fear, fright, horror, scare
भीती दाखवणे intimidate
भीतीदायक scary
भीती वाटणे fear
भीषण appalling
भुंकणे bark
भुकटी powder
भुकेला hungry
भुकेलेली व्यकी ravenous
भुणभूण लावणे pester
भुतांनी झपाटलेले haunted
भुताटकी करणारी व्यकी sorcerer
भुयारी रस्ता subway

भुयारी रेल्वे underground
भुयारी रेल्वे स्थानक underground station
भुवई eyebrow
भुसा bran
भूक appetite, hunger
भूकंप earthquake
भूक न लागणारा anorexic
भूक न लागणे anorexia
भूखंड plot
भूगर्भशास्त्र geology
भूगोलशास्त्र geography
भूत ghost
भूतकाळ past
भूतकाळातील past
भू-मध्य समुद्र Mediterranean
भूमिका role
भूमिगत underground
भूलथापा bluff
भूलभुलैय्या maze
भेग crack
भेट visit
भेटकार्ड greetings card
भेटणे meet, see
भेटण्याचे संकेतस्थळ rendezvous
भेट देणे go round, visit
भेटवस्तू गुंडाळण्याचा कागद wrapping paper
भेटवस्तू gift, present
भेटवस्तूंचे कूपन gift voucher
भेटायला येणारा visitor
भेदाभेद discrimination
भोंगा horn, siren
भोक hole
भोक पाडणे drill
भोगणे (दुःख) undergo
भोपळा pumpkin
भोवताली around
भोवळ आल्यासारखे वाटणे dizzy
भोसकणे stab
भौतिकशास्त्र physics
भौतिकशास्त्रज्ञ physicist

भ्याड coward, cowardly
भ्रमणध्वनी mobile phone
भ्रष्ट corrupt
भ्रष्टाचार corruption
मंगळवार Tuesday
मंच stage
मंडळ board
मंत्र spell
मंत्रालय ministry
मंत्री minister
मंद slow
मंद उकळणे simmer
मंदिर temple
मंदी recession
मंदीचा हंगाम low season
मऊ soft
मकर रास Capricorn
मका maize
मक्का Mecca
मक्तेदारी monopoly
मक्याचे पीठ cornflour
मखमल velvet
मग then
मगर alligator, crocodile
मगूर rude
मच्छिमार fisherman
मच्छिमार होडी fishing boat
मजकूर text
मजबूत sound, strong
मजबूत करणे strengthen
मजबूतपणे strongly
मजबूत मोटरसायकल mountain bike
मजला floor
मजुरी/वेतन wage
मजकूर content
मजूर labourer
मजेशीर funny, great
मज्जातंतू nerve
मणका spine
मणी bead
मत comment, opinion, view, vote
मतदान poll

मतदारसंघ constituency, electorate
मतदारसंघातील जागा seat
मत देणे vote
मतप्रणाली ideology
मत्सरी envious, jealous, spiteful
मत्स्यालय aquarium
मथळा caption, headline
मदत assistance, help
मदत करणे help
मदत करण्यात तत्पर helpful
मद्य alcohol
मद्य न पिणारा teetotal
मद्य न प्यायलेला sober
मद्यपान केलेली व्यक्ती drunk
मद्यपानगृह bar
मद्यपी alcoholic
मद्ययुक्त alcoholic
मद्यरहित alcohol-free
मद्यविरहित पेय soft drink
मद्यार्कनिर्मिती कारखाना distillery
मध honey
मधमाशी bee
मधला intermediate
मधला काळ interval
मधील असणे belong
मधुचंद्र honeymoon
मधुमेह diabetes
मधुमेहसंबंधी diabetic
मधुमेही diabetic
मधून from
मधून जाणे go through
मधे समाविष्ट among
मध्य mid
मध्यंतर interval
मध्य पूर्व Middle East
मध्यम medium, modest
मध्यम आकाराचा medium-sized
मध्यममार्ग moderation
मध्यमवयीन middle-aged
मध्यमवर्गीय middle-class, moderate

मध्ययुग Middle Ages
मध्ययुगीन mediaeval
मध्यरात्र midnight
मध्यवर्ती central
मध्यवर्ती संकल्पना theme
मध्यस्थी arbitration
मध्यान्तर half-time
मध्यान्ह midday, noon
मध्यान्हपूर्व a.m.
मध्यावर halfway, middle
मध्ये between, in
मन mind, spirit
मनगट wrist
मन:चक्षूसमोर आणणे visualize
मनमोहक glamorous
मन वळवणे persuade
मन वळवील असे persuasive
मन शांत करणारे औषध tranquillizer
मनस्थिती spirits
मनाई करणे prohibit
मनाची अवस्था mood
मनात हेतू असणे mean
मनावर घेणे bother
मनुका plum, prune
मनुष्य bloke
मनुष्यनिर्मित man-made
मनुष्यबळ manpower
मनोबल morale
मनोरंजक entertaining
मनोरंजक विनोदी कार्यक्रम comedy
मनोरंजन उद्योग show business
मनोरा tower
मनोरुग्णालय mental hospital
मनोरुग्णालयातील रुग्ण inmate
मफलर muffler
ममताळू affectionate
ममतेने kindly
मयत late

मरणे die
मर्यादा limit, range
मर्यादित qualified
मलई cream
मलम ointment
मलमपट्टी bandage
मलमपट्टी करणे bandage
मला me
मळमळ nausea
मळलेला dirty
मवाळ moderate, moderation
मशीद mosque
मसाला spice
मसालेदार spicy
मसुदा draft
मसूर lentils
मस्करी करणे kid
महत्कृत्य achievement
महत्त्व importance, significance
महत्त्वपूर्ण crucial, vital
महत्त्वाकांक्षा ambition
महत्त्वाकांक्षी ambitious
महत्त्वाचा important
महत्त्वाचा major, momentous
महत्त्वाचा अधिकारी mandarin
महत्त्वाचे significant
महत्त्वाचे असणे matter
महत्त्वाचा क्षण critical
महत्त्वाचा क्षण landmark
महत्त्वाचे relevant
महसूल revenue
महाकाय giant
महाग dear
महान great
महापौर mayor
महाविद्यालय college
महाविद्यालयीन परिसर campus
महाविद्यालयीन शिक्षण further education
महाशय sir

महासागर ocean
महिना month
महिलांचे अंतर्वस्त्र slip
महिला खेळाडू sportswoman
महिला पोलीस policewoman
महिला वर्ग female
महोगनी लाकूड mahogany
मांजर cat
मांजराचे आनंदाने गुरगुरणे purr
मांजरीचे पिल्लू kitten
मांडी lap, thigh
मासाचा तुकडा chop
माकड monkey
मागची बाजू rear
मागच्या बाजूला backwards
मागणी demand
मागणी करणे demand
मागणी नोंदवण्याचा अर्ज order form
मागणे ask for
मागील back
मागील बाजू back
मागे back
मागे जाणे (काळ) go back
मागे राहणे lag behind
मागे रेंगाळणारा reclining
मागे वळणे turn back
मागे सरकणे move back
माजी पती ex-husband
माजी पत्नी ex-wife
माझं mine
माझा my
माणुसकीच्या नात्याने humanitarian
माणूस chap
मात करणे overcome
मातब्बर veteran
माती earth, soil
मातीची वस्तू pottery
मातृभाषा mother tongue
मातेच्या भावना maternal
माथा top
माथेफिरू maniac

माध्यमिक शाळा secondary school
मान neck
मानव human being
मानवजात mankind
मानववंशविषयक ethnic
मानववंशशास्त्र anthropology
मानवी human
मानवी हक्क human rights
मानसन्मान glory
मानसशास्त्र psychology
मानसशास्त्रज्ञ psychologist
मानसिक mental, psychiatric, psychological
मानसिकता mentality
मानसोपचार psychotherapy
मानसोपचारतज्ज्ञ psychiatrist
मान्य असलेले agreed
मान्य करणे admit, agree, own up
मापाचे असणे fit
माफ करा! sorry
माफी apology
मामी auntie
मामे भाऊ/बहीण cousin
मारणे beat
मार्क्सवाद Marxism
मार्ग course, route
मार्गदर्शक guide
मार्गदर्शक कुत्रा guide dog
मार्गदर्शक पुस्तक guidebook
मार्गदर्शन directions
मार्गदर्शिका directory
मार्गे via
मार्च महिना March
मालक boss, master, owner
मालकी असणे possess
मालकीचे असणे belong, own
मालमत्ता asset, property
मालाची वाहतूक freight
मालावी Malawi
मालिका serial
माल्डोव्हा Moldova
माळ necklace
माळी gardener

मावरी Maori
मावरी जमात Maori
मावशी aunt, auntie
माशी fly
मासा fish
मासिक magazine, monthly
मासिक स्राव (पाळी) menstruation
मासेमारी fishing
मासेमारी करणे fish
मासेमारीचा गळ fishing rod
मासेमारीची साधनसामग्री fishing tackle
मासेविक्रेता fishmonger
माहिती data, information
माहिती कार्यालय information office
माहिती देणारे informative
माहिती देणारे केंद्र visitor centre
माहिती देणे inform, notify, report
माहितीपट documentary
माहितीपुस्तिका brochure, handbook, leaflet, manual, pamphlet
माहीत असणे know
माहीत असलेला known
मिटवणे settle
मिठाई sweets
मिठी hug
मिठी मारणे cuddle
मितभाषी reserved
मितव्ययी economical
मित्र friend, mate, pal
मित्रत्वाचा friendly, playful
मिथुन रास Gemini
मिनिट minute
मिरची chilli
मिरवणूक procession
मिरी pepper
मिरीची भाजी pepper
मिळकत income
मिळणे get, receive
मिळवणे add up, gain

मिळालेली पदवी graduation
मिशी moustache
मिश्रण mix, mixture
मिश्र सलाड mixed salad
मिसळणे add, mix
मिस्किलपणे हळूच हसणे snigger
मी I
मीठ salt
मीन रास Pisces
मी स्वत: myself
मुंगी ant
मुका dumb
मुकुट crown
मुक्कामाचा कालावधी stay
मुक्त liberal
मुक्त करणे free
मुक्ती liberation
मुखवटा mask
मुखवटा चढवलेली व्यक्ती masked
मुख्य chief, main, principal
मुख्य आहार staple
मुख्य कार्यकारी अधिकारी CEO
मुख्य कार्यालय head office
मुख्य गायक lead singer
मुख्यत: mainly, primarily
मुख्य भूप्रदेश mainland
मुख्य भूमिका lead
मुख्य भूमिका करणे star
मुख्य रस्ता main road
मुख्य विषय focus
मुख्याध्यापक headteacher
मुख्यालय headquarters, HQ
मुतारी loo
मुदतपूर्व premature
मुदत संपण्याची तारीख expiry date
मुद्दा issue, point
मुद्दाम deliberately
मुरगळणे sprain
मुरमे pimple
मुरूम acne
मुलगा boy, lad
मुलगी girl, lass

मुलाखत interview
मुलाखतकार interviewer
मुलाखत घेणे interview
मुळा radish
मुष्टियुद्ध boxing
मुष्टियोद्धा boxer
मुसंडी dash
मुसलमान Muslim
मुसळधार पाऊस downpour
मुसळी नावाची वनस्पती asparagus
मुस्लिम Moslem, Muslim
मूठ fist, handle
मूठ (दरवाजाची) knob
मूत्रपिंड kidney
मूत्राशय bladder
मूर्ख fool, idiot, silly, stupid
मूर्खपणा madness
मूर्खपणाचा absurd
मूर्खपणाचा daft
मूर्खपणाची ridiculous
मूर्खपणाचे idiotic
मूर्ख बनविणे fool
मूल child
मूलत: basically
मूलभूत basic
मूलभूत बाबी basics
मूल वाढवणे foster, upbringing
मूल्य value
मूल्य वर्धित कर VAT
मूल्यांकन करणे judge
मूळ origin, root
मूळचा original
मूळ पदावर येणे relapse
मूळव्याध haemorrhoids, piles
मृत dead
मृत्युपत्र will
मृत्युलेख/मृत्युवार्ता obituary
मृत्यू death
मृत्यूच्या कारणांची चौकशी inquest
मॅडम/बाईसाहेब madam
मेंढा ram

मेंढी ewe, sheep
मेंढीची लोकर fleece
मेंढयाचे वा बकरीचे मांस mutton
मेंदू brain
मेंदूज्वर meningitis
मेंदूला झालेली इजा concussion
मेज table
मेजवानी bash, party, treat
मेण wax
(मेणकापडाचा) रेनकोट mac
मेणबत्ती candle
मेणयुक्त रंगखडू crayon
मेद fat
मेळावा rally
मेष रास Aries
मेहनत करणे slave
मेहनतीचा hard
मेहणा brother-in-law
मैत्री friendship
मैदानी outdoor
मैल mile
मैल प्रतितास mph
मॉर्फिन morphine
मोकळा liberal
मोकळी जाग room
मोकळी मार्गिका aisle
मोकळेपणाने frankly
मोकळ्या जागी outdoors, out-of-doors
मोजणी करणे quantify
मोजणे count, gauge, measure
मोजपट्टी scale, tape measure
मोजमाप measurements
मोटरगाड्यांची शर्यत motor racing
मोटर दुरुस्त करणारा motor mechanic
मोटरसायकल motorbike
मोटरसायकलस्वार motorcyclist
मोठा great, high

मोठा big, large
मोठा (आवाज) loud
मोठा आवाज bang, crash, shout
मोठा आवाज करणे bang
मोठा गोल चमचा ladle
मोठा चढाव steep
मोठा चमचा tablespoon
मोठा वाडा mansion
मोठा ससा hare
(मोठी) कामगिरी achievement
मोठी केसाळ माशी bumblebee
मोठी पेटी trunk
मोठी संख्या host
मोठे broad
मोठे अक्षर capital
मोठे आतडे bowels
मोठे काळवीट reindeer
मोठे प्रवासी जहाज liner
मोठे वादळ hurricane
मोठे शहर city
मोठे स्मित करणे grin
मोठे हसू/स्मित grin
मोठे होणे grow up
मोठ्या आकाराची वस्तू outsize
मोठ्या आवाजात loudly
मोठ्या आवाजात ओरडणे shout
मोठ्या कोळंब्या scampi
मोठ्याने aloud
मोठ्याने ओरडणे call, yell
मोठ्याने बोलणे speak up
मोठ्याने वाचन करणे read out
मोठ्या प्रकाशझोताचे दिवे floodlight
मोठ्या प्रमाणात वाढविणे multiply
मोठ्या प्रमाणावर extensively, fairly, largely
मोठ्या प्रमाणावरील massive
मोडलेले हाड fracture

मोतिबिंदू cataract
मोती pearl
मोफत free
मोबाईल क्रमांक mobile number
मोबाईल फोन mobile phone
मोर peacock
मोर्चा rally
मोलकरीण maid
मोह temptation
मोहर seal
मोहात पाडणारे tempting
मोहात पाडणे tempt
मोहिनी घालणारा fascinating
मोहीम campaign, expedition
मौल्यवान precious, valuable
मौल्यवान पुराण वस्तू antique
मौल्यवान वस्तू valuables
म्हण proverb
म्हणजे so
म्हणजेच i.e.
म्हणणे statement
म्हणून as, so, therefore
यंत्र machine
यंत्रनौका motorboat
यंत्रमानव robot
यंत्रसामग्री machinery
यंत्राची मूठ वा दांडा lever
यंत्राच्या भागाची रचना mechanism
यंत्रातील किंवा योजनेतील बिघाड break down
यंत्राने गवत कापणे mow
यकृत liver
यजमान host
यथातथा so-so
यश success
यशस्वी successful
यशस्वीपणे successfully
यशस्वीपणे हाताळणे cope
यशस्वी होणे succeed
यहुदी Jew

यहुदी धर्मियांचे प्रार्थनास्थळ synagogue
यहुदी धर्मीय Jewish
यांत्रिक impersonal
यांत्रिक नांगर tractor
याआधीचा last
याचना करणे beg
याचिका petition
यात्रा कंपनीचे कार्यालय tourist office
यादवी युद्ध civil war
यादी list
यादी तयार करणे list
यादीत समावेश नसलेला unlisted
याहृच्छिक random
यान craft
(युएफओ) उडती तबकडी UFO
युकी tactics
युकी शोधणे devise
युती alliance
युद्ध war
युद्धकाळातील प्रकाशबंदी blackout
युद्धबंदी ceasefire
युरोप Europe
येणारा coming
येणारा following
येणे come, show up, turn up
येथे here
येशू ख्रिस्त Jesus
योग yoga
योगदान contribution
योगायोग accident
योगायोग coincidence
योगायोगाने होणे coincide
योग्य appropriate, decent, fair, fit, okay, proper, reasonable, suitable
योग्य आकाराचा गालिचा fitted carpet
योग्य जागी असणे belong
योग्यपणे correctly, properly, reasonably, rightly
योजना plan, scheme

योजना आखणे plan
रंग colour, paint
रंगछटा colouring
रंगछटा असलेला tinted
रंगद्रव्य dye
रंग लावणे paint
रंग लावण्याचा ब्रश paintbrush
रंगविणे dye
रंगसंगती matching
रंगांधळा colour-blind
रंगीबेरंगी colourful
रंगीबेरंगी काच stained glass
रंधा plane
रक्कम amount, sum
रक्त blood
रक्तक्षयी anaemic
रक्तगट blood group
रक्तदान transfusion
रक्तदाब blood pressure
रक्तधानप्रयोग transfusion
रक्तपिपासू भूत vampire
रक्तवाहिनी vein
रक्तस्राव होणे bleed
रक्ताची चाचणी blood test
रक्षक guard
रक्षण करणे guard
रक्षापात्र ashtray
रखवालदार doorman
रचना composition, structure
रचनात्मक constructive
रजई duvet
रजा leave
रडणे cry, weep
रणगाडा tank
रत्न gem, jewel
रद्द करणे call off, cancel, scrap
रबर rubber
रबरी हातमोजे rubber gloves
रमदान Ramadan
रविवार Sunday
रस juice
रसायन chemical

रसायनशास्त्र chemistry
रस्ता passage, path, road, way
रस्ता चुकलेली व्यक्ती lost
रस्तादुरूस्तीचे काम roadworks
रस्त्यांचा नकाशा road map
रस्त्याचा नकाशा street map
रस्त्याचे शेवटचे टोक dead end
रस्त्यावरचा अडथळा roadblock
रस्त्यावरील दिव्याचा खांब lamppost
रस्सा gravy
रस्सीखेच tug-of-war
रहदारी traffic
रहिवासी inhabitant, resident
र्हास होणे deteriorate
रांग queue, rank, row
रांगणे crawl
रांगेत उभे राहणे queue
राक्षस Devil, monster
राखणे maintain
राखून ठेवणे reserve
राग temper
रागाने पाहणे glare
रागाने सांगणे tell off
रागावणे cross
रागावलेला mad
राजकन्या princess
राजकारण politics
राजकारणी politician
राजकीय political
राजकीय विरोधक opponent
राजघराण्याचा royal
राजदूत ambassador, consul
राजदूतावास consulate
राजधानी capital
राजपुत्र prince
राजवाडा palace
राजहंस swan
राजा king, monarch
राजाश्रय asylum
राजीनामा देणे resign

राजेशाही monarchy, royal
राज्य kingdom
राज्य करणे rule
राज्यकर्ता ruler
राज्यघटना constitution
राणी monarch, queen
रात्र night
रात्रपाळी night shift
रात्रशाळा night school
रात्रीची मेजवानी dinner party
रात्रीचे जेवण dinner, supper
रात्रीच्या जेवणाची वेळ dinner time
रानगवत weed
रानगवत नाशक weedkiller
रानटी barbaric
राळ resin
राशिचक्र zodiac
राष्ट्र nation
राष्ट्रगीत national anthem
राष्ट्रवाद nationalism
राष्ट्रवादी nationalist
राष्ट्राध्यक्ष/अध्यक्ष president
राष्ट्रीय national
राष्ट्रीय उद्यान national park
राष्ट्रीयत्व nationality
राष्ट्रीयीकरण करणे nationalize
रास्त reasonable
रास्तपणा fairness
रास्तपणे reasonably
राहणीमान standard of living
राहणीमानाचा खर्च cost of living
राहणे keep, live, stay
राहण्याची व्यवस्था accommodation
रिकामा vacant
रिकामे empty
रिकामे करणे empty, vacate
रिमझिम पाऊस drizzle
रिले शर्यत relay
रीळ reel
रुंद wide

रुंदी width
रुग्ण patient
रुग्णवाहिका ambulance
रुग्णालय hospital, infirmary
रुमाल scarf
रूग्णालयातील कक्ष ward
रूढी custom
रूप बदलणे turn
रेकॉर्ड करणे record
रेखांश longitude
रेखाचित्र sketch
रेखाचित्र तयार करणे sketch
रेचक laxative
रेझर razor
रेझरचे पाते razor blade
रेडा buffalo
रेडिओ radio
रेणू molecule
रेनकोट raincoat
रेल्वेचे फाटक level crossing
रेल्वेचे रूळ railway
रेल्वे स्थानक railway station
रेशीम silk
रेषा line
उपाहारगृह restaurant
रॉकेल kerosene
रोखठोक blunt
रोखपाल cashier
रोख रक्कम cash
रोग disease
रोगजंतू germ
रोगप्रतिकारक शक्ती immune system
रोगाची साथ epidemic
रोप plant
रोमन Roman
रोमांच goose pimples
रोषणाई lighting
रोहित पक्षी flamingo
लंगडत चालणे limp
लंगडा lame
लंडन London
लंबगोलाकार oval
लक्ष attention

लक्ष केंद्रित करणे focus
लक्ष ठेवणे watch out
लक्ष ठेवण्याची क्रिया oversight
लक्षण symptom
लक्ष दुसरीकडे वळविणे distract
लक्ष देणे listen
लक्षात न येणे miss
लक्षात येणे notice
लक्षाधीश millionaire
लक्ष्य target
लखलखाट flash
लगाम reins
लगेच नजर फरविणे look at
लग्न करणे marry
लग्न/विवाहसमारंभ wedding
लग्नाचा वाढदिवस wedding anniversary
लग्नाची अंगठी wedding ring
लग्नापूर्वीचे नाव maiden name
लघवी urine
लघुकथा short story
लघुदृष्टी असलेली व्यक्ती near-sighted
लघुलेखन shorthand
लचक sprain
लज्जास्पद disgraceful
लज्जित ashamed
लज्जित/पंचाईत होणे embarrassed
लटकणे hang
लटकावणे hang
लठ्ठ fat
लढा fight
लढाई battle, fighting
लढाऊ जहाज battleship
लपंडाव hide-and-seek
लपणे hide
लपलेला hidden
लपविणे hide
लबाड insincere
लय rhythm

लळा attachment
लळा असलेला attached
लवंग clove
लवकर early, fast, soon
लवचिक flexible
लवाद tribunal
लव्हाळे reed
लसीकरण vaccination
लसीकरण करणे vaccinate
लसूण garlic
लहरी moody
लहान little, miniature, small, younger
लहान घर cottage
लहान तीक्ष्ण तीर dart
लहान तुकडा scrap
लहान तोफ mortar
लहान थेंब drip
लहान दगड pebble
लहान प्रतिकृती miniature
लहान मुलांचा कागदी टॉवेल baby wipe
लहान मुलांची बाटली baby's bottle
लहान मूल kid
लहान वयाचा कोंबडा cockerel -at
लांडगा wolf
लांब long
लांब अरुंद खड्डा ditch
लांब उडी long jump
लांबच्या रस्त्याने जाणे detour
लांबी length
लाकडाचा भुसा sawdust
लाकूड wood
लाकूडकाम woodwork
लाख lacquer
लागण होणे have
लागवड करणे plant
लागोपाठचा consecutive, successive
लाच देणे bribe
लाच लुचपतपणा bribery
लाज shame

लाजणे blush
लाजाळू shy
लाट wave
लाटणे rolling pin
लाडामुळे बिघडलेले मूल spoilt
लाथ kick
लाथ मारणे kick
लादी tile
लादीवरील ठिपक्यांची नक्षी mosaic
लाद्या/कौल बसवलेली tiled
लाभांश bonus
ला महत्त्व देणे emphasize
लाल red
लालजर्द scarlet
लालबुंद होणे flush
लालसर तेजस्वी ginger
लाली flush
लाळ saliva
लाव्हारस lava
लाह्या popcorn
लिंग gender, sex
लिंबाची साल zest
लिंबू lemon
लिंबू सरबत lemonade
लिखाण text, writing
लिखाणासाठी वापरायचा कागद writing paper
लिनो (जाजम) lino
लिफाफा envelope
लिफ्ट देणे lift
लिलाव auction
लिहिणे write
लिहून घेणे note down, write down
लीप वर्ष leap year
लुकडा thin
लुच्चा crook
लुटणे rob
लुटारू robber
लुट्रपुट्रचा mock
लेख article
लेखक author, writer
लेखनसामग्री stationery

लेखनसामग्रीचे दुकान stationer
लेखाधिकार copyright
लेखी हमी warranty
लॉरी चालक lorry driver
लोक people
लोककला folklore
लोकप्रिय fashionable, popular
लोकप्रियता popularity
लोकप्रिय नसलेला unpopular
लोकमत opinion poll
लोकर wool
लोकरीचे कपडे woollens
लोकरीचे मऊ कापड flannel
लोकशाही democracy
लोकशाही राज्यपद्धती democratic
लोकसंख्या population
लोकसंगीत folk music
लोकापवाद scandal
लोखंड iron
लोणी butter
लोभी greedy
लोशन lotion
लोहचुंबक magnet
लोहमार्ग railway
वंगण grease
वंगण लावलेली वस्तू greasy
वंध्यत्व असलेली व्यक्ती infertile
वंश race
वंशद्वेष/जातीयवाद racism
वंशवादी/जातीयवादी racist
वकिलात embassy
वकील lawyer, solicitor
वक्तशीर punctual
वक्ता speaker
वखार warehouse
वगळून excluding
वचन promise
वचन देणे promise
वजन weight
वजन करणे weigh
वजने scales

वजा करणे deduct, minus, subtract
वटवाघूळ bat
वडील dad, father
वन wood
वनस्पती vegetation
वनौषधी herbs
वय age
वयस्क elderly
वयाचा aged
वयाने मोठा elder
वयोमर्यादा age limit
वर above, on, onto, over, up
वरचढ superior
वरचा upper
वरच्या दिशेने upwards, vertical
वरच्या मजल्यावर upstairs
वरवरचे casual
वरिष्ठ senior, superior
वर्ग category, class
वर्गखोली classroom
वर्गखोली सहाय्यक classroom assistant
वर्गणी subscription
वर्गमित्र classmate
वर्ण colouring, complexion
वर्णन description, outline
वर्णन करणे describe
वर्णमाला alphabet
वर्तणूक करणे behaviour
वर्तमान present
वर्तमानपत्र newspaper
वर्तमानपत्राचे दुकान newsagent
वर्तवता न येणारे unpredictable
वर्तुळ circle
वर्तुळाकार circular
वर्धापन दिन anniversary
वर्ष year
वर्षा ऋतू monsoon
वल्हे oar
वल्हे असलेली नौका rowing boat

वळण bend, turn, turning
वळण घेणे wind
वळणे turn, turn around
वळणी washing line
वसंत ऋतू spring
वसंत ऋतूचा कालावधी
  springtime
वसतिगृह hostel
वसतिगृह असलेली शाळा
  boarding school
वस्तरा razor
वस्तुसंग्रहालय museum
वस्तुस्थिती fact
वस्तुस्थितीची जाणीव नसलेला
  unrealistic
वस्तू goods, item, object,
  stuff
वस्तूंची देवाणघेवाण करणे
  swap
वस्त्र garment
वही notebook
वांशिक/जातीय racial
वाईट awful, bad, dreadful,
  nasty
वाईट कृत्य करणे commit
वाईट भाषेचा वापर करणे
  swear
वाईट रीतीने badly
वाईट शब्द swearword
वाकलेला bent
वाकुल्या दाखविणे mock
वाक्प्रचार phrase
वाक्प्रचारांचे पुस्तक
  phrasebook
वाक्य sentence
वागणूक देणे treat
वागणे behave
(वागण्या-बोलण्यात) पटाईत
  tactful
वाग्दत्त वधू fiancée
वाग्दत्त वर fiancé
वाघ tiger
वाङ्मय literature
वाचक reader
वाचणे read, survive

वाचता न येण्याजोगे illegible
वाचन reading
वाचणे save
वाजणे ring
वाजवणे play
वाटणे feel, reckon, seem,
  send out, think
वाटप circulation
वाटप करणे distribute, give
  out
वाट पाहणे wait
वाटा share
वाटाणे peas
वाटी bowl
वाट्टेल ते करायला तयार
  असणारा desperate
वाङ्निश्चयाची अंगठी
  engagement ring
वाढ gain, growth, increase,
  rise
वाढणे go up, grow, mount
  up, rise
वाढत्या प्रमाणावर
  increasingly
वाढदिवस birthday
वाढवलेले मूल foster child
वाढविणे grow
वाढ होणे increase
वातानुकूलन air conditioning
वातानुकूलित air-conditioned
वातावरण atmosphere
वादक player
वाद घालणे argue
वादळ storm
वादळी stormy, thundery
वादळी वारा gale
वादविवाद argument, row
वादविवाद करणे row
वाद्य instrument
वाद्यवृंद orchestra
वाद्यवृंदाचे संगीत symphony
वापर use
वापरणे use
वापरण्यास सुलभ user-
  friendly

वापरलेले used
वापरून संपवणे use up
वाफ steam
वायफळ बडबड nonsense
वायव्य northwest
वायुवीजन ventilation
वायू gas
वारंवार घडणारा frequent
वारंवारता frequency
वारस heir
वारसाहक्क inheritance
वारसाहक्काने मिळणे inherit
वाऱ्याचा जोरदार झोत gust
वाऱ्याचा झोत draught
वाऱ्याची झुळूक breeze
वारा wind
वार्ताहर correspondent
वार्षिक annual, yearly
वार्षिक सर्वसाधारण सभा
  AGM
वाळलेले गवत hay
वाळवंट desert
वाळवंटातील हिरवळीची/
  पाणथळ जागा oasis
वाळू sand
वाळूचा खडक sandstone
वाळूची टेकडी sand dune
वाळूचे खडे grit
वावडे allergy
वावडे असलेला allergic
वास smell
वास घेणे smell
वास येणे smell
वासराचे मांस veal
वासरू calf
वास्तव वाटावे असे virtual
  reality
वास्तववादी realistic
वास्तवात reality
वास्तविक actual, virtual
वास्तू premises
वाहणे blow, flow
वाहतुकीच्या खुणा road sign
वाहतूक transport
वाहतूक करणे transport

वाहतूक कोंडी traffic jam
वाहन transport, vehicle
वाहन खेचून नेणे tow away
वाहनचालक प्रशिक्षक driving instructor
वाहन चालवणे drive
वाहन चालविण्याचा धडा driving lesson
वाहन चालविण्याची चाचणी driving test
वाहनाचा बंपर bumper
वाहनाची पुढची काच windscreen
वाहनाचे अपहरण करणे hijack
वाहनाचे पुढील दिवे headlight
वाहनात इंधन भरणे refuel
वाहनातला प्रवास drive
वाहनाने ठोकर मारणे run over
वाहिनी channel
वाहून नेणे bear
विंचू scorpion
विंचरणे comb
विकणे sell
विकत घेणे buy
विकसनशील देश developing country
विकसीत करणे develop
विकास development
विकून टाकणे sell off
विक्रम record
विक्री sale
विक्रीची किंमत selling price
विक्री प्रतिनिधी sales rep
विक्री सहाय्यक sales assistant
विक्रेता salesman, salesperson, vendor
विक्रेती saleswoman
विक्षिप्त absent-minded, eccentric
विखारी भावना venom
विघटनयोग्य biodegradable
विचार thought
विचार करणे consider, think
विचारणे ask

विचारधारा ideology
विचारमग्न thoughtful
विचारार्थ पुढे मांडणे put forward
विचित्र odd, strange, weird
विजय triumph, victory
विजय होणे triumph
विजेचा electrical
विजेचा झटका electric shock
विजेचा दिवा light bulb
विजेचे काम करणारा electrician
विजेता champion, winner
विजेतेपद championship
विजेरी torch
विज्ञान science
विझणे out
विटलेला fed up
विटलेले worn
विणकाम knitting
विणकाम करणे crochet
विणकामाची सुई knitting needle
विणणे knit
विणलेले कपडे textile
वितरक distributor
वितळणे melt
वितळवणे melt
वितळू लागलेला बर्फ slush
विदूषक clown
विदेशी exotic
विद्यापीठ uni
विद्यार्थी pupil, student
विद्यार्थ्यांना दिलेली सूट student discount
विद्युत electric
विद्युतजनित generator
विद्युतभार charge
विद्युतभारित करणे charge
विद्युतशक्ती electricity
विद्राव्य soluble
विद्रूप hideous
विधवा widow
विधूर widower

विधेयक bill
विध्वंस destruction, sabotage
विध्वंस करणे sabotage
विनंती request
विनंती करणे request
विनाविलंब prompt
विनिमयाचा दर rate of exchange
विनोद humour, joke
विनोद करणारा comedian
विनोदबुद्धी sense of humour
विनोद सांगणे joke
विनोदी hilarious, humorous
विभक्त होणे split up
विभाग department
विभाग/क्षेत्र zone
विभागणे divide
विभागून घेणे share
विभाजन division
विमा insurance
विमा उतरवणे insure
विमाकृत insured
विमान aircraft, plane
विमान जमिनीवर उतरवणे touchdown
विमानतळ airport
विमानतळावरील धावपट्टी runway
विमान लागणारा airsick
विमान हवेत उडणे take off
विमानातील सेवकवर्ग cabin crew
विमानोड्डाण flight
विमा पॉलिसी insurance policy
विमा प्रमाणपत्र insurance certificate
विरघळणारा soluble
विरघळणे dissolve
विराम pause
विरामचिह्नांचा वापर punctuation
विरुद्ध against, opposite, versus

विरोध opposition
विरोधक adversary
विरोध करणे fight, oppose
विरोध न करणारा passive
विरोधात opposed
विरोधाभास contradiction
विरोधी opposing
विरोधी गट rival
विरोधी प्रचार propaganda
विलंबित delayed
विलक्षण fantastic
विलासी luxurious
विवस्त्र करणे strip
विवादास्पद controversial
विवाह marriage
विवाह करणे marry
विवाह प्रमाणपत्र marriage certificate
विवाहित married
विविध various
विविधता variety
विवेक discretion
विव्हळणे groan, moan
विशाल broad
विशिष्ट particular, peculiar, specific
विशिष्ट जागा spot
विशिष्ट प्रदेशातील प्राणिजात fauna
विशिष्ट प्रदेशातील वनस्पतीजात flora
विशिष्ट मर्यादेत बदलणे range
विशिष्ट वंश breed
विशेष अधिकार privilege
विशेषज्ञ specialist
विशेषण adjective
विशेषतः especially, particularly
विश्रांती घेणे rest
विक्षेषण analysis
विक्षेषण करणे analyse
विश्व universe, world
विश्व चषक World Cup
विश्वविद्यापीठ university
विश्वसनीय credible

विश्वास confidence, faith, trust
विश्वासघात करणे betray
विश्वास ठेवणारा trusting
विश्वास ठेवणे trust
विश्वास न ठेवण्याजोगा unreliable
विश्वास न बसण्याजोगे unreal
विश्वास वाटणे believe
विश्वासू reliable, reputable
विष poison
विष देणे poison
विषप्रयोग करणे poison
विषबाधेवरील उतारा antidote
विषम odd
विषमज्वर typhoid
विषय subject
विषयपत्रिका agenda
विषयी regarding
विषाणू virus
विषादजनक offensive
विषारी poisonous, toxic
विषारी अळंबी toadstool
विषुवृत्त equator
विषुववृत्तीय tropical
विषुववृत्तीय गिनी Equatorial Guinea
विसरणे forget
विसावा twentieth
विस्तारणे stretch
विस्तारित कक्ष extension
विस्मयकारक fabulous, wonderful
विस्मयचकित stunned
विस्मयचकित करणे amaze
विस्मृतीत गेलेला forgotten
विहीर well
वीज lightning
वीट brick
वीस twenty
वृत्तपत्र paper
वृद्ध old
वृद्ध निवृत्तीवेतनधारक old-age pensioner
वृश्चिक रास Scorpio

वृषण testicle
वृषभ रास Taurus
वेंधळा clumsy
वेग speed
वेग कमी करणे slow down
वेगमर्यादा speed limit
वेगळा different
वेगळा distinctive
वेगळे separate
वेगळे करणे separate
वेगळेपणाने उठून दिसणारे striking
वेगळे होणे separation
वेगळ्या रंगाचा पट्टा stripe
वेग वाढवणे speed up
वेगाने जाण्याची क्रिया speeding
वेटरला दिलेली बक्षिसी tip
वेटरला बक्षिसी देणे tip
वेडपट nutter
वेडपिसा frantic
वेडसर crazy, insane, lunatic
वेडा mad, madman
वेडेपणाचे unwise
वेड्यासारखे madly
वेढणे surround
वेणी pigtail, plait
वेदना ache, pain
वेदनामय painful
वेदनामुक्त करणे relieve
वेदनाशामक painkiller
वेदना होणे ache, suffer
वेधशाळा observatory
वेळ time
वेळ घालवण्याचे साधन pastime
वेळ टळून गेलेली गोष्ट overdue
वेळ वाया घालवणे mess about
वेळापत्रक timetable
वेळेवर on time
वेळोवेळी occasionally
वेषभूषा costume
वेषांतर करणे disguise

वेष्टन काढून टाकणे unwrap	व्यवहार deal, transaction	शकणे can
वेष्टनातून बाहेर काढणे unpack	व्यवहार करणे deal with	शकलो could
वैज्ञानिक कल्पित कथा sci-fi	व्यवहारचातुर्य tact	शक्तिवर्धक औषध tonic
वैद्यक शास्त्र medicine	व्यवहारचातुर्य नसलेली व्यक्ती tactless	शक्तिशाली powerful
वैद्यकीय medical	व्यवहारचातुर्यपूर्ण tactful	शक्ती energy, power, strength
वैद्यकीय इलाज treatment	व्यवहारज्ञान common sense	शक्य possible, probable
वैद्यकीय प्रमाणपत्र medical certificate	व्यवहार्य feasible, practical	शक्यता possibility, probability, prospect
वैध valid	व्यसनाधीन addict	शक्य तेवढ्या लवकर asap
वैमानिक pilot	व्यसनी addicted	शक्यतो possibly, preferably, probably
वैयक्तिक personal	व्याकरण grammar	
वैयक्तिक सहाय्यक PA, personal assistant	व्याकरणविषयक grammatical	शतक century
	व्याकरणातील धातूंचा गण conjugation	शताब्दी centenary
वैर उत्पन्न करणे antagonize	व्याख्या definition	शत्रुत्व rivalry
वैवाहिक जोडीदार spouse	व्याख्याता lecturer	शत्रुभावाचा unfriendly
वैवाहिक स्थिती marital status	व्याख्यान lecture	शत्रू enemy
	व्याख्यान देणे lecture	शनिवार Saturday
वैविध्यपूर्ण varied	व्याज interest	शनिवार-रविवार weekend
वैशिष्ट्य speciality	व्याजदर interest rate	शपथ oath
व्यंगचित्र cartoon	व्यापक comprehensive	शब्द word
व्यंगपट cartoon	व्यापार business, trade	शब्दकोडे crossword
व्यंजन consonant	व्यापारी businessman, dealer	शब्दकोश dictionary
व्यक्त करणे express		शब्दचित्र portrait
व्यक्तिचित्र portrait	व्यापारी चिन्ह brand	शब्दसंग्रह vocabulary
व्यक्तिनिरपेक्ष impersonal	व्यापारी बँक merchant bank	शयनकक्ष bedroom
व्यक्तिमत्व personality	व्यापारी स्त्री businesswoman	शयनकक्षातला दिवा bedside lamp
व्यक्तिशः personally	व्यायाम exercise	
व्यक्ती person	व्यायामशाळा gym	शयनकक्षातले टेबल bedside table
व्यग्र busy	व्यावसायिक professional	
व्यग्र संदेशयंत्रणा busy signal	व्यावसायिक दृष्ट्या professionally	शरण जाणे yield
व्यतिरिक्त except		शरणागती पत्करणे surrender
व्यवसाय career, occupation, profession	व्यावसायिक विश्रांती commercial break	शरीर body
	व्यावसायिक संस्था agency	शरीर कमावणे bodybuilding
व्यवसाय बंद करणे closure	व्यास diameter	शरीराचा अवयव organ
व्यवसायातील नेहमीचे खर्च overheads	व्यासपीठ stage	शर्करा glucose
	व्रण scar	शर्यत race
व्यवस्था arrangement	व्रात्य brat, naughty	शर्यतीचा घोडा racehorse
व्यवस्थापक manager	शंका doubt, query, reservation	शर्यतीची कार racing car
व्यवस्थापकीय संचालक managing director		शर्यतीची धावपट्टी/मैदान racetrack
	शंका उपस्थित करणे query	
व्यवस्थापन management	शंका घेणे doubt	शर्यतीत भाग घेणारा racer
व्यवस्थापन करणे manage	शंकू cone	शर्यतीत भाग घेणे race
व्यवस्थापिका manageress	शंभर hundred	शवपेटी coffin
व्यवस्थित लावणे arrange		शवागार morgue

शस्त्र weapon
शस्त्रक्रिया operation, surgery
शस्त्रक्रिया करणारे डॉक्टर surgeon
शस्त्रक्रिया करणे operate
शस्त्रक्रियागृह operating theatre
शहर town
शहराचा मध्यवर्ती भाग city centre
शहरातील मध्यवर्ती विभाग town centre
शहरापासून दूरवरचा भाग outskirts
शहराबाहेरची दूरवरची रपेट hike
शहाणपण common sense, wisdom
शहाणा wise
शहामृग ostrich
शांत calm, easy-going, patient, quiet, silent
शांतता discretion, peace, silence
शांततापूर्ण peaceful
शांतपण quietly
शांत स्वभाव patience
शांत होणे calm down, relax
शाई ink
शाकाहारी vegetarian
शानदार elegant
शारीरिक physical
शारीरिक क्षमता stamina
शारीरिक शिक्षा corporal punishment
शाल shawl
शाळकरी मुलगा schoolboy
शाळकरी मुलगी schoolgirl
शाळकरी मुले schoolchildren
शाळा school
शाळा/महाविद्यालयाचे माहितीपत्रक prospectus
शाळेचा गणवेश school uniform

शाळेतील शिक्षक schoolteacher
शाळेला दांडी मारणे play truant
शास्त्रज्ञ scientist
शास्त्रीय classical, scientific
शिंकणे sneeze
शिंग horn
शिंगरू foal
शिंग (वाजवायचे) cornet
शिंतोडे उडवणे splash
शिंपला oyster
शिंपी tailor
शिकणारा learner
शिकणे learn
शिकवणी tuition
शिकवणे teach
शिकाऊ apprentice
शिकाऊ चालक learner driver
शिकार hunting
शिकार करणे hunt
शिकारी hunter
शिकारीची मोहीम safari
शिकारी पक्षी bird of prey
शिक्का मारणे stamp
शिक्षक teacher
शिक्षण education
शिक्षा penalty, punishment, sentence
शिक्षा करणे penalize, punish
शिक्षा सुनावणे sentence
शिखर परिषद summit
शिट्टी whistle
शिट्टी वाजवणे whistle
शिडाची नौका sailing boat
शिडी ladder
शिफारस recommendation
शिफारस करणे recommend
शिलाई यंत्र sewing machine
शिल्प sculpture
शिल्पकार sculptor
शिल्लक left
शिळा stale
शिवण seam
शिवणकाम sewing

शिवणे sew, stitch
शिवाय apart from, besides, without
शिवून एकत्र जोडणे sew up
शिव्याशाप curse
शिव्याशाप देणे slag off
शिष्ट snob
शिष्टाचार manners
शिष्यवृत्ती scholarship
शिसारी आणणारा sickening
शिसे lead
शिसेरहित lead-free, unleaded
शिसेरहित पेट्रोल unleaded petrol
शिस्त discipline
शीख Sikh
शीड sail
शीर्षक title
शुक्रजंतू sperm
शुक्रवार Friday
शुद्ध pure
शुद्धिकरण कारखाना refinery
शुद्धीवर येणे come round
शुभारंभाचा प्रयोग premiere
शुभेच्छापत्र card
शुल्क fee
शून्य nil, nought
शून्य अंश zero
शूर brave
शेंग bean
शेंगदाणा peanut
शेंगेतच मोड आणलेले धान्य beansprouts
शेंदरी scarlet
शेअर दलाल stockbroker
शेअर बाजार stock exchange, stock market
शेकोटी fireplace
शेजारचा भाग neighbourhood
शेजारी neighbour
शेत farm, field
शेतकरी farmer
शेतावरील झाप barn

शेती agriculture, farming
शेतीविषयक agricultural
शेपूट tail
शेवंती chrysanthemum
शेवट end, ending, finish
शेवट करणे finalize
शेवटचा last
शेवटची कालमर्यादा ultimatum
शेवट होणे end
शेवटी finally, lastly, ultimately
शेवाळ moss
शैक्षणिक academic, educational
शैक्षणिक वर्ष academic year
शैली style
शॉटगन shotgun
शोक mourning
शोकात्म tragic
शोकान्तिका tragedy
शोध invention, search
शोध घेणारा explorer
शोध घेणे explore, search
शोधून काढणे find out, hunt, look for, seek
शोध लावणे discover, invent
शोधून काढणे track down, work out
शोभून दिसणे suit
शोषण exploitation
शोषण करणे exploit
शौचालय lavatory
शौर्य bravery
श्रद्धा belief
श्रद्धा/विश्वास ठेवणे believe
श्रम labour
श्रवण hearing
श्रवणयंत्र hearing aid
श्रावण घेवडा French beans
श्रीमंत rich, wealthy
श्रीमती Ms
श्रीयुत Mr
श्रीलंका Sri Lanka
श्रोता listener

श्रोते वा प्रेक्षक audience
श्वास breath
श्वास अडकणे wind
श्वास घेणे breathe in
श्वास सोडणे breathe out
श्वासोच्छवास breathing
श्वासोच्छवास करणे breathe
संकटात लोटणे endanger
संकटातून वाचलेली व्यक्ती survivor
संकटातून सोडविणे rescue
संकीर्ण miscellaneous
संकुल complex
संकेत signal
संकोची reserved
संक्रमण transition
संक्षिप्त concise
संक्षिप्त रूप abbreviation
संख्या number, quantity
संगणक computer, workstation
संगणक विज्ञान computer science
(संगणकाकडून) माहिती मिळवणे access
संगणकाचा वापर करणे computing
संगणकावरील खेळ computer game
संगमरवर marble
संगीत music
संगीतकार composer, musician
संगीत नाटक musical
(संगीत) वाद्य musical instrument
संगीताचा musical
संगीताची धून tune
संगीताची लिखित स्वरावली score
संगोपन करणे bring up, upbringing
संग्रह album, collection
संग्राहक collector
संघ team

संघटना organization, union
संघर्ष conflict, struggle
संघर्ष करणे clash, struggle
संच kit, set
संचय pool
संचलन parade
संचारबंदी curfew
संज्ञा term
संत saint
संतस irritable
संताप आणणारे infuriating
संताप आलेला resentful
संतापजनक irritating
संताप येणे resent
संतापलेला furious
संतुलित balanced
संत्रे orange
संत्र्याचा रस orange juice
संदर्भ context, reference
संदर्भ क्रमांक reference number
संदिग्ध dubious, vague
संदेशवाहक messenger
संधिवात rheumatism
संधी chance, opportunity
संध्याकाळ evening
संध्याशाळा evening class
संप strike
संपणे expire, run out
संपत्ती fortune, wealth
संपदा estate
संप पुकारणे strike
संपर्क contact
संपर्क करणे contact
संपर्क तोडणे disconnect
संपलेला over
संपवणे finish
संपवलेले finished
संपादक editor
संपावरील व्यक्ती striker
संपूर्ण thorough, whole
संपूर्णतः absolutely
संपूर्णपणे completely, thoroughly, totally

संपूर्ण विकली गेलेली sold out
संपूर्ण वैद्यकीय चाचणी medical
संप्रेरक hormone
संबंध connection, relation
संबंधी about, concerning
संभाषण conversation, talk
संभ्रमित baffled
संमती approval
संमती देणे approve
समिश्र mixed
संयुक्त joint
संयुक्त खाते joint account
संयुक्त राष्ट्रसंघ UN, United Nations
संयोग conjunction
संयोगचिन्ह hyphen
संयोजक conductor
संरक्षक चष्मा goggles
संरक्षण conservation, defence, protection
संरक्षण करणे defend, protect
संलग्न adjacent
संवाद communication, dialogue
संवाद साधणे communicate, talk to
संवेदनशील sensitive
संवेदना वा शुद्ध हरवणारा पदार्थ anaesthetic
संशय घेणे suspect
संशयवादी sceptical
संशयास्पद doubtful, suspicious
संशयित alleged, suspect
संशोधक inventor
संशोधन research
संसद parliament
संसर्ग catching, infection
संसर्गजन्य contagious, infectious
संस्कृती culture
संस्था association, institute, institution

संहिता code
सकाळ morning
सक्रिय active
सक्षम able, capable, competent
सखल भूप्रदेश plain
सखोल intensive
सख्य communion
सगळीकडे around, everywhere
सचिव secretary
सजवणे decorate
सजावटकार decorator
सजावटीची वस्तू ornament
सजीव live
सज्ज ready
सज्जा balcony
सटकणे dodge
सडणे rot
सडपातळ slender, slim
सडलेले rotten
सतत constant
सतत उणेदुणे काढणे nag
सततचा continual
सतरा seventeen
सतरावा seventeenth
सत्तर seventy
सत्य truth, truthful
सत्र semester, session, term
सदनिका flat
सदैव forever
सदोष faulty
सद्वर्तनी well-behaved
सद्सद्विवेकबुद्धि conscience
सध्या currently
सध्याचा current
सनसनाटी sensational
सन्मान honour
सपाट even, flat, plain
सपाट माथ्याची टाचणी thumbtack
सपाट/समतल जागा plane
सफरचंद apple
सफाई करणारा cleaner

सबब excuse
सभा meeting
सभासद member
सभासदत्व membership
सभासदत्वाचे कार्ड membership card
सभोवती around
सभ्य gentle, polite, sober
सभ्यकुलीन गृहस्थ gentleman
सभ्यपणा politeness
सभ्यपणे politely
सभ्य स्त्री lady
सम even
समकालीन contemporary
समज असलेले sensitive
समजणे realize, regard, understand
समजण्याजोगे understandable
समजावून सांगणे explain
समजूतदार considerate, sensible, understanding
समजून चालणे suppose
समझोता करणे compromise
समर्थक supporter
समर्थन करणे excuse, justify
समर्पण dedication
समर्पित devoted
समवेत among
समस्या difficulty, problem
समस्या सोडवणे tackle
समस्या सोडविणे solve
समांतर parallel
समाज community, society
समाजवाद socialism
समाजवादी left-wing, socialist
समाजशास्त्र sociology
समाजसेवा social services
समाधान satisfaction
समाधानकारक rewarding, satisfactory
समाधानी content, pleased, satisfied, self-contained

समान equal, equivalent
समानता equality
समारंभ ceremony
समालोचक commentator
समालोचन commentary
समाविष्ट inclusive
समाविष्ट असणे include, involve
समिती committee
समीकरण equation
समीक्षक critic
समुदाय host
समुद्र sea
समुद्रकिनारा beach, coast, seashore
समुद्रपर्यटन sailing
समुद्रप्रवासामुळे उलट्या होणे seasick
समुद्रसपाटी sea level
समुद्रसपाटीपासूनची उंची altitude
समुद्राची भरती-ओहोटी tide
समुद्राच्या काठचा प्रदेश seaside
समुद्रात वाढणारे गवत seaweed
समुद्रातील धक्का jetty, pier
समुद्री चाचे pirate
समूह bunch, party
समोर opposite
समोरासमोर opposite
सम्राट emperor
सर sir
सरकणे shift, slide
सरकार government
सरणे go by
सरपटणारा प्राणी reptile
सरपटणे creep
सरमिसळ mix up
सरळ straight, straight on, upright
सरहद border
सराव practice
सरासरी average
सरुवात करणे start

सर्जनशील creative
सर्दी cold
सर्दी-पडसे flu
सर्व all, every
सर्वत्र throughout
सर्वत्र पसरलेले widespread
सर्वनाम pronoun
सर्ववेळ throughout
सर्वसाधारण common
सर्वसाधारण विधान generalize
सर्वसामान्य general, ordinary
सर्वात चांगला best
सर्वात लहान youngest
सर्वात वरचा top
सर्वाधिक maximum
सर्वाधिक वाईट worst
सर्वेक्षक surveyor
सर्वेक्षण survey
सर्वोच्च बिंदू peak
सर्वोत्कृष्ट superb, unbeatable
सर्वोत्तम best
सर्शत qualified
सलगचा consecutive
सलाम करणे salute
सल्ला advice, tip
सल्ला घेणे consult
सल्ला देणे advise
सल्ला देण्याजोगे advisable
सवड time off
सवय habit
सवलत concession, discount
सव्य clockwise
सशर्त conditional
सशस्त्र armed
ससा rabbit
सस्तन mammal
सहकारी associate, colleague
सहकार्य cooperation
सहजगत्या निवडलेला random
सहचारी companion
सहज casual, easily

सहजगत्या अस्वस्थ होणारे touchy
सहज घेता येण्याजोगा accessible
सहज दिसणारा noticeable
सहजपणे casually
सहज पहाणे browse
सहन करणे bear up
सहनशील patient, tolerant
सहभागी होणे get into, participate
सहमत न होणे disagree
सहल outing, picnic, trip
सहस्रक millennium
सहा six
सहाजिक understandable
सहानुभूतिपूर्वक वागणारा sympathetic
सहानुभूती sympathy
सहानुभूती दाखविणे sympathize
सहायक assistant
सहाय्य aid
सहारा वाळवंट Sahara
सहावा sixth
सहित included, including, with
साहित्य material
सही autograph, sign, signature
सांगणे state, tell
सांजवेळ dusk
सांडणे spill
सांधा joint
सांधेदुखी arthritis
सांस्कृतिक cultural
साक्षीदार witness
साखर sugar
साखरयुक्त मिठाई toffee
साखररहित sugar-free
साखळी chain
साचा mould, pattern
साजरा करणे celebrate
साठ sixty
साठवून ठेवणे store

साठा storage
साठा करणे stock
साठा करून ठेवणे stock up
सात seven
सातत्यपूर्ण consistent, persistent
सातत्याचा अभाव असलेले inconsistent
सातत्याने constantly
सातवा seventh
सातवा भाग seventh
सादर करणे present
सादरकर्ता presenter
सादरीकरण performance
साधने means
साधू monk
साधेपणा austerity
साधेसरळ straightforward
साप snake
सापडणे find
सापळा trap
साफ clear
साफ करणे clean, clear, clear up
साफसफाई cleaning
साबण soap
साबण चुरा soap powder
सामग्री material
सामना match
सामना अनिर्णित रहाणे draw
सामाजिक social
सामाजिक कार्यकर्ता social worker
सामाजिक सुरक्षितता social security
सामान luggage
सामान उतरवून घेणे unload
सामान ठेवण्याची रॅक luggage rack
सामान भरणे load
सामानवाहू नौका barge
सामानसुमानाने सज्ज furnished
सामानाची बांधाबांध करणे pack

सामानाची यादी inventory
सामान्य normal
सामान्य ज्ञान general knowledge
सामान्यत: generally, normally, usually
सामावलेले असणे contain
सामावून घेणे accommodate
सामील करून घेणे rope in
सामील होणे join
सामुदायिक collective
सामूहिक collective
साम्यवाद communism
साम्यवादी communist
साम्राज्य empire
साय cream
सायकल bicycle
सायकलचालक cyclist
सायकल चालवणे cycle
सायकलचा हॅंडल handlebars
सायकलस्वारी cycling
सारखा like, similar
सारखेच same
सारखेपणा resemblance, similarity
सारस crane
सारांश summary
सारांशरूपाने सांगणे summarize, sum up
सार्वजनिक public
सार्वजनिक मालमत्तेची नासधूस vandalism
सार्वजनिक वाहतूक व्यवस्था public transport
सार्वजनिक सुट्टी bank holiday, public holiday
सार्वत्रिक निवडणूक general election
साल skin
साल काढणे peel
सालीसहित भाजलेले बटाटे baked potato
साळू hedgehog
सावकार pawnbroker
सावत्र आई stepmother

सावत्र बहीण stepsister
सावत्र बाप stepfather
सावत्र भाऊ stepbrother
सावत्र मुलगा stepson
सावत्र मुलगी stepdaughter
सावध alert, cautious
सावध करणे alert
सावधपणे cautiously
सावधानता caution, precaution
सावधानतेने carefully
सावरणे get over
सावली shadow
सासरची माणसे in-laws
सासरा father-in-law
सासू mother-in-law
साहजिक naturally
साहस adventure, courage
साहसी adventurous
सिंह lion
सिंह रास Leo
सिंहासन throne
सिंहीण lioness
सिद्ध करणे demonstrate
सिद्ध होणे prove
सिद्धांत theory
सी.ई.ओ. CEO
सीक नोट sick note
सीमा border, boundary
सीमाचिन्ह landmark
सुंदर beautiful, lovely
सुंदरपणे beautifully
सुई needle
सुईण midwife
सुकवलेली पांढरी द्राक्षे sultana
सुका dried
सुके प्लम फळ prune
सुखवस्तू well-off
सुगंध aroma, scent
सुगंधोपचार aromatherapy
सुगी harvest
सुजलेला swollen
सुटका escape, release, relief
सुटका करणे release
सुटसुटीत compact

सुटे करणे take apart
सुटे घर detached house
सुटे पैसे change
सुटे भाग spare part
सुट्टी holiday
सुतार carpenter, joiner
सुतारकाम carpentry
सुती कापड cotton
सुती धागा cotton
सुदान Sudan
सुदैवाने fortunately, luckily
सुदैवी fortunate
सुद्धा also, too
सुधारणा improvement, modification, revision
सुधारणा करणे modify, revise
सुधारणा होणे improve
सुधारणे correct
सुधारलेले better
सुनामी tsunami
सुपीक fertile
सुप्रसिद्ध famous, renowned, well-known
सुप्रसिद्ध व्यक्ती celebrity
सुमारे about, nearly
सुयश चिंतणे toast
सुरई jug
सुरकुतलेला creased, wrinkled
सुरकुती crease, wrinkle
सुरक्षारक्षक security guard
सुरक्षाव्यवस्था security
सुरक्षित safe, secure
सुरक्षितता safety
सुरक्षितता पट्टा safety belt
सुरक्षित स्थळी हलविणे evacuate
सुरवंट caterpillar
सुरी knife
सुरु ठेवणे pursue
सुरुवात beginning, kick off, start
सुरुवात करणे begin, start off
सुरुवात होणे start

सुरुवातीचा initial
सुरुवातीपासून outset
सुरुवातीला initially, originally
सुरु होणे kick off
सुळका cliff
सुवाच्य legible
सुविधा amenities, facilities
सुविधाजनक convenient
सुशिक्षित educated
सुसंगत rational
सुसंबद्ध relevant
सुसज्ज equipped
सुस्पष्ट glaring, vivid
सुस्वभावी good-natured
सुस्वरूप good-looking
सूंसूं करणे sniff
सूक्ष्म subtle
सूक्ष्म जीव organism
सूक्ष्मदर्शी microscope
सूचक इशारा cue
सूचक गोष्ट clue, hint
सूचना directions, instructions, notice, suggestion
सूचनांचे पालन करणे obey
सूचना करणे suggest
सूचना देणे instruct
सूचनाफलक noticeboard
सूचनाफलक bulletin board
सूट rebate
सूत्र formula
सूत्रधार compere
सून daughter-in-law
सूर जुळणे get on
सूर (पाण्यातला) dive
सूर मारण्याची क्रिया diving
सूर्य sun
सूर्यप्रकाश sunlight
सूर्यफूल sunflower
सूर्यमाला solar system
सूर्यस्नान करणे sunbathe
सूर्यास्त sunset
सूर्योदय sunrise
सेंद्रिय organic
सेंद्रिय खत manure

सेकंद second
सेनापती general
सेवा service
सेवा आकार service charge
सेवा करणे serve
सेवा केंद्र service station
सैनिक soldier, troops
सैनिकी military
सैन्यदल army, troops
सैन्याची तुकडी regiment
सैन्यातील माणूस serviceman
सैन्यातील स्त्री servicewoman
सैल कपडे baggy
सैल सोडणे undo
सोंड trunk
सोटा club
सोडणे leave, undo, untie
सोडणे (अवकाशात) launch
सोडत raffle
सोडवणे sort out
सोडून देणे abandon, give up, leave out, parting, quit
सोडून येणे leave
सोने gold
सोनेरी golden
सोनेरी मासा goldfish
सोन्याचा मुलामा दिलेले gold-plated
सोपा simple
सोपे easy
सोपे करणे simplify
सोपेपणाने simply
सोप्या रीतीने simply
सोबत along, with
सोबत करणे accompany
सोमवार Monday
सोमालिया Somalia
सोमाली Somali
सोळा sixteen
सोळावा sixteenth
सोसाट्याचा वारा सुटलेला windy
सौ Mrs

सौंदर्य beauty
सौंदर्यप्रसाधनगृह beauty salon
सौंदर्यवर्धक शस्त्रक्रिया cosmetic surgery
सौंदर्यस्थळ beauty spot
सौंदर्यप्रसाधन cosmetics
सौदा bargain
सौदेबाज negotiator
सौम्य dilute, mild
सौम्य करणे dilute
सौम्यपणे politely
सौर solar
सौर ऊर्जा solar power
स्टॉल stall
स्तंभ column
स्तन breast
स्तनपान देणे breast-feed
स्तुतिगीत anthem
स्तुती करणे hail, praise
स्तुती/ कौतुक करणे admire
स्तुतीपर complimentary
स्त्रियांचा पोहण्याचा पोशाख bikini
स्त्रियांची ऋतुसमासी menopause
स्त्रियांना गौण समजणारा sexist
स्त्रियांना गौण समजणे sexism
स्त्रियांसंबंधित feminine
स्त्रियांसाठी feminine, ladies
स्त्री female, woman
स्त्रीरोग विशेषज्ञ gynaecologist
स्त्रीवादी feminist
स्त्री वारसदार heiress
स्थलांतर immigration
स्थलांतरित immigrant
स्थानक station
स्थानिक local
स्थापत्य शास्त्र architecture
स्थापत्य शास्त्रज्ञ architect
स्थित situated
स्थिती condition

स्थिर fixed, motionless, stable, steady, still
स्थिरस्थावर होणे settle down
स्थूल chubby, obese
स्थैर्य stability
स्नातकोत्तर postgraduate
स्नायुबंध tendon
स्नायू muscle, tissue
स्नायूंचा muscular
स्पर्धक competitor, contestant
स्पर्धा competition, contest, tournament
स्पर्धा करणे compete
स्पर्धात्मक competitive
स्पर्श करणे touch
स्पष्ट apparent, clear, obvious
स्पष्ट करणे define, specify
स्पष्टपणे clearly, frankly, obviously
स्पष्टपणे उघडपणे apparently
स्पष्टवक्ता outspoken
स्पष्टीकरण explanation
स्पष्टीकरण देणे clarify
स्फटिक crystal
स्फोट blast, explosion
स्फोटक पदार्थ explosive
स्फोट होणे explode
स्मरणिका souvenir
स्मशान crematorium
स्मारक memorial, monument
स्मृतिचिन्ह memento
स्मृतिशिला plaque
स्मृती memory
स्रोत resource
स्वच्छ clean, clear, spotless
स्वतः oneself
(स्वतःचे) मूल वाढवणे upbringing
स्वतंत्र free, independent
स्वतंत्रपणे separately
स्वतःचा own

स्वतःचा मुलगा son
स्वतःची मुलगी daughter
स्वतःच्या मालकीच्या वस्तू belongings
स्वतःवरील ताबा self-control
स्वतःविषयी जागरूक असलेला self-conscious
स्वतःशीच विचार करणे wonder
स्वदेश homeland
स्वदेशी domestic
स्वप्न dream
स्वप्न पाहणे dream
स्वयंकेंद्री self-centred
स्वयंचलित automatic
स्वयंपाक cooking
स्वयंपाक करणे cook
स्वयंपाकघर kitchen
स्वयंपाकाची क्रिया cookery
स्वयंपाकी cook
स्वयंरोजगार असणारा self-employed
स्वयंशिस्त self-discipline
स्वयंसेवक volunteer
स्वर vowel
स्वरचाचणी audition
स्वरपट्टी pitch
स्वरावली note
स्वर्ग heaven
स्वल्पविराम comma
स्वसंरक्षण self-defence
स्वस्त cheap
स्वाक्षरी autograph
स्वागत welcome!
स्वागत/अभिवादन करणे greet
स्वागत असो! welcome!
स्वागत कक्ष reception
स्वागत करणे welcome!
स्वागतकार receptionist
स्वागतपर greeting
स्वातंत्र्य freedom, independence
स्वाद flavouring
स्वादिष्ट delicious

स्वायत्त autonomous
स्वायत्तता autonomy
स्वास्थ्य interest
स्वास्थ्य असलेला interested
स्वार्थी selfish
स्वीकार करणे accept
स्वीकारार्ह acceptable
स्वेच्छेने readily, voluntarily, willingly
स्वेटशर्ट sweatshirt
हंगाम नसलेला काळ off-season
हंगामी acting, seasonal
हंगेरी Hungary
(हक्क) सोडून देणे waive
हजार thousand
हजारावा thousandth
हजेरी roll call
हट्टी obstinate, stubborn
हडकुळा skinny
हत्ती elephant
हत्याकांड massacre
हद्दपारी exile
हनुवटी chin
हप्ता instalment
हमी guarantee
हमी देणे guarantee
हरकत objection
हरकत घेणे mind
हरणाचे मांस venison
हरणे lose
हरवणे lose
हरवलेले missing
हरिण deer
हरितगृह greenhouse
अंतर्गळ hernia
हलकट mean
हलका faint, light
हलक्या प्रतीचा second-rate
हलणे shake
हलवणे move, stir
हलविणे shake
हल्ला attack
हल्ला करणे attack, strike
हल्ली presently

हळू आवाजात बोलणे mutter
हळुवारपणे gently
हळुवारपणे चालणे creep
हळुवारपणे हात फिरवणे stroke
हळूहळू gradual, gradually, slowly
हळूहळू धावणे canter, jog
हवा air
हवाई टपाल airmail
हवाई दल air force
हवाई वाहतूक नियंत्रक air traffic controller
हवाई सुंदरी air hostess
हवाई हद्द airspace
हवाबंद airtight
हवा भरणे pump up
हवामान climate, weather
हवामानाचा अंदाज weather forecast
हवामानातील बदल climate change
हवे असणे ask for, want
हसणे laugh, smile
हसू laugh, smile
हस्तलिखित प्रत manuscript
हस्तांतरण transfer
हस्ताक्षर handwriting
हस्तिदंत ivory
हा this
हाक मारणे call
हाड bone
हाडांचा सांगाडा skeleton
हात hand
हातभार लावणे contribute
हातमोजे glove
हातरुमाल handkerchief, hankie
हाताचा फटका मारणे smack
हाताने बनविलेली वस्तू handmade
हाताळणे handle
हाती घेणे mount
हातोडा hammer
हादरलेला shaken

हानिकारक harmful
हानी damage, loss
हानी पोहोचविणे damage, harm
हार necklace
हालचाल movement
हावभाव expression, gesture
हास्य smile
हास्याचा आवाज laughter
हिंदू Hindu
हिंदू धर्म Hinduism
हिंमत करणे dare
हिंसक violent
हिंसा violence
हिम snow
हिमकण snowflake
हिमनग glacier, iceberg
हिमवर्षाव होणे snow
हिमवादळ snowstorm
हिरवळीचे मैदान lawn
हिरवा green
हिरा diamond
हिवताप malaria
हिवाळा winter
हिवाळ्यातील खेळ winter sports
हिशेब ठेवणारी व्यक्ती accountant
हिशेबतपासणी audit
हिशेबतपासणी करणे audit
हिशेबतपासनीस auditor
हिसकावून घेणे snatch, wrench
हिस्सा section
हिस्सा असणे make up
हिस्सा देणे share out
हुंगणे sniff
हुंदके देत रडणे sob
हुकूमशहा dictator
हुकूम सोडणे boss around
हुतात्मा martyr
हुबेहूब प्रतिकृती dummy
हुशार clever
हृदय heart
हृदयदाह heartburn

हृदय विकाराचा झटका heart attack
हँडल handle
हे these
हेतू intention, purpose
हेर spy
हेरगिरी espionage, spying
हेरगिरी करणे spy
हेरसंस्था secret service
हेलकावा swing

हेलकावे खाणे rock, sway
हेलावून गेलेला touched
हेलावून टाकणारा moving, touching
हेवा envy
हेवा वाटणे envy
हैती Haiti
हॉटेलात साफसफाई करणारी स्त्री chambermaid

हॉटेलातील स्वयंपाकी chef
हॉर्न horn
हॉलंड Holland
हो! yes!
होंडूरास. Honduras
होकायंत्र compass
होकारार्थी मान हलविणे nod
होणे become, get
हौद tank
हौशी amateur